Hills of Conflict

The Basque Series

JAMES E. JACOB

Hills of Conflict

Basque Nationalism in France

University of Nevada Press   Reno   Las Vegas   London

Basque Series

Editor: William A. Douglass

A list of books in the series

follows the index.

University of Nevada Press

Reno, Nevada 89557 USA

Copyright © 1994 by the

University of Nevada Press

Book design by Richard Hendel

Jacket design by Heather Goulding

Printed in the United States of America

The paper used in this book meets the

requirements of American National

Standard for Information Sciences—

Permanence of Paper for Printed Library

Materials, ANSI Z39.48–1984. Binding

materials were selected for strength and

durability.

9 8 7 6 5 4 3 2 1

Library of Congress

Cataloging-in-Publication Data

Jacob, James E.

Hills of conflict : Basque nationalism in

France / by James E. Jacob.

   p.   cm. — (Basque series)

Includes bibliographical references

and index.

ISBN 0-87417-220-9

1. Pays Basque (France)—History—

Autonomy and independence

movements.   2. Nationalism—France—

Pays Basque.   3. Government,

Resistance to—France—Pays Basque.

I. Title.   II. Series.

DC611.B318J33   1994

946'.6—dc20   93-14730

                               CIP

Dedicated to the memory of Professor Eugène Goyheneche

scholar, mentor, and friend

Contents

Acknowledgments

This book is the result of nearly twenty years of interest in the politics and society of the Pays Basque Français. It first began when I was a student at the University of Bordeaux in 1970 and at the University of California at Berkeley and continued as part of my graduate work at Cornell University. As with many such journeys, it started as a book project and ended as a way of life. As Frank Kermode once wrote, "We bring ourselves and our conflicts to our words, to poems and pictures, as we bring them to the world; and thus we change the poems and pictures, or perhaps it is ourselves we change."[1]

I am deeply indebted to a number of people who have helped me bring this project to fruition. I would like to express special thanks to Professor William Douglass, director of the Basque Studies Program of the University of Nevada at Reno, for his encouragement and support over several years. I want to express my thanks to the University of Nevada for a generous Research Professorship in the summer of 1981 which permitted me to extend my library research in Basque history, and to the staff of the Basque Studies Center, including Jill Berner, for their great professionalism and bonhomie over the years. I would also like to acknowledge the courtesy of the reference staffs of the Bibliothèque Nationale in Paris, the Bibliothèque Municipale in Bayonne, France, the New York Public Library, the Newberry Library of the University of Chicago, and the Library of the Hoover Institution of War, Revolution and Peace at Stanford University.

Earlier versions of chapters 4, 5, 6, 8, and 9, submitted as *Basque Nationalism in Iparralde, 1947–1991*, shared the second annual José Antonio Agirre Prize awarded by the Fondación Sabino Arana in Bilbao, Spain, in 1991 for the best unpublished manuscript on the subject of Basque nationalism. Parts of chapters 2, 4, and 5 appeared in an earlier incarnation as part of my doctoral dissertation at Cornell University. I greatly benefited from the guidance of my thesis committee, which included Sidney Tarrow, Davydd Greenwood, Peter Katzenstein, and Milton Esman. Milton Esman in particular has had a major impact on my thinking about the nature of communal conflict and I am indebted to him for his kindness and rigor. Part of the research on which this book is based was funded by the Council for European Studies; the Western Societies Program and the Center for International Studies of

Cornell University; and the Faculty Research Development Fund, Faculty Research Incentive Fund, and the College of Liberal Arts of Wright State University. I owe a particular debt of gratitude to Dean Perry Moore of the College of Liberal Arts of Wright State University, who made it possible to combine research and writing with my service as chair of my department.

I have greatly benefited from a number of individuals and institutions in the Pays Basque Français during the course of several research trips and nearly a year and a half of residence there. One of the finest collections of Basque material in the world is the Musée Basque in Bayonne, France. I want to acknowledge in particular the consistent support of its staff, especially that of Manex Pagola, *conservateur adjoint* and now himself a doctoral candidate in ethnography. The magnificent building by the Nive River housing the Musée was closed temporarily several years ago for renovations, and I have lent my voice to those of scholars around the world who have urged the municipality of Bayonne to speed the reopening of this scholarly treasure at the same site as a museum devoted to Basque culture alone.

I am also deeply indebted to the French newspaper *Le Monde* for opening its archives to me on numerous occasions. I am grateful to *Le Monde*'s archivist Michel Tatu and his staff, especially Liliane Thouvenot, for assisting me in my research. Their archives are a chronicle of contemporary French history and were invaluable to me in my work.

I cannot acknowledge or name many of the individuals who over the past twenty years have given freely of their opinions and documents on the modern Basque movement. Several did so at some personal risk, and all honored me by their openness to a foreign scholar in a time of growing violence and repression. Above all I owe a tremendous intellectual debt to the late eminent Basque historian and nationalist Professor Eugène Goyheneche. He was a splendid mentor and guide, opening his home Uhaldea and his considerable personal archives for me to use in their entirety. His militancy reads like a road map of Basque nationalism in the twentieth century and his passing has impoverished the movement and his friends. I have been honored by the willingness of a host of Basque militants over four generations to welcome me despite their natural suspicions of a foreign scholar and the sensitivity of my subject matter in recent years. I truly regret not being able to thank in print several close personal friends who have followed and critiqued my work for nearly twenty years. I have chosen to leave them anonymous. But I offer a sincere and collective thank you (*mil esker!*) and, to one in particular, *Quand même*. Thanks also to Joelle and Camille Jaille of Halsou and to MéMé and the girls, who made their first renter one of the family in ensuing years.

Working with the editorial staff of the University of Nevada Press has been a fit and pleasant ending to this project. My thanks to Tom Radko and

Nick Cady for their interest in my work, and to Sara Vélez Mallea and my copy editor Kathy Lewis, whose superb editorial work greatly improved the finished product.

I owe a special thanks to Patricia Browder, Joanne Ballmann, and Joan Mullins for their great patience and professionalism in preparing my manuscript for publication. Patt in particular has been a technical wizard with WordPerfect, and a tough taskmaster. All have undoubtedly learned more about the Basques than they ever wanted or thought possible. Finally, my wife Kathy, daughters Lisa and Lindsey, and stepdaughter Amanda have been sources of love and support throughout this journey. I hope I have imparted some small part of my love for the Basques to them in return. As I bring this project to a close, I am reminded of one of the oldest Basque proverbs, *Ibia duena igaren, daqui ossina sein den barrhen* (Only he who has passed the quay knows how deep the river is).

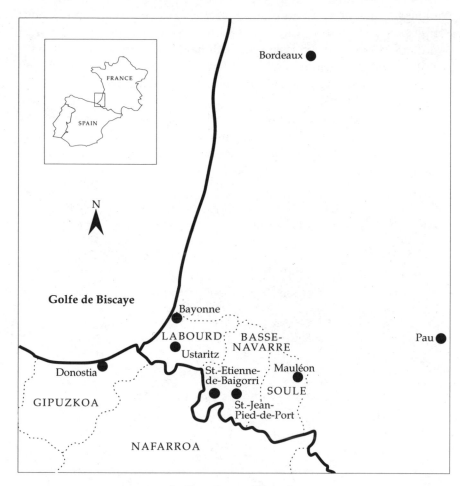

Le Pays Basque Français

Introduction

Lehen hala
Orai hola
Gero ez jakin nola.

Once it was like that
Now it is like this
In the future, who's to know.

Basque proverb

During the Middle Ages, pilgrims to the sepulcher of Saint James at Santiago de Compostella in Galicia reported encountering a people in the Pyrénées mountains who "understood no language."[1] They were not the first to encounter the Basque people, whose presence in these mountains represents a living link between prehistory and the modern age. Early Roman histories describe a warlike people whose resistance to the Roman occupation prevented the complete pacification of Gaul.[2] Scholars now believe that the massacre of the rear guard of Charlemagne's army in A.D. 778 which was immortalized in "The Song of Roland" was the revenge of the Basques for Charlemagne's sacking of Pamplona (Iruñea).[3] In 1833 Victor Hugo wrote during a journey through the Pyrénées:

> I add that here a secret and profound tie . . . which none can break, unites, despite treaties, these diplomatic boundaries, despite the Pyrénées, these natural boundaries, all members of the mysterious Basque family. . . . One is born Basque, one speaks Basque, one lives Basque, and one dies as a Basque. The Basque language is a *patrie*, I almost said a religion.[4]

For Hugo, "Neither France nor Spain was able to break up the Basque [people]. Under the new history which has imposed itself for four centuries, it is still perfectly visible like a crater under a lake."[5]

One of the mysteries of European anthropology was the origins of the Basques. Writing in the *Revue des Deux Mondes* in 1867, the geographer Elisée Réclus called the Basques "the descendants of a mysterious race of which no other nation on earth can call itself the sister."[6] Beginning in the years immediately following World War II, scientific interest shifted to the study of Basque blood typologies. In 1974 the physical anthropologist Morton Levine of the American Museum of Natural History and his colleagues reported on their hemotypological research of blood types in the remote French Basque village of Macaye. They found that the Basques showed no similarities in culture, language, or blood typologies to any other known population. Levine concluded, as had others before him, that the Basques were the indigenous population of Europe which had passed down from prehistoric times.[7] Repeated studies have confirmed that the "pure" Basque blood type of which Levine spoke included a nearly 60 percent incidence of type "O" blood (compared to 40 percent in the general population), almost total nonexistence of "A" and "B" types, and an incidence of the Rh-negative factor ranging between 27 percent and 35 percent, which is the highest in the world.[8] The previously known highest incidence of Rh-negative was 17 percent. Since the populations of Asia and Africa are highly Rh-positive, and also high "B," these findings led A. E. Mourant and others to conclude that the Basques were descendants of the original European population from which the Rh-negative factor in the current European population was derived.[9] Emmanuel Le Roy Ladurie joined José Miguel de Barandiaran and others in stating flatly that the Basques were the descendants of Cro-Magnon man.[10] Moreover, there is substantial corroborative linguistic evidence of the paleolithic origins of the present-day Basque language, with many words containing the root word "stone": axe (*aitz-kor*), knife (*aitz-tto*, and arrowhead or stone point (*aitz-kon*).[11] Basque is the only non-Indo-European language native to Europe and occupies a separate place in most linguistic atlases.[12]

The ability of the Basques to maintain the distinctiveness of their language and traditions is all the more remarkable given the chronicle of nearly two thousand years of invasions, consolidation of states, royal domination, and pressures of cultural assimilation. It suggests the staying power and adaptability of a once-prehistoric and now modern people, who over millennia retreated behind the defensive barriers of their mountainous Pyrenean reaches and their impenetrable tongue.

If scholars believe that the territory of the Basques extended as far north as present-day Poitiers in France, today the limits of the Basque country extend across the Spanish and French border, a territory of approximately 20,000 square kilometers. The Basque linguistic space in northern Spain extends across four provinces: Bizkaia (Vizkaya), Araba (Alava), Gipuzkoa (Guipúzcoa), and Nafarroa (Navarra). The Basque region of France includes the ancient provinces of Labourd (Lapurdi), Basse-Navarre (Nafarroa Beherea), and Soule (Zuberoa), which today cover approximately two-fifths of the land area of the French Department of the Pyrénées-Atlantiques. The seven historic Basque provinces symbolize one of the historic slogans of the Basque movement: *Zazpiak bat* (The seven are one, that is four Spanish Basque provinces plus three French Basque provinces equals one Euskadi or Basque nation). The Basque language is called Euskara and the Basques refer to themselves as Euskaldunak (Those who possess Euskara). While Prince Louis-Lucien Bonaparte found eight primary dialects and as many as twenty-five subdialects between 1860 and 1870, today from a literary perspective there are four broad dialectic groups: Biscayen, Guipuzcoan, Labourdin, and Souletin.[13] The renaissance of Basque culture has fueled a large literary outpouring: according to the late Chanoine Pierre Lafitte, more books were published in Basque in 1972 alone (sixty-two) than were published between the sixteenth and eighteenth centuries put together.[14] By 1991 more than seven hundred books per year were being published in Basque.[15]

According to Jean Haritschelhar, president of Euskaltzaindia (the Basque Academy), former director of the Musée Basque in Bayonne and former professor and chair in Basque literature at the University of Bordeaux, the number of people who speak Basque as a vernacular language totals approximately 800,000 or about 30 percent of the 2,800,000 people who live in the seven Basque provinces in Spain and France.[16] In both cases, nearly all Basque speakers are now bilingual with either French or Spanish. Basque speakers in Spain represent nearly 90 percent of the total Basque-speaking population in these two countries. Historically, there has been less scholarly attention to the 10 percent of the Basque population which resides in France.

In modern France the Basque population is to be found in the Department of the Pyrénées-Atlantiques, where the western terminus of the Pyrénées mountains along the French-Spanish border reaches the Atlantic Ocean. Our ability to estimate the number of Basque speakers in France has been hampered by the French government's long-standing refusal to ask questions concerning language use on its official censuses, a situation which has provoked scholarly complaints since at least 1851.[17] Nonetheless, in 1806 the statistical office of the French Ministry of the Interior estimated the number of Basque speakers in France at 108,000, according to the departmental prefect, M. Castellane.[18] In 1991 the private French survey research group SIADECO estimated with a predicted accuracy of 95 percent the number of current Basque speakers in the Pays Basque Français at 75,000, approximately one-third of the total population, with another 55,000 having some incomplete knowledge of the language.[19] Three years before, Haritschelhar had estimated the number of Basque speakers in the rural interior alone at 70,000, based on his survey of rural mayors.[20]

The problem confronting the survival of the Basque language in France has been that those areas with the greatest concentration of Basque speakers (in rural Soule and Basse-Navarre) are also the areas where the extent of depopulation has been the greatest. The population of Soule was 21,693 in 1817, and only 15,404 in 1982.[21] In Basse-Navarre the population declined from 43,684 in 1817 to 26,148 in 1982. The market village of Saint Etienne-de-Baigorri in Basse-Navarre lost 833 people, or 12 percent of its population, between 1968 and 1975 alone. Only in Labourd was there substantial population growth: from 69,498 in 1817 to 194,937 in 1982. The problem, however, was that most of this population growth in Labourd was accounted for by non-Basque speakers, thus further diluting the Basque linguistic space in the cities along the Atlantic coast. So while the overall population of the Basque country increased 75 percent between 1817 and 1982, and Labourd tripled in population, Soule lost 30 percent of its people and Basse-Navarre lost a full 40 percent. These population trends have grown worse in the years following World War II.

In the two centuries before the French Revolution, the survival of Basque culture and traditions in France was threatened by the steady growth of monarchical incursions into local privileges and customary law. The process of state- and nation-building in France, which I would argue continued well into the Third Republic in the early twentieth century, has resembled what Joseph LaPalombara has called the "crisis of penetration," the territorial and psychological penetration of the central government into areas under only nominal control.[22] Since the early Constituent Assembly of the Revolution, the Basques mounted a conservative resistance to the growing threats to their religion and way of life. Beginning in the late nineteenth century, a political sense of Basque distinctiveness and destiny, of nationhood, motivated the Spanish Basque Sabino Arana Goiri to develop the first doctrine of Basque nationalism.

This book is about Basque nationalism in France, tracing the idea of Basque political mobilization from before the French Revolution to the present day. While this book is about Basque political resistance to the processes of state- and nation-building in France, it is also about France as well. For it is clear that the real differences in the nature of Basque politics in Spain and France have been strongly influenced by the different sociopolitical and historical conditions each movement had to face.

Chapter 1 describes the nature of traditional Basque customary law, the body of privileges in the three French Basque provinces, and the growth of royal intrusions into these liberties in the centuries leading up to the French Revolution. We will examine the question of "collective nobility," inheritance law, political participation, and the role of religion in traditional Basque society. With the advent of the Revolution, the Basques represented one of those conservative provinces which resisted the leveling promise of the

Revolution, and whose *Cahiers de doléances* expressed the desire to maintain their traditional privileges. The Basque resistance to French threats to their religion and language which emerged in the late revolutionary era defined the nature of Basque mobilization until the twentieth century.

Chapter 2 examines the nature of Basque resistance to the public policy initiatives of the early Third Republic and the role of the clergy as the primary Basque ethnic elite, who used the Basque language and religion as the main tools for political mobilization. *Eskualdun, fededun* (He who is Basque is a believer) captured the symbiosis between Basque identity and Catholicism that culminated in the Basque resistance to the crisis of separation of church and state in 1905–1906. Yet, despite the intense level of Basque mobilization in this period, the French Basque population remained largely cut off from the development of Basque nationalism in Spain under the aegis of Sabino Arana Goiri, and we will consider this separation as well.

Chapter 3 examines the rise of clerical regionalism under the leadership of Abbé and later Chanoine (Canon) Pierre Lafitte in the interwar years. Through the Eskualerriste movement and his newspaper *Aintzina*, Lafitte recruited the first true generation of Basque nationalists in France and propelled that generation to ascendance in the years after World War II. We will examine in particular the militancy of Eugène Goyheneche and his role in a number of initiatives in this period, including contacts with other ethnic movements in France, and the gamble which Lafitte and Goyheneche took in pursuing parallel paths of resistance and collaboration. The Spanish Civil War in the 1930s had a profound impact on the Pays Basque Français and served to stigmatize the cause of Basque nationalism among this conservative population by intertwining it with "Godless communism" and anarchism. We will examine the impact of the Spanish Civil War on the French Basque community, as well as the presence of Spanish Basque refugees as important political and cultural role models in this period, despite the efforts at neutrality by the Basque government in exile.

Chapter 4 analyzes the rise of the first generation of secular French Basque nationalists after World War II, around the newspaper *Enbata*. We will examine the influence of Euskadi Ta Askatasuna (ETA) on the ideological development of successive French Basque movements and their ties with ETA beginning in the 1960s. Like its namesake, *Enbata* appeared like a wind which rose up off the ocean to signal an approaching storm and was thus a harbinger of more radical movements to come.

Chapter 5 examines the rise of Euskal Herriko Alderdi Sozialista (EHAS), which was far more committed to socialist revolution than *Enbata* and which attempted to ally itself for the first time with a Basque political party in Spain.

Chapter 6 discusses the rise of Basque violence in France in the early 1970s, in particular, the creation of Iparretarrak, "Those of ETA of the North." Iparretarrak's appearance represented a revolutionary expropriation of the terrain of Basque nationalism in France; its use of violence was as much a weapon against the French state as it was a tool to capture control of the Basque political terrain. We will examine the nature of Iparretarrak's relationship with ETA over time. On one level, Iparretarrak's violence was a serious threat to the sanctuary of ETA refugees in France and led to serious tension between the two movements which lasted until the mid-1980s.

Chapter 7 analyzes the rise of ETA's refugee community in France beginning in the 1960s and its impact on French-Spanish diplomacy. France constituted ETA's northern sanctuary for more than twenty years and served as a rear base for violent attacks mounted against the Spanish state and its agents. Beginning in the mid-1970s, the Spanish government mounted a counterattack against ETA's leaders in France and sought by raising the level of violence in the Pays Basque Français to force the French to change their policy on asylum and begin extraditing ETA militants to Spain. This period of state-sponsored terrorism was the greatest domestic political violence France had known since World War II, leading to a reversal of French government policy and a growing cooperation between the two governments in the 1990s.

Chapter 8 discusses the descent of Iparretarrak into a cycle of violence which largely cut it off from Basque public opinion. As a result, Iparretarrak itself led to the rise of a number of moderate Basque political movements which sought to emerge from the ghetto of violence and reclaim the legitimate Basque political center.

Chapter 9 summarizes the major arguments made in the book and discusses the factors affecting the future of Basque nationalism in 1994. We will situate the idea of Basque nationalism in a broader historical context defined by European unification, the discrediting of communism, and the rise of nationalist violence as one of the major elements in international politics on the eve of the twenty-first century.

Finally, I am obliged to offer a short note at this point on Basque language use and terminology. In describing the Basque region of France, the French and Basque texts use a number of terms, including Pays Basque (Basque country), Pays Basque Français (French Basque country), Iparralde (Basque for the northern part of Basque territory in France, Hegoalde being the South, in Spain), or simply "the North." I have generally used Pays Basque Français [pay-ee' baahsk-frawhn-say]. However, in translating Basque texts, I have chosen to translate Iparralde as the northern Basque country or the North depending on the context. *Abertzale* [ab-bert-zah'-lay], which appears frequently in later chapters, is the Basque word for a Basque patriot. Used as an adjective (e.g., the *abertzale* movement), it means "Basque nationalist." In quotations I have left "Euzkadi," the name Arana Goiri gave to the Basque nation in the nineteenth century. Basque proper names generally appear in the united Batua dialect of Basque developed by the Academy of the Basque Language. I have chosen to leave familiar cities and place names, like Biarritz and Bayonne, in French for purposes of clarity.

Chapter One

The French Revolution and

the Basques of France

They find themselves well enough off in this [ancien] régime;
they would be fearful to change from it.
Cahier de doléances of the Third Estate of the
Basque Province of Labourd, 1789[1]

Federalism and superstition speak low Breton; emigration and
hate of the Revolution speak German; the counterrevolution
speaks Italian, and fanaticism speaks Basque.
Bertrand Barère de Vieuzac for the
Comité de Salut Public, 8 pluviôse, An II[2]

On January 24, 1789, Louis XVI, king of France and of Navarre, called for
the first meeting of the Estates General of France to be held in 175 years.[3]
Scheduled to begin in Versailles the following April, it represented an end
to the absolutism of the French kings and an admission of the growing fiscal problems facing the state. We now see in this innocuous beginning a
harbinger of profound changes in Western political institutions.

The French Revolution, as Crane Brinton reminded us, is one of the few
events in modern history which provokes a feeling of awe. Yet few could
have anticipated that the Estates' intended purpose of fiscal reform would
give way to paroxysms of regicide and Revolution. The king, faced with the
specter of state bankruptcy, was forced to convene the Estates and to solicit
lists of grievances (*Cahiers de doléances*) from his subjects, "in order to aid us
in surmounting all the difficulties in which we find ourselves, relative to the
state of our finances, and to establish . . . a constant and invariable order in
all parts of the government."[4]

Beatrice Fry Hyslop's painstaking analysis of the surviving 522 of the 615
Cahiers prepared for the Estates General reveals once more a France of overwhelming disunity, a patchwork quilt of local interests.[5] The success of the

Revolution meant challenging and overcoming this social and territorial diversity. The triumph of the republican camp, however incomplete, would
come only at the expense of the provincial liberties, local privileges, and
linguistic heterogeneity which were lumped together with feudalism as a target of the early Constituent Assembly. In this way, the Jacobin urge toward
centralization and uniformity sacrificed liberty in the pursuit of equality.

The revolutionary period is an important chapter in the political history
of the Basques of France.[6] Linguistic particularism, clericalism, economic
defense of provincial privileges, and the defense of traditional, democratic
Basque institutions all figured in the Basque reaction to the unfolding Revolution. The *Cahier* of the Third Estate of Soule spoke for a Basque population
in 1789 that felt itself "as foreign to [France] as if it were situated in Turkey."[7]
The reactions of the Basques of Labourd and Basse-Navarre, in particular,
were reflective of the conservative reluctance of many provinces to see dismantled a substantial body of customary laws—many formally recognized
by royal charter. In some cases the embodiment of royal concessions granted
before the consolidation of the modern French state (many inherited from
English rule under the Plantagenets), in later times these royal grants reflected local economic circumstances or, in frontier regions such as the Pays
Basque, actual or promised services to the crown in case of foreign aggres-
sion. These *fors* granted important concessions or exemptions in the areas
of taxation, customs duties, military service, hunting and fishing rights,
civic obligations, and the degree of autonomy of local self-government. In
the Pays Basque, as elsewhere, as they entered into the collective memory
of historic, customary law, they became a reflection of the political self-
perceptions of local populations and, as such, jealously guarded privileges
as much symbolic as real.

The Basque reaction to the Revolution was conservative—especially in the
province of Labourd and the portion of the Kingdom of Navarre which had
passed to France as Basse-Navarre with the accession of Henri III, duc of
Béarn and king of Navarre, to the throne as King Henri IV of France in 1589.
The provinces of Soule and Labourd had passed earlier to the French with
the Treaty of Ayherre in 1451 as part of the spoils of the Hundred Years' War.
In each case, successive monarchs had sworn loyalty or acquiesced in fact to
these local privileges perfected over time. So, as the Revolution threatened
to abolish these provincial liberties in its Jacobin and republican zeal, the
Basques reacted conservatively, because tradition had given them much to
conserve. Thus, Basque reaction from the convocation of the Estates General
through the early Constituent Assembly is an example of provinces where
the burden of feudalism was virtually nonexistent and where the commit-

ment to existing traditions was preferable to the uncertainties of evolving revolutionary change. The revolutionary period is an important chapter in the political history of the Basque people, even if it represented a futile resistance to the Jacobin republicanism ascendant in Paris and Versailles.

In this chapter, I intend to examine the nature of the integration of the Basque provinces of Labourd, Soule, and Basse-Navarre under the French crown and the nature of the local rights, privileges, and *fors* behind which Basque culture and local political institutions had developed. Second, I intend to trace the elements of Basque resistance during the early French Revolution which manifest themselves in the *Cahiers* drawn for the Estates General and the parliamentary debates within the early Constituent Assembly. Finally, I will examine the impact which these forces would have on the nature of subsequent ethnic mobilization among the Basques of France.

The Question of the *Fors*

The basis of political and social organization in the three Basque provinces was a diverse body of customary and later written law known variously as *privilèges, la coutume, observances, fueros* (charters) or *fors*.[8] The content of these *fors* was different for each province, and coexisted with particular local *fors* which governed social and economic life in individual villages, valleys, or parishes.[9] These traditional and highly legitimate understandings covered diverse aspects of daily communal life, regulating everything from local economic and social customs concerning common pasturage, hunting, fishing and water rights to the nature of political representation and economic obligations to the monarchy.

The first of these understandings predated the consolidation of the monarchy and were, as in Navarre, sets of guarantees to ensure the preservation of these privileges, which were sworn to by successive monarchs upon accession to the throne. In this way, Louis XIII accepted his role as sovereign, "however without deviating from the *fors*, exemptions, liberties, privileges, and rights of his subjects of the Kingdom of Navarre," a commitment remembered by the Estates of Navarre in their letter of protest to Louis XVI in 1789.[10] In some cases, these *fors* originated in the *carta de población*, or royal letter of settlement, which granted certain privileges and immunities in order to encourage settlement in particular areas.[11] Other *fors* were granted, as the Bilçar of Labourd pointed out in 1789, as a payment for services to frontier provinces in time of war,[12] and "for their poverty, the infertility of their soil, in order to aid them to live, and to send them back to their land."[13]

It was perhaps this fact more than any other—the overwhelming complexity of local privileges accepted through tradition or through royal charter—that stood as an obstacle to the revolutionary desires for *égalité* in 1789.

The written texts of Basque customary law were codified by the sixteenth century, generally at the request of a monarch interested in systematically recording this welter of customary privileges and exemptions. For example, the first written *Fuero general* of Navarre is believed to have been drafted in 1155, long after the emergence of the kings of Navarre, and further still from the origins of the *fueros* which recognized privileges and exemptions granted to houses for services dating back to the Moorish resistance.[14] Under the reign of Henri IV, king of France and of Navarre, the Estates of Navarre drafted a new written version of the *fueros* in order to clarify confusing elements in existing customary law. Henri IV balked at accepting this unrequested document and charged royal *commissaires* with drafting an official version in a letter dated March 14, 1608. This royal version contained 450 articles, of which more than 100 were judged by the Estates of Navarre to be injurious to the interest of Navarre. Still other customs had been omitted altogether. Despite Navarrese protest, Louis XIII ordered in 1611 that these *Fors et costumas deu royaume de Navarre* become law, and they were only belatedly registered in the Chancellery of Navarre in 1622. Substantial disagreement over the nature of Navarre's relationship with France emerged again during the early Revolution and lasted until December 30, 1789, when Navarre capitulated and accepted its amalgamation with France.

SOULE

The Basque provinces of Soule and Labourd passed along with Gascony under English rule in 1152 with the marriage of Henry Plantagenet to Eleanor of Aquitaine. The royal practice of granting autonomy in exchange for money had been recognized as early as 1106 and recodified by King Edward II of England in 1311.[15] In 1341 Labourd received assurances from Edward III to (1) render justice according to the *fors* and customs of the country; (2) never alienate his rights held over the land of Labourd; and (3) keep this land always attached to his own.[16]

In 1358 conflict arose between the residents of Soule and the chatelain of Edward III, who the residents accused in a letter to the king himself of violating customary law and exceeding his royal mandate.[17] Edward's response is a classic in English justice and indicative of the reciprocal obligation which bound a monarch to his subjects. In a letter delivered by royal emissary to the chatelain, the king said, "If we find you guilty of that, we will proceed in your regard in such a way that others will be deterred by fear and by terror from imitating you."[18] Four days later the king affirmed to "nobles and non-nobles, to each and every inhabitant of Soule," the preservation of their secular liberties, their right to continue to possess land as they had always possessed it in paying ancient rights to the king, and the maintenance of their other privileges including pasturage, millage of grain, and so forth. These rights were reaffirmed again in 1377 and, according to Goyheneche, were included nearly verbatim in the *Custom of Soule* drafted in 1520. The problem with this early version was that it was drafted not in Basque, but in the Béarnais-Gascon dialect of the *Sénéchausée* of Lannes.[19] Resulting problems in interpretation led the Estates of Soule to order a French translation in 1766. Among the privileges guaranteed the Souletin population were freedom from servile obligations, freedom of movement, the right to carry arms, right of political assembly, and unrestricted hunting and fishing privileges. Indeed, one of the most violent examples of Basque resistance under the *ancien régime* began in 1639 when the king sought to sell common land near Tardets which the Souletins regarded as their own.[20] The land was purchased for 70,000 livres by Jean de Peyrer, son of a merchant from Oloron, who became Arnaud-Jean de Troisvilles, later inspiration for Alexander Dumas's character in the *Three Musketeers*. So great was the popular outcry that the king eventually annulled the sale, but required the population of Soule to reimburse Troisvilles and the cost of litigation, a sum exceeding 150,000 livres. Popular discontent found a leader in Bernard de Goyheneche, *curé* of Moncayolle, who, as "Matalas," led a lengthy revolt which ultimately cost more than four hundred lives and was not ended until Matalas was caught and beheaded in 1661.

The problem in Soule, as elsewhere, in this period was the steady erosion of local privileges at the hands of royal intendants between the seventeenth and eighteenth centuries.[21] Between 1742 and 1762 alone, taxes levied in Soule increased from 8,000 to 30,000 livres.[22] They symbolized the intrusion of the absolutist state into local liberty and the steady onslaught against foral privilege.

LABOURD

The nature of the *fors* of Labourd was also clarified at the behest of King Edward II of England in 1311.[23] Later, in 1341, Edward III swore neither to violate the fors of Labourd nor to alienate the land from his crown. The *fors* were again renewed by King Henry IV, as duc de Guienne, in 1413 near the end of English rule.

During the winter of 1450, French forces led by Gaston IV, comte de Foix, crushed the last English support in the Basque countryside and forced the

English forces into Bayonne, which ultimately fell on August 15, 1451.[24] On March 18, 1450, a delegation of Labourdin Basques went to the Chateau of Belsunce at Ayherre in order to sign a loyalty oath to the kings of France.[25] From this time, the province of Labourd was exempted from a number of other taxes, duties, and feudal obligations known elsewhere in France. As the Bilçar of Labourd noted in 1789:

> The *aides, tailles, crues,* etc. [common forms of taxes], were already known in the kingdom. However, these impositions were never intro- duced to the land of Labour. To the contrary, every king through the middle of the last century continued and renewed the privilege of ex- emption from all these impositions for the Labourdins.[26]

The strongest royal pledge of privilege came from both Henri IV and Louis XIV, who exempted Labourd from all sorts of impositions, "as much ordinary as extraordinary, done and to be done."[27]

Indeed, by the middle of the seventeenth century, the single royal tax on Labourd was 253 livres! With the introduction of a new form of taxa- tion, the *vingtièmes* (or twentieths), the tax burden on Labourd grew steadily in the ensuing century until it reached more than 70,000 livres on the eve of the Revolution.[28] In 1784 the debt of the province of Labourd to the Royal Treasury equaled *140,000* livres. The venality or sale of offices by the crown forced the province to pay in order to prevent non-Basques from occupying these offices. In order to lobby effectively, the province was paying per- manent representatives in Paris to represent its interests.[29] This lobbying then increased taxes even more. The onerous impact of central authority continued to affect the three Basque provinces until the Revolution.

The reaction of the Basques, in particular those of Labourd and Basse- Navarre, is instructive. Unlike the other provinces in France, which called for an end to feudal obligations, fiscal equality, and a new constitutional order, the conservative response of the Basques was to call for the return of their traditional customary privileges. Theirs was, as Hannah Arendt noted, the older sense of revolution: a return to what had been.[30] Indeed the Basque expression for revolution, *iraultza*, suggests a timeless agricultural rhythm of the tilling of the soil or the orbiting of the planets in the sky.

Feudalism and "Collective Nobility"
among the Basques of France

The nobility of the Basques is national and collective.
Augustin Chaho (1836)[31]

The *Cahier* of the Third Estate of Labourd was an example of the conservative reluctance of some provinces to accept the uncertainties of revolutionary change. This reluctance stemmed in large measure, as we have seen, from the body of customary privileges or *fors* which had generally spared the Basques of Labourd the onerous burden of feudal obligations reflected in the grievances of many other provincial *Cahiers* at that time. Indeed, the Basque provinces (particularly Labourd) were distinguished from much of prerevolutionary France by the weak implantation of feudalism and the relative impotence of feudal nobles in local political assemblies.

The whole of the nobility of Labourd which gathered on April 19, 1789, in Ustaritz to elect a deputy to the Estates General numbered twelve nobles, in addition to three widows holding fiefs and four other representatives for a total of *nineteen,* in a province whose population exceeded forty-five thousand people.[32] Prominent in the *Cahier* drawn up by these nobles was the complaint of overtaxation (paying one-eighth of the taxes while owning but one-twentieth of the property), and their constraint to sit as mere property owners, and not as nobles, in the provincial assembly of Labourd, the Bilçar.[33]

One of the explanations for the near-absence of the feudal *franc-fief* lies in the particular body of *fors* concerning land tenure, inheritance and succession, economic tax exemptions, and social privileges granted by the king. Reasoning from these royal concessions, successive generations of Basque scholars have suggested the incompatibility of the logic of feudalism among a people which considered itself collectively noble. Yet few problems in the study of Basque political culture in France are as vexatious as the concept of collective nobility.

Successive Basque sources including Sanadon (1785);[34] Polverel, *syndic* of the Estates of Navarre (1789); Garat, deputy of Labourd during the Revolution, twice minister, senator, and count of the Napoleonic Empire (1808); Chaho (1836); Belsunce (1847); Françisque-Michel (1857);[35] Tessier (1918); and Harispé (1929)[36] have supported the concept of collective nobility among the Basques of France. These arguments derive from two root assumptions: first, that the collective nobility of the Basques derives from their racial purity of blood preserved over the centuries in the face of threats of assimilation by Romans, Moors, and French; and/or second, that the specific privileges granted by the kings and embodied in 'the *fors* granted nobility on the Basques by extending to them as a provincial population privileges reserved elsewhere in France for nobles alone. In either case, the argument reflects an early awareness of the question of collective nobility in the Basque provinces of Gipuzkoa and Bizkaia in Spain.[37] As Garat wrote in an early project for the unification of the Basque provinces of France and Spain, "In France as in Spain, the Basques believe themselves, declare themselves, and proclaim themselves all noble." [38] Belsunce wrote in 1847:

> The privilege of nobility attributed to the Souletins in the written cus-
> tom, recognized by the kings of France and assimilating each of these
> mountain men as gentlemen and owners of fiefs in the kingdom, was
> common to the Basques of the seven provinces, as much in France as
> in Spain.[39]

From Sanadon's analysis in 1785 onward, one sees the use of reason by analogy to the Gipuzkoan and Bizkaian examples in order to extend the concept of collective nobility to the Basque provinces in France, as well.

The problem is a complex one, turning as much on the province involved as on the period, and greatly complicated by the differing perceptions of the Basques and the crown and its agents. Documentary evidence on the eve of the Revolution indicates fairly conclusively the presence of a deeply held particularism among the political classes which emerges from the Basque *Cahiers*, a proto-nationalistic ethnic pride occasionally expressed as a belief in the nobility of the Basques. This belief is based in part on traditional, customary law. Let us examine in more detail the nature of the ennobling privileges in the customary law of the three Basque provinces in France and the extent of the actual first estate of the three provinces at the convocation of the Estates General in 1789.

SOULE

The extent of feudal obligation in Soule was ill defined with the ceding of the Vicomté de Soule to King Edward II of England by Louis-le-Hétin in the fourteenth century. The only property or privilege mentioned in the act of transfer was the deed to the chateau of Mauléon. No mention was made of the Souletin countryside or of its people.[40] As previously noted, the body of Souletin customary law, *La coutume*, was codified in 1520. One of the most complete recitations of its privileges occurred in 1667 when Isaac de Bela, *syndic* of Soule, presented its elements to the *commissaire des partis* of the province of Guienne who was charged with investigating usurpations of the privileges of nobility. According to Sanadon, the verification of the rights and privileges listed in *La coutume* of Soule was followed by their recognition by the provincial authorities of Guienne. Among elements of Souletin customary law were elements first codified at the time of François I with the consolidation of the French monarchy. Among the most important of these rights was the recognition "that all Souletins are free, of free condition, and with no trace of servitude."[41] Other elements of *La coutume* of Soule included the right to bear arms at all times and in all places; the exemption against any forced conscription except that ordered by the monarch in time of war; the right to create marriage contracts involving hereditary provision of property, a privilege which, according to Sanadon, "cannot take place in France except between nobles";[42] the right to execution by beheading in the event of grave crimes or treason, which, according to Sanadon, "belongs only to the nobility";[43] the right to hunt and fish freely; the right to construct and operate gristmills, provided they harm the water rights of neither the public nor their neighbors; and the exemption from such forms of taxation as the *gabelle*, the *droits de foraine* levied on the sale of produce in the regional capitals, the *taille*, and any other imposition with the sole exception of the *capitation*.

It was the issue of taxation as no other which fueled the antagonism of the Estates and which reappeared in successive provincial *Cahiers*. As Manex Goyhenetche points out, taxes levied against Soule increased from 8,000 livres to more than 30,000 between 1742 and 1762 alone.[44] Taxes were a symbol of the steady erosion of provincial privileges before the often arbitrary onslaught of absolutist monarchy. This fiscal capriciousness struck at the very heart of historic provincial relations with the sovereign for, following *La coutume*, "Soule owes nothing to the king, so long as she recognizes no other *seigneur* but the king."[45] Finally, as Sanadon noted, should any Basque from Soule establish residence in Spain, it sufficed for him to prove four generations of Basque descent to be received as a gentleman in the courts and to be admitted to military orders requiring proof of nobility.[46]

Crucial to these privileges was a system of land tenure recognized by royal authority, which guaranteed the alodiality (from the Latin: *usu allodium* as opposed to *feodum*) or free ownership of land with no duties or obligations owed any superior whatsoever. In Soule the ancestral home determined the political and administrative duties of its owner; ownership of houses carrying patents of nobility conferred nobility upon their owners.[47] There were two degrees of nobility in Soule.[48] The superior title of *potestat* corresponded roughly to the *ricombre* of Navarre. Below the *potestaterie* were the *cavers* or knights and the *domengers* or captains of infantry. Each category of noble sat in the Estates of Soule without distinction between them.

By the end of the tenth century one finds the occasional large property next to small plots owned by freeholders free from any vassalage. Often the question of nobility itself was relative, for, as Tessier argues, "They weren't in reality but property owners a little richer than the others."[49] Though later confusion emerged with the practice of the French kings of granting nobility not upon houses but upon individuals, the traditional prohibitions in customary law against the sale of the ancestral home outside the family effectively limited the size of the Souletin nobility by the fourteenth century. Though some noble houses had special privileges, such as the right to occupy the first row of the church (with the responsibility to maintain the church and lodge the *curé*) or to sit more often in the decision-making Cour de Licharre, Nussy-Saint-Säens argues that "Souletin nobles did not exercise at all the attributes of public power."[50] Even this latter symbolic privilege— entry to the Cour de Licharre—was usurped with the suppression of the Cour by royal decree in 1776.[51] Ultimately, fifty-five Souletin nobles met on May 18, 1789, to elect representatives to an Estates General already in session since May 5; they nearly decided against sending a delegate because of the expense.[52]

BASSE-NAVARRE

The question of privileges and the extent of the nobility in Basse-Navarre is a more difficult question than in the other Basque provinces of Labourd and Soule. As Eugène Goyheneche points out, what emerges in Basse-Navarre is a more complex set of institutions, owing in part to the history of the partition of the ancient kingdom of Navarre and to the geographic dispersion of the population among isolated *pays* and valleys, each with its own set of traditional, customary laws reflected in particular *fors*.[53] Goyheneche argues:

> Differing from Labourd and Soule, which constitute geographic political and administrative units, Basse-Navarre is a federation of small *pays*, of valleys, each of which from an institutional point of view is the equivalent of Labourd or Soule; their unity rested only in a common allegiance to the King of Navarre, represented by the *capitaine-châtelain* of St.-Jean-Pied-de-Port.[54]

It was the nature of earlier privileges recognized by kings of Navarre which colored the nature of nobility in Basse-Navarre, the one province of the three, according to Tessier, where the nature of legislation was the least Basque.[55] The extent of the nobility in Basse-Navarre at the time of its unification with France was the greatest of any of the three provinces, *one-sixth* of the population, according of Nogaret.[56] The nature of this Basse-Navarrese nobility in 1789 reflected a customary law and a system of land tenure that predated the consolidation of the kingdom of Navarre itself.

Before the consolidation of the kingdom of Navarre, when the country was a congeries of independent valleys and *pays*, its residents had already begun to recognize the authority of one landowner in their midst, generally considered wiser, richer, or more experienced than the rest.[57] The title given these individuals was *ricombre*, apparently a derivation from the Spanish *rico hombre* or "noble" in historic usage. The authority of the *ricombres* grew during the Moorish invasions when they formed small bands of troops for mutual defense. The selection of a king, or *primus inter pares*, came out of the uniting of these armies. The solemn oath of successive kings of Navarre was to preserve the privileges of the *ricombres* who elected him. In that reciprocal act of feudal obligation was the recognition of a body of customary privileges or *fueros* that predated the state and monarchy of Navarre. Below the *ricombres* were *caballeros* or knights and below the *caballeros* were *infançons* or captains of infantry. Each realized real privileges, which varied according to the locality. However, these privileges, vestiges of a military kingdom, became diluted with time, by the conquest of Navarre by Castille as well as by the annexation of Basse-Navarre by the kingdom of France. By the sixteenth century the title of *ricombre* had disappeared.

The nobility grew under the Navarrese kings, with the granting of privileges, exemptions, or nobility to certain houses as a repayment of favors or services to the crown. Occasionally, entire villages or valleys were so favored, as was the case of the village of Arberoue in 1435, when the king exempted 110 houses from payment of taxes in exchange for a payment of 240 livres.[58]

The basis of Navarrese nobility was the ownership of houses or property which carried patents of nobility. According to Goyheneche, there were 150 noble houses in Basse-Navarre by the end of the sixteenth century.[59] Class differences in Basse-Navarrese society were based on the ownership of noble houses. The possessor of such a house was himself noble, regardless of his previous social class, and continued to enjoy the prerogatives of nobility as long as the property remained in his possession.[60] But it was possible to pass from a nobility of ownership to a hereditary nobility: after holding a noble property within one family for 100 years, the family was considered "gentlemen of race and extraction." The result, as Nogaret indicated, was that one-sixth of the population was noble at the time of the annexation of Basse-Navarre to France. Many of these privileges were symbolic and uncodified; as the Basque historian and *notaire* from Saint-Etienne-de-Baigorri, Jean Etcheverry-Ainchart, points out, by the eighteenth century on, it was difficult to distinguish between homes by their original status.[61]

Despite the existence of a substantial number of noble houses, Basse-Navarre, like Labourd and Soule, was a land of *franc-alleu*, alodiality or the freeholding of property.[62] This system of land tenure assured the humblest of property owners the same privileges enjoyed by the king over his own land. The resistance to feudal law and the encroachment of royal authority characterized the relationship between the Estates of Navarre and the French kings from the edict of union through 1789. To the feudal maxim *Nulle terre sans seigneur* (No land without lord), the Basse-Navarrese responded *Nul seigneur sans terre* (No lord without land).[63] The Navarrese pledged to render respect to the king, but this was not fully feudal; for as the viceroy of Navarre had written to Philippe the Hardy during the regency of Queen Jeanne, "The King will receive no other fealties or other homages from the Navarrese."[64]

A chronicle of this struggle for provincial privileges is to be found in an important letter to Louis XVI commissioned by the Estates of Navarre on March 31, 1789, on the eve of the Estates General, which called for "the maintenance of their violently attacked franchises and liberties."[65] The Estates of Navarre provide in this letter a historical recitation of the recognition of the rights and privileges of Basse-Navarre by successive French kings. The Navarrese argued that the establishment of the feudal *franc-fief* dated from the time of the crusades and, as a law based on the right of conquest, had little in common with Navarrese customary law and a Navarrese monarchy founded on popular consent and not on conquest. The letter noted:

> One knows that the feudal law which covered all parts of France produced that of *franc-fief*; but Navarre being in *franc-alleu* from its origins, one does not find there any vestiges of this [feudal] law, which was never recognized or even known.[66]

They reminded the king that, from the time of his forebear Louis XIII onward, successive French kings had pledged to respect this system of land tenure and "to maintain the Basse-Navarrese in all their *fors*, rights and privileges, etc."[67] Accordingly, the Estates of Navarre continued in this letter to Louis XVI:

> One cannot eliminate the immunities [of *franc-alleu*] by establishments which would be diametrically opposed, such as the right of *franc-fief*, without reversing the law which unites the two crowns.[68]

The right of alodiality and *franc-alleu* was further clarified for the Navarrese at the time of Louis XIV, when concern was expressed by the Navarrese Estates over the purview of the king's edict of August 1692 governing *franc-fief* and *franc-alleu*. The king issued a further edict in April 1694 in response to Navarrese concerns. The edict reported that Louis XIV:

> extinguishes, suppresses, and revokes, for that which concerns Navarre, these edicts . . . and in consequence, keeps them able to hold in *franc-*

alleu . . . all their goods noble and common, individual and collective, and all their other rights, privileges, exemptions, and liberties.[69]

The Navarrese were thus "exempt from all acts of vassalage, of all seigneurial rights, and notably that of *franc-fief*." [70]

Despite these guarantees, the Estates of Navarre evoked in 1789 a period of increasing and arbitrary taxation which threatened the noble privileges of the Basse-Navarrese:

> The laws of Navarre, as old as the monarchy itself, and in contrast to that which the kings introduced in France, ennobles each owner of room, or house decorated with the right to take part in the estates, provided however, that those so covered live nobly. So much is the nobility real in Navarre. . . . One cannot presume, sire, that the intention of your majesty would be to contest to owners of houses, living nobly from father to son, the right of nobility.[71]

The problem of the Navarrese, and the reason for the letter to Louis XVI on the eve of the Estates General of France in 1789, was their inability to prove their nobility (and hence privileges and tax exemptions) through reference to any documents, census, or deeds beyond the fact of possession of their property. As the Navarrese pled their case to the king:

> The nobles, living under the faith in their laws, have neglected to conserve the titles justifying their ties, such that the nobles, even of extraction, can hardly produce the proof.[72]

One senses the extreme concern of the Navarrese Estates anxious to preserve their privileges with a French king only marginally also king of Navarre. Their futile efforts were directed at the preservation of *fors* which predated their union with France. As one Navarrese delegate exhorted his colleagues during their deliberations:

> I propose to you to return to what you once were, what you should never have ceased to be, a free and independent people, exercising by its Estates General, by its representatives, legislative power, offering to its kings only voluntary givings, imposing on itself and recognizing the right of no other power to impose upon it. . . . There is nothing to fear being accused of sedition, since you are only asking for the execution of the *fors*; the *fors* are the common titles of the kings and of the nation.[73]

LABOURD

Of the three Basque provinces, Labourd was the one where the impact of the feudal nobility was the weakest. On the eve of the Revolution, the nobility owned one-twentieth of the land in Labourd, yet paid one-eighth of the taxes in the province, a burden mentioned by the nobility of Labourd in its *Cahier* in 1789.[74] So weak was the impact of feudalism in the province that the *Cahier* of the Third Estate added as its final grievance:

> Finally, the inhabitants of Bonloc and Lahonce are saddled with enor-mous seigneurial obligations. These are the only traces of oppressive feudalism that one remarks with affront in the pays of Labourd, noble for all time, that is to say, free and alodial.[75]

It is significant that the feudal lords of Bonloc and Lahonce were, in fact, clerical orders and not *nobles de l'épée*. So inhospitable were the residents of Espelette to the implantation of a feudal barony there that one of the daugh-ters of the late baron willed her rights to the townspeople in totality.[76] The implantation of feudalism in the entire province of Labourd was so weak, as we have seen, that only twelve nobles and a handful of other widows and representatives met in 1789 to draw up their *Cahier*. Thus, it was indicative of the balance of power in Labourd on the eve of the Revolution that the *Cahier* of the nobility petitioned the king for a voice in the administration of the province.[77] Here, too, the weakness of the nobility owed much to the nature of the *fors*.

The early *fors* of Labourd remained uncodified during the imposition of royal authority in the province. The Vicomté de Labourd was founded in 1023 by Sanche le Grand, king of Navarre, for his cousin, Loup Sanche.[78] Labourd passed under English rule in 1152 with the marriage of Eleanor of Aquitaine to Henry Plantagenet. The province was later pacified by Richard the Lion-Hearted, to whom the eighth vicomte of Labourd, Guillaume Raymond de Sault, sold his rights. Consequently, the juridical situation of Labourd was better known than in Soule or Basse-Navarre thanks to the previously dis-cussed study ordered by King Edward II of England in 1311 to clarify his rights over the land.[79] As Goyheneche points out, if this document indicated the presence of some feudal fiefs in this period, "they were exceptional and late [in appearing]."[80]

The nature of land tenure in Labourd was an obstacle to the implanta-tion of the feudal *franc-fief*. Labourd was recognized as a land of alodiality and *franc-alleu*, elements which contributed to its predominant character as a province of small, divided freeholdings with an occasional noble estate. The particular privileges of Labourd extended them to all inhabitants, prevent-ing the appearance of class divisions similar to those existing in Soule and Basse-Navarre.[81]

The *fors* of Labourd were repeatedly recognized under English kings through Henry IV in 1413. Under French rule, these privileges were further recognized by Charles VII, Louis XI in 1473, and Louis XII in 1513. The *Coutume* of Labourd was finally codified in 1514. As Tessier notes, "It had existed for a long time, but it wasn't written and was transmitted by tradition."[82]

Many of the early *fors* concerned quotidian rights to bear arms, free travel, transport of goods, the rights of each parish to assemble in order to deal with matters of common interest and to make agreements with other parishes governing pasturage, and so forth.[83] More significant were the tax exemptions granted to the province, for these, along with the defense of *franc-alleu*, were the subject of the most pointed claims by the *Cahiers* of Labourd during the Revolution and not simply, in the words of the Bilçar in 1789, some attachment "to the vainglory meant by the word privilege."[84] They pointed to the series of royal recognition of these foral immunities, privileges, and exemptions stretching from François I in 1542 to Louis XIV in 1683.[85]

The ensuing century was a chronicle of the decline of Basque privileges, the augmentation of taxation, the limitation of local political liberties, and the venality of offices. As in the other provinces, the decline of these privileges was accompanied by an increase in the power of the monarchy and its *intendants*. One of the most significant losses of privilege concerned the limitation in power of the Bilçar, a representative local decision-making body referred to by Garat in 1808 as an assembly of elders.[86] In the Bilçar sat the elected representatives of the landowners of thirty-five municipalities or voting parishes. Clergy and nobility were prevented from sitting in the Bilçar except as simple landowners elected by their parishes. This no doubt contributed to the observation of one royal *intendant* who claimed that Labourd was a "land hostile to nobles."[87] The Bilçar was led by a *syndic-général* and met in Ustaritz, provincial capital and seat of the royal bailiwick. The relationship of these local administrative units to the royal administration was a matter of considerable confusion, owing to the changing of administrative units and boundaries. Basse-Navarre was regrouped under eight different *généralités* (usually the territory corresponding to the authority of a royal *intendant*) between 1631 and 1789, and Labourd was under five.

In 1660 Louis XIV journeyed to Saint-Jean-de-Luz to marry Princess Marie-Thérèse of Spain. While there, he presided over a Council which seriously changed the political freedom of Labourd.[88] He decreed that henceforth the Bilçar could meet only in Ustaritz, in the locale of the royal authority of that bailiwick. The Bilçar would still be convened by its *syndic*, but only at the order of the royal *bailli* and meeting only in his presence. The order further stipulated that anyone taking part in assemblies exercising customary rights over justice and other matters would be punished by detention and confiscation of property. Despite pitched resistance, the tide had begun to turn away from the *fors*.

The traditional foral exemptions from taxation began to give way to increasing royal taxation. The total taxation of the province had risen to more than 70,000 on the eve of the Estates General in 1789,[89] and the total debt of Labourd to the royal treasury exceeded 140,000 livres by 1784. Typical of the local reaction was the near riot in Hasparren in 1784 at the attempted imposition of the *gabelle,* in direct violation of the *furs.*[90] As royal *intendant* Neville remarked in 1787, the populace of Labourd "is naturally disquieted and jealous of what it calls its privileges."[91] It was this concern over the steady erosion of foral privileges, the precipitous increase in taxation, and the vitiating of local political liberties which reflected itself in the Basque reaction to the convocation of the Estates General.

The Convocation of the Estates General

Cy veult le roy, cy veult la loy.
What the king wants, the law wants.[92]

By the summer of 1788 the fiscal crisis of the state made the convening of the Estates General of France—the first in 175 years—a political necessity. So far had the representative process fallen into desuetude that Louis XVI, in an *Arrêt du conseil* of July 5, 1788, ordered officials and archivists throughout France to collect and send to Versailles any information regarding the calling of previous Estates General.[93] An edict of August 4, 1788, set the opening of the Estates for April 1789. On October 4, 1788, an assembly of notables met to discuss representation and recommended that: (1) representation should be by bailiwick, as was the case in 1614, but proportionate to population; (2) the representation of the nobility and that of the clergy together should equal that of the Third Estate; and (3) each group would elect its representatives from among its own members. On December 27, 1788, the Council accepted the first two of these recommendations. The election of members of the Estates was a novelty, even in provinces where the provincial estates had continued to meet.[94] Representatives usually sat ex-officio or were appointed. The need to elect representatives, and to draft lists of local grievances, led to the holding of more than 40,000 local meetings in the months preceding the Estates General. While elections were supposed to take place during February and March, administrative confusion and petitions for special exceptions (including those of Labourd and Basse-Navarre) forced the delay of the opening of the Estates until early May.

According to Crane Brinton, the political class of France was clearly divided as to the purpose of the coming Estates.[95] On the conservative side, including the king and his court as well as most of the nobility and upper clergy, the feeling was that the Estates would confine itself to ways of forestalling the budgetary crisis and the specter of state bankruptcy. On the other side was the reformist camp which wanted a constitution to replace constitutionless absolutism. Many of the subsequent *Cahiers* would attest to the popularity of the constitutional idea.

France at that time was a rural society of significant inequalities. Its total population was approximately 26 million people.[96] The nobility totaled no more than 400,000 people or less than 2 percent of the population. According to Palmer, priests, monks, and nuns numbered approximately 100,000, or proportionately fewer than the Protestant clergy in England at the time. The aggregate population of the fifty largest French cities was only 2,200,000, but all of these fifty cities were larger than Boston at the time of the Boston Tea Party.

Nor was the distinction between the Estates indicative of a clearly defined social hierarchy. The impoverishment of many of the landed nobility contrasted with the growing wealth of the urban merchant class. Moreover, as Palmer notes, after 1783, *every one* of the 135 French bishops was a nobleman.[97] If occasional challenges were made of the credentials of deputies elected in the local assemblies, the Third Estate which ultimately gathered in Versailles included three priests and approximately twelve nobles. The result of these local elections was the composition of an Estates General in 1789 of 1,248 delegates, including 300 nobles, 300 clergy, and 648 from the Third Estate.[98] The occupational profile of the Third Estate in 1789 is not dissimilar to that of most Western parliaments in the twentieth century: more than half were lawyers; 278 held some kind of government office; 85 were merchants or businessmen; 67 lived off income, generally from land; and 31 were from professions, usually doctors.[99] It is hard to identify a single peasant or worker. As Palmer speculates, the presence of peasants in the Estates would doubtless have made it more docile.

The content of the surviving 522 of the total 615 *Cahiers de doléances* prepared for the Estates General shows a France of great diversity and provides a remarkable cross section of the hopes and aspirations of local France during those few months in the spring of 1789. As Brinton notes:

> Village cahiers almost wholly eschew, not only metaphysics, but all general ideas; they demand concrete, specific reforms—abolition of various dues, which are named (almost never do they ask for the abolition of the feudal system as a whole), abolition of game laws, monopolies, and so on.[100]

Hyslop's painstaking analysis of the *Cahiers* shows that the most frequent demand was an equal tax liability, a renunciation of privileges, or both.[101] Many called for administrative and legal uniformity. Only thirty-seven of the *Cahiers*, generally of the clergy or Third Estate, manifested a regionalism or provincial consciousness greater than a national spirit. Among them were *Cahiers* in Béarn, Labourd, and Navarre. As Hyslop points out:

> The cahiers of Navarre, Béarn, and of the clergy and third estate of Ustaritz looked upon their respective territories as separate entities. The Clergy of Ustaritz were particularly vehement: they spoke of the purity of their blood, of the military vigor of the Basques, of the Basque language, customs, and traditions.[102]

The defense of regional identity and privileges was more characteristic of border than interior provinces. If this was a minority position in the early Revolution, it was nonetheless a strong one among the Basques. Hyslop argues that "regionalism was stronger on the Spanish frontier than anywhere else in France. . . . None were more separatist than the territories of Béarn and Navarre."[103]

The Basque Reaction to the Convocation of the Estates General

A complete analysis of the events surrounding Basque reaction to the Estates General lies outside the scope of this chapter. A number of excellent English and French sources exist on this period (among those already cited: Castelli, Goyheneche, Etcheverry, Darricau, Yturbide, and Haristoy). However, several of the issues which emerged in this period are important defenses of traditional Basque privileges or *fors*. Still others strike at the very heart of the philosophical arguments surrounding the unification of republican France and its division into *départements* during the early Constituent Assembly.

LABOURD

On January 1, 1789, a young salaried lobbyist in Paris (and later deputy) for the Bilçar of Labourd, Dominique-Joseph Garat, asked for the right of Labourd to have its own representation in the coming Estates General.[104] Despite his entreaties, the royal decree of January 24, 1789, amalgamated Labourd with Bayonne, itself a secondary unit within the *sénéchaussée* of Lannes, under the *généralité* of Bordeaux. The other provinces of Soule and Basse-Navarre were under the *généralité* of Auch. The *syndic* of the Bilçar of Labourd, M. Haramboure, protested this decision in a letter to the king dated March 8, 1789:

But considering . . . that Labourd forms in itself a province which has its leaders, its assemblies, its constitution, its particular law . . . it had to think that it should have been treated as his majesty intended. . . . Considering finally that the interests of Labourd are in formal and constant opposition with those of its neighbors . . . one cannot disguise the evident danger to which it would have been exposed, a more particular danger for a *pays* of which the administration, the customs, the mores, the languages, in a word, everything which constitutes it, are absolutely unique in the kingdom and can only be developed for the Estates General by Basque deputies.[105]

On March 28, 1789, the crown reversed itself, announcing "sufficient motives for according to the Basques a direct deputation" of four deputies, one each from the nobility and clergy, and two from the Third Estate.[106] Elections began in the parish church of Ustaritz on Sunday, April 19, 1789, at 10 A.M., presided over by Joachim D'Urtubie, baron of Garro, age sixteen, and last royal *bailli* of Labourd.

Among those present were 12 nobles, in addition to 7 representatives of noble holdings (including 3 widows), 69 members of the clergy; and 124 members of the Third Estate.[107] The Third Estate soon moved its meetings to the locale of the Bilçar and spurned requests to meet in common session with the clergy and nobility.

The nobility elected as its deputy M. Caupenne, nobleman of Saint-Pée, with M. Haraneder, vicomte de Macaye, as his substitute.[108] Caupenne withdrew upon his election in favor of the vicomte de Macaye. The clergy, in an apparent split between parish priests and the high clergy, elected the *abbé* of Saint-Esteben, *curé* of Ciboure, by one vote. The election of the two deputies of the Third Estate seemed predestined with the candidacies of Dominique-Joseph Garat, agent of the Bilçar in Paris, and M. d'Ithurbide, his benefactor and architect of Labourd's successful plea for a separate delegation to the Estates General. Ultimately, Dominique-Joseph Garat was elected, as was his older brother, Dominique Garat, both of whom were lawyers admitted to the bar before the Parlement of Bordeaux. The elder Garat represented Labourd in the Revolutionary Assembly through September 30, 1791, before returning to Ustaritz, where he led the municipal administration before his death in 1799.[109] His fame was eclipsed by that of his son Dominique, who was reputedly the most famous singer of his time and a favorite of the queen and royal court.

The younger Basque deputy, Dominique-Joseph Garat, was one of the most illustrious figures in Basque political history.[110] After representing Labourdin interests (futilely, as we will see) in the early Constituent Assembly, he was twice appointed minister (first of justice, then of interior). After succeeding Danton as minister of justice on October 12, 1792, Garat was charged with informing Louis XVI of his impending execution, though having opposed it himself:

> What! You're going to take a move as cruel as death, a move which has a hundred inconveniences and not a single advantage? . . . As for me, I would have Louis led by gendarmes until the frontier; and there, I would say to him: "You are king by the law of the sword, here is your own; go, if you want, the way of emigrants. You are king by the grace of God, he will be the judge between us." [111]

In 1793 Garat was appointed minister of interior; in 1795 member of the French Institute; and in 1798 ambassador to Naples. He was later appointed one of the first sixty senators under Napoleon, count of the empire, and commander of the legion of honor. In his later years, he approached Napoleon with plans for the unification of the Basque provinces of France and Spain, though no evidence remains of his reception.[112] He died in Ustaritz on December 9, 1833.

SOULE

On February 19, 1789, the king issued regulations for the election of four deputies from Soule to the Estates General, still intended to begin the following April 27 in Versailles.[113] The province responded, in a March 15 letter from Clément de Meharon de Maytie, counselor to the king and lieutenant-general in Mauléon, to the keeper of seals, asking for a delay in the selection of deputies and preparation of *Cahiers:* "We will not imitate our Basque neighbors; . . . our customs and language are different." [114] It was not until May 5, the day the Estates General began in Versailles, that Maytie convened the Souletin assembly for the election of deputies and the drawing up of the *Cahiers.* The assembly met from May 18 until July 3, 1789. It was due to the lateness of the gathering in Soule that Hyslop includes the *Cahiers* from the three Souletin estates among seventeen she found suspect. She is, however, of the opinion that Soule is indicative of those remote provinces where news of Paris and Versailles had not penetrated, so that the *Cahiers*—though drafted while the Estates General was already in session for some weeks in Versailles—are uncontaminated and hence valid indicators of provincial sentiment. In addition to the demands for preservation of the customary privileges described earlier, one rural *Cahier* asked for the integration of Mauléon, its largest town, into Soule, since currently "Mauléon is as foreign to Soule as if it were in Turkey." [115]

Among the demands of the Souletins were abolition of the royal decrees of

June 28, 1730, which practically abolished the Estates of Soule, and the preservation of Souletin privileges, which the *Cahier* of the nobility argued had
been granted to Soule for the defense of the frontier and were now needed
due to the poverty of the province.[116] The nobility called for the retention
or reinstitution of a number of their privileges and exemption from others
found onerous. Among the latter was the ritual payment to the owner of the
Chateau of Mauléon the sum of three thousand livres for providing protection of justice in the province and a request that the level of support for the
clergy be proportionate to the "amount of really useful work they do."[117]

The *Cahier* of the Third Estate called for the equal sharing of the tax burden among the three orders and asked that those taxes collected were to go
directly into the royal treasury and not for the benefit of local tax collectors.
The Third Estate demanded that its members be eligible for civil, clerical,
and military positions and that promotions be based on merit and ability
alone.[118] Occupants of common lands were to be driven off, and the lands
were again to be used for common benefit. In short, one sees in the Souletin
Cahiers, as in those of Labourd, a welter of discrete local interests embroi-
dered onto a fabric of provincial demands asserted by all three orders for the
defense and enhancement of traditional privileges.

The representatives of the three Estates gathered in the Capuchin church
in Mauléon on May 18, 1789 (fully two weeks after the Estates General had
been convened in Versailles). The nobility was represented by 48 nobles,
1 priest, 1 female holder of a fief, 4 women of undetermined civil status,
and 1 woman serving as guardian of her children.[119] The clergy was represented by 47 priests, 25 holders of benefices, 1 deputy from a monastery,
and 2 priests and a commander of the Order of Malta. The Third Estate
numbered 142 deputies, representing 69 towns, parishes, or communes.

The nobility elected as its representative the marquis d'Uhart, after ascer-
taining in a written correspondence with Versailles that minors under the
age of twenty-five were indeed eligible to serve if deemed capable.[120] The
clergy elected Monseigneur Villoutreix de Faye, bishop of Oloron. The Third
Estate elected M. d'Arraing, mayor of Mauléon, and M. d'Escuret-Labourde,
a *notaire* from Mauléon, later replaced by M. d'Etcheberry, *curé* of Mauléon.[121]

BASSE-NAVARRE

As we have seen, the constitutional status of Basse-Navarre was completely
different from that of either Labourd or Soule. On the eve of the Revolution,
Basse-Navarre remained a separate kingdom, ruled by the king of Navarre,
who had also been king of France since the time of Henri IV. As a result,
the status of Navarre in the Estates General of France was particular, since
it was not a French province like the others. Thus, Navarre had refused to

be represented in the Estates General of 1649, a political precedent which the Navarrese believed would have been "contrary to their rights and privileges." [122]

So the Navarrese reacted with understandable alarm to the royal letter of February 19, 1789, convening Navarre *as a province like others* to elect deputies to the forthcoming Estates General of France. By March 27 the clergy and nobility of Navarre had declared that it was not a province of France. [123] Resisting demotion to the status of province, the Navarrese Estates argued to their king, "To the contrary, following the edict of 1620, Navarre must always be considered a distinct and separate kingdom in that which touches its primordial freedoms." [124] The three Navarrese Estates argued that their convocation as a province was "as to Navarre, irregular, illegal, and anticonstitutional." [125] As the momentum of the coming Revolution would demonstrate, Navarrese confidence in the king was, at best, naïve:

> But a reflected examination of the constituent rights of your kingdom of Navarre dissipated their alarms. They quickly saw reborn from their assemblies the feelings of confidence which your justice and your paternal goodness cease not to inspire in them. It is to your majesty, sire, to justify their security, it is to warn you against new surprises that they pass themselves before the foot of the throne. [126]

In response to the Navarrese protests, the king issued a proclamation on April 1 clarifying his earlier decree of February 19, which stated that Navarre "cannot be bound by the rulings made for the provinces of France." [127]

Even these reassurances did little to calm the Navarrese disquiet, and the constitutional theme dominated their *Cahier* to the king, which exceeded 100 pages in length. As the Navarrese Estates argued in their unified *Cahier* to the king, "Navarre is not a province of the kingdom of France . . . but distinct and independent of the kingdom of France." [128]

The resolution of Navarre was thus hardened, tempered by the historic defense of their privileges and *fueros,* and compounded by the isolation of distance and delayed communication with Versailles. Meeting the evening before, and a world away from the king's concession of April 1, the Navarrese Estates decided on March 31 to send deputies to Louis XVI, as king of Navarre, in order to argue for the preservation of their traditional liberties. As to the relationship of Navarre to the Estates General of France, one Navarrese delegate argued before the Estates of Navarre of March 31:

> The same deputies will be charged with the powers of the Estates of Navarre in order to present themselves to the Estates General of France, to make known to them the constitution and independence of Navarre,

the impossibility . . . of renouncing this constitution and this independence and by consequence to declare themselves members of the Estates General of France, until these Estates General have given themselves a constitution as good or better than that of Navarre. . . . They declare . . . that they can neither ask for nor accept a deliberative voice in the Estates General of France . . . because to deliberate on the form of the French constitution would be . . . to renounce the constitution of Navarre.[129]

These arguments formed the heart of Navarrese strategy during late summer and early fall of 1789 as the Estates General of France was transformed into a National Assembly, the Constituent Assembly of the early Revolution. This argument would later be made in a letter written by M. de Polverel, *syndic* of the Estates Navarre, and read before the Constituent Assembly on October 12, 1789, before the suppression of the title "king of Navarre."[130] Their futile defense of privilege would ultimately give way before a tide of revolutionary change.

It was not until June 15, 1789, that the Estates General of Navarre finally met in Saint-Jean-Pied-de-Port. Two days later the Estates General of France, in session since May 5, declared itself the National Assembly of France. It was not until July 4 that the Navarrese proceeded to elect a delegation "to the king." Making one concession to the king, the Estates Navarre agreed to elect two representatives from the Third Estate to join one each from the clergy and nobility, as well as a *syndic*, a secretary, and a guard to complete the Navarrese delegation to the king. The nobility elected M. de Logras, marquis of Olhonce; the clergy elected the nineteen-year-old bishop of Bayonne, Monseigneur Pavée de Villevielle; and the Third Estate elected Arnaud de Vivie, of Garris, and Jean-Baptiste de Franchistéguy, notary from Saint-Jean-Pied-de-Port. M. de Polverel was chosen as *syndic*.[131]

From the Estates General to the National Assembly of France

The actual opening of the Estates General on May 5, 1789, was surrounded by the signs of political and economic collapse. The mood of the common people and nature of the fiscal crisis were a somber backdrop for the pageantry and gaiety of the royal procession that opened the Estates in Versailles.[132] Despite nearly a year of anticipation since the previous July, neither the king nor Jacques Necker, his chief advisor, had prepared any program of their own to control events. This proved to be a fatal strategic error because it not only forced the crown into a defensive posture, but gave the advantage to the reformist camp and to popular passions as events unfolded. Second,

the harshness of the winter of 1788–1789, and the accompanying poor harvest, lent a personal immediacy to the general economic crisis of the French
state. In the Basque country, as elsewhere in France, the poor harvest struck
most harshly in the urban area along the coast where the population was dependent on the surplus agricultural production of the rural Basque interior.
In Bayonne in 1788–1789 the problems of hunger, shortages, and hoarding
were reflected in bread riots, theft, and unrest.[133] Bread riots demanding a
fixed price for bread at three sous occurred in late September. Forty peasants were arrested in Boucau in October trying to loot a grain boat. Along
the Basque coast in 1789 a kilo (2.2 pounds) of wheat cost one-quarter of
a typical day's salary. The Estates General which convened that spring in
Versailles was a house whose windows opened onto a population needing
economic and institutional change.[134]

   That institutional change came not with the storming of the Bastille prison
on July 14 and the liberation of its *seven* prisoners, but with the decision of
the Third Estate on June 17 to constitute itself as a "National Assembly" bent
not on fiscal but on constitutional reform. Soon elements of the clergy and
the nobility rallied to the side of the Third Estate. On June 27 the king was
obliged to ask the three Estates to merge to form a French National Assembly. Forces were now unleashed which would leave revolutionary changes
in their wake. Implementation of the constitutional idea came through a host
of economic and social reforms throughout late summer and into early 1790
as the republican camp applied its measures of "liberty, equality, and fra-
ternity" to the welter of social, economic, and political inequalities that was
France of the *ancien régime*.

From August 4, 1789, to January 15, 1790:
The End of Provincial Privileges

Despite the transformation of the Estates General into the National Assembly
in late June 1789, the duty of the Labourdin Basque deputies remained unchanged: to defend and enhance the province's privileges and *fors*. Their conservatism also was manifested in their regard for the king. On July 15, 1789,
the day after the fall of the Bastille, M. Haraneder, the vicomte de Macaye,
representative of the nobility of Labourd, found himself near Louis XVI as
the king returned on foot to the palace after having addressed the National
Assembly. The Basque nobleman, in a voice which carried to the king, flat-
tered the monarch by reporting that his Basque compatriots were unhappy
at being unable to see "so good a king."[135] The king responded by saying

the people should not give up hope of seeing him one day. Haraneder then received the king's permission to report their conversation in his province and concluded by asking the king to accept his sincerest wishes and remembrance of his fellow Basques. The chance encounter was then reported back to the Bilçar of Labourd in Ustaritz in a letter dated July 27, 1789, and signed by all four Basque deputies in the new National Assembly: the vicomte de Macaye, the *abbé* of Saint Esteben and the brothers Garat.[136] The optimism of this chance and superficial encounter would be eclipsed within the week by the assembly's actions of August 4, which would themselves cast doubt upon the judgment and loyalty of Labourd's deputies at Versailles.

AUGUST 4 AND THE END OF PROVINCIAL PRIVILEGES

Throughout July and early August a number of philosophical and practical debates centered on the question of a new constitution, individual political rights, the status of the three Estates in a combined assembly, and the electoral process needed for the abolition "of ancient and established laws." [137] Should a two-thirds majority be required, as the bishop of Chartres proposed, then the nobility might reasonably hope to attract sufficient support from the high clergy (every bishop in France on the eve of the Revolution was of noble origins) and the Third Estate to prevent the dismantlement of the existing system of orders and privileges.[138] As M. Parisot, deputy from Bar-sur-Seine, wrote on the morning of August 5:

> Persuaded as we were that the nobility and clergy were only trying to delay matters and do nothing . . . we felt that as long as the two privileged classes had any privileges whatsoever private interests would overrule the general good.[139]

The decision to assault these privileges was orchestrated by the Breton Club, a caucus of Breton deputies which began in late April and swelled as the Breton deputies admitted other like-minded deputies to their council.[140] To be led by the duc d'Aiguillon, one of the largest landowners in France, the Breton Club showed a notable political acumen in using liberal members of the nobility to attack the privileges of their own class. The club resolved to use, in one participant's words, "a kind of magic," employing a truce on the constitutional question in order to eliminate the privileges of classes, provinces, towns, and corporations.[141]

These discussions were taking place in a climate of increasing civil insurrection throughout France, settling a host of local accounts which masqueraded behind a façade of revolutionary redistributive justice unleashed with the fall of the Bastille barely three weeks before. The deputies who gathered on the evening of August 4 were well aware of the threat posed by the growing climate of public disorder.

Despite the plan of the Breton Club to use the duc d'Aiguillon to initiate its "magic," he was beaten to the podium by the opportunistic vicomte de Noailles. Noailles was hardly the symbol of a nobility willfully renouncing its privileges since, being referred to as "Jean-sans-terre" as the youngest son of a noble family and without significant holdings of his own, his gesture was made without any personal loss.[142] But Noailles was warmly received, and his genius lay in evoking the cause of the public "effervescence" outside the Assembly. Noailles pointed out that the Assembly had been debating the public good for three months while the peasantry waited impatiently for relief from specific grievances. As Noailles argued, for the peasantry, "the public good is, above all, the definite objects they desire."[143] Thus, the Assembly could calm them not with words, but with the abolition of the feudal system. Brinton notes:

> So began the night of August 4; before it was over dozens of deputies had appeared at the orator's desk and given up privilege after privilege—some of which, indeed, they had hardly been authorized by their constituents to give up. When early in the morning of the 5th the tired president had succeeded in stopping the flow of sacrifices, the old regime had been in principle destroyed.[144]

While the National Assembly no doubt perceived that the peasantry was leading the charge for the abolition of feudal dues, as Hyslop points out, more *Cahiers* of the nobility had called for either abolition of privileges or equality in taxation (or both) than had the *Cahiers* of the Third Estate.[145] As Barère reported in his memoirs, Noailles had come to him before the debates on August 4 and argued the political necessity for a member of the nobility to propose the abolition of feudalism.[146]

By all accounts, a kind of contagion spread through the assembly that evening, as speaker after speaker came forth to make sacrifices in the spirit of *égalité* and *fraternité*.[147] Barère noted in his own detailed minutes of the session, "The most generous propositions succeeded themselves with a rapidity of which only an understanding of the French character can give an idea."[148] Before the evening was over, nearly thirty resolutions had been passed, nearly all in unanimity. Their goal was the elimination of feudal and class privileges and provincial liberties as well. Before the Assembly adjourned at 2 A.M., the deputies had put to rest the *ancien régime*. As the first article of the official decree of these decisions states, "The National Assembly destroys the feudal regime entirely."[149]

The provincial liberties which the Basque deputies had been charged with defending were very much caught up in the general contagion. It was article 10 of the official decree of the events of August 4 which spelled the end of provincial liberties and particularisms:

A national constitution and public liberty being more advantageous to the provinces than the privileges enjoyed by some of them and of which the sacrifice is necessary for the intimate union of all parts of the empire, it is declared that all the particular privileges of the provinces, principalities, lands, cantons, towns, and communities of inhabitants, be they pecuniary or of all other natures, are abolished without return and will remain included in the common law of all the French.[150]

So complex were the issues involved that the welter of decisions made on the evening of August 4 were not fully codified until August 11. A number of committees were created to oversee the decrees, including the Comité des Droits Féodaux created on August 12 to implement the redemption of former feudal rights.[151] By August 20 the Assembly was able to turn again to discussion on the proposed "Declaration of the Rights of Man and of the Citizen." The revised text which passed on August 26 was the long-awaited constitution and the "death certificate" of the *ancien régime*.[152]

BASQUE REACTIONS TO THE EVENTS OF AUGUST 4

Despite the republican zeal which animated the Assembly on the night of August 4, in the clear light of morning it was evident that many delegates had exceeded or violated their mandates in voting to dismantle the old order. Still, many delegates who spoke on August 4 took pains to state that they spoke in their own names alone and that any actions taken by the Assembly would have to be ratified by their constituents. This was the position taken by the Souletin deputy who spoke that night, the *only* Basque deputy to participate in the debate surrounding the elimination of provincial liberties.[153] The record reveals that the Labourdin Basques were silent throughout the debate and acquiesced to the will of the majority—both actions in apparent violation of the mandate of the Bilçar. The delegation from Navarre refused on principle even to enter the chamber as observers. As M. de Logras, deputy of the Navarrese nobility, explained their refusal: "It is an established principle in the National Assembly that the simple presence of deputies is an acquiescence to all that which might be determined by the Assembly."[154]

The news of the Assembly's actions was passively received in Soule. But they provoked a quick and hostile reaction from the Bilçar of Labourd. On September 1, 1789, the Bilçar sent an extraordinary letter to the president of the National Assembly effectively repudiating the action of its delegation:

The French Basques of Labourd have never ceased repeating . . . to the government that their present constitution is the only one under which they can exist. Commanded by this imperious law, they ordered . . . their deputies to maintain it. A decree of the National Assembly has just informed them of the general abolition of the privileges of the provinces. . . . If their deputies voluntarily sacrificed their privileges or were forced to do so . . . it was in being too caught up by the *élan* of patriotism: they forgot the limits of their mandate, or they didn't have the courage to present this opposition. . . . The Bilçar doesn't fear saying that the voluntary abandonment that their representatives made of their privileges is radically and essentially *null* as contrary to their mandate. . . . Their regrets are even stronger since each of the benefits that the decrees of the National Assembly has so wisely determined for the state not only misses its mark in their regard, but evidently even worsens their lot.[155]

Four days later, on September 5, 1789, the Bilçar drafted a letter to the Labourdin deputies in Versailles, enclosing a copy of their recent letter to the president of the National Assembly. This second letter constituted a harsh reprimand for their silence on August 4:

We must not omit repeating to you that there is no other means for you to rehabilitate yourselves in the opinion of your constituents than in the complete success of your demands. . . . We must not hide from you, sirs, that the question of your removal had begun to appear in the Bilçar; we thought it better to quell it, but we only did so in the hope of more obedience on your part; we will also not hide from you that if you betray this hope no consideration will prevent us from carrying out this humiliating threat.[156]

Clearly, the Bilçar in Ustaritz had begun to have doubts about how representative the Garat brothers were of their province of birth: "the Labourdins would have had little to say if . . . their deputies had been able to add an understanding so precious of the locality; of a *patrie* in which they have never lived."[157]

The Bilçar then turned to the preparation of the detailed, if futile, rebuttal to the actions of the National Assembly and to the criticism levied against the province in the contemporary press. This pointed summary of the *fors* and privileges of the province was drafted on November 18, 1789. Among its more lyric passages:

The National Assembly will have difficulty in believing that there exists a single canton in the kingdom that could not feel the happy influence of the benevolent star which lit the night of August 4. How will it believe that there is one which its actions harm so painfully? All seems thus lost for the Labourdins, all seems to chase them from a land on which from father to son they let fall their sweat and their tears.[158]

The Bilçar thus failed in convincing the National Assembly to maintain its provincial liberties and *fors*. The only further issue concerned the imminent territorial redivision of France. Basing its desire on cultural and linguistic affinities, the Bilçar asked, if its current status could not be maintained, "to be united with the provinces of Basse-Navarre and Soule *only*, with the condition nonetheless that the assemblies of the department be alternated among the three Basque provinces."[159] Following this meeting on November 18, 1789, the Bilçar of Labourd met no more.

THE NAVARRESE REACTION

The nature of the Navarrese response was more complex, given the mandate of its delegation and its refusal to participate in the Assembly's debates. The deputies had been appointed by the Estates of Navarre as a delegation to Louis XVI, as king of Navarre. Their charge was to submit their lengthy *Cahier* to him and to ask that he swear once more as king to uphold the privileges and *fors* of his subjects. The king, reluctant to inflame the Assembly by making the pledge and recognizing the quandary posed by the actions of August 4 taken in the absence of the Navarrese delegation, called for another meeting of the Estates of Navarre in a letter on September 8.[160] The Estates of Navarre reconvened on September 19 in Saint-Jean-Pied-de-Port. The king's agent, the marquis de Lons, had been instructed to suspend the Navarrese Estates if it appeared the Navarrese would act against the decrees passed by the National Assembly on August 4. Thus, when the Navarrese nobility and clergy refused to accept the actions of the National Assembly—and thereby refused union with France—Lons temporarily suspended the meeting of the Navarrese Estates on September 22, after only three days in session. In fact, this would be the last meeting of the Estates of Navarre.

Meanwhile, the National Assembly had begun debate on a proposal to suppress the title "king of Navarre." Heretofore the title used in common currency was "king of France and of Navarre." It was the Labourdin Basque deputy Garat (the elder) who defended the rights of the Navarrese in their principled absence:

It is not without good reason that our kings have kept the title "king of Navarre." That province has no deputies here; however, it named some who came to size up the situation but did not present themselves; it claims to have the right to hold its own Estates General; it considers itself a separate kingdom, etc.[161]

Garat further warned that suppression of the title king of Navarre would encourage Spanish ambitions in that area.

On October 11 the king refused again to meet the Navarrese delegation, citing their refusal to participate in the deliberations of the National Assembly. For the Navarrese, this was tantamount to refusal to retake the pledge of loyalty to his subjects.

During the session of October 12, the Assembly heard read the defense of Navarrese privileges drafted by Polverel, its *syndic*, at the request of the Navarrese Estates.[162] The Navarrese declared:

> The Estates of Navarre believed they should not combine themselves with France and renounce their constitution until France could offer them a constitution as good as their own; in waiting they offered and asked of the National Assembly a treaty of federation [between France and Navarre].[163]

Polverel excused the absence of the Navarrese from the Assembly, arguing that the Assembly would have interpreted their presence as an act of adhesion to its decrees and as a renunciation by Navarre of its "constitution, its independence, and its privileges."[164]

A number of arguments were advanced in the succeeding debate that suggested how central was the question of the status of Navarre to the *novus ordo saeculorum* being constructed by the Assembly. M. Salicetti of Corsica stated that if the Navarrese demand was honored, preserving the title "king of France and of Navarre," his *Cahier* ordered him to demand that "king of Corsica" also be added. Other deputies extended the logic, demanding the addition of their constituencies: Guyenne, Marseilles, the duchies of Lorraine and Barrois. As the count of Mirabeau cautioned the Assembly:

> Nothing is more contrary to the unity of the monarchy than this variety of titles; instead of being a fusion of homogeneous parts, this empire would be composed of isolated and disparate little parts, which would not wait long to become divided.[165]

The Assembly then brought cloture to its debate by deciding that nothing should be added to the title "king of the French." The debate on this topic ended with cries of "Long live the king of the French."

Meanwhile, Polverel persisted in his stalwart defense of Navarre's privileges. In a manuscript on Navarre's constitution published in late 1789, which attempted to rebut the actions of the Assembly and the king, Polverel argued passionately:

I say it with regret, but there remains for Navarre but one move to make, and that is to declare itself an independent republic and to govern itself by itself. One has given it abundantly the right. The Ministers who dissolved its Estates violated its constitution. By this fact alone it would be released from its pledge of fidelity if there were a pledge. . . . There cannot exist a tie between Navarre and the king except by a pledge of reciprocal fidelity. . . . The king cannot be proclaimed, recognized, except after the pledge. The refusal of the pledge has prevented there from being any tie between Navarre and the king. . . . Those that doubt that Navarre can conserve its independence do not know either its mountains, or the intrepidity of the Basques, or their love of liberty.[166]

Despite these sentiments, which were undoubtedly widely shared in Navarre, the ancient kingdom capitulated, and the National Assembly learned on December 30, 1789, that "Navarre adheres to the decree integrating it with France."[167]

The Division of France into Departments

Since November 11, 1789, a committee of the National Assembly had been preparing the administrative redivision of France into *départements*. As Mazure noted in 1839:

The division of the kingdom of France into *départements* was the great measure of the Constituent Assembly. . . . To find a secret for reducing to unity all this . . . matter so complicated, this network of links without end, which each had their character, their own physiognomy, their laws, their rights, that was to accomplish the Revolution.[168]

As M. Duqesnoy pointed out, it was clear that one goal of this reorganization was to combat the persistence of provincial loyalties and localism: "The division of France . . . must have as its goal to mix spirits and mores, in such a manner that there will only be Frenchmen in France, and not Provençaux, Normands, etc."[169]

In fact, as the Abbé Grégoire found in his detailed survey of language use in France in this period, the existence of a homogeneous "French" nation was clearly more hoped for than fact:

One can assure without exaggeration that at least six million Frenchmen [of a total French population of twenty-five million], especially in the provinces, are ignorant of the national language; that an equal number are nearly incapable of holding a sustained conversation; that in the last analysis, the number of those who speak it fluently does not exceed three million, and probably the number of those who write it correctly is smaller still.[170]

Thus, Grégoire argued that France, with more than thirty languages, dialects, or *patois* spoken on the eve of the Revolution, was a "linguistic tower of Babel."[171] What Grégoire favored in reality was bilingualism, a knowledge of *both* French and local languages, which would aid in the development of a national spirit.

Others of the Jacobin persuasion were less generous. As the Revolution stalled and began to turn back upon itself, an increasing preoccupation lay in identifying enemies of the Revolution as causes of its failure. Caught up in this revolutionary paranoia, Bertrand Barère de Vieuzac gave his famous report for the Comité de Salut Public to the Convention on 8 pluviôse An II (January 27, 1794): "federalism and superstition speak low-Breton; emigration and hate for the Revolution speak German; the counterrevolution speaks Italian; and *fanaticism speaks Basque.*"[172] Ironically, the timing of early revolutionary policy on language use in 1790 suggests that it may have been the most lasting contribution of the protest the Basque deputies made over the division of France into *départements*. For it was two days after Basque arguments against their inclusion in the department of the Basses-Pyrénées (on linguistic and cultural grounds) that the Assembly grudgingly gave way to linguistic reality and ordered on January 14, 1790, that all revolutionary decrees be translated into local languages and dialects and no longer appear only in the still largely unintelligible French. Thus, for example, the statement from the Declaration of the Rights of Man "La loi est l'expression de la volonté générale" was followed, in this case in Gascon, with "La loi est l'expression de la bolontat générale."[173] On November 7, 1792, the Assembly ordered the minister of justice, the former Labourdin Basque deputy Dominique-Joseph Garat (the younger), who had replaced Danton on October 12, 1792, to translate laws, "en langues allemande, italienne, catalane, basque et bretonne."[174]

On January 12, 1790, the National Assembly turned to discussion of the proposed *département* of the Basses-Pyrénées, which would include Béarn, Soule, Labourd, Basse-Navarre, and Bayonne. The Labourdin Basque deputy, Garat the Elder, was the first to speak:

My request interests but a people poor and hardly numerous. . . . The difference in languages [between the Basques and Béarn] is an insurmountable obstacle. The assemblage that is proposed is physically and morally impossible. Reunite those who speak one language with others who speak another . . . they will finish by separating themselves, like . . . the tower of Babel.[175]

Despite the eloquence of the Garats, and the vicomte de Macaye, who also evoked the differences in languages, the Assembly was impatient to proceed to approve the committee's recommendation. This was done; no sooner than was the vote completed than Garat the younger took the podium to protest one last time in vain:

There remains for me one duty to fulfill; it is demanded by my constituents, by my reason, by my conscience: nothing in the world could make me forget it. In a unanimous deliberation, my province protests![176]

Yet, over Basque opposition, the National Assembly voted on January 15, 1790, to divide France into eighty-three administrative departments, including the Basses-Pyrénées, which would combine the Pays Basque with Béarn.[177]

Less an Ending Than a Beginning: The Revolution and Its Aftermath

By January 1793 the Jacobin revolutionaries in Paris had succeeded in eliminating most symbols of the *ancien régime;* to the early legislation of the Constituent Assembly abolishing provincial liberties and feudal rights were added the civil constitution of the clergy in 1790; revolutionary laws mandating equal inheritance among heirs; the declaration of the First Republic on September 21, 1792; and finally the beheading of Louis XVI on January 21, 1793. Then, on May 31, 1793, began the Terror.

THE TERROR

Guillotines functioned on the Place de la Liberté in Bayonne and the Place de la Liberté (now Place Louis XIV) at Saint-Jean-de-Luz.[178] More than sixty death penalties were pronounced in Bayonne, most for complicity in illegal emigration or correspondence with priests in exile. M. Cavaignac, agent of the revolutionary Convention in Bayonne, wrote in 1793:

There no longer exists a functioning priest in this department. The land of liberty was soiled there more than elsewhere by the presence of resistant priests. Seven or eight *misérables* paid for their infamous projects with their heads.[179]

The revolutionary attack on the church and its clergy was the source of much unrest in the Pays Basque, given the historic centrality of the Catholic faith to Basque identity in France. It was the barrier of language use which permitted the resistance of Basque populations led by Basque priests against the insurgence of the radical and anticlerical republic. As we will see in chapter 2, this confrontation would become one of the central themes in subsequent Basque political culture: virtually identical issues were raised more than a century later during the crisis of separation of church and state of the Third Republic.[180]

Using language as a tool for the exhortation of the faithful against the republican Terror, Basque priests were singled out as explicit targets by the Jacobin camp. As the Abbé Grégoire argued:

> Those that found themselves in the Pyrénées-Orientales in October 1792, will write you that, among the Basques, a gentle and good people, a great number were susceptible to fanaticism, because the [Basque language] is an obstacle to the . . . enlightenment. The same thing has happened in other departments, where the [clergy] based the success of their counterrevolutionary machinations on the ignorance of our language.[181]

Bertrand Barère de Vieuzac voiced similar concerns for the Comité de Salut Public:

> But they have priests, and the priests employ the local languages in order to fanaticize them; but they are ignorant of the French language and the language of the laws of the Republic. It is therefore necessary that they learn it, because despite the differences of language and despite their priests, they are devoted to the Republic.[182]

If the clergy of Soule demonstrated less opposition to the government's legal onslaught against the clergy, the clergy of Basse-Navarre and Labourd were far more hostile. A report from the Directory in Ustaritz on October 14, 1791, found only 26 priests conforming to the state's decrees out of a total of more than 180.[183] On August 26, 1792, the Assembly decreed the banishment of unreconstructed clergy, with a fifteen-day delay. Those attempting to hide would be deported to French Guyana. In some cases, whole clerical orders went into exile, and most Basque clergy leaving the Pays Basque Français crossed the border into Spain. A rich history remains of the local priests and populations who chose to defy, even openly, the anticlerical initiatives of the Revolution.

As we will see in chapter 2, even the much-vaunted revolutionary laws mandating equal inheritance, first passed in 1793, further strengthened the rate of the clergy and Basque customary law. Far from bowing to the Revolution's demands, the voluntary acquiescence of nonheirs to the custom of a single heir kept the ancestral home intact. As chapter 2 shows, the decision of many nonheirs either to emigrate or to enter clerical orders not only reinforced the strength of the clergy but also protected the conservative rural Basque society from the pressures of economic and demographic change occurring elsewhere.

As the Revolution became more fulsome in its ideological purity, it ordered the renaming of local towns and communes throughout France, just as it had earlier issued its calendar (pluviôse, ventôse, brumaire, etc.). Among the more curious of these short-lived name changes in the Pays Basque were Ustaritz (Marat-sur-Nive), Urt (Liberté), Arbonne (Constante), Cambo (La Montagne), Saint-Jean-de-Luz (Chauvin-Dragon), Villefranque (Tricolore), Itxassou (Union), and Baigorri (Thermopyle).[184] Little used or respected, they remain as only curious historical footnotes today.

THE DEPORTATION

The most tragic episode of the revolutionary period in the Pays Basque involved the forced deportation of more than *three thousand* Basques from towns along the Spanish frontier, accused by the Comité de Salut Public of treason with Spain. The immediate justification for the deportation was the desertion of forty-seven young Basque soldiers from Itxassou who bridled at the law mandating universal and forced conscription passed by the Convention in 1793. As the Convention's decree of August 23, 1793, put it, "From this moment and until that when our enemies have been chased from the territory of the republic, all the French are in permanent requisition."[185] The suspicion that the young deserters were exhorted by an exiled priest only stoked the antagonisms of more than a year of war along the Spanish frontier. In reality, however, a number of other factors influenced the severity of the reaction: the revolutionaries' expectation of insurrection or treason by a Basque population still resentful over the loss of its privileges; the inability of agents of the Revolution to proselytize among a Basque population isolated by linguistic barriers; the historic desire of the rural Basque peasantry to be left alone to farm or tend their flocks; and the consuming hostility of the Revolution to a resistant clergy still unusually strong in the Pays Basque. As M. Antoine Richard put it: "The Pays Basque, poorly assimilated, closed in by its language, its mentality, and its mountains to new ideas, was pushed into the arms of Spain by its priests and its nobles."[186]

His statement only echoed the formal accusation made by local agents to the Comité de Salut Public:

You have been instructed for a long time that a large part of the land that was previously called Pays Basque, and principally the part which borders on the Spanish frontier, is inhabited by men that superstition, fanaticism, and love of gold have sold to the Spaniard. This land offers the spectacle, rare elsewhere and particularly odious, of simple farmers and grazers detesting liberty and equality, wishing for the success of the arms of Spain, to which they pass clandestinely their animals and for which they serve as spies against us. This land is so gangrenous that one cannot hope for any progress of the public spirit there so long as the present generation exists; it is the Terror alone that can contain these men.[187]

As a result, the Convention decreed on 13 ventôse An II (March 3, 1794) that the entire populations of the frontier communities of Sare, Itxassou, Ascain, Espelette, Ainhoa, and Souraide and elements of the populations of towns further to the interior like Louhossoa, Cambo, Macaye, and Mendione were to be deported a distance of twenty leagues from the frontier and that their possessions were to be seized and sold to pay for the cost of their deportation and internment.[188] Accordingly, by the end of March, more than three thousand Basques had been forcibly removed from their homes, their possessions confiscated, and deported throughout southwest France, Les Landes, Gers, Lot-et-Garonne, and Béarn. Subsequent provision was made to employ them in public works projects for the good of the Revolution. However, on September 28, 1794, the Basque internees were ordered freed and given permission to return to their homes. If a subsequent decree on September 30 ordered their property returned to them, those returning faced total economic ruin with little remaining but empty homes and land devoid of crops or livestock to survive the coming winter. In fact, of the more than three thousand deportees in March, fewer than *half* survived the interment to return to their homes. More than sixteen hundred Basques died during their exile, included six hundred from Sare alone. Philippe Veyrin calls this the worst episode of the Revolution in southwestern France.[189]

Conclusion

So passed the Revolution among the Basques of France. The end of the Terror and the advent of the Napoleonic Empire returned a measure of calm to the Basque country largely unknown since 1789. Though the land was traversed by French, English, and Spanish armies for a time, these latter-day invaders seemed no more successful in assimilating the Basques than the

Romans, Moors, Richard the Lion-Hearted, or Charlemagne before them. The aftermath of the Revolution found the material and linguistic reality of rural life largely unchanged. As Garat wrote Napoleon in 1803, "The French Revolution even passed over them like a great phenomenon which they little understood and which left them what they were before." [190]

Yet, as we have seen, the Revolution did real violence to Basque institutions and social values. Despite its fraternal intentions, the Revolution served to destroy a highly participatory Basque political culture through abolition of the *fors* and suppression of the Labourdin Bilçar and the Estates of Navarre and Soule. As Goyheneche points out, fewer Basques were eligible to vote in 1830 than had been voting *in a single village* before the Revolution.[191] Hence, the conservative political culture which had greeted the Revolution in 1789 was hardly disabused of its skepticism by its outcome: the suppression of tradition foral liberties, pitched anticlericalism, new laws of inheritance, and the Terror. Religion, Basque language, and private property—the pillars of Basque culture—were all threatened by the republican Revolution. The attack on these dominant ethnic values reinforced the hostility of the Basques and their historic tendency to retreat behind the linguistic barriers of their isolated villages.

Few political avenues were open to the Basques for their political aspirations in postrevolutionary France. To be sure, Garat had approached Napoleon with a proposal to unite the Basque provinces of France and Spain in 1808.[192] Garat mentions in his text the earlier proposal of the Spanish Basque Jesuit Larramendi in 1756,[193] which called for preservation of the *fors* and the creation of united Basque provinces in the Pyrénées.[194] Yet Garat clearly weakened the force of his proposal by identifying the Basques as descendants of the Phoenicians and suggesting that the newly created Basque *départements* be called "New Phoenicia" and "New Tyre." While Napoleon's reaction to the proposal is not known, it is reported in another context that Napoleon greeted Garat, senator, count of the empire, and trusted ambassador, by asking, "Well now, Mr. Garat, how goes the ideology?" [195]

Virtually alone during the empire, Garat was followed by J. Augustin Chaho, who called for Basque national unification and a Basque federation in various writings between 1836 and 1847.[196] Chaho's works remain among the most detailed histories of the Basque resistance to the Romans and offer an early version of many demands of the contemporary Basque movement. But like the earlier Garat, Chaho's rambling theology and mystic cosmology probably prevented his ideas from receiving the serious consideration they merited in his own time.[197] One Spanish scholar referred to Chaho as an amalgam of romanticism and socialism, of the revolutionary, carlist, and encyclopedist.[198] Active during the Revolution of 1848 in Bayonne, and the first

Basque to be buried in a civil ceremony among this Catholic people, Chaho the man and the author provided the bridge between the Revolution and the century to come. For Chaho's vision of *iraultza* was a fitting metaphor for this rural, agrarian people—suggesting revolution not as innovation, but as a cycle of nature, a *return* to a better time.

The French Revolution was an important chapter in the political history of the Basque people. Viewed in hindsight, the Revolution was less a conclusion than an introduction of new and secular forces which would further erode the strength of Basque culture and language use in France. Seen in this light, the revolutionary ideals of 1789—however incomplete—were important as harbingers of things to come. Given the persistence of Basque culture, and the absence of any effective Basque political mobilization, the first three quarters of the nineteenth century seem a scant apostrophe to the republican agenda which would resume under the Third Republic. What was once reality was soon relegated to history, as the *fors* and their privileges entered into the collective memory of the Basque people and as the pressures for cultural assimilation inevitably and inexorably began to grow.

Chapter Two

Clericalism, Cultural Preservation,

and the Tensions of Church and State

in the Pays Basque, 1870–1906

Especially now when so many dissolute elements conspire against our religious mores and the preservation of our Basque language, it is important to defend our poor but noble country against any foreign invader, be it doctrine, legislation, or even manners, which tends to take away the distinction of our nationality. It falls to the clergy, to all the cultured spirits of our country . . . as well as to all men of honor who have not degenerated among foreign races. . . . It falls to all true Basques to support and encourage all that which tends to conserve these two treasures of our ancient family: Catholicism and our language.
Chanoine Adema, 1890[1]

Eskualdun, fededun.
He who is Basque is a believer.
Basque proverb[2]

Despite the lofty aspirations of the Revolution now a century old, by the beginning of the French Third Republic in 1870, travelers would have seen much the same cultural milieu in the rural Basque interior as existed during the Revolution. The interior was still an area of predominant Basque monolingualism, where the social order revolved around the church and the Basque clergy remained the primary ethnic elite. More than a century after the Revolution, the intrusion of the authority of the state remained largely incomplete. In the language of political development, France in the early Third Republic was on the eve of a state-initiated crisis of nation-building. The crisis of separation of church and state which culminated in France in the first years of the twentieth century was but one of several crises of nation-building which marked the politics of the Third Republic. Taken together,

39

they represented the unfinished work of the French Revolution: the pressing
need to create the unified (and still fictive) nation from which the revolutionary state claimed its legitimacy. To paraphrase what Count Massimo
d'Azeglio said of the Italian *risorgimento*, "We have created France. Now we
must create the French."

In the last two decades of the nineteenth century, roughly from 1879 onward, a multifaceted series of policy initiatives emerged from within the
republican camp whose Jacobin motivation represented the most deliberate attempt to implement the principles of the Constituent Assembly since
the Revolution itself. Yet, in the early Third Republic as before, cleavages
persisted between Catholic and anticleric, left and right, and between Paris
and the peripheral provinces, among a host of others. The persistence of
these striated political and social identities and the historic inability of the
French to arrive at community through consensus is further evidence that
the Revolution has never really ended.

The bulk of France's efforts at nation-building in the early Third Republic
took the form of remedial legislation in the fields of education, transporta-
tion, church-state relations, and military conscription. Taken together, these
policy initiatives represented a deliberate attempt by the state to penetrate
a rural society which was, at best, ignorant of the republican state and, at
worst, abidingly hostile toward it. The success of the state in these circumstances would be measured by its ability to effect the social and political
homogenization of rural France in the last years of the nineteenth century.

The Pays Basque in the early Third Republic offers a predominantly stable
pattern of social and political authority which became an increasingly isolated and defensive bastion of conservative clericalism in the anticlerical and
radical policy climate of the new republic. An understanding of the depth
of Basque religiosity is central to the nature of Basque political mobilization in the early Third Republic. Ethnic issues were largely subordinated to
religious ones, and there was no mobilization of the population as Basques
outside of the aegis of the local church. The closeness of this identification
between Basque culture and religion was both the strength of the Basques
during the Third Republic and also their undoing. Should the state break that
link between Basque culture and Catholicism, then Basque culture would
lack both a unifying ethnic elite and the traditional issues of their political
mobilization against the state. In fact, that was the genius of the crisis of
separation of church and state of 1905–1906 in the Basque country. For with
the subsequent neutralization of the Basque clergy in the interests of epis-
copal *Realpolitik*, Basque culture was effectively cast adrift at the turn of the
century; this rudderlessness, in contrast to the rise of Basque nationalism

in Spain in this period, retarded the rise of a secular doctrine of Basque nationalism in France.

In order to explain the nature of Basque political mobilization in this period, in this chapter I will consider the persistence of Basque language use in the Third Republic and its politicization in the hands of the Basque clergy; the nature of the Basque *famille souche*, the way Basque customary law served to thwart revolutionary laws on inheritance, and the resulting importance of emigration and religious ordination in reinforcing the conservative social structure in the Basque interior; the nature of the crisis of separation of church and state and its aftermath in the Basque country; and, finally, the factors which explain the weak impact of Sabino Arana Goiri's doctrine of Basque nationalism, which arose in the Spanish Basque provinces in this period.

The Persistence of the Basque Language in Third Republic France

As we saw in chapter 1, one of the greatest challenges facing the Constituent Assembly in the early years of the Revolution was to reduce the sheer diversity of local dialects and customs in order to extend the control of the French state into areas previously only nominally under central control. In fact, the linguistic fragmentation of France remained substantially unaltered for much of the century following the Revolution, despite much-vaunted Napoleonic reforms in education. Concern over this state of affairs represented a common thread in the fragmentary remains of the reports of the *inspecteurs d'académie*. Maps included in Eugen Weber's magisterial study of peasant society in the Third Republic show how marginal was the hold of French on its territory on the eve of this century.[3] The limits of the *patois*-speaking *départements* reproduced the linguistic boundaries of France's seven minority language groups and covered a territory in 1870 equal to, at minimum, one-half of France.

In a climate of accelerating anticlericalism, suspicions were raised concerning the role of the church and its local clergy in exhorting the faithful against the republic. Of special concern were the minority regions of France, in particular the Pays Basque, Brittany, and Alsace, where the level of religious practice was and remains the highest of any populations in France.[4] In these regions, minority language use remained a barrier behind which the clergy exhorted the faithful against republican values.

In truth, few inroads would be made on the hold of the Basque language in the rural Basque countryside in the century following the Revolution.[5]

In 1806 the Ministry of the Interior under the First Empire estimated the number of Basque speakers, based on the reports of departmental prefect Castellane, at 108,000.[6] *Le Mémorial des Pyrénées* on February 26, 1835, reported that fully one-half of the mayors in the *arrondissements* of Mauléon and Bayonne did not know a word of French.[7] Apparently the level of fluency in French among schoolteachers was no better, and the general level of illiteracy among rural Basques was taken at the time as a surrogate indicator of the weak position of the French language, especially in comparison with neighboring Béarn.[8] At mid-century the situation remained unchanged.[9]

On the eve of the Third Republic, Réclus estimated the number of individuals using Basque as their common language at 120,000.[10] This is based on a total population, enumerated commune by commune, of 123,810 in 1866, including French-speakers who resided in the cities of Mauléon and Saint Palais in the interior, and in Saint-Jean-de-Luz and Hendaye on the coast. The linguistic boundary Réclus offered, paralleling work done by Prince Louis-Lucien Bonaparte, is used with minor adjustments to this day.[11]

The subsequent political turmoil in the Pays Basque in the early Third Republic is understandable in this light: for while the political coloration of the republic was changing considerably from that of the Second Empire, the political and social order of the Pays Basque remained much the same. The dominance of Basque language and customs through this period can be attributed in large measure to the control of the Catholic clergy in the Basque countryside. In their hands, the Basque language became an instrument of clerical reaction which politicized the Basque population behind a phalanx of local notables and the clerical elite.

The Church and Traditional Basque Culture

The proverb *Eskualdun, fededun* (He who is Basque is a believer) which prefaced this chapter captures the relationship between the church and Basque culture in the nineteenth century. The church, through the manipulation of ethnic symbols, achieved a predominance in the Basque country that surpassed the level of religiosity of nearly every other region of France during the Third Republic.[12]

Social relations, political attitudes, reactions to social and economic dislocation—all were infused, collectively and at the level of the individual, with the philosophic imprint of the church. If this state of affairs held the potential for passionate (and, occasionally, violent) political mobilization against the state, it also served to enforce and legitimate a passive social order at the local level based on traditional Basque customs. For the Catholic faith served to instill in the Basque individual "an attachment to his duties which supports him during his trials and makes the task of the authorities easier."[13] What was reactionary elsewhere represented welcome conservatism and social tradition within these mountainous reaches.[14]

THE FAMILLE SOUCHE

What was it about traditional Basque culture that made it so amenable to clerical control? One element was the stability of the Basque family and property over time. Based on a prerevolutionary customary law with distinctly radical components (female suffrage as head of household,[15] as well as political participation based on landownership deriving from a concept of collective nobility), the traditional structure of the family and property was maintained through distinctly conservative and highly legitimate elements of Basque customary law concerning inheritance and the inalienability of property.[16]

One of the great thrusts of the revolutionary urge to *égalité* concerned the question of inheritance law. Revolutionary decisions to mandate the equal division of property among heirs were contained in the law on inheritance passed in 1793, softened by subsequent legislation, and modified further still in the *Code civile* of 1803.[17] The thrust of this legislation was to challenge one of the most fundamental of Basque customary laws: the passing of the *etche-ondo*, or ancestral family home, intact and undivided from generation to generation. This custom lay at the core of Basque family tradition. As the proverb put it, *Herriek beren legea, etcheek beren astura* (Every land has its law, every house has its custom).[18]

While laws passed under the Revolution sought to distribute inheritances equally among heirs, open collusion between Basque families (and their heirs) and local *notaires* served to preserve landholdings and to ensure the heritage of the land over generations by one heir, not necessarily the eldest or a male.[19] Basque tradition was unique in its treatment of inheritance, based on the right of primogeniture without distinction between the sexes. The highly legitimate traditional Basque custom was for the eldest child to inherit the land in its entirety, whether the firstborn was male or female. Acquired property (e.g., savings, livestock, etc.) was generally divided equally. Female heirs exercised all the political and social rights of Basque freeholders, and children born in houses of female heirs through the seventeenth century took the name of the house and not that of their father. It is for this reason that common Basque family surnames today contain the root *etche* (house) or refer to geographic locations of those houses. Basque customary law strongly discouraged both the intermarriage of heirs (which would lead to the accumulation of property and the shrinking of the number of

family units) and the intermarriage of nonheirs, since this would create a
new family unit without land and lead, as was the case in Saint-Etienne-de-
Baigorri, to the appropriation of common grazing lands previously used by
all. By the end of the nineteenth century the custom of primogeniture had
evolved so that, while one child still inherited the family land intact, it was
no longer necessarily the eldest. In fact, today it is frequently the youngest
child who is designated as heir as the older siblings announce their intention to pursue education, learn a trade, and often move to the coastal cities.
Despite the thrust of these revolutionary laws mandating equal inheritance,
the strength of Basque tradition was such that nonheirs nearly always voluntarily acquiesced to this pattern of undivided inheritance in order to protect
the ancestral home and property over time.

This stable familial and social order attracted the attention of the social
philosopher Frédéric le Play, who adopted the Basque family as a model for
his ideal *famille souche*—an enduring nuclear family which maintained traditional values of home, family, and religion in the face of the increasing
onslaught of modernity.[20] As Le Play's followers argued:

> In addition to their particular attachment to religion, they have an orga-
> nization of the family and of property which permitted them to pass
> through the centuries . . . without losing . . . a fragment of their nation-
> ality. . . . And the secret of their vitality is in the constitution of the
> family and property.[21]

The smooth functioning of such a system depended on the acquiescence of
the younger heirs. Historically, four alternatives were open to them. First, if
they sought to remain in the village, their strategy was to marry an heir. In
many cases, despite their hopes of remaining, this often meant leaving the
village and settling elsewhere. Second, others chose to remain unmarried
and to live in their family home under the direction of the sibling heir. So
long as they remained unmarried they had the right to remain in the home.
It was not unheard of for unmarried siblings to return to the family home
later in their lives and to reassume a subordinate role there.[22] The nature of
familial authority would slowly pass with the infirmity of the parents to the
heirs and their spouses, who by this time were the primary economic exploi-
tants of the land and parents of children themselves. Third, from the middle
of the nineteenth century onward, increasing numbers of French Basques
chose to emigrate to the New World. Finally, a disproportionate number of
young Basques chose to enter religious orders, accounting for one of the
highest rates of ordination of any population in France. These two latter outlets were of particular historical importance to Basque society and served as

safety valves to siphon off economic and demographic conflict and leave the traditional authority patterns of the church and traditional law intact.

THE TRADITION OF BASQUE EMIGRATION

Had these outlets not existed, others would have had to be created or Basque tradition would necessarily have been altered. For at a time when single heirs received property intact from their parents (effectively destituting siblings), the incidence of large families among the Basques was one of the highest in France. Louis Etcheverry reported in 1898 that, while the average French family in the late nineteenth century had 3.5 children, families in the Department of the Basses-Pyrénées averaged 4.5 children and had two and one-half times the national incidence of families with 6 children or more.[23] In another context, Etcheverry claimed that, if 19 out of every 100 families in France in 1890 had 4 or more children, the figure was 30 out of 100 for the Pays Basque as a whole, and 50 out of 100 for the *arrondissement* of Mauléon, which later experienced the greatest population decline.[24]

With communal common lands rapidly developed, and with few economic alternatives in the Basque interior which would have permitted the capital accumulation necessary for nonheirs to purchase their own farms, emigration appeared to offer an infinitely elastic outlet for the shortfall. While many men and women left for the large provincial cities of Bordeaux and Toulouse and for Paris, Basque population movements during the nineteenth century differed qualitatively from those elsewhere in France by the disproportionate number of departees to the New World, especially to South America and the western American states of California, Wyoming, and Nevada.[25] This emigration began in earnest in 1832, when English firms began to recruit agricultural workers for colonies in Uruguay. Many of these emigrants stayed on in the New World, furnishing the countries of South America with some of their most notable political and military figures.[26] Often these early Basque emigrants returned, as was their original intent, with sufficient capital to purchase farms or small businesses and marry, and their example served to provoke new and important depopulation trends in the most economically stagnant rural areas.[27]

Table 1 shows the aggregate figures for (non-direction-specific) emigration for the Department of the Basses-Pyrénées for the years 1832–1891. Etcheverry, in interpreting these figures, claimed that, while Basques accounted for one-quarter of the departmental population during this period, they furnished fully two-thirds of all emigrants.[28] The number of agricultural emigrants from the Basses-Pyrénées in this period was one and a half times the national average. Rural communes were particularly heavily affected by

TABLE 1

Emigration from the Department of the Basses-Pyrénées, 1832–1891

Years	Number of Departures	Average Yearly Departures	Total Departmental Population
1832–1835	828	208	428,401 (1831)
1836–1845	10,162	1,016	
1846–1855	16,111	1,614	
1856–1864	12,833	1,425	
1865–1874	17,750	1,775	
1875–1883	5,157	573	
1884–1891	16,421	2,052	423,662 (1891)
Total:	79,262		

Source: Louis Etcheverry, "L'émigration dans les Basses-Pyrénées pendant soixante ans," p. 2.

the outmigration. The commune of Saint-Jean-le-Vieux was typical of many, losing 40 percent of its population by the end of the century.[29] Even important market towns were unspared: Mauléon, a *subprefecture*, lost twelve thousand inhabitants in this period. Overall, the two Basque provinces of the interior, Soule and Basse-Navarre, lost 20 to 25 percent of their population in twenty-five years.[30] Indeed, Etcheverry asserted that virtually the *entire* population growth in the French Basque provinces in the last half of the nineteenth century was canceled by emigration, leaving a more elderly population of approximately the same size on the land in 1910 as lived there in 1840.[31]

Important sociodemographic transformations affected the remaining population: the number of married individuals increased in proportion to the total population, reflecting the departure of young, and unmarried, males. In later years the emigration of Basque women to French cities reversed the earlier male/female imbalance and gave rise in this century to the common phenomenon of bachelor male heirs unable to find Basque women willing to accept the hardship of small-scale, frequently subsistence farming. In some cases Spanish Basque wives were found for farming lives which, if Spartan, were acceptable to rural Spanish Basque women without the alternatives now afforded to young women in the French Basque interior.

THE RATE OF BASQUE ENTRY INTO RELIGIOUS ORDERS

In addition to this high rate of emigration among Basques, the second great outlet for rural overpopulation was entry into the clergy. The historic extent of clerical ordinations among the Basques is an additional indicator of the strength of religious sentiment among the Basque people. Vincent Wright reports that they were among the most fervently religious of any peoples in France before 1870.[32] A century later Chanoine Boulard found their level of religiosity to be virtually unchanged, despite the secular decline in religious sentiment for France as a whole.[33] Moreau reports that survey findings in 1951 of weekly attendance at mass and partaking of Easter communion showed that the religious practice of rural Basques was unequaled by any other religious people in France, though here, as elsewhere, religiosity dropped off in urban areas.[34]

Figures for religious ordinations parallel general findings for religiosity. Indeed, the tradition of Basque entry into clerical or religious orders has been a major force in Basque religion, which has furnished the church with ecclesiastics of the order of the Jesuit Saint Francis Xavier from Basse-Navarre, as well as the contemporary Michel Cardinal Etchegaray from Espelette in Labourd.

Globally, for the department of the Basses-Pyrénées, the rate of clerical ordination constantly exceeded that for France as a whole and was *triple* the national rate of ordination for the years 1886–1890. Moreau reports that, while Basque ordinations grew steadily upward between 1870 and 1913, the curve for the department as a whole is much more irregular, due to the irregular, and lower, rates of ordination in Béarn.[35] If one effect of the crisis of the separation of church and state in 1905–1906 was the precipitant decline in ordinations in France by over 40 percent (nearly 50 percent in Béarn), the rate for the Basque interior *increased* by nearly 14 percent during the same period. Not only were Basque ordinations already substantially higher than the national average during the nineteenth century, but they would continue at such a rate as to represent, from the beginning of the twentieth century until the present, a proportionally greater contribution to the total number of church ordinations in France than they had even during the previous century. Since the beginning of the twentieth century, while representing a fairly constant one-quarter of the departmental population, the Basques have furnished one-half of the priests and two-thirds of the nuns of the Diocese of Bayonne.[36]

Emigration and clerical ordination served as important outlets for social and economic tension in the Basque interior—each arising from elements of the traditional social order (Basque customary law in the former case, the popular legitimacy of the clergy in the latter). Etcheverry, as a spokes-man for the conservative social order, argued that in a broader climate of threatening economic and social change the continued survival of Basque village life depended on the continued vitality of the church and the Basque language.[37] The ability of these twin pillars of the social order—the church and Basque customary law—to create the safety valve through which social and economic conflict might be controlled served to reinforce the legitimacy of their own authority and to pass it unchallenged over generations. As H. Descamps de Bragelongne described it:

> It's that external influences strike the triple wall of culture, family, and Catholic church. The essential characteristic of the Basque is his attach-ment and the very clear awareness he has of his duties in regard to this social trilogy. This attachment and this awareness determine his entire social activity.[38]

The revisionist Basque sociologist Pierre Bidart argues that the power of the clergy in Basque culture was itself a manifestation of the conservative social structure and not an independent influence upon it.[39] So central was their cultural role that some saw the clergy as *the* primary motive force of Basque culture.[40] As Gaetan Bernoville argues:

> The parish is the true unit of the Pays Basque, the center of life there is the church, and the supreme authority [*chef*] the priest. Nothing can dispute it and the Pays Basque would cease to be itself were it to be otherwise. . . . That being so, everything, in spirit and in life, is orga-nized in consequence. . . . The traditional and instinctive statute of the Pays Basque is the patriarchal and religious statute with, as its center, the steeple.[41]

Indeed, so intertwined is the spiritual and political role of the clergy in Basque culture that the Basque word for "mayor" translates as *curé du quartier* (*hauzaphez*, "mayor"; *aphez*, "priest").[42]

The influence of the clergy on Basque culture should be understood in two contexts: first, as an organic relationship that developed in the Pays Basque over centuries; and, second, as a form of social and political authority which developed in the virtual absence, as we saw in chapter 1, of the feudal struc-ture and royal control common to other areas of France from the Middle Ages until the Revolution, including neighboring Béarn.[43]

The church first exerted its influence among the Basques during the great medieval pilgrimages to the sepulcher of the disciple Saint James at Compos-tella in Galicia in Spain.[44] Geographic considerations made the Pays Basque a natural funnel for the myriad pilgrimage routes which crisscrossed the maps of Europe. In conjunction with these great population flows, religious orders were established, offering succor and military protection to pilgrims. Long after the passage of the pilgrims, these religious orders remained as a visible and wide-ranging form of social and communal organization. It was in part due to this early implantation of the church among the Basques that the boundaries between the secular and religious in the Pays Basque were poorly defined. Indeed, the inhabitants looked to the clerical orders for physical as well as spiritual protection. So it was that in the threatening climate of the crisis of separation of church and state the Basques turned to the clergy for political guidance and rallied behind the church and the Basque language in opposition to the state.

The Politicization of Language and the Incipient Conflict between Church and State

The end of the nineteenth century was characterized by the persistent use, in the France of the countrysides and small towns, of local languages and dialects. . . . In the majority of these cases, the defense of regional languages was supported by the conservative spheres who see in these latter a means of opposition to the Jacobin concentration denounced by Le Play and an instrument of social or political influence—notably in electoral matters—on the peasant world.
Pierre Tauzia[45]

By the mid-1880s, corroborative reports reaching Paris affirmed the persistent usage of the Basque language and the continued marginality of French in the Basque interior. In tone and substance, these reports differ little from similar texts circulated during the Revolution and its aftermath. In the Pays Basque, as elsewhere, agents of the French administration again identified as their main obstacle the symbiotic relationship of the church and indigenous local culture. The Basque language was the barrier behind which, in both social and geographical terms, lay a population which was, at best, indifferent to central institutions and, at worst, politically hostile to them. As *inspecteur* Felix Pécaut described it:

> The Pays Basque merits a special study . . . their national language is nearly the only one which they use: it's the language of common [*vulgaire*] and everyday needs, as well as of the feelings of the family; it is above all that of religion, that is to say of the whole order of beliefs, of moral traditions, of rules of conduct, of high hopes, and of intimate emotions.

[The attitude of the clergy] . . . is eminently national and doubly Basque, hardly favorable to the spread of French, which is in its eyes the vehicle of foreign and suspect ideas, of the spirit of insubordination and of disbelief.[46]

Common was the opinion of *inspecteur d'académie* Fauré, who wrote in 1892 that "the use of a distinct idiom, ancient traditions, the spirit of resistance to all penetration have rendered more difficult the propagation of the French language."[47]

By the dawn of the twentieth century not even the local mayor could be considered an agent of central authority. This was unexpected at so late a date, which explains the wonderment of departmental prefect Francière, who wrote to the minister of religion in 1901 that "I've even encountered during my rounds of inspection mayors who don't speak French."[48] Hourmat had found earlier that even the local *instituteurs* charged with the teaching of French were themselves only marginally literate. In fact, in many villages, the only individual who could converse (and read and write) in French was the local priest. Ironically, it was the priest who was identified in successive reports by agents of the ministries of Education, Religion, and the Interior as the source of primary opposition to governmental authority in the village. Using their role of interlocutors to mobilize the population against the Republic, the local clergy employed the Basque tongue, as Tauzia argues, in their

> struggle against liberal and secular ideas, conveyed, in French, by the school and the press, their desire to maintain over rural populations an influence permitted by the perfect knowledge of a language with which, most often, agents of the republican administration remain unfamiliar.[49]

The problem which confronted the administration was how to move against the clergy, and their teaching of Basque, without provoking further electoral losses in this already predominantly conservative and clerically rightist electorate.[50] In the Basque interior, however, the republic had little to lose, so negligible was its support in local and national elections. As Bidart writes of Saint-Etienne-de-Baigorri:

> In this region, militant clericalism which [notables who were candidates] displayed in an election guaranteed their election in advance. There did not exist the phenomenon of political bipolarization . . . in the Pays Basque, except in some villages. In Baigorry, to be sure, there always were some reds (essentially construction workers, of the S.N.C.F. [French National Railways] but they remained mired in political powerlessness and isolation.[51]

In order to avoid further hardening of opposition to central institutions, successive departmental prefects recommended that, whatever measures were instituted against the teaching of Basque by the clergy, they be timed in such a way as to not coincide with local or national elections in the Pays Basque.[52] Prefect Francière, writing in 1901, reflected this caution:

> The population of the Basses-Pyrénées has remained attached to its ancient customs and a thousand traits reveal the conservative spirit with which it has remained imbued. This observation applies with a rigorous exactitude to the Basques. So it would be imprudent, in my opinion, to clash with the sentiments of these populations, at so close a distance to the departmental and legislative elections, in forcing them to renounce some of the customs which they have observed for so long.[53]

In fact, the ultimate measures taken by the government were postponed until after the legislative elections of 1902, but, from the results registered, little more could have been lost by adding the emotional issue of language to an already mobilized rural population.[54]

Because the clerical defense of regional languages was not unique to the Basques, the ultimate measures ordered by the minister of religion repeated those first instituted in the Flemish-speaking area of the Département du Nord, along the French-Belgian border. Coming after the legislative elections of June 1902, the decree issued from the prefecture in Pau stated that from January 1903 French would be the only language permitted in the teaching of catechism, upon penalty of suspension of government stipends to the clergy who violated the decree.

Local reaction to the decree varied. Not surprisingly, the most vehement reaction came from the clerical press, which reacted with strongly worded editorials, including one which defended the rights of fathers and which evoked the ancient *fueros*.[55] Moderately worded petitions were sent to the prefect by local elites who, while entreating the administration to protect the Basque language, expressly rejected any accusation of separatism. Responding in conciliatory terms, the prefect, while refusing to permit any exceptions to the decree, admitted the need to employ Basque for explanations in those (all too many) cases where knowledge of French was woefully inadequate.[56]

Given the pacifism of elected elites, attention was rapidly focused on the target of the decree, the clergy.[57] If widespread resistance was expected from them, little transpired. The immediate reaction of fifty-two of the ninety-four affected clergy was to inform their parishioners of their intention to comply with the decree and cease offering catechism in Basque. Despite isolated instances of discontent and attempts to circumvent the intent of the law, by the summer of 1903 only ten priests remained intransigent.[58] This led the prefecture, in the autumn of 1904, to declare the situation stabilized and to recommend that no new reprisals be taken on the eve of upcoming cantonal elections as "local resistance bends more every hour before the continued and determined action of the Administration."[59]

The capitulation of the clergy can be attributed to a number of factors, among them the schism which separated the local clergy from the republican bishopric in the Diocese of Bayonne and the ultimate recognition that a battle on two fronts, against the enemies of the church and against its own hierarchy, could not be won. A new bishop, Mgr. Jauffret, had arrived in Bayonne in early 1890, and the conciliatory position he took in regard to the republic was accompanied by disciplinary action against local clerics who were outspoken in their hostility to the government.[60] Whether he acted with the blessing of the pope is a matter of some dispute. Goyeneche writes of the church hierarchy and of Jauffret:

> From 1877 to the beginning of the twentieth century, this was perhaps the most lamentable period of the religious history of France: deceitful or sordid attacks by bourgeois "republicans" for whom democracy became incarnate in anticlericalism, more comfortably than in the social sense . . . conservatives who each day had less to conserve led or held back by concordant bishops . . . sorts of spiritual prefects but inferior in rank to prefects. . . . Catholics of this era espoused a nationalist mythology which was—unbeknownst to them—but a pale dilution of Jacobinism, they sacrificed all to a "fatherland" which turned its back. The depths of lowness were attained by Mgr. Jauffret, otherwise, we're told, a saintly man.[61]

Having already moved to sanction certain particularly antirepublican clergy, Jauffret succeeded, in effect, in divorcing their cause from the legitimating embrace of the hierarchy of the church. By undercutting the local alliances formed around the church-language issue, he hoped to mute that conflict and avoid further, and more serious, reprisals from the government.

If this proved to be an effective barrier to organized political dissent by the local clergy and their supporters, it would not prevent the already looming conflict which culminated in the separation. Moreover, Jauffret's death in 1902 added a further dimension of confusion to the relationship of the local clergy to the church hierarchy. Having effectively quelled early dissent among the most nationalistic priests, he departed on the eve of increased government hostility to religious education, depriving the diocese of the leadership and unity it needed in this period of crisis. His seat remained empty from 1902 until the process of the inventories of church property contained in the law of the separation of church and state had already begun in early 1906.

With the clergy in disarray, and in the absence of any effective political mobilization around the issue of language without them, even the most militant of antirepublicans seemed resigned to their inability to counter the growing authority of the administration. As the longtime clericalist deputy Louis Etcheverry described it:

> Paris exercises over the rest of France a dictatorship absolutely incompatible with public sovereignty, and this dictatorship is periodically expressed in violently imposed revolutions. . . . Familial and religious influences are not effective enough to resist governmental coercion.[62]

As Chanoine Lafitte later wrote, "The Basque public, it must be said, [was] strongly sensitized by the dramatic circumstances of the epoch, circumstances which directly threatened their identities as Catholics and as ethnic Basques."[63] At the same time, however, both in terms of electoral choice and by other informal indicators of political mobilization, the Basque public remained hostile to the initiatives of the government and lacked only the leadership necessary to articulate grievances which struck so centrally to their identity as Catholics and as Basques.

As one indicator of the rising frustration of the Basque electorate, the conservative clerical weekly *Eskualduna* (The Basque), founded in 1887 under the leadership of Louis Etcheverry, experienced steadily rising subscriptions during this period, which rose dramatically on the eve of the separation and coincided with the neutralization of the local clergy.[64] Secular only in origin, the doctrinal content of *Eskualduna* apparently closely reflected the sentiments of rural Basque Catholics and molded them, in turn, because of its singular impact in remote areas of the provinces of Labourd and Basse-Navarre.[65] The extremely powerful deputy and later minister under Vichy Jean Ybarnégaray was first elected in this period, campaigning on the nearly ritual theme of free religious education using the slogan *Eskualdun, fededun* made popular by *Eskualduna*.[66] It was in this climate of growing anticlericalism from without and popular disarray within that the crisis of the separation of church and state burst forth in 1905.[67]

The Crisis of Church and State in the Pays Basque, 1905–1906

If the closing of religious schools and the forced exile of some clerical orders to Spain had already mobilized the population, the decision by the govern-

ment to proceed in early 1906 to an inventory of church possessions at the
local level gave many villagers their first direct contact with agents charged
with carrying out the letter of the law of separation. Departmental maps
showing sites of significant local opposition to the inventories essentially reproduce the linguistic boundary separating the Pays Basque from Béarn.[68]
Though the nature of local protests varied in scope and scale, the popular
fervor and the clearly spontaneous nature of many of the scenes underscored
once more the depth of religious feeling at the local level. That the protests
were no more violent than they were was due in part, certainly, to the spontaneity caused by lack of warning. In some villages the local priest could not
be found, while in others his absence was a deliberate attempt to thwart the
inventory.

If the burden was generally heavy throughout, it fell particularly harshly
on those teaching orders in respected seminaries in the region, such as
the Grand Séminaire at Bayonne, the Petit Séminaire at Larressore, and the
Benedictine Abbey at Belloc. Though the clerics at Belloc were forced into
exile in Spain, by a "jesuitical" manipulation of deeds the physical property
was sold to a Benedictine, and the teachers of the Petit Séminaire were able
to move there. They were joined by the Benedictines who were able to return from Spain after World War I. They coexisted at Belloc until the new
Petit Séminaire was built on the southern outskirts of Ustaritz in 1926. The
property of the old Petit Séminaire was transformed into the state mental
hospital which it remains today.

Owing, in part, to this experience, the Petit Séminaire became a seedbed
of subsequent Basque nationalism, as we will see in chapter 3, under the
guidance of Abbé (later Chanoine) Pierre Lafitte.[69] In the aftermath of the
crisis of separation, most Basque clergy did in fact return, but the memory
of that period did nothing to improve relations between the state and the
Catholic population, and the hostilities which gelled in this period became
a part of Basque political culture which endures to this day. At the same
time, profound changes were occurring in the coastal cities as the republic began to insinuate itself among the working class and civil service. The
urban-rural cleavage which appears here is not a new one, but it, too, is one
which persisted until the mid-1970s.

But the grist of a true nationalistic sentiment is absent in all this; once
having occurred, these popular demonstrations of hostility to the state rapidly subsided. The neutralization of the clergy deprived the Basques of their
natural and traditional ethnic elites. Without leadership, much of the rural
Basque population descended into a resolutely apolitical Catholicism from
which they were reluctant to stir. Ironically, however, some of the objectives
of the clergy had in fact been met. Now freed from their concordat with the

state, and no longer dependent on it for stipends, the clergy, in the aftermath of the crisis, could return in an informal way to their role as purveyor and interpreter of Basque language and culture in the villages. In the secular trends of this century, the level of religiosity of France as a whole has changed. But now, as then, the Basques remain among the most devout of any Catholic population in France. Soon a confluence of other factors was to emerge, among them the cultural consequences of World War I and the cumulative impact of modernization. Their impact would irremediably alter the village unit as the cradle of Basque culture and change the basis of Basque political culture in the twentieth century.

World War I and the Staying Power of Basque Culture

Coming in the aftermath of the separation, World War I provoked profound and irreversible demographic and psychological changes in rural France, disrupting the harmony and continuity of life for a generation of young Basques, many of whom had never before left their village and the shadow of its steeple.[70] Thrown into units with young Bretons, Auvergnats, and Corsicans, they turned to French out of necessity as a *lingua franca*.[71]

The war proved to be a watershed for the Basques in two essential ways. First, unlike earlier or later wars, the demographic effect of the carnage of this war was overwhelming, as peasants became cannon fodder in so many trenches, bogged down through the inclement weather and the sodden immobility of ill-planned strategy. For many rural Basque villages, the war simply severely reduced two generations of males and, with them, the reproductive capacity of the village.[72] In the first instance, then, the demographic effects of the war served to disrupt the stability of life in many rural villages. With the youth went the economic future; if the losses of war were not already enough, many of those who remained migrated to the coastal cities and elsewhere and would not return.

The second consequence of World War I was its impact on Basque culture. In these villages of the interior lay the vitality of Basque culture and the burden of its linguistic population. Loss by death was sudden and abrupt. But the return of demobilized Basque soldiers now committed to cultural assimilation into French society posed a longer threat to Basque culture. For those who returned from the war, the cultural perspectives they brought with them spread like an infection, assaulting the remaining enclaves of Basque monolingualism. Bilingualism among Basque children increased in this period as parental opposition to republican, francophone schools changed, often as a result of the taunts and scorn experienced by Basque males during the war.[73]

In an interview in Ustaritz on December 2, 1975, Pierre Bidart argued that in Saint-Etienne-de-Baigorri the linguistic change was slow in coming and that it originated with young Basque women:

> Each study confirmed even more the particular attitude of girls, who from whatever milieu they were from, were situated at a higher level of acculturation. They internalize more rapidly the system of symbols, of objects, of values emanating from urban society. Similarly girls have a tendency to almost ignore the local tongue. During recreation, at least half of the boys still continue to converse in Basque whereas all the girls speak in French. Curious scenes thus occur, as widespread in agricultural as in nonagricultural families where children and parents carry on dialogue in different languages, one wanting to ignore the language of the other. More complicated situations occur: such as in one family, one of the boys, ten years of age, received a slap from his mother who reproached him for speaking in French. Now this same boy found himself with a teacher who forbade him the use of the Basque language.[74]

Coupled with the economic marginality of life in rural villages, the incentive to speak French was doubly persuasive; many parents viewed it as the key to success and upward mobility.[75] As Weber puts it, "The situation in 1920 was just the reverse of what it had been in 1880; bilinguals were more awkward in *patois* than in French; the majority and, most important, the young were on the side of the national language."[76] Arnold Van Gennep states succinctly, "French pays, *patois* doesn't pay."[77]

By the end of the war the most profound of these changes were already apparent. Albert Tessier noted in 1918, "Moreover, our region has not escaped the common fate of the ancient French provinces. Roads, railroads, contact with the large cities, obligatory education, and military service are so many causes of weakening of the local and particularistic spirit."[78] To be sure, these trends had been apparent even earlier. The geographer Elisée Réclus captured in his prescient analysis in 1866 much of what has come later to be called the syndrome of modernization.[79] Yet the tenacious persistence of Basque culture has thwarted the predictions of doomsayers and Jacobin centralizers alike. The linguistic population on the land in 1945 approximated what it was in 1849 when Karl Marx and Frederick Engels referred to the Basques as one of a number of Europe's historyless (*geschichtslose*) peoples, ethnic leftovers or national ruins whose counterrevolutionary nature threatened the unity of existing states.[80] Confidently, Marx and Engels asserted, "The next world war will result in the disappearance from the face of the earth . . . of entire reactionary peoples. And that, too, is a step forward."[81] Certainly Basque political culture has indeed been hostile to revolution and resolutely anti-Communist in the modern era. Far from facing extinction, though, the Basques retreated to the cultural bedrocks of tradition and piety, as bastions from which to await the new century and its onslaughts.

Sabino Arana Goiri, the Origins of Basque Nationalism in Spain, and Their Impact on the Pays Basque Français

Several explanations have been advanced to explain the failure of an ethnically based political movement to coalesce behind a Basque clerical elite. Inevitably, given the richness of the opportunity, latter-day militants have asked what combination of leadership, issues, and strategy might have altered this outcome and led to the appearance of a true nationalist movement among French Basques.

Accordingly, much attention has been paid to the example of Sabino Arana Goiri, creator of the original doctrine of Basque nationalism in Spain during this period and founder of the Basque Nationalist Party.[82] At first glance, the failure of Arana's ideas to attract a following in France seems paradoxical, given the ideological congruity of Arana's doctrines and the values of family, religion, and traditional Basque culture which were common currency among French Basques at this time. What prevented the extension of Arana's thought, by demonstration, to his ethnic kin in France? For all available evidence suggests that his impact in France was virtually nonexistent at this time, though the Spanish example in later generations would have a distinct impact on the nature of ethnic militancy in France. It appears that the failure of Arana's ideology of Basque nationalism to spread among French Basques can be explained by three factors: his marginal concern for the Basques of France in the body of his political writings; the lack of congruence between his view of the role of the clergy in a Basque nationalist movement and the underlying political and social realities of life in the Pays Basque Français; and, finally, nearly total unfamiliarity with his ideas by French Basques during his lifetime.

In the years preceding World War I, when the level of popular mobilization among French Basques around the conflict of church and state was most suited to the appearance of an ethnic nationalist movement, the insularity of life among rural French Basques was matched by the "ethnocentrism" of Arana's own writings—each contributing to the isolation of the French Basque case and to the retarded appearance of a nationalist sentiment there. The geographic concentration of Arana's doctrine might be most fruitfully understood as a series of concentric circles representing three levels of his concern: at the center, and most important, was Arana's concern for his native province of Bizkaia; next was his emphasis on conditions in the four Spanish Basque provinces; and finally came mention of the three French Basque provinces as part of his view of an independent Basque state, which he called, for the first time, "Euzkadi."

In its earliest statement, Arana's evolving ideology was concerned primarily with his native province of Bizkaia, a position he outlined in *Bizkaya por su independencia,* first published in 1893.[83] Explaining how Arana's early emphasis on Bizkaia could affect the spread of his ideas into the other Basque provinces of Spain, Da Silva writes:

> Initially Basque nationalism was limited to the province of Vizkaya, Arana's home province. When he published *Bizkaya por su independencia,* he concentrated on defending what he conceived to be the historical rights of that province, although reference was also made to the Basque region as a whole. But because initially he addressed himself mainly to the independence of Vizkaya, early Basque nationalism was also referred to as *bizkaitarrismo.* It was not until after his death that his ideas began to find support in the other three provinces.[84]

To be sure, there was nothing incompatible between this emphasis on his native Bizkaia and the larger political structure he envisioned for his homeland. In order to maintain the particular autonomy and traditions of each Basque within his vision of Euzkadi, Arana foresaw the development of a federal structure,[85] patterned in part on the American example, which he outspokenly admired.[86] Reflected in the expression *Zazpiak bat* (The seven are one), Arana foresaw the unification of the four Basque provinces of Spain and the three of France in a larger Basque confederation. He put it this way:

> Alava, Vizkaya, Guipúzcoa, Labourd, Navarre, Basse-Navarre, and Soule brother-peoples by the natural ties of race, of language, of character and customs; according to the nationalist policy, they are called on to form a confederation.[87]

This goal did not translate itself in Arana's lifetime into any organizational work in France or any particular attention devoted to problems there, despite his residing there in his youth and during later exile for his nationalist activity in Spain.[88] Exceptions to this statement must exist within the body of his voluminous writings, but statements made with particular reference to conditions in the Pays Basque Français are rare and unsystematic.[89] One notable exception which warrants citing at length was directed specifically to the crisis in church-state relations taking place in the Pays Basque Français at that time. Published in *La Patria* in 1902 on the eve of his death, it was too little, in too obscure a source, and too late to influence events substantially:

O, you Basques of the right of the Bidassoa and the north of the Pyrénées! Our brothers who suffer the yoke of this impious France! Tell me:
will you accept it resignedly and feel happy under it? Do you want to
be more French than Basques, even at the risk of no longer being Christians? Or is it that you have already lost the memory of your origin,
you no longer recognize your mother? Are you unaware, by chance,
that you are neither Gauls nor Latins, but Basques? Have you forgotten
your history, and has the word independence no longer any meaning
for you? Wake up, and last! If you do not awaken, it is not that you are
asleep, but dead![90]

The condition of the Basque provinces of France was of secondary importance to Arana, unable by choice and circumstance to devote to them the
time and organizational skills necessary to create a political movement like
that which was still only incipient even in Spain. Reinforcing the natural
insularity of life among rural French Basques, a nearly hermetic conceptual
curtain separated these two segments of the same ethnic culture. It would
not be opened until the Spanish Civil War, when an influx of more than
100,000 Spanish refugees upset the calm of the Pays Basque Français—a
disruption which would provoke a debate over identity which Arana might
have favored, but whose outcome he could not accept.

A second substantive problem exists within Arana's doctrine, which raises
questions about its applicability to the underlying political and cultural conditions among French Basques: the role of the clergy. Reflecting the strong
religious dimension of his ideology and the widely held Basque belief in the
moral impact of family, tradition, and the church, Arana felt that the sole
role of the clergy should be to teach and preserve this moral order, while
eschewing any political activity whatsoever.[91] Goyheneche writes:

> Let us add that if Arana Goiri devotes Euzkadi to God and the Basque
> state to the accomplishment of divine will, he establishes as a precept
> the separation—otherwise traditional with the Basques—between the
> church and the state, and forbids the clergy any action or any influence
> that is not purely religious.[92]

This was an understandable element of Arana's ideology in theory, but
an ironic one in light of reality, for in Spain as well as in France the local
clergy was a major segment in Basque nationalism, and perhaps its most
effective recruiter. What has emerged from an analysis of the role of the
French Basque clergy in the early Third Republic is a persistent and unmis-
takable involvement in local and national politics. This political involvement
was not necessarily a matter of choice, though it was greatly aided by both

the authoritative role of the clergy in Basque culture and the politicization of religion in Third Republic France. In a climate of accelerating anticlericalism, with early challenges to religious teaching in vernacular languages evolving into the later crisis of separation involving the seizure of church property and the exile of religious orders, the local clergy found that their traditional concerns—piety, religious education, and the continuity of local traditions— had themselves become politicized, drawing the clergy into the vortex as political actors. As nominal service-sector intellectuals, or as Machiavellian manipulators of cultural symbols, the central role of the clergy in the maintenance of the Basque language became politicized as the French state sought to supplant these languages, dialects, or vulgar *patois* with French. Their role in preserving their culture, and their reaction to the threat of French institutions, marked them as ethnic militants. Their traditional position in Basque culture made them ethnic elites, unchallenged in this period by secular counterparts who could divorce ethnicity from clericalism among the Basques. They were the only ethnic elite in the Pays Basque Français and the only militants capable of creating a popular nationalist movement at the turn of the century.

Wide circulation of Arana's doctrine among French Basques probably would have hindered the creation of a Basque nationalist movement by circumscribing the role of the clergy in the absence of any other potential ethnic elite—in effect perpetuating the status quo. Arana's doctrine ironically jibed with the pitched effort of the French state in this period, committed to the neutralization of the clergy and their elimination as political actors at the local level. By isolating the most militant elements of the clergy before World War I, the collusion of the church hierarchy and the state was able to forestall the appearance of a separatist or nationalist movement by depriving it of its potential leadership. Never again would popular grievances be so widespread and so ripe for political manipulation; never again would ethnic elites enjoy the natural position of legitimacy and respect given the clergy at the turn of the century. New issues, and new elites, would emerge in the French Basque case before the appearance of a true nationalist movement. Arana's doctrine would be more influential then, as would the example of Basque nationalism in Spain.

The third and final element of this discussion of Arana's impact among French Basques is the most telling—their unfamiliarity with his writings during his lifetime. The major indicator of this is the virtual lack of subscriptions to nationalist newspapers begun by Arana and his followers in Spain.[93] *Bizkaitarra* (The Bizkaian), the first Basque nationalist newspaper to appear in Spain, published from June 1893 until 1895, had an extremely low subscription rate in France. Number 15 (September 20, 1894) lists two subscriptions in Labourd; one, in the name of "J. de U.," can be assumed to be a Spanish Basque because of the rarity of that form among French Basque names.[94] Number 17 (November 30, 1894) lists a subscription in Saint-Jean-de-Luz in the name of "Dr. G." The weekly *Baserritarra*, which began in 1897 and had an eventual press-run of eighteen issues, listed five subscriptions in the Pays Basque Français—at least one of which ("J. de U.") was also a subscriber to the earlier *Bizkaitarra*. All five subscribers were residents of the coastal cities of Saint-Jean-de-Luz or Hendaye near the Spanish border.[95] For the first time in the Biskaian nationalist press, news was given of Labourd and Basse-Navarre in *El Correo Vasco*, a daily published in Bilbao from June through September 1899.[96] *La Patria*, source of Arana's previously cited impassioned pleas to French Basques, had only three subscribers in the Pays Basque Français.[97]

Ultimately, the contribution of these publications to the development of Basque nationalism in Spain must be measured in terms of their content and ideological development, even in Bizkaia. What emerges, however, from a study of their subscribers is that their presence among French Basques is nearly nonexistent and that most of the few copies which did trickle across the French-Spanish border appear to have been destined for transplanted Spanish Basques. Those subscriptions which did arrive in France were confined to the coastal cities near the border, areas with little contact or impact with the rural interior, where the strength of Basque culture in France had always remained.

Conclusion

In this chapter, I have touched on certain aspects of the nature of Basque mobilization in the early French Third Republic. Crucial to an understanding of Basque political culture in this period is the inseparable link between Basque ethnic identity and Catholic religiosity. The imprint of the church molded all aspects of social and political life at the local level, and the clergy served as an unchallenged ethnic elite.

The Pays Basque in the Third Republic was able to preserve a stable pattern of social and political authority because of the way in which the clergy and local customary laws combined to deflect the real social and economic problems in the rural Basque economy. By effectively exporting the potential sources of discontent, the Pays Basque was spared the economic problems which afflicted rural France in this period. As a result, it was able to present a nearly homogeneous clerical and conservative opposition to the dominant political tendencies of the Third Republic.

The politicization of Basque cultural symbols and language use was ma-nipulated by the clergy as an instrument of popular exhortation against the increasingly hostile anticlericalism of the republican government. Ethnic mobilization among the Basques in this period was effectively subsumed within the rife question of church-state relations in France.

The ultimate neutralization of the local clergy came not as the result of successful governmental initiatives, but as part of a series of conciliatory gestures by the French episcopate, which hoped to placate the republican administration and so forestall the separation which loomed on the hori-zon. The elimination of the clergy as a protonationalist ethnic elite served to deprive the Basques of the ethnic and political leadership they had tra-ditionally known. Accordingly, if hostility toward the state was accentuated throughout the crisis of separation, it was deprived of the coherence and leadership it had enjoyed among a population guided by a legitimate clerical ethnic elite.

The neutralization of the overwhelming majority of the Basque clergy in this period effectively separated the political defense of Basque cultural tradi-tions and language use from its traditional clerical defenders and so opened them up to later manipulation by secular Basque movements. The greatest obstacle these later movements would face would be to legitimize their role among the still conservative rural Basque clergy. For the social power of the clergy continued in the rural Pays Basque, and their retreat from political action also represented an obstacle to the rise of a secular strain of national-ism. It meant that henceforth secular movements which attempted to defend Basque traditions and language use would arise from outside the accepted limits of traditional political culture. Indeed, the greatest obstacles to the further political mobilization of the Basques around ethnic issues came not from the state but from the bearers of those cultural symbols and the mass of native Basque-speakers. This chapter has laid the groundwork for an under-standing of the early ethnic mobilization of the Basques during the Third Republic and of the tenets of traditional Basque political culture. By refer-ence to each, we may understand the problems associated with the secular expressions of nationalism to come.

Chapter Three

The "Red" Fish in the Baptismal Font:

Clericalism and Nationalism among the

Basques of France, 1920–1945

Young people, everyone to work! If politics happen without you, they will
happen against you. Young people, march without fear and in full awareness:
it is on you that the whole future of the Pays Basque rests.
JEL (*Jainkoa eta legea* [God and the law];
pseudonym of Abbé Pierre Lafitte ca. 1933)[1]

Regionalism, centralization, religious liberty, restoration of our ancient laws,
feminism, antistatism . . . those are . . . the diverse
political points . . . of our program.
Kapito Harri (pseudonym of Abbé Pierre Lafitte, 1935)[2]

Pierre Lafitte is a red fish swimming in a baptismal font.
Jean Ybarnégaray, Basque deputy[3]

By the end of World War I, profound and irreversible changes were apparent
on the social horizon of rural, local France.[4] If the demographic effects of
the war were not devastating enough, the rise of French nationalism in the
war's aftermath was of a magnitude never before seen in minority regions,
including the Pays Basque. As we saw in chapter 2, the crisis of separation of
church and state at the beginning of the century represented the most threatening intrusions of the secular French state into the historic ties between the
church and Basque culture. With the neutralization of the Basque clergy as
its natural elite, Basque political culture found itself bereft of its traditional
defenders and buffeted by a climate of threatening republican change. The
Basques in this interwar period remained suspicious of change and hostile to the signs of corruption and immoral modernity encroaching upon
them. It was in this context between the two world wars that we witness

63

the appearance of the first generation of secular French Basque nationalists. Born of the regionalism and clericalism of the late dynamic Abbé (later
Chanoine) Pierre Lafitte and his Eskualerriste movement, this young generation launched two series of the Basque nationalist newspaper *Aintzina*,
was profoundly influenced by the Spanish Civil War and its refugees, and
experienced again the ravages of world war now compounded by German
occupation. Some latter-day Basque critics would dismiss this young movement (and its newspaper *Aintzina*) as a timid and retrograde expression of
clerical regionalism. In reality, with its young members like Eugène Goyheneche and Marc Légasse and the influence of Abbé Pierre Lafitte, Abbé Pierre
Larzabal, and Abbé Jean-Pierre Urricarriet among others, it represented the
bridge between past and future across which the later nationalist movement
of the 1960s would come.

The generation of young French Basque nationalists which emerged in
the 1930s and 1940s was important to the history of Basque nationalism in
France for a number of reasons. First, they represented the first generation to transcend the reflexive conservative clericalism which had dominated
Basque political culture since before the Revolution. Second, their early writings show the first wakening awareness of the common cause shared with
other budding ethnic movements elsewhere in France. Third, with the advent of the Spanish Civil War and its stream of refugees into the Pays Basque
Français, one sees the first awareness of a common cause between Basques
in France and Spain that even Sabino Arana Goiri could not instill. The
result was the first stirring of a Spanish Basque "demonstrator effect" on
French Basque movements and nationalist doctrines that continues to this
day. Taken as a whole, the political and cultural hopes of this first generation
of French Basque nationalists provide a clear polar star for later generations
of Basque militants to follow.

In this chapter I will examine the rise to political awareness of this generation of young Basque militants, including their contact with other ethnic
movements in France. Second, I will consider the circumstances surrounding
the creation of the Eskualerriste movement and the Basque newspaper *Aintzina* under the aegis of Abbé Pierre Lafitte. Third, I will discuss the impact
of the Spanish Civil War and the influx of refugees. Fourth, I will examine
the strategy of the Basque movement during the German occupation during
World War II and the choice between resistance and collaboration. Finally, I
will discuss the legacy of this first generation of secular nationalists for later
Basque militancy to come.

The Pays Basque Français in the Aftermath of World War I

The prevailing social order in the Pays Basque between 1920 and 1940 remained a rural, agrarian society with an overwhelmingly clerical and conservative political culture.[5] Political elites came predominantly from the bourgeoisie and their tenure in office was generally long-term. Jean Ybarnégaray, for example, remained the deputy of the Basque interior from the pre–World War I era until World War II, when he served briefly as Vichy minister of sports and youth.[6] Similarly, at the local level, the town of Ustaritz had only two mayors between 1910 and 1939.[7] Elected officials often increased their political power through the *cumul de mandats*, a French tradition permitting officeholders to hold multiple political offices at the same time. In this way, deputies were usually also either mayors or departmental *conseillers généraux* (or both), and *conseillers généraux* were usually mayors. A surprising number of these local officials, as elsewhere in rural France, were medical doctors or *notaires* by profession.

The nature of Basque political elites was thus a self-perpetuating and stable order in which the church played an important role. The primary conduit of socialization remained the system of Catholic education. The first socialization of Basque youth was in the Petit Séminaire, which in the Pays Basque included both students destined for the clergy and a larger number destined for a host of secular occupations. As Theodore Zeldin describes the typical education in the Petit Séminaire, it was determined to cut children off from the pleasure of the world and to "instill principles in them."[8] The education in these establishments was a strict one and slow to modernize. Zeldin describes an unreconstructed conservative style of Catholic education in the *séminaires* at the turn of the century:[9]

> At the turn of the century, three-quarters of the eighty-four *grands séminaires* taught no science nor mathematics; ecclesiastical history was only a recent addition, and considered of secondary importance; there was very little critical study of the Bible, and no effort was made to introduce pupils to the modern world. The Middle Ages were held up as the ideal period of Christianity.[10]

The two primary religious institutions in the Pays Basque were the Petit Séminaire at Larressore (and later at Ustaritz, historic capital of the Basque province of Labourd) and the Grand Séminaire at Bayonne. Especially important was the socializing role of the Petit Séminaire at Larressore in the Basque interior. In the aftermath of the crisis of separation, the Petit Séminaire had its property definitively confiscated by the state in 1919 and was ultimately transformed into the state mental hospital it remains to this day.

Not until 1926 was a new facility constructed some kilometers north of its former site, this time on the southern outskirts of Ustaritz.

Through the doors of the Petit Séminaire passed successive generations of young Basque elites whose early Basque and Catholic education served as a foundation for young men who went on to distinguish themselves not only in the clergy but in a variety of secular occupations, among them politics, medicine, and law. The Petit Séminaire was the early training ground of the Basque bourgeoisie and its political and social elite. As Bernard Ménou put it, all of the sons of the Basque bourgeoisie were there; it was a veritable laboratory for the creation of Basque elites.[11]

The *Bulletin* of former students of the Petit Séminaire for the year 1931 alone lists among its names such later notables as: deputies Jean Ybarnégaray and Jean Lissar and *conseillers généraux* Adrien Barnetche (Saint-Jean-de-Luz), Alexandre Camino (Cambo), Albert Constantin (Tardets), Désiré Etcheverry-Ainchart (Saint-Etienne-de-Baigorri), Dr. Edmond Goyheneche (Ustaritz), and Louis Inchauspé (Saint-Jean-Pied-de-Port).[12]

"Father" and "Son": The Impact of Abbé Pierre Lafitte and Eugène Goyheneche

Among the early generation of Basque militants in the 1930s, two individuals contributed more intellectually to the fledgling Basque movement than any others: Abbé (later Chanoine) Pierre Lafitte and Eugène Goyheneche. To be sure, the archival evidence from this period shows a number of important individuals: the *abbés* Urricarriet, Larzabal, and Aranart; and young militants like Pierre Amoçain, Jacques Mestelan, and Madeleine de Jaureguiberry in the 1930s and later Marc and Jacques Légasse in the 1940s. But for the seed that slowly germinated and flowered into the Basque militancy of the 1930s, the role of Lafitte and Goyheneche was paramount.

PIERRE LAFITTE, 1901–1985

Chanoine Lafitte remains today one of the great figures in Basque letters in this century: member of the Académie Basque, founder of the Basque newspaper *Aintzina;* director of *Herria;* longtime co-editor and contributor to *Gure Herria*, the sole and influential Basque language weekly in the rural interior; and *chargé de recherche* by the French Centre Nationale de Recherche Scientifique (CNRS) in biblical Greek. Among his many works were *Lexique français-basque, La grammaire basque,* and *Dictionnaire basque-français* (co-authored).[13] He was a professor at the Petit Séminaire, religious guide, political mobilizer, cultural militant, and mentor of the first generation of secular Basque nationalists.

Lafitte was born in the Basque province of Labourd at Louhossoa in 1901, the son of a Basque customs agent.[14] Orphaned by the death of his parents in 1907 and 1908, he was raised by an uncle and aunt who spoke only the Béarnais dialect of Occitan in the home. He entered the Petit Séminaire, where he found at play that his schoolmates spoke freely in Basque. At the Petit Séminaire his mentor was Abbé Bastinçorri. In 1920–1921 he studied at the Grand Séminaire at Bayonne, where he was greatly influenced by the Basque language militancy of his mentor, Mgr. Saint-Pierre. The latter intervened with one of Lafitte's aunts in order that he learn Basque and further reproached the young Lafitte for preaching in Béarnais and not Basque. From 1921 onward Lafitte began to write in Basque and set out to read everything that had been written between 1545, the date of the first Basque-language confessional, and 1920. According to Chanoine Lafitte, more books appeared in the Basque language in any one year during the 1970s than were published between 1545 and 1920.

In 1921 Lafitte began his studies for the *licence ès lettres* at the Institut Catholique de Toulouse, where he remained until he was ordained as a priest in 1924. During that time Lafitte was troubled by the low level of religious practice among the people of Toulouse and saw his mission to nourish them, marry them, and otherwise regularize their lives. He also maintained that one had first to feed an individual before converting him. Among the early elements of his thought which would reappear repeatedly in his later Basque militancy were a suspicion of the anticlericalism and centralization of the French state; the liberation of women, especially regarding salaries and the right to vote; and the defense of unions and corporate groups. He attempted, at least in part, to relate all these efforts to the body of ancient Basque customary laws or *fors*, which he felt would have a purifying influence in a morally threatening age. In relating his program to past customary law, he deliberately sought to make them seem less revolutionary in scope. Still, Lafitte remembered being called "le rouge et le noir" after Stendhal's novel of the same name, a (Communist) red in priestly black. Between 1928 and 1933 he contributed to a fledgling Catholic newspaper in Bordeaux called *Le Carillon des Jeunes* in which, writing under the pseudonym Pierrette Labbé, he advanced many of his earlier themes, especially regarding the liberation of women and the defense of the family. He came to see the revival of Basque culture and traditions as one means for the solution of the social ills afflicting France in this period.

Lafitte returned to his alma mater, the Petit Séminaire, as a professor in

1926, soon after it opened its new campus in Ustaritz. It was from this position that he came to influence virtually the entire generation of young Basque
militants in the 1930s and 1940s. Much of his own distinctive political philosophy emerges clearly in his Basque newspaper, *Aintzina*, whose pages
were filled by a variety of articles under his many pseudonyms. *Aintzina*
was a product of its times, and we can identify some of the crises within
the church and within French ideas at the time which suggest the origins of
Lafitte's thought.

FRENCH CATHOLIC DOGMA AFTER THE SEPARATION: MODERNISME, SILLON, AND L'ACTION FRANÇAISE

One of the earliest and most direct responses to the anticlericalism of the
radical Third Republic was the appearance and popularity of a number of
new Catholic movements which sought to reinstill vigor and dynamism in
now challenged dogma. Three of the most important of those movements
were *modernisme*, Marc Sangnier's *Le Sillon*, and especially Charles Maurras's
L'Action Française.[15] To these were added the philosophic influence of Max
Scheler and the later Ordre Nouveau.

   Le Sillon was the name of a Christian social journal created in 1894 by Paul
Renaudin as a response to the anticlericalism rampant in France in the aftermath of the Dreyfus Affair.[16] In 1902 its control passed to Marc Sangnier and
it became the primary publication of the Christian Democratic movement in
France. In 1904 his weekly, *L'Eveil Démocratique*, had a press-run of 50,000
copies. *Sillonisme* was criticized by the Catholic Church as an instrument
of "politicization" and "social modernism," and Pope Pius X condemned
Sangnier in August 1910. Though Sangnier denounced the pope in a letter
to French bishops later that month, he nonetheless submitted to papal authority. Despite the disapproval of the church, according to some sources,
his disciples remained among the front rank of the social Catholic movement
after World War I. Sangnier remained active. Among his later works, he created the network of youth hostels (*auberges de jeunesse*) in France and was
elected a deputy in 1946, shortly before his death in 1950.

   Le Sillon enjoyed a notable success in the Basses-Pyrénées, and Moreau reports that its organ in Pau, *Le Patriote*, had a larger readership than all three
Catholic newspapers in Bayonne.[17] One important supporter in the Pays
Basque was Abbé Sebastian Hiriart, known as Hiriart-Makola, who served
on the teaching faculty at Larressore and then at Belloc until 1918. According
to Moreau, *Le Sillon* was violently opposed by the "concordant" bishop of
Bayonne, Mgr. Gieure, but supported by others, including the superiors of
certain Catholic colleges, among them Larressore. Despite Sangnier's sub-

mission to papal authority in 1910, the impact of his ideas continued among the Basque teaching faculty and was one element in the Catholic socialization of Basque youth, among them Pierre Lafitte.

Second, *modernisme* was, according to Moreau, a doctrinal amalgam of "the religious symbolism of Hébert, the moral dogmatism of Labretonnière, the pragmatism of Edouard le Roy, the liberal exegesis of Loisy, and the theological modernism of Tyrrell."[18] What is noteworthy is that the Institut Catholique of Toulouse was suspected of being a seedbed of *modernisme* by Mgr. Gieure. Pierre Lafitte enrolled there in 1920 after graduating from the Petit Séminaire at Larressore and the Grand Séminaire at Bayonne.

Third, and most important of all, was the impact of L'Action Française, symbol of the complex figure of Charles Maurras on French nationalist and intellectual life. As Chanoine Etienne Salaberry put it:

> Around the year 1920, when I was awakening to the life of the spirit, Charles Maurras wielded an absolute dictatorship over French intellectualism. His power wasn't the lesser on the left than on the right. . . . At a certain epoch, France was Maurras, and Maurras was France.[19]

L'Action Française found its foothold in the Basses-Pyrénées between 1906 and 1909 and was seen as one means of undercutting the anticlericalism of the period.[20] Fifteen hundred people attended a reunion in Pau in 1911, including the future Basque deputy Jean Ybarnégaray. According to Moreau, L'Action Française targeted the Catholic teaching institutions, in particular the Petit Séminaire of Larressore. Among its participants was Abbé Laurent Apestéguy, *aumonier* of Basque Catholic Youth between 1919 and 1924. The followers of L'Action Française at the Grand Séminaire at Bayonne were, according to Moreau, "a very little group, of a very riled up and evil spirit."[21] On September 7, 1910, the bishop of Bayonne wrote to one of its followers, a professor at the Petit Séminaire:

> After having long reflected, consulted, prayed, I have decided to relieve you at the Seminary. You know in what trouble, what agitation one has lived there; divisions between teachers, between students. I would like to bring back peace and union.[22]

The decision of the pope to condemn L'Action Française and place it on the Index threw French Catholicism into great disarray.[23] According to Jacques Maritain:

> By this fact, a good number of young Catholics found themselves without a cause, demobilized, while in other times they would have found

in the Maurrassian troops an outlet for their need of action and their re-
volts. This no doubt explains in part the relatively important role Catholics played in the birth of several of the youth movements of the 1930s.[24]

This crisis in 1926 came at the same time that the Petit Séminaire was
finally able to return to new quarters at Ustaritz, after twenty years of exile
at Belloc. According to Lafitte, other important influences on the ideology
of these young Basque militants of the 1930s were the philosophic writings
of Scheler, and (in its concept of *personnalisme*) the doctrines of Ordre Nouveau asserted by such writers as Henri Daniel-Rops, Dandieu, Alexandre
Marc,[25] and Emmanuel Mounier.[26] While Jean-Paul Malherbe sees in this
migration the melding of Maurrassian ideas with the influence of Proudhon or M. A. Bakunin, it is clear that the result in Pierre Lafitte's political
philosophy was a distinct amalgam of personal freedom, Basque tradition,
progressive Catholicism, and suspicion of the state. As Lafitte identified his
philosophy in the prefatory quotation to this chapter, it included such political platforms as "regionalism, decentralization, religious liberty, restoration
of the old laws [*fors*], feminism, antistatism."[27] For his later critics, in particular Marc Légasse, who figured in the life and death of the second series
of *Aintzina* during World War II, Lafitte would be dismissed as a fanatical reactionary of the mold of the founder of Basque nationalism in Spain, Sabino
Arana Goiri, albeit with progressive elements.[28] The parallel seems particularly apt. For, as Lafitte himself notes in regard to the life and work of Sabino
Arana Goiri:

> I don't believe in spontaneous generation. If Sabino de Arana Goiri was
> the master we celebrate today, it is that his personal genius found a
> propitious milieu for its blossoming and its development.[29]

As Lafitte cites Sabino's own words, "I had the impression that God wanted
to save me for something . . ."[30]

EUGÈNE GOYHENECHE (1915–1989)

Central to the circle of young Basque militants around Abbé Pierre Lafitte
was Eugène Goyheneche.[31] Goyheneche's militancy reads like a road map
of French Basque nationalism and represents the vitality and variety of a
political idea over more than fifty years. Goyheneche was successively a student briefly at the Petit Séminaire; a student at Saint Louis de Gonzague in
Bayonne; a student in Paris at the Sorbonne and the Ecole Nationale des
Chartes; prominent in the team of young Basques who created the newspaper *Aintzina*; later closely associated with the expatriate Spanish Basque
population exiled in France after the Civil War; an accused collaborator with

Nazi occupational forces, condemned to life at hard labor after the war, pardoned, then appointed departmental archivist in the overseas department of Martinique; historian; and associate professor (*maître Assistant*) of Basque Studies at the University of Pau until his retirement in 1983. Goyheneche's ideological contribution to the Basque idea in the 1930s rivals Lafitte's own, and he remains one of the most important intellectual figures in the French Basque movement in the twentieth century.

Goyheneche was born in 1915 into the elite bourgeois family of Dr. Edmond Goyheneche of Ustaritz. The elder Goyheneche was well respected as a Basque social and political notable, a doctor of medicine in the local community and elected *conseiller général* from the *circonscription* of Ustaritz for forty-five years from 1919 to 1964.

Like his father before him, Eugène entered the Petit Séminaire for preparatory study in that doctrinally turbulent time of exile from Larressore, continuing through the return to its new location near Ustaritz. Receiving his *baccalaureat* from Saint Louis de Gonzague in 1932, he left to pursue his studies for the *licence* in history at the Sorbonne in Paris as well as to study later at the national school for archivists, the Ecole Nationale des Chartes. It was in that distant atmosphere, conceptually and geographically separate from the foothills of the Pyrénées, that his sense of Basque identity became most real.[32]

In the 1930s the Sorbonne was already experiencing the overcrowding that would give way in the 1960s to university reforms and the construction of new campuses throughout France. To be at the Sorbonne in the 1930s was to be immersed in a teeming cauldron of French intellectual life. Here diverse ideas, movements, and traditions met and interacted. This spirit of challenge and inquiry no doubt contrasted with the rote dissertation style of French academics in the jam-packed amphitheaters of the Sorbonne. It should not be surprising that this vibrant, impersonal, and intellectual Parisian milieu should affect the identities of young Basques—albeit sons of the bourgeoisie—from the rural Basque interior. As Goyheneche wrote around 1933, "Often our compatriots, parting with great hopes, find themselves upon their arrival . . . in a French city absolutely deprived of all, isolated, and disarmed for the hard combat they will have to undertake."[33]

In this Parisian "exile," Goyheneche began to communicate with other young Basques in Paris and in the Pays Basque, as well as with young militants from other minority groups in France. An as yet ill-defined sense of nationalism began to emerge in Goyheneche's thinking that would accelerate in 1932 and 1933 through his correspondence with Lafitte, Abbé Urricarriet, G. Mendiboure, Pierre Amoçain, Michel Diharce, Jacques Mestelan, and a number of militants of other ethnic groups, among them the Breton militant Yann Fouéré, and the circle of federalists and regionalists around Jean Charles-Brun.

In 1932 Goyheneche wrote of his political beliefs to G. Mendiboure in Saint-Jean-de-Luz. At first confusing Eugène with his father Edmond, Mendiboure then went on in a letter dated July 28, 1932, to discuss the political philosophy of Charles Maurras and speak of the potential for political mobilization in the Basque country of France:

> Until the present moment of Transpyrenean nationalism it could seem chimerical to preach nationalism in our land [*pays*]. I admit that it is possible now. . . . But I am well afraid that all these votes, counter-projects etc. . . . of the Spanish Basque country won't come to harden things in such a way as to sap the enthusiasm and absorb all the energies to the profit of the politicians in Madrid and their creatures. This has happened in France. However, I congratulate you on your ardor as a Basque and, as I told you, if it is impossible to be a good Frenchman as a result of the breaking up of France by democracy, be good Basques. For that, propaganda is needed. I am sure you will do your utmost possible. . . . Politics first and foremost.[34]

THE CREATION OF THE PARISIAN CHAPTER OF THE ESKUAL-IKASLEEN BILTZARRA, 1933

This call to Basque political mobilization found its first stirring in the area of language and culture. Heretofore the primary focus for the preservation of Basque language and culture in both France and Spain had been the conservative and traditionalist Eskualzaleen Biltzarra (Association of Basque Studies), founded on September 11, 1902, in Fontarrabie in the Spanish Basque province of Gipuzkoa.[35] Based on the linguistic inspiration of Sabino Arana Goiri, the association sought to revitalize the use and study of the Basque language. In its avowed apolitical nature, it was reminiscent of the Provençal movement, the Felibrige, of Frédéric Mistral. The Eskualzaleen Biltzarra served as the major point of contact for culturally concerned Basques on both sides of the border.

Affiliated with the Eskualzaleen Biltzarra was a student organization known as the Eskual-Ikasleen Biltzarra (Association of Basque Students), with chapters in university towns such as Bilbao, Madrid, Barcelona, and Brussels.[36] The idea came to Goyheneche and others in December 1932 to begin a chapter of the Eskual-Ikasleen Biltzarra in Paris. It was thus founded by Goyheneche, Alamon, and Gaillasteguy on February 2, 1933, with Goyheneche as its first president. It had thirty to forty members from

France and Spain, of which at least five were Basques from Spain.[37] Among its members was later deputy Jean Etcheverry-Ainchart.

According to *Le Courrier de Bayonne*, the goal of the new group was to further the study and love of the Basque land and its traditions.[38] In fact, the motivations were more complex and turned as much on the nature of the individuals involved, as on the perennial desire of youth for political action.

A major theme in the writings of Goyheneche during this time was the danger to Basque culture posed by the defeatism of certain popular authors, among them the article entitled, "Les Basques: Un peuple qui s'en va," by the geographer Elisée Réclus in the *Revue des Deux Mondes* in 1867.[39] Responding to Réclus's prediction of the disappearance of Basque culture, Goyheneche wrote: "This odious blasphemy toward our race and our people has been repeated often since."[40] Thus, Goyheneche captured a major reason for the founding of the Paris chapter of the Eskual-Ikasleen Biltzarra:

> It is to struggle against the double danger of defeatism . . . and of indifference on the part of youth that we had decided in January 1933 to found a section of the Association of Basque Students.[41]

Another major theme in Goyheneche's writing at this time was the role of youth in nationalist movements:

> In every national renaissance, youth, and especially intellectual youth, have played a preponderant role. They have been above all the avant-garde of magnificent, heroic movements which have illustrated the illustrious history of the nineteenth and twentieth centuries; one could not fail at such a glorious mission in the Basque country.[42]

Thus, as the news was later transmitted in *Aintzina* in 1935, "it was necessary for the intellectual elite of the Pays Basque to stay united in the work and love of the country."[43]

Still, Goyheneche worried about the "elite" nature of nationalism as a political phenomenon cut off from everyday reality. Does this tendency to differentiate oneself from one's neighbors "manifest itself spontaneously and clearly in the people? Or then is it vague in the people and isn't it only expressed by some intellectuals?"[44] Sharing these same ideas with Abbé Pierre Lafitte at the Petit Séminaire back in Ustaritz, Goyheneche received the following reply:

> It is difficult to guide our people. That is in part what has made them last. I am of the same opinion as you on the import of our relations with the countryside. They should serve all the more for "internal use":

make people aware of their particular nature, give importance to this particularism. In sum, give them pride in being Basque.[45]

Goyheneche described the fine line which the movement would walk:

The intellectuals will be destined to compose the cadres of the party. . . . But our party must not be a party of intellectuals, it must be a popular party. Without that . . . certain failure . . . without the people we can do nothing. What good is it if our language and our traditions are cultivated by some scholars if they are abandoned by the people?[46]

The resulting statement of goals by the young organization Eskual-Ikasleen Biltzarra was an effort to depict as moderate certain ideas which had been seen as nationalist among Spanish Basques since 1931, if not since the time of Arana Goiri decades before. Among its elements were the commitment to conform to the traditional principles of the Basque country, submitting itself in all cases to the rules and interests of Catholic morality (art. 2, para. 1) and asserting that it had no political tendencies (art. 2, para. 2).[47] Far from abandoning Catholicism as its doctrine became more explicitly nationalistic, Goyheneche described the thematic unity of Basque nationalism and Catholicism in a letter to one of his priestly mentors, a man whose ideas on nationalism and race had profound effects on Goyheneche's thinking, Abbé Jean-Pierre Urricarriet:

For a Basque is no longer a Basque if he ceases to be a believer. Religion is an essential element of our nationality . . . the Basque, in remaining a believer in the midst of pagans, will find in his religion an element which will distinguish him from his neighbors. For the moment, the three poles of Basque nationality are *Religion, Race, Language*.[48]

In Urricarriet's few remaining letters (he died during World War II), one sees a greater insistence on race as a defining characteristic of Basque nationality than in any other nationalist of his generation. In one letter to Goyheneche, Urricarriet says:

Man is not one. A white has nothing in common with a black. A German with a Latin. They are elected races, *races* destined to rule and others to obey. In each people what must be cultivated and retained is that which differentiates them from their neighbors. Language, folklore. Each particular language supposes a particular manner of expression and thus of feeling. What is this particular *kultur?*[49]

The logical conclusion of this nationalist self-differentiation was evident. As Goyheneche wrote to Urricarriet, in clearer terms than in any of his other public writing of the period:

In my opinion, the only workable solution, the only lasting, the only one which will satisfy our dignity as Basques is *separatism*. . . . This solution alone will permit us to protect our Religion, our Race, and our Language. So long as we remain tied to the French state, this latter will assail our religion. But it is evident that this *necessary* separatism can only be envisioned in the long term—a whole mentality must be created, a new mentality which I see with joy appearing in the youth.[50]

Goyheneche's pointed defense of separatism in private contrasted neatly with the moderation and denials of separatism he maintained in public, including one notable exchange with the Basque deputy Jean Lissar. Having written Lissar asking for his moral and financial support of the new group, Goyheneche received the following reply on June 20, 1933:

It is with all my heart that I would accept the honor that your kind Association has given me if you would first have the goodness to reassure me on the ideas of separatism which, it seems, figure in the program of your group.[51]

Goyheneche responded to the deputy by return mail the same day, denying any separatist intention:

From the point of view of separatism, it will never figure in the program of the Association of Basque Students. . . . We have decided that never under any pretext will we engage in politics. The diversity of our political and even for some religious ideas was the best guarantee that this decision would be respected.[52]

Goyheneche then went on to assure Lissar that the group had the same cultural goals as the Eskualzaleen Biltzarra. Moreover, Goyheneche noted, his own father *conseiller général* Dr. Edmond Goyheneche had the same fears regarding separatism; as Goyheneche reassured Lissar, "he would never have permitted me to take part in any separatist movement." Goyheneche continues: "You know the most part of these young people: in general they are all Catholics, of the [political] right, without political ideas."[53] Goyheneche concluded his reassurance by stating, "I am not separatist . . . I am simply a regionalist . . . separatism . . . is a madness, a dangerous utopia."[54]

Goyheneche's eloquence evidently succeeded, for on June 23, 1933, Lissar replied, "It is with pleasure that I read your kind letter whose frank explanations dissipated the only hesitations I could have in being one of yours."[55] On July 5, 1933, Lissar contributed 200 francs to the group to permit it to air its existence on Radio-Paris.[56] Despite the frankly misleading nature of this exchange, as Goyheneche would laugh forty years later, "One never tells the truth to a deputy, and especially not when asking for money!"[57]

By 1935 the group's goals in Paris included radio interviews, articles for magazines and newspapers, relations with student groups in Paris, and fraternal collaboration with the young peninsular Basques (of Spain), who, Goyheneche wrote, "remain still too much strangers and from whom we have all to learn."[58]

At the same time, the effort at mobilization was continuing in the Basque country as well. A critical mass of young Basque militants both in Paris and in the Basque country around Abbé Lafitte was beginning to coalesce. As one young militant wrote repeatedly to Goyheneche during 1932:

> There is one thing which we always lack; it is a small association of *abertzale* of the three Basque provinces called French: you who know him better than I, M. Lafitte, you could speak to him about it; maybe he will come [up with] something. It wouldn't even be impossible to publish a monthly magazine, for example. If we lack a little money at the beginning, the Basques of Spain would give us a little. . . . Maybe what I'm saying to you doesn't have any reason for being yet: you have but to see for yourself with M. Lafitte.[59]

The Eskualerriste Movement and the Creation of the Basque Newspaper *Aintzina*

By 1932 Pierre Lafitte had begun to gather around him a number of young Basques who seemed ready for the kind of organization which would give structure to their identities as young Basques. In holographic and unpublished manuscripts from this period, Lafitte proposed creating a party which would seek to recruit young Basque intellectual "emigrants" in the university cities and in *lycées* and *collèges* within the Pays Basque itself.[60] Members would be eligible if they were born of Basque parents or had lived in the Pays Basque for ten years and were nominated by two members. The goal of this party would be to learn, recruit, organize, and teach.

These ideas formed the basis of the Eskualerriste movement which Lafitte created in 1933.[61] Its published program included fifteen points, among them:[62]

—The Eskualerriste program is summarized in the slogan God and the ancient law (*Jainkoa eta lege zaharra*).
—A commitment to work for political decentralization and against the modern unitary state.

—A call for Basque to be made a co-equal official language alongside French.
—A defense of Basque culture in its many manifestations.
—The defense of women's rights, and the recruitment of women in the movement.
—A "foreign policy" toward Basques in the four provinces within Spain.
—Support of the demands of other regionalist and federalist movements in France.

In an accompanying narrative to the Eskualerriste program, Lafitte discusses the particularly political nature of the group's platform.[63] First and foremost, he makes clear: "We are not separatists."[64] While maintaining close ties with Basques in Spain, Lafitte argued that each group should remain master of its own house, they in Spain, we in France. Moreover, he claimed that the real separatist is the one who would divide the Basques on both sides of the frontier, a theme later often repeated by the contemporary Basque movement. As he wrote, "We don't want to break either with France (political separatism), nor with Spanish Basques (ethnic separatism), nor with Catholicism (religious separatism), nor with the past (historical separatism)."[65]

In a contemporaneous unpublished and handwritten manuscript entitled "Réponses," Lafitte dwelled at length on the political doctrine of the young movement.[66] The Eskualerriste movement would be above all regionalist, democratic, and antistatist, with the commune as its basic unit of organization. Lafitte believed the regionalist sentiment to be a real one among the people, but both an advantage and a risk, for as he put it:

> The regionalist sentiment is very real among the people and it would suffice to excite them but a little in order to transform it into a separatist élan. . . . The new party intends to remain on the regionalist terrain, considering separatism unrealizable.[67]

The conclusion for Lafitte was a statute of autonomy within a federal French state:

> Certainly a Basque statute which would attach our two *arrondissements* to a federal French state would be desirable from a cultural, linguistic, educational, and religious point of view: it is just this necessity which renders any separatist dream utopian in our eyes. No, the logic of the movement does not imply separatism: for this logic applies to the real and reality attaches us economically to France.[68]

Yet, at the same time, Eugène Goyheneche's thinking was progressing in even more radical directions, a sign that the movement was already succeeding like the sorcerer's apprentice in unleashing forces of Basque nationalism beyond its control. For Goyheneche would write in late 1933 that the goal of the movement was to work for the unity and independence of our "Patrie Euzkadi."[69] The means of this action were threefold: (1) wholly support the work of the Parti Eskualerriste as a first indispensable stage in the evolution of the Pays Basque toward independence; (2) render the output of the party more radical and more extremist, by propaganda and by flooding separatist elements into the interior of the party; and (3) a secret, violent, electoral and indefatigable action without mercy against French domination and all it represents. This was in clear contrast to Goyheneche's public assurances to Jean Lissar. Yet Lafitte's moderation clearly won out; while Goyheneche's attention would soon turn to the Spanish Basque cause during the Spanish Civil War, Lafitte's small group embraced a confessional regionalism whose slogan *Jainkoa eta lege zaharra* (God and the ancient law) flowed directly from Arana Goiri's writings and appealed for mainstream public support.

Central to the Eskualerriste appeal was the use of religious symbols among this devoutly Catholic population. In their publications, the Eskualerristes insisted that God was the basis of their politics and the Catholic Church was God's interpreter on earth. But to avoid papal bans on explicit political activity by the concordant church, the Eskualerristes denied being a Catholic party, and at least publicly forbade ecclesiastics from being active or dues-paying members, though they played an important role below the surface.

The Eskualerriste movement was thus formally announced as a movement of Basque youth: "The Eskualerristes are young French Basques having decided to spread their political ideas, and above all to organize for a methodical labor on the electoral terrain."[70] But as Lafitte noted:

> The Eskualerriste movement was not created by intellectuals properly speaking, but by the middle class (the young militants emerge for the most part from primary school . . .). Certainly, one finds certain more educated elements (a lawyer, a professor, a doctor, students in law or medicine).[71]

Any movement seeking to represent Basque cultural symbols legitimately would live or die in the rural countryside where Basque ethnic identity and language use had always been strongest. As Goyheneche put it, "The movement doesn't need militants of the pavement, it needs militants of the barnyard [*fumier*]."[72] The movement thus slowly began to form from these beginnings. As Lafitte recollected, the movement began as a study circle in Ustaritz—not as a movement, but as "a little minority of nothing at all."[73]

But it was hardly a popular movement because Basque political culture remained suspicious and hostile to new ideas. What was lacking was a means of spreading the word. To be sure, *Eskualduna,* the dominant Basque newspaper of the time, with a weekly readership of more than 8,700, gave the movement publicity, as did the bimonthly review *Gure Herria,* with a readership of 700.[74] But, as Lafitte noted:

> The newspaper [*Eskualduna*] reaches the farmer and very few the bourgeoisie. The journal [*Gure Herria*] reaches clerics, doctors, notaries, and other bourgeois. We are planning a more particularly political newspaper.[75]

And while the movement in reality had fewer than twenty members according to both Goyheneche and Lafitte, in order to suggest a public groundswell, Lafitte wrote circa 1932: "The still young movement has but several hundred adherents."[76]

The Creation of the Nationalist Newspaper *Aintzina,* 1934

The hour seems to have come to take a step forward and to give all our care to a political organization. That is why Aintzina risks the light. It wants to be a humble lantern which helps to move forward in the night.
—*Aintzina* 1, no. 1 (October 1934)

By late 1933 it was apparent that the young Basque movement needed its own newspaper through which to propagate its ideas. Again Lafitte gently planted the seed. As the young militant Jacques Mestelan wrote to Eugène Goyheneche on November 16, 1933:

> Regarding the press, here is a newspaper which would be very useful in our movement. As Pierre Lafitte said, it needs a young man with the head of a journalist who can take on the newspaper. But who? I would like to be ten years older and I would do it. Because that would be an important stage in our game. We'll think about it again I hope.[77]

Later, on February 16, 1934, Mestelan again wrote to Goyheneche to reveal the planning already taking place:

> And we also have another path; it's still a vague project, but I hope it will happen: that of founding a newspaper or a monthly or bimonthly bulletin. In having it printed at the Orphanage in Tarbes, M. Lafitte calculated that that would come to . . . fifteen francs per column, thus 90

francs for one page of six columns. Only where is the money? . . . Also, that's not all, we must assure an ongoing publication since M. Lafitte cannot do this job alone. Beyond that, I think that we could make it with 800 subscriptions or newspapers sold, paying the costs of printing. And we could write in it what we want. I just made a discovery that maybe you have already made: . . . I saw that the ideas [of *La Revue Française*] were nearly the same as ours: they seem to be fairly strong, nearly in the same sense as *l'Esprit* and *L'Ordre Nouveau*.[78]

In the early fall of 1934, an announcement appeared regarding the coming appearance of *Aintzina*. While the common definition of *Aintzina* in the French Basque Labourdin dialect is "forward," it is also interesting to note that among Spanish Basques the word also meant "ancient" or "a long time ago." Here, as with the dual sense of revolution (*iraultza*), meaning both "change" and "return," the very word *Aintzina* suggested a movement forward into the purity of the past.[79] As Lafitte would later write in *Aintzina*, "The past is our guide."

The announcement said that *Aintzina* would discuss in Basque and in French the personalist, familial, and social doctrine of young Basques; give news of other regionalist movements in France; and finally and above all interest itself in civic, union, and artistic activity of organizations in the three French Basque provinces. Subscriptions were offered for three francs, five francs for supporting members. "Again a Basque newspaper? . . . finally a Basque newspaper! That was lacking in the Basque country, a truly Basque newspaper, a newspaper of living, interested, and courageous youth!"[80]

Accordingly, volume 1, number 1 of the new paper appeared in October 1934. Its nominal editor was a 29-year-old baker from Ustaritz, Jean Duboscq. According to Duboscq, 1,200 copies of *Aintzina* were printed.[81] Of the 300 subscriptions, more than half were held by members of the clergy, but a particular part of the clergy, as Duboscq recollected—the teaching clergy—for he argued that the parish priests of the time were less free to deal with ideas and so viewed *Aintzina* with suspicion. Within two months of the newspaper's first edition Mestelan wrote:

The number of subscriptions has increased . . . but it's not yet sufficient . . . M. Lafitte says that we need 500 to balance our accounts for next year . . . I've just learned that the exact number of subscriptions is 230. It's meager. We must make the number climb to 300 by summer vacation.[82]

THE POLITICAL GOALS OF AINTZINA

The goal of the newspaper became clear from its first issue: to serve as a focal point for Basque mobilization and a source for the propagation of Lafitte's particular political doctrine. As *Aintzina* printed in its first edition, "If men are isolated, their action will be nearly null. An organized party is more stable: men pass on, the party remains; a collective doctrine evolves more slowly than individual opinion." [83]

Foremost in the early editions of the paper was a call to moral and spiritual purification on the part of Basque youth:

> The old proverb is right. "Let each person sweep before his own door and the street will be clean. . . ." That is why we are regionalists. . . . We believe we're better able to know our Pays Basque and give it the medication it needs. This little newspaper would like to lead the youth in the sense of a great renovation which would touch in part on eternal principles, the only solid foundation of all moral construction, and on the other hand on the concrete resources of the individual, the family, and the region.[84]

Much of this moral crisis to be combated lay in the nature of French society:

> They imposed on us a decadent, materialist, irreligious, antifamilial Latin civilization. . . . The remedy for so great an evil is the awakening of a Basque consciousness in all the Provinces, under the sign of our ancient slogan *Jainkoa eta lege zaharra:* "God and the ancient law." Basque people, awaken yourselves! Don't forget your past, keep your spirit of independence, and react against the sacrileges of those who don't want to understand you.[85]

The goals of the Eskualerristes was morally to resist the corruption of French society:

> The essential task which falls to the true Eskualerriste: maintain the Basque soul at the moral level of his ancestors while not permitting it to decline or become corrupted in contact with the nefarious influences of modern society.[86]

THE MEMBERSHIP OF AINTZINA

The group which surrounded Abbé Lafitte was a small but dedicated one. Lafitte himself, however, continued to write much of the content of the monthly editions, using multiple pseudonyms like "JEL" or "Junior." Among the young militants around Lafitte were Eugène Goyheneche; Jacques (Jakes)

Mestelan, who wrote under the pseudonyms "Jakue" and Jakes Lehuntze (the village where he lived); Pierre Amoçain, a dedicated young militant who later emigrated to Chile; Jean Duboscq, the nominal editor of *Aintzina* whose militancy was short-lived and who remained a baker in Ustaritz, a Gaullist, and Eugène Goyheneche's next-door neighbor for the next fifty-five years; Mayi Diharce, one of the few women in *Aintzina;* Jean de Jaureguiberry, an aristocratic young doctor from Sibas, near Tardets in the interior of Soule; and his sister, Madeleine de Jaureguiberry, who was secretary to the Begira-leak, the women's group within *Aintzina,* under the pseudonym of Augusta Larralde. Mademoiselle de Jaureguiberry, as she was known throughout her life, became active along with Jacques Maritain in the ardent defense of Spanish Basque Catholics in their Republican alliance with Communist and anarchist forces during the Spanish Civil War. In addition to the dominant influence of Lafitte on the young movement, Abbé Léon Lassalle of the Petit Séminaire also contributed to *Aintzina* under the pseudonym "News Politic." According to Lafitte, one young Basque lawyer, Jean Biatarana, later adjunct to the mayor of Bayonne, was associated with the nascent movement for a short period.

The movement was thus created for Basque youth: "Our movement is made up above all of the young; it is in their hands. Aren't they the future?"[87] As Jean Duboscq mused in 1975, reflecting back on his short-lived and idealistic militancy more than forty years before: "We were young. We needed a cause, something to believe in."[88]

THE DOCTRINE OF AINTZINA: SOCIAL, POLITICAL, AND REGIONALIST

The political philosophy which thus emerges from *Aintzina* was an evolving discussion based on the personalist political philosophy of Pierre Lafitte which guided the Eskualerriste movement. The three broad elements of the ideology of *Aintzina* were its Christian social and family policy, its political tradition and view of the French state, and its awareness of the activity of other regionalist movements in France. Curiously absent was any ongoing coverage of the emerging Spanish Civil War and the plight of the Spanish Basque people.

CHRISTIAN SOCIAL AND FAMILY POLICY

Central to the ideology of Aintzina was the slogan *Jainkoa eta lege zaharra* (God and the ancient law). It reflected, as had Basque militancy in the late nineteenth century, the symbiosis between Basque cultural symbols and religiosity. As the Eskualerriste program put it, "God served first, . . . and it is the church that we will demand, like our ancestors, to teach us to serve Him in our political life as in our private life."[89] Moreover, "We suffer morally and politically. We will not heal politically without healing morally."[90]

The basis of this moral action would be a new unity of the individual, family, and region under this Christian doctrine:

> This little journal would like to lead youth in the way of a great renovation which will touch in part on eternal principles, . . . and in another part on the concrete resources of the person, family, and region.[91]

Each was tied intimately into the "personalist" political philosophy of Pierre Lafitte:

> If one doesn't make men good individually, no good families; without good families, no good communes; without good communes, no good regions; without good regions, no good nations, without good nations, no peace on earth.[92]

The family was the primary unit in this cultural and moral struggle: "We are Basques and by consequence of a race where the rights of the family are sacred."[93] As the Eskualerriste program argued, "Our party doesn't forget that for a true Basque the center of all interests is the home, *etchea:* . . . our program is essentially familial."[94] Such was the intent of Madeleine de Jaureguiberry's Begiraleak movement, part of the young group around *Aintzina*, which saw itself as a Basque regionalist and feminist group dedicated to saving Basque language, faith, and institutions.[95]

The solution to these problems for Lafitte involved a number of positions, some familiar, including the defense of the Basque language and the defense of private Catholic schooling. According to Jean-Paul Malherbe, other positions taken by Lafitte in *Aintzina* reflected papal encyclicals of the time, such as the defense of a "family vote" and "family salary" from the encyclical *Rerum novarum* of Leon XIII and the defense of corporatism (as an alternative to class struggle), which appeared in the encyclical *Quadragesimo anno* of Pius XI.[96]

Whether the threat was to language, religion, family life, or the commune—all pillars of Basque cultural traditions—the source of that threat was seen as the French state.

THE POLITICAL PHILOSOPHY OF AINTZINA: ITS VIEW OF CENTRALIZATION AND THE STATE

The treatment of the French state in the pages of *Aintzina* is central to its philosophy, owing as much to the inheritance of religious antipathies in the aftermath of the crisis of separation as to the defense of Basque language

and culture. The criticism took the form of resistance to Jacobin ideology, a
pointed critique of centralization, and a growing hostility to the French left
on the eve of the legislative elections of 1936.

One of the most urgent political criticisms in *Aintzina* involved the Jacobin
socialization of the state:

> History is also a school of patriotism, on the condition that it be true.
> Let it not be said to our kids: "Our fathers the Gauls" or "our French an-
> cestors" since in reality the Basques haven't ever been included under
> this label, and have even fought against the Gauls and the Francs.
>
> Nothing captivates the young more than the pure and simple tell-
> ing of the struggles waged by the Basques with diverse outcomes for
> the preservation of their independence against the Romans, Spanish,
> English, against . . . still others.[97]

The tradition of republican socialization was perhaps the greatest legacy
of the Third Republic, as it sought to forge the unified French *nation* from
which the republican state claimed its legitimacy. For *Aintzina*, the obstacles
were great:

> The task is difficult for us, for not only is the ignorance great, but it has
> been supported for a long time by the primary prejudices of the Jacobin
> education that was imposed upon us.[98]

One of the greatest dangers to Basque identity was the centralizing tendencies of the French state:

> One of the great illusions that has precipitated the world in ruin is the
> mirage of centralization. Under the pretext that "union makes strong,"
> they have said "unity makes strong," and they sought no longer to unite,
> but to unify. They subordinated instead of coordinating. . . . Central-
> ization equals confusion, and confusion is disorder . . . instead of thus
> concentrating forces, why not decentralize them?[99]

The result was a call by Lafitte for resistance against the state: "For we are
antistatists, and my word!"[100] As it sought to organize itself into a political
movement, *Aintzina* called for passive resistance against the Jacobin state:

> Basques, continue to do the minimum demanded by civic duty toward
> a government which does not inspire any confidence; but reserve to our
> customs and our ancestral liberties the clearest and surest of our forces
> and our resources.[101]

The young group therefore called itself to political action: "The hour seemed
to have come to take a step forward [*Aintzina*] and to give to our efforts a

political organization." [102] Their goal: "to act on the political terrain in order to properly influence the general decisions of France." [103]

THE COMING OF THE FRONT POPULAIRE

The political activity of *Aintzina* was limited, however, to Christian, conservative, and regionalist editorializing and the support of conservative candidates, given the threat of the Popular Front looming in 1936. A conflicted Lafitte called for the support of the longtime deputy from the Basque interior, Jean Ybarnégaray, "who, it seems, doesn't like us very much." [104] Ybarnégaray was the lesser of two evils; the greater danger was the coming to power of the French left.

One thus witnesses in the months before the legislative elections of 1936 the most hostile and pointed commentary in *Aintzina* reserved for the Popular Front and for Léon Blum. Lamenting the lack of a true Christian party in France, Abbé Lassalle, writing in *Aintzina* as "News Politic," bitterly attacks the French left as:

This gangrene which festers in France from one end to the other of this land, as much among the workers in our factories, as in the middle of the populations in our countryside, it is necessary at any cost that we preserve our children and young people. [105]

Following the legislative elections in 1936, he wrote:

Blum has come to power. . . . Every regionalist who knows what he thinks must cry everywhere: "Down with Blum, the tyrant of the popular masses who enslaves us in the name of liberty." [106]

Then, echoing the symbolism of Dostoevsky's Grand Inquisitor, the editorial continues: "He enslaves us, but he feeds us, a worker from Bayonne told me, happy with a salary increase." [107]

After a year in power, *Aintzina*'s hostility remained undiminished and increasingly anti-Semitic:

There are moments in life where memory blooms in the soul with the power . . . of an obsession. For those who lived the years of the separation of the Church and state, [before] the comedy which is playing under the reign of the Jewish internationalist Léon Blum. . . . Thus it was then during the vote for this despoiling and hateful law of separation which accumulated ruins throughout France. Thus one proposed to destroy the religious armor of our traditionally Christian land. [108]

In reality, the Basque electorate in 1936 rallied as rarely before in opposition to the Popular Front, revealing once more the persistence of an unreconciled clerical electorate disaffected with the Third Republic.

AINTZINA, THE BASQUE ELECTORATE, AND THE
ELECTIONS OF 1936

In 1934 the "Affaire Stawisky" struck the political consciousness of France. Under the administration of Mayor Joseph Garat of Bayonne, it involved the mismanagement and fraud perpetrated on the Crédit Municipal in Bayonne by its cosmopolitan promoter, Alexandre Stawisky. According to René Cuzacq, the resulting conspiracy between certain leftist politicians and figures in high finance became a national scandal.[109] The result of this scandal was the alleged "suicide" of Stawisky and the political ruin of Mayor Garat. Deputy Jean Ybarnégaray had demanded that blame go right to the top,[110] and the municipal elections of 1934 brought Garat's defeat, a political result which demonstrated to Cuzacq that "the consequences of Stawisky were not yet exhausted."[111]

This scandal was transformed by *Aintzina* in its early issues into one more example of the moral crisis facing French politics and society. The intertwining in this case of moral decay, the political duplicity of leftist politicians, and the fact that Stawisky was a Jew of Hungarian extraction began to fuel themes which later would spring full-blown in *Aintzina*'s treatment of Léon Blum and the Popular Front. As a new religiously oriented political movement, choosing not to field its own candidates, but rather attempting to influence the electoral process, *Aintzina* insisted on the moral integrity of Basque candidates:

> The vote is not a question of interest or of parties; the least one can demand of the candidates is competence and propriety. Only in this way will dissipate this mystery which would make one believe in the fiscal perversion of our people or in its incorrigible cheating.[112]

Following the senatorial elections of late 1934, *Aintzina* reported the election of candidates Georges Champetier de Ribes and Jean Lissar at the polls, claiming, "We are happy to salute two new senators equally convinced of the danger of centralization."[113]

In fact, what became increasingly clear in this period was the bifurcation of Basque political culture into two phenomena: a persistent clerical conservatism on the part of rural Basques and a growing leftist vote in the linguistically heterogeneous cities on the Basque coast. The looming threat of a leftist victory in France began to mirror itself in *Aintzina*'s growing stridency: "During the last municipal elections in Bayonne, which were, as one knows, a triumph of popular stupidity . . . these imbecilic voters."[114]

Thus, the need to spread the Eskualerriste doctrine became the focus of *Aintzina*'s strategy for the upcoming legislative elections of 1936:

The legislative elections are approaching. We haven't assembled a sufficient organization in order to present Eskualerriste [candidates] and to pay for their electoral campaign.

That will come in its own time. We want to penetrate the municipal elections before attacking the . . . deputation.

Our friends shouldn't only vote for Ybarnégaray (who, it seems, doesn't like us very much), but struggle seriously.

We ask our Eskualerriste youth to profit from the electoral campaign by spreading their ideas while working for the triumph of Ybar . . . against the Popular Front.[115]

In the countryside, the threat of the Popular Front was real enough for *Aintzina* to caution the rural populations against those teachers who were

more or less revolutionary, adherents of masonic leagues . . . [and who waged] an active campaign in order to win our rural populations to communism. There exists in our dear Pays Basque an *arrondissement* . . . which is the especially coveted prey of the social-communists.[116]

JEAN YBARNÉGARAY

Faced with the threat of a Socialist victory, *Aintzina* supported the reelection of Jean Ybarnégaray, the longtime deputy from Basse-Navarre and one of the most important political figures in modern Basque history. Elected deputy between 1914 and 1940, he more than any other Basque politicians of his age had succeeded in championing the reality of rural Basque tradition. His political career culminated under Vichy, where he briefly served as minister of youth and sport. Charged with treason following the liberation, he was released because of his service to the Resistance. Nevertheless, he was forbidden from running for office for ten years. He ran for deputy again in 1956, but lost, and died shortly thereafter.

Bernard Ménou argues that Ybarnégaray was the product of a conservative and patriotic rural France, spared the effects of evolution:

This France is a closed world where traditional hierarchies perpetuate themselves. In the Pays Basque more than elsewhere, in the first half of the twentieth century, the organization of society seemed frozen. The Catholic clergy enclosed people, whereas the family constituted the most important milieu . . . in the life of the individual. It seemed that this society would not evolve.[117]

Ybarnégaray understood this rural society and remained an extremely popular political figure. Speaking of the illiteracy of this rural Basque population,

Abbé Mongaston claimed that Ybarnégaray once said that "it's better that way, otherwise they'd go live somewhere else."[118] Ybarnégaray's undeniable strength came from his ability to defend the traditions and thought of the rural Basque population and to serve as a voice capable of making itself heard in the highest councils of the state.

Thus, in the legislative elections of 1936, Ybarnégaray's overwhelming victory in the rural interior was hardly surprising. Of 12,918 valid votes cast, in the first round, Ybarnégaray received 11,043 votes to 1,875 for his Socialist adversary Alliez, whose votes came nearly entirely from Mauléon and Tardets, reflecting in part a radicalization of the shoe industry in Soule.[119] He virtually wiped out his opponent in his native Basse-Navarre, though in Saint-Etienne-de-Baigorri, railway workers and others gave the Communist candidate, a local teacher, 10 percent of the vote.

In the second *circonscription,* M. de Coral defeated M. Lannepouquet, mayor of Hendaye. René Delzangles, a strong opponent of the Popular Front, narrowly defeated the radical mayor of Bayonne, M. Simonet.[120] Yet, in the elections for *conseil général* the following year, in October 1937, Delzangles defeated Simonet by a margin of more than two to one, reflecting growing disenchantment with the Popular Front. It was in this context that *Aintzina* inveighed against the "gangrene" threatening France, led by the "tyrant" and "Jewish internationalist" Léon Blum, another radical French Republic which again threatened Basque faith and traditions.

The Regionalism of *Aintzina:* A Common Cause with Other Minority Groups in France

One of the most important legacies of *Aintzina* to the modern Basque movement was its awareness of the struggle of other ethnic minorities in France: Bretons, Flemish, Alsatians, Catalonians, and so forth. The heady discovery that took place in Paris in the 1930s gave rise to a host of regionalist and federalist movements and journals and ideas that continue to have force to the present day.

Among the most important influences on regionalist and federalist thinking in this era was that of Jean Charles-Brun. In his central work *Le régionalisme,* published in 1911, Charles-Brun provided the bridge between the federalist ideas of the nineteenth century and the regionalism of the twentieth.[121] His writings and gatherings in Paris socialized a whole generation of young militants and continued through World War II. He gave selflessly of his time in his devotion to the regionalist cause. Charles-Brun conceived of regionalism as more than just folklore, as he wrote in *Aintzina*:

> However, I would want that one not forget this: regionalism is a complete method, which applies to administrations, the economy, to pedagogy, to letters, to arts. The festivals, so brilliant and so useful as they are, do not constitute the whole and perhaps we should restrain ourselves a little . . . rather than to become the simple organizers of *spectacles*. I wouldn't have written these lines if the indifferent and the ignorant weren't inclined to hasty generalizations and if our adversaries didn't profit from them.[122]

Among the veritable explosion of groups and newspapers in this period were Charles-Brun's Fédération Régionaliste Française and his *L'Action Régionaliste; Esprit* and *Ordre Nouveau;* Erwin Reifenrath's Centre d'Action et d'Union des Régionalistes et des Fédéralistes Français (CAURFF); Marcel Peguy's *Le Fédéraliste* and Foyer des Etudes Fédéralistes; and young militants like Alexandre Marc (*Ordre Nouveau*) and Yann Fouéré (Breton nationalist and later exile) who would later give life along with Guy Héraud to the Mouvement Fédéraliste Européen, an influential force on ethnic movements in France in the 1960s, as we will see in chapter 4.[123]

One of the central elements in this regionalist thought was the distance it took from separatism. Unlike separatist thought which called for the right of national self-determination and political independence (influenced no doubt in part by the dismantlement of the Austro-Hungarian Empire at Versailles after World War I), regionalism called for greater autonomy within the reality of the existing French state and society and sought to render its regionalism compatible with greater French patriotism. Erwin Reifenrath wrote in an open letter of July 15, 1935, offering his services to "unify all federalists and regionalists as long as they don't attempt to harm national unity—that is, they can't be anti-French."[124] Similarly, in *Aintzina*, an article on Alsace-Lorraine argued that it was possible to serve one's "nationality" and the "grande patrie" at the same time,[125] an important proviso in an Alsace which had been separated from France between 1870 and 1914 and remained an object of Hitler's irredentist thought. This moderate regionalism was the doctrine which was embraced by Pierre Lafitte in the Eskualerriste platform and in the pages of *Aintzina*.

As Robert Audic wrote to Eugène Goyheneche on March 21, 1934:

> Everyone understands that the diverse minority groups governed at the present time by the French state would have an advantage in uniting

in order to resist the encroachments of central power, but it would be necessary, in order to do this, to have . . . a certain mutual knowledge of each other.[126]

It was in Paris that the first stirring of mutual awareness took place. Goyheneche wrote of this Paris of the 1930s:

> But the principal interest of Paris rests in the great exchange of ideas, in the innumerable political formations of all lands which are formed there and by which we should profit for our propaganda. The minority associations were the first to attract our attention: from February 1933 our brothers in the Paris section of the Parti National Breton gave a conference on Basque nationalism, and since then our association has collaborated with the Breton newspaper *Breiz Atao* and has undertaken the same ongoing relationships with the Alsatians, Flemish, and the French Catalans . . . we have made contact with national minorities oppressed by the Soviets, especially the Ukraine.[127]

The interethnic contacts developing between the Basques and other minorities in France took various forms. Much was informational and involved sharing details about history and common political hopes. Thus, members of the Flemish student movement Katholiek Vlaamsch Hoogstudenten Verbond, wrote that they were "vibrating with the same proud ideal which is also yours; we feel ourselves very close to you despite the distances."[128] Goyheneche, in turn, was able to channel much of the shared information back to the Pays Basque, where it appeared in *Aintzina*. Jacques Mestelan wrote to Goyheneche on December 13, 1934:

> Can you send me a copy of *Feu*, the regionalist newspaper of the Midi? Can you also give me precise information on the existence or nonexistence of regionalist movements in Auvergne? Finally, could you indicate to me a brochure where I would find an exact exposé of the situation of the regionalist movement in Flanders and of regionalist newspapers from the North written in French?
>   You see why I am asking you these questions. It's to continue a series of articles on the diverse regionalist movements of France that I am [writing] in *Aintzina*.[129]

At the same time, information about the Basque movement was also being shared with other federalist and regionalist movements. Thus, Charles Iriarte, secretary of the Foyer d'Etudes Fédéralistes in Paris, wrote to Goyheneche on September 19, 1934, of the example of the Pays Basque where there exist two Catholic movements: in the Spanish Basque Country Basque Nationalist Party (separatist), in the French Basque Country the Eskualerriste Party (regionalist).[130]

Iriarte had unknowingly posed one of the great ironies of *Aintzina* and for French Basque mobilization in the 1930s. For despite the proximity of their Spanish Basque brethren, and the full impact of the Spanish Civil War on France at this time, *Aintzina* continued to deal monthly with news of other minority groups in France, while treating with virtual silence the plight of the Basques of Spain.

The Basques of France and the Spanish Civil War

There are two Frances. . . . The eternal France counted and will always count on all our sympathies. . . . But there is another France that we can only view with displeasure. . . . This other is united with Spanish Marxism and cooperates by all means with its nefarious work. This France, we consider as one of our greatest enemies. . . . Anti-Marxist France is with us and we are with her.
Le Courrier de Bayonne,
September 22, 1936

Basque Nationalists, no one would have believed that you could have united in arms with the supporters of the Moscovite barbarism and fought your brothers of race and those who hold your own religious principle.
General Béorlégui in *La Presse,*
August 5, 1936

Shortly after the founding of the Spanish Republic in 1931, the Catalans were granted a Statute of Autonomy which greatly increased their domestic control within the context of Spain. In the case of the Basques, a similar status was not forthcoming until after the beginning of the Spanish Civil War. Thus, the Basques had every interest in remaining loyal to the Republic when faced with the Francoist uprising which led to the Spanish Civil War between 1936 and 1939.[131]

Despite the historically incomplete contact between Basques in France and Spain, the Basque population of France was strongly affected by the Spanish Civil War from its earliest days. In the early campaigns of the Civil War, troops of General Emilio Mola brought the Civil War to the very borders of France, as they laid siege to and claimed the cities of Irún and Donostia

(San Sebastián) and the province of Gipuzkoa. France, claiming to respect
the dictates of the Committee on Nonintervention (already violated by Italy
and Germany), closed its frontier, which accomplished Mola's goal of preventing escape into France. From safe vantage points across the Bidassoa
River, French Basques gathered to watch the panorama of war unfold before
them, much as had Americans in the early campaigns of the American Civil
War. But the hermetic frontier soon gave way before a massive onslaught
of refugees into France, an influx which would not only engender a pitched
political debate within France at the time, but would forever change the
political sociology of the Basque country of France.

According to José M. Borrás Llop, the refugees flowed into France in
three stages, corresponding to the battles occurring in the Basque country
of Spain.[132] The first stage involved approximately 10,000 refugees who fled
across the nearby frontier during the bombardment and ultimate surrender
of Donostia and the border town of Irún in August and September 1936.
According to press accounts, masses of refugees descended on the French
border town of Hendaye and the coast, perhaps as many as 9,000 on the
evening of August 31, 1936, alone.[133] *Le Courrier* of September 7, 1936, wrote,
"If our city isn't rapidly emptied of all the troubled elements which has
just invaded it, we will take part in demonstrations which could become
bloody."[134] From July 23 onward there was a severe shortage of bread along
the coast. Yet, in a theme later taken up by the deputy Delzangles, the concern of the local *La Gazette* was the effect of the refugees on local business:
"Seven hundred families who live on border traffic . . . are going to rapidly
find themselves without resources."[135] The concern reflected the realities of
a local economy which already lived on tourism.

The second stage, and far greater, involved as many as 160,000 refugees
from the northern campaign of 1937. The third and final stage brought 24,000
refugees from the Battle of Northern Aragon in April–June 1938. Of these
nearly 200,000 refugees who fled into France seeking temporary sanctuary,
Javier Rubio estimates that as many as 40,000–45,000 remained in France,
though not all in the French Pays Basque.[136]

The reaction of French Basques took two forms. The first, and by far
smaller, was an effort to aid the refugees and to criticize the Francoist/Nazi
alliance. An early Comité d'Aide aux Basques was created by such notables
as Mgr. Mathieu, bishop of Dax (the Diocese of Bayonne would not participate); Michel d'Arcangues; Mademoiselle Madeleine de Jaureguiberry and
Dr. Jean de Jaureguiberry, her brother; and Dr. Edmond Goyheneche of
Ustaritz.[137] Though soon forced to disband, this early effort gave way to the
later Ligue Internationale des Amis des Basques.

In *Aintzina*, one finds only a few references to the growing conflict in Spain:

The sacrifice of our fathers promised us peace and happiness. . . . Over there [among the Basques of Spain] it is Hitler, always menacing, who waits with impatience. Perhaps, in a very near time, we will have to leave our mountains and our valley and, after a last look at the little village where the pelote strikes against the fronton, go in the mud and under the machinegun to oppose the invader. Happy will be those who return. Defending our little *patrie,* preparing from this moment the work of future reconstruction in beginning at home, we will see our hope realized. The somber clouds will have passed; on our Basque earth will fall the first rays of a new sunlight.[138]

In other contexts, Lafitte criticized the treatment of Basques by the government of Gipuzkoa and insisted that there was no separation between "continental" and "peninsular" Basques.[139] But beyond that *Aintzina* would not or could not go. Much of the reason for its silence is to be found in the hostility of the church and Basque elites both to the refugee problem and to the controversial if instrumental alliance made by Spanish Basques with Communist and anarchist forces in defense of republican institutions in Spain.

THE REACTION OF BASQUE ELITES TO THE CIVIL WAR AND ITS REFUGEES

The early reaction of French Basque elites was to seek an early end to the conflict, while distancing themselves and their constituents from it. Thus, deputy Delzangles spoke before the Chamber of Deputies in Paris on July 31, 1936:

I have the honor of representing in this Assembly populations which are united by ties of blood to their brothers on the other side of the Pyrénées. They are now haunted by the desire to see finished as quickly as possible a savage and fratricidal struggle. They also have the legitimate concern to see ended certain scandalous reports which would tend to make one believe that the Pays Basque Français is an extension of the theatre of Spanish revolution. These populations are waiting for a gesture of pacification from you.[140]

Yet, within a year, the attitude of Delzangles had changed, reflecting an anger toward the refugees and an impatience to see their presence brought to an end. In a letter to M. Yvon Delbos, minister of foreign affairs, Delzangles wrote:

Every nation and interested faction is letting flow freely toward France individuals or groups judged undesirable by all . . . [France] must not become the dumping ground of Europe.[141]

Delzangles was attacked by some for his defense of tourism and the local economy over the human plight of the victims of the Civil War.[142] Yet he was not alone in this attitude: even local social service agencies protested over the unfair burden they were forced to assume in dealing with the influx of refugees.[143]

Students of the *Mariel* boat lift from Cuba to the United States in the 1980s will see familiar themes in the images of the refugees held by elements of the French national press and population:

> We are experiencing, at the present moment, an invasion of Spaniards who are exercising, in the regions where they camp, a veritable terror. . . . The defeated militias have been accompanied not only by the pitiable army of unfortunates, that of women, of the old, but by cohorts of banditism, those of Communist and anarchist hoodlums where one found men who refused to fight, and, who, in the rear, did criminal deeds robbing homes, sacking churches, killing civilian populations.[144]

In the same vein:

> It is not the elite of the country which is coming into France, but the criminal element, and often the very lowest; France, which voluntarily accepted the elite, wouldn't, without danger, be able to digest this criminal element.[145]

Other deputies denounced the danger to France of thieves, looters, assassins, and common law criminals. Even the eventual return of most of the refugees after hostilities ceased was little cause for comfort, for as the *Bulletin Quotidien* lamented:

> The worst has arrived, since the border of the Pyrénées has become for us a reverse filter, which lets flow out harmless elements in leaving as our share a residue of toxins and poisons.[146]

The great danger was that the virus of civil war introduced by these refugees would spread its virulence within France:

> It is necessary to watch inside our borders so that the leprosy and the spleen which were unleased on us from over the Pyrénées are strictly overseen and prevented from spreading themselves, so that the scourge conjured up in Spain is not reborn on the soil of France.[147]

THE BASQUE CATHOLIC ALLIANCE WITH COMMUNISTS
AND ANARCHISTS

The single most important explanation for the virulence of these attacks lay in the French Catholic reaction to the tactical alliance entered into by Spanish Basque Catholics with Communists and anarchists in defense of the Spanish Republic.

It was the perception of this alliance which served in the Pays Basque Français—as few other issues could—to galvanize public opinion and contaminate the very idea of Basque nationalism. As Généviève Marre put it:

There existed in nineteen hundred and thirty-six a collective unconscious which created among the public a true feeling of panic faced with pagan and blood-thirsty bolshevism.[148]

Jean Ybarnégaray described the stakes:

The uprising has taken on the character of a religious war. One thus cultivates the vision of a Spain divided into two camps: on one side the *franquistes*, soldiers of God, who are waging a crusade for faith, on the other side the "Popular Front," herald of pagan anarchy.[149]

The Basque nationalism of José Antonio Aguirre was a particular *bête noire* of Ybarnégaray, and Spanish Basque priests who supported the cause of Basque nationalism were dismissed by Ybarnégaray as goldfish (in French literally, red fish) swimming in baptismal fonts, an image he also used for Abbé Pierre Lafitte.[150]

Much of the local Basque press expressed similar sentiments to those of General Béorlégui who, in a prefatory quotation to this section, expressed amazement that Basques could have so betrayed their religious principles in allying themselves with Moscow. As *La Presse* wrote on August 6, 1936: "For among them [Basques] there are a lot of Catholics and one can't imagine that they would long support fraternizing with . . . the sacrilegious Communist assassins." Condemning the Spanish Basque bishops who permitted this alliance, *La Presse* wrote again on August 11, 1936:

It is they who wanted to separate the Basque people from Spanish unity. It is they who assured, by their alliance, the success of the Popular Front at the last elections. They no longer recognized the authority of the Pope in order to unite with the Communists whose doctrines irreducibly oppose the religious, political, social and economic doctrine.[151]

As *Le Courrier* editorialized on November 21, 1936, "It is nonetheless surprising to realize that the Basques, ardent Catholics, are associated with the worst enemies of the Church and of civilization." *La Gazette* warned on September 9, 1936, "may the Basque nationalists regret their pact with the devil."

Sometime between the beginning of hostilities in mid-1936 and 1937, the labels given to the respective sides shifted in an important way in the French press. At the beginning of the conflict, the republican side was known as the "nationalists" and the forces of Franco as the "insurgents." But as the force of this tactical Spanish Basque alliance with Communists and anarchists sunk into the French public consciousness, the labels changed, and Franco's forces became the "nationalist" cause.[152] Moreover, history itself was rewritten to justify opposition to the republican cause. As *La Gazette* wrote on November 23, 1936: "It is only too evident that the aid furnished to the government forces by Russia will increasingly cause the Germans and Italians to lend, privately, aid to the nationalists." The perception is revealing, for the facts were exactly the opposite. Yet this perceived Communist threat was a central one. As Ybarnégaray argued before the Chamber of Deputies on December 5, 1936, "whether it be in Spain or among us communism is war." [153] Thus, Ybarnégaray spoke in the Chamber of Deputies in favor of the exile of Spanish Basque refugees from the border provinces. While hundreds ultimately were sent to camps at Gurs near Pau, or north of the Loire, Paul Jourdain insisted, "I ask that one give them asylum where they want it, in Moscow, for example, but that one limit their stay among us." [154] So strong was the French Basque passion against the Communist cause, according to Goyheneche and Oyhamburu among others, that General Mola was able to finance his northern campaign against republican forces by borrowing money from politically well-connected French Basque capitalists.[155]

THE CATHOLIC REACTION IN DEFENSE OF THE BASQUES

If the popular press of the epoch is to be believed, the struggle of 1936–1937 was between Catholic and pagan. In fact, considerable differences of opinion existed within the Catholic world over the alliance of the Spanish Basques. Gaetan Bernoville joined the debate, writing in the Catholic journal *Etudes*, on October 5, 1936:

> From the first days, the Basque Nationalist Party rallied to the *Popular Front*. This paradoxical and shameful alliance provoked a universal stupefaction. The immense majority of the public, in France and in Europe, didn't understand, and still don't understand.[156]

Bernoville rejected the alliance—even for instrumental reasons, because he suspected the Basques would always be used as dupes by their Communist allies. In response, Pedro Duhalde found Bernoville's analysis timorous and lacking in "critical spirit".[157] For Duhalde, it was a simple material coincidence that these disparate defenders of the republic found themselves allied in the same camp against Franco, politics making strange bedfellows indeed.

In December 1936 a delegation of Young Spanish Basque Nationalist Catholics defended their actions at a conference in Paris:

> You all know that we, Basque Nationalist Catholics, are struggling today with all our energy, with all our ardor, against the fascist conglomerate of the military, carlists, and Spanish phalangists. And we are in the trenches with young antifascists who, by their ideology, are far from our religious ideal. The entire world has the right to ask us the reason for this attitude. We will respond to you in all loyalty like the Basques that we are.[158]

They justified their tactical alliance: (1) by the right of self-defense; (2) as democrats and enemies of governmental violence; and, (3) for God and the ancient laws.

Still the Basques found themselves abandoned, as Victor Monserrat argues, "the victim of incomprehension on the part of those who falsely accused them as reds."[159] The Basque National Council in diplomatic representations to the Vatican made every effort to convince the Holy See that the Basques remained devoted Christians and Catholics.[160] Georges Bernanos in his famous pamphlet of 1938 entitled "Les grandes cimetières sous la lune" drew the contrast between the solicitude of the Vatican for the plight of German Jews and its silence about Spanish Basque Catholics. As Pierre Lafitte wrote Eugène Goyheneche, circa 1936:

> These stories of Spain have perverted all our ideas: we don't even have the right to call ourselves Basque without risking being called Communist. React as much as we can against all statist tendencies. . . . Catholicism is incompatible with totalitarian systems whatever they may be, and regionalism also.[161]

Forty years later Mademoiselle Madeleine de Jaureguiberry, avid supporter of Jacques Maritain, spoke of this same logic that motivated her efforts in 1936:

> To say that the Basques were Communists? This lie . . . was taken up . . . the following days by the Catholic press of the whole world. Catholics in their great majority turned indignantly against the Basques, treating their exiled priests as addled. They abandoned to its sad fate the little people more attached to its liberty than to the faith of its ancestors.[162]

During the spring of 1937 two eminent French Catholic men of letters, Jacques Maritain and François Mauriac, spoke out in defense of the Basques,

a position considerably strengthened with the destruction of the Basque
town of Gernika (Guernica) by aerial bombardment.[163] Writing in the Dominican journal *Sept* in June 1937, François Mauriac made this appeal on behalf
of the Basques:

> A little people is agonizing on the side of the road. It is not the moment
> to ask them the reasons which led them to make their choice in the camp
> of the enemies of the faith, but to give aid to our brothers in Christ.[164]

At the same time, pro-Franco forces in Spain were attempting to show the
destruction of the church at the hands of the "red-separatists."[165] Others, including the archbishop of Westminster, called the struggle "a furious battle
between Christian civilization and the most cruel paganism that has ever
darkened the world."[166] The pope, in a gesture of appeasement, declared that
all the clergy who lost their lives were martyrs.[167] Yet the Spanish Bishopric
in a letter addressed to "Bishops of the Whole World" argued that the nature
of Spanish institutions under the republic since 1931 had sought to change
"Spanish history in a way contrary to the needs of the national spirit."[168] The
civil war was thus theologically just. Others called it a duty.

On August 28, 1937, the pope recognized the Francoist "Burgos authorities" as the legitimate government of Spain and thus put Mauriac and others
in the position of being rebels against the decision of Rome. But the war of
pamphlets continued throughout the rest of the war, especially in France.
As Mauriac wrote in 1939:

> There is no one in France any longer ignorant of the fact that, before the
> Civil War, not only was there no alliance between the Basque Catholics
> and the Communists, but that, in the electoral field . . . they remained
> irreconcilable opponents. Attacked by the rebels from the first day, the
> Basques found themselves fighting side by side with the Spanish left,
> just as in September, an attack by Germany would have placed us, along
> with conservative England, in the same field with Soviet Russia!![169]

History, of course, would soon prove Mauriac correct.

The Basque Government in Exile, 1939

Despite French government efforts to avoid antagonizing the new Franco
regime in Spain, France's traditional commitment to political asylum com-
pelled it to accept Basque political refugees.[170] It also accepted the presence
of the Basque government in exile, which opened government offices, a con-

sulate, a hospital, and an orphanage in the Pays Basque Français. The Basque Nationalist party dominated the government in exile.

The Basque government in exile walked a fine line, however, and it soon became apparent that the price it paid for sanctuary in France was a pledge of absolute nonintervention in French Basque affairs. As Paul Sérant explained it:

> The Spanish Basques kept themselves, during the war, from making an appeal to the solidarity of French Basques. If they had done so, they would have immediately lost the support of the French government, which would not tolerate evoking the existence of a Basque problem inside its borders.[171]

The Autonomous Government of Euzkadi, as it called itself, took pains to reassure French public opinion:

> The best of relations exist between the Basque and French Governments. The Basque regions in France are directly under the French Government and do not play any politically important part in the affairs of the Autonomous Basque Country.[172]

Indeed, in 1940, the Basque National Council defined the territorial limits of "Euzkadi" in such a way as to eliminate the three Basque provinces of France altogether.[173] This did not appease the hard-line Bayonne newspaper *Le Courrier*, which wrote on February 25, 1937: "The Basque separatists, with the authorization of the amiable Monsieur Blum, have installed a propaganda office in Paris."[174] A week later, on March 3, 1937, *Le Courrier* wrote:

> Without the participation of French Basques, a Republic of Euzkadi cannot be envisioned. And yet we maintain and we tolerate in Bayonne the considerable center of this French-Spanish separatist propaganda; it is at the same time a scandal and a danger.[175]

Grateful for the *concordat*, the Autonomous Government in Exile settled near the French-Spanish border and seemingly acted as if it was not among a Basque population at all.

The Basque government offered to organize Spanish Basque refugee units to fight within Free French Forces, but the British urged de Gaulle's government in exile in London to integrate Spanish Basques into heterogeneous units and to avoid creating uniquely Spanish fighting units.[176] The British position was that the French were free to enter into such diplomatic relations as they chose when back on French territory, but so long as both French and

Basques were in exile on British territory, the British were reluctant to give any signal which might be interpreted as supporting Basque separatism.

De Gaulle's government further requested that no individuals with Communist sympathies be included in the Basque levies.[177] As further proof of the temporary and instrumental nature of the Basque-Communist alliance during the recent Civil War, the Basque National Council readily agreed to this French demand. During the German occupation individual Spanish Basque refugees later distinguished themselves in the Resistance, and not a single one was charged with collaboration at the end of World War II.[178] This was despite confusing comments to the contrary by the deputy mayor of Biarritz and later Senator Guy Petit during a press conference in Madrid in 1948, retracted shortly thereafter.[179]

Of more lasting importance to the cultural and later political regeneration in the French Basque provinces was the spontaneous appearance of a number of cultural groups—dance, theater, folklore—created by the refugees which served as the first means of mobilizing young French Basques as Basques.[180] Prime among them was the folklore group Elai Alai, composed of children of Gernika, which founded in Biarritz the group Olaeta which later became the dance group Oldarra, one of the greatest avenues of ethnic socialization for the later *Enbata* in the 1960s. One remembers Mao Zedong's assertion that the revolution would be made in dancing or not at all.

Behind the scenes, Abbé Urricarriet described to Eugène Goyheneche in a private letter in March 1943 the way nationalism might grow:

> In leaning on the Basque refugees to organize nationalist sections everywhere. In order not to frighten away anyone these would be simple courses in Basque dances, or courses in the Basque language. But behind the scenes, good men . . . aided financially . . . could do stupefying work in a very short time. . . . In conclusion make known: . . . the urgent necessity not to disperse the already existent groups of dancers, which are all foyers of nationalism. The Basque people will open its eyes in dancing. Unique and marvelous instrument of propaganda.[181]

Publicly, however, the Autonomous Basque Government in Exile steered resolutely clear from any political activity among the French Basque population. Others saw the natural tie between the two populations. In an important series of remarks in Paris on March 3, 1944, "M. Olamendia" (probably a pseudonym during the war) sought to subordinate the content of French Basque nationalism in support of the Basque struggle in Spain:

> I firmly believe the only means of saving the Pays Basque [in France] is to be nationalist, to want Basque as [the] only language, the rebirth

of Basque civilization in art as in thought. There exists a Basque genius which explodes in dances, songs, painting. . . . However, alongside this nationalism of feeling, I think that there is a possible political nationalism for the Basques [in France]. It consists very simply in aiding with all our forces the [Spanish] Basque country in considering that if it is free one day we will finally have our homeland in the world. . . . And . . . alongside this peninsular Euzkadi strong and free, the attraction for the three other provinces of the North will happen by itself and that finally the seven in one will be so truly . . . *Gora Euzkadi Azkatuta!!* [Long Live the Basque Country Free!!] [182]

The Phoenix in Basque Nationalism: The Death and Rebirth of *Aintzina*, 1937–1942

By the middle of 1937 the fortunes of the small newspaper *Aintzina* were being influenced by the larger public attitudes toward Basque nationalism brought about by the Spanish Civil War. Thus, Goyheneche saw a more political reason for the paper's ceasing existence after its issue number 32 of May 1937: "*Aintzina* had to disappear for two reasons: because it was Basque nationalist, and because it was Christian Democratic." [183]

For Pierre Lafitte, the paper ceased to exist because of exorbitant increases in the cost of printing and the impact of inflation on French currency. According to Lafitte, the first issue of *Aintzina* cost 65 francs to print and the last issue, number 32, cost 600 francs, an increase of nearly a thousand percent in less than three years of existence. Its nominal editor, Jean Duboscq, recollects that *Aintzina* ceased publishing because of the cost of printing and the inevitable departure of its young militants who left home for school or work. Abbé Urricarriet, however, in a later letter to Eugène Goyheneche, suggested something of the ecclesiastical pressure that Abbé Lafitte must have experienced from a church hierarchy in Bayonne clearly hostile to the idea of Basque nationalism. For Abbé Urricarriet, the church's pressure on Lafitte demonstrated the need for a secular generation of Basque nationalists to emerge:

They would create secular cadres who should at the earliest possible moment open the bishop's shutters, who are all old "habit-wearers." This is something which underscores this affair of *Aintzina* when analyzed from close up. An ecclesiastic is the least free man in the world. It is in the universities of Bordeaux and Paris, and in the cities like Bayonne, Biarritz, Saint-Jean-de-Luz and Saint-Jean-Pied-de-Port where nationalists must be formed, the true ones. . . . It is they who should have in hand the only French [Basque] newspaper of the region.[184]

So it was for reasons of finances, internal church politics, and an accelerating climate of hostility to Basque nationalism on the part of the church hierarchy, local notables, and the local press that *Aintzina* ceased publication in May 1937. Lafitte would soon become editor of the more traditional Basque journal *Gure Herria*, and still later editor of the new newspaper *Herria*, which took over from the discredited *Eskualduna* at the end of the war. It would be five years, well into the German occupation of France, before a new vehicle of Basque themes would appear.

THE SECOND SERIES OF AINTZINA (1942–1943): REGIONALISM VS. SEPARATISM IN THE CLIMATE OF WORLD WAR AND OCCUPATION

In 1942, five years after the end of the first series of *Aintzina* and well into the Nazi occupation of France, the second series of *Aintzina* appeared. This effort was led by Abbé Pierre Larzabal and Marc Légasse, and its maximum affiliation of sixty-five young Basques included as active contributors Abbé Diharce of the monastery at Belloc writing under the pseudonym Iratzeder; Jean Duboscq; Marc's brother Jacques Légasse; André Ospital; later deputy and senator Michel Labéguerie; and M. Dutournier. The two central forces in this second *Aintzina's* life and death were Abbé Pierre Larzabal and Marc Légasse.

PIERRE LARZABAL

Larzabal was ordained a priest in 1939 and served in the army between 1939 and 1940, when he was captured and made a prisoner of war.[185] He was sent to hard labor and, falling ill, was evacuated to Switzerland and to a hospital in Lyon in 1942. Recovered, he returned to the Basque country, where he was made vicar in the Basque town of Hasparren and editor of the reborn *Aintzina* he had proposed in mid-1942. He was also later active in the founding of *Enbata* in the early 1960s, *curé* of Socoa near the Spanish border, and so active in defense of Spanish Basque refugees in the 1970s that he was called the "confessor of terrorists" by the French press.

MARC LÉGASSE

Few figures in the modern Basque movement are more enigmatic than Marc Légasse. The son of a wealthy Basque shipbuilding family in Saint-Jean-de-Luz, Légasse began his militancy with *Aintzina* and at the end of World War II ran as a Basque nationalist in the municipal elections of 1945.[186] He was the most radical nationalist of his generation. He reminisced in 1991 in *Enbata* that he had intended to restart publication of *Gure Herria*, which had been defunct since 1939. When the editorial board opposed him, Chanoine Lafitte offered the use of the title *Aintzina*.[187] Légasse later referred to Lafitte's first *Aintzina* as "the venerable literary, musical, and historical chronicle of Ustaritz."[188] While Légasse had little patience for the regionalist timidity of Lafitte's earlier *Aintzina*, it is interesting to note that this biting comment was made *fifty* years later. Shortly after forming the second *Aintzina* with Larzabal, Légasse quarreled with him in turn, and contemporaries of both men insist today that Légasse's attitude led to Larzabal's departure.

Légasse was the author of the project for a Basque Department presented in the National Assembly by deputy Jean Etcheverry-Ainchart in 1945. As we will see below, Légasse, in a famous letter, would criticize President Aguirre of the exiled Basque republic on the Basque government's collaboration with the French state and its indifference to the French Basque movement. During the 1960s Légasse's writings resembled a twentieth-century Chaho in works like "Words of a Basque Anarchist" and "Smuggling as an Act of Conscience." He freely admitted the fanciful nature of his work and claimed he was dismissed by many as being a rich dilettante, but he insisted that all his work had a core of political seriousness. He began a small newspaper, *Hordago*, in the 1960s and a small press of the same name. Today Légasse remains extremely close to the exiled members of ETA in France and their families and vocal in his radical defense of his homeland. In the late 1980s he began to contribute a weekly column to the nationalist newspaper *Enbata*.

Regionalism-Separatist Debate of the New *Aintzina*

Unlike the overt regionalism of Pierre Lafitte's first *Aintzina*, the *Aintzina* of Larzabal and Lafitte remained purely cultural and literary in nature, owing to its publication in the occupied France of 1942. Moreover, it recognized the failure of its predecessor to win over public opinion, which "isn't yet ready."[189] So if the reborn *Aintzina* was regionalist in nature, its regionalism was only latent in the Basque content of its literary articles.

In his proposal for the rebirth of *Aintzina*, dated July 14, 1942, Larzabal wrote:

> We must see that one day or another we will clash with the clergy in the countryside. With foresight, we will begin by positioning ourselves strongly in the "atheist" cities . . . here we will easily earn the sympathies

of the Basque clergy which suffers in isolation. . . . Once established
in these centers, we will impose ourselves on the rural clergy in such a
way that they will prefer to use us rather than excommunicate us.[190]

Yet, while Larzabal could speak of a Basque nationalist movement, even *Aintzina II*'s regionalism remained implied and not explicit under the German
occupation. Indeed, in a manuscript entitled "Notre programme," written
after the new *Aintzina* had been in existence for more than a year, Larzabal
insisted:

> *Aintzina* doesn't want to be a political party. Let no one ask us to sup-
> port candidates in the elections. . . . France and Spain don't have to
> worry about us. . . . The enemies of the true France and the true Spain
> are ours as well.[191]

According to Larzabal, in this climate of accelerating occupation *Aintzina*
should not even be considered an organized movement. Reflecting back
thirty-five years later, Larzabal denied that *Aintzina* was nationalist and insisted it was a regionalist movement with strong ties to France. What preoccupied its members was "what was good and beautiful in the past, a
nostalgia to fill the emptiness of our thoughts."[192]

Be that as it may, it was clear that strong and real disagreements already
were dividing Abbé Larzabal and Marc Légasse by the end of 1942. On
February 18, 1943, having just resigned as editor-in-chief of *Aintzina*, Larzabal wrote to Eugène Goyheneche in Paris, its correspondent in the French
capital: "M. Légasse finds my program too regionalist and not separatist
enough. . . . Without doubt, *Aintzina* will fall! Or it will be a sheet of literature, but not a movement, as I intended."[193]

Larzabal should hardly have expected a sympathetic ear in Goyheneche.
First, Goyheneche's nationalist sentiments were already well known. Second, in his program for the founding of the new *Aintzina*, Larzabal had
referred to Goyheneche in the context of the German occupation: "Toward
Eugène Goyheneche, intimate union at all costs in JEL. Even with the devil
if necessary."[194]

Thus, Goyheneche responded to Larzabal with strong personal respect,
but with a clear rejection of the cautious regionalism Larzabal had in mind.
Among the points he made in his letter of March 29, 1943 were that his
position was clear and he could not subscribe to Larzabal's position; that,
whatever the politics of *Aintzina*, they should be first and foremost Basque
politics, with the precise label "nationalist, regionalist, autonomist, or separatist"[195] mattering little, as the Basques should count only on themselves
and not on a French or Spanish civilization which had trampled on their

rights for generations. Goyheneche still insisted that *Aintzina* appear, as it represented the only proof of the existence of the Basque people under the occupation.

Larzabal replied to Goyheneche in turn on April 7, 1943, clarifying the dispute between regionalism and separatism that led to his departure and the ultimate decline of the paper sometime later. He claimed that because he had said that *Aintzina* was not separatist the separatists had decided he was against them. Running afoul of the separatist position of Légasse, Larzabal resigned, having lost their confidence. In fact, as Larzabal added in a postscript to his letter to Goyheneche of April 7, 1943, the political content of the new *Aintzina* had been submitted to Abbé Pierre Lafitte and approved by him. Larzabal was surprised to learn Lafitte had named him editor, and Légasse made it clear to Larzabal that this had happened over his own objections. For Larzabal, this explained much of the animosity between himself and Légasse, which ultimately led to the collapse of the second *Aintzina* in 1943.

Yet, with Larzabal's departure, the editorial line of the paper hardly changed; certainly no radical assertion of Basque nationalism or separatism was ever seen. As a result, Larzabal wrote:

> I deplore the lack of a doctrine brought about by the lack of an editor. When one reads *Aintzina*, one asks, "But where do these guys want to go?" What rhyme is there in this series of articles? And then without doctrine, no movement is possible, and without a movement it will come to nothing from the Basque point of view.[196]

In fact, given the lack of change in the doctrine of the newspaper after Larzabal's resignation, it appeared to be more a conflict over personalities— only the first of many involving Légasse—than a reflection of a genuine separatist turn.

As Abbé Urricarriet wrote to Goyheneche at this time, as seen from afar:

> The *Aintzina* Affair, whose dossier I'm going to continue to address, is significant. Here's what we must avoid quickly and at any cost. The separatists-nationalists are the infinite minority. Included within them are all the Spanish-Basque refugees; thus no need to worry . . . to the contrary they must be given the means to push their work further. The French separatist-nationalists must not exceed two dozen. Besides Abbé Charritton and [Père] Diharce . . . of the Benedictines of Belloc, there are no priests included. On their side, this group of French nationalists, under the influence of voguish ideas and the war in Spain, are turning their ideas toward England.[197]

As Larzabal watched the young movement flounder without direction, he still cautioned against a premature political strategy which, in attempting to obtain a Basque state, would moderate 99 percent of French Basques. But even the cautious alternative of education and consciousness-raising would fail without a leader. As Larzabal wrote Goyheneche:

> In brief, we lack a leader who will take over the leadership of the Basque movement. . . . The Basque people are waiting for a leader. Will you be one? If I weren't a priest I think I would have sacrificed my life to the cause.[198]

But Goyheneche was hardly the candidate for leadership of the movement, for, in this Basque country in the midst of the German occupation, he was carrying out a lonely strategy designed to ensure the best possible outcome for the Basque people regardless of the outcome of World War II.

Ethnic Strategies under Vichy and the Nazi Occupation

As France began to recover from the shock of the rapid defeat of the French army in 1940, hope began to emerge for a new status for France's ethnic minorities under Vichy and the German occupation. For some, as in the case of Brittany, this was the unfolding of long planning. For all, it raised intense and sometimes fractious debates about ethnic self-interest and the wisdom of collaboration versus resistance.

THE REGIONALIST PROMISE UNDER VICHY

Regionalism will be the strength of our country.
Marshal Pétain [199]

In July 1940 Marshal Pétain greatly encouraged the regionalist idea in announcing the *necessity* of creating regions which would permit the rebirth of the old French provinces within the modern French state.[200] In so doing, Pétain gave legitimacy to an idea which Doyen Barthélemy had evoked in 1925 when he claimed that "the problem of regionalism was that it gave . . . the impression of an empty agitation and of an electoral bluff."[201] Pétain's "Révolution Nationale" raised provincial hopes in a way that had not been felt since the first moments of the Constituent Assembly of the French Revolution more than 150 years before.

During the spring of 1941 a Vichy Commission chaired by Lucien Romier, which included Jean Charles-Brun among its members, was studying the administrative and economic organization of France and the limits of its regions. Pierre Lafitte wrote to Eugène Goyheneche (then studying in Paris at the Ecole Nationale des Chartes) on May 14, 1941, to request his urgent participation in the Basque response to Vichy's plans: "At the moment when Vichy is discussing the new organization of France, it is important that we not be absent. . . . If you know something on the memoranda sent by the Flamands and the Bretons."[202] Meanwhile, Lafitte had developed a Basque position paper and arranged with Chanoine Lamarque to have it published in *La Presse du Sud-Ouest* on May 15, 1941. As Lafitte's article noted, "No one could misunderstand the importance of these works [of Vichy], which are going to give to the France of tomorrow its new physiognomy and fix the boundaries in which its life will take place from now on."[203]

The Romier Commission openly solicited ideas and proposals from each province in order to clarify its work. As Lafitte saw the implication, "It would mean in sum the drawing up of *cahiers* analogous to those of the Estates General."[204]

In fact, Lafitte's position elaborated in *La Presse* was clearly inspired by the revolutionary *Cahiers*, specifically in demanding that Soule not be separated from Labourd and Basse-Navarre; that the Basques not be combined in an economic or administrative region with Béarn (as they had been in 1793); and that Bayonne be made the administrative center of the Basque region.

On the question of language, Lafitte proposed that Basque be recognized and be made an examination option in French education. A year later, on March 13, 1942, the secretary general of the Ministry of Public Instruction addressed a circular to the *inspecteurs d'académie*,[205] in which the Vichy administration proposed financial incentives for instructors who, outside of normal classes, would offer elective classes in regional languages. Though further hopes were raised by the Carcopino Decree on regional language of March 13, 1943, as Goyheneche noted, it was no more implemented than other decrees before it or after.[206] In fact, it soon became evident that Vichy's regionalism was as Jacobin as any which had come before it. As Robert Paxton simply noted in his study of Vichy, the regionalist aspirations of France's minorities were "severely disappointed."[207]

Ethnic Collaboration with the Nazi Occupation of France

If the Vichy government eventually proved to be as unsympathetic to ethnic demands as its predecessors, hope nonetheless continued to rest on the German Occupational Administration and the German Foreign Ministry on Wilhelmstrasse in Berlin. In fact, since World War I Germany had shown itself willing to aid restive minorities in order to weaken its enemies, which only added to a long-standing German scholarly interest in the ethnography and linguistics of Europe's minorities. Thus, those movements which hoped for German assistance in their goals of independence—primarily in Brittany and French Flanders—were encouraged by reports of the kaiser's earlier plan to dismember France. One of the resulting entities would have been a "Principality of Vasconia or Navarre" with Bilbao as its capital.[208] They were further encouraged by the historical record of German aid to the Irish in 1916, to the Finns against Russia in 1918, and to French Flemish collaboration during World War I.[209] The *New York Post* in 1940 spoke of the dismemberment of France as part of the Nazi version of the "New Europe."[210]

It was clear, however, that German willingness to exploit ethnic discontent was a tool of German *Realpolitik* and neither a permanent nor a universal policy commitment by any German government. Thus, one reads in the newspaper *Stur* (January 5–6, 1936) that "the idea of creating internal difficulties in France could only develop after a reversal of its Western policy, which wasn't in sight."[211] Moreover, *Stur* addressed the specific idea of aiding either Breton or Alsacian autonomism in 1936:

> Germany, whose soldiers are studying every technical possibility of a war with France, has political leaders who would make disappear quickly in a concentration camp anyone who permitted themselves to advocate the support of Breton or Alsatian autonomism.[212]

In 1938 J. Von Ribbentrop, German minister of foreign affairs, further clarified this policy, asserting that Germany accepted the frontiers of its neighboring states as given and that it had foresworn any effort to Germanize neighboring populations:

> As a consequence, we no longer know the concept of "Germanization." The particular mentality of the last century, by virtue of which one could imagine one's self transforming Poles or Frenchmen into Germans, is as foreign to us as would be passionate our resistance to any inverse effort. We consider the European nations surrounding us as constituting given realities.[213]

Ribbentrop's policy was certainly at odds with the attitude Hitler expressed throughout *Mein Kampf*, written thirteen years before when France still occupied the Ruhr, in addition to having reclaimed Alsace-Lorraine, annexed by Germany after the Franco-Prussian War of 1870 and remaining in German hands until Versailles.

Hitler insisted that Alsace-Lorraine had been stolen by France.[214] "France was tearing piece after piece out of the flesh of our national body."[215] According to Hitler, France's goal was "the dissolution of Germany into a hodgepodge of little states"[216]—in effect, "the balkanization of Germany."[217] He continued the argument:

> This French war aim would have been attainable by the War alone if, as Paris had hoped, the struggle had taken place on German soil . . . this would have offered a possibility of breaking up Germany. It is very questionable whether our young federative state could for four and a half years have survived the same test of strain as rigidly centralized France, oriented solely toward her uncontested center in Paris.[218]

As a statement of his offensive strategy toward his neighbors, Hitler asserted, "State boundaries are made by man and changed by man."[219] Thus, force is the handmaiden of *Realpolitik* and the midwife of change:

> We must clearly recognize the fact that the recovery of the lost territories is not through solemn appeals to the Lord or through pious hopes in a League of Nations, but only by *force of arms*.[220]

According to Von Ribbentrop, when asked by Bertrand de Jouvenel in 1936 if he wished to offer a rectification to these harsh words toward France, the *Führer* responded, "My rectification, I will write it in the great Book of History."[221]

According to M. Georges-Anquetil, the newspaper *Excelsior* of March 13, 1938, reproduced a map of German territorial claims which had allegedly been posted in German schools since 1935.[222] Figuring in the territories to be joined to "Greater Germany" by the Anschluss were Alsace and Lorraine. This mirrored the belief of the Vatican, expressed by the Papal Nuncio Borgongini Duca to Cardinal Maglione on June 22, 1940, that among the conditions the Axis would impose on the Allies as a condition for peace would be, among other territorial transfers, the return of Alsace-Lorraine to Germany and of Corsica to Italy.[223]

According to Rita Thalmann, in 1940 the German government was considering a proposal to reduce French territory to the boundaries of the Treaty of Westphalia in 1648.[224] General Jodl called it "restitution of territories stolen for four hundred years from the German people."[225] In October 1940 Hitler is reported to have said that Germany would be satisfied with Alsace-Lorraine, the Bassin de Briex, and a corridor south of Belfort.[226] Yet, according to Thalmann, in his *Propos de Table* (1941–1944), Hitler included the ancient kingdom of Bourgogne as well.[227] However, other than these territorial aspirations, as Dr. Werner Best (himself close to these minority groups) claimed as early as 1940, there was no real interest in supporting "völkisch or national" forces in France.[228]

In July 1940 world press attention focused on Brittany—a nonculturally

Germanic region of France which had not publicly figured in any of Hitler's previous grievances against France. The *New York Times* of July 26, 1940, reported that Berlin had recognized Brittany as an autonomous unit, including Breton desires to form an independent state.[229] The next day, however, the *Times* reported that the German Foreign Office denied the report of the German News Agency DNB that Germany had given such recognition to Brittany. German sources claimed Breton militants had "slipped this idea through when nobody was looking" and that DNB in turn had circulated it without authorization.[230] Meic Stephens believes that the speed with which the German government reacted in denying the report is explained by German desires to do nothing to upset French support of the war with Britain and attributes this belief to Otto Abetz, the German ambassador to France.[231] Be that as it may, British newspapers in July mused over reports of a new state of Brittany and suggested this was either to create neutral buffer states or, as the British press speculated:

> It was considered more probable, however, that the Nazis would seek to prevent France from becoming unified to the point where she could become strong again as she did after the Franco-Prussian War of 1870.[232]

THE EXAMPLE OF BRETON COLLABORATION

Brittany was the most serious case of collaboration by an ethnic movement with the Nazi occupation. While Robert Lafont would later seek to minimize the importance of these events, claiming, "It was an era of 'marking time' ideologically and of grave dangers warded off,"[233] it was clear in the case of Brittany that collaboration was a deliberate strategy, planned well in advance, and involving more than a few militants by 1943. As an indication of how seriously France took Brittany's efforts at collaboration, while many collaborators were charged with treason at the liberation in 1945, two leading Breton nationalists, Olier Mordrel and François de Debauvais, were charged with treason in 1940.

The central figures in Breton collaboration were men such as Olier Mordrel, François de Bauvais, Yann Fouéré, and Célestin Lainé.[234] Their efforts began long before the war, as early as 1927, with the founding of the Parti Autonomiste Breton.[235] According to the *New York Times* in 1940, the Breton movement was strongly influenced by the Irish example of the Sinn Fein in its newspaper *Breiz Atao* (Brittany Arise), and the organization Gwenn-ha-du was said to be patterned after the Irish Republican Army.[236] Gwenn-ha-du was blamed for the bombing plot against French premier Edouard Herriot's train when he came to Brittany in November 1932 to celebrate Brittany's union with France.

Olier Mordrel's autobiographical account of the history of the Breton movement, *Breiz Atao* (named after the movement's newspaper), reveals an early interest in Germany. Indeed, as Mordrel points out, the oldest subscriber to *Breiz Atao* was the German federalist Dr. Hans Otto Wagner. Between 1933 and 1937, during the course of several trips to Germany, Mordrel and his associates were able to expose Breton desires to officials of various German ministries.[237] Mordrel claims that if Admiral Canaris of German intelligence was interested, foreign minister von Ribbentrop, faithful to his previously cited public pledge, was not.

Why would the Breton movement risk discreditation and possible death by considering collaboration with the Nazis? As Mordrel admitted: "The principles on which the Third Reich was built are in good part the negation of the values for which we fought, but the other side refused to give us the right of life."[238] As Célestin Lainé said at the Congrès du Guingamp of the Breton movement on August 28, 1939, "not a further drop of Breton blood should be spilled for foreign causes."[239] The Parti Nationalist Breton took a stance of neutrality at the outbreak of hostilities between Germany and France, and Mordrel counseled Bretons to consider themselves "freed from any commitments vis-à-vis France."[240] In part as a result of these positions, the Parti Nationalist Breton was dissolved by the French state in October 1939; Olier Mordrel and François de Bauvais were condemned to death for treason, fleeing into exile. As Mordrel explained the gamble, he knew people would reproach the Breton movement for "having stabbed France in the back"[241]; if they won they would be heroes, and if they lost, traitors. As one Breton militant put it:

> What does it matter if we're ten or ten thousand or a million! We represent the Breton nation because we are the Breton movement in the flesh. We are at war with France, a war we have regularly declared. The countries who would enter into war with her will be . . . our allies.[242]

Thus went the logic that led to Breton collaboration with Germany during the war. Yet not all elements of the German government were sympathetic to the Breton cause. Mordrel labeled Ribbentrop and the German ambassador in Paris "Francophiles," and to the Bretons only Admiral Canaris and the SS were truly pro-Breton. As Mordrel wrote, "The other Germans who understood nothing, learned nothing, were contemptible beings."[243] Indeed, later postwar translations of the monthly intelligence reports emanating from the Headquarters of the German army's 25th Corps in Brittany reveal that, while mention is made of the Breton movement, the German army remained more preoccupied with the Communist underground as the greater threat.[244]

In 1943 the most nationalist part of the Breton movement split away and, around Lainé and Guiyesse, founded a second PNB and a second *Breiz Atao*, each more radical than its predecessor. Their platform favored "in foreign policy a sincere and complete collaboration with Germany, and in domestic policy, a struggle against Gaullism, communism, and terrorism." [245] By early 1944 the conflict came to pit Breton against Breton. More than 150 volunteers joined the Formation Perrot, organized by the Germans and named after the nationalist Abbé Perrot assassinated by the Resistance in December 1943.[246] Mordrel personally traveled to German prisoner of war camps vainly trying to recruit French soldiers of Breton origin to take up arms against France.

The last months of the war were thus characterized by this pitched conflict between Bretons in collaboration and others in the Resistance. In February 1945 Mordrel signed a pact with Doriot in Germany in which Doriot pledged to recognize a Breton state as head of France at the successful conclusion of the war.[247]

The resulting purge at war's end touched literally thousands of Breton militants and largely discredited the ideal. Mordrel was condemned to death two times: in 1940 for desertion, and in 1945 for collaboration.[248] From the French perspective, Jacques Kermoal writes of this period:

> A very ugly page was turned. The purging is going to do its cleansing. Thirty leaders of the P.N.V. will be shot or killed. Hundreds of militants will be imprisoned. Mordrel is condemned to death in absentia, and finds himself, with Tann Goulet, [Yann] Fouéré, and [Célestin] Lainé in exile in Ireland, where they brood, bitter, over their lost illusions.[249]

During the course of the war events in Brittany were hardly occurring in a vacuum. Similar efforts at collaboration would also occur in French Flanders and Germanic Alsace-Lorraine—and in the person of Eugène Goyheneche in the Pays Basque. There was substantial interethnic contact among these minorities in this period, continuing from the 1930s, in Paris and beyond. The Basque National Council conceived of contacts between the Basques and other minority groups collaborating with the German occupation as a means of keeping itself informed:

> An excellent means of informing ourselves of the actions of the enemy consists of entering in contact with the pseudo-nationalist Breton, Alsatian, and Flemish elements who are working in close collaboration with the invader. Here the Basques can again serve us. In the name of solidarity of "minorities," certain Basque elements with our complete confidence could enter into contact with these small groups without any political importance, but susceptible of being used for the ends of an

espionage service. This would be even easier since it seems that the Germans are seeking to create a center of dissidence in the Basque countries. We can furnish precise proof of this fact.[250]

Basque Contact with Ethnic Collaborationist Movements

One of the primary agents of the PNV in this effort was Eugène Goyheneche, who was studying in Paris at the Ecole Nationale des Chartes in the early war years. He continued during the war to correspond with other ethnic movements, including the Flemish and Yann Fouéré in Brittany. Fouéré had begun to correspond with a number of other Basque militants by this time, including Pierre Lafitte and Marc Légasse. Thus, in the midst of the Breton movement's radicalization in 1943, Fouéré wrote to Marc Légasse, inviting Basque militants to Brittany:

> Don't you think it would be possible to send to Rennes for the first time . . . some delegates . . . from the French Pays Basque? Naturally, the Conference will have a cultural scope above all, but I am very certain that it would inevitably have a great consequence from the political point of view.[251]

One week later, Fouéré wrote to Abbé Lafitte, evoking the "community of demands which unites on the cultural plane the different minority people of France . . . the work of coming together . . . which had already been prevented before the last war."[252] Writing to Pierre Landaburu on November 30, 1943, Fouéré discussed a meeting to be held at the home of Jean Charles-Brun in Paris, which would include two delegates from each minority group in France.[253]

In a series of manuscripts from the war years, Goyheneche reflected on the lessons of Breton nationalism. Cynically, Goyheneche insisted:

> The politics of France toward the little nationalists is very clever and scarcely loyal . . . after having proclaimed the right of peoples to dispose of themselves she adds prudently "but at home the question of national minorities does not pose itself; the autonomist movements of our country are the work of unscrupulous agitators under the hand of Germany (sic) or the eye of Moscow (resic)."[254]

Later, speaking of the ideological example of the Breton case, Goyheneche wrote:

See in Brittany: for years different Breton parties elaborated mirific theories in test tubes, reconstructing Brittany, France, Europe . . . letting,
without being aware, the national spirit and the language disappear,
misery grow, assimilation succeed. The young Bretons abandoning the
scholarly and sterile theories of their elders are content to affirm that
Brittany is a nation, without worrying to distinguish autonomism from
regionalism or federalism—a summary program, if you want, but one
which has proven itself and which is bearing fruit.[255]

Thus, Basque reaction to the coming of the German occupation hardly occurred within a vacuum, or, in Nathan Leites's felicitous phrase, from within
a house without windows.

Collaboration and Resistance among the Basques of France

But listen. You can keep a secret, I suppose? We, the Basques of France, cannot
remain neutral after the defeat. Either accept it, with Pétain, Vichy, and the
Germans, or refuse it with de Gaulle. Well, to speak frankly, we don't know which
will be the better for the future of the Pays Basque.
Christian Rudel, *Les guerriers d'Euskadi*[256]

If the specter of collaboration was a difficult one anywhere, it was doubly
so among the Basques due to their recent defeat by German-assisted Francoist troops during the Spanish Civil War. Moreover, it was German planes
in Franco's service which bombed the Basque capital of Gernika, an event
which inspired Picasso's epic mural.

In fact, German scholarly interest in the Basque people was of long standing by the eve of World War I. Some of the German officers sent to the Basque
country were in fact professors of linguistics or anthropology with serious academic interests and occasionally ties with the Basques. As François
Pranzac described the German strategy, "They sent us charming and flatter-
ing scholars."[257] Professor Ewald Ammende had attended the Aberri Eguna
(Basque national holiday) in 1933. But among all others, the figure of Professor Karl Budda (later of the University of Erlangen) stands out. According to
Pranzac:

His science of Basque, it must be recognized, astonished many basco-
philes. . . . Of the language, he possessed all the nuances of terms and
of accent whether it were in Navarais, the dialect of Biscaye, of Gipuzkoa or of Labourd. In such a way, he created a small legend of virtuosity
around his person. It was a means of contact.[258]

For reasons of *Realpolitik,* German strategic interest in the Basque country of Spain was also long-standing. In 1911, for example, maps of Euskadi existed in Germany stamped with the imprint of the Service of Mines of Prussia. Access to Basque mines, especially iron ore, was regarded as a major strategic asset in the event of war.[259] As an anonymous pamphlet mused around 1938:

> Having in mind the circumstances which have given dramatic actuality to this millenarian people and the German intervention in the Spanish Civil War, and especially their interest in Euzkadi's economy, one wonders what can be the real reason for the curiosity that is now to be observed in Germany regarding the Basque people.[260]

Pranzac asserts that between 1914 and 1918 German agents based in Bilbao and Donostia had attempted to foment unrest in French regions bordering on Spain. Some even believed that Germany sought strategic advantage over France by making a buffer state of the Basques. For Dumas, this was an article of faith: "No one could deny that Germany has not always wanted to put France in a vise, in creating itself a friendly or allied state."[261]

After the fall of France the German occupation began in a far less intrusive way than elsewhere in France, but accelerated as the war progressed and as the Germans became aware of the large-scale traffic in Allied pilots passing through the Basque Resistance network and into safety in Spain. In fact, the Hotel Eskualduna at Saint-Jean-de-Luz served two purposes: upstairs was the billet of German officers in the city while in its basement was a stop on the underground railroad for downed Allied flyers on their way over the mountains to safety in Spain. Yet, according to Eugène Goyheneche, not a *single* German was killed by the Resistance and the Basque population was spared the divisive choice between collaboration and resistance experienced in Brittany at the same time.

Representatives of both the Vichy administration and the victorious French nationalism at the liberation believed that *Aintzina* was held in favor by the Nazi occupational administration. During the time that Basque deputy and notable Jean Ybarnégaray was Vichy minister of sports and youth, the following anonymous letter was sent to Goyheneche:

> I have just learned that the Services of the Ministry of Youth is following with "interest" the development of the young Basque movement. They received a report from Bayonne on the [French] Basque nationalist movement. . . . They are completely against it, but they dare not voice this, as they swear that the Occupation views it with pleasure.[262]

As the French nationalist Pranzac wrote in 1946:

At the same time [as Professor Budda's activity] Sonderführer Jantzen had installed the Services of the Propaganda Staff in Biarritz, at the Hotel Aranoa, where Hauptmann Professor Meyer would succeed him later. . . . It is in these services that a Basque journal, "Aintzina," received with discretion but with certainty the benediction and all the sacraments of the Propaganda Staff.[263]

The Basques between Resistance and Collaboration

The Basques were largely spared the fractious debate over collaboration versus resistance that shattered the Breton movement at war's end. In the Basque case, the overwhelming majority of militants who became active in the struggle aided or were themselves members of the Resistance. The Basque clergy was particularly active, including Abbé Pierre Lafitte at the Petit Séminaire, who, under the *nom de guerre* "La Croix," provided maps of German troop movements and sent them into Spain and North Africa.[264] Other clergy along the border became active in the smuggling of people and information across the Pyrénées into Spain.[265] Besides historically having elevated smuggling to an art form, the Basques greatly benefited from the rough and inaccessible terrain of the Pyrénées along the French-Spanish border.[266] Roland Moreau, in his history of the Basque faith, mentions the special role of several clergy along the border in the passage of aviators and others. But, according to Moreau, "None however, among the Basque clergy, rendered as signal a set of services to the resistance as the Benedictines of Belloc."[267] The Resistance at Belloc continued despite the Gestapo's sending several of its leaders into detention at Buchenwald and Dachau (from whence they returned at war's end). The Benedictine Abbey of Belloc was recognized by the French army in 1951 for having smuggled more than a thousand individuals across the border to safety.

According to Pierre Lafitte, however, the vast majority of Basques were either pro-Vichy (and the role of Jean Ybarnégaray as a minister under Vichy aided this support) or accommodated themselves to the Nazi occupation and sought simply to endure.[268] In fact, only one individual, Eugène Goyheneche, chose a path that some would later call collaboration.

Basque Nationalism and "Collaboration" in the Ideology of
Eugène Goyheneche, 1940–1945

*A handful of us took risks in the name of the future of all Basques. Some are
going to work with the men of de Gaulle and others with Germany.
There will be conquerors and conquered, but those who will be
with the conquerors will try to save, if it's still possible, those of
their brothers who will be on the side of the conquered.*
Christian Rudel, *Les guerriers d'Euskadi*[269]

By the early 1940s three formative influences on the thinking of Goyheneche
would push his militancy in the same direction: his acute understanding of
Basque political history; his position in Paris as interlocutor with other ethnic
movements in France, including Breton and Flamand; and the ongoing impact of Abbé Jean-Pierre Urricarriet and others on his thought.

In March 1943 Urricarriet wrote to Goyheneche, describing the political
choices made by the Basque movement and offering a utopian plan:

> Those who are ready to play the German card—and who think it urgent
> to do so in the manner of the Flamands in 14–18—can be counted on the
> fingers of the hand. All the rest are behind "collaborationist" *Eskualduna*
> and *Aintzina*, in the manner of Larzabal, 100%, but above all no politics,
> and let's do nothing to hurt the injured France.
>
> 1. What to do? One terrific solution: under the pretext of a Pyrenean
> border to guard, establish a military government in Bayonne. . . . Chase
> away Vichy and its offices, government by protectorate, newspapers
> in Basque . . . schools in Basque, courts and city council meetings in
> Basque. That would be radical. All non-Basque civil servants out the
> door; they are all Communist and Gaullist. And the people would ac-
> commodate this regime very well, which would be profitable to the
> Germans and would leave indelible traces in our future. But it's too
> beautiful.[270]

Urricarriet from behind the scenes represented an unflinching source of
nationalism and radical thinking which influenced Goyheneche from the
time he first settled in Paris in 1932. The influence German philosophy had
on Urricarriet, in turn, was clear in his letters to the young nationalist:

> Another difference is the role accorded to sciences, for French scientific
> research must be disinterested and its only goal to discover truth. . . .
> For a "racist" scientific research must be above all practical and oriented

toward that which will increase the well-being and the industrial power of a people which lets itself be respected and admired by the others, in waiting for the moment when it can dominate them.[271]

To this influence of Urricarriet was added Goyheneche's close knowledge of the well-developed body of collaborationist logic in both Brittany and Flanders.

In a never-published document from his archives entitled "Quelques idées" (ca. 1942–1943), Goyheneche laid out a Basque strategy toward the war:

> Our position: NEUTRAL
> Side to take: With that one which offers freedom to our [Basque] *patrie*.
> A fact: The crisis or failure of Latin civilization. Let it not take us with it. Win who may, a new Europe is being born where Latin ideas and civilization will be excluded or at least relegated to a secondary rung, ceding priority to Nordic peoples. Let us profit from this![272]

In 1946, in his now famous letter to José Antonio Aguirre, president of the Basque government in exile, Marc Légasse identified a Spanish Basque exile in France, M. Epalza, as another influence on Goyheneche's thought, particularly on his relations with the German occupational authorities. Légasse complained bitterly about Epalza:

> I don't want to end this letter without drawing your attention to the case of M. Epalza, one of our most mettlesome adversaries. During the years of the occupation, this very notorious Germanophile didn't cease preaching a basque Nationalism with Hitlerian sauce to young continental Basques. The unfortunate Goyheneche paid with hard labor for the lessons and encouragements of M. Epalza. I am unaware of the reasons which have pushed you to appear in public with a man whose activities during the war were so contrary to yours and which could have been prejudicial to the Basque cause, but we are many here, after having deplored that Goyheneche was the only one to pay for the criminal follies of M. Epalza, not to accord to the latter but a single right after all that he did, and that is the right to silence himself.[273]

According to Goyheneche, in retrospect, three goals became paramount: (1) preserve the Pays Basque from the consequences of occupation; (2) protect the Spanish Basque refugees from the common effort of French and German police; and (3) recognize the possibility that Germany might well win the war.[274] In that case, Goyheneche favored the creation of a Basque buffer state which would proportionally weaken both France and Spain.[275]

Since the Basque government in exile had already developed close ties with London and Washington, it was important now to cover the options in working with the occupational forces in the protection of Basques and the Pays Basque. According to Abbé Lafitte in 1973, Goyheneche bet on the German side, and Lafitte on the side of the Resistance. They agreed that the winner would try to save the loser.[276]

It is significant that Goyheneche has hardly written about this period, not even in his masterwork of nearly a thousand pages, *Le Pays Basque*.[277] His silence stands in contrast to Olier Mordrel, who, in *Breiz Atao*, goes to great lengths to defend and explain his position. Goyheneche has spoken quite freely, however, about that period; perhaps the best account of Goyheneche's strategy during World War II is to be found in the fictionalized account of the work of "Professor Henri Etchebarne" in Christian Rudel's *Les guerriers d'Euskadi*.[278] In addition to the two prefatory quotations in the previous sections, the fictionalized Etchebarne speaks of the "chance which the Germans represent."[279] But to cover all bases, he goes on:

> To hide nothing from you, we are prudent, we mustn't put all our eggs in the same basket, thus we will protect our chances at de Gaulle's side. There will be Basques in the Resistance.[280]

In later years both Lafitte and Goyheneche would use virtually identical language in explaining their logic: each would work on different sides for the future of the Pays Basque, and at war's end the winner would try to help the loser. The hope, of course, was for the creation of an independent Basque state:

> I told you, do not let any opportunity pass by. If they give us a Basque state, here in France, or if they judge that they should impose a Basque state on Franco, then their most devastating defeat will never be able to erase this decision, and we will have profited by them to the maximum.[281]

Goyheneche's path was a lonely one. As we have seen, even Abbé Larzabal, then editor of *Aintzina*, urged that groups should maintain close ties with Goyheneche or even with the devil if necessary in order to serve the Basque cause. Pranzac wrote of Goyheneche in 1946:

> A young intellectual, a fanatic of autonomism, frequented the [Propaganda Staff] on a regular basis and he paid dearly since, by long years at hard labor for his relations . . . with the occupants. From the beginning, for the rest, after having been alerted, . . . the committee of sponsors of *Aintzina* abandoned him at full speed.[282]

The German occupation of the Pays Basque ended in September 1944, and Goyheneche was arrested fifteen days later.[283] As elsewhere in France, some individuals brought out shotguns and claimed membership in the Resistance when they had been absent during the occupation. France became a *country of resistants* at the liberation with old grievances and feuds to settle. On January 10, 1945, Goyheneche was brought to trial before a jury of twelve members of the Resistance. Goyheneche's main accuser was a policeman from the rural interior who claimed to have been arrested after Goyheneche denounced him to the Germans. Despite testimony on his behalf, at the age of twenty-nine, Goyheneche was found guilty and sentenced to life at hard labor. He ultimately served thirty-seven months before being freed in November 1947.

Even the Basque radical left would later insist that Goyheneche was hardly a collaborator.[284] Perhaps the greatest testimony to that effect would come from Marc Légasse almost thirty years later, despite animosities which had divided them for decades:

> Goyheneche was very nationalistic. He did the most of anyone for the Spanish Basque refugees during the war. He didn't do propaganda for the Nazis; he contacted them to help his fellow Basques. During this time he maintained close ties with the Basque Government in Exile. His imprisonment was a monumental injustice. He cannot be reproached for anything.[285]

The Basque Idea at the Liberation: Three Faces of the Militancy of Marc Légasse

With the liberation in 1945 came three different initiatives on the part of Marc Légasse which demonstrated the reaction of the public, the French government, and the Basque government in exile toward Basque nationalism in France. These initiatives, before the hiatus which would soon follow, pointed the direction in which later Basque militancy would flow.

The three episodes are, in chronological order, the candidacy of Légasse and several others as Basque nationalists in the cantonal elections of September 23, 1945; Légasse's proposal for a Basque department presented to a Commission of the Chamber of Deputies in Paris in 1946 by Basque deputy Jean Etcheverry-Ainchart; and, finally, the letter Légasse wrote to President José Antonio Aguirre of the exiled Autonomous Government of Euzkadi in which he criticized the attitude of the Spanish Basque refugees toward the French Basque movement. All of these issues—the electoral support of the

Basque movement, the question of the creation of a Basque department in France, and the ties between French Basques and the refugee community—remain central in the Basque movement to the present day.

The Presentation of Basque Nationalist Candidates in 1945

Hardly had the heady triumph of ascendant French nationalism consolidated itself in 1945 than France returned to free elections. In the cantonal elections of September 23 and 30, 1945, four Basque candidates presented themselves to the electorate: Marc Légasse running as a "Basque Nationalist" in the canton of Saint-Jean-de-Luz in the first round on September 23; Joseph Darmendrail as a "Basque Nationalist" in the second round of the canton of Bayonne Nord-Est; Pierre Landaburu as a "Nationalist Basque" in the second round in the canton of Biarritz; and André Ospital as an "Independent" in the second round in the canton of Bayonne Nord-Ouest.[286]

The results of the election indicated sparse public support for the idea of Basque nationalism in 1945. Légasse polled a total of 95 votes along the southern Basque coast. Landaburu polled 59 votes in Biarritz. Ospital received 57 votes in Bayonne Nord-Ouest. Darmendrail received a surprising total of 549 votes in Bayonne Nord-Est, with 300 coming from Bayonne alone. These results did not surprise Légasse, who had intended these candidacies to be symbolic in nature all along:

> Precisely at this epoch, the continental Pays Basque, after four years of German occupation under which the French authorities were degraded at will, found itself in full spiritual, moral, political, and even patriotic disarray, while a very clear movement of Basque renaissance was taking place in all domains. One was the logical consequence of the other . . . but passing. Was it necessary despite these eminently favorable circumstances that the Basque Nationalists of continental Euzkadi hold themselves long apart from the movement of emancipation of peoples not only of France but of the world? . . . We didn't think so. And it was also without waging an electoral campaign that we presented ourselves symbolically in the elections, in order to deploy our banner . . . in a wind which seemed to us propitious.[287]

But the autonomism implied in these candidacies—greater freedom within the context of France—was already a pale imitation of Légasse's own political credo, which he readily admitted was separatist[288] or Basque anarchist,[289] depending on his mood. At base, however, his political tendency was Basque:

"I am neither anti-French nor anti-Spanish. I mean simply to be able to remain Basque."[290] In the first issues of his "nonperiodical" *Hordago* and later articles in the local press and in his antics at his trial in 1947 (discussed below), Légasse often used the absurd as a method for making his political points. He would say later, "My writings, even if comical, had some element of seriousness, and that was to beware the threat of government."[291]

The low electoral turnout for Légasse and his compatriots led many to declare the threat of a Basque nationalism in France ended. Gaetan Bernoville wrote in 1946:

> That which interests us here is to note that the autonomist claim of the other side of the mountains hasn't affected the Pays Basque Français, profoundly integrated, thank God, in [French] national unity. . . . The *Zazpiak bat*—"The seven provinces are one"—remains an ideal line, a salute to the community of origin and of mores.[292]

Philippe Veyrin could write a year later, in 1947:

> If the sympathy of the French Basques has always been with their brothers in Spain, one must nevertheless recognize that they were never tempted to imitate their action of a political nature. Autonomism is not appropriate here. The beautiful efforts—especially over the past fifty years—to maintain traditions, save the language, enrich literature and art, to develop in a word a culture properly Basque, arise only from a genuine regionalism, perfectly legitimate. It would therefore be completely erroneous to see the least anti-French claim in the spread . . . of symbols such as the Basque cross, the shield of the three or seven provinces of the Basque country, and the green, red, and white flag.[293]

Yet that is precisely what happened in 1948, during an international folklore festival, when Guy Petit, deputy-mayor of Biarritz, forced the removal of a Basque flag in order not to offend Spanish participants. In response to the pitched opposition of such figures as former deputy Jean Etcheverry-Ainchart, Abbé Pierre Lafitte, Marc Légasse, and Dr. (future senator) Michel Labéguerie, Petit remained uncontrite:

> But if it means a flag, then there is only one for the Basques of Labourd, Basse-Navarre, and Soule, as for the Alsatians, [or] Bretons: the tricolored flag: Blue, White, Red. To pretend to assign to the same rank a regional emblem is to engage in separatism and threaten the unity of the fatherland.[294]

Multiple responses pointed out that de Gaulle himself had recognized the Basque flag. As Légasse pointed out, "It's not necessary to be more Gaullist than de Gaulle, more opposed to the Basque flag than Spanish carlists, and more 'little' than Monsieur Petit."[295]

Yet this fear of separatism continued to influence French governmental reaction to the Basque movement in the immediate aftermath of the war. When, during the legislative elections of June 1946, Légasse published a poster calling for Basques to abstain from participating in "the affairs of a people to which you don't belong" and "to keep apart from these sordid electoral melees during which these Punch and Judy puppets bitterly fight over the politico-touristic exploitation of Euzkadi," he was arrested and charged with activity threatening the security of the state.[296] The newspaper *Résistance Républicaine*, which carried the account of Légasse's arrest in 1946, went on to add:

> Let us add that the Basque Nationalist Movement has not benefited from public favor. In a population of around one hundred thousand French Basques, only several dozen seem to be interested in it. The other French Basques very attached to the mother-fatherland disapprove any spirit of autonomy and don't take seriously the activity of some young fanatics, whom they consider jesters besides.[297]

Légasse spent nineteen days in jail in Bayonne and underwent psychiatric exams which found him capable of standing trial. During the process, however, he underwent a hunger strike (the first of what later would be many by *abertzale* in the 1970s and 1980s), and became a sudden embarrassment to a French state, which faced the specter of Légasse dying, as one newspaper feared rural Basques might see it, "for Basque independence."[298] He was soon released. Ultimately brought to trial nine months later, in March 1947, Légasse was finally fined fifteen hundred francs under a law dating back to Napoleon III which forbade certain forms of abstentionism. What was most interesting about the trial, however, was not the "*Canard Enchaîné* defense" of Légasse's posters, but that the judge really put on trial the *statut de loi* Légasse had written in favor of a Basque department, which had been introduced in a committee of the National Assembly by the Basque deputy Jean Etcheverry-Ainchart in 1945.

Légasse's Proposed Law Creating a Basque Department

In 1945, in the first legislative elections for the postwar Constituent Assembly, Jean Etcheverry-Ainchart of Saint-Etienne-de-Baigorri, *notaire* and scion of a family of political notables from Basse-Navarre, decided to run as a "Basque independent." When some objected to the word "Basque," Cuzacq claims he dropped the word "independent" and thus appeared on the ballot as "Candidat Basque."[299] Shortly after the election, Légasse and others approached Etcheverry-Ainchart and asked him to introduce a *projet de loi* entitled "Statute of Autonomy for the Pays Basque within the French Republic," before the National Assembly.[300] Etcheverry-Ainchart did, in fact, introduce this bill before a committee of the National Assembly working on the new French constitution. Légasse recollects that Etcheverry-Ainchart laughed at many of the details, which Légasse freely admits were a bit "absurd" or "crazy"; but other aspects called for the recognition of Basque as a co-equal language with French. According to Légasse, "We asked for the maximum short of separation."[301] Légasse's proposal for the creation of a Basque department would later be taken up again in the 1970s and made a major element of Basque mobilization, greatly buoyed by François Mitterrand's inclusion of a Basque department in his platform for the 1981 presidential elections (see chapter 6).

Writing to President Aguirre in his famous letter of 1946, Légasse spoke of the *projet de loi* following on his earlier electoral campaign:

> Some time later our minimal demands were given a legal form under a proposed Statute that M. Etcheverry-Ainchart presented to members to the Constitutional Commission. I have at hand the responses of several deputies, members of that commission who are not wholly unfavorable. [But when the Constitutional Commission voted on several laws] . . . the simple demand for Basque courses in school were rejected.
>
> . . . all this received the approval of people as reflective as Abbé Lafitte, who in the sole Basque newspaper *Herria* valiantly supported our point of view and made the project for a statute his own—M. Etcheverry-Ainchart, who strongly encouraged us to create an extremist party clearly nationalist, which would facilitate the task of more moderate Basques and accustom the Basque public to claims that until that point had not been publicly expressed. Evidently, the French reacted much differently and since the month of September we have been the brunt of surveillance by the special police of the subprefecture of Bayonne. Sanctions were even envisioned and then abandoned.[302]

Yet, with Légasse's arrest in mid-1946, charged with threats to the security of the state for his posters recommending abstention in the legislative elections of June 1946, the question of his treatment by the state remained. Thus, when Légasse was brought to trial in March 1947, it is significant that the judge wanted to discuss not the posters but the *projet de loi*.

Abbé Pierre Lafitte covered the trial for *Herria*, and his account is of interest.[303] If Légasse could claim that the posters were just a joke, "the judge found that the *projet de statut* wasn't a joke, and was disturbing to the unity of France."[304] The judge went on to ask Légasse: since the law proposed a division of the existing department, wasn't that a menace of territorial redistribution? The judge claimed to see no use for a Basque department and in fact raised the danger of separatist tendencies which might try to unite the seven Basque provinces. "The judge found that a movement might easily become a party of treason, as was seen in other circumstances, particularly in Brittany and Flanders."[305]

Though it appeared through 1948 and 1949 that France was considering the creation of a new department called Bas-Adour, Côte Basque, Nive-Adour, or Pyrénées-Atlantiques, there was apparent reluctance to tamper with existing territorial boundaries. So skittish was French reaction that one editorial writer bridled at the innocuous cry of M. Inchauspé upon his election in 1949 as president of the Conseil Général des Basses-Pyrénées: "Vive le Pays Basque!"—falsely seeing in this emotion Légasse's plan coming to life.[306] Not until the advent of the French Fifth Republic was the Department of the Pyrénées-Atlantiques created, subsuming in its entirety the old department of the Basses-Pyrénées, product of the French Revolution, dominated by Béarn and still situated in Pau. Thus, this period revealed the state's persistent suspicion of suggestion of separatism, an institutional obstacle compounding the earlier public indifference at the polls. It was in this climate of institutional hostility and public indifference that Légasse wrote to Aguirre in 1946.

Marc Légasse's Grievances against the Basque Government in Exile

The final element of this trilogy—the alienation which French Basques felt from the Spanish Basque militants now political refugees in France—was revealed in the letter written by Marc Légasse to José Antonio de Aguirre Lecube on March 25, 1946. In this extraordinary document Légasse put aside the anarchist humor of *Hordago* and provided a mordant critique of the Spanish Basque government in exile. Given its historical importance, the letter merits quoting at length:[307]

Mr. President,

I have the regret to protest to you by this present letter the attitude adopted by diverse influential members of the Basque Nationalist Party, certain ministers and functionaries of the Basque Government, and yourself toward the Basque nationalist movement in continental

EUZKADI. The press as a whole has shown itself hostile. The right accuses us even of playing the game of the Communists, and these latter accuse us of being disciples of Ybarnégaray. The clergy in certain cases has taken a clear position against us. However, despite it all . . . one can say without exaggeration that the Basque Nationalist idea, whether of the autonomous form like the *projet de statut* or of the separatist form as conceived by the small group to which I belong, is an idea which counts at the present time in the Basque country and which remains for many people without a precise opinion (the great majority) a possibility which in the bottom of their hearts they would like to caress.

It is thus that we have noticed that while we resist the pressure of the French administration . . . certain influential members of the Basque Nationalist Party are carrying out a work of sabotage behind our back which strangely seems to coincide with the maneuvers of the subprefecture in Bayonne. . . .

In the refugee milieu has been created slowly but surely a psychology of fear and dread about the possible consequences of our action. They first told us that our action risked compromising your diplomatic activities and in particular your relationship with the French government. . . . [But] what does the French government and especially French public opinion see in you? A Spaniard, a republican Spaniard, a Basque political leader who is at the same time a Spanish functionary. . . . They also told us that sanctions could be taken against the Basque refugees as a result of our nationalist action . . . I don't believe it. . . .

In truth, Mr. President, I think that the reasons that you pushed the Basque Nationalist Party to adopt a hostile attitude toward us are quite other than those alleged and come in reality from a low and very sad spiritual and moral evolution. The party of Sabino [Arana Goiri— founder of Basque nationalism], also ferociously separatist . . . has lost in growing up and . . . has forgotten a little, in aging and working, of the very heart of its doctrine. The separatism has fallen by the wayside. . . . And today one witnesses the bewildering but so sad spectacle of the disciples of Arana Goiri collaborating with their enemies the Spanish . . . and . . . with the French administrations in the smothering and dispersion of the Basque nationalist movement [in France]. It is a very old truth that when one begins to cheat on principles one always ends up by betraying them.

You will excuse, Mr. President, this letter so long, so violent, and so little respectful. . . . It is true that the foolish sometimes speak the truth; thus I hope that you will take count of that which seems to you foolish, in order to consider only what may seem to you true.

Please accept, Monsieur, the assurance of my devotion in the cause of the independence of Euzkadi.

Marc Légasse

P.S. Given the notoriety of the criticisms that you and your friends have uttered against our movement, you will not see any inconvenience if some copies of this letter of justification are transmitted to diverse Basque parties and to diverse Basque nationalist personalities.

Conclusion

Thus ended an era of Basque nationalism in France which had stretched from the founding of the Eskualerriste movement in 1933 to the French nationalist resurgence in the years following World War II.

This was an important chapter in the history of the Basque movement in France for a number of reasons. First, it represented the emergence of the first generation of young secular Basque nationalists—products of the church, but able to transcend its clerical regionalism in aspiring toward true political self-determination. Second, it was in this period, in the heady atmosphere of Paris between the wars, that the first sustained contact began between militants of various ethnic movements—Basque, Breton, Flemish, Occitan—making them aware of a common cause and a common destiny. Third, the advent of the Spanish Civil War accelerated the ideological debate regarding Basque nationalism which had just begun in France and, for many in this conservative and traditional rural political culture, contaminated the movement and challenged its effort to represent ethnic cultural symbols legitimately. Thus, to the extent to which the Basque movement began to move away from the church and then became more nationalist, it came to be seen as less Basque. This was driven home further by the alliance of Basques, Communists, and anarchists in the Spanish Civil War. The civil war also brought the massive influx of refugees into France, whose leaders, far from embracing the nascent French Basque movement, seemed willing to sacrifice it in order to preserve their own sanctuary in France. Fourth, the Nazi occupation raised further fears of collaboration and separatism in the local population, press, clergy, and French administration. The question of ethnic self-interest and Basque mobilization was lost on most individuals preoccupied with simple survival.

Thus, in those heady days of triumphant French nationalism in the years immediately following World War II, the French Basque movement was confronted by three related obstacles: public suspicion and electoral indifference; government hostility; and rejection by many in the Spanish Basque refugee population, a painful realization fraught with images of fratricide and abandonment.

It was in these circumstances that the movement entered a hiatus that would last until the creation of *Enbata* in the early 1960s. By then many of the lessons of this earlier generation would be lost or obscured. Abbé Lafitte became editor of the traditional Basque newspaper *Herria* and was later appointed a canon (*chanoine*) of the cathedral in Bayonne. He remained at the Petit Séminaire until his death in the spring of 1985. Goyheneche was rehabilitated and appointed archivist in the overseas department of Martinique. He would later return to a similar position in the contiguous department of Les Landes. Active behind the scenes in the founding of *Enbata*, he was appointed *maître assistant* (associate professor) of Basque at the University of Pau in 1968, retiring in 1983. Goyheneche died on January 11, 1989. Abbé Larzabal headed the church of Socoa; from that pulpit he helped found *Enbata* and became a strong defender of the rights of the refugee population until his death in 1988. Marc Légasse continued his particular philosophy in *Hordago* and in the 1960s became one of the closest French Basque defenders of the more radical Spanish Basque refugees of ETA. In 1993, the last of his generation, he continued to write weekly columns in *Enbata*. New faces and new names would emerge from the universities of Bordeaux, Paris, and Pau and from the rural interior.

However, many of the problems of the interwar years remained: how to promote secular Basque nationalism among a conservative and clerical rural population, especially at the polls; how to win concessions from the French state; and what role to play vis-à-vis the more serious and accelerating Basque conflict in Spain.

Of particular note is the frequent failure of the latter-day Basque movement to recognize the ideological contributions of its forbears. Seen from the safety of today's vantage point, the ideologies of the 1930s and 1940s have been stigmatized as timid, reactionary, and weak. They were quite otherwise, when judged by the standards of their day.

History, we are reminded, is the product of the human ability to shape events. The generation of the interwar years produced important role models for later Basque nationalists: men of the caliber of Pierre Lafitte, Eugène Goyheneche, Pierre Larzabal, and Marc Légasse. Without their militancy, the modern Basque movement would have been greatly impoverished, if not stillborn. Their beliefs—regionalism, nationalism, separatism—became woven into the fabric of the slowly unfolding tapestry of Basque nationalism in France. As T. S. Eliot reminds us, "Time present and time past are both perhaps present in time future, and time future contained in time past."[308]

Chapter Four

The Wind before the Storm:

Enbata and Secular Nationalism,

1960–1974

Often, in the evening of a burning hot summer day, a fresh ocean breeze—the
Enbata—*rises up briskly, making the shutters bang and transforming the*
atmosphere from one moment to the next. The arid sky is covered with faint vapors
which, by themselves, will vanish in the night.
Philippe Veyrin, *Les Basques*[1]

The ideal of the Basque fatherland is forgotten, neglected, fought, swept aside,
replaced. The ideal of a foreign nationality is proposed as the fatherland for the
Basques. . . . It is time to react. It is time for the mother to be returned to the
child. . . . It is time that the Basque fatherland gives itself a
nationality of its own choosing and at its service.
Embata 1, no. 1
(September 1960)[2]

How to admit that the Basque nation existed on the other side of the Pyrénées
without recognizing for "our" Basques the right to integrate with them? And
Alsace? Was it necessary to rewrite the history of France in reverse?
Jean-Paul Sartre[3]

In 1960 the publication of a small nationalist newspaper, *Embata*—soon to
be *Enbata*—marked the beginning of the modern era of ethnic mobilization
among French Basques. *Enbata* served as a harbinger of changing times,
an internalization of the lessons of Algeria and the crises of decolonization
which had so traumatized the French political landscape during the late
Fourth Republic and early Fifth Republic.[4] In the history of Basque political ideas, *Enbata* served as the transition from the conservative clericalism
and regionalism of *Aintzina* to a modern and self-conscious secular doc-

trine of ethnic nationalism and self-determination. Its appearance marks the beginning of the modern era of Basque militancy in France.

In this chapter I will consider the origins of *Enbata* and the sources of its early ideology; the decision to field candidates in local and national elections and the effects this would have on the movement's organization and ideology; the mobilization strategy of a nationalist movement among a profoundly conservative rural population; the influence of the Spanish Basque case and especially the Spanish Basque movement ETA (Euzkadi Ta Askatasuna, Basque Homeland and Freedom); and finally the differences between *Enbata* and the French state which led to the dissolution of *Enbata* as a political movement in 1974 and set the stage for the violence to come.

Enbata: Its Origins and Early Ideology

> *Gu gira Euzkadiko gazteri berria*
> *Euzkadi bakarra da gure aberria.*
> We are the new Basque youth
> Euzkadi alone is our homeland.
> *Enbata* co-founder Michel Labéguerie
> (original song sung the Monday of Pentecost, 1961)[5]

In the years following World War II the traditional avenue of upward mobility for the sons (and later the daughters) of the Basque bourgeoisie had been the pursuit of university studies, often in law, medicine, or pharmacy. Since the Basque country had no university, and the University of Pau would not be built until the 1960s, the most frequently chosen universities were in Paris, Toulouse, or Bordeaux. Two hours by train or car to the north, the University of Bordeaux was the closest. University studies represented for the Basque elites, as for France as a whole, the primary method for the bourgeoisie to replicate itself and to socialize its sons and daughters into the French fabric of economic and social success. In the years immediately following World War II it was still most common for university studies to be confined largely to the sons of the aristocracy and the doctors, *notaires*, and *commerçants* who made up the political and economic classes of rural France. To be sure, while the brightest of other students were joining them as merit challenged social class as a means of upward mobility in France, as late as the 1960s children of the working class still represented only a few percent of the total French university enrollment, a political *revendication* which would emerge as a major issue during the French student revolt in 1968.

THE FOUNDING OF EMBATA

In 1947 Abbé (later Chanoine) Pierre Lafitte created three small groups which served to bridge the interregnum of the war years and to continue the work of Basque and Christian socialization he had begun in the 1930s with *Aintzina I* and the Eskualerriste movement.[6] The first and most important of these groups was the Association des Etudiants Basques (Association of Basque Students), which held for the first time in 1947 a series of what would later become annual summer gatherings at Hasparren known as "Basque Student Days." In the same spirit he created the dance group Irrintzi for Basque university students at Bordeaux. The groups included later *Enbata* founder, doctor, *député*, and senator Michel Labéguerie, as well as later *député* Michel Inchauspé of the banking family of Saint-Jean-Pied-de-Port, Abbé Pierre Charritton, and Henri Mathieu. During this same year, 1947, a small chorale group was created within the Basque student community in Paris, L'Ochote Ernandorena.

According to Charles Arribillaga, the author of *Embata*'s first and now forgotten history of its creation in 1958, this phase of the Association of Basque Students was at the stage of "folklore" where many of these young assimilated Basques could discover their roots.[7] "Folklore" would soon give rise to a broader "cultural phase."

The purpose of the Basque Student Days was to create a climate of fellowship and instruction in which these students could grow as Catholics and Basques. Among the individuals who gave presentations during the first several Basque Student Days in the late 1940s and early 1950s were Abbé Lafitte, Manu de la Sota, Abbé (later Chanoine) Etienne Salaberry, Abbé André Hiriart-Urraty; Abbé Idiartegaray; Père François; Rev. Père Gachitéguy; Michel Inchauspé; Marc Légasse (who, as we saw, had led the more political *Aintzina II* during the early war years); and Telésforo de Monzón of the Basque Nationalist Party (PNV) and Basque government in exile. Abbé Thomas Dassance, speaking at the Basque Student Days in Saint Palais in 1949, chided and exhorted the students in attendance by calling them "intellectual tourists" who only related to Basque culture three days a year.[8] He also suggested somewhat apocryphally that the salvation of the Basques might not itself be Basque.

The role of Abbé Lafitte in creating these organizations and the early preponderance of clergy in the guise of early teachers and guides demonstrate the Basque movement's slow transition toward a later secular statement of Basque nationalism. While *Enbata*'s own later histories have chosen to date its origins from the date in 1953 when the Association of Basque Students changed its name to *Embata*,[9] it is clear that its roots lie directly in the three groups created by Lafitte in 1947. It is thus important to underscore that

Embata's origins were not a sudden and abrupt change from the Christian Democratic tradition which had preceded it and which characterized the essence of legitimate Basque political culture in France since the early Third Republic.

The photo taken at the Basque Student Days at Saint Palais in 1949 demonstrates the tie to Lafitte's efforts in the 1930s, as well as the strength of the clerical influence in the early postwar years. Sitting in the front and center of the photo were Abbé Etienne Salaberry, the Benedictine Père Thomas Dassance, and the elderly *curé* of Espelette, Curé Chilibolost. In the photo were six other actual or future priests, including a young Père Pierre Charritton. In the center of the photo is the elderly Mademoiselle Madeleine de Jaureguiberry, who, as we saw earlier, led the Begiraleak, the female wing of Lafitte's Eskualerriste movement in the 1930s. In fact, nearly half of the students in the photo were female. All were representatives of the Basque bourgeoisie, upwardly mobile youth who would go on to distinguish themselves in careers in medicine, science, or business. Two of the first members of these groups, Michel Labéguerie and Michel Inchauspé, would later be elected *députés* to the French National Assembly. It would be wrong to state that these students were pre- or proto-*abertzale*, imbued with a sense of Basque identity that would grow into nationalism. This conservative, bourgeois generation of young educated Basques was still solidly within the embrace of the church and its Christian Democratic tradition. But within this group were individuals like Dr. Michel Burucoa or Dr. Michel Labéguerie who spun the cocoon from which the chrysalis of secular nationalism would soon rise.

By the early 1950s the Association of Basque Students had two strong poles in its groups in Paris and Bordeaux. Paris had taken the lead in the organization's early years and included such members as Michel Inchauspé, Charles Arribillaga, Henri Mathieu, and Basque students from Spain. Bordeaux's group included Michel Burucoa and his brother, Ximun Haran, François Mendy, Jean Fagoaga, Laurent Darraidou, and M. Pariès.

In 1953, at the urging of the group from Bordeaux, the Association of Basque Students took the name *Embata*, the Basque word for the ocean breezes which precede the storms which rise up along the Pays Basque's Atlantic coast.[10] The choice of the very name was a symbol of coming change, the rise of this generation to political and nationalist consciousness. As much as the first stirring of the storm-laden breezes over the Atlantic, *Embata* was a harbinger of things to come.

The first president of *Embata* was Michel Burucoa, and its twenty or so members included former world pelote champion and later pharmacist Ximun Haran, and Doctor Michel Labéguerie, who had already returned to

Cambo to open a medical practice in 1948.[11] All three would join to usher in *Enbata*'s creation as a political movement in the early 1960s. Under the influence of three priests, Abbés Abeberry, Gachitéguy, and Harguindéguy, the young members of *Embata* began to interest themselves in economics and questions of rural sociology. In February 1956 the association transferred its headquarters to the Musée Basque in Bayonne.

In 1960 the death of the revered former president of the Basque Republic, José Antonio de Aguirre, and his funeral in Saint-Jean-de-Luz attracted more than 5,000 people. According to Malherbe, this was one of the events which spurred Haran to action.[12] A meeting of *Embata* attended by Burucoa, Labéguerie, Haran, Jean Fagoaga, Abbé Lécuona, and J. Iturria, among others, held in Espelette on July 24, 1960, represented a turning point in the rising political consciousness of the young movement. At this meeting it was decided to create a newspaper, elect a slate of officers, and open an office in Bayonne to be run by Dr. Burucoa. *Enbata*, in its self-history,[13] asserted that the seven figures who served as the heart of the movement were already clearly visible: Jacques Abeberry, Dr. Michel Burucoa, Jean-Louis Davant, Michel Eppherre, Ximun Haran, Dr. Michel Labéguerie, and Abbé Pierre Larzabal.

The first issue of the newspaper *Embata* was distributed in September 1960, at the meeting of the Eskualzaleen Biltzarra in Arbouet. The much more frankly political tone of the newspaper provoked dissent within the cultural association—a conflict which came to a head during a meeting at the Musée Basque at Christmastime, 1960. It was decided to change the name of the newspaper—if only slightly—from *Embata* to *Enbata*, in order to placate the more timid members who were opposed to the frank politicization of the new publication. The first issue of the newspaper to reflect the new spelling *Enbata* appeared in February 1961.

The rise of the young association to political consciousness was a natural reflection of the crises taking place in Basque society at that time: the decline of the rural economy, the need for youth to leave the familiar embrace of rural values for study and work in the city and to find a new social identity when confronted with the rhythms and values of a threatening French society, and the constant pressures of assimilation.[14] Their espousal of traditional Basque values and their defense of the Basque language were elements in a nationalist consciousness-raising which created its own myth and sought to manipulate the symbols of Basque ethnicity in order to mobilize the rural Basque population. There was in this romanticism a certain Freudian undertone, reflected in the appeals framed in the first issue of *Embata* in September 1960:

Euzkadi . . . you, my mother, there you are transformed into a prosti-
tute. Men coming from everywhere have defiled your home. . . . You, so
serious, you so beautiful, you have denied your soul to please them.[15]

Then, in the same first issue, one reads the lamentation of "an epoch where
the Basque was ashamed to speak Basque. He didn't yet have pride in his
race" (p. 2). Moreover, one finds the symbolic imagery of trees brought to
fruit within the benevolent embrace of nature, of culture as symbolic mother,
and of father figures deserving the respect and pride of young Basques.

The emergent nationalism of the young militants was apparent from the
first issue. If hardly more than a flyer, it nonetheless revealed the general
orientations around which the later political movement would coalesce. It
included emotional appeals to the Basque people and nationalist appeals
for the unification of the Basque provinces of France and Spain and for the
inclusion of this unified "Euzkadi" in a federated Europe of ethnic peoples.

Much of the early nationalist sloganeering of the young militants came
from five sources. First, the writings of the founder of Basque nationalism
in nineteenth-century Spain, Sabino Arana Goiri, served as the sacred texts
to which all Basque patriots referred. His flag, his name for the country, and
his dream of a Basque homeland became rooted in the Basque ideal in much
the same way that Americans revere Washington or Lincoln or the Soviets
revered Lenin and Marx.

Part of the making of nationalist myths, however, involves the selective
borrowing and interpreting from sacred texts. Accordingly, Arana Goiri
would serve as a spiritual father, but his clerical regionalism and conservatism would be glossed over in favor of nationalist themes more in vogue in
the 1960s. Moreover, Arana never held the place among French Basques that
he had among Spanish Basques and especially those of the PNV, as we have
seen previously.

Second, the historical memory of Basque resistance during the French
Revolution and during the French Third Republic became a symbol of inspiration for modern Basque resistance to an encroaching French state. Of
particular interest was the Basque demand during the Revolution for a distinct Basque department separate from Gascony or Béarn. The same demand
for a separate Basque department is still being heard today. A hundred years
after the Revolution Basque resistance to the anticlerical French Third Republic was a defense against a Catholic way of life deeply embedded in
Basque tradition. The example of Basque protests in these two periods was
part of a self-written history of resistance to the French state which would
continue into modern era. This history became a familiar vineyard for the
young political journalists of *Enbata*.

Third, the influence of the Spanish Basque movement Euskadi Ta Askatasuna (ETA, Basque Homeland and Freedom), founded in 1959, would
become increasingly important in the ideological growth of the young movement and serve as a major justification for its repression by the French state
throughout its history.[16] As ETA's own struggle shifted to violent resistance
against Franco's Spanish state, growing numbers of its militants began to
seek temporary or permanent asylum in France. Many were seen by eager
young French Basques as war heroes, who exposed young French Basques
to the language, literary tradition, and dance which the refugees brought
with them. Jacques Abeberry was but one of his generation to be influenced
by the culture of the refugee community, which found outward expression
for him as much in his association with the Basque ballet troupe Oldarra
as in his later editorializing for *Enbata*. One of *Enbata*'s earliest causes was
the treatment of the growing Spanish Basque refugee community in France.
Enbata would closely follow the ideological development of ETA—a fact
recognized by ETA as much as by the French state. The crucial exception
in *Enbata*'s political doctrine was its refusal to espouse the use of violence
as a tool of political struggle. It would follow ETA, however, as the latter
organization splintered in a dispute over the primacy of national liberation
versus Socialist class struggle. ETA remained an important "demonstrator
influence" for *Enbata* as it struggled to define its own political line.

Fourth, the contacts between Basque militants and militants of other ethnic
peoples had continued since Eugène Goyheneche's contacts with students
from other French minorities in university circles in Paris during the 1930s.
After World War II a network of "nations without states" under the umbrella
of the Mouvement Fédéraliste Européen arose which gave common cause
to the idea of ethnic self-determination and independence in a Europe of
ethnic peoples.[17]

Fifth, these young Basques could hardly remain apart from the most important questions among contemporary French political ideas: the role of
colonialism and France's anguished self-reconceptualization following Algerian independence. The French Fourth Republic finally fell over this issue,
as had Pierre Mendès-France over Tunisia only a few scant years before. De
Gaulle's reversal on the issue created enmities that marked the politics of
the early French Fifth Republic, itself the child of the crisis of decolonization. Through these influences, *Enbata* borrowed the phraseology of national
liberation, internal colonialism, and oppressed peoples. According to Abbé
Pierre Larzabal, the lessons of the Third World and Fourth World (the poorest
of the poor) in their struggles for independence raised a number of parallels with the aspirations of submerged minorities in France.[18] Above all, the
crises of decolonization demonstrated the weakness of formerly "impreg-

nable" states and suggested that existing political structures were transitory and not durable. As Chanoine Etienne Salaberry put it simply:

> The French provinces are the colonies of the Parisian metropole. . . . Colonialist exploitation projects itself on the plane of consciousness where it engenders a complex of inferiority. The inferiority complex is the reflection, at the bottom of the soul, of an inferiorized situation, accepted as such in passivity and abandon.[19]

By early 1960 seven former French colonies in Africa had become independent. Seeing the irony of independence for ethnic peoples less economically or politically developed than France's own internal minorities, *Enbata* asked, "Aren't we evolved enough to be able to govern ourselves?"[20] In fact, as the young militants first tentatively approached the idea of nationalism, they asked, "Will it be nationalism? Who would dare to reproach it in an epoch when all the ethnic groups are awakening?"[21] For French nationalists across the political spectrum, movements like *Enbata*—and others in Brittany, Corsica, and Occitanie—represented not simply *le trahison des clercs*, but the lessons of Algeria, Tunisia, and Vietnam brought home with a vengeance.

THE TENSION BETWEEN CLERICALISM AND SECULARISM

As we have seen, it is clear that *Enbata*'s origins lay in the legitimate tradition of Basque Christian Democracy. Larzabal, Labéguerie, and Burucoa were clear bridges back to Lafitte's initiatives in the 1940s. But most of the other early members of *Enbata* were also of this Christian Democratic tradition, among them Michel Eppherre, Jean-Louis Davant, Ximun Haran, Ramuntxo Camblong, and Jean Etcheverry-Ainchart. In a personal as well as national sense, to espouse a secular statement of Basque nationalism was to recast the tradition of Basque identity in France.

Enbata's greatest risk lay in its decision to embark on a secular political path and to neutralize the conservative and clerical rural political culture which had marked the history of Basque politics in France. In so doing, *Enbata* rejected the slogan *Eskualdun, fededun* (He who is Basque is a believer) which was popular, as we saw previously, during the nineteenth century, and Arana Goiri's own slogan of "God and the ancient laws," which Chanoine Lafitte had made the slogan of *Aintzina* during the 1930s. To succeed, *Enbata* would have to recast what it meant to be Basque in France.

The desire to develop a secular strain of Basque nationalism reflected a number of circumstantial factors proper to the Pays Basque of the 1960s. First, it was a challenge to the Christian Democratic moderation of Arana Goiri's tradition and, as such, a reflection of a political movement not of maturity but of youth.

Second, it reflected the neutralization of the Basque clergy as the unchallenged ethnic elite after the crisis of separation of church and state in France in 1905–1906 and the absence of a self-proclaiming nationalist elite among older generations. While some clergy were overtly nationalistic in sentiment, they were a minority both among Basque clergy and among Basque militants in France. So the decision to embark on a secular path of nationalism was a product of historical circumstances in the era of Algeria and the trauma of decolonization; an absence of attractive alternatives, with the neutralization of the clergy as the traditional ethnic elite; and a natural generational conflict, which brought with it a rethinking of Basque values and the future of Basque identity by a new generation of Basque youth.

THE ROLE OF ABBÉ PIERRE LARZABAL

Nowhere was the tension between secularism and clericalism more evident than in the role played by the Abbé Pierre Larzabal, who constituted an important bridge between the militants of the 1940s and those of the 1960s. Larzabal took over from Chanoine Pierre Lafitte as editor of the second series of *Aintzina* in the 1940s. He remained in that capacity until conflict with Marc Légasse led to his departure. Larzabal, like Lafitte before him, was a "fisher of men," and his self-effacing talent lay in his ability to plant the seeds of nationalism and retreat into the background to await their maturation.

Larzabal's role in the founding of the young organization and its early direction is a matter of some dispute.[22] Nowhere does he appear in *Enbata*'s early histories except as "a Basque priest," despite the naming of all of the other founders.[23] Yet, according to Larzabal himself, he was one of the three founders of the young association and virtually the sole author of its early editorials and statement of principles.[24] Ironically, as Larzabal pointed out, this was despite the erroneous impression on the part of its critics that *Enbata* had been created by ETA refugees—who had, in fact, not yet arrived in France.[25] In fact, some latter-day Basque militants, including later members of *Enbata*, see the influence of Telésforo de Monzón behind Larzabal's role in creating *Enbata*. This would have afforded de Monzón the plausible deniability he would have needed in order to maintain the PNV's stance of political neutrality in France, especially toward the French Basque population.

Larzabal soon withdrew into anonymity at his own request in order to force the young movement away from what he called "the skirts of the church."[26] As Larzabal explained it, if the movement was perceived as being in the hands of a priest, then other priests would join, the youth would depart, and the movement would either be stillborn or sink slowly into conservatism. Thus, Larzabal—having pointed the movement in the right direction—chose to leave in order to ensure the development of a secular nationalism free from the stifling apolitical embrace of the church. It was apparent, however, that the bishop of Bayonne was beginning to grow concerned by the politicization of Basque youth and had, in fact, dissolved the Movement of Rural Christian Youth (MJRC) during this same period for being too politicized.[27] Simon Haran revealed in 1991 that, shortly following the appearance of the first issue of *Enbata,* Marc Légasse hastened to submit an article strongly attacking the bishop of Bayonne, which *Enbata* rejected for publication.[28] It was one thing to chart a secular political course vis-à-vis the bishop; it was apparently quite another to send so vehement a shot across his bow. Haran later called Légasse's rejected article "an inopportune critique totally misplaced and, as was his habit, without logical proof [*argumentaire*]."[29] For Haran, Légasse remained a "humorist of demolition."[30]

Larzabal was thus probably under the same constraints as Lafitte had been a generation before as a young nationalist priest. His work done, he retreated into the background rather than risk an overt conflict with the bishop. Interestingly, if anything Larzabal became even more outspoken in his defense of nationalist causes in his later life and would firmly say, "I am with ETA-militar,"[31] earning him the popular French press's title of "confessor to terrorists."

TOWARD A STRATEGY OF POPULAR MOBILIZATION

Given the overwhelming Catholicism of French Basques in 1960 and the fundamental conservativism of their political culture, the decision to embark on a secular political path in the 1960s reflected a clear risk. It meant attempting to change a rural culture which continued to exist linguistically, culturally, and spiritually through its ability to resist and manage change.

As the Communist historian Henri Lefebvre put it, "The ancient community folds back on itself, it tries to oppose [the flow of] history. It functions like a mutual aid society against historical accidents."[32] For *Enbata* to succeed meant circumventing the traditional structure of politics in the Pays Basque and depended on the acquiescence or defeat of firmly entrenched conservative Basque elites supported by the church.[33]

The conflict *Enbata* thus posed was not simply one of political doctrine, but one of generations as well. As the late Chanoine Etienne Salaberry put it, in defending *Enbata* against its critics:

> Someone like me from the beginning of the century can speak without foregone conclusions about a movement of the end of the century, the movement *Enbata.* It represents an age which I am no longer; a party of which I am no longer. The wrath which the word *Enbata* provokes among

certain Basques demonstrates to a power of nine, if that were necessary, the depth to which the virus of alienation has penetrated them. . . . The members of *Enbata* are the Young Turks of the Pays Basque. . . . [It would be] a land indeed as poor in truth as would be a land deprived . . . of Young Turks. The Pays Basque proves its vitality in offering itself this luxury. The hostility toward the youth of *Enbata* comes from a general hostility toward youth. . . . This attitude isn't Basque.[34]

Crucial to *Enbata*'s political strategy would be its ability to popularize itself among a generally skeptical Basque electorate.

The problem which confronted *Enbata* was not simply a widespread suspicion of nationalism—tainted in most minds with the violence of the Spanish Civil War—but the reality that the young militants of *Enbata* would have to pry the mantle of cultural legitimacy from the hands of deeply entrenched rural Basque notables and thus defend their claim to be legitimate representatives of Basque culture and traditions. The terrain of cultural legitimacy and thus of political orthodoxy was well occupied and had been for generations. *Enbata* recognized early on the necessity of legitimating its enterprise through the association with ethnic cultural symbols and the Basque language. Thus, *Enbata*'s insistence on the cultural genius of the Basque people was made evident from the first issue of the newspaper.

The Aberri Eguna of 1963: Transformation into a Political Movement

It would be two more years before the young militants of *Enbata*—now transformed into journalists—would realize their ambition of creating a true political movement. That moment came in the winter of 1963 with notices in *Enbata* announcing the celebration of the first Aberri Eguna, or Day of the Fatherland, among French Basques. The symbolism of the Aberri Eguna and the planting of a symbolic "Oak Tree of Gernika" that day in the churchyard of Itxassou were a direct link back to the time of short-lived Basque autonomy during the Spanish Republic before the Spanish Civil War. According to *Enbata*, "The Aberri Eguna of 1963 must be the striking demonstration of our political maturity."[35]

THE POLITICAL REPORT

The Aberri Eguna took place on Easter Monday, April 15, 1963, in the small village of Itxassou, alive with the blossoms of the cherry trees for which it is famous. The first Constitutive Congress of *Enbata* began at 9 A.M. in the

FIGURE 1

Charte d'Itxassou

En ce jour de la Patrie, quinzième d'avril 1963, les BASQUES rassemblés autour du jeune chêne de Gernika planté à ITXASSOU en Province du Labourd, déclarent:

Nous Basques

SOMMES:

UN PEUPLE par la Terre, la Race, La Langue, les Institutions.

UNE NATION par notre Volonté passée et présente.

UNE DÉMOCRATIE par notre Nature et notre Histoire.

COMME PEUPLE, NATION, DÉMOCRATIE.

AFFIRMONS:

notre Droit à l'UNITÉ.

à la LIBRE DISPOSITION individuelle et Collective.

FORTS DE CES RÉALITÉS, CONSCIENTS DE CES DROITS et de celui, universellement reconnu, des peuples à disposer d'eux-mêmes,

PROCLAMONS:

NOTRE DÉTERMINATION—A RÉALISER, par l'ORGANISATION DE LA NATION ET SA RECONNAISSANCE par le PLEIN EXERCICE DE LA DÉMOCRATIE la CONTINUITÉ et la VIE DU PEUPLE BASQUE RASSEMBLÉ.

village's parish hall. The assembly heard three reports: on the Basque language (in Basque), on economics, and on politics. The assembly unanimously adopted the movement's charter, *La charte d'Itxassou,* presented by the respected former deputy and *conseiller général* from Saint-Etienne-de-Baigorri, Jean Etcheverry-Ainchart (see fig. 1). The final Basque-language version of the *charter* was overseen by Chanoine Lafitte himself. *La charte d'Itxassou* argued that the Basque people were one by virtue of their land, race, language, and institutions.[36] On that objective bedrock lay the sentiment of a Basque nation, legitimated by past and present will. Asserting that the Basques were one people, nation, and democracy, the charter called for the right to unity and the individual and collective right to self-determination, which were held to be universal.

The associated political motion went further. It held that the Basque nation was divided in half by the present French and Spanish states.[37] Yet, in a self-conscious effort to avoid any mention of separatism, the movement called first for the creation of a Basque department with a statute for the Basque language—in a manner respecting the constitution and laws of the French republic. In a second stage, it called for a culturally, politically, and administratively autonomous Basque region regrouping the Basque regions of France and Spain together in a united Europe, tied through federalism to other European entities.[38] Neither of these goals was terribly extreme. The existing departmental structure of France which dated from the Revolution had been revised barely five years before with the beginning of the Fifth Republic, and the dream of a United Europe had been popularized by Jean Monnet and Robert Schumann since the end of World War II.

It was Jacques Abeberry's political report, not submitted for a public vote, that extended the political goals of the movement and revealed the natural outcome of the goal of national self-determination. In his report Abeberry said, "The Basque nation must realize its right of self-determination . . . it must give itself a political structure of Basque society, that is to say a State.[39] The stages described by Abeberry were more specific than those submitted for public approval. While the first stage shared the call for a Basque department with a special statute for the Basque language, the second step called for the creation of an independent Basque state:

> the total liberation of our people in its unity remains our final goal; only the constitution of a Basque state will permit the full realization of the aspirations of the Basque people and will permit free rein to its genius.[40]

Abeberry's schema then called for the uniting of this Basque state with other states in a federal or confederal Europe.

THE ECONOMIC REPORT

What clearly differentiated *Enbata* from the movements which preceded it was the extent of its economic analysis and the link made between economic decline and the cultural threats to the Basque people. The economic report at Itxassou was made by Jean-Louis Davant, who would continue to influence the movement's economic analyses for most of the ensuing decade.[41] Davant's analysis, later extended in the movement's first economic *cahier*, touched on the problems of rural agriculture and its resulting depopulation and the need both for cooperative action and the modernization of agricultural holdings too small to be economically viable. He also called for mutual action between Basque fishermen from Bayonne to Bilbao in Spain in order to protect their livelihoods.

His analysis was one of the first to point out the dangers of the tourism that threatened to reduce Basque culture to that of an Indian reservation, and to lead to an employment/unemployment cycle of feast and famine around a seasonal tourist industry marketing folklore and lasting barely three months a year.

Finally, Davant saw little chance of industrialization coming from the French region of Aquitaine centered in Bordeaux. For the Basques, the potential for industrialization would best be realized along the axis stretching from Lacq (the natural gas exploitation near Pau) to the industrial centers of Spain's northern Basque coast, which were the most highly industrial areas in Europe west of Paris. Basque economic development and industrialization would come not from France, but from a new Europe with the Pays Basque in its midst.

This brief analysis set forth themes which would be repeated widely until the present day. What *Enbata* did in 1963 was to add economic factors to the traditional list of linguistic and cultural grievances and to situate the question of ethnic mobilization in a broader context of political economy.

Among the five hundred people in attendance were a number of Basque elected officials, including Senator Jean Errecart, newly elected deputy Michel Labéguerie (who was already distancing himself from his former allies in *Enbata* who had helped him get elected), former deputy René Delzangles, and numerous *conseillers généraux* and mayors. Representatives of a number of other nations without states included delegates from Catalonia, Brittany, Occitanie, Flanders, Wallonia, and Quebec. Telegrams were received from Bavaria and Wales. Most of the prominent Spanish Basque refugees in France were also in attendance.

PRESS REACTION

Despite the care with which the public motions were framed, the conservative and influential daily newspaper *Sud-Ouest* titled its account of the previous day's assemblage: "A Itxassou (Basses-Pyrénées) rassemblement de séparatistes qui demandent la création d'un département basque." [42] *Côte-Basque Soir* was more objective and matter of fact in reporting the event, as was *Le Courrier*.[43] *Côte-Basque Soir*, for example, estimated the audience that attended the assembly and picnicked outside at several hundred more than the five hundred who dined inside.[44] The leftist and Gascon-oriented account of André Graciannette in *Le Travail* admitted its ambivalence toward a dynamic young movement critical of the existing political situation, yet based on disturbing theories of race, economics, and theories of colonialism.[45] *Le Monde* pointed out the new form of these Basque particularist sentiments and distinguished them from the separatism of Marc Légasse's team "before the war [sic]," [46] though claiming the event sought to unite all those movements—more or less autonomist and more or less separatist—in Europe. *Le*

Monde's account noted in particular the youth of those attending, estimating that three-quarters of the five hundred were less than thirty, and the number of delegations from other European minorities.[47]

The skepticism of *Sud-Ouest* was seconded by a later editorial in *Le Travail*, entitled, "*Enbata* is promising them a prefecture." Its biting tone mocked the idea of a "pure Basque race" and condemned it at last as a "puerile agitation whose slogans of nationalism and racism cover regrettable regressions" and as "insane political ambitions."[48]

Yet Michel Labéguerie, in an interview in *Paris-Presse* picked up in a later editorial of the local *Le Courrier*, called the demands presented at Itxassou "very modest" and stated, "The demands were made very calmly; it is not among us that one will find excited individuals throwing bombs."[49] As the editorialist Fernand Laurens concluded, "It's sometimes necessary to shout loudly to make oneself heard."[50]

It was thus with this public beginning that *Enbata* offered itself as a political movement to the Basque people. In terms of its political ideology and goals, *Enbata* had staked out a clearly nationalist position far out on the margins of existing Basque political culture. On the level of cultural practice and language use, there was clearly a bedrock reality of Basque culture in the Pyrenean foothills. Whether or not *Enbata* as a nationalist movement could move these conservative rural Basques and transform them into foot soldiers of a nationalist movement was another question.

The Question of Basque Identity and the Use of French

In order to win this ethnic legitimacy, *Enbata* adopted a mobilization strategy which predated its transformation into a political movement. It elements were understandable, if paradoxical. First, the group made the deliberate decision to appeal to as large a potential following as possible, a strategy confirmed by public documents and by the private correspondence of its militants. Paradoxically, then, this strategy forced adoption of French as the vernacular language of Basque nationalism in France.[51]

This strategy was justified in part by the extent of linguistic assimilation of most ethnic Basques in the urban, coastal cities where *Enbata*'s early militants were most concentrated. Indeed, the greatest struggle faced by the movement in seeking to popularize itself was to bridge the gap between its early militants raised in a climate of French assimilation and cultural integration along the coast and the reality of overwhelming Basque language use in some cases only a few miles inland. What was left unsaid, until the movement later wrote its own history (read *auto-critique*),[52] was that many of its most active militants, though Basque in origin and accepted as Basque, were not themselves fluent in the Basque language. The choice of French, then, also corresponded to the needs of the organization. Throughout its history, *Enbata* would be at least bilingual in French and Basque, though frequently printing short articles in Spanish, and even letting the odd word in English slip through.

As a result, *Enbata* was led to a flexible definition of what constituted a Basque, both for the purposes of its inclusive mobilization strategy and reflecting an instrumental awareness of its members' own backgrounds as they teetered along the path between Basque culture and assimilation into dominant French culture. In the range of ethnic barriers to be traversed, *Enbata*'s was loose and inclusive, perhaps a psychological balm for the unsettling passage of their own individual self-definitions. As Jacques Abeberry pointed out in his political report at the Aberri Eguna in 1963, "A Basque, in the national sense of the term, is he who, accepting the Basque ethnic factors, desires to be one."[53] For a movement which spoke of "race" as a distinct marker of Basque historical distinction, *Enbata*'s own political use of ethnic barriers was virtually nonexistent. Paradoxically, former members of *Enbata* (presumably including Jacques Abeberry himself) who were now members of Euskal Batasuna argued erroneously in 1988[54] that *Enbata*'s ethnic self-definition manifested in the *Charte d'Itxassou* was close to the definition of Joseph Stalin, in his 1913 work *Marxism and the National Question:*

> A nation is a historically constituted, stable community of people, formed on the basis of a common language, territory, economic life, and psychological make-up manifested in a common culture.[55]

In fact, Stalin's definition remains one of the most uncompromising and demanding in the historical literature on nationalism. As Stalin put it, "it is sufficient for a single one of these characteristics to be lacking and the nation ceases to be a nation. . . . *It is only when all these characteristics are present together that we have a nation.*"[56] In reality, many of the first generation of *Enbata*'s militants who did not speak the Basque language might well not have been considered Basque by Stalin. And by Stalin's rigorous definition the Basques themselves might well not have been considered a nation, an idea Abeberry did not intend to advance.

The psychological motivation of young Basques whose maternal language was not Basque, or who were the product of mixed marriages, is an important question in national movements in general. For it raises the question of the displacement of inner tensions and insecurities into public action. This is particularly true in Robert Clark's excellent analysis of ETA militants, in which he finds that while only about 8 percent of the total population of the Basque provinces of Spain is of mixed ancestry (one parent is Basque and the other non-Basque), fully *forty percent* of ETA members come from such mixed families and *one out of every six* male members of ETA is the son of two non-Basque parents.[57] Not unheard of in the Basque movements of Spain or France is the example of José Luis Alvarez Emparanza ("Txillardegi"), one of ETA's founders and later a member of the elite Basque literary academy, who did not learn Basque until he was seventeen.[58] This was a frequent occurrence among French Basque militants from the coastal cities who rose to political consciousness during the 1960s.

Confronting the Issue of Separatism

One of the earliest and most clearly self-conscious decisions of the young movement was its explicit desire to avoid French charges of sedition or separatism. Thus, *Enbata* made a deliberate decision to channel its militancy in conformity with the French laws of association of 1901, as modified in 1936. This explicit desire to avoid legal problems with the state was made clear in a letter from the late Michel Labéguerie to Eugène Goyheneche (ca. 1961):

> It is well understood that you will be assured anonymity. For the moment, only [Ximun] Haran will appear. You know the others all very well, and they are not numerous. They are serious and discreet. They are a little vague from an ideological point of view, but that is going to clarify itself, I hope, very soon, and in such a fashion that there will be publicly defined an irreproachable and unassailable line of conduct from the point of view of legality. It is necessary that all intentions be put in plain daylight in a very loyal and serene fashion. It is the best means to ensure that the young ones have no worries, and also that they attract numerous hesitants, who remain hesitant because of the suspicion of unacknowledged goals.[59]

Labéguerie's concern must have been to reassure Goyheneche and the public of the movement's rejection of the use of violence—a position maintained by *Enbata* throughout its existence. Otherwise, what hidden threats might there have been, given an open expression of nationalism in the group's writings—unless it was the fear of "separatism"?

Whether these early goals could be characterized as separatist, in the historical sense in which that term is used in France, is uncertain. Calls for self-determination and the recognition of Basque ethnic distinctiveness were

couched in more palatable terms, with reference not only to the French Declaration of the Rights of Man, but also to the Encyclical of the late Pope
John XXIII, *Pacem in terris,* in which the pope argued:

> One must categorically affirm that everything done to stifle the vital
> potential and the development of these minorities gravely violates jus-
> tice and much more if these blows have as a goal to destroy the race.
>
> It is altogether just that public authorities apply themselves effec-
> tively to favor the human values of these minorities, in particular their
> language, culture, traditions, and economic development.[60]

Calls for self-determination and the creation of a Basque "nationality"
were not accompanied by calls for secession from France, even in appealing
for the uniting of the Basques in a new Europe, and hence did not strictly
qualify as threats to the integrity of French territory under the French laws
of association of 1901 and 1936.

The Doctrine of "Ethnic Federalism" and the Mouvement Fédéraliste Européen

Indeed, in its first *cahier*—as at the Aberri Eguna in 1963, *Enbata*'s dominant demand had been the creation of a separate Basque department within
France, a demand as old as the French Revolution itself. Only in a later
phase would one witness the creation of a politically, culturally, and administratively "autonomous" region composed of the seven Basque provinces of
both France and Spain in a Europe of other federated "entities," in a *Europe es
Ethnies.*[61] The concept of a Europe of ethnic peoples was the platform of the
Mouvement Fédéraliste Européen, inspired by the writings of law professor Guy Héraud. The MFE, whose other primary theorists included Breton
militant Yann Fouéré and Alexandre Marc, represented the fruition of interethnic contacts which stretched back to Paris in the 1930s, whose spiritual
bases lay in the revolutionary Giroude as well as in the writings of P. J.
Proudhon.

The MFE's doctrine of ethnic federalism was the basis of *Enbata*'s "Pourquoi Enbata?" Basque nationalism, as defined by *Enbata*, embraced federalism *in opposition to* separatism and thus sought to ally itself with an idea
which, if still suspect, had been a part of the historic French political vocabulary since the time of the Revolution. As we will see below, however, these
jesuitical semantic maneuvers did not placate either the departmental ad-

ministration or the French press, whose journalistic shorthand, or log line, reduced *Enbata* to "the Basque autonomists" or "the Basque separatists." In reply to these charges of separatism, *Enbata* stated that the *true separatism* was the concerted policy of the existing state system to separate members of one ethnic group by outmoded state borders or the attempt to prevent the creation of a united Europe.[62] The semantic legerdemain surrounding this definition does real violence to the common usage of "separatist," even if this is understandable given the emotion-ridden connotations of the term in the history of political ideas in France.

In reality, both the dream of the unification of the seven Basque provinces of France and Spain into Euskadi and the creation of a Europe of ethnic peoples presupposed the end of existing state sovereignty and frontiers. Thus, even before its transformation into a political movement in 1963, *Enbata* provoked clear suspicion on the part of the French government. Intelligence documents from this time focused on the threat posed by *Enbata* to the sovereign authority of the French state. Challenges to the integrity of French territory were now specifically contrary to the constitution of the Fifth Republic, as well as to the familiar French laws of association of 1901 and 1936. Far more ominous to the French government than the beliefs espoused by *Enbata* was the link between it and the Spanish Basque movement, ETA. Despite *Enbata*'s overt sympathy with ETA and its struggle for independence in Spain, it had never advocated the use of violence as a tool of Basque politics in France. Indeed, in the aftermath of the Aberri Eguna in 1963, reports to the French government made clear that *Enbata*'s words were carefully chosen and that ultimately whatever illegality might be advocated by *Enbata* would not be violence, but rather passive resistance and civil disobedience. Nevertheless, French government suspicion persisted undiluted for over a decade of *Enbata*'s existence and would ultimately constitute the primary rationale for banning the movement in January 1974.

In the end, however, it was less the state which was an obstacle to the spread of Basque nationalism in France than the reaction of the Basque electorate itself. Indeed, the nearly insurmountable obstacle facing these young nationalists was the overwhelming Gaullism of the Basque electorate—a wholesale rallying to the French state and nation, as fervently as their ancestors had opposed it less than two generations before. For the Basque interior was, like other minority-language enclaves in Brittany and Alsace, among those electorates where the percentage vote for de Gaulle and his referenda surpassed that in any other areas of France in the Fifth Republic.[63] Ethnic France was Gaullist France, and the Basques remained overwhelmingly faithful to de Gaulle throughout his stay in office and beyond.[64] Indeed,

President Valéry Giscard d'Estaing made a short visit in 1974 to the Basque village of Arhansus, which had given him fifty-nine of its sixty-one votes in the second round of the 1974 presidential elections.

The Basque electorate had found in de Gaulle and his "certain idea of France" a congenial defender of their traditional and conservatively clerical political culture. De Gaulle's choice between himself and Communist disorder was no choice at all in these mountain villages. It was not that the Basque electorate had changed substantially from that of a century before, but rather that the French political context had changed around them. Gaullism was an infinitely more palatable political option than the conjured threat posed by the French left in these rural, mountainous reaches.

Basque nationalism was contaminated by the distaste for communism before it ever appeared in France. Older French Basques' suspicion of the idea of Basque nationalism dated from the conduct of the Spanish Republic during the Spanish Civil War. Given the tactical willingness of the republican forces—including the Basques—to enter into temporary alliances with Communists and anarchists who also opposed Franco, it fell victim to an international media barrage led by the French Catholic press of the time. Transfixed by the spectacle of open warfare in Irún from their vantage points across the Bidassoa River, and buffeted by the massive influx of Spanish Basque refugees who fled into sanctuary in France, the French Basque population was led by conservative elites to equate Basque nationalism with violence and Godless communism. It was the paradox of Basque political mobilization in France, as Chanoine Pierre Lafitte pointed out, that those most ethnically Basque were the most adamant opponents of Basque nationalism.[65] What, then, were the factors which led *Enbata* to espouse a doctrine of Basque nationalism which the Basque electorate had long ago found suspect?

The Influence of the Spanish Basque Case on the Ideological Development of *Enbata*

Truth on this side of the Pyrénées, error on the other.
Pascal

As we have previously seen, one explanation for the failure of a nationalist movement to emerge in Third Republic France along the lines of that which began in Spain in the 1890s was the almost total lack of contact between Basque movements on the two sides of the border. By the years immediately prior to World War II this parallel developmental process had been fundamentally and irrevocably altered. Indeed, during the Spanish Civil War, it is clear that the influx of thousands of Spanish Basque refugees into France following the fall of the Spanish Republic, and the decision of many to settle permanently there as Franco consolidated his power in Spain, brought the seeds of a genuine nationalist sentiment which stood in contrast to the timid regionalism in vogue among French Basques of the era.

Many of the Basque nationalists of the 1960s were exposed to the vitality of the culture and politics of this refugee community as young people, and this early influence had a seminal impact on their own political development as Basques. Later nationalists, among them *Enbata's* Jacques Abeberry, frequently dated their rise to political consciousness to their association with the refugees in 1936. In Abeberry's case, it came through contact with the Basque tradition of dance. He would later become a leader of the Basque ballet troupe Oldarra. Along with the tradition of dance, the refugee community was also transmitting a latent political message about the vitality of Basque culture and its political history in Spain.[66] Yet the first stirring of a genuinely French Basque nationalism was a worrisome development to a refugee community now dependent on the grace of the French administration for continued apolitical asylum in France.[67]

In truth, the Spanish Basque case surrounded and contaminated *Enbata* from its origins. *Embata's* appearance in 1960 was preceded in 1959 by the creation of the Spanish Basque separatist (and later terrorist) organization ETA from an earlier movement called *Ekin* (Action).[68] ETA's own history describes the evolution of the movement and the first rudimentary violence in 1961—bombs against a train near Donostia—which provoked the arrest of 130 Basque militants in Spain. By 1961, then, ETA had adopted a tactic of terrorist violence directed at the symbols and agents of Spanish authority in the Spanish Basque provinces, whose goal was the eventual liberation of Euzkadi. In a classic display of action/reaction, the clarification of ETA's separatist ideology provoked an accelerating cycle of repressive measures by the authoritarian Spanish government. In such a climate of mounting violence in the South (which would increase nearly exponentially into the 1970s), it was inevitable that the Basque provinces of France would again experience another influx of political refugees from Spain.

Unlike the quiescent generation of refugees in the post–Spanish Civil War years who remained largely apolitical because of their status as refugees, the young refugees of ETA who crossed the border into France in the 1960s continued their militancy in many cases. This took many forms. Ultimately, the French Basque provinces came to serve as a border staging area, a kind of Cambodian sanctuary for terrorist attacks directed against Spain. While many refugees sought permanent asylum as political refugees, others went underground and crossed the border as had the Basque smugglers smuggling Allied flyers into Spain during World War II. For ETA, the question of permitting its militants to give up the armed struggle was one of the most sensitive issues the organization would confront. As late as the early 1980s ETA militants who responded to Spanish offers of amnesty (for other than crimes of "blood") risked being assassinated by ETA in their home villages in the Spanish Basque country, sometimes in front of their children, as was the case of "Yoyes" (discussed below). Yet it was manifestly through appeals to the deep loyalties and convictions of its militants that ETA built a substantial logistical infrastructure among the refugee community in France,[69] buttressed by growing numbers of French Basques who offered support to the soldiers of the armed struggle in the South. So firmly rooted was the concept of asylum in the French political conscience that it would take more than ten years of debate within the government before France would take active measures against the refugee community and begin deporting refugees to Spain.

From the earliest association of French Basques with the refugee community, and certainly well before the Aberri Eguna of 1963, the French government viewed with concern the ties between the refugees of ETA and the fledgling militants of *Enbata*. At their most innocent, these contacts involved the humanitarian resettlement of refugees and their families and finding employment for them. Of more concern for the French state, little secret was made of the contacts between the militants of *Enbata* and ETA theoreticians from the earliest planning reunions of the young movement.[70] As ETA stated:

> Others were obliged to seek refuge in the northern Basque country, under French domination. By then ETA was collaborating with what was going to be transformed into the sole nationalist movement existing at the present time in northern Euzkadi: *Enbata*.[71]

Enbata's self-history reveals that in October 1962, in order to celebrate the opening of his pharmacy, Ximun Haran invited the *Enbata* "team" and sympathizers to a cookout at a farm in Espelette.[72] Among the invitees were ten ETA refugees and their spouses. They had just learned the day before of the French government's decision to force four refugees to leave the Pays Basque for residences elsewhere in France. It was decided that *Enbata* would do everything possible in order to reverse the government's decision.

Throughout this period the contacts between *Enbata* and the ETA refugee community increased. Labéguerie was said to be particularly close to four of ETA's first leaders, Benito del Valle, José Luis Alvarez Emparanza ("Txillardegi"), Irigaray, and Julen Madariaga, and this on the eve of his decision to run for the Chamber of Deputies.[73] Government reports maintained that the ties between the ETA and *Enbata* were now daily and ongoing. Haran is re-ported to have visited Caracas, a center of ETA's organization in exile. Upon his return, a number of commercial enterprises are said to have been created and controlled jointly by members of both ETA and *Enbata* for the benefit of ETA refugees now residing in France. The government felt Haran, Davant, Burucoa, and Abeberry were particularly close to ETA; Jacques Abeberry was said to be the "hinge" between the two movements, as well as the workhorse of *Enbata*. The closeness of these ties was made evident by *Enbata*'s transformation into a political movement at the Aberri Eguna in 1963. Among the nearly five hundred participants were most of the ETA refugees in France at that time; indeed, the departmental prefect estimated that more than one hundred attendees were Spanish Basque refugees.[74]

The greatest symbolic public moment that day was the planting of an oak tree of Gernika to symbolize the Basque institutions destroyed by Franco during the Spanish Civil War. The tree was planted jointly by Ximun Haran, representing *Enbata*, and Julen Madariaga, representing ETA. For the French government, the gathering represented the identification of the goals of *Enbata* with those of ETA, notwithstanding the issue of the use of violence. Evidently the Spanish government was similarly concerned, since an under-cover Spanish police colonel was discovered among the crowd at the Aberri Eguna and roughed up until rescued by the organizers. In 1966, when *Enbata* militant Patxi Noblia was arrested at the Spanish border by Guardia Civiles for having copies of *Enbata* in his car, he later claimed that the Spanish offi-cials "were only interested or gave the impression of only being interested in *Enbata* in relationship to ETA."[75] If this ceremony represented the sym-bolic commingling of the roots of *Enbata* and ETA, the absence of any official representative of the Basque government in exile at the festivities at Itxassou underscored the real generational differences between the elder members of the PNV—clinging to the diplomatic custom of neutrality—and the "Young Turks" of both ETA and *Enbata*.[76]

ETA gave prominent coverage to the Aberri Eguna in its publication *Zutik*.[77] For ETA, the appearance of *Enbata* represented a new and loud battle cry (*irrintzina*): the creation of a "true and complete BASQUE NATIONAL UNION,"[78] which could then proceed immediately to the "total liberation of our people."[79] According to historian Jokin Apalategi, in contrast to the opposition of the PNV, the first exiles of the "Basque Revolutionary Move-ment of National Liberation [ETA]" did their utmost to encourage the first small nucleus of *Enbata*.[80] As Apalategi pointed out, this support was public and found echo in ETA's own publications.[81] ETA's journal *Zutik* solicited its readership from its own offices in Caracas to subscribe to *Enbata* as early as 1961.[82] It also regularly published extracts from *Enbata* in the interest of what it called "a true national dialogue" and entered the fray on *Enbata*'s behalf on the charges of separatism.[83]

By 1966 one begins to see increasing discussions within *Enbata* concerning the creation of a "Basque National Front" with ETA and other parties. During the fall of 1966 *Enbata*'s internal newsletter for its militants, *Ekin*, carried an ongoing discussion of the merits of creating a Basque national front, based on the proposal of Txillardegi, one of the founders of ETA now legally residing in France.[84] Yet *Enbata*'s problems were closer to home, involving consciousness-raising among the French Basque population itself. As *Enbata*'s Bordeaux section noted in *Ekin*, "The Basques on the whole don't realize that the existence of *Enbata* is tied to that of Euzkadi South [Spain]; moreover, they are ignorant of the existence of the Basques in Spain."[85] Having made their nationalism a matter of public record, it remained for the militants of *Enbata* to forge a constituency at home among French Basques. In that endeavor, the aid of the refugee community mattered little. Indeed, it was one of the major handicaps that *Enbata* would face.

Nationalism and the Polls: *Enbata*'s Electoral Strategy

Even before its transformation into a political movement in 1963, *Enbata* had long discussed the idea of fielding Basque candidates for elective office at the local, cantonal, and legislative level. The group was strongly encouraged by the election of one of its founders, Michel Labéguerie, as a deputy to the National Assembly in 1962 and the re-election of longtime Basque militant Jean Etcheverry-Ainchart as a *conseiller général* from Saint-Etienne-de-Baigorri, for the first time under the party label of *Enbata*.[86] Yet it would be incorrect to interpret these as victories for Basque nationalism.

Etcheverry-Ainchart, at least, had a strong local following, which, in the tradition of the politics of *notabilisme* in rural, local France, eschewed partisan labels and asked voters to support individuals first and only secondarily parties. For that reason, one can still see in many village elections today party labels such as "independent" or "Defense of Local Interests." In the case of Etcheverry-Ainchart, he was a third-generation notable of this interior market center in Basse-Navarre, a *notaire*, elected deputy to the National Assembly for one term in 1946 (where he introduced a bill written by Marc Légasse, calling for a Basque department), and successor to both his father and his grandfather before him as *conseiller général*. It was clear in this case that Etcheverry-Ainchart was offering his legitimating imprimatur to *Enbata* and not vice versa.

THE LINGERING LABÉGUERIE CONFLICT

In the case of Labéguerie, the strong public attacks on him as a separatist and the resultant retreat of his fellow *Enbata* militants to low-key, behind-the-scenes campaign work could hardly be interpreted as an electoral victory for nationalism. Indeed, so effectively was the charge of separatism used by his opponent to stigmatize Labéguerie that it would be more correct to state that he won *despite Enbata*'s support and not because of it. The posters of Labéguerie's opponent in the election, Dr. Camino, said, "Vote Basque, vote French, vote antiseparatist."[87] The mayor of Hasparren voiced his support for Camino against "federalists for whom the destiny of France is secondary."[88] After the election, in responding to a protest filed by five *conseillers généraux* supporting Labéguerie against Camino's charges of separatism, the departmental prefect responded blandly that it was unthinkable that there could be separatists in this beautiful Basque country.[89] No sooner than he had been elected than Labéguerie began to mark his distance from *Enbata* and eventually came to renounce even those platforms which he had written himself for the movement a few scant years before. In fact, by the Aberri Eguna of 1963, when Labéguerie was asked directly whether he would advance the theses of *Enbata* in his role as deputy in the French National Assembly, his response was a simple "no."[90] In 1964, as a direct reflection of Labéguerie's action, came one of the first efforts to co-opt the theses of *Enbata* in the effort of the Mouvement Démocrate Basque to take up *Enbata*'s earlier theses regarding economic development. This led to the creation of Indar Berri, a regionalist economic development association.[91] By attempting to co-opt the economic issue, the goal was to divorce it from the nationalist camp and return it to the political mainstream. In this way, *Enbata*'s platform passed into political legitimacy.

In 1967 Labéguerie would speak in favor of an association of Basque elected officials and a Basque economic region, but against the idea of a Basque department.[92] By 1974 Labéguerie had been elected to the French Senate and spoke in favor of teaching Basque in public education.[93] But his opposition to his previous nationalism would not change before his premature death in 1980, and it became apparent that there was a strong personal dimension to his conflict with his former allies.

Though the split between him and *Enbata* was clear by his first electoral campaign in 1962, it was still preoccupying *Enbata* three years later. In the fall of 1965, in *Enbata*'s internal publication *Ekin*, Jean-Louis Davant in a characteristically nuanced and reflective *tribune libre* nonetheless conceded: "Others will doubtless appraise the behavior of our deputy according to criteria of morals or of psychoanalysis."[94] For Davant, who chose to focus on the sociology of the long dispute, Labéguerie was of another generation than the majority of militants in *Enbata* by 1962. While his action converged with *Enbata* for a short while, according to Davant, clear differences were apparent from the beginning. As Davant put it, "I am more and more convinced of it when I analyze the 'clandestine' reunions which our group of 'seven historic leaders' held."[95] For Davant, it did not suffice to simply feel nationalist: "one must believe in the chance of success, one must risk a lot in order to obtain it."[96] Appearing between 1960 and 1962, these differences between Labéguerie and the other militants seemed to Davant to be as permanent as they were evident. As a result, he argued that Labéguerie emerged as a "French Basque" who, after his election, became verbally and overtly critical of *Enbata*. This ongoing dispute with Labéguerie was, for Davant, the last fruit of an ill-considered electoral strategy adopted in 1962:

> In 1962 we committed a double error. In one way, we threw ourselves too early into the electoral arena—even if in the shadows—without sufficient preparation. Moreover, we signed a blank check to someone over whom we lost any means of pressure or control.[97]

Labéguerie may have felt himself a nationalist, but he refused to manifest it in his public life. *Enbata* was thus at war with a former ally who was now a French deputy. In the ongoing struggle with Labéguerie, Davant suggested that *Enbata* had lost sight of its goal. As he put it, "It's a question of knowing what we want: shock the bourgeoisie or liberate Euzkadi. For some time now, we have done a lot of shocking, but it doesn't seem that that will advance the movement."[98]

The whole episode between Labéguerie and *Enbata*, which had continued more than three years after his election as deputy in 1962, suggested the force of passion and interpersonal conflicts which remained a part of *Enbata* from its origins until its dissolution. As Davant put it, "Personal questions play too big a part in Basque nationalism in general and in *Enbata* in particular."[99]

Thus, in the long aftermath of this electoral turmoil, *Enbata*'s first electoral forays could not be considered unqualified successes or gauges of the level of public support for nationalism. In fact, the second Aberri Eguna to be held in the North, again in Itxassou, on March 30, 1964, attracted only about 250 people or half of the attendance the previous year. This stood in clear contrast to more than 25,000 Basques attending parallel festivities in Spain the day before. Yet *Enbata* was determined to continue down the electoral path and began planning for the French legislative elections of 1967.

By late 1965 *Ekin* reported on the organization of the movement. Sections had been created in Bordeaux, Cambo, Saint-Jean-de-Luz, Bayonne (two), and Paris.[100] The number of militants reported in these sections totals just over 60, though *Enbata* claimed 250 as the total "enrolled."[101] In 1965 the newspaper had a press run of as many as 3,200 copies. By 1968, however, *Ekin* reported that there were only 350 subscribers and that more than a thousand copies were being given away free to local mayors and members of the clergy.[102] The remainder were sold by hawkers during demonstrations or otherwise distributed without charge.

THE FRENCH LEGISLATIVE ELECTIONS OF 1967

There appear to have been two main arguments behind *Enbata*'s decision to field candidates in the legislative elections of 1967. First, and for public consumption, *Enbata* wanted to offer a "Basque" alternative to an electorate which was still deprived of clear political choices. This was due as much to the historic weakness of the French left (except in coastal cities like Bayonne or Hendaye where the Basque population was most diluted) as it was to the stranglehold some traditional notables had on some public offices. In offering a Basque alternative, *Enbata* reasoned, the greater the number of votes received, the greater the impact it would have on a recalcitrant French administration.[103]

The second argument for fielding candidates was that *Enbata* needed a strong forward impetus as a movement; if it failed to participate in these elections after four years of existence, it might well disintegrate. Opponents countered by evoking the risk of alienating the Basque electorate either through too weak a showing or by too extreme a platform. As Patxi Noblia and *Enbata*'s section at Bordeaux had argued as early as 1965, premature entry into the electoral arena risked discrediting the movement before it even began:

> *Enbata* cannot . . . emasculate itself prematurely. It suffices to see the program of the cantonal elections in order to perceive what degeneration elections will cause for a political movement whose implantation isn't yet complete.[104]

The decision to field candidates was not made in unanimity. As Jean-Louis Davant argued:

> Don't start over in 1967, whether in presenting a candidate from the movement or in supporting [another] candidate, unless we are clearly more strong then than we are today. To my way of thinking, the ELECTORAL struggle is for *Enbata* the most dangerous of all, that which most risks separating us from the Basque people. We don't have any interest in counting our votes as long as they don't have any chance of winning.[105]

In the end, the hope of a credible showing quieted the movement's internal critics.[106]

The platform which *Enbata* adopted for the election was by now a familiar one, based on the *Charte d'Itxassou* adopted in 1963. The ethnic federalist argument became more coherent as contacts with the Mouvement Fédéraliste Européen increased. Yet the tone of the electoral appeals in the issues of *Enbata* prior to the March 1967 election was strangely defensive in nature, as if the election involved less the discussion of substantive issues than a defense of the movement's own legitimacy and ideology.[107] Attempts to make direct appeals to specific conditions or issues of concern to French Basques were often fragmentary or contradictory.

For instance, a major effort was made to draw attention to the stagnating economy of the rural interior. Yet, in a full-page chronology of the history of Euskadi preceding the election, the last mention of the French Basques was in 1839, concerning the quixotic visionary philosopher Augustin Chaho and his position on the First Carlist Wars in Spain. Given that Chaho was also the first Basque to be refused burial in a churchyard upon his death, his example was hardly a rallying point in the religious interior. It appeared in 1967 that *Enbata* was still falling back on the experience of the Spanish Basques in its inability to popularize issues of widespread appeal to the very different conditions in the Pays Basque Français.

There was also an evident frustration among these young militants, who were casting about for the right appeal to gain popular support among the conservative Basque electorate. Patxi Noblia, in a report prepared by *Enbata*'s section at the University of Bordeaux for the 1965 congress of the movement, wrote:

> We are at the center of discussions by all Basques. There isn't a day that goes by in the villages where there aren't questions about *Enbata*, whether favorable or hostile (Espagnoleak) [Spaniards].[108]

In fact, the questions were generally negative, constituting a virtually impassable barrier to the political culture of the rural interior. As Noblia concluded rather plaintively, "We are neither clandestine nor leprous." [109]

THE CHOICE OF CANDIDATES

Beyond the construction of an electoral platform, the choice of particular candidates was also crucial, given the differences in climate of the two legislative *circonscriptions* which covered the Basque electorate. The area around Mauléon in the interior province of Soule was the Pyrénées-Atlantiques 3ème, and the coastal cities around Bayonne were in the Pyrénées-Atlantiques 4ème. In the rural interior *Enbata* first sought to present a well-known nationalist priest. The advantages of such a candidacy were clear: beyond the obvious appeal to the Catholic population, it was hoped he might rally the clergy to his campaign, thus undercutting the criticism of conservative elites and countering the charge of extremism likely to greet any candidate *Enbata* might choose to field.

When predictable objections were voiced by the Catholic diocese in Bayonne, *Enbata* turned instead to a young female militant, Christiane Etchalus. Her nomination posed still other problems. She had just finished serving an eighteen-month prison sentence in Spain for alleged possession of explosive detonators and ETA propaganda during a border crossing. She clearly ran the risk of being discounted as too revolutionary. Moreover, it was argued that as a woman she might not represent a credible alternative in the male-dominated electoral arena.[110] Her running mate was a young Basque farmer, still underrepresented among Basque militants in France.

Prior to the election, however, the most prominent coverage was devoted to the more populous coastal fourth *circonscription,* where the movement fielded as candidates its director general, the former national pelote champion Ximun Haran, with Dr. Michel Burucoa as his running mate. The emphasis on the coastal district reflected the weak penetration of *Enbata* into the interior, outside of the province of Labourd and a pocket around the Basse-Navarrese market town of Saint-Etienne-de-Baigorri. In order to effect that penetration rapidly, *Enbata* sought to publicize itself through other means. Accordingly, of the 181 public meetings *Enbata* held before the election, more than 130 were held in the *circonscription* around Mauléon.

The results of the election were surprisingly similar in both *circonscriptions,* given the differences in context and in the nature of the candidates and campaigns. In the interior, Etchalus polled 1,879 votes (4.72 percent), while on the coast Haran received 3,156 (4.57 percent).[111] In each *circonscription,* only a larger vote in two cantons made the overall percentage figure as high as it was.[112] From this election on, a popular vote of 5 percent of total votes cast became the symbolic threshold each succeeding candidate and movement sought to surpass. While *Enbata* did not admit publicly to a total defeat, it did concede a victory to Parisian centralization.[113]

For Jean-Paul Malherbe, however, Etchalus's showing in the interior was not wholly a defeat. He argues that her image as a result of her recent arrest and imprisonment for aiding ETA impressed certain segments of Basque youth who had previously viewed *Enbata* as a bourgeois organization and who now saw it through new eyes.[114] Whether *Enbata* could exploit this new image or would lose this newly mobilized youth to another style of movement was a question central to its survival.

Privately, the size of the defeat revived the differences within the movement about the wisdom of the electoral strategy. Personality conflicts were growing, and fissures threatened to split the group apart.

Fifteen months later, in the immediate aftermath of the disorder of May 1968, new legislative elections were called by General de Gaulle to renew his choice between himself and disorder. *Enbata* naïvely seized on the opportunity to test its electoral strength once again. Not surprisingly, the pervasive Gaullist coloration of the Basque electorate responded overwhelmingly to the general's call, just as it had faithfully at each election and referendum during the Fifth Republic. Deputy Michel Inchauspé, incumbent in the third *circonscription*, won re-election with a majority in the first round. The "parachuted" former international rugby referee Bernard Marie polled 49 percent in the first round in the fourth *circonscription* and won handily in the second. In both cases, the number of parties fielding candidates increased over 1967. Despite fielding two of its most visible militants, Dr. Burucoa in the third and Jacques Abeberry in the fourth, *Enbata*'s share of the total vote fell to 2 percent in the third *circonscription* and 1.4 percent in the fourth.

In absolute terms, this represented a decline from 5,035 to 1,711 votes. In its defense, *Enbata* was simply buried in the Gaullist landslide which followed the events of May. But *Enbata* seemed to shock rural sensibilities. Its campaign arrived in rural villages with loudspeakers, tracts, and slogans painted on walls. This offended the natural reserve of the conservative villagers and led in more than one case to counterslogans of *Espagnoleak kanporat* (Spaniards get out). As one militant put it, "They seemed to speak well with the people in power, but they couldn't talk to the base. They seemed to be more bourgeois than truly Basque. The irony was that they had to relearn Basque in order to make Basque political demands."

The magnitude of this second consecutive defeat threw the movement into disarray. Fundamental differences emerged over strategy and tactics. As the internal bulletin *Ekin* reported in a clear understatement, "As a result of the meeting of the Board of Directors, several currents seem to differ on some fundamental points."[115] According to participants involved, Haran asked for sole authority to direct the movement for one year in order to try to refocus its energies in the wake of the failure of the electoral strategy. When a majority of the others refused to acquiesce, Haran resigned as director, as did the entire executive committee. He remained on the executive committee and was responsible for *Enbata*'s external relations into the early 1970s. He ultimately left the movement entirely, as did others. This was undoubtedly a difficult decision for him to make: in an account of this period written twenty years later, Haran stated that the original newspaper was created by him and was his own "personal property."[116] Haran helped found Euskal Elkargoa and continued to militate for the condition of the refugee community.[117] He would later grow closer to the efforts of the Basque Nationalist Party (PNV) and lead its first section in France created in the 1990s. The tension between Haran and Jacques Abeberry which dates to this period continues to the present day.

Enbata as a newspaper ceased to be published during a hiatus of four months between June and October 1968 during which the remaining militants reflected on the nature of the movement and the potential for effective political action in the Pays Basque. From interviews with participants five years later comes a near-universal admission that what led to the fragmentation of the movement in 1968 even more than the electoral defeats was a question of personalities that had been brewing since the Labéguerie affair. As Dominique Aligner argues, the stormy arguments over policy and tactics which characterized this period were exacerbated by the frustration of personalities who had worked together for most of the decade without any concrete result.[118] A word often used by the militants involved to describe their interpersonal relationships in this climate of organizational disarray was "psychodrama."

FRAGMENTATION AND DIASPORA

In the wake of the twin electoral defeats, *Enbata* turned back upon itself. Old quarrels which had surfaced around the conflict with Labéguerie—and which intensified as a result of the movement's inability to attract a broad following—led to recriminations and accusations. Many militants joined Haran in departing in 1968, as much in exasperation as in despair.

The Impact of the Events of May–June 1968

The internal disarray of *Enbata* came at an important time in the political development of the Fifth Republic. The paralyzing events of May and June 1968 represented the most concentrated, extrasystemic assault on French institutions since the Commune of Paris in 1871.[119] From rather banal beginnings as one of the peripatetic student strikes which periodically mark the French political landscape, within three short weeks the student revolt had spread to disaffected workers and union members and had ground the French economy to a halt. What was new in the events of May–June 1968 was the specter of a new tactical alliance between students and young workers pursuing different grievances in common cause against the state. So threatened was de Gaulle by the accelerating economic paralysis and street demonstrations that, when summoned home from an aborted state visit to Rumania, he disappeared en route. It emerged that he had flown home by way of West

Germany to visit General Jacques Massu, in command of all French forces in West Germany, in order to assure that his troops would remain loyal to the government in the event of the collapse of political order. De Gaulle's private reaction was far from his contemptuous public dismissal of the events as "la chienlit" (defecating in one's own bed). Perhaps de Gaulle remembered the exchange between Louis XVI and the duc de Liancourt de la Rochefoucault on the eve of the Revolution: "It's a riot then? No, sire, it is the Revolution."

The impact of the strikes of May 1968 in the Basque country was varied. If the workers in the area itself were less prone to strike than those nationally, the Pays Basque could not avoid the impact of national work stoppages which affected the delivery of gasoline and halted train travel and mail delivery and local work actions which ended newspaper publication and the collection of garbage (which led to a great increase in the number of rats on the streets of Bayonne).[120] By May 25 the large department stores were all closed, raising fears about the availability of food.[121] Some would not reopen until June 4. The only collective public services which did not join the strike were the national electricity and natural gas authority, municipal and departmental water services, and automatic telephones. While 4,000 protesters marched on May 12 in support of the strike,[122] the number pales before the 150,000 demonstrators in Brittany five days earlier,[123] and the mass demonstrations in major French cities from Paris to Marseilles. Three weeks later, on June 5, another 4,000 people marched in Bayonne in support of General de Gaulle, carrying banners which read "De Gaulle Isn't Alone," "No to Disorder," "For a Free France," and, in a reference to the student strike leader, "Cohn-Bendit to Peking."[124]

Having restored political order in early June, de Gaulle called for immediate legislative elections. His campaign theme offered the people of France the now-familiar choice between himself and disorder. The French people as a whole, and the Basques among them, rallied once more behind the general in reaction to the economic and social threat posed by the paralyzing strikes from which the country had just emerged. According to Catherine Mas, the Pays Basque was only superficially affected by the events of May 1968 and thus its population was left apart from the sense of the protest involved.[125] The Basques remained in 1968 one of the most profoundly Gaullist electorates in France. Their vote was hardly unexpected, as the conservative reflex of a rural region which had no trouble choosing between the now-familiarly broad Gaullist brushstrokes of order and chaos.

What was left unsettled in the uneasy aftermath of the events of May was the political fallout of the mobilization of literally tens of thousands of youths whose rise to political consciousness had been at the barricades—a political mobilization against the traditional French political spectrum as a whole.

This youth protest stood as much in opposition to the French Communist Party as it was to the rightist government of de Gaulle.

The French Communist Party made a serious tactical blunder in 1968 by vainly opposing the workers' strikes which began in support of the students. These were largely young workers at the large assembly plants who were not yet fully integrated into the discipline of Communist labor organization under the Confédération Générale du Travail (CGT). The Communist Party opposed the strikes because it had not called them and was more concerned with maintaining its monopoly over labor discipline than in opportunistically seizing the initiative from the student and worker revolt. The PCF emerged from 1968 with a reputation not as the vanguard of the proletariat but as a conservative and aging bureaucratic organization, preoccupied with self-interest and hardly attractive to those who sought an effective institutional home for protest against state and society in France.

In the aftermath of 1968, therefore, came widespread dissatisfaction with the alternatives posed for militancy in the Fifth Republic, a perception on the part of French youth which stigmatized the range of traditional political choices in France. *Enbata* fell victim to this rejection, as did more formal French political parties. It was in this climate that *Enbata*'s departing militants found themselves along with a host of newly mobilized young Basque militants searching for what the French call a *chapelle politique* (political chapel)—a new vehicle for their newfound or revitalized militancy.

Within the larger French political spectrum, one major set of beneficiaries of the alienation of leftist youth were the French parties of the extreme left such as the Ligue Communiste Révolutionnaire or Parti Socialiste Unifié (PSU).[126] Their focus was on revolutionary change, in contrast to the image of the rigid and ossified PCF. What most of these parties shared in common was the notion of militancy on a human scale, principled stands against the rote impersonalization of traditional French political parties. But the most dynamic ideology among French student circles in the aftermath of 1968 was Maoism. It offered a "color your own" approach to doctrine, combined with a focus on social struggle over organization and bureaucracy—in short, an attractive alternative to the traditional French Communist left. While Maoism was certainly in vogue on university campuses in the wake of 1968, it competed with a range of other leftist political splinter groups. In 1970, for example, there were three separate Trotskyist groups on the campus of the University of Bordeaux alone. While George Lichtheim referred to this process of splintering and fragmentation of radical movements as "tiny mites devouring themselves in a drop of water," what all these movements shared in common was an opposition to the institutions of the Fifth Republic, from right to left. Their weakness lay in their perennial inability to unite in common cause against the state. They remained marginal due to their insistence on doctrinal purity over political reality. What they represented was the vehicle for the inclusion of new political grievances in French politics, only the latest in a history of "surge" political movements in France. In the aftermath of May 1968 they added to the national agenda such issues as ecology, anti–nuclear power protests, and the rights of women and minorities. In this way they represented the "greening" of French politics.

In the Pays Basque leftist parties made a real effort to recruit militants now departed from *Enbata* as well as the newly mobilized and previously unaffiliated youth in the wake of 1968. According to Beñat Urgarbi, one of the greatest threats to the creation of a true Front of Basque National Liberation in this climate was the efforts at co-optation of Basque issues by leftist French political parties.[127] He alleged that the situation was particularly complicated in the French Pays Basque due to the presence of a number of Spanish Basque militants who were proselytizing for French leftist organizations, among them Secours Rouge or the CGT.[128] Following *Enbata*'s internal explosion, several of its militants gravitated toward the Maoists or the PSU. For Urgarbi, however:

> These militants, not knowing how to go beyond the electoral defeat, finally thought that there was only combat to pursue in Euzkadi Nord and that this combat was very simply that of class struggle. In thus neglecting the national question, they lost the essence of what personalized their combat as patriotic Basque militants. A good number of these former militants of *Enbata* purely and simply abandoned political combat, while others sought refuge in activity of a cultural character. All these latter, after having militated within the movement for the national liberation of Euzkadi, seem to have definitively abandoned the Basque political combat to which they had been considered committed.[129]

If the events which occurred in 1968 in France itself were not already serious enough, two additional events occurred in Spain which hardened the nationalist feelings of the period. The first was the killing of ETA militant Txabi Etxebarrieta by the Spanish police in June 1968. This was followed in August 1968 by ETA's assassination of Spanish police captain Melitón Manzanas in Irún, an event widely understood by ETA and the Spanish government alike as representing an intensification of the Basque struggle with Spain.

It was in this climate in 1970 that *Enbata* and ETA sought to rally Basque public opinion against the trial of ETA militants opening in Burgos in Spain and against the treatment of ETA refugees in France. The subsequent demonstrations in Bayonne took on a diverse coloration, with non-Basque groups like the PSU or Secours Rouge seeking, according to Urgarbi, to claim credit for Basque mobilization against French and Spanish repression.[130] The situation was one of considerable ideological and organizational flux.

The Rise of the New Basque Youth Movements

One of the greatest fronts of the events of May 1968 was the appearance of a host of political groups, many short-lived or stillborn, which reflected the climate of political and intellectual upheaval. In that sense, 1968 was reminiscent of the Revolution of 1848 in Paris, which saw nearly three hundred newspapers created within a few weeks, most of which published an issue or two before disappearing.

In the Pays Basque the primary spiritual offspring of 1968 was Amaia, though other short-lived groups included Beltza and Aski. Aski never surpassed the level of *travail en chambre* and was thus stillborn.[131] Several of these groups were less important as actual political structures than as evanescent rest stops along the road to political consciousness and self-awareness. Many of these splinter groups or political ideas were what the noted French political scientist Maurice Duverger refers to as *partis passoires* (parties of political transit or passage).[132] They reflected the energy of the politicization of 1968, an energy not yet of being but of becoming. Like other short-lived movements such as the first Etorkizuna in the 1960s and EKA in the 1970s, Aski and Beltza were shadows on the wall—a flickering reflection of a greater militancy to come.

AMAIA

Amaia was one of the most important movements to rise as an alternative to *Enbata*.[133] It would serve as the root organization from which many of the most significant movements of the 1970s, including those devoted to violence, would evolve. It took its name from the mythological Basque goddess of the earth, Amaia, the mother figure from which all life emerges.[134] Amaia grew out of *Enbata*'s section at the University of Bordeaux and also recruited from within Ikasle, the student movement created by *Enbata* in an attempt to increase its appeal to Basque students. Founded some time before the events of May 1968, Amaia was begun by former *Enbata* militants who believed that *Enbata* held little appeal to Basque youth, given the generation gap of its older and more successful bourgeois militants. This was despite *Enbata*'s considerable efforts to stage Basque summer "universities" and its publication of Ikasle *cahiers* directed specifically to students. Amaia's critique asserted that *Enbata* was not radical enough and had become just another movement of notables whose militancy was leading to nothing. As Amaia wrote in one of its first tracts:

> The members of Amaia intend to try to emphasize and develop this culture, which, for the present moment, belongs but to a very small group of erudites. These latter, despite their incontestable goodwill and all their love for Basque culture, haven't been able . . . either to attract or to interest the youngest elements of the population in whom reside . . . the whole future of Basque culture.[135]

Born in this climate characterized by ethnic violence and government repression, Amaia was sensitive to the terms of French laws of association and defined itself as a cultural association according to the law of 1901 in order to avoid problems with the police. Internally, it was more overtly political in focus and tone. Its goal was to use cultural militancy as a path to nationalism—a fabian-like strategy in which Amaia would serve as ideological midwife to high school and university students as they rose to political awareness.

Amaia was organized around the personality of one charismatic leader, Peyo Oyharçabal; while numbering as many as one hundred militants, it functioned due to the contributions of a small core of committed militants who provided its structure and *cahiers*, among them Eñaut Haritschelhar, Xan Coscarat, Peyo's brothers Gabi Oyharçabal and Beñat Oyharçabal, the brothers Lucien and Dominique ("Txomin") Etxezaharreta, Xarles Videgain, and Yon and Margaita Etcheverry-Ainchart, son and daughter of Jean Etcheverry-Ainchart. Amaia held that the ultimate liberation of the Basque country would come about through a certain number of militants—that an independent Pays Basque would be created through deliberate acts of political will. One of the sources of Amaia's appeal was that it was organized, hierarchical, and secret, in contrast to *Enbata*, which one Amaia militant called something of a "carnival" at the time. Indeed, one of Amaia's major criticisms of *Enbata* was its spontaneity and lack of organization. The down side of this tight discipline and centralization was the extent of control Amaia came to exercise over people's lives. According to one former militant, Amaia's internal structure bordered on the totalitarian or, as he put it, ran "like a machine out of control." Still others referred to it as fascist and authoritarian and claimed that its leaders sought to create a cadre of "militant monks." Its leaders adopted a kind of revolutionary asceticism in opposing the tradition of partying (*faire la fête*), so its militants reluctantly followed suit. Oyharçabal is remembered frequently referring to "the sacrifice." Malherbe described Amaia's internal discipline as that of a secular monastery and its impact on the individual militant:

It was demanded of the militants to abdicate any individual dimension, any personality, and to integrate into the group as one would enter into a religion, body and soul. The discipline is scary, exercising itself . . . day and night. The member of Amaia no longer belongs to himself, no longer lives save for the organization, always at its service and at its orders. The most servile obedience is demanded.[136]

Its leaders spoke of it as "the fortress" and defined Amaia as an elite *école de cadres* which would train the future leaders of the Basque nation. According to former militants, the role models for Amaia's political action were said to be the Jewish agency, the Irgun, and the Algerian movement, among others. The image of the kibbutz became real when many of the militants came to stay together during summer breaks.

Amaia created sections within the communities of Basque university students in Paris, Pau, Bordeaux, and Toulouse. Its focus, however, remained in Bayonne; if Aski was primarily a dream of young workers, Amaia's militants were more bourgeois in background. Amaia probably numbered around fifteen core militants in Bayonne at its height. Characteristic of what Duverger calls the *parti passoire*, Amaia's importance was not in the number of its militants, but as an indicator of the growing radicalization of an important segment among Basque youth.

Amaia lasted from 1968 until 1970–1971 when it, too, fell victim to internal quarrels which led to its rupture. The terms were by now familiar: the inevitability of personality conflict in small militant groups of this kind; the growing doctrinal and definitional tension, which first led to ETA's splintering in two—ETA-V, which continued the primacy of the struggle for national liberation, and ETA-VI, which defined it in terms of Marxist-Leninist class struggle and which was fragmenting the Basque movement in France in its wake, and finally an undercurrent which was attracted toward clandestinity and violent action.

Several militants of a more Marxist orientation rejected the nationalism and cultural militancy of the others and left the movement in 1971 seeking a more classically Marxist focus on popular mass action. Many of the non-Marxists who remained flirted with the idea of "military action," which meant in this context the use of terrorist violence against the state and its symbols. Amaia already practiced the internal discipline and secrecy of a clandestine organization, while publicly conforming to the French laws of association. In fact, for certain of its militants, Amaia was an important organizational and ideological way station on the road to the clandestinity and violence which would appear during the 1970s. Amaia already functioned as a disciplined and homogeneous group of militants, small enough to avoid the infiltration by French police informers prevalent in or near other movements in this period, including *Enbata* and allegedly even ETA. As one militant put it, "You are never betrayed by your enemies, but rather by the ones you love." According to former militants who rejected this fascination with violence, it grew in part out of the fascination with clandestinity, the guerrilla as Robin Hood, which the others stigmatized as more "elitism" than anything else. The difference between the two conceptions of militancy turns on the Marxist distinction between a genuine mass action by the working class versus the efforts of an elite vanguard party who would act for the working class. The conflict between these two differing directions of militancy were tearing apart the movement internally. Gabi Oyharçabal left on Christmas in 1970. By Easter of 1971 it was clear that the movement no longer existed.

MENDE BERRI

Following his departure from Amaia, Gabi Oyharçabal created Mende Berri (New Century), adopting the name of the Basque-language bookstore first opened by Amaia.[137] Mende Berri's militancy focused on the survival of Basque culture and language. He was joined by Eñaut Haritschelhar (whose father was a true Basque notable: former mayor of Baigorri, holder of the chair in Basque at the University of Bordeaux, and director of the Basque Museum in Bayonne), Xan Coscarat, and others. Oyharçabal continued his efforts at recruitment within Basque student circles, which had been a focus of his militancy in Amaia. Malherbe, for one, calls the success of Oyharçabal's cultural militancy and recruitment efforts "remarkable." [138]

According to a former member with access to the rolls, Mende Berri was set up with a three-tiered membership structure, "one" being the highest level of commitment and "three" being the lowest. The membership rolls for the second or intermediate tier of membership were said to contain 280 names. Other militants placed the number of true militants between 60 and 70, with 30 percent of those being fluent in Basque.

Mende Berri styled itself the voice of Basque youth and reflected their worries and preoccupations, ranging from concerns over language and cultural preservation to the growing ecological consciousness to emerge from 1968, which in the Pays Basque took the form of a hostility to the seasonal tourism which threatened the region's culture and economic stability.[139] As its ideology developed, it also espoused a *socialisme autogestionnaire* or self-managed socialism based on the Yugoslavian model, which was as much in vogue in progressive and academic circles in the United States as in Western Europe at the time.

Within three years, then, *Enbata* was challenged by a second-generation movement which was cutting *Enbata* off from the regenerative effect of youthful militants which it needed to attract or die. Mendi Berri's importance was less on the level of doctrine, for according to some critics it had no real program. What Mende Berri offered was a shelter of ethnic awakening for Basque youth struggling against the inexorable process of assimilation by French culture.

THE HUNGER STRIKES OF 1972

The growing problems of the refugee community and repression by the French state gave Mende Berri an issue around which it could express its militancy. In October 1972 four members of Mende Berri began a hunger strike in the main cathedral of Bayonne in support of the refugees: Eñaut Haritschelhar, Beñat ("Nini") Oyharçabal (who would be elected to the elite Basque Academy twenty years later, following a doctorate in linguistics and a postdoctoral teaching stint at MIT), Martin (Mattin) Larzabal, and Jacques Sallaberry. They represented the nationalist tendency within Amaia and Mende Berri, and militants close to them claimed that their decision to embark on a hunger strike was heavily influenced by Julen Madariaga and the nationalist ideology of ETA-V. Shortly after the beginning of the hunger strike in the main cathedral a second strike group composed of refugees close to ETA-VI and led by one of its leaders, José Iriarte, occupied the nearby church of Saint André. Even on the level of hunger strikes, then, it appeared that the internal conflict within ETA was playing itself out within the Basque community in France as well as in Spain. Controversy increased when police entered both churches, throwing tear gas in the main cathedral. The hunger strikes ended in early December amid concern for the health of the strikers. While the strikes became a *cause célèbre* and a focus of public demonstrations in their support, the government's policy of assigning ETA refugees to residency outside the Basque country (for example, Iriarte was assigned to residence in Lille) continued without change when the strikes finally ended.

DIVISIONS WITHIN MENDE BERRI

As a result of the hunger strike, French Basque nationalist circles reached a new political high-water mark, now fully engaged in the debate swirling around theses of nationalism, class struggle, and violence. As one of Mende Berri's militants recalled fifteen years later, "these issues were fairly bubbling within the *abertzale* zone of Mende Berri's headquarters on the Rue Bourgneuf in Bayonne." To some extent this was natural, he continued, since "the preoccupation of youth is to be in regular crisis. That's their job." In Mende Berri's case, Oyharçabal had brought with him from Amaia the penchant for rigidity and control which many ultimately found oppressive. One segment of Mende Berri's militants was pushing for more political and spontaneous action. These militants, associated with the hunger strikers in the cathedral of Bayonne, were also keen on associating with the Basque struggle in Spain. In contrast to the hunger strikers in the cathedral, there was another more apolitical current within Mende Berri, which focused less on the fate of the refugees and more on the conditions among French Basques. Moreover, since Oyharçabal was anti-Marxist, the Marxist militants were outgrowing Mende Berri and were now anxious to seek a more congenial institutional home.

Mende Berri broke apart as its members pursued two clearly different visions of Basque militancy. Mende Berri had been on the very frontier between the "cultural" and the "political," and the tension over its insistent apolitical nature led to its fragmentation. Those who wanted to pursue a more political militancy created Ezker Berri (New Left), a political group of ten to twenty members which lasted from 1976 until around 1982 at the latest. As one of its former militants put it, "If Aski was stillborn, Ezker Berri was a newborn which died shortly after birth." Ezker Berri was under strong pressure to join with HAS (as we shall see in the next chapter), which Ezker Berri criticized as having ideological blinders and a *gueule de bois* or wooden ideological tongue that drunkenly spouted Marxist slogans as a substitute for more sensitive political analysis. In the words of one former member of Ezker Berri, HAS "simply trotted out canned words and threw them at situations. It was not for us."

Those members of Mende Berri who left due to its anti-Marxism joined former members of Amaia in founding Euskal Gogoa (Basque Spirit). Like Ezker Berri, Euskal Gogoa was part of a nebulous set of currents that swirled around the successive scissions of Mende Berri. The irony of this period of personal and organizational flux was that many of those militants who left Mende Berri during an earlier splintering would find themselves reunited two years later in a different political vehicle.

Euskal Gogoa focused more on the plight of the refugees and was thus more politicized than Mende Berri. Euskal Gogoa ultimately foundered on its resistance to a formal organizational structure (as an understandable reaction to the rigidity of Amaia and Mende Berri), preferring more spontaneous political action. This led the group to dissolve in 1975, according to Malherbe,[140] and many of its militants subsequently created the loosely structured Jazar (Combat or Struggle), which appeared in 1974. Jazar enjoyed short-lived autonomy and melded itself, in turn, into Herriaren Alde (On the side of the people). Perhaps nine out of ten of its militants had come along the route from Amaia through Mende Berri. Many of these, in turn, would gravitate later toward the Herri Taldeak movement (discussed below).

In each case, these groups were generally unstructured and in a state of political and ideological flux. They were characteristic of a period of "youth in crisis," out of whose struggles a new generation of *abertzale* youth was beginning to emerge. Many were content to define themselves as *abertzale de gauche* (Basque patriots of the left) without any longer-range strategy. These movements were children of the 1960s, living in the 1970s—often with a communal and bohemian life-style—and quick to reject other Basque groups, including their contemporaries, as "too fascist, too structured."

The hunger strike in 1970 was a major avenue for political consciousness-raising among Basque youth dissatisfied with *Enbata* in the climate of post-1968 France. The more clearly nationalist group surrounding the hunger strike had become more radical as a result of exposure to various theses swirling within ETA's refugee community during the strike, microcosms of the debates within ETA-V and ETA-VI at the time. On May 19, 1971, a second hunger strike began over the rights of the refugees to live in the Pays Basque without fear of expulsion. One of the causes of the second strike was a report in the Spanish paper *ABC*, on May 16, announcing the imminent expulsion of eighteen Basques from the Pays Basque to residences elsewhere in France. Since the French government itself did not announce the news until two days later, this was widely seen as concrete proof of the collusion between the French and Spanish governments over the Basque question.[141] The strike over the right of the refugees to live in the Pays Basque began the day after the French government announcement.

As a result of their exposure during the first hunger strike to the doctrine of class struggle associated with ETA-VI, Eñaut Haritschelhar and others, including Liliane Hirigoyen, began the small monthly *Koska* ("Crack") while pursuing their studies at the *facultés* of the University of Bordeaux in early 1973. *Koska* justified its existence by the lies of the official French press in covering the Basque question.[142] It spoke of the problem of oppression in the Basque country and adopted an ideological line embracing the notion of both nationalist and social oppression,[143] which reflected the evolution in ETA-V's doctrine by this time. As they wrote in *Koska*'s first issue, "We will never say that the two aspects of the social and national struggle are anything but two sides of the same coin." Virtually the entire first issue was devoted to an explanation of ETA's recent kidnappings of Spanish industrialists Huarte and Zabala. On the cover was the slogan *Gora Euzkadi Askatuta*, now firmly associated with ETA in the public's (and government's) mind. *Koska*'s overt support of violence set it distinctly apart from *Enbata*, Amaia, or Mende Berri. It reflected the hardening of political beliefs among the most politicized segment of Basque youth and the growing influence of ETA as a symbol. As *Koska* declared in its second issue:

The political awareness of the youth from all milieux has greatly advanced in the sense of a solidarity between the South and the North, and also . . . that constitutes a novelty for the North, the mobilization of youth is greater and greater.[144]

As *Koska* proclaimed in its first issue, "In these conditions, only armed struggle can bring a solution to the problem."[145] Even the names chosen for these new groups (Jazar/Combat or Struggle) and publications (*Koska*/Anger) reflected the hardening of their political sentiments. For one segment of the Basque movement, then, the embrace of political violence similar to that of ETA was a natural progression in the Basque struggle in France. It was in this climate that the first act of violence was claimed by a new movement on the outskirts of Baigorri in the summer of 1973. As we will see in later chapters, its name was Iparretarrak: "Those of ETA of the North."

ENBATA MOVES LEFTWARD

As we have seen, in the wake of its twin electoral defeats in 1967 and 1968, *Enbata* was thrown into considerable internal disarray. Many of its militants left the movement entirely; some, like Haran, would continue to militate for the Spanish Basque refugee community, while many of the younger militants who left gravitated to one of the leftist movements described above.

After four months of silence the first issue of the newspaper *Enbata* reappeared in October 1968. While masking the evident conflicts which were tearing the movement apart internally, *Enbata* nonetheless proceeded to a postmortem of its electoral defeats. It specifically attributed them to three factors: (1) the hostility of the French state; (2) the treason and cowardice of the alleged Basque elites; and (3) the profound alienation of the Basque people.[146] In an apparent gesture of reconciliation toward its recently departed militants, *Enbata* conceded the legitimacy of alternative types of *abertzale* activity. For itself, however, *Enbata* vowed to continue in the spirit of its old principles and within the framework of French law.[147] Regardless of these affirmations of doctrinal faith, it was clear that *Enbata* would have to evolve in political strategy or fall by the wayside.[148] The ideological changes which followed the electoral defeats of 1967–1968 did not become fully apparent until 1972. Nonetheless, elements of a change in emphasis were already percolating as early as mid-1967.

In the wake of the failure of this strategy of moderation, *Enbata* appears to have splintered internally between those who held to the old definition of nationalism/federalism and growing voices of support not only for socialism, but for ETA as well. According to Malherbe, it was the issue of contact with ETA which led to the rupture within the executive committee in 1967.[149] Haran, as director general, allegedly forbade any contact with ETA; in a showdown at the movement's congress on April 30, 1967, Haran's decision was overturned by the movement's militants.[150] In fact, as early as February 1968, well before the events of May and before the rupture following the abortive 1968 legislative elections, voices were beginning to rise within *Enbata* calling for it to become a shock movement, willing to use terrorism if necessary to achieve its political goals:

> With a small number of voters, an even smaller number of militants, we must be a shock movement. . . . If we are Basque patriots, if we are militants, it is necessary to be ready for a long struggle leading to terrorism if need be, in order for our children to be able to live free, and not have to blush in shame at their fathers. GORA EUSKADI ASKATUTA [Long live the Basque Country free].[151]

At the same time, a growing minority were espousing a radical socialism which also challenged the dominant ideology of the group. The appearance of *Etorkizuna* (The Future) in 1967 represented the crystallizing of this socialism and an explicit criticism of *Enbata*'s direction: "We no longer believe in the flow of words and formulas which amount to nothing." [152] *Etorkizuna* was particularly harsh in its criticism of *Enbata*'s electoral strategy:

> One can now pose the question: how can this people, apolitical at base, having never had to confront or debate a political thought of any sort, how could it embrace as its own a Basque nationalist ideology. . . .
>
> This can't be the case of a political party which intended, with some seriousness, to make accepted an ideology which challenged all the political and economic institutions of our country. Such is the goal, however, of nationalism. We want to convince the Basque people of the excellence of our ideology, to effect a profound revolution in its institutions, give it a new direction, a new spirit, and engage it in an adventure which, to say the least, must seem perilous and of which the absolute necessity doesn't seem evident. . . . We will become in several years a marginal party, isolated from the people, definitively filed away and rejected. Let's avoid at all costs the trap of electoralism. . . . Here we are turned toward an electoralism which, as intoxicating and exalted as it may seem, is essentially noxious to our cause.[153]

For *Etorkizuna*, the only serious alternative ideologies to attempt to alter Basque political culture were socialism and communism. The appearance of *Etorkizuna* represented what Malherbe calls a "fierce" socialism,[154] which *Etor-*

kizuna itself called, "a socialism which rejects any compromise." [155] It would be nearly three years before *Enbata* would embrace this socialism as its own, but the direction in which the wind of Basque nationalism was now blowing was clear as early as 1967.

ETA'S GROWING INFLUENCE

In retrospect, the influence of ETA on *Enbata* in its early development appears to have been, in addition to the electoral defeats, an important contributory factor in the internal conflict which fractured *Enbata* between 1967 and 1968. According to Ximun Haran, writing in *Ager* in early 1988, there were two opposing tendencies that manifested themselves at *Enbata*'s national congress on April 30, 1967.[156] One group, composed of many of the more long-standing militants, wanted to focus more on the context of Iparralde, the Pays Basque Français. The other camp, composed mainly of newer militants, held that *Enbata*'s priority lay in supporting the struggle of ETA. With Haran's departure in 1967, so his argument goes, the pro-ETA camp within *Enbata* became ascendant; not until the creation of Herri Taldeak in the late 1970s and early 1980s (discussed in later chapters) did a movement appear in the North focusing first on issues proper to the Pays Basque Français. In fact, according to Haran, ETA's influence on *Enbata* really dated to the time of the first expulsion of refugees in the fall of 1962:

> From then on, the whole history of *Enbata* was dotted with demonstrations . . . over the hunger strikes, the house arrests, and the expulsions. The problems of the Northern Pays Basque became secondary. . . . In a parallel fashion, and as a result of these demonstrations, ETA little by little penetrated the movement *Enbata* so as to infiltrate it to the core by 1967.[157]

For Haran, the announcement of the Aberri Eguna at Itxassou in 1963 "was the last act of independence of *Enbata*." [158]

Consistent with Haran's interpretation, virtually the entire first issue to appear following the hiatus of 1968 is devoted to an interview with a leader of ETA.[159] The interview exposed a number of themes which explained the evolution of Basque nationalism in Spain at this time, particularly the distinction between goals of national liberation (by armed means if necessary) and Socialist revolution which had led to ETA's second splintering, into ETA-V Assembly and ETA-VI Assembly beginning in the summer of 1970.[160] The motive force of this pitched debate within ETA over national liberation (ETA-V) versus Marxist-Socialist revolution (ETA-VI) arose around the trial of Burgos, a *cause célèbre* for ETA in 1970.[161] The recriminations in this period scarred ETA and led to a generational warfare, perhaps best expressed in the letter of denunciation signed by the sixteen defendants of the Burgos trial against the five historic leaders of ETA who criticized the ideological shift reflected in ETA's Sixth Assembly.[162] The five targets of this letter—Madariaga, Etxave, Arregui, Beltza, and Krutwig—were denounced for "handing out folklore calendars or writing novels,"[163] for being bourgeois bystanders to the Socialist transformation of the Basque struggle. According to Clark, by 1971 ETA-VI controlled the organization's apparatus and most of its rank-and-file members.[164] Yet ETA-VI would fritter away its control over the next two years as it moved away from the stuff of traditional Basque nationalist mobilization in Spain, erroneously choosing a class-based struggle over an ethnically based one.[165] The result, according to Clark, was that "by the end of 1972, ETA-VI had effectively destroyed itself as a major force in Basque politics."[166] Thus, in a near-total reversal of fortune, if "ETA-V in early 1971 had few members, scant resources, and no reputations to speak of. . . . By 1972 . . . ETA-V had become the stronger of the two groups."[167] So by early 1973 ETA-V had outlived its rival and came to be known simply as "ETA."[168] A major result of this organizational weakness within ETA-V was its need for sanctuary within the French Basque country, a fact which explained its opposition to the rise of "armed struggle" among the French Basque movement, which would certainly provoke a cycle of French government repression.

In reality, the clear distinction between these two poles of ethnic organization within ETA—based primarily on national liberation or Socialist revolution—had begun to blur within a matter of months. As Julen Madariaga, one of ETA's founders and one of the five critics of ETA-VI's socialism, is quoted in early January 1971:

> We believe that class struggle and the national question are two sides of the same problem; that, in a country like ours, cut into two halves, oppressed culturally and linguistically, the national contradiction is the principal contradiction, and that it is only after having resolved it that one can concentrate on class struggle.
>
> Better: we believe that the struggle for national liberation, and thus the independence of our country, is automatically going to lead us to the establishment of a Socialist régime . . . because, today, in the twentieth century, and in Western Europe, one cannot conceive that a country can liberate itself nationally without effecting, at the same time, Socialist revolution.[169]

It was this emphasis on Basque ethnicity over social class that made ETA-V popular with a rising generation of Basque youth.[170] Nonetheless, its five platforms adopted in 1971 included democratization of the basic industries, as well as their nationalization.[171]

The first two platforms of ETA-V's suggested program in 1971 were:

1. The unification of the Basque ethno-nation by separating its two halves from both France and Spain, and the creation of a new political entity.
2. The sovereign independence of this new state from both France and Spain.[172]

Among the platforms adopted by ETA at its "legitimate sixth assembly" in 1973 were pledges to gather together and train all exiled ETA members in France and to maintain close contact with *Enbata*.[173]

Enbata's decision to mirror ETA's "socialism as the flip side of nationalism" argument was a major ideological shift for the French Basque movement. While the primary impetus indisputably came from ETA, other ethnic movements in France were wrestling with these same issues, notably in Brittany and Occitanie.[174] *Enbata's* attempt to reconcile its newfound socialism with its earlier nationalism (or even federalism) would be a major ideological preoccupation in the early 1970s.

The second major import of the ETA interview published in *Enbata* in October 1968 was the question of the coordination of struggles in France and Spain, specifically regarding the creation of a Basque national liberation front. In regard to such a front and ETA's own role in France, the spokesman is quoted in *Enbata* as saying:

> In those zones which pose the most grave problems of survival, zones little touched by traditional nationalist parties, where the revolutionary praxis is still weak, I think . . . of the French Pays Basque, where the most progressive groups evolve toward a rapid awareness of the revolutionary contradictions of their people. Thus in these zones, E.T.A. presents itself as the sole organization which, by its total action, hard and revolutionary, can offer a solution to the people.[175]

ETA would thus offer itself as a political example, and a partner in the creation of a Basque front of national liberation:

> E.T.A. believes that it must aid the nationalists of the French Pays Basque to develop among themselves a similar ideology to that of its own and E.T.A. hopes that from the experience that will ensue, there will result a unity of organization and of struggle, that is a Front of National Liberation.[176]

In the aftermath of Indochina and Algeria, the value of such a national liberation front seemed an incontestable article of faith. According to Beñat Urgarbi:

> Every liberation has been made by Fronts of National Liberation. The necessity of such a Front of National Liberation of the Pays Basque makes itself felt more than ever at the present time.[177]

In the organizational disarray which characterized this period, it was natural that a reconstructed *Enbata* would turn to ETA's socialism for guidance. For Malherbe, ETA was the only model in existence on which *Enbata* could pattern its new doctrine.[178] As he put it, "This project . . . shows the fascination which ETA exercises on certain spirits."[179]

Thus, this newfound Socialist coloration was eagerly embraced and extended so far as a rewriting of the history of the movement from the perspective of its Socialist *auto-critique*.[180] Seen in this light, *Enbata* would assert that its socialism had been latent in its long support of ethnic federalism.[181] Moreover, its support of rural agriculture or the strikes by shoe workers in Hasparren were latent reflections of its own entry into class struggle.[182] By early 1971 *Enbata* was calling itself in *Ekin* a "Basque Socialist Party,"[183] what Malherbe considered a reflection of the "growing radicalization" of the movement.[184]

Others were not so generous in their assessment of the "progressive" nature of *Enbata*'s ideology. One of ETA's historic theorists, Sarrailh de Ihartza (Federico Krutwig), provided the purest critique of *Enbata*'s ideology, which he dismissed as mere political regionalism:

> No outstanding ideologue has followed Marc Légasse in the Northern Country [French Pays Basque]. The movement *Enbata*, founded later, in no sense offers any ideological contribution, even after reaping the fruits of Légasse's labor.
>
> . . . we cannot deny that we also find some progressives in *Enbata*, but this in no way hinders the movement *Enbata*, so that it, in itself, has no social or national ideology. The ideological output of *Enbata* is nonexistent. Since, moreover, the new generations still have not come forth with their contributions, the monthly *Enbata* has clearly demeaned itself before our very eyes.[185]

The seeming incompatibility between socialism and its early nationalism did not seem to faze *Enbata*. Responding to those leftist purist critics who asserted the primacy of class struggle above all, *Enbata* maintained much as had ETA before it that "as in any oppressed country, in the Pays Basque, social alienation and national liberation are two sides of the same coin."[186] The text which consecrated *Enbata*'s shift toward socialism, *Objectifs et stráte-gie*, published in 1972, explicitly claimed to be convergent with the analysis of ETA, notwithstanding the refusal of violence.[187]

The decision to embrace ETA's socialism held at least three dangers. First, it risked inviting increased repression by a French state determined to prevent ETA's influence on the French Basque movement. As it turned out, this is exactly what would transpire. Second, it risked offending the Basque electorate, which could hardly be expected to embrace socialism any more warmly than it had nationalism. Socialism seemed foolhardy as a strategy of popular mobilization among French Basques who still equated the Basque nationalism of the Spanish Civil War with civil war and communism. It is hard to see how adding a socialism borrowed from the Spanish Basques would increase *Enbata*'s appeal among conservative Basque voters. Indeed, it seemed to invite the very opposite effect.

Third, if *Enbata* was instrumentally motivated by the desire to appeal to Basque youth who had outgrown the movement after 1968, then it was clearly a case of too little, too late. As we have seen, many of *Enbata*'s departed militants joined with newly mobilized Basque youth in affiliating with parties of the extreme French left. For them, socialism smacked of Leninist rigidity and thus tainted *Enbata* as it would even more strictly Socialist movements to come. Still others were hardening into a militancy much closer to that of ETA and were ready to embrace the violence and clandestinity which *Enbata* had always rejected. Stigmatized as *dépassé* or "johnny come lately" in its newfound socialism, *Enbata* never regained the momentum it lost. Deprived of a continual infusion of new militants and new blood, *Enbata* was cut off from precisely those young Basques who were most ripe for recruitment into the cause. Other movements would reap the harvest. When one later Socialist militant was asked why he had formerly been a member of *Enbata*, he responded, "There wasn't anything else at the time."

Seen in this perspective, *Enbata*'s increasing embrace of ETA's socialism was a sign not of ideological growth, but of the defeat of its strategy of popular mobilization. By 1973 the newspaper had approximately five to six hundred subscribers. A survey done by *Enbata* of 275 subscribers in 1973 found the following characteristics: 85 percent were male; 60 percent were over forty; and, while 85 percent of readers were native to the Pays Basque Français, 10 percent were native to the Spanish Basque region.[188] Table 2 shows the occupational breakdowns of the 275 subscribers surveyed.[189] The movement still suffered from an inability to expand its support into either student circles or farmers from the interior, two groups which had been a traditional if unsuccessful target of *Enbata*'s efforts.

TABLE 2

Occupations of Enbata *Subscribers in 1973*

Occupation	Percent
White-collar salaried	17
Non-white-collar salaried	15
Commerçants or artisans	16
Students	2
Clergy	11
Liberal professions	9
Retired	10
Farmers	6
Diverse	14

A bold plan was discussed beginning in September 1973 to increase the size of the four-page paper to twelve to sixteen pages and to increase the press run from 1,200 copies to more than 3,000.[190] With two paid positions, an editor-in-chief and a secretary, the total cost would run more than 214,000 francs a year. To raise this sum would require doubling the number of subscribers from 500–600 to 1,000–1,200 and tripling the number sold in newsstands from 500 to 1,500.

While the movement was still concentrating on increasing its public support, it was clear that the adoption of socialism symbolized a growing disillusionment with the prospects for Basque political action in France and a resultant preoccupation with the political circumstances of the Basque movement in Spain. As Jean-Louis Davant conceded, "On the quantitative plane, the future of the Basque people is playing itself out essentially in [Spain] because of its demographic, industrial, and political force."[191] He concluded, "It's above all ETA which is animating the Basque resistance."[192] As French interior minister Raymond Marcellin put it:

> Basque nationalism in the North [France] is a vast bluff. We are dealing with a dozen agitators totally cut off from the Basque population. It suffices to isolate them in order for the whole charade to be debunked.[193]

In this climate of ideological flux, the French government increased its repression of the Spanish Basque refugee community. It was this issue which would become the primary vehicle for Basque popular mobilization in France in the 1970s.

To be sure, there was nothing new about government measures against the refugee community. The French government had moved in certain cases in the early 1960s, when the flow of ETA refugees in France had just begun.[194] But by the 1970s the scope and implications of the problem had greatly increased. Now the refugee community numbered well over a thousand; the level of violence between ETA and the Spanish government had intensified continually over the ensuing decade; and, far from accepting French government requirements of political neutrality, many of these ETA militants were using French territory not as a retirement colony, but as a sanctuary from which to continue the armed struggle against Spain. The problem weighed heavily on the diplomatic agendas of the French and Spanish states and risked impeding the progress of political and economic ties between the two countries in the twilight of Franco's rule.[195]

The demonstrations of solidarity by French Basques in support of the refugees were among the largest ever seen in the region, ranging from the unexpected support of many local elected officials in representations to the departmental prefect to the highly publicized hunger strikes in the main cathedral of Bayonne.[196] Yet the pattern of these demonstrations was important, because it served to underscore once more the perennial problems confronting the nationalist camp in France. Despite the high level of activity by Basque militants in the coastal cities, regardless of the issue, attempts to mobilize the predominantly rural and conservative Basque population in the interior were admittedly unsuccessful.[197] Heated debates about basing a mobilization strategy on national liberation or Socialist revolution were largely moot: neither was part of the conceptual universe of traditional Basque culture in France. As Descamps de Bragelongne explains it:

> It is this spirit of submission to authority, of spontaneous adherence to social hierarchies, which excludes any sentiment of nationalism; even today, a handful of youths dream of autonomy, under the influence of the autonomism of the Spanish Basques opposed to Franco; it finds no echo among the [French Basque] masses or among the notables. But, ever respectful of authority, the Basque is intransigent about his traditions and his customs—he has a keen awareness of belonging to a very old community of people, and he intends to maintain that community by all means necessary.[198]

As one farming wife put it in Itxassou, "We are poor. Poor people should be quiet and not speak out."[199] Christian Rudel expressed the same idea: "You understand, all that is vague, it's abstract and they have never had the occasion to see what that could give them in reality. And then there's the force of habit."[200] Extremism was simply extremism among this conservative population, regardless of its coloration. With the practicality born of generations of fending off the intrusions of an unwanted state, the Basque farmer believed that troublemaking would only invite unwanted trouble. Dominique Aligner captures the practicality of this conservative logic:

> The great mass [of Basques] is made up of skeptics, of critics . . . but rarely those who would permit themselves being recruited. They admit the good intentions of the movement but refuse to take part out of laziness or lack of courage. They prefer the order imposed on them, even if it's unjust: it tranquilizes them. And then, above all, they are suspicious of *Enbata:* its militants, didn't they have some run-ins with the law, and numerous prison terms? As soon as there are any disputes in a meeting, the reaction is immediate: "It's *Enbata.*" They fear the name *Enbata,* because a whole counter-propaganda has been created on the subject: to walk with *Enbata* is to risk retirement pensions for the elderly, the family allocations, social security. . . . The population is convinced of it.[201]

In the end, *Enbata* was blamed for the political violence it had steadfastly opposed throughout its existence. In the conceptual shorthand of the peasantry, it was simply "*Enbata.*" As one Basque farming wife exclaimed in her seventeenth-century farmhouse:

> Bah. These people of *Enbata.* What do they think they're doing? Going around planting bombs and killing people, what's the point? It doesn't have anything to do with the people here. Look at them, do you see any support? Well, I say if they don't like things here they can go back to Spain where they can be more comfortable, and leave us the hell alone [*foutez-nous la paix*]. *Enbata?* Bah! [gesture of finality].

A farmer from Ustaritz put it less harshly: "We're simple people. We don't get involved in politics here. *Enbata,* well, you know."

Beyond a certain bedrock of public support, then, the movement could progress no further.

The Decline and Demise of *Enbata,* 1973–1974

The common struggle against repression in the South [Spain] is the occasion for us for a true awakening. From now on, Enbata *is going to resume life and activity on new themes. The essential theme from now on is self-management. . . . Our path toward socialism will be that one, based on the example of what our comrades in the South are doing. . . . And we are going to emerge from our isolation.*
Jacques Abeberry, founder of *Enbata* [202]

By 1973 a number of factors had combined to underscore the marginality of *Enbata* as a political movement. The much-vaunted bunting of its ideological "transformation" tried to obscure the inescapable fact that the movement itself was nearly moribund, clinging to organizational life behind the façade of an ongoing newspaper. The high-water mark of *Enbata* as a newspaper reveals a press run of 2,000 copies, with approximately 500 subscriptions. Only a handful of militants continued to work on the newspaper,[203] and meetings witnessed in 1973 were marked by interpersonal hostilities and disarray.

Enbata's self-identification with the refugee problem and its overt sympathy with ETA's struggle with the Spanish government invited the increased hostility of the French government. Early pressure, in the form of fines and court trials both for the content of the paper and for its sponsorship of the Aberri Eguna, was only a harbinger of things to come. The immediate consequence of this institutional hostility was to force the movement into a beleaguered, defensive posture. The heaviness of the fines imposed on its leaders led *Enbata* to quiz its supporters in public meetings as to whether the movement should continue, in open legality or not.[204] For Maurice Abeberry, brother of Jacques and Koko and the attorney representing *Enbata*, the government's strategy demonstrated "a relentless determination to attack *Enbata* in order to make it disappear."[205]

The movement's response was to announce plans for a new and enlarged newspaper in the fall of 1973. This decision reflected a number of factors, including the declining number of active militants in the movement; the inability of *Enbata* to define for itself any role in Basque politics in the mid-1970s except as a "Basque Press Service" in France; and, finally, the realization that the tide of ethnic mobilization had left the movement behind.

By the end of 1973, as one of its founders would later remark, *Enbata* for all intents and purposes no longer existed as a political movement.[206] What remained of its sincere ambition were a statement of principles and a newspaper—the same conditions from which the movement began hardly a decade before.

DISSOLUTION AND BEYOND

Because of the marginality of the movement, near-universal surprise greeted the decision of the French government to ban four ethnic movements which threatened the unity of French territory.[207] First among the four was *Enbata*. The others included two Breton movements and one from Corsica. Of the four, *Enbata* was the only one which had not engaged in terrorist violence against the French state.[208] However, the judgment of the French Council of Ministers was uncompromising. It charged that *Enbata* was a publicly declared separatist organization; that its contacts with foreign political parties and assistance rendered to them constituted an essential conspiracy against the French government and its agents; that its contacts with ETA, an organization forbidden on French territory, made *Enbata* the spokesman for ETA in France—a position further substantiated by the material aid given to ETA refugees in France; and, finally, that the militants of *Enbata* made themselves a party to violence by their refusal to condemn it. As a result, these four groups, and *Enbata* first among them in the government decree, were dissolved according to authority established in article 1, paragraph 3, of the law of association of January 10, 1936, concerning groups threatening the unity and integrity of French territory.[209]

The reaction of the press was mixed. *Le Figaro* saw in the government's action a sea change in its traditional tactical denial or outward indifference to these movements.[210] It was joined by *L'Aurore* in urging the government to deal with the underlying socioeconomic causes of these movements. As *L'Aurore* put it, "Violence is certainly condemnable, but, too often, alas, it remains the ultimate recourse of those who one doesn't want to hear."[211] For *Combat*, "If autonomist pressures appeared, it's because of a lack of dialogue. To want to repress all regionalist manifestations at any price, one embarks obligatorily on the path of the worst violences. We are there today."[212]

Why the government should have chosen to act at this time is open to question, especially since in the case of *Enbata* the statements on which its decision was based had been made publicly for most of the previous decade. If the magnitude of its electoral defeats was not proof enough, its marginality as a political movement among the French Basque electorate was cemented by its conversion to socialism. At the moment of its dissolution, *Enbata* had effectively ceased to exist as a political movement other than in name alone, a point of which the government was well aware.

Despite legal appeals which would continue for over a year, *Enbata* announced in early February 1974 its intention to acquiesce to the government's decree.[213] The government's appellate brief, signed by minister of the interior Michel Poniatowski and dated July 24, 1974, clarified the government's case against *Enbata*.[214] The case was based on four elements. First, the government alleged that *Enbata* manifested a public and ongoing device to create a Basque state separate from France. Second, *Enbata* was alleged to justify the use of violence. Third, *Enbata* had attacked French administrators, including the prefect and subprefect of the Department of the Pyrénées-Atlantiques, as well as the police. Finally, *Enbata* was alleged to maintain "close" ties with the "Spanish Revolutionary and Basque Separatist Group" as well as with other French autonomist movements. In all cases, the government's case was based on extracts from the newspaper beginning in 1970, as well as on the text of the *Charte d'Itxassou* which appeared in 1963. Among the quotations used by the government was: "We are pursuing our path, which converges with that of ETA."[215]

With the advantage of hindsight, a real question persists about the goals which the government sought to accomplish in banning this largely ineffectual and stagnating group of militants. If the government's goal was to eliminate the force of Basque nationalism in France, it risked just the opposite. Specifically, in contrast to *Enbata*, which had always rejected the use of violence, the government's decree risked driving the Basque idea in France into clandestinity and terrorism, an option that a small but growing minority of militants in and out of *Enbata* had been pressing for for a number of years. Indeed, given the nature of the charges and the violent company with which *Enbata* was grouped in the dissolution decree, it seems that *Enbata* was largely a surrogate for the real target of the French government action— ETA—and the terrorist violence which was now upsetting France's diplomatic agenda with Spain. The greatest example of the diplomatic problem which ETA posed for France was the press conference held in the French Basque country by ETA commandos who had just assassinated the Spanish premier, Admiral Carrero Blanco, in downtown Madrid, postponing their bombing attack a day in order to spare the life of Henry Kissinger, who was riding in the car with the admiral the day before.[216] Finally, as with the demonstrations in support of the refugees, the government's decision did what *Enbata* had not succeeded in doing—popularizing the nationalist cause as a result of heavy-handed efforts to suppress it. The calm which settled over the region was artificial, the calm before the growing storm to come.

Conclusion

Enbata, in its short history, represented one of the most coherent examples of Basque political mobilization since the French Revolution. Its daring as a political movement lay in its deliberate decision to transcend the conservative and clerical regionalism which had characterized Basque politics in France since the early Third Republic. *Enbata*'s failure to win popular support reflected the suspicions of a conservative rural electorate which equated Basque nationalism with "Godless communism" and which refused to recognize *Enbata* as a legitimate ethnic elite. Inability to win public support threw the movement into internal disarray and ultimate collapse. As Jokin Apalategi put it, *Enbata* was already unraveling by 1968, and the government decree in 1974 rendered official what was already true in fact—*Enbata* no longer existed as a movement.[217]

Enbata foundered on the now familiar problems of personality conflict and intergenerational struggle which characterize Basque nationalism in France. Freudian concepts of parricide may be most helpful in explaining not only the internal conflicts within the movement, but also *Enbata's* rejection and ultimate neglect by its successors. *Enbata* demonstrated one of the tragedies of the Basque movement—the resistance toward any leadership by this people whose democratic, communal tradition is as old as any in Europe. The lack of an accepted leadership, or perhaps an unwillingness to be led, would immobilize the movement and keep it in a permanent state of disorder.

In reality, *Enbata* set the stage and largely defined the theoretical terms for much of the modern-day debate over Basque nationalism in France. The corpus of Jacques Abeberry's editorials in *Enbata* have defined the terrain of Basque political thought for the past thirty years. *Enbata* would emerge some months later as a newspaper without a movement, a documentary witness to the spiraling vortex of violence and marginality to come. Viewed against the current backdrop of violence and internecine struggle, *Enbata* appears to be what its name suggests: the wind that precedes the storm. As one of its leaders remarked in 1975:

> A movement may overcome us, surpass us; a violent movement and it can't be ruled out that the hard-line tendency which is probably going to constitute itself, led by the young of *Enbata*, will enter into clandestinity. But tell you what we're going to do at present—that I cannot. We have been the wind that precedes the tempest. Let the tempest come.[218]

Chapter Five

Socialism and Autonomy: EHAS Confronted

by the Rise of Young Radical *Abertzale*,

1974–1981

> *Those who make peaceful revolution impossible*
> *will make violent revolution inevitable.*
> John F. Kennedy
>
> *We are dancing on a volcano.*
> Comte de Solvandy, on the Revolution of 1830

In the aftermath of the dissolution of *Enbata* in January 1974, the French government witnessed the growth of two parallel tendencies within the nationalist community which would define the nature of Basque militancy in France throughout the 1970s. The first was the rise of an avowed Socialist party which was as frank and uncompromising in its Socialist commitment as *Enbata* had been self-serving and late-coming in its own. Like *Enbata*, the Basque Socialist Party, Herriko Alderdi Sozialista (HAS) would militate in open legality, field candidates in French elections, and condemn the violence which was threatening the nationalist cause. But for the first time in French Basque politics, HAS would organically unite with a Spanish Basque Socialist Party to form the first political movement militating jointly in both halves of the Basque community for Basque independence.

The second tendency which marked French Basque politics in the 1970s was the rise of a number of clandestine movements which grew out of the radical political ferment after 1968 and willfully embraced the overt use of terrorist violence as a tool of revolutionary politics. The greatest of these movements appeared in 1973, when an attack on a medical center in Banca on the outskirts of Saint-Etienne-de-Baigorri in Basse-Navarre was acknowledged by a heretofore unheard-of group, Iparretarrak (Those of ETA of the

North). Iparretarrak's violence has polarized the Pays Basque as has no other issue, and its continued violence into the 1990s marks the tormented path of modern Basque militancy in France.

In this chapter I will examine the shift leftward in Basque nationalism beginning in the mid-1970s with the creation of HAS/EHAS, the development of its ideology, its running dispute with *Enbata*, and the response of the Basque electorate to the growing radicalization of Basque nationalism in France. Second, I will discuss HAS/EHAS's relationship with the French left, and other ethnic movements, and its inability to create a Basque Socialist Coordinating Committee (KAS) based on a Spanish model, due to its rejection by other Basque movements wary of electoral cooperation with HAS/EHAS. Finally, I will describe EHAS's rejection of violence and the act of "revolutionary expropriation" by which the clandestine terrorist movement Iparretarrak eliminated EHAS as a moderate competitor in order to assert itself as the preeminent Basque tendency in France.

Herriko Alderdi Sozialista (HAS): The Rise of the Basque Socialist Party

Within two months of the dissolution of *Enbata* in January 1974, and coincidentally on the day of the death of French president Georges Pompidou, the first issue of a new Basque monthly, *Euskaldunak*, appeared, announcing the formation of a new Basque Socialist movement, Herriko Alderdi Sozialista (HAS). Reading between the lines, even the announcement of HAS's appearance was a contrast with *Enbata*'s internal disarray:

> For our part, we wanted to break the silence. We know well that people will sneer at our possibilities of success. We know that our possibilities are modest, but we are a homogeneous and determined team, with very precise objectives that we want to attain.[1]

The monthly *Euskaldunak* was central to HAS's militancy. One reads in HAS's internal bulletin, *EHASKIDE:*

> Can we consider the newspaper *Euskaldunak* as the organ of EHAS? And in this perspective, can we consider the newspaper as a tool of choice for the political work with the masses? Let's say that in every revolution and in the life of every party, the press has held a fundamental role which is summed up in the slogan of Lenin: "The press constitutes the powerful arm of the people."[2]

HAS was also clear from the very beginning that it would be a political party:

> We wanted to create a political organization called a *party*, not a group
> or a club. One doesn't join EHAS in order to do no matter what, no
> matter when, no matter how. Our objective is to create a party that has
> consistency, duration, and credibility.[3]

EXORCISING THE GHOST OF ENBATA

HAS sought to gather the remnants of *Enbata* following its dissolution and
create a truly Socialist Basque political party. As HAS put it, "By its evolution
these last years, sanctioned by the French governmental interdiction, *Enbata*
has fallen to the left. From its fall is born a Basque Socialist force."[4] In fact,
virtually all of HAS's founding members had passed through *Enbata* at one
time or another. Some left in the wake of the electoral defeats in 1967 and
1968, frustrated by *Enbata*'s inability to attract a public following and turned
off by the personal conflicts which siphoned off the movement's creativity.
Others remained with *Enbata* to the end, including Jean-Louis Davant, the
architect of Enbata's Socialist self-transformation, who became a member of
HAS's *comité directeur* from the very beginning. For F. B. (Battitta) Larzabal
(Larçabal), one of HAS's founders, those more leftist militants who stood
on the sidelines as *Enbata* evolved during the early 1970s were expecting
it to develop ultimately into a conservatively nationalist Basque patriotic
party along the lines of the contemporary Basque Nationalist Party (PNV)
in Spain.[5] In reality, as Larzabal continued, *Enbata* dissolved in 1974 into
three different factions: one an "opportunistic rightist faction" (undoubtedly
around the Abeberrys) which sought temporary refuge in a kind of Giscar-
dian/centrist Christian democracy; the second culturally and economically
oriented, which began Basque businesses and supported the Ikastola (private Basque primary school) movement; and, finally, those whose early and
more fluid attraction to self-managing socialism (*socialisme autogestionnaire*)
would "naturally evolve" into a true revolutionary socialism. It was from
this latter group that HAS would emerge.[6]

According to Manex Goyhenetche, another of HAS's founders and perhaps its greatest ideologist,[7] the movement began with four militants who
sought to fill the void caused by *Enbata*'s collapse, soon growing to eight.[8]
HAS's first *comité directeur* included Manex Goyhenetche, F. B. (Battitta) Larzabal, Jean-Louis Davant, (Jakes) Eyherampunho, J. Etchebarne, Ch. Etxezaharreta, Raoul Reinares, Etienne Arotçarena, and Osane, a young woman
otherwise unidentified.[9]

According to Larzabal, the movement had one hundred militants at its
height, with between fifty and eighty actually active and spread out in local

party sections in Bayonne, Saint-Jean-de-Luz, Soule, Hasparren, Saint-Pée-sur-Nivelle, Hendaye, and Paris.[10] As in other such movements, there was a natural ebb and flow of members. Malherbe estimates that HAS had twenty militants at the beginning and fifty by the end of 1976.[11] The movement's internal publication, *EHASKIDE* (March 1978, p. 2), reveals "a total of 69 militants. In the weeks which come we can very well arrive at 100 militants if everyone sets about it."

HAS's center, like that of *Enbata* before it, was the coastal city of Bayonne. Unlike Mende Berri and the other catchment basins for young militants which dotted the Basque political landscape, HAS's militants were older, generally from twenty to forty-five, and already embarked on careers. Most of its leading members were teachers or salaried workers, like Larzabal, Goyhenetche, or Davant.[12] The primary attraction of HAS was not an appeal to youth, but the intensity of its commitment to Socialist revolution blended with the traditional stuff of nationalism. While the movement had unusually active sections in the Basque interior, notably at Hasparren and in Soule, according to Larzabal it was difficult to claim it had truly broken through into the interior, anymore than had *Enbata* before it.[13]

As HAS strove to identify itself, it was clear that *Enbata* was both a historic adversary against which criticism was fair and a preoccupying incubus which would have to exorcised for HAS to look forward. In fact, throughout most of HAS's existence *EHASKIDE* periodically repeated the suspicion of *Enbata*'s hostility or of its efforts to minimize HAS. For instance: "One mustn't delude oneself on the good which our confrère wishes us: in the articles appearing in *Le Monde* which were done by people in contact with *Enbata* or of *Enbata*, not a single time was EHAS mentioned."[14] In its public and private pronouncements, HAS clearly sought to define itself in a different way than had *Enbata*, in terms of both internal structure and ideology. Reflecting the view that *Enbata* had become a right-wing party of nationalist notables, HAS criticized *Enbata*'s drive to monopolize the political landscape:

> In Euskadi North as well, there is bipolarization. Here as well, there is an effort in some sense *gaullien*—though clearly anti-Gaullist—which is coming to an end as the fundamental effort of the Basque movement which it created: that of *Enbata*, which wanted to gather together the Basques around a certain idea of Euskadi, in a single organization.[15]

According to Larzabal, if *Enbata* wanted to be the "holy union" of all Basque militants, HAS saw itself as a stage which would clearly mark the Basque transition toward socialism. With the recruitment of Jean-Louis Davant from the now-defunct *Enbata*, HAS would boast of its own commitment to socialism in contrast to *Enbata*, which HAS stigmatized as bourgeois and right-wing, a thinly disguised attack on Jacques Abeberry and others who refused to join HAS, even after *Enbata*'s dissolution.[16] Deprived of the use of *Enbata* as a forum for a response to HAS's attacks, Jacques Abeberry chose to respond in a letter to the editor in *Euskaldunak* itself, in which he criticized the ideological posturing and rigidity he already saw emerging within HAS:

> The Pays Basque Nord has no need of theoreticians nor of theologians but of leaders capable of resolving its problems. Your publication can aid in the blossoming of these leaders on the condition that you avoid the dangers I just described. . . . In hoping that the next issues will indicate an effort in this direction and will make of your publication that of all Basques, I wish long life to "Euskaldunak."[17]

Abeberry then signed his letter "Former editor of a recently disappeared Basque newspaper."[18] He subsequently elaborated on his criticism of HAS, describing it as ideologically rigid and lacking the openness necessary to expand the base of Basque militancy.[19] Abeberry claimed that one of HAS's fundamental errors was its insistence on a rigid organizational style which was unlikely to attract new blood into the movement. He reproached HAS's willingness to criticize mayors and other local elected officials. He challenged HAS's ideological dismissal of *Enbata* as "right-wing," insisting that in reality the doctrinal differences between Basque nationalists were quite narrow by this point and that the ideological spectrum within the *abertzale* camp in France really *began* at the center left and moved leftward from there. For Abeberry, the test of HAS's structure and organization would be its ability to attract previously unmobilized Basque youth who had been unwilling to join a Basque organization before, including *Enbata,* as well as those young Basque militants already fragmented in a host of extreme left *splinter groups* in the aftermath of 1968. What was needed, then, was a broad Basque movement committed to *opening,* and not closed into a tight, hierarchical organization with a rigid ideology. HAS's problem, in Abeberry's view, was one of tactics and organizational style.

For its part, HAS, in a clear demonstration of *Schadenfreude,*[20] described the circumstances of *Enbata*'s demise:

> Disheartened and harassed by the multiple trials, vexations, hazings, fines, police harassment, stays at the police station, suspended prison terms striking most of its leaders and a number of its militants, faced with prospective financial disasters and the risks of seizure, in a total juridical uncertainty, they stopped the publication of the weekly . . . the [government interdiction] attained through its ambiguity what it intended above all: to silence the newspaper.[21]

HAS was thus glad to see *Enbata* disappear as a competing movement, but ambivalent about the disappearance of the newspaper as a source of information:

> As for us, not being masochists, we are not especially seeking competition from another Basque movement—the newspaper, that's another thing . . . —what we're having a hard time seeing is where it would situate itself.[22]

It would take over a year for HAS to clarify its basic argument with *Enbata*, by which time *Enbata*, having received government assurances, had reappeared as a newspaper without a political movement behind it.[23] *Enbata* saw itself at this time as something of a foil for a new movement anxious to define its own ideological space. This was undoubtedly aided by an increasing ambivalence, if not outright hostility, to socialism expressed by the newly resuscitated *Enbata*. For HAS, the distinction between them was the timeworn debate between nationalism and socialism which continued to torment ETA in Spain. Referring to a text which appeared in *Enbata*, HAS responded:

> But we no longer follow "Enbata" when it claims that "the Basque nationalist sentiment is, regardless of what the Marxists say, independent of the social and economic structures of Basque society, because its bases are above all ethnic and cultural . . ." And further on ". . . we hope that a self-managed socialism will prevail in Euzkadi, but that is independent of the Basque national problem."[24]

HAS seized on the evident discrepancy between this text and the Socialist platform adopted by the now-defunct *Enbata* in 1972:

> One has the impression that the texts were never fully digested by the totality of its militants, nor even by its leaders, who contented themselves with having their heart to the left, without forcing themselves to rigorous socioeconomic analyses.[25]

In contrast, HAS attempted to resolve the dilemma between nationalism and socialism in much the same way that ETA had before it:

> The national question and the social question are linked. . . . It is thus as Basque Socialists that we fight for the national rights of the Basque people, at the same time as for the international victory of socialism. It is certainly not by chance that the axis of the *abertzale* movement tips squarely to the left.[26]

HAS's solution to the national/social dilemma had been to define it away, freeing the party to pursue both goals in tandem. This was underscored by HAS's declaration in its ideological platform that it would serve, "a Basque people denied its national rights and exploited in its social categories." [27] But the same strain of nationalism which had sustained *Enbata* from its origins was also present in *Euskaldunak* from its first issues: "The Basque people like all nations large and small have the right to constitute an entity enjoying its political, economic, and cultural rights." [28] One of HAS's objectives was the reunification of the Basque provinces in France and Spain, "on the model of Vietnam or Ireland." [29] Others pointed to the impact of the Algerian war on this generation of militants and to the fact that some had seen military service there.

THE DIMENSIONS OF HAS'S SOCIALISM

Despite its criticism of *Enbata*'s ideological shortcomings, as late as 1978 HAS (by then EHAS) was still preoccupied with the fear that *Enbata* would arise like the phoenix and create a new political movement to compete with it.[30] HAS went to great lengths to distance itself from the image of disunity which had characterized *Enbata* from 1967 until its demise. What clearly distinguished HAS was the strength of its Socialist self-definition. The extent of its commitment to socialism was clear:

> We have demonstrated . . . a fundamental aspect of our engagement: the establishment of a reunited Pays Basque with a democratic and popular government in which the working classes will take power. This presupposes the necessity of the destruction of all capitalist and imperialist structures, the appropriation by the people of all means of production, of distribution, of credit.[31]

If the strength of this Socialist statement reflected the hand of Manex Goyhenetche, others shared it to varying degrees, though Battitta Larzabal in 1987 remembered HAS's socialism as more non-Marxist in nature, influenced primarily by events in the Spanish Basque country.[32] In the fifth issue of *Euskaldunak* HAS laid out the outlines of a broad Basque Socialist movement.[33] It had four major dimensions: (1) the construction of a true socialism implying: (a) the appropriation of the means of production, credit, and exchange; (b) establishment of a democratically planned Socialist economy; and (c) the establishment of a democratic regime when the working classes assume power; (2) the reestablishment of the national rights of the Basque people, including a defense of Basque language and culture and the affirmation of their rights to self-determination; (3) the support of revolutionary violence when buttressed by popular support and harnessed to a revolutionary strategy. This, following Lenin, was to be distinguished from the nihilistic and premature terrorism of impotent intellectuals who underestimate the revolutionary potential of the working class. ETA, as the prime practitioner of Basque revolutionary violence and with substantial public support in Spain at that time, would presumably warrant the support of the Basque left, while Iparretarrak and other fledgling terrorist movements in France would not. Indeed, HAS's rejection of Iparretarrak's use of violence would be a major factor in the dispute between these two movements and lay at the center of EHAS's later demise. (4) Finally, HAS's socialism involved the call for international solidarity and cooperation between antiimperialist and progressive forces, including solidarity with French and Spanish leftist organizations, in its goal of building a Socialist Europe of equal partners.

As HAS explained the need for this international Socialist movement:

> Euskadi North: its colonization. For the French state, the Basque people doesn't exist. The little Basque farmer is victim of a growing proletarianization without end: his land, his products, his channels of sale are more and more controlled by European monopolies and the multinational firms. The Basque workers, [who are] often products of this rural world condemned by capitalism, arrive in industrial society without professional training, without a tradition of struggle. . . . yes, Socialist internationalism must suppress the nation-states inherited from the bourgeoisie. The Europe of peoples and workers is in progress.[34]

This last element, the notion of Socialist internationalism, was the most problematic of the four, because it raised the question of relationships with mainstream working-class parties of France and Spain, which, like the French Communist Party, had always opposed ethnic demands in its own French nationalist zeal.[35] HAS's position vis-à-vis the French left was more ambiguous, if not contradictory, in practice than it was in theory. On the one hand, HAS *had* espoused a tactical, if optimistic, strategy of working-class solidarity in supporting Socialist François Mitterrand in the first round of the 1974 presidential elections.[36] HAS's electoral strategy in 1974 seemed to reflect a pragmatic tilt toward French socialism in the electoral arena as the lesser of two evils. Yet, if cooperation with progressive leftist parties was the goal, how could HAS justify splintering the Socialist vote by presenting itself as a separate *Basque* Socialist Party, rather than militating within the traditional French left, such as the Parti Socialiste (PS), the Parti Communiste Français (PCF), or even the extreme left, in the PSU? As Goyhenetche explained their unsuitability, "The P.S., the P.S.U., and the P.C.F. are hexagonal parties, that is to say representing a dominating state which has always colonized us."[37] HAS then justified its existence as a separate Socialist Party because the Basque people were deprived of their legitimate national rights.[38] In this light, it argued, the Basques were unlikely ever to receive them from a French left too long committed to the perspective of the traditional nation-state system.[39] The fact that the French left had lately discovered the nationalities problem and was now seeking to co-opt it made Basque Socialists temporary—and wary—bedfellows, at best.[40] As Goyhenetche noted of the PS:

> The Socialist Party for some time now has begun a policy of opening toward the national minorities. . . . But we are obliged to recognize that this policy at times stems from co-optation and electoral opportunism.[41]

Cooperating with other progressive parties was one thing; seeking a French solution to the Basque problem was quite another:

> No regionalization in the context of the [French] hexagon can resolve the Basque problem which passes inexorably by the reunification of the North and South. *Therefore no hexagonal solution can satisfy us.*[42]

The Creation of EHAS: The First Interstate Basque Political Party

By 1975 HAS's rejection of an alliance with the traditional French left and its continuing opposition to the use of violence as a tool of the Basque struggle led it to consider a wholly new form of political organization and militancy, one which would bridge the border and unite Socialist militants of similar persuasions in both France and Spain.

Around the time of the death of Franco in November 1975 there was considerable ideological ferment on both sides of the border. In Spain discussions were occurring between groups across the political spectrum, ranging from social democrats to Trotskyists, while omitting "militarist" groups. The result was the distillation of an ideological position which excluded "reformers" and social democrats and gathered together progressive elements willing to pursue a strategy of Socialist revolution without armed struggle.[43]

At the same time, HAS's first tentative contacts with Spanish Basque Socialists ultimately bore fruit:

> The objective was to arrive at [their] merger, given that their ideological and political positions resembled each other a lot and their common objective was the construction of a socialism in the Basque social reality

starting with a national strategy, in going beyond the divisions imposed by the border between the two states.[44]

In November 1975 HAS announced its decision to combine with its Spanish Basque counterpart, Euskal Alderdi Sozialista (EAS), to create the first Basque political party to straddle both sides of the border.[45] The new party took the name of Euskal Herriko Alderdi Sozialista (EHAS). HAS's interest in such an alliance paralleled that of Euskal Alderdi Sozialista (EAS), itself created by elements of ETA's Frente Cultural, which had earlier broken with ETA's Frente Militar over the issue of violence. According to Jokin Apalategi, the desire to find a type of militancy other than the armed struggle lay at the heart of their union.[46] The question of support for ETA and the armed struggle among French Basque militants is complex. According to several former militants of HAS who were aware of the organizational flux which had led to the creation of EAS, it was clear that EHAS included many former members of ETA. While one leader of HAS estimated that as many as 80 percent of French Basque nationalists sympathized with ETA and its use of violence, HAS nevertheless recognized the difficulty which an overt support of ETA and the armed struggle would pose for HAS, just as it had for *Enbata* before it. In fact, within a year of its reappearance as a newspaper alone without a political movement, *Enbata* was once again pursued by the French state for "grave presumptions of apology for murder" arising from an interview with a leader of ETA in its March 25, 1976, issue which described the killing of police informers.[47] This was the climate in which EHAS was born. According to one of HAS's founders, the use of violence was a function both of the structure of the state and of the support of the people, and both clearly distinguished the French Basque context from that of Spain.

At the same time, EAS was the product of the rejection of the armed struggle by dissident members of ETA. According to Robert Clark, ETA's Frente Cultural split from the Frente Militar early in 1974 and joined with dissident members of the Basque Labor Union, Solidarity of Basque Workers (Solidaridad de Trabajadores Vascos, STV) to form the Basque Socialist Party (EAS).[48] Clark attributes the conflict within ETA in early 1974 (which would lead to the formation of EAS some months later) as a reaction to the assassination of Admiral Carrero Blanco in Operation Ogro the previous year. This spectacular action crystallized the growing tension within ETA between the hard-line Frente Militar and others more willing to pursue a traditional, nonviolent political strategy within the legal mainstream of Spanish politics, especially in the new context after Franco's death on November 20, 1975.[49]

In December 1975 *Euskaldunak* included a flyer in its monthly edition which was the first communiqué of the newly created EHAS.[50] It was also included in a longer manifesto in which the outlines of EHAS's new political strategy were made clear. Among its elements were:

—to serve as an organizing party for the Basque masses in order to create a Basque Socialist state, based on the right of self-determination.
—to view as inseparable the struggle for the national and social liberation of Euzkadi.
—to constitute itself as the first political party to act in the entirety of the Basque nation, thus destroying the division imposed by the French and Spanish states.
—to denounce the oligarchies responsible for national division and socioeconomic exploitation.
—to denounce French and Spanish leftist organizations which through their insolent ignorance of Euzkadi, blinded as they are by the state imperialism, reproduce the national oppression of the oligarchy.
—to denounce in the same way the Basque right wing which asserts the formal liberation of Euzkadi, refusing the real liberation of the Basque Working People.[51]

As a consequence, the goals of EHAS included:

—reunification of the two parts of the Basque country;
—the constitution of a Socialist and nondependent state;
—the implementation of the Basque language as the expression of national culture;
—the solidarity with working classes and oppressed people throughout the world, and especially in the French and Spanish states; and
—the creation of a Koordinadora Abertzale Sozialista (KAS) as an indispensable instrument of liberation.[52]

The list of objectives concludes with the slogans *Gora Euskadi Askatua* (Long Live the Basque Country Free) and *Gora Euskadi Sozialista* (Long Live the Basque Country Socialist).

If ETA's view of the French HAS in 1974 was unenthusiastic, describing its ideology as only "a little more progressive" than that of *Enbata*,[53] ETA's reaction to the creation of the new composite and transnational EHAS was more generous, claiming the new party had:

all the possibilities of transforming itself in a large mass party, capable of surpassing the PNV and playing an important role in the political future of Euskadi. Its strong implantation in the Basque cultural milieu through publishing houses and the Basque primary schools [Ikastolas] seems evident.[54]

During this same period profound changes were occurring within ETA which would affect the organization until the present day. In October of 1974 ETA split again, this time into two factions: ETA-pm (poli milis), who, according to Clark, embraced a more radical Marxist-Leninist view of military strategy tied closely to proletarian revolution and were thus closer to the Tupamaros of Uruguay in their admixture of military action and ideology; and ETA-m (growing out of the now-extinct Frente Militar), a much smaller group dedicated to clandestine armed struggle which split off from ETA in November 1974 and which was allegedly influenced by the strategy of the Palestinian movement Black September.[55] If ETA-pm's Marxist revolutionary ideology was the most threatening to the Spanish state, according to Clark, the spectacular armed actions of the much smaller ETA-m began to attract the more radical members of ETA-pm so that, by the early 1980s, ETA-m outnumbered ETA-pm by more than three to one, and the tide had shifted decidedly in its favor.[56] The continued survival of these organizations, especially ETA-m, gave renewed vitality to the armed struggle and its role as either inspiration or antagonist for other movements in both Spain and France.

TENSIONS BETWEEN NORTH AND SOUTH

In the months following the creation of the joint party, considerable effort and expense was devoted to producing trilingual publications (Basque, French, and Spanish) which would be relevant to both sides of the border. The early issues of the joint publication were smuggled clandestinely into Spain in the continuing climate of Francoist censorship. In reality, the unanticipated and substantial political and linguistic differences (for francophone as well as for hispanophone readers) between the two Basque populations were forcing EHAS to reconsider the strategy of joint publication. Accordingly, the November 1976 issue of *EHASKIDE* announced:

> The November issue will be the last which will be done for the South and the North [together]. The reason is that EHAS has a sufficient structure for publishing *Euskaldunak* clandestinely in the South. The same problem is posed in the South as in the North: the militants [there] find that there is too much French just like here the readers find that there is too

much Spanish. . . . We'll see later the consequences of this decision. . . . EHAS south is very active and things are moving very quickly there.

By May 1977 the separate pace of political development in the two divisions of the party were now overtly acknowledged. *Euskaldunak* stated:

The national congress of Pamplona of March 13, 1977, marks a date in the evolution of our party. E.H.A.S.-Sud is in the process of becoming a mass party. For the moment, E.H.A.S.-Nord is a party of militants even though it has always had the ambition of transforming itself into a mass party, but that which is possible today in the South is not necessarily possible in the North.[57]

In fact, the French party was almost broke by this time and was living hand to mouth, depending on paid orders from Spain in order to pay the newspaper's bills:

Henceforth, the time of "fat cows" is over. In effect, for several months now, *Euskaldunak* has lived on artificial financing; the bills being paid at the same time as orders [came in] from the South. And during the same time:
—street sales have fallen
—subscriptions are null
—subscription renewals are at the point of death
—the sole little paid advertisement hasn't been renewed.[58]

Part of the problem seemed due to an overly ambitious press run, reaching a peak of 6,500 for the October 1976 issue (due to distribution in Spain),[59] before falling back to a level of 1,500–1,700 which it maintained for the rest of its life.

But many of EHAS's financial problems were due to a poor level of domestic subscriptions, renewals, and sales of *Euskaldunak* in France. By November 1976 *Euskaldunak* had 569 paid subscribers, of which 385 were current, 184 were lapsed, and 177 had renewed.[60] By January 1977 the party estimated that fully 31 percent of its subscribers were not renewing their subscriptions.[61] Goyhenetche took pains to point out that even some of the movement's own militants were not subscribing to *Euskaldunak* and threatened to publish their names.[62] By 1978 the monthly had 671 subscribers (of which 130 were past due). Out of a total press run of 1,700, 671 copies were sent to subscribers, 85 were distributed free of charge, and an average of 610 were being sold each month in newsstands.[63] The precarious state of the newspaper's finances became a regular feature in *EHASKIDE* and led to constant appeals for contributions in *Euskaldunak*.

As a result of these pressures, signs of dissension were beginning to grow within HAS's *comité directeur*. In the November 1976 issue of *EHASKIDE*, the following cryptic comment appeared in the minutes of the October 29, 1976, meeting of the *comité directeur*:

> At the beginning, there was a violent incident between two members of the CD. . . . In the future we ask that you explain yourself before leaving the meeting so that the other members can understand what's it about exactly.

Friction between militants was beginning to develop as a result of the unremitting conflict with *Enbata*, the weak implantation of the movement, the poor state of its finances, and the looming pressures of an electoral campaign. By the end of 1977 Manex Goyhenetche's leadership style was under attack as being too autocratic; one militant in *EHASKIDE* referred to it as the style of a "Wild-West sheriff."[64] For his part, Goyhenetche conceded:

> One must know how *to be political*, that is to say to accept flexibility and compromise, without yielding on the essential. And from this point of view, there are some skills which we lack.[65]

The conflict belied the public statement EHAS made in 1979: "Decisions are made by the majority, after a discussion that is settled by a democratic vote."[66] In fact, in 1976, HAS made it clear that it differed from its Spanish counterpart in a number of ways, and one major difference was in the nature of internal decision-making: "But the working principles of HAS and EHAS are not the same. HAS affirmed that it applied democratic centralism, EHAS not. In fact, we are content to have a sure practice."[67] This is ironic since its counterpart, having become HASI and part of the Herri Batasuna coalition in Spain, is widely viewed as the most Stalinist party of the Basque nationalist left. Of all the aspects of Leninist practice, democratic centralism is one of the most contentious, forming the basis for the hierarchical and autocratic decision-making style characteristic of the Leninist party. It was this style, attributed to Goyhenetche, which lay at the heart of many of the persistent internal conflicts within HAS/EHAS. As Jean-Louis Davant wrote in a letter to militants on April 30, 1979:

> I find that there is much too much personal polemics these days within EHAS. That reminds me desperately of the last moments of the movement *Enbata*, where one threw in each other's faces failures real or imagined in a kind of suicidal delight. I place myself in no way as judge, but as a simple militant who this bothers more than it is possible to say and

who wishes this would cease. The enemy is on the exterior, and let's not forget it.[68]

Davant urged the militants not to attack the members of the *comité directeur* and urged its own members to be a little thicker-skinned in turn in the face of criticisms, however excessive. He sought to redirect the focus of this energy: "Once again, this tone should be reserved for our enemies, and we have enough of them without searching for more among and around us."[69]

THE CREATION OF KAS

In September 1975, shortly before HAS and EAS combined to form EHAS, the mass public protests surrounding the Spanish trial of two ETA militants, Angel Otaegi and Juan Paredes Manot ("Txiki"), galvanized Basque public opinion on both sides of the border as had few issues in recent memory. HAS joined ETA, Langile Abertzale Iraultzalean Alderdia (LAIA), and Euskadiko Langileen Indarra to issue a communiqué on the Spanish repression on behalf of a newly formed ad hoc Patriotic Basque Socialist Committee (Comité Abertzale Socialiste). It said, in part:

> Once more, the majority (the working class of Euskadi) represented by *Garmendia ("Tupa")* and *Otaegi*, are going to be cruelly repressed by a minority of repressors represented by the fascist Spanish court. . . . *It's the Basque proletariat which is going to be judged*, it the undiminished fighter, for which the only crime is the following: to struggle and demonstrate its will to constitute an *Independent and Unified Basque Socialist State*, in which there will be no more social classes nor exploitation of man by man. That is its only crime.[70]

The mobilization of organizations and militants surrounding this trial demonstrated the force of a combined militancy and led to the creation of the Patriotic Socialist Coordinating Council (Koordinadora Abertzale Sozialista, KAS), which was composed of the newly formed EHAS and Spanish groups, including the Patriotic Revolutionary Workers' Party (LAIA), the Patriotic Workers' Committee (Langile Abertzale Komiteak, LAK), and ETA-pm.[71] Additionally, KAS was supported—though not joined—by the Patriotic Workers' Council (Langile Abertzalean Batzordea, LAB) and ETA-m. Beyond its importance as a joint guideline for action, KAS would serve repeatedly as the umbrella organization or vehicle which made possible broadly based political protests which crossed partisan lines in Spain.[72]

Given the organizational complexities involved in the uniting of the two wings of the party, and no doubt as a reflection of the greater success of the movement in Spain compared to that in France, it was inevitable that

EHAS would not last long as an integrated political party. In 1977 the Spanish wing of EHAS changed its name to the Popular Revolutionary Socialist Party (Herriko Alderdi Sozialista Iraultzalea, HASI) and ultimately become one of the core parties of Popular Unity (Herri Batasuna, HB), the legal political party which was the most intransigent supporter of ETA-m in Spanish politics, in much the same role that Sinn Fein plays for the IRA.[73] ETA-pm in turn would be supported by the Basque Left Party (Euzkadiko Ezkerra, EE). EHAS was unwilling to admit the failure of its strategy of union, and stated in 1979 that "we kept a common structure with H.A.S.I. within [the umbrella group] Buru Bateragile, [Joint Summit]. And now, we have clearly affirmed our support, our participation in Herri Batasuna."[74] In 1977 EHAS would reject the proposal of ETA-pm through its political movement, ELAI, for the creation of a large mass nationalist movement known as the alternative KAS.[75] EHAS explained its rejection of ETA-pm's alternative program by reaffirming that:

> E.H.A.S. refuses this perspective, which aims at the formation of a national front on the base of nationalism but without any class content. . . . For E.H.A.S. the only "front" which can have any reality whatsoever is. . . . K.A.S. . . . the choice of E.H.A.S. goes to K.A.S.[76]

THE INFLUENCE OF THE BRETON MOVEMENT ON EHAS

If the greatest influence on EHAS's early political development was the Spanish Basque experience, another direct and important influence on HAS's early socialism was the long stay in Brittany by its founder and primary theoretician, Manex Goyhenetche, and his effort to model HAS along the lines of contemporary Breton militancy, especially the Union Démocratique Bretonne (UDB) in which Goyhenetche had been active during his years of study there.[77] The parallels between the militancy of the UDB and that of HAS are instructive. The UDB began in late 1963 as a leftist offshoot and criticism of the Mouvement pour l'Organisation de Bretagne (MOB) founded by Yann Fouéré, who had been in contact with Eugène Goyheneche in Paris during the 1930s as part of the first real period of contact and consciousness-raising between ethnic minorities in France. Fouéré was a Breton regionalist and, along with Guy Héraud, one of the primary theorists of the Mouvement Fédéraliste Européen, the source of *Enbata*'s doctrine of ethnic federalism.[78] In fact, according to Ronan Roudaut, with most of its progressive militants departed by 1966, the MOB then changed its name to Mouvement National Breton et Fédéraliste Européen.[79] Criticizing Fouéré's MOB for its "lack of political clarity," the UDB defined itself as "a party gathering together Bretons and friends of Brittany [who are] conscious of the national calling of

Brittany and convinced of the need to build socialism in their country."[80] In this way, HAS's rejection of *Enbata*'s federalism paralleled the UDB's similar rejection of the federalism and regionalism of MOB. Each would assert a self-conscious socialism in their steads.

The UDB's development was greatly influenced by two phenomena which also paralleled the Basque experience: the appeal of the theses of the extreme French left to young and impatient militants in the aftermath of the events of 1968 and the rise of "the armed struggle" as a tool of Breton nationalism by the Front de Libération de Bretagne (FLB). Both of the wings of the FLB would be dissolved in 1974 by the French Council of Ministers along with *Enbata*.[81] The reaction of the UDB to the FLB's violence would influence HAS's own opposition to the armed struggle, which HAS would make explicit from the first issue of *Euskaldunak* in March 1974. But the principled rejection of violence had its own costs, as the Breton UDB found in criticizing the FLB:

> The wave of attacks by the FLB beginning in 1966 was condemned by the leadership of the UDB but the size of popular support . . . led numerous militants seduced by the most violent forms of action and by revolutionary romanticism to rethink their conceptions of an intransigent scientific socialism vis-à-vis activism and adventurism.[82]

Stigmatized as a "subversive myth,"[83] the FLB insisted as did Iparretarrak later that "the FLB was born . . . of the necessity to respond by . . . armed struggle, and not of an individualist despair, nor of some revolutionary romanticism."[84] The UDB, for its part, continued to reject this nationalist violence and reaffirmed its own commitment to Leninist democratic centralism, which other ultra-leftist Breton militants would denounce as "Stalinist" in form.[85] It continued the difficult reconciliation between a militancy based on class struggle and national liberation, while more extreme movements were attempting a flanking maneuver to its left.[86] Many of these themes would be familiar to HAS as well.

HAS's earliest organizational contacts with the UDB were based on the *Charte de Brest* of February 4, 1974, which sought to codify the basis of a common cause among several of Europe's minority regions. Signing the charter were groups from Catalonia (Parti Socialiste de Libération Nationale des Pays Catalans Provisoire, PSANP, and Gauche Catalan des Travailleurs, ECT); Ireland (Sinn Fein and Official IRA); Euskadi (Euskal Herriko Alderdi Sozialista, EHAS); Brittany (Union Démocratique Bretonne, UDB), Galicia (Union du Peuple Galicien, UPG); and Wales (Pays de Galles Rouge, CG). The charter was subsequently modified on April 18, 1976, to alter the descriptions of the situation in Spanish Catalonia and the Spanish Basque country.[87] The purpose of the original joint declaration was to "solemnly declare the necessity of a union between the oppressed people of Europe." Among its conclusions were affirmations of:

—the inalienable right of national self-determination;
—the struggle against economic, social, political, and cultural oppression, and the rights of peoples to be masters of their own land;
—the need for each oppressed people to create its own revolutionary organization, in order to wage a national and revolutionary struggle;
—the struggle against all forms of alienation, exploitation, and human degradation, including racism, fascism, and sectarianism;
—the need to destroy all capitalist and imperialist structures, and for the people to appropriate the means of production, distribution and credit;
—the establishment of a planned Socialist economy, and political system, under the control of the working class;
—the struggle for the official recognition of national languages and cultures, which are an integral part of the construction of socialism in our countries;
—revolutionary solidarity with the worldwide struggle against colonialism and imperialism;
—the establishment of a Socialist Europe of ethnic peoples on the basic of reciprocal equality, respect, and recognition.[88]

The document concludes with the slogans "Proletarians of all Countries and Oppressed Peoples: Unite!" and "Long Live Proletarian Internationalism."[89]

In fact, actualizing the interethnic cooperation envisioned by the *Charte de Brest* was harder to accomplish than its framers undoubtedly had intended. HAS's Paris section was in charge of negotiating joint political action with their UDB counterparts in Paris, but it was a "delegated" authority, and multiple issues of *EHASKIDE* chronicled the fact that the Paris section did not have the authority to speak for HAS, nor for KAS, and was thus directed to speak in the name of "some Basque collective" rather than for HAS itself.[90] The frustration of the Parisian militants was palpable.

Throughout its organizational life, EHAS maintained closer organizational ties with the UDB than it did with any other political movement outside of the French and Spanish Basque countries. EHAS saw the UDB as the same type of movement pursuing the same kind of struggle. As Goyhenetche put it, "All the oppressed people of the hexagon have elaborated institutions adequate for their decolonization and the construction of socialism: U.D.B. in Brittany, H.A.S. in Euskadi."[91] In 1976 Ch. Etxezaharreta and Battitta Larzabal were HAS's official delegates, along with one Spanish Basque delegate,

to the Twelfth Congress of the UDB, which took place on April 17, 1976, in
Brest. Their glowing report appeared in the next issue of *Euskaldunak*. The
delegation

> was impressed by the seriousness and sense of organization of the UDB.
> It's true that it's a party which is already at its twelfth congress, but age
> alone doesn't explain the number of militants and the progression of
> the party's action in all domains. . . . The UDB perfectly understands
> the relative side of electoral results, but even so they have a significance
> because they prove that the parties of oppressed nations aren't sworn
> to perpetual marginality and that the national and social awareness of a
> colonized people can happen at the price of an arduous labor. This is an
> encouragement for other parties of the same type and thus for EHAS.[92]

EHAS, then, took courage from the UDB's example and made it a role model
for its own political efforts in the Pays Basque. During the UDB's congress,
the signatories of the *Charte de Brest* held their annual meeting and gave the
newly united party its imprimatur, endorsing the membership of the Spanish EHAS as well as the principle of a single political party representing an
ethnic people divided between two states.[93]

HAS's Electoral Strategy in the Presidential
Elections of 1974

Though HAS defined itself as a political party from its origins—which implied the intention to field candidates in French elections as *Enbata* had before
it—its birth in the weeks preceding the French presidential election of May
1974 obliged it to make an early choice from the sidelines from a range of
possible candidates. The choice was essentially between the ethnic federalist
candidacy of Professor Guy Héraud or Socialist François Mitterrand as the
candidate of the combined left. According to HAS, the only other alternatives were abstention or silence: in either case a choice of cowardice. Neither
rightist candidate, Jacques Chaban-Delmas or Valéry Giscard d'Estaing, was
likely to receive HAS's support. As we saw above, HAS chose to support
Mitterrand as the lesser of evils, without diluting its skepticism regarding the
ethnic commitment of the traditional French left. HAS's decision to support
Mitterrand was in direct contrast to leading ex-militants of the now-defunct
Enbata, who supported Guy Héraud as they had in the presidential election
of 1969.[94] Héraud's candidacy seemed an artifact of the symbolic politics of
interest-group expression in France.

It is an artifact of the electoral system in the Fifth Republic that a two-round, "winner take all" electoral system encourages the proliferation of symbolic candidacies in the first round, before settling down to the horse trading involved in the alliance formation, tactical withdrawals, and majority-building involved in the actual electing of a candidate in the second round. The use of two-round elections thus makes the first round a kind of low-cost beauty contest in which voters vote their emotional preferences. As Pierre Bidart explains it:

> The French electoral tradition intends that one chooses on the first round and elects on the second. This is to say that the first vote occurs, at the same time, in the perspective of the least political risk, and with the goal of demonstrating one's own political convictions. The interest of the first round resides precisely in the fact that each candidate can measure his political "weight" or at least the impact of particular themes (for example . . . the federalism of Héraud), the presidential candidacy serving as a pretext for a political soapbox, in the French electoral system.[95]

HAS deliberately chose not to support Guy Héraud as the candidate of minorities, even in the symbolic arena of the first round:

> The presidential campaign represents for the workers a very important stage in the conquest of their demands and their rights . . . any candidacy of the minorities risks seeming in [the] eyes [of French left parties and unions] to be a candidacy of division and this from the first round. There is why we decided to provide a tactical support to the common candidate of the left.[96]

HAS's logic was that the French right had had its chance to deal with the problem of France's minorities without success, and now it was the turn of the left. A vote for the left was justified in order to counter the French right, with its reign of big capital, disastrous economic policies for the Pays Basque, and attacks on the freedom of expression and on minorities.[97] Moreover, the coming to power of the left would be an important stage on the path toward a Socialist society in France. In any case, HAS's support of Mitterrand was for overtly tactical reasons—less a rallying to the theses of the French left than a conditional support of Mitterrand, while reminding him of his responsibilities toward France's national minorities.

The results of the first round revealed both constancy and change in the political culture of the rural Basque interior.[98] Though trailing Giscard d'Estaing by 73,798 to 76,720 total votes in the two Basque *circonscriptions*, Aquitaine's Chaban-Delmas won in Baigorri, Saint Palais, Ustaritz, Labastide, Hasparren, Iholdy, Espelette, and even Saint-Jean-de-Luz on the coast.

HAS noted this traditional Basque vote: "It seems there is enough there to show that the most traditional Basques are always behind in the electoral battle. The people erred to the right."[99] Mitterrand's total vote in the first round as the unified candidate of the left was 101,536 votes, but this was a distant second to the certain combination of Giscard's and Chaban's votes in the second round.[100] Héraud received a scant 1,135 votes in the Pyrénées-Atlantiques, half the score of Jean-Marie Le Pen, whose racist National Front was just beginning to attract public attention. More disappointing, Héraud's showing was barely greater in the Basque interior than it was in Béarn, where he was less familiar as a candidate. Nationally, Héraud received fewer votes than any other candidate in the first round, polling 19,281 votes or 0.7 percent of all votes cast. For HAS, the greatest damage done by Héraud's candidacy was that it might well serve to make the problem of minorities in France seem "negligible" in its wake.[101]

The national electoral results confirmed the victory of rightist Valery Giscard d'Estaing over Mitterrand in a surprisingly bipolar election. The Basques still voted overwhelmingly to the right in the rural interior. After being elected president, as we saw in chapter 1, Valéry Giscard d'Estaing paid a brief visit in 1974 to the interior village of Arhansus, which had given him 97 percent of its votes.

As it turned out, the greatest surprise of the second round was not that Mitterrand won relative majorities along the coast, especially in Bayonne and Biarritz, because the strength of leftist organization there had been long-standing since the time of the Popular Front. Surprisingly, he won in the rural areas of eastern and southern Soule in the Basque interior, primarily as a result of discontent with the decline both of the traditional shoe industry in Mauléon and of the rural agricultural economy, which provoked a hemorrhage of depopulation in excess of 17 percent in the remote mountain area of Soule and approaching 21 percent around Tardets.[102] Following the first round, *Euskaldunak* predicted:

> The second round is going to finally unfold in the best Basque political tradition: the "reds" against the "whites." . . . Very happily the results in St.-Jean-Pied-de-Port, Soule, Baigorry, and Anglet and Hendaye mark the beginning of an awareness of the misdeeds of the right.[103]

For HAS, the results of the second round showed the first fissures in the conservative political barrier which the clergy and local notables had erected in their defense of traditional customs and politics. The appearance of flyers during the election evoking the closure of religious schools, using contrasting quotes from Mitterrand and Giscard, showed the continued salience of religiosity as a political issue in the late twentieth century. The strategy of using the religious issue seems, in retrospect, to have been important in areas of strong conservative strength, given its support by Giscard and the near-unanimous support of local notables and elected officials.[104] Yet the credible showing of the Socialist Party (PS) along the coast and especially in the rural interior of Soule seemed to reflect a new circumstance of political bipolarization within the Basque electorate.[105] These new Socialist inroads in the interior encouraged HAS in its intention to field Basque Socialist candidates in future elections.

HAS'S CAMPAIGN AGAINST CONSERVATIVE LOCAL NOTABLES

Rather than seeking an accommodation with its adversaries, HAS began a public program of vilification of political opponents, seeking to sharpen the bipolarization which emerged in the 1974 presidentials. Not surprisingly, an early target of HAS's effort to build public support were the local notables, pillars of the traditional conservative social order. In a 1975 editorial entitled "The Putrefaction of Local Notables" HAS criticized local elected officials for remaining silent in the face of Spanish terrorist attacks in France and for creating a local electoral arena for Giscardian reformism.[106] This attack came in the wake of allegations that Spanish police agents were carrying out attacks on the ETA community in France, perhaps with the tacit cooperation of French police and customs officials, who knew who they were. In the wake of these charges, French minister of the interior (Prince) Michel Poniatowski paid an official visit to the Pays Basque in late May 1975 and condemned not only the actions of Spanish police in France, but also the use of French territory as a staging ground for ETA violence as well. As Poniatowski insisted, "I will not accept that French territory serves as a staging area for illegitimate actions."[107] In the wake of his visit, HAS attacked the local officials who had remained silent on the issue of Spanish police violence against the refugee community.

In a later issue HAS published the names of local officials who favored improving local roads in order to improve the tourist economy, to the political profit of the conservative government in power.[108] For HAS:

> The lesson is clear. For us the mass of classes who undergo the domination of capitalism, colonial exploitation and the reign of electoral notabilism, to us farmers, shepherds, seamen-fishermen, workers, artisans, shopkeepers, intellectual workers, students . . . it is up to us to regroup in order to construct the Socialist revolution in Euskadi.[109]

In another editorial entitled "The Bankruptcy of the Basque Bourgeoisie" HAS encouraged the people to rise up:

And this role, the bourgeoisie Basque plays it very well. It holds power within the municipalities. . . . The Basque bourgeoisie plays the tourist card to the hilt against the interest of the Basque working classes . . . all in playing the game of imperialism in accordance with its role as "valet" . . . BASQUE PEOPLE, WHEN THEN WILL YOU RISE UP?[110]

THE 1976 CANTONAL ELECTIONS AND THE
IDEA OF A BASQUE DEPARTMENT

The run up to 1976 cantonal elections, which elected members to the departmental *conseil général*, turned in part on the issue of the creation of a Basque department. A diverse coalition of Basque nationalists and representatives of the local chambers of commerce, including Jacques St. Martin, director of the Izarra Distilleries, combined to create an Association pour la Création d'un Département Basque. This was as contentious an issue in local politics as it was on a national level. Didier Borotra, conservative *conseiller général* from Biarritz, presented a motion before the *conseil* in January 1976 on the eve of the elections in March protesting against the tendency to privilege the points of view of what he called "autonomist or separatist" movements.[111] At the same time, Dr. Lastrade, the Basque *conseiller général* from Ustaritz, announced his resignation from the Association for the Creation of a Basque Department.

The press looked upon the candidacy of Jean Haritschelhar, secretary of the Association for the Creation of a Basque Department, in his hometown of Saint-Etienne-de-Baigorri as a test of strength of the idea of a Basque department. When Haritschelhar lost the election, the regional newspaper *Sud-Ouest* interpreted his defeat as a defeat for the departmental idea:

> The divisions in this canton worked against Mr. Haritschelhar. Moreover, he, in his role as secretary of the Association for the Creation of a Basque Department, spoke a little like the standard bearer of this movement. This test was settled by a defeat. (As a general rule, it seems that the population was hardly aware of this move.) The road will be long for its partisans.[112]

The newspaper *Enbata* was an ardent supporter of the idea of a Basque department and rejected the point of view of those who saw the results of the first round of the cantonals as a defeat for the creation of a Basque department.[113] *Enbata* supported André Luberriaga in Ustaritz and the Socialist Jean-Pierre Destrade, who beat Didier Borotra, an ardent opponent of a Basque department, in Biarritz.[114] With the conclusion of the second round of the cantonals, the Basque representation numbered three *conseillers* from the left and sixteen from the right, including seven from the Gaullist UDR, which was consolidating its support in the interior. One high point of the election was the subsequent election of Basque *conseiller général* Franz Duboscq as president of the departmental *conseil général*, only the third Basque ever elected to head a *conseil* dominated by the larger delegations from Béarn.[115]

Duboscq himself waffled in his support of the idea of a department, alternating between communiqués supporting the idea as well as professions of support to Jacques St. Martin, head of the association, and other statements mentioning the "necessary unity" of Basques and Béarnais and the "two peoples" of the Pyrénées-Atlantiques.[116] As *Enbata* interpreted the results, "In this regard, the Pays Basque seems now like an island of the right in an ocean of the left."[117] The quandary now posed for the supporters of a Basque department was the need to gain the support of the predominantly conservative Basque *conseillers généraux* who had been most opposed to the idea in the first place.

Despite the long-standing support for the idea of a separate Basque department within the nationalist camp, HAS/EHAS opposed it, even as (and perhaps because) *Enbata* strongly supported it. This opposition dated from its origins in 1974. HAS/EHAS explained its position this way:

> At the same time, let's be realistic: the creation of a prefecture at Bayonne is the reinforcement of the central administration, an additional prefect, additional powers, a fussy, hairsplitting administration, closer surveillance, a more efficient police. We are in no way interested in the perpetuation of the Napoleonic administration. Maybe the commercial bourgeoisie will find it to its profit; but will the interest of the popular masses be better defended for all this?[118]

What HAS/EHAS did favor was the creation of a Basque department/region, "a stage in the establishment of the national rights of the Basque people and the construction of socialism,"[119] a goal which considerably upped the ante and the fears of separatism present in both Pau, the departmental capital, and Paris.

For the longtime nationalist Marc Légasse, who offered a symbolic candidacy in Hendaye, the results of the election were simply one more way station on the long road to the fulfillment of Basque goals. In an open letter to his supporters after the election, he said:

> I thank the voters of the canton of Hendaye who voted for Basque autonomy and make an appointment with them for the legislative elections of 1978. As Arana-Goiri put it: what is lamentable in politics is not being beaten, it's not to fight. The combat continues.[120]

THE 1977 MUNICIPAL ELECTIONS

With the opening of the nationalist camp to socialism, the French left continued its efforts to co-opt the Basque issue by offering EHAS two places out of its list of seventeen which included candidates from the PS, PSU, and PCF in the 1977 municipal elections in Bayonne, as well as on the list of Hasparren in the interior.[121] *Le Monde* identified EHAS for its readers as Basque nationalist and described it as a Socialist Party representing the three Basque provinces in France and four in Spain.[122]

Given that less than eighteen months before EHAS was referring to the French left's attitude toward the Basque problem as "social imperialism,"[123] and to the PCF as "Gaullists of the left,"[124] EHAS sought to explain the thinking behind its decision to cooperate with the French left in the municipal elections or even to field candidates at all. EHAS continued to maintain that the solution to the Basque problem would not come through the ballot box:

> First of all, there is a principle which it is fitting to pose clearly: one mustn't believe that ballot boxes can save the Pays Basque Nord and bring a definitive solution to the Basque problem. This must be clear: the electoral system cannot constitute a goal in and of itself for us.[125]

At the same time, election campaigns offered the chance to proselytize and bring the movement out of its isolated ghetto:

> The time of elections, whether they be municipal, cantonal, or legislative, constitutes a strong time in political life that it would be a shame not to use in order to advance our cause . . . in short, to use it as a tool of propaganda . . . we believe that the political isolation of the Basques has lasted too long; the ghetto has lasted too long; we refuse to withdraw into an elitist attitude, we the "pure and the hard." The Basque movement must be brought out of its marginalization . . . we mustn't overlook every chance, every occasion which is offered us.[126]

While EHAS's calls to other elements of the *abertzale* community went largely unheeded, it began a series of negotiations with the French left based on their points of common interest. As EHAS put it:

> We are mindful of our orientation as Basque patriots of the left; as such our Socialist obligation is a common denunciation with the parties of the French left; as Socialists, we have a common interest. . . . We believe that this manner, at the present moment, is a concrete means of serving the interest of the workers and reunite their hopes.[127]

EHAS was particularly hopeful of its chances in Hasparren, a light industrial town in the Labourdin interior which had lost more than 20 percent of its population since 1876.[128] For the first time in its history, a list of the left ran in its municipal elections, and the results of the first round gave it an encouraging 8 percent of the vote. This was a hopeful sign and, for EHAS, a call for dialogue with a French left which "has every chance of winning the legislative elections of 1978."[129] In Bayonne the joint list of the left, which included EHAS, polled 38 percent of the vote.[130] Robert Hirigoyen ran alone against two conservative lists in Larressore and won 19 percent in the first round; Manex Pagola won 15 percent in Urcuit. In the village of Chéraute in Soule two militants were reelected on the mayor's list. The surprise of the election in Soule was that a list of young people supported by EHAS won the election in Larrau on a campaign against tourism and for access to communal land.[131] Finally, the election gave encouragement to those continuing to push for the creation of a Basque department.

THE 1978 LEGISLATIVE ELECTIONS AND THE ATTEMPT TO CREATE A KAS IN THE PAYS BASQUE NORD

On July 3, 1977, the Spanish half of the unified EHAS met with militants of Eusko Sozialistak in the first general assembly of a new political party, the Popular Revolutionary Socialist Party (Herriko Alderdi Sozialista Iraultzalea, HASI), which would become a central part of the Herri Batasuna coalition supporting ETA-m in Spain.[132] EHAS claimed to fully support this effort to orient the Basque Socialist left following the disappointing outcome of the Spanish elections on June 15. As HASI explained in a press release following its constituent assembly, on an organizational level, what it meant for EHAS was that the party would now be a federal association of two national parties for the foreseeable future:

> Given that the rhythm of the convergence is different in these two parties, at present, we are constituting ourselves as a federal party, in the North with the name E.H.A.S., until integration with other groups takes place or until the Constitutional Assembly where it will be integrated in H.A.S.I.[133]

EHAS pledged to continue its contacts with HASI in the newly created coordinating group, Buru Bateragile. With the creation of HASI, EHAS turned its attention to the Basque political context in France and sought to begin a "process of convergence," with the goal of creating, if not a new and broader political organization, at least a KAS similar to that which was created in Spain in 1975:

> E.H.A.S. North for its part said yes to the process of convergence, that is, that it is willing to disappear as an organization, with its name and

emblem, in order to create a stronger, more reinforced party . . . with the others. A first informational meeting took place in Bayonne; delegates of E.H.A.S. North, Jazar, Herriaren Alde, Ezker Berri, [and] independent militants attended; it's up to each and all now to move on to action.[134]

In reality, EHAS's first effort at bridging the gap between the various groups and *splinter groups* which made up the French Basque movement in the 1970s began in 1975 with a public analysis in *Euskaldunak* of the splintering of the *abertzale* camp:

> Since May 1968 youth have regularly questioned the capitalist society in which they find themselves confined. For that, '68 brought a different political mentality based on spontaneous actions and the refusal of a "party" as such. This leads in Euzkadi to a profusion of small groups of youths which, consumed by internal discussions, can't manage a coherent labor of mass consciousness-raising. These vaguely politicized factions only unite during periods of agitation (hunger strikes, support committees, etc.). Their refusal to integrate themselves in a party, to follow a discipline of labor and to accomplish a daily militancy, shows that the Basque patriotic youth aren't yet ready for a realistic politics, their analysis being for the most part utopian. The actions which such groups lead are incidental and touch the population only superficially.[135]

According to former militants of Mende Berri, EHAS seemed particularly threatened by Mende Berri and sought to co-opt it by subsuming it within EHAS. They felt that EHAS wanted to be *the* Basque political party; it had a desire for hegemony "like any self-respecting party." This is an ironic charge, given HAS's bitter criticism of *Enbata* in 1974 for the same behavior. EHAS condemned Mende Berri for not being clear in its political line. Mende Berri, in turn, criticized EHAS for being too sectarian, too ideological, too Marxist. This did not stop the two groups from some joint efforts, notably the distribution of handbills at rallies, but these efforts were at arm's length. According to these ex-militants of Mende Berri, the real problem with EHAS's political seduction was that those most politicized militants in Mende Berri by the mid-1970s were leftist Christians: "anti-Marxist" may have been too strong a term, but "class struggle" was definitely not an appealing battle cry. Finally, another obstacle for EHAS to overcome was Manex Goyhenetche's style, which seemed too critical and overbearing to attract these younger militants already suspicious of organized partisan activity.

The *Pindar* Initiative

In December 1976 the first issue of a new nationalist publication *Pindar* (Flame) signaled the intensification of contacts between the various Basque groups and the search for a common ground between them. *Pindar* argued that Basque political militants in 1976 were divided into three broad tendencies: a Basque nationalist current, a patriotic Basque Socialist current, and finally a current of the extreme French left. *Pindar* sought to bridge the gaps within the Basque Socialist camp in order to find a more effective means of joint action:

> What preoccupies us is the patriotic Basque Socialist current. All the organizations, associations, or groups in this current are aware today of their limited capacity to lead struggles. Having become aware of their respective roles, a will seems be emerging to move toward more coordination between all. Everyone recognizes the weakness in the development of the theoretical arguments on which our action rests.[136]

Pindar thus proposed a joint theoretical publication which would publish the texts on which these various groups' political action was based:

> In addition, [*Pindar*] may contribute to the existence of regular contacts between the different groups and militants, which is desirable. It is in this state of mind that the principle of *Pindar* was retained during a discussion between militants notably of MENDE BERRI, EHAS, JAZAR, HERRIAREN ALDE, and the GROUP OF HENDAYE. [137]

To begin that debate, *Pindar* sent out a questionnaire covering the broad aspects of Basque militancy and political beliefs and then published the responses received from the Group of Hendaye, Jazar, and Mende Berri.

By February 1977 reports in *EHASKIDE* confirmed the largely symbolic nature of the ties with HASI and the need to find ways to make these ties real and dynamic.[138] As EHAS was forced to admit, "Let's say that the relationships are evidently good but that they are essentially episodic. . . . The HASI-EHAS tandem can only work if there is something to do in common."[139] Rumors were spreading in Spain at this time about conflict between EHAS and HASI. EHAS sought to put these rumors to rest in an interview in *Egin* affirming EHAS's federal relationship with HASI since its constituent assembly. At the same time, the Spanish Basque party close to ETA-pm, Basque Left (Euzkadiko Ezkerra, EE), had asked EHAS to take part in work on a statute for the Spanish Basque country. While EE insisted it was not asking EHAS to break with HASI, EHAS knew that any agreement would have been used against HASI in internecine quarrels in the South and so refused.

If EHAS's relationship with HASI was in flux, its relationship with other European minorities, especially the Breton movement UDB, was essentially moribund. As EHAS noted:

> The idea of the *Charte de Brest* is excellent on the level of principles, but it is, for the moment, scantly operational. Each of the signatory parties seems completely submerged by its own problems.[140]

While each party was united in its commitment to the struggle against imperialism, EHAS noted that "it seems that their strategies differ, notably concerning the recourse to violence."[141] This same concern also complicated EHAS's relations with HASI, which EHAS now saw as supporting the armed struggle of ETA in Spain.

TOWARD A FRENCH BASQUE KAS

The natural remaining avenue of political alliance was with the other groups and militants of the *abertzale* left in France. But as late as February 1977 EHAS reported to its militants: "There hasn't been carried out a policy determined in advance but simply a steering in that direction."[142]

In a report prepared for its general assembly in 1977, EHAS sought to define its own militancy in regard to both ETA and the *Pindar* initiative:

> One of the constituent parts of the Basque patriotic left is EHAS. . . . But this leftist current has considerably enriched itself starting with ETA's own fief. This new current is in the process of affirming its own personality and it is concretizing itself through movements rich in potential and which are, in reality, much more complementary than antagonistic. This is the idea of those who launched *Pindar* and we should profit from this spark in order to make the light shine. . . . In this sense, the initiative of *Pindar* is largely positive, even if we only weakly supported it—let's admit it![143]

EHAS saw itself at a crossroads in 1977 which led to two possible alternative relationships with these other groups on the Basque left:

> EHAS finds itself currently adrift of this bloc and has the frightening possibility of making it burst apart into antagonistic factions or, to the contrary, actively contributing to transform it into a revolutionary movement.[144]

Battitta Larzabal urged his fellow militants to embrace the politics of union as the sole way of creating a genuine mass party like HASI in Spain. It would have no excuses if it missed this historical rendezvous:

If we don't play this unitary politics we will have a good part of the responsibility for the crumbling of the Basque Socialist forces in the North, and we will not have the excuse of forty years of [Franco] or of clandestinity.[145]

Based on this logic, at the General Assembly of the party in 1977 at Itxassou Larzabal proposed the constitution of a Patriotic Socialist Coordinating Council (Koordinadora Abertzale Sozialista, KAS) for Ipar Euskal Herria or the Pays Basque Français. This coordinating body would include EHAS, Jazar, Herriaren Alde, and Mende Berri but be open to any groups defining themselves as patriotic Basque Socialists.

While the militants' response was unanimously favorable, a number of concerns were nonetheless raised: Would the KAS in fact weaken EHAS as a party? Would it be based on a clear set of guidelines? Might the other groups see this as a thinly veiled attempt at co-optation of their militants? Would this risk diluting the clarity of EHAS's Socialist analysis should it have to compromise in order to bring other movements into the KAS? Unless the KAS was built on organization-to-organization contacts, it risked developing a "carnival-like" atmosphere hardly conducive to effective action. Finally, given the predominantly rural milieu in the North, it was important that groups of militant farmers from the interior be included in KAS, as well as traditional Basque militants from the coastal urban areas.

Larzabal's proposal anticipated many of these concerns. First, the KAS would need to be explicit in not threatening the autonomy of any group choosing to take part: "The KAS must constitute itself without any preliminaries on the basis of the complete autonomy of each group. The progression of the KAS cannot be programmed."[146] Second, in contrast to the decision-making style adopted by the KAS in Spain, the northern version would be based on a unity which began at the grassroots and not at the political summit. Third, the KAS would be broadly constituted and invite the participation of all Socialist *abertzale* groups, as well as farmers' groups from the interior. In fact, Larzabal envisioned a corporatist decision-making structure within the KAS, with a weighted system of voting based on occupations to ensure that workers and farmers would hold power in this "avant-garde of the revolutionary Socialist Party." In Larzabal's scheme, workers and farmers would each receive 38 percent of the votes in this vanguard, with students receiving 12 percent, as would "independents" (which would include artisans, shop owners, and liberal professions combined). Such a weighted voting system would ensure that the numerical combination of votes arriving at the 75 percent threshold necessary for passage of important decisions could only come from the joint agreement of the workers and farmers.[147] Finally, Larzabal proposed launching the KAS in a broad electoral campaign around the theme of a Basque department-region, a goal he saw as feasible and not the least utopian.

ABERTZALE REACTION TO THE KAS PROPOSAL

Goyhenetche gave a brief report on the first preliminary reactions of the *abertzale* milieu to cooperative action of this kind. He reported that Mende Berri had voiced no objections, but other militants questioned Mende Berri's credentials in the first place, some seeing it as a "right wing" movement by this time. EHAS had cast its net widely after the legislative elections and had contacted extreme left-wing French parties, including the Communist Revolutionary League (LCR), PSU, and OCT. Each had absolutely refused to join the KAS. By the end of the General Assembly, it was agreed that approaches would be made to Jazar, Herriaren Alde, and Mende Berri. Significantly, the question of including Iparretarrak in the KAS was discussed, but it seems that Iparretarrak's commitment to violence and clandestinity risked contaminating the whole effort, and it was decided not to include it.[148] Larzabal was given responsibility for developing the creation of the KAS.

Six months after HAS's General Assembly endorsed the principle of a KAS for the French Basque left, it emerged in October 1977 as the linchpin of HAS's electoral strategy for the upcoming 1978 legislative elections. *EHASKIDE* reported on the tepid reaction of the other groups to the idea of a KAS and to a joint effort for the legislative elections:

> As well as our documents from the Assembly at Itxassou, our "propositions for the legislatives" appearing in the last issue of *Euskaldunak* were sent to Ezker Berri, Herriaren Alde, Jazar. . . . Herriaren Alde is opposed to participating in the elections; in fact, this group seems reduced at present to 2–3 militants, the others having departed. Ezker Berri would be favorable but isn't strong about it and the theme "Département-Région Pays Basque" doesn't provoke much enthusiasm; in fact, this group is breaking apart as well: the majority just left it, and there remains a minority in Ezker Berri, a total of 4 to 5 militants. Jazar continues to remain without reply: for the six months that we've sent texts, organized reunions for HASI, thrown out propositions for the elections (and before the legislatives, for the municipals), Jazar hasn't responded to the idea of a detailed discussion.[149]

As we have seen, Ezker Berri was a political group created by Mende Berri for imprecisely defined political action. It would last until about 1982. The number of militants involved in all these splinter groups by this point brings to mind Malherbe's argument that they really resembled clubs more than anything else.[150] However, in *Pindar* as elsewhere one is struck by the depth of their political analysis and the sincerity of their militancy. Having no response to its repeated approaches, EHAS could only surmise the reasons for Jazar's lack of response. EHAS attributed this indifference to the fact Jazar was working at the same time to create a competing campaign against unemployment which would exclude existing Basque political organizations (read EHAS): "This amounts to wanting to isolate EHAS and demonstrate our electoralist approach, thus reformist and petit bourgeois, etc., etc."[151] Jazar's and Herriaren Alde's point-by-point rebuttals of EHAS's arguments came a month later in *Pindar*.[152]

Jazar's reaction closely paralleled Davant's lone voice within EHAS itself when it predicted that *abertzale* Socialist candidates would only receive the votes of their fellow Basque leftists and sympathizers, that is, a minority of votes leading to a reduced result. As to the argument that it was important to view the elections as a platform for propagating nationalist ideas, Jazar said: "This is one of the worst platforms that one could hope for, given the context and material conditions."[153] As a result, Jazar concluded:

> Taking account of the possible evolution of Euskadi Nord . . . it seems to us necessary to steer us to a strategy of rupture. FOR ALL THESE REASONS, THE GROUP JAZAR HAS DECIDED TO NOT PARTICIPATE IN THE ELECTIONS OR TO SUPPORT ANY CANDIDATE. We have also decided that we will refuse to disparage EHAS's candidates.[154]

For its part, Herriaren Alde argued that it was illusory to think that the power of the Basque people would come through the ballot box. The true liberation of the Basque people would come through reinforcing popular struggles and allying itself with the people. Finally, in a statement rife with anarchist tones, Herriaren Alde asserted, "For the *abertzale* movement in '78 the watchwords 'Elections, traps for fools' 'The power is in the street' and 'decolonize Euskadi' have never been as true."[155]

Finally, in a short communiqué, Ezker Berri protested against the manner in which EHAS unilaterally designated its candidates at the same time it was soliciting the participation of other groups. This, for Ezker Berri, was all the more "shocking" given the presence of *Pindar* as another avenue for discussing the issue of candidates in an open way.[156] Even *Enbata*, committed to supporting the *abertzale* party line, was troubled by EHAS's refusal to solicit advice from others on whose support it depended:

The tally of the actions carried out these past years precisely should have led EHAS to limit its ambitions and to relativize its role. When one bases one's undertaking on a labor done in large part outside of self it would be good to solicit from these "others" their opinion.[157]

At the same time, *Enbata* criticized EHAS for limiting its dialogue to two or three leftist groups and ignoring the rest of the nationalist camp.[158] The irony was that the attention of several of these groups was already gravitating elsewhere. Jazar would soon join the remnants of Herriaren Alde to become one of the first elements of the Herri Taldeak movement, close to Iparretarrak and formed from the Comités Xan (see the next chapter). In the final analysis, hostile reactions to EHAS's electoral initiative were received from Jazar and Herriaren Alde, joined by other groups including Eibat and MAT and the clandestine and violent movements Iparretarrak and Euskal Zuzentasuna (EZ, Basque Justice).[159] Based on the biting tone of these other movements' critiques, it appeared that the idea of creating a KAS for the 1978 legislatives was out of the question.

EHAS AND THE 1978 LEGISLATIVE ELECTIONS

The other major piece of business to be transacted at the General Assembly of the Party at Itxassou in the spring of 1977 was the party's own position on whether to participate in the elections or not. The militants were by no means united in their view of such a campaign. Many of their reservations echoed those the other movements would frame six months later. The most vocal opponent was Jean-Louis Davant, who, in a spirit of *déjà vu*, saw in such a campaign a repetition of the errors of *Enbata*, whose weak electoral showing weakened the *abertzale* movement. He argued that the votes received were always fewer than the movement's actual audience—hence the chance of discrediting the cause. Larzabal was one of the strongest voices in favor of making a run for the legislative elections. Among his arguments was the need to prevent the French left from harvesting the fruits of EHAS's grassroots political activity. Other militants voiced their support for fielding candidates under the KAS label, and not that of EHAS alone.

In the end, it was decided to poll the movement's militants by mail ballot, given "the few militants present."[160] The results of the mailed ballot were surprisingly one-sided. Of thirty-five responses to its questionnaire about an EHAS candidacy for the 1978 legislatives, the clear majority opposed the party label "EHAS" alone and favored a more generic "Patriotic Basque Socialist Movement." Only one (in all likelihood Davant) was opposed to participating in the elections under any circumstance. In the end, the decision to participate in the election was sealed.

THE 1978 LEGISLATIVE ELECTIONS

EHAS announced in the November 1977 issue of *Euskaldunak* that it would participate in the 1978 legislative elections;[161] not until two months later, in January 1978, did it announce who its standard-bearers would be.[162] The party's two leaders were announced as the candidates: F. B. Larzabal in the third *circonscription* (Mauléon), with Manex Lanathoua as his *suppléant*, and Manex Goyhenetche in the fourth *circonscription* (Bayonne), with A. Massigoge as *suppléant*. At the same time, a support committee was announced for the campaign in the interior. Among its members were Jean-Louis Davant, who, having expressed his reservations, nevertheless loyally supported the decision once it was made. Nine of the fourteen names had occupations of worker or farmer, including one priest who was identified as a shepherd. Five were *conseillers municipaux*, including three on the farmers/workers list.

The bases of EHAS's campaign were by now largely familiar—a Socialist mobilization strategy directed at those most afflicted by the nature of colonial exploitation:

> We want to respond to the hope of the whole of the classes [who are] victims in diverse degrees of colonial exploitation: workers, shepherds, farmers, seamen-fishermen, artisans, small shopkeepers, students, etc., and who by their struggles are in the process of creating Euskadi by socialism. That's what it is to be an *abertzale* Socialist.[163]

Among the familiar issues addressed by EHAS were the creation of jobs and a true policy of industrialization; reinforcement of the rural agricultural economy and a reversal of its decline in population; halt to tourist construction threatening to Basque culture and its year-round economy; and the defense of the Basque language, including support of the Ikastola movement.

The one new twist in the campaign was the way EHAS chose to frame its long-standing demand for a Basque department-region. In an article entitled "Statute of Autonomy," the terms "department" or "department-region" were never mentioned. This time EHAS called for the creation of an "autonomous territorial collectivity composed of Soule, Basse-Navarre, and Labourd."[164] Creating such a collectivity would necessitate an "administrative recarving" of France. The new Basque collectivity would be governed by a Bilçar or sovereign Basque assembly elected by direct universal suffrage and based on proportional representation. The Basque collectivity would have complete autonomy in the areas of education, culture, and radio and television. The Basque language would become the co-equal official language of the area along with French. The collectivity would have the right to limit the purchase of land by nonusers and to nationalize enterprises and transfer their property to the collectivity. Finally, the banking and productive sector would be transferred to worker control.

If EHAS seized on the electoral campaign as a means of spreading its ideas, according to Christian Bombédiac writing in *Le Monde,* the election would provide an important indication of the degree of public support for the Basque cause:

> We are present at a period of consciousness-raising of Basque patriots. The next elections (they will be represented by the Basque Socialist Party EHAS) will show their real influence on the population. What matters most to this movement is to open a [campaign] in order to sensitize public opinion. Little by little the Basques of the North are thus inspired by the work accomplished by their brothers in the South. And it is true that, from now on, they can no longer be ignored. They must be reckoned with.[165]

Later in February, *Le Monde,* in its preelectoral analysis, referred to "a Basque nationalist whose candidacy seems symbolic."[166] Once more, EHAS took the high-risk strategy of strongly attacking the conservative Basque political notables, including deputies, senators, and members of the *conseil général:*

> What have they done? Have they contributed to returning its dignity to the Basque people? No! . . . These notables have maintained the Pays Basque in underdevelopment. These notables favor real estate speculation, tourism. . . . This is a parasitic bourgeoisie, unproductive, a valet of the existing power structure, and finally, ANTI-BASQUE, which has led the Pays Basque for more than twenty years ADRIFT. WE MUST BE DONE WITH IT![167]

THE RESULTS

Despite its every effort, the results were disappointing. Larzabal and Lanatua received 4.76 percent of the vote in the interior, and Goyhenetche and Massigoge polled 3.02 percent on the coast.[168] *Enbata* asked, "Why hide our disappointment?" at a level of nationalist support that was at best stagnant, and declining along the coast.[169] According to the Basque historian Jean-Claude Larronde, EHAS's vote on the coast did not equal the 4.6 percent that Ximun Haran achieved in 1967, and its vote in the interior barely equaled what Christiane Etchalus got in 1967.[170] *Enbata* suggested that EHAS's greatest support came in the rural areas most affected by depopulation and economic decline.[171] In its internal publication, EHAS insisted, "These results aren't a failure, nor a spectacular success."[172] While admitting the weakness of the score, EHAS saw it as a militant vote and the first time the electorate was offered the combination of a Basque Socialist and autonomist platform.[173] *Enbata*, however, noted, "We can measure today the damage caused by our divisions. . . . One day could we be more patriotic than partisan?"[174]

In addition to the prior conflict over the KAS initiative, EHAS had abundant reason to resent the behavior of other Basque movements during the election. First, EHAS noted the sudden appearance of spray-painted inscriptions on walls which irritated the local population. Moreover, there was a sudden increase in the very number of names on the walls, "MAT, HAT, EX-EZKER BERRI . . . [until] the population loses itself and diminishes our credibility; the Basque movement appears too much to public opinion as if it's composed of jerks."[175] Once more, it was claimed that *Enbata* had not done EHAS's campaign any favors.

Most importantly, EHAS's campaign was already being effaced by the Comités Xan in the first stirrings of the militancy to come. The arrest on December 23, 1977, of Jean-Claude ("Xan") Marguirault, a young militant charged with aiding and abetting Iparretarrak, and his detention without bail during the ensuing months led to the creation of a committee in support of Xan that soon became multiple grassroots committees as the issue galvanized local Basque communities in a way EHAS had not been able to. Strong support for Xan was voiced by groups across the political spectrum, but in particular those leftist groups like Herriaren Alde, Ex-Ezker Berri, or Euskal Zuzentasuna (EZ) which had refused to support EHAS's campaign.[176]

EHAS charged that during its poster campaign certain members of the Comités Xan had "sabotaged" EHAS's posters by spray painting "Xan" on the wall and sometimes falsely signing it "EHAS."[177] Moreover, "one would say that sometimes their authors followed on the very heels of the . . . EHAS militants."[178] The inscriptions appeared throughout the Basque country in the nights before the election. In several cases the inscriptions were painted on the walls of homes or apartment buildings and had to be removed at the residents' expense. EHAS interpreted this as "one way like another to establish a strategy of rupture with the people."[179]

A year later EHAS again presented a slate of candidates in eight cantons for the March 1979 cantonal elections in the Pyrénées-Atlantiques.[180] Its campaign was based on the same basic themes as in the legislative elections of the previous year, though with some notable changes. First, the French government treatment of the Spanish Basque refugee population became an issue, as was cooperation between the French and Spanish governments. While the vague idea of the creation of an "autonomous collectivity" was maintained, it was concretized by the call for the immediate creation of a Basque department. The results indicated declining support for EHAS and its program in the rural interior, where EHAS fell from 6.43 percent to 4.60 percent in the canton of Tardets, from 5 percent to 2.5 percent in Labastide, and from 6 percent to 5.5 percent in Iholdy. The results in the urban coastal cantons showed slight progress, but were hardly more than moral victories: from 2.36 percent to 3.24 percent in Bayonne-Ouest, 1.8 percent to 3.47 percent in Bayonne-Est, and 1.9 percent to 3.13 percent in Biarritz-Ouest. The total number of votes EHAS received in the cantonals (1,361) was virtually identical to that received in the legislatives a year before (1,376). But after five years of militancy and two consecutive electoral campaigns the results indicated a defeat for the party and its hope to unite the Basque electorate in a Socialist political movement.

The electoral terms for the European elections of May 1979 effectively prevented minority candidates by mandating national electoral lists of eighty-one candidates for the whole of the French territory. EHAS, like the UDB and other minority parties, was thus deprived of the chance to present its case at the level of a greater Europe.[181] Given its inability to win support even among the Basque electorate, this seemed a fortunate respite. As Jean-Louis Davant explained EHAS's showing in the cantonal elections:

> E.H.A.S. doesn't represent the whole of the Basque patriotic [forces]. Everyone knows that certain groups were cool (at the very least) toward our candidacies: some, those of refusal, because they don't believe in using elections to resolve the Basque problem; others, the moderates, because they believed in them too much and would have wanted to present themselves in our place.[182]

To the very end of its electoral strategy, EHAS continued to battle *Enbata* for self-respect. It seems fitting that EHAS wrote the obituary of its own electoral strategy in 1979: "Whether one likes it or not, and whether *Enbata* likes it or not, the era of the assembling of all the Basques is over."[183]

The Rise of the Comités Xan and the Eclipse of EHAS

In October 1978 EHAS received an invitation from the Comités Xan to a day of *luttes et fêtes* on the theme of "Struggles in Northern Euzkadi" scheduled for November 5 in Hasparren. The problem with the Comités Xan's invitation was that it was extended to *Euskaldunak* and not to EHAS on the pretense that political parties were not invited. After some debate within the *comité directeur*, Larzabal was instructed to respond favorably, while informing the Comités Xan that EHAS would come in full and that it was not up to other militants to impose limits on the nature of EHAS and its activity.[184]

Two members of the *comité directeur* opposed accepting the invitation since it might appear to endorse the use of violence. In the end, the majority nonetheless decided to accept. The Comités Xan soon evolved into the Herri Taldeak (singular Herri Talde) movement, which was widely viewed as the open side of the terrorist movement Iparretarrak, as Sinn Fein was to the IRA in Ireland or as Herri Batasuna was to ETA-m in Spain.

Speaking for Herri Talde, Richard Irazusta leveled a devastating series of critiques of EHAS in *Egin* between 1978 and 1980. EHAS was something of a helpless target at this point, no longer able to grow and now clearly outdistanced in popular support by the new Herri Taldeak movement. EHAS became an obstacle in the eyes of Herri Talde; in the words of a former EHAS militant, "We became the fronton against which they played pelote." Or, as he continued in a more Freudian vein, it was a clear case of the patricidal urge to kill the father. EHAS was no more successful in attracting youth than *Enbata* had been.

THE REJECTION OF VIOLENCE

On the other hand, Iparretarrak had committed its first act of violence in 1973 and by 1980 was on the verge of greatly expanding its use of the armed struggle. In the eyes of many Basque youth, if EHAS was too staid and structured in its organization, Iparretarrak projected a Robin Hood image that was undeniably attractive. EHAS continued to oppose the recourse to violence, as it had from the first issue of *Euskaldunak* in March 1974. EHAS's opposition to the use of armed struggle in France turned on four interrelated points: (1) the situation in France was different than in Spain and therefore the use of ETA's example did not apply; (2) the use of violence risked turning off the very Basque population on whose support the movement must depend; (3) violence risked provoking a massive French retaliation in response; and (4) the very use of violence invited fascist groups to up the ante:

> Moreover, [violence] is an open door to the action of fascist or irresponsible groups who would quickly begin to commit some attack whose odious nature would have discredited the [Basque] revolutionaries even if these latter denied responsibility.[185]

In a major article in *Euskaldunak* in April 1978 EHAS repeated its longstanding opposition to violence in the French Basque case and described the conflict preventing a united front: "The most important disagreement exists, in fact, over the means of struggle."[186] It based its opposition on several related concerns. First, the decision to use violence would invite a massive response from the French state. As EHAS described it:

When one opts for violence, one must accept the entire logic of such a choice, that is to say, the fact that one is going to find oneself sooner or later face to face with the enormous arsenal of violence at the disposal of the modern state. In such a ratio of forces the governors know all too well that in Euskadi North they will easily have the upper hand.[187]

Second, any reference to ETA's use of violence in Spain ignored the essential difference between the two cases: the degree of public support which sheltered ETA from the Francoist state. Echoing the classic Marxist-Leninist position on violence, EHAS insisted that the violence must emanate from the support of the working class and that a premature use of violence might turn the working class against an isolated Basque movement. As the parties of the *Charte de Brest* asserted, premature violence risked becoming elitist and isolated, an ill-advised effort to substitute rhetoric and adventurism for the unavoidable stages through which a revolutionary movement must pass.[188] Finally, EHAS rejected what it called the inappropriate use of the Spanish Basque experience to justify extending the armed struggle into France. As EHAS insisted, "For the use of violence in Euskadi North any reference to Euskadi South is absurd."[189]

But could violence "wake up" the people to the logic of the Basque cause?

Nothing is less sure. Well to the contrary, exactly the opposite result might be obtained in the sense that only a minority of the Basque people is wedded to its own cause and that [with violence] a majority may be turned against them. In the actual state of things, the wager on violence is very simply suicidal.[190]

The bottom line for EHAS was that violence was unlikely to lead to greater public support for the movement or a greater accumulation of progressive forces and that it would play into the hands of the authorities, who would see the very use of violence as a pretext for further repression. In the final analysis, "The great danger is that a 'politics of rupture' theoretically engaged against 'the system' may become, in practice, a rupture pure and simple with the people."[191]

Iparretarrak and the Act of Revolutionary Expropriation

Otsoac estu caussizen mandatariric bera iduriric.
The wolf never uses a messenger who looks like himself.
Basque proverb

On March 26, 1980, in one of the most spectacular actions yet attempted by Iparretarrak, two of its young militants, Dominique ("Txomin") Olhagaray and Raymond ("Ramuntxo") Arruiz, were killed when a bomb prematurely exploded as they tried to install it in the car of the wife of the French subprefect in Bayonne, Mme. Biacabe, parked outside the Hospital of Bayonne.[192] The nature of the attempted action and the manner of the deaths of the two youths greatly polarized Basque public opinion. EHAS chose to release a communiqué to the press in the aftermath of their deaths once again opposing the use of violence because it served to contaminate all forms of Basque militancy:

> In any case, E.H.A.S. cannot but disapprove of this type of armed struggle which places the civilian population in danger. . . . This form of action remains for us a political error. . . . The solution to the Basque problem will not come suddenly, but will be the result of a long struggle carried out patiently through mobilizations, failures, defeats . . . obstinately. Nothing can be undertaken, nothing can progress without the support of the people.[193]

Though EHAS took pains to salute the memory of the two dead militants, its persistent criticism of the armed struggle was poorly taken by Iparretarrak as well as by Herri Taldeak, whose attacks on EHAS accelerated from this point on.

In the spring of 1981 EHAS was essentially dead in the water. The biggest issue at that point was the upcoming presidential elections in May. EHAS endorsed the candidate of the left in both rounds, and François Mitterrand would, in fact, be elected president. The great challenge for the PS and its Basque supporters in the 1980s would be to carry out the promises included in Mitterrand's platform, including the creation of a Basque department.

EHAS as a movement and *Euskaldunak* were being carried by Goyhenetche and Larzabal and a small group of others who remained faithful to its abrupt end. As one of its militants expressed EHAS's internal climate in the spring of 1981:

> There was finally a sense of turning in circles, accomplishing nothing. Even the alliance with other ethnic movements wasn't working. And the conflict within the *abertzale* camp was beginning to sap our spirits.

EHAS found itself being increasingly confronted for leadership of cultural movements like the Basque primary school (Ikastola) movement controlled by Seaska. EHAS's primary competitor was the Herri Taldeak movement which grew out of the Comités Xan. HT came to position itself as a kind of front organization of Iparretarrak. EHAS greatly resented this effort to co-opt Seaska, all the more so since its co-founder, Manex Goyhenetche, was also secretary general of Seaska at the same time. The other faction was led by Xan Coscarat, who worked for Seaska and represented the HT camp. Both Goyhenetche and Seaska's president, Jean-Pierre Seiliez, denounced the HT/ IK campaign at the meeting of Seaska's *comité directeur* before its upcoming General Assembly in early 1981. According to participants, Goyhenetche was particularly incensed that Seaska had recently printed an open Iparretarrak tract on the cultural policy of Seaska. Moreover, he is said to have charged that labels for Iparretarrak's publication, *ILDO*, were being printed from the mailing list of Seaska's newsletter. Seiliez and Goyhenetche were both denounced by the hard-line camp as a result.

In a set of confrontations which remain cloaked in mystery to this day, it is widely understood that both Jean-Pierre Seiliez and Manex Goyhenetche were threatened by armed and masked Iparretarrak militants. Seiliez's attack came first, when he was confronted by a masked and armed Philippe Bidart. As we will see in the next chapter, Bidart was the presumed leader of Iparretarrak by this point and soon the author of its greatest acts of violence. Both Seiliez and Goyhenetche had to have known who he was, if for no other reason than that Bidart had been active in the Ikastola movement as head of its school at Blancpignon in Anglet for three years during the late 1970s while Seiliez was president and Goyhenetche was secretary general of Seaska. Moreover, along with Coscarat, Bidart had been a major force in the effort of the Herri Taldeak group (as a thinly disguised front for Iparretarrak) to take over or, as one militant called it, to tender "a public purchase offer" for the Ikastola movement.

According to informed sources, Seiliez was physically hurt in the resulting confrontation. Some days later Goyhenetche returned home to find a hooded and armed figure waiting for him in his garage. Here again, the universal opinion within Basque circles is that it was Philippe Bidart. Aware of Seiliez's injuries, Goyhenetche attempted to flee by jumping over a nearby wall, breaking his foot in the process.

Neither has ever said publicly what transpired that night. But it appears clear that in an act of parsimonious revolutionary expropriation Bidart made each man an offer that he could not refuse. That choice was apparently between his life or abandoning the field of battle to Iparretarrak alone. Seiliez resigned as president of Seaska at its General Assembly, which took place soon thereafter. The muting of Seiliez and Goyhenetche gave Iparretarrak's theses free rein in Seaska. In contrast to the earlier strategy of dialogue ·

with the French state regarding the integration of Basque-language instruction into the French Ministry of Education and the regularizing of the contracts of its teachers, Iparretarrak's strategy involved "rupture" with the state and with the previous moderate strategy. With Seiliez's departure, many of Goyhenetche's generation swung over to the theses which Coscarat had championed for HT/IK. This sea change in Seaska led to a hardening of its bargaining position with the state. The French government, for its part, was if anything even more reluctant than before to grant concessions to a seemingly "innocuous" cultural group which it saw increasingly as a major source of sympathizers for Iparretarrak's violence.

The End of EHAS

Iparretarrak's physical intimidation of Goyhenetche had the desired effect on EHAS. Within a matter of weeks, the eighty-first and last issue of *Euskaldunak* appeared, announcing the end of EHAS as a movement:

> This Tuesday, May 5, 1981, we have decided to stop the activities of E.H.A.S. and the publication of *Euskaldunak*. The date was chosen not as a function of the politics of the French state with the possible accession of the left to power, but as a function of the evolution of the *abertzale* world in the Pays Basque Nord.[194]

When HAS was created in March 1974 Iparretarrak had already committed its first act of violence in Baigorri. Throughout its existence, other groups would rise up in violence and then disappear, many into Iparretarrak. EHAS maintained to the very end its principled opposition to the armed struggle despite growing criticism within the radical camp. EHAS's path was not an easy one:

> But we were obliged to navigate against the current within the Basque movement. Today . . . many of our analyses and our ideas are accepted and taken up [by others]. But for them to blossom and become concrete required without a doubt the death of the father or the big brother. Why do the Basques escape the laws of psychoanalysis? And the *abertzale* militants who will rejoice at the disappearance of EHAS and *Euskaldunak* will only serve to confirm that the *abertzale* milieu often reacts as a function of psychoanalytical behaviors. . . . EHAS constituted a target against which converged shots from *Enbata* to Jazar, Herriaren Alde, *Pindar*, Ezker Berri, without speaking of the Comités Xan then Herri

Taldeak. In effect, the *abertzale* movement has turned on itself . . . it will be psychologically easier for many to join a new organization that they'll create themselves than to come to EHAS.[195]

With these words, EHAS was no more.

Chapter Six

Radicalization and the Rise of

Basque Violence in France: Iparretarrak, or

"Those of ETA of the North"

For they have sown the wind, and they shall reap the whirlwind.
Hosea 8:7

Today violence is the rhetoric of the period.
José Ortega y Gasset, *The Revolt of the Masses*

All modern revolutions have ended in a reinforcement of the power of the state.
Albert Camus, *The Rebel*

The considerable ideological flux which characterized France and the Pays Basque in the aftermath of 1968 led to an ideological crossroads for the French Basque movement. One path, that of EHAS, sought to move beyond *Enbata*'s Christian democratic nationalism and build the basis of a radical Basque Socialist Party. While EHAS espoused the language of Marxist revolution, it nonetheless rejected the use of violence as a tool of Basque nationalism in France. At the same time, in the early 1970s, a second tendency began to manifest itself among Basque youth—a generation which, like their Spanish Basque brethren, readily defended the use of political violence.

Their decision to embrace violence at that time emerged from a number of factors surrounding the French Basque movement itself and the historical context. These "demonstrator influences" helped frame the ideological universe of ethnic movements in France in the 1960s and 1970s. Among the influences which led to the emergence of French Basque violence, four were especially important. First, the Spanish Basque movement writ large remained the prime political inspiration for French Basque nationalists, as it had been since the Spanish Civil War. With the emergence of ETA in the 1960s, its violence exercised an undeniable attraction for many French

Basque youth who had grown impatient with their fathers' political hesitancy. The most politically mobilized of French Basque youth in the early 1970s were molded in the crucible of the hunger strikes in the cathedral and churches of Bayonne and strongly influenced by the swelling ETA refugee community. On a doctrinal level, the ideological splintering of ETA along lines of nationalism and class struggle (ETA-V vs. ETA-VI) had ripple effects across the French border as well. What would not become clear until much later was that, while ETA's violence influenced the appearance of violence in France, it also led to the recruitment of a number of French Basques into ETA itself, including the most deadly of ETA's itinerant commandos, that of Henri Parot (see chapter 7).

The second set of ideological influences on the growth of Basque violence in France flowed out of the trauma of decolonization. As the tides retreated from the height of France's colonial empire, one of the greatest victims was, in Charles de Gaulle's felicitous phrase, the historic "certain idea" of France and its indivisibility. The cumulative impact of Dien Bien Phu and the loss of Indochina, Tunisia, and the Algerian conflict ruined political careers and led to the collapse of the Fourth Republic. De Gaulle's about-face on Algerian independence profoundly marked the politics of the early Fifth Republic, overshadowing the steady independence of most of France's subsaharan African colonies. France's colonial grandeur in the 1960s was sorely tarnished, and with it the invincible image of the French state. Robert Lafont and François Fontan's several works on internal colonialism brought the language and imagery of colonial struggle back home and nurtured a new generation of ethnic youth in the heady hopes of independence and, at the extreme, struggles of national liberation. This influence was particularly strong among movements in the Pays Basque, Brittany, and Corsica.

Third, the events of May–June 1968 discredited much of the formal French political establishment, from Gaullism to a hesitant and bureaucratic French Communist Party. This latest generation to emerge from the barricades was profoundly influenced by the intellectual Maoism sweeping French intellectual circles at this time, coincident with the height of the Chinese Cultural Revolution itself. Prime among Mao's influences were his writings on guerrilla war.

Finally, the generation of young Basques who became politicized in the aftermath of 1968 showed a marked impatience and anger toward the older generations of Basque nationalists in France. *Enbata*'s successive electoral failures and its more bourgeois demeanor failed to recruit a new generation of youth necessary to give the movement vitality. At the same time, the rigidity of EHAS's militancy seemed out of step with the lessons of 1968 and the desire for a new form of militancy.

For these reasons, among others, the rise of Basque violence in France in the 1970s was a natural, if by no means inevitable, product of the historical context in which the Basque movement found itself. The decision to resort to violence, however, was not a complete break with the past. In many ways it borrowed and extended language and values which had been a familiar part of French Basque militancy for more than a decade. The terrorist groups which arose in the 1970s rejected the hesitancy of their predecessors' practice, and, following ETA, grafted a commitment to "armed struggle" onto the socialism much in vogue in this period. Yet, as we saw in chapters 4 and 5, socialism was even more suspect than nationalism among the rural Basque electorate. With the rise of the armed struggle, the appearance of indigenous Basque violence in France polarized the Basque community there as had no other issue, and its continued use defines the tormented path of Basque nationalism in France.

In this chapter I will examine the growth of several indigenous terrorist movements in France, the greatest of which was Iparretarrak (Those of ETA of the North). Second, I will chart the intellectual sources of the armed struggle and how these movements justified their use of violence within the Basque community, examining the nature of the violence itself and demonstrating how the choice of targets reveals the progression of the movements' ideology over time. Third, I will describe the rise of other legal movements which were created to serve as the public face or front for banned movements, like the Herri Taldeak movement which grew out of the Comités Xan in the early 1980s. Finally, I will discuss the spiraling vortex of Iparretarrak's violence, which estranged it even from ETA and gave rise to a series of moderate Basque movements which sought to reoccupy the legitimate Basque center in the 1980s and undercut the radical camp.

The Rise of Iparretarrak: Those of ETA of the North

Atzerri, otserri.
A foreign land is a land of wolves.
Basque proverb

By the beginning of the 1970s for all practical purposes the only real foyers of Basque militancy in France were *Enbata* and Amaia. *Enbata* had lived the crisis of its electoral defeats and subsequent internal disarray. Despite its effort to regroup, it was losing militants, stagnating ideologically, and was still two years from its "conversion" to socialism. Amaia was riven with the

internal conflicts over leadership style and purpose that would soon lead to
its fragmentation and the rise of Mende Berri.

A major part of *Enbata*'s difficulty in this period was its inability to appeal
to younger Basque militants. In addition to this generational gap, *Enbata* also
fell victim to the patricidal tradition within the Basque movement, which
either rejected the political contribution of earlier movements or sought to
bury them with invective and passionate criticism. Viewed from the slowly
developing radical perspective in the early 1970s, from which violence would
soon emerge, *Enbata* was stigmatized and ultimately rejected as "chauvin-
istic, pacifist, legalistic, and petit bourgeois."[1] Within this swirling state of
flux, the hunger strikes which took place in 1970 in defense of the ETA refugees represented a focus for a still inchoate sense of *abertzale* activity and
a chance for these Basque youth to prove their commitment to the idea of
Basque nationalism. Through these strikes, as we have seen, yet another
generation of young French Basques were exposed to the Spanish Basque
guerrilleros of ETA.

The French government was intensely concerned with the spillover of
ETA's militancy into France, and its repression and later dissolution of *Enbata*
was an effort to truncate the growth of Basque nationalism and isolate the
nationalist fringe from the political mainstream. It was in this spirit that the
government banned any celebration of the Aberri Eguna in France during
both 1971 and 1972. Yet, in a self-inflicted Hobbesian choice, the outlawing
of the Basque national day celebration forced the government either to back
up its decree with the provocative use of force or to stand by and watch a
scantly observed holiday become a rousing celebration of defiance against
the state. In this way, the repressive measures of the French state often
served to popularize the Basque cause and thus became the grounds for new
efforts at Basque political mobilization.

Despite its relative lack of competition, Enbata was not in a position to
take advantage of this rise in consciousness, despite its best efforts. Looking
back, Iparretarrak would write:

> The petit bourgeois nationalism of *Enbata* is more and more contested by
> a new tendency, still poorly defined, somewhat tributary to the events
> of May 1968. This dispute aiming to take even more radical positions
> would see the light of day at the time of the Aberri Eguna of Mauléon
> in 1972.[2]

By the summer of 1973 accelerating government repression of *Enbata,* in the
form of trials and fines for its leaders, led to a crossroads. When *Enbata* called
a public meeting attended by two hundred people in July in order to ask its

supporters how to proceed, several voices were clear in arguing that the time had come for the movement to pass into clandestinity. While it remained a distinctly minority position, even within *Enbata* the appeal of clandestinity and a hardened struggle was beginning to stir.

As we saw in chapter 4, some months earlier, in January, 1973, the first issue of *Koska* appeared within the Basque student community at the University of Bordeaux.[3] Growing out of the experience of both Amaia and Mende Berri, and nourished by the hunger strikes of 1970, *Koska*'s overt support of the armed struggle demonstrated the extent of ETA's influence on this next generation of French Basque youth. It was a sign of their willingness to graft ETA's theses—especially concerning the armed struggle—onto the Pays Basque Français. Many of the students surrounding *Koska* at Bordeaux were from the interior market town of Saint-Etienne-de-Baigorri in Basse-Navarre, whose socioeconomic and demographic decline mirrored that of the Basque interior as a whole. Between the years of 1968 and 1975 alone Baigorri lost 833 inhabitants or 12 percent of its population. With the decline of local industry and agriculture, the Valley of Baigorri risked being reduced to a picturesque "Indian reservation" for a summer influx of tourists. From their vantage point in Bordeaux, it must have been clear to these Basque students that most of them would never be able to live or find work in their villages again.

IPARRETARRAK'S FIRST OPERATION

In later 1973 the residents of Baigorri received a long tract in the mail which claimed responsibility for the recent break-in and theft of financial records from the Institut Medico-Pédagogique "La Rosée" in nearby Banca. Responsibility was claimed by a group called Iparretarrak (IK), heretofore unheard of in the Pays Basque Français.[4] Even the group's name was a matter of some controversy at the beginning, leading some, including a persistent *Le Monde*, to translate it as "Those of the North."[5] In fact, Ipartarrak would mean Those of the North. But with the inclusion of the *e* in correct Basque grammar Iparretarrak could only mean Those of ETA of (Etarrak) the North (Ipar).[6]

From a reading of its early texts, it is apparent that IK was aware of the risk that its use of violence might well alienate the Basque population, thereby condemning itself to marginalization. IK stated its intention to adhere closely to the working class, to complement existing struggles:

> The struggles taking place legally in Euskadi North are, although absolutely necessary, limited by the very nature of the law, which is bourgeois and which go counter to the interest of the workers. This argument

made, it was decided to create a complementary link to the forms of already existing struggles, in order to aid in their radicalization and to break the pillory of bourgeois law.[7]

IK's operation against "La Rosée" was a Robin Hood exploit in which the movement entered into an existing dispute on the side of the working class against the forces of bourgeois capitalism. In the case of "La Rosée," the effort of local Basque workers to unionize were strongly opposed by the institute's administration, led by M. Toureng, one of the richest and most prominent men in Baigorri. The purpose of the break-in was to seize and publicize financial records which would discredit management's position and debunk its arguments against unionization. IK described M. Toureng and the stakes of the conflict in broad brushstrokes:

> You all know this rich Monsieur . . . who wants to earn even more by any means on the back of the people. . . . This Monsieur isn't just anybody. Because of his money, he's one of the biggest personalities, one of the bourgeois of the valley of Baigorri. . . . The whole Pays Basque Nord is under the domination of these rich, of these bourgeois. It is they who say that the Pays Basque is made for "tourism" and then the factories are less and less numerous. In order to live the young are obliged to move far away from [their] country. Our culture is under the control of money, a tourist trinket, used to pass the time. . . . Our country is in the process of dying and will die. In several years our land will be the paradise of the retired, the sick, and foreigners. . . . If we want to have our rights, if we want our liberty, we only have one path: STRUGGLE. Henceforth, we will not be quiet, we will not stop, we will not have peace until these bourgeois and their friends are chased from the Pays Basque.[8]

Following the action against "La Rosée" IK returned underground and was not heard from for more than a year, until October 1974, with the appearance of the first issue of *ILDO* (Furrow), its periodical for public distribution. IK also began publishing an internal newsletter for its militants called *Erne* (Vigilant).[9]

In this first issue of *ILDO*, IK defined itself as "a Basque revolutionary Socialist organization of national liberation."[10] IK's political line was a radical expression of doctrinaire socialism and asserted its desire "to overturn capitalism and to destroy all social relations inherited from bourgeois society and to install socialism."[11] In October 1974 IK represented a dogmatic version of socialism, inherited for the most part from ETA. Its socialism was even more hard-line than that of EHAS, which had just appeared the previous March following *Enbata*'s dissolution in January, but its theoretical foundation was still superficial. The one crucial difference between IK and EHAS was the fact that IK justified its adoption of the armed struggle—the use of violence as a tool of Basque politics in France—from its very beginning.

The Justification for Violence

The question of violence concerns its efficacy as much as its ethics. There is no more one point of view on violence than there is a solution to the problem of just and unjust wars. Isn't every act of creation, of birth, necessarily an act of violence— symbolic, philosophic, real—against the society which precedes it?
Anonymous Basque militant, 1987

You search for bombs, but you won't find them, because they're in my mind.
Anonymous Basque militant, 1987

The use of violence was central to IK's self-definition as a movement and set it apart from every movement which preceded it. IK's use of violence flowed clearly from the classic Marxist understanding of violence as a progressive tool when tied to the legitimate struggle of the working class against capitalism. IK's main-line Socialist analysis of modern capitalism led to two observations:

1. The bourgeoisie will never accept seeing its interests and domination challenged.
2. The present legality serves as a screen for the daily violence which it exercises in order to exploit and oppress us.[12]

IK's defense of the use of violence therefore rested on two assertions that find historic grounding in the literature of Marxism as well as anarchism: that the nature of bourgeois society is itself a daily exercise in violence against the working class and that no bourgeoisie is going to give up its privileges without a fight:

One doesn't see by what magic spell the ruling class will effectively commit suicide in permitting a government to legislate which little by little will trim away all its powers in order to establish socialism. Reformism leads to an impasse. It is evident that the reversal of the bourgeois order will be violent or it won't happen.[13]

The use of the armed struggle thus becomes a necessary complement to working class organization in order to overthrow bourgeois capitalism and create a Basque Socialist system. This same insistence on the need to ground the use of violence in the concrete needs of the people was repeated four years later when IK's second issue of *ILDO* appeared in 1978:

> This violent activity is subordinated to the political struggle of the Basque people . . . violent action isn't the sole means of liberation, it is a necessary means. . . . The liberation will be accomplished by the Basque people, by its struggle. Violent action is the guarantor of the gains of this struggle. Our organization practices violent action. It doesn't intend to stop this activity but rather to develop it. But violent action alone cannot resolve the liberation of the Basque people. It needs popular political support. It will be the guarantor, the support, the prod, the detonator. It's in this sense that we count on acting, including by violent action, in support of a popular political struggle.[14]

For IK, the closer the violence was to the struggles of the people, the more it would be understood and supported. For that reason, IK insisted that its actions were chosen with care, in order to advance the people's cause:

> We do not choose our actions in just any way; they are always tied to a very precise problem of the northern Pays Basque and they have two goals: (1) Make the people aware of this precise problem. (2) Make the cause advance in helping in particular those who are struggling and in giving them more strength.[15]

IK's choice of violence was also based on its view of the institutional violence wreaked by the modern industrial state:

> Faced with institutionalized, legalized violence, we must react with all means, including revolutionary violence. We will not accept limiting our means of action to legal bourgeois paths alone. Our sole objective is popular power, our means of action the popular struggle, and the people know that at certain moments the struggle will be violent.[16]

In such a climate of ethnic violence IK insisted that the firm support of the working class was the best arm against the certain efforts of the state to isolate the movement: "we have already said that the system always seeks to isolate those who struggle against it."[17]

VIOLENCE AS A STRATEGY OF POPULAR MOBILIZATION

Ser da mira, ardiac otsoari ihes ari badira?
Is it surprising that the lamb should flee the wolf?
Basque proverb

Regardless of the dangers associated with the introduction of the armed struggle among this conservative Basque population, IK was willing to gamble that the Basque public would accept its violence more easily than it had the petit bourgeois militancy of Enbata:

> The reaction of the French proletariat and of working-class organizations in general to the (ex) movement *Enbata*, as well as the welcome which the Basque people itself gave it, is sufficient to demonstrate that the exploited classes don't intend to support movements of a petit bourgeois ideology, even when these latter claim to defend their interests. By contrast, the reaction of the workers to the demands of ETA and the reaction of the Basque people in particular demonstrate that just demands, which in their practice makes their truly revolutionary content apparent, are understood, if not supported, even when they are the work of a revolutionary Basque patriotic movement.[18]

Looking back from his later vantage point in the 1980s, a rural Basque priest described the attitude of his villagers toward IK this way:

> We aren't in agreement, the people here. Their analysis is false and we feel that they're going to cause harm. But we don't criticize them. If you have a child who does something stupid you don't reproach him for it. He's of the household. "Eh beh," it's the same thing with Iparretarrak. Even if we don't agree, they are part of the household here, they are at home.[19]

Ultimately, the use of violence was a deliberate strategy directed more at Basque youth than at older and more conservative generations. IK sought to use violence as an instrument of political socialization of Basque youth, on whom the future depended. As one militant put it:

> The real long-term question is to see the influence of Iparretarrak violence on the very young. Their logic, their "rationality," may be something completely different from that of their elders. The gamble is on the ability of violence today greatly to expand the national consciousness of the generations to come.

While this strategy was one thing in theory, in reality it involved declaring war on the French state and its symbols. This was a real and present danger. As one militant familiar with French counterinsurgency in Indochina and Algeria argued:

> Random and small acts of violence are one thing, like burning down an unpopular building in a village. But attacking the French state is quite

another thing, because the state has the means to defend itself. Even ETA in the South, in a far weaker state and with a far more intense use of violence, has been unsuccessful in forcing negotiations [with the Spanish government]. Here in the northern Pays Basque, in considering the use of violence, you have to consider that the population is against it, the state is clever, and the police force is strong.

THE ATTACK ON TOURISM AND UNEMPLOYMENT

Herriak bizi behar du.
The people must live.
IK slogan

A major target of IK's first verbal and physical attacks was the economic warfare waged on the Basque economy in the guise of tourism and the progressive decline of local industries, especially the shoe industry in interior towns like Hasparren, Louhossoa, or Mauléon.

IK's attack on tourism was an intensification of a theme which IK shared with virtually every movement to appear in the French Basque country since 1960. Situated where the Pyrénées mountains meet the Atlantic Ocean, the Pays Basque offers visitors a panorama of unsurpassed scenic beauty. Green foothills are punctuated by centuries-old white farmhouses with beamed façades and red tile roofs. Flocks of sheep graze by fast-moving trout streams. On Saturday mornings old Basque farmers and their wives gather on the bridges in Bayonne in the miasma of the Nive River in the gray predawn darkness to sell cheeses, produce, and live animals destined for the tables of Bayonne. In the summer the beaches are sunny and warm, and the village festivals offer diversions for natives and tourists alike. The problem is that tourism has become the most dynamic element of the Basque economy, meaning that the people experience a boom economy for two months a year, followed by ten months of unemployment. The cultural and demographic consequences of tourism are overwhelming: every summer the population of the Basque country *doubles* during the summer season, a Nantucket or Martha's Vineyard on a larger scale. In Biarritz, more than 40 percent of the residences are vacant nine or ten months a year. Farmers are unable to purchase land at auction in competition with "fruppies"[20] from Paris seeking vacation homes for the month of August. Particularly objectionable to the nationalist camp is that the local population has been led to package their culture as a photo opportunity: displays of woodchopping, dance, or the village pastorales are replete with Basques in the costumes of the Corsairs. For IK, tourism was a cultural and economic threat to the survival of Basque culture in France and thus a mortal enemy of the cause.

In attacking the tourist infrastructure of the Basque country, IK especially targeted the large real estate development and land speculation firms which were profiting from the spectacular rise in purchases of retirement or vacation homes by non-Basques who first discovered the beauty of the region during summer vacations. Even long-abandoned hay barns or *cayolars* were transformed into vacation *pieds à terre* and then lived in only one month a year. As IK explained its particular ire toward touristic speculation: "The development of tourism, we repeat, is the pure product of imperialism. We will treat it as such."[21]

A protest against tourism and the complicity of the local bourgeoisie figured, as we saw above, in IK's very first attack on "La Rosée" in 1973. IK then lay dormant for the next four years; not until 1977 would IK again claim responsibility for acts of violence. Its greatest acts of violence were yet to come. For that reason, as late as 1977 as sensitive an observer as Malherbe could make passing mention of "a reduced group which is entitled Iparretarrak."[22]

The first two attacks which ended this hiatus in 1977 were against exclusive real estate developments on the coast. In a press release, IK claimed responsibility for the attack by Molotov cocktail carried out on April 8, 1977, against the sales office of the "Hameau de Socoa" development in coastal Socoa.[23] It justified its attack in this way:

> The only solution which they pose for us is that of tourism, and this tourism mocks our true needs. We want to live in our country and to be able to live in one's country is a right. For that there must be a useful job for each and all. TOURISM ALONE WILL NOT GIVE IT. While one [sells] luxurious houses like "Le Hameau de Socoa" for those who have millions, our jobs for us are disappearing. . . . FACED WITH THAT, THE TOURISM THAT THEY IMPOSE ON US, RELYING ON OUR RAPACIOUS LOCAL NOTABLES, CAN BRING US NOTHING, EXCEPT TO MAKE US DIE.[24]

The second attack followed on June 1, 1977, with the firebombing of the offices of the modern Victoria-Surf apartment development in downtown Biarritz. Echoing the justifications of its attack in Socoa two months before, IK explained its choice of the Victoria-Surf as a target: "Because it is the detrimental consequence of an exclusively touristic and disastrous development imposed by the current power structure with the complicity of rapacious local notables."[25] To the now-familiar criticism of tourism was now added an ecological concern over these "concrete monsters" which were destroying the environment of the Basque coast. Finally, IK underscored its political opposition: "By this action, we manifest our disagreement with a politics which isn't solving any of our problems. The politics we need and want is very different."[26] These attacks were followed by others in the same vein, including the first of IK's declared "Blue Nights" of multiple attacks on March 12–13, 1978, followed by one the night of March 25–26, 1981, which targeted vacation homes, tourist and economic development offices, a ski cabin, and the Yacht Club at Ciboure.[27] For older Basque militants, many of these actions were less political statements than acts of vandalism. As Jean Haritschelhar wrote in a letter in *Sud-Ouest* protesting vandalism during a meeting of the Jeune Chambre Economique of Baigorri in June 1978:

> Why? Exaltation of anarchism with the Red Brigades as model, exal-
> tation of Euskadi at the same time? Does one have something to do
> with the other? Are we defending Euskadi by pillage? . . . The cultural
> militant that I am and will continue to be . . . employs for his combat
> other arms than those of the nocturnal vandals who only use the arms
> of cowardice.

At the same time, IK chose to protest the closing of the Ttikia shoe factory in Hasparren, a symbol of the process of economic decline and depopu-lation that constrains Basque youth to leave the Pays Basque for work. IK attributed this to the deliberate decision of factory owners: "Those who hold power (the rich, the bourgeois) have decided to empty the Pays Basque North of all its force and all its life in order for them to be able to use the open spaces . . . however they want." This Basque bourgeoisie became the avowed class enemies of IK and the legitimate target of their violence:

> If we want to keep the Pays Basque North alive, we must, ALL TOGETHER,
> cry ENOUGH!, and not only cry it, because as for TTIKIA, that isn't
> enough, but also to show it, by acts, even violent. That's the only lan-
> guage that they understand. It's they who first employed violence in
> obliging us by their corruption of money to leave our cities and our
> villages.[28]

Continuing the campaign against unemployment and underemployment, during 1981 IK began to target "temporary employment" agencies which placed employees in hotels and restaurants for the two-month tourist season each July and August.

THE CHOICE OF POLITICAL TARGETS

But the most important trend in IK's targeting was its move toward political targets, including the subprefecture in Bayonne, the car of the wife of the subprefect, and housing of the French Compagnie Républicaine de Sécurité (CRS) in Hendaye. The most important action of IK in this period was in fact aborted before it took place, with the arrest on December 23, 1977, of a young Basque named Jean-Claude Marguirault ("Xan") for using a stolen car to transport arms, Molotov cocktails, and gasoline destined for an IK attack. IK steadfastly insisted that Xan was only a sympathizer and not an actual member of the movement himself:

> J.-C. Marguirault was stopped by the police while he was carrying out an assignment that had been asked of him. He was not a member of Iparretarrak. He was a sympathizer with the struggle of the patriotic Basque left and it was in this capacity that he had accepted to serve as a liaison. We publicly declare that J.-C. Marguirault is a militant fallen in the service of the Basque cause. We ask that the whole of the patriotic Basque left, that the whole of the Basque people, support him and mobilize against the repression he's going to undergo.[29]

The government suspected Marguirault of involvement in recent IK attacks, including those on the La Feria cinema and temporary employment agencies in Bayonne.[30] His arrest finally appeared to give the movement an issue around which it might increase its public support.

The Rise of Herri Taldeak and the Comités Xan

Xan is neither a criminal nor a terrorist. . . . Xan is a brother in combat,
we are all Xans.
Iparretarrak[31]

The armed struggle is the best guarantee of the national struggle.
Herri Taldeak[32]

The arrest of Jean-Claude Marguirault or Xan became the issue around which previously unaffiliated militants could unite. Statements of support were made by existing Basque left movements, including EHAS, EZ, Herriaren Alde, and others, as well as the PSU, even while denouncing the rise in political violence.[33] A mass demonstration in support of Xan was cleverly set for May 1, 1978, in order to benefit from the traditional leftist labor rallies which occur on that day. Approximately 800 people demonstrated for Xan, and a petition calling for his release was signed by 3,500 people.[34] When Xan was eventually released from detention on August 23, 1978, IK attributed his freedom to the level of popular support manifested on his behalf.[35]

Given the intensity and breadth of support for his cause, it seems as if his plight was the pretext for a popular mobilization waiting to happen. What was unusual about this wave of mobilization was that multiple support committees grew up at the local level, even in the interior. They constituted a loose-knit coalition of groups which grafted support of Xan onto other grievances of a purely local nature. Collectively they became known as the Comités Xan. What is all the more significant about their appearance is that the energy they channeled did not disappear after Xan's release. The nature of their early coordination was free-form or situational in nature, and it took more than two years before the energy which these decentralized committees represented coalesced in an organizational focus.

As we saw in chapter 5, in November 1978 the Comités Xan organized a day of discussion at Hasparren in order to assess the future direction of Basque militancy. This was a meeting to which *Euskaldunak* was invited, but not EHAS, on the pretense that political parties were not included. That meeting determined that the energy subsumed in the Comités Xan had not dissipated and was searching for an appropriate expression. The search for an institutional focus led to the creation of the idea of a Herri Talde (Village Group) in 1980. The agency for the coordination of these local movements became Herri Taldeak (the plural of Herri Talde), meaning a collection of village groups. The idea for the Herri Taldeak did not spring from thin air. IK had called for just such a movement in the second issue of *ILDO*, which appeared in the summer of 1978, several months after Xan's arrest. At that time IK called for the creation of "groups of local struggle" as a means of advancing the process of consciousness-raising at the grassroots.[36] The mass meeting called at Hasparren in November 1978 to set that process in motion was the fruit of IK's plan.

THE COMPOSITION OF HERRI TALDEAK

Herri Taldeak coalesced from a number of different sources. The first of these were the seven village committees which grew up in support of Xan, the Herri Taldes of Biarritz, Saint-Pierre-d'Irube, Saint-Jean-de-Luz, Baigorri, Saint-Palais, Garazi, and a final grouping of Espelette-Itxassou-Cambo.[37] As HT described these local groups in its own early history, "The Herri Taldes don't have a single history because each Herri Talde started in a different fashion."[38] The earliest of the village committees was not surprisingly the Baigorriko Taldea in Baigorri, which was the center of Iparretarrak's early development and the site of its first action. While at least one source erroneously traced the union of the seven village groups to Baigorri in 1974,[39] there was at the very least a halo effect spreading outward from there through the force of IK's tracts and actions. IK represented something new: the novelty of the armed struggle combined with the appeal of the *guerrillero* as Robin Hood. Born in Baigorri, IK then created HT as a means of recruitment. By conceiving the idea of "militancy" as progressive layers of commitment, HT could serve as an intake group from which the most suitable recruits could be invited to pass into the inner sanctum of armed struggle.

The second component of Herri Taldeak were the previously mobilized militants and groups which encompassed their activity in Herri Taldeak between 1978 and 1980. Among these groups were Jazar, Herriaren Alde, and Miarritzeko Abertzale Taldea (MAT).[40] These groups contained only a handful of militants each, and the creation of HT was more fortuitous for them than simply withering away. Jazar is said to have joined Baigorriko Taldea as the first component of the future Herri Taldeak.

The first phase of HT's growth culminated at the first general assembly of the Herri Taldes at Saint-Jean-le-Vieux in 1980. It was decided to create a coordinating structure between the local committees. This Herri Taldeak, or coordinating body of the village committees, defined itself at its general assembly in 1980:

> Herri Taldeak is the name which is given the organization which regroups the whole of the Herri Talde. A Herri Talde is an organization of struggle which has the will to gather together the militants of a geographic sector desiring to participate in Basque Socialist struggles and causes such as culture, tourism, employment, land-ownership, repression, nuclear.[41]

Not surprisingly, the membership in HT at the beginning was as fluid as its as yet imprecise ideological goals. Militants came and went for personal reasons. Some gravitated to Laguntza (see below) which also flirted with violence before 1981. The problems in organizing a clear path in this first period were due, according to one HT militant, to the diversity of people and causes involved.

The second phase of HT's development occurred around its second general assembly on May 24, 1981, and involved the politicization of the movement. By the second general assembly, the ideological line of HT had grown explicitly closer to that of IK:

> Herri Taldeak is a Basque Socialist Organization of the left which, in the political, social, and cultural struggles in Euskadi North, agitates for the national and social liberation of the Basque People, in order to arrive at a Socialist and reunited Euskadi. Our combat for the Basque People is inseparable from our combat for socialism. Our combat for socialism is inseparable from our combat for the Basque People.[42]

By HT's own admission, this phase of politicization was marked by a clearer statement of support for the armed struggle which emerged from the 1981 general assembly. This direction led to the departure of militants who were uncomfortable with the direction HT was headed.[43] Some of these militants would later join ELB.

Following the 1981 general assembly, *Samatsa,* HT's internal newsletter for its militants, reported that HT had created eleven local sections: Amikuze, Baigorri, Bayonne, Donibane Lohitzun (Saint-Jean-de-Luz), Garazi (Saint-Jean-Pied-de-Port), Hiriburu, Zubero (Soule), Uztaritze (Ustaritz), Kanbo (Cambo-les-Bains), Miarritze (Biarritz), and Hendaye.[44] Only Hendaye was absent from the meeting.

On January 27, 1982, HT held its first public press conference and further clarified its structure and goals:[45]

> The militants who created HT never had the will to create a party. We define ourselves as being more like a movement, an assembly, with a will to react against the traditional definition of parties: centralized organization, precise doctrine . . . HT isn't structured . . . the local work must define the sense of HT, its politics. . . . It's this practice, and the development of struggles on the local level, which defines HT.[46]

In contrast to the electoral strategies of both *Enbata* and EHAS before it, HT kept its distance from the French electoral system, arguing that "any participation in these elections will be a vote of support given to this system."[47] Given the choice of electing a leftist president or abstaining on principle from a political spectrum unlikely to view Basque issues with sympathy, HT made clear its preference for abstention. By early March of 1982 the upcoming cantonal elections gave HT the opportunity to assess the conduct of the French left after a year in power. What it saw was a Socialist government which had reneged on its promises of a separate Basque department and whose socioeconomic policies had failed to implement a clearer break with the capitalism of the previous rightist government. Once again HT recommended that its supporters abstain from voting.[48]

HERRI TALDEAK AND THE QUESTION OF THE ARMED STRUGGLE

The first news conference held by HT in January 1982 revealed no trace of the internal split over support of the armed struggle which had occurred at the second general assembly several months before. When asked by a journalist about the attitude of HT toward armed clandestine groups, HT responded by claiming:

> There is no official position, but we can give an indication of the dominant opinion. HT is a political movement having defined its objectives . . . whereas other organizations having the same objectives as us

have chosen the armed struggle as a means of action. It is not for us to judge the opportuneness of these means of action and of the use of the armed struggle. We have chosen to carry out our combat on a political terrain with other means but with common motivations . . . we will support . . . the Basque militants who will be victims of repression. These armed organizations are a reality.[49]

By 1985 its attitude toward the armed struggle had somewhat hardened; it claimed that the struggle for the creation of socialism is an absolute necessity for the survival of the Basque people and that "the armed struggle is an integral part of this struggle. In this sense, Herri Taldeak refuses to condemn an organization whose practices subscribe to this struggle."[50]

By the time the mass meeting called Ipar Euskadi Gaur was held in 1985, bringing together Basque militants across the political spectrum for a dialogue on the future direction of the Basque movement in France, HT's publicly supported theses on violence were virtually indistinguishable from those of IK. Xan Coscarat was the spokesman for HT at the meeting;[51] he was quoted by more than one participant as having said openly, "The armed struggle is the best guarantee of the national struggle." Later in the debate these same participants insisted that Coscarat asserted, "Every struggle for national liberation needs violence," to which Jacques Abeberry rejoined, "But here . . . and now?" *Herriz Herri* described the differences of opinion on the correctness of the armed struggle as "profound."[52] HT's position follows closely that taken by IK in *ILDO* in 1979:

> Violence alone can't make much of anything advance, but revolutionary violence is necessary in order to make struggles succeed. Without revolutionary violence, struggles stop quickly and are co-opted by reformists. Struggles will succeed thanks to revolutionary violence. We practice revolutionary violence in order to arouse, to support, and to make succeed the struggles of the workers and of the Basque people.[53]

HERRI TALDEAK'S MILITANTS

HT claimed around one hundred militants at the beginning. As public opinion clamored over the arrest of Xan, two or three times that number were at least episodically mobilized. A better indicator of strength of commitment was the fact that the two general assemblies of 1980 and 1981 were attended by approximately one hundred militants and that by 1983 *Samatsa*, its internal newsletter for militants, had a press run of one hundred copies.

The problem with HT, according to one militant, is that it was not always clear who was in and who wasn't. Without early membership rolls, and with open invitations to rallies and demonstrations, the early membership in HT was informal and in a constant state of flux. Second, HT demanded a less faithful or time-consuming militancy than did a self-conscious political party. This was clearly a lesson learned from the more rigidly structured EHAS and had been the source of many of its internal conflicts, as well as the reason why potential younger militants were turned off from joining EHAS in the first place. The deliberate result of this strategy is that HT became what one older Basque militant called "a movement of the very young." According to one former HT militant, by setting the membership barrier low enough, HT could keep the interest of quasi-politicized young Basques who saw the Basque movement as a festive thing. "Doing the festivals"—the annual round of nearly week-long village celebrations which occurred one after the other in summer months in the rural interior—was a highlight of the social life of young Basques. For much of this century these festivals have also served as matchmakers, as the vehicle for youths from isolated farms or small villages to meet future spouses. In this value system, Basque rallies or demonstrations were politicized quasi-*fêtes*, but still anticipated events in the absence of anything better. By deemphasizing rigor and loyalty, HT had a better chance of keeping the interest of these youths, in the hopes of further socialization. For those whose attention was captured by HT, their politicization came quickly. According to one close observer, "Given their lack of experience in political culture, it was startling to see how fast they moved to the defense of radical solutions, that is, the choice of violence as the only solution." Many of these young militants were products of social and economic classes which, if not in decline, confronted precarious futures.

HT's LEADERS

An important element in the analysis of HT and its thought is the nature of its leaders and where they came from. The most visible of HT's leaders and those who were responsible for its doctrine and organization were Xan Coscarat, Eñaut Haritschelhar, and Michel Bergougnian.

Xan Coscarat flowed along the familiar stream of militancy described in chapters 4 and 5. As a young seminarian in the late 1960s, he joined Amaia in the aftermath of 1968 and became one of its central members, honing the craft of his militancy in its structure of hierarchy and secrecy. With the internal schism of Amaia, Coscarat followed Oyharçabal and Haritschelhar to Mende Berri. By the mid-1970s Coscarat had found a paying position within Seaska during the time when it was locked in a bitter conflict with the French government for official recognition and funding. With the formation of HT, Coscarat became Manex Goyhenetche's antagonist within Seaska, which he fought to radicalize and bring under HT/IK's control. As we saw at the end of chapter 5, the rise of HT/IK's influence within Seaska was characterized by an intransigent position vis-à-vis the government and the increasing radicalization of the movement. The government came to see Seaska as an emanation of both the ETA refugee community and HT/IK and so was reluctant to make concessions to Seaska for fear of entering into an accelerating spiral of nonnegotiable demands. For moderates within Seaska, the fate of Basque language instruction hung in the balance. As one of them put it, "It is the ruination." Coscarat was a leader of this hard-line faction in Seaska after 1981.

Eñaut Haritschelhar was the son of Jean Haritschelhar, holder of the chair in Basque at the University of Bordeaux, director of the Musée Basque, president of the Basque Academy, and elected mayor on an insurgent opposition list in Baigorri in 1982. Eñaut Haritschelhar grew up in one of the most intellectually nationalistic of Basque households in the village of Baigorri at a time when its conservative unity was fragmented under the pressure of economic and demographic decline in the 1960s. He was part of the generation of the 1960s mobilized by the events of 1968 and first militated within Amaia. Following Oyharçabal to Mende Berri, Haritschelhar was a central figure in its recruitment of high school youth. He was one of the "political wing" of Mende Berri who were dissatisfied with its cultural focus and looked for other alternatives. As we saw in chapter 4, he was one of the first four hunger strikers who occupied the main cathedral of Bayonne in 1970 in defense of ETA refugees. Moving to Bordeaux for university studies, he was the editor of the journal *Koska* which had defended the armed struggle as early as 1973. He was later active in both Euskal Gogoa and Herriaren Alde, as well as the original Baigorriko Taldea which lay at the origins of the eventual Herri Taldeak movement. Haritschelhar graduated from Bordeaux and returned to teach in a Lycée Agricole in rural Basse-Navarre not far from Baigorri.

The third recognized leader of HT from its beginnings was Michel Bergougnian, a farmer from Baigorri whose 100-hectare holding was larger by an order of magnitude than most Basque farms in the interior. Bergougnian had also been a member of Amaia. He represented the politicization of rural Basque agriculture and the cohort of young modern farmers who sought to reverse the decline of the agricultural Basque economy. HT then attracted elements of a generation of young farmers whose first exposure to political and economic reflection had come from the Catholic Mouvement Rural de Jeunesse Chrétienne (MRJC) during the 1960s.

THE SCHISM OVER VIOLENCE

HT's ideology was weak and derivative, reflecting the influence of multiple influences: IK and ETA's link between socialism and armed struggle; a critique of tourism which it shared with *Enbata* and EHAS before it; and even the sloganeering of the Occitan movement: *Volem viure al païs* (We want to live on our land). From sources which stretch across the Basque political spectrum, not all of whom were hostile to HT and its goals, there emerges a picture of HT as a movement in the full and optimistic blush of youth. Its ideology often seemed a very simplified and impoverished Maoism, with schematic slogans and an impatient, adolescent willingness to adopt a utopian line without reflecting on its implications. The widespread criticism of HT from across the *abertzale* spectrum was that it was an adolescent movement with adolescent analyses.

With the killing of two French CRS in Baigorri in 1982, the issue of IK's violence left the realm of the hypothetical and became a real issue which fragmented HT internally. Many of its moderate voices left after 1982, which meant ironically that those who remained were often more vocal in their support of IK than before. There was a growing government perception that the inner core of HT were in fact members of IK, whose relationship to simple militants was like that of the Albigensian (or Cathar) *parfaits* to the uninitiated. According to these ex-militants, this inner core of IK militants within HT had created HT and were manipulating the idealism and naïveté of the HT converts for their own agenda. This attitude slowly began to estrange the movement from the reality of village people as well. As one priest of a rural village put it:

> The other thing is that they don't want to have a dialogue with the people. Without finding out the feelings of the rural Basques, they've embarked on this cycle of violence. Who does it benefit? Themselves. As I told one Herri Talde recently, when they have rallies, why is it always him who speaks? Why? Well, because it gives his ego pleasure. And the others, why won't he let them speak? His militancy only benefits him. Well, it's like that with their violence. It is very poorly supported by the people in my village, very poorly.

By this time many of those active in IK had withdrawn from other forms of Basque militancy and, behind the scenes, functioned as puppet masters of the open movement, serving, in the words of one former HT-militant, as "these illustrious unknowns."

In the aftermath of IK's killing of the CRS in Baigorri in 1982, the fall-out for HT was real. Some close observers estimate that, as the extent of IK's control over HT became clear, the number of HT militants who left the group in disillusionment ranged from one-half to two-thirds. For one of these ex-militants:

Herri Taldeak missed its historical opportunity. It had a free terrain after the fall of EHAS. HT's willingness to participate in the political process was openly appreciated. But the decline of HT began when they began to openly defend IK. They blew their own future. It's lost.

With the aggravation of the armed struggle, and with the growing willingness of the government and Basque public to equate HT with IK, former militants report that a paranoid climate of suspicion and denunciation began to develop within HT's meetings. One ex-militant remembered not being able to express free thoughts. Another explained the reason for his departure from the movement:

> Gradually, however, I began to notice a strange thing in their meetings: fewer and fewer of the people that I knew were speaking. And when I asked why not, they responded by saying that there were those within the movement who were taking down what they said, especially any criticisms, and would use them one day against them, whether by a visit by a masked group brandishing pistols or otherwise.

He concluded this visit by saying, "It's better that you not use my name or things could happen to me. It's better if you deny you ever saw me." This climate of threat and suspicion indicated the degree to which HT was being slowly subsumed by IK and its style.

THE CONNECTION BETWEEN HERRI TALDEAK AND IPARRETARRAK

One of the greatest truisms in the study of the Basque movement in France was a belief which stretched across the political landscape—shared by officials of the Police Judiciare and the gendarmerie, the local and national press, and Basque militants across the political spectrum—that the leaders of Herri Taldeak and Iparretarrak were one and the same.

Within four days of the killing of the CRS in Baigorri in 1982, the government sought to round up "the usual suspects"; ten of HT's militants, mostly from Baigorri, were questioned by French police. It was clear that the government's suspicions were based on extensive surveillance of the movement. HT denounced the government's attitude: "Here again the will is clear: to facilitate the amalgamation between IPARRETARRAK and HERRI TALDEAK."[54]

It was the militancy of Xan Coscarat during the 1980s which gave added force to what were initially unconfirmed suspicions of the tie between HT and IK. In March 1982, in the aftermath of the attack in Baigorri which killed two members of the French CRS, Coscarat was detained following a search of the offices of Seaska. He was suspected of having aided Philippe Bidart in that attack, as we will see below. Then, on January 10, 1984, four militants of Herri Taldeak were arrested while transporting seven journalists in the back of a moving van to a clandestine press conference with members of IK.[55] The four militants arrested were Xan Coscarat, Betti Bidart (brother of Philippé Bidart, presumed killer of the CRS in Baigorri in 1982, and in hiding since 1981), Manex Borda, and Alain Mateo.[56]

Initial police euphoria at their arrest gave way to regret that the actual IK members giving the press conference had not also been arrested, since it was felt that they were the likely authors of IK's recent killing at Léon, in Les Landes. Herri Taldeak held a press conference on Friday, January 13, to discuss the arrest of its four militants. The five spokespersons included Michel Bergougnian.

When a journalist raised the natural connection that would be made in public opinion between HT and IK, HT's response was (1) it has not been proven yet that they were members of IK; and (2) "We are not inquisitors [able] to know the degree of engagement of each one of us." [57]

The four were kept in custody pending the state's verdict. Their imprisonment led to the creation of a Commission Anti-Répression Herri Taldeak and demonstrations until the court issued its finding in June.[58] It was not until the following January, a year after their arrest, that the appellate court in Pau issued its finding of guilt:

> The organization of a press conference by a movement which only commits and claims credit for crimes in order to reinforce the credibility of its own political discourse is not a harmless act.[59]

The four were then sentenced to two-year suspended sentences and five years of probation for association with criminals.

Coscarat came to trial again in January 1990, charged with a series of crimes including membership in IK, association with criminals, and tax evasion. Extraordinary evidence was presented in open court detailing the degree of French police surveillance of Coscarat (by both the Police Judiciare and the gendarmerie) dating as far back as his time as a seminarian in 1969. The circumstantial evidence contained in these chronological surveillance reports greatly helped to explain the government's suspicion of Coscarat as a leader of IK. However, the greatest revelation of the data produced in court was the sheer extent of government surveillance of the Basque movement since the 1960s. Some of the notations are innocuous ("1978: found himself at a meeting in Hasparren"), but others confirmed the government's suspicions of guilt by association. Among them were statements that Coscarat had founded the journal *Oiharzuna* with "Filipe" Bidart in 1978, that since 1978 he had been at the origin of such activities as the Herri Talde, Seaska,

Estalgi, Mintza, Ateka, Ekaintza, EMA, and Ahaideak; that he crossed the French-Spanish border at Biriatou with "Filipe" Bidart in 1981; and so forth.[60] The report of the gendarmerie's Commandant Barthes detailed a range of activities beginning in 1980, ranging from his association with IK militants and the dates and his companions when his car was stopped for I.D. checks to his sexual partners. The report included mention of police surveillance of Coscarat's multiple visits to what the report discreetly calls "Mademoiselle . . ." in Bordeaux during 1985. Commandant Barthes's report concludes by listing the organizations whose meetings Coscarat attended and the number of each, including Seaska (ten) and Herri Talde (twelve), as well as nine demonstrations and ten judicial actions.[61] The sheer degree of detail in these reports revealed the long-standing government surveillance of the Basque movement and raised the clear possibility of undercover infiltration of the groups involved, as we will see below. The only surveillance evidence not presented openly at the trial was telephone wiretaps, which were an extensive element of the government's strategy to surround the movement.

The report of Commissaire Pasotti of the Police Judiciare left no uncertainty about the government's view of Coscarat's importance to IK. Following the arrest of Lucienne Fourcade and Philippe Bidart in 1988, Pasotti alleged that IK's attacks had become more amateurish, with some devices failing to explode due to a lack of technical expertise. But, according to Pasotti:

> By contrast, the intellectual who wrote the texts of demands remained active since the same style was maintained and an identical typeface was observed on the letters examined. After the incarceration of Coscarat, the Pays Basque knew several months without violence. . . . After the middle of the month of June 1989, attacks were committed with totally new means. The demands . . . the typeface were radically different, their content and style new. Jean Etienne Coscarat, member of I.K., tried, during the first three months of the year 1989, alone or very likely while poorly surrounded, to "keep afloat" an organization which weathered a difficult passage.[62]

The Rise of Other Violent Movements

The choice of political violence reflected the ratcheting upward of *abertzale* youth to a new level of political militancy. Iparretarrak was only the first of the movements to use violence and served as an example for the others. The first to emulate IK was the short-lived Lutte pour la Liberté et Socialisme en Euskadi, which appeared in 1976, committed two attacks, and disappeared.[63]

The next movement using violence was Euskal Zuzentasuna (Basque Justice). Its initials "EZ" also meant "no" in Basque. Like IK, EZ defined itself as a "revolutionary organization of national liberation."[64] Its first action occurred on the night of November 22, 1977, with the firebombing of two temporary employment agencies. Between 1977 and 1979 EZ claimed responsibility for eleven attacks in all, at least two of which were joint operations with IK.[65] EZ's last operation was a machine-gun attack on the "Puerta del Sol" train as it passed near Guéthary in 1979. According to militants close to this tendency, there was contact between EZ, IK, and the later Hordago during this early period, but some competition as well as each tried to outdo the other. Police investigators believe EZ was ultimately absorbed into IK itself. In July 1977 a small group calling itself Herritarrak (Defenders of the Country) committed one attack against the Tour de France bicycle race in order to demonstrate that the Pays Basque was not France.[66] As Moruzzi and Boulaert point out, IK criticized this action for not targeting what it called "the true responsible [parties] of the economic situation in the Pays Basque," but this did not stop IK from attempting to attack the Tour de France itself in July 1987.[67]

HORDAGO

The greatest alternative movement to IK to appear in this period was Hordago (All or Nothing),[68] which borrowed the name of Marc Légasse's earlier nationalist/anarchist/phantasmagoric publication of the same name. Hordago's leader was Jacques (Jakes) Borthayrou, who, like nearly all others of his generation, had passed through Mende Berri. Like others of his generation after 1968, he was antiauthority and left-wing by emotion, "one of the *zonards*" as another militant called him, who were involved in radical rock music and had come out of the more urban Basque factions on the coast.

According to the recollections of Jakes Borthayrou in 1987, Hordago was motivated by the belief that the use of violence against symbols of the state and capitalism could mobilize people and advance the cause.[69] According to him, Hordago was less a vanguard movement than an instrument of the struggle: "Hordago had no real long-term vision; what was important above all was to act, to do something in the immediate." He continued:

> There was especially a desire to act. It was based on the belief that controlled, careful, and symbolic violence could advance the cause. It was not the result of a super-theoretical discussion. "Enough blah, blah, blah—action!" The theory then followed.

Borthayrou made a distinction between the "armed struggle" and Hordago's use of violence: "We didn't use armed struggle, but rather acts of violence or illegal acts. . . . For a long time it was said that we had to limit ourselves to nonviolence in order to not shock people, but the *abertzale* movement was withering."

In November 1979 Hordago published the first issue of its pamphlet *Eduki*, closely resembling IK's *ILDO*. Its primary motivation was to respond to criticisms levied against it by other *abertzale* during its first year of existence, which stigmatized it variously as "anarchist," a more or less fascist movement seeking to instill a climate of fear in the community and thus torpedo the Basque movement, and a group of "unreal actions and . . . urban language."[70] According to Borthayrou, *Enbata* felt Hordago's violence threatened the refugees and EHAS considered it "adventurist" and "a fascist action that attracted the police."

For Hordago, the Basque movement was divided into two broad tendencies: one, legitimist, was characterized by cultural or electoral action within the mainstream of French politics. For Hordago, the recent appearance of the group IZAN carried on a tradition first maintained by *Enbata*.[71] IZAN was a pressure group created in 1978 with less focus on ideology than on those issues on which *abertzale* circles could agree, such as creation of jobs, the cooperative movement, and the Basque department. IZAN said its own motivation was to "render credible the *abertzale* movement in its capacity of leading and saving the Pays Basque North."[72] Ultimately, IZAN participated in the 1983 municipal elections on the list of Herritarki.

In justifying its use of violence, Hordago maintained in 1979 that "*revolution is more agreeable . . . and . . . to live in our country means 'let's revolt.'*"[73] As Borthayrou put it, "Violence is the midwife of history." Hordago's first action was on June 19, 1978, against the *syndicat d'initiative* in Hasparren, followed by four others within the next two months. The police attribute fifteen total attacks to Hordago between 1978 and 1981.[74] Like IK, it attacked the tourist infrastructure and attacked local Basque notables as "the gravediggers of the Pays Basque."[75] Its most visible attack was against the Palais Justice in Bayonne on August 11, 1979.[76] Hordago had a maximum of thirty sympathizers, but the number of militants actually carrying out its actions was only a handful.

In late March 1981 police investigations against one of IK's "Nuits Bleus" led to information about Hordago. On April 3, 1981, police arrested six Hordago militants—Jakes Borthayrou (24), Jean-Pierre Halzuet (22), Jean-Marc Cazaubon (23), Isabelle Etxeberria (31), Renée-Christine Canales (22), and Andrée Etxeberria (25)—and brought them before the Cour de Sûreté de l'Etat on April 8.[77] They were charged with possession of explosives and with the destruction of public and private buildings. The six apparently admitted committing eleven attacks between June 20, 1978, and September 8, 1979.[78]

According to Borthayrou, at the time of their arrest, four of the six were no longer part of Hordago.

With the election of François Mitterrand in May 1981, Borthayrou and the other militants benefited from the traditional amnesty granted to people convicted of crimes other than those of "blood." Five were released in June, and Borthayrou on July 6, 1981.

THE APPEARANCE OF LAGUNTZA

Borthayrou and other ex-Hordago members who had given up the use of violence soon created Laguntza (Help or Aid), formalizing a group which had formed to support them after their arrest.[79] According to a former member, it was less a movement than a political committee against repression. It was composed of about twenty militants in all, including those from the ex-Hordago. Others came to Laguntza from an earlier secession from Mende Berri. As one participant put it, "At each secession, the latest secessionists found themselves reunited with the previous secessionists." What distinguished Laguntza from Hordago and IK was its rejection of the use of violence: "The armed arm substitutes itself for the movement." Laguntza not only criticized some of IK's armed operations, but also criticized it for its "imperialistic, hegemonic attitude." The issue of violence also led Laguntza later to break with Herri Taldeak, with whom it had collaborated in *Ateka*. Yet it also strongly criticized the press for its conduct following the killing of the two CRS in Baigorri in March 1982.[80] Following IK's attack on the "Talgo" in 1984, Laguntza, in a long and nuanced discussion of revolutionary violence, ultimately criticized IK's action as less a popular action than one of a small group of clandestine "specialists" who were above all seeking "a military confrontation with the power."[81] For Laguntza, IK's "actions don't correspond to the terrains of struggle of the movement but they take [the *abertzale* movement itself] hostage since it itself is now directly attacked. It is in this way that the action of Urrugne [against the "Talgo"] . . . contributed to justifying the offensive of the notables against the *abertzale* movement."[82] Regarding IK itself, Laguntza maintained, "Insofar as there only exists one armed group in Euskadi North the calling in to question of this group may lead to a calling in to question of the very idea of the utility of the armed struggle in Euskadi North."[83]

With the election of Mitterrand in May 1981 and his amnesty for the Hordago six as well as the dissolution of the Cour de Sûreté de l'Etat, it appeared that many of the underlying problems which had led to Laguntza's creation were resolved.[84] Laguntza then dissolved. Some of those closest to Hordago began a small publication, *KATZAKA*, whose two issues (ending in 1982) were put out by a small group of ten people bringing together ex-militants from Hordago, Herri Taldeak, and Ezker Berri.

As they began to clarify their opposition to the IZAN initiative, which they saw as an emanation of the *abertzale* right, it was clear that reasons still existed for Laguntza and it began anew in the fall of 1981.[85] Its first tract appeared on December 15, 1981, calling, among other things, for the self-organization of the Basques; support for the Spanish Basque struggle; criticism of government policy against the refugees; and the defense of the Basque language and the Ikastolas. By May 1983 it was also supporting the first "Squatt," a movement of urban homesteaders seeking to occupy vacant urban lodgings, similar to other such movements in the Netherlands and Germany.[86] By 1985 Laguntza had disappeared into EMA, the umbrella group HT proposed for the legislative elections of 1986.

OTHER SHORT-LIVED VIOLENT GROUPS

Among the other short-lived groups using violence were Iparra Borrokan (Fighters of the North), which attacked the police station in Saint-Jean-de-Luz in May 1980 before disappearing in turn.[87] Five years later, Indar 7 (Force 7) committed five attacks against tourist targets. According to Moruzzi and Boulaert, police suspected it to be composed of members of Laguntza.[88] A group with the self-explanatory name Zilatu (To Bore or To Pierce) began a campaign of puncturing the tires of tourists' cars in the region. The puncturing of tires appeared off and on during the 1970s and 1980s as either a low-risk expression of hostility to tourism or simple vandalism by barely politicized youth. A group calling itself Cellule Enbata—Gora Euskadi (Enbata Cell—Long live Euskadi) committed one attack on September 30, 1984, placing a bomb against a storefront in Paris. According to Moruzzi and Boulaert, this was the only Basque attack in Paris between 1973 and 1988.[89] In the region around Mauléon in Soule, a group called Hexa was formed to protest the increasing emphasis on tourism as an answer to the decline of local industries, especially the shoe industry. Hexa included within it a "secret action group" called Matalaz after the Souletin priest who led a peasant revolt against the monarchy before the Revolution.[90] Matalaz was particularly active in 1984, committing a number of attacks, including attacks against the *syndicat d'initiative* of Tardets, the gendarmeries of Tardets and Mauléon, the customs post at Larrau, and setting tires aflame on the main rail line between Bayonne and Pau.[91] According to Matalaz, "There where they are, the Socialist *abertzale* militants must . . . react against the criminal franco-espagnol collaboration and face up to the repression which is falling on the *abertzale* movement."[92] A group called Zutik (Upright) staged two attacks in the evening of April 3, 1985, and nothing since. Finally, on July 15, 1985, an unexploded bomb was found against the wall of the tax office in Biarritz. On a nearby wall was found the inscription "Enough GAL," signed "EEE."[93]

All of these groups reflected the socializing effect of IK's early use of violence. Those militants who continued their taste for violence probably gravitated toward IK or, scared of the consequences, returned to a less dangerous militancy. But in the period which began in 1973 and continues today the only movement to maintain a sustained commitment to violence and a demonstrated ability to recruit new generations of militants is Iparretarrak.

The Acceleration of Iparretarrak's Violence

Gaiz oroc du bere gaizagoa.
Every evil has its worse.
Basque proverb

In 1979 Iparretarrak embarked on a new phase of the armed struggle, adding political targets to the softer real estate, employment agencies, and tourist targets that it continues to target. On June 29, 1979, IK detonated a bomb outside the office of the subprefect in Bayonne, one of the most secure government compounds in the region.[94] The bomb was placed and detonated in such a way as to target the subprefect's office and not the living quarters and was timed to explode when the office was empty after midnight. The office was completely destroyed, as were adjacent rooms. This marked the beginning of a campaign to target the French state and its agents. As IK announced in the fourth issue of *ILDO*, "Our action against the SUBPREFECTURE is a response when faced with the violence of the State, economic, political, cultural violence, violence against the revolutionary Basque Socialist militants."[95]

Then came the premature explosion of a bomb on March 26, 1980, which literally blew apart two young militants, Dominique Olhagaray ("Txomin") and a naturalized Spanish Basque, Raymond Arruiz ("Ramuntxo"), as they sought to place a time bomb in the car of the wife of subprefect Biacabe in the parking lot of the Hospital of Bayonne, where she worked.[96] It was apparently IK's intention for the bomb to explode later that night once the car was parked under the office back at the subprefecture.

It was in the aftermath of this attack, as we saw in the last chapter, that EHAS voiced its opposition to this event in specific and to the use of violence in general as a tool of the Basque struggle. This provoked accelerated attacks against it by both HT and IK and eventually led to its demise. HT, for its part, while claiming that the use of violence was not its own choice, supported those who did use it in pursuit of the same goals.[97] While criticism against the bombing continued to pour in from across the political spectrum, estimates claimed that as many as twelve hundred people attended the funeral services of the two militants jointly celebrated by twelve Basque priests in their hometowns of Baigorri and Itxassou.[98]

The French Cour de Sûreté de l'Etat took up the dossier on this attack in the days which followed the bombing.[99] This court, charged with state security, had been created by the French Parliament in 1963 in the aftermath of Algeria in order to deal with the still real threat posed by the Organisation de l'Armée Secrète or OAS. Composed of three civilian judges and two military judges, it had wide authority and autonomy to pursue its charge. Following the OAS, it has been used during the Fifth Republic to pursue cases against extreme leftists, as well as against militants from Guadeloupe, Brittany, Corsica, and the Pays Basque, among others.[100]

Yet, as former *Enbata* founder and now senator Michel Labéguerie said in the days following the burials:

> One cannot let a people plunge themselves into an idiotic violence . . . [but] . . . there are hardly any villages which don't count their small nucleus of youth committed to the maximum. And these are our sons, and we don't have any power over them. . . . This Pays Basque, which was conservative, is in the process of veering to the left. If we continue to do nothing, we will be in store for another twenty years of difficulties and attacks. And if the thousand or twelve hundred youths who were at the burial of Olhagaray at Itxassou are as committed as they say, then all the more reason to be apprehensive, because it won't be the C.R.S. who will solve this problem.[101]

Following the deaths of Olhagaray and Arruiz, IK ceased its attacks for the following year. As *ILDO* 6 explained the silence:

> The death of Txomin and Ramuntxo showed us the necessity of radicalizing the armed struggle, that is to say, to define clear objectives, to support with greater efficacy all the struggles. . . . That's why, in the days after the death of our two comrades, we decided to stop our interventions and to devote a year to reinforcing ourselves, and to preparing us to carry out our task better.[102]

On the first anniversary of the deaths of Olhagaray and Arruiz, on March 26, 1981, IK marked their loss with a series of six bombs, two of which did not explode. Among the targets were the now-familiar temporary employment services, tourist facilities, and the Yacht Club at Ciboure, for the second time since 1978. For the first time, IK targeted the French Ministry of Education, bombing the local office of public school inspectors (as an opponent of Seaska).[103] In the week leading up to the French presidential elections of 1981 IK claimed responsibility for three different bombing attacks, including one against the helicopter of Souletin industrialist Charles Etchandy, as the "very symbol of the profit earned on the backs of the workers."[104] At the same time a veritable "who's who" of Basque militants called for the election of François Mitterrand as president.[105] When *Enbata* questioned the political value of attacking this helicopter and its owner, who was an employer in a declining region, IK retorted by pointing out the irony of Basques like *Enbata* who support Mitterrand and traditional Basque capitalism at the same time: "This leads us to denounce the game of certain *abertzale* [read *Enbata*] who call for voting for Mitterrand but want to conserve and reinforce the structures of our domination."[106]

In reality, the presidential elections of 1981 unfolded in a climate of great optimism among mainstream Basque militants. Polls showed that Mitterrand had a good chance to win, and among published Socialist platforms were pledges for the creation of a Basque department, the end of the prefectural system, the teaching of the Basque language as an elective in public schools, and the end of the Cour de Sûreté de l'Etat.

IK held its first clandestine press conference on April 3, 1981, based in part on the recently published sixth issue of *ILDO*, and explained its intention to carry its struggle to a "new level."[107] Within three months the seventh issue of *ILDO* appeared, containing a series of communiqués explaining the increase in attacks by IK during the ensuing months of March and April 1981 as part of IK's strategy of rupture with even a Socialist French government.[108]

THE ATTACK AT BAIGORRI

Lan gaxtoa, borxascoa.
It's a bad job, that which is done by force.
Basque proverb

On March 19, 1982, IK elevated its use of violence to a new level by ambushing and killing one member of the French CRS on patrol on the outskirts of Saint-Etienne-de-Baigorri and wounding his colleague, who would die of his wounds within a month.[109] Two days later two different organizations claimed responsibility for the attack: the Spanish extreme rightist group Spanish Basque Battalion (Bataillon Basque Espagnol) and Iparretarrak. The second phone call, in the name of IK, was by a man speaking French with a heavy Spanish accent, which might have been false,[110] who claimed the attack was an error, intended instead to punish "two traitors." [111] Investigators lent more credibility to the claim by IK, especially since this was within days of the anniversary of the deaths of Olhagaray and Arruiz in Bayonne two years before. In fact, the getaway car found six kilometers from the scene contained chains, padlocks, and handcuffs—as well as a scuba knife missing a crucial piece—leading investigators to believe the killings were in fact an attempted kidnapping gone awry. Within three days of the attack investigators had questioned six residents of Baigorri, including two brothers of Philippe Bidart, a fugitive since a holdup at Saint-Paul-des-Dax on November 7, 1981.[112] According to Moruzzi and Boulaert, it was common knowledge in Baigorri that Bidart returned frequently to the village to see his wife and daughter.[113] During the police search of Bidart's home, a scuba bag was discovered containing an adhesive band missing from the end of the diver's knife found in the abandoned getaway car.[114] In the ensuing confusion, IK denied responsibility for the attack, and rumors arose suggesting that it represented an extracurricular operation by Bidart without IK's blessing, including the suspicion that it represented his effort to force the struggle to a higher level. From the account of the wounded CRS before his death, it appeared that two masked and armed men had attempted to stop the CRS vehicle on the outskirts of Baigorri. When the driver accelerated toward them, they opened fire with Sten guns, killing the driver and wounding his colleague.[115] Whether the killings were deliberate or an error, the public reaction was swift and hostile.

Indicative of the protest which the murders provoked in *abertzale* circles was the public statement of Hitza Hitz (The Given Word), a group of moderate nationalists which had supported Mitterrand the previous year: "The act of criminal madness of Friday night, from wherever it comes, seems to us like a gross provocation, inadmissible in the current situation in the Pays Basque Nord." [116] In a front-page editorial, *Herriz Herri* wrote, "This grave act, difficult to explain, [and] the political use which has been made of it these last days, have conjured up a gross provocation whoever the authors or their silent partners were. Who could it profit from it?" [117] The Baigorri newspaper *Berriak* claimed that "the killers are completely marginalized." [118] The killings provoked a real political upheaval in Baigorri. Jean Haritschelhar was strongly criticized by his municipal council and had to resign both as mayor and as a member of the council.

Herri Taldeak continued to denounce the campaign of lies against Bidart and pointed out the lack of an official claim of IK's responsibility or any other "tangible proof": "We want to denounce here how, without formal proof, and while his organization has denied [responsibility for] the attack, a veritable enterprise of lies has developed in order to sully Philippe Bidart." [119] On behalf of the government, interior minister Gaston Defferre, speaking at the funeral of the CRS who was killed instantly in the attack, declared:

> The recourse to violence is indefensible and unacceptable when the country is a democracy offering to everyone the right and the actual possibility to express themselves and to convince [others]. The government will not let itself be drawn into an infernal cycle of provocation and repression toward which the terrorism seeks to draw it. [120]

As part of the intense police investigation of the killing, the government proceeded to a careful search of the headquarters of Seaska, seizing documents and employee records and taking examples of the typefaces of its typewriters. [121] Bidart's wife Maialen worked as a secretary for the association. [122] As we saw above, this led to the arrest and custody of Xan Coscarat, [123] one of HT's leaders and an employee of Seaska, who had known Bidart since childhood. As Coscarat declared to the judge during his 1990 trial, "Filipe Bidart? We were both born in Baigorri, three months apart. We grew up together, we have always known each other. I have always been his friend." [124] According to reports of the Police Judiciare given during his 1990 trial, Coscarat had crossed the frontier at Biriatou in the company of Bidart in 1981, a short time before Bidart passed into clandestinity. [125] The government issued an arrest warrant for Bidart on April 10. [126]

IK laid low for a time and did not claim responsibility for an attack until nine months later, this time a holdup in January 1983 netting 800,000 francs. [127] But within two months the violence began again in earnest with an attack in March against property belonging to the *conseil général*, [128] followed by an attack on a temporary employment agency in April. [129] In May an attempt was made on the Palais de Justice in Bayonne. In June 1983 IK launched an attack on a patrol of the gendarmerie that caused no injuries, but destroyed a vehicle by explosives. These actions made clear that the attack in Baigorri of the previous year was not an isolated act and raised the specter of a new level of political violence directed at the law enforcement community, akin to ETA's persistent attacks on the Guardia Civil in Spain.

In what was by now an intense campaign, IK turned against tourist targets in July as the tourist season began in earnest, attacking the Comité de Coordination Touristique du Pays Basque in Biarritz on July 9. It failed twice that month (on June 9 and 17) in attacks on the tourist office of Saint-Jean-Pied-de-Port, but succeeded in destroying the *syndicat d'initiative* in Saint Palais on June 17. [130] In fact, IK claimed in a communiqué that, after realizing the bomb in Saint-Jean-Pied-de-Port hadn't exploded, they called the gendarmerie to warn them. IK attributed the gendarmerie's failure to act as an effort to discredit IK: "All means are good in order to discredit our struggle."[131] By early August IK had added to this campaign a new target: destroying tourists' cars with plastic explosives, as part of its campaign "Turismo . . . Aski."[132] *Enbata* saw the accelerated pace of IK's bombing attacks as signs that the movement had entered into a new phase of its struggle, which *Enbata* called the "Corsica-zation" of the Basque struggle.[133] *Enbata* plainly asked if this level of violence was suited to the Basque struggle and understood by the Basque people. Moreover, it wondered whether it might harm the struggle of ETA for the liberation of nine-tenths of the Basque people in Spain. For *Enbata*, the time had come for a debate on the use of violence in the North.[134] Yet IK's violence continued at a greater pace.

Philippe Bidart and the Reign of Seminarians

Elisaren hurren-ena, aldarearen urrun-ena.
The closest to the church is the furthest from the altar.
Basque proverb

On August 2, 1983, police arrested Xan Marguirault, whose earlier arrest in 1977 led to the creation of Herri Taldeak, this time as a suspect in the bombing of a tourist's car in Ascain.[135] Marguirault had been previously sentenced in July 1979 to thirty months in jail (of which twelve were suspended) for the 1977 offense.[136]

On August 5, 1983, police in Bayonne arrested Jean-Paul Hiribarren, who brandished a pistol but did not fire.[137] In his car police found guns and ammunition, explosives, handcuffs, and hoods. Most significant, police found a receipt from a miniature golf course in the nearby department of Les Landes. At the same time that Hiribarren was being arraigned in Bayonne, the gendarmerie of Montfort in Les Landes received a telephone call informing them that a suspicious car was just leaving the "Lou Pantaou" campground. Strangely, only two gendarmes answered the call and confronted the car as it was leaving the campground. As they approached the car, the driver got out with his hands in the air, but two of the four men opened fire, with one gendarme being killed instantly and the other wounded. A home movie made by a nearby camper indicated that two of the men were IK militants Jean-Louis ("Popo") Larre (the driver) and Gabi Mouesca. The two others were thought to be Philippe Bidart and Joseph Etxebeste (a.k.a. Etcheveste). The four disappeared into thin air, and Jean-Louis Larre was never heard from again.[138] Investigators speculate that Larre panicked following the shootout and, not having fired on the officers, decided to surrender. According to this version, the others killed Larre either to cover their trail or in the panic of the moment. In *ILDO* 9, which appeared in April 1984, IK accused the French police of having assassinated him.[139]

If IK had fooled anyone by its silence over the killing of the CRS at Baigorri, the shootout at Léon made it clear that IK had made a quantum leap in militancy. IK continued to insist that it had been a regrettable accident, but that it reflected once more the fact that the choice of the armed struggle was a "total commitment" for some militants.[140] Herri Taldeak stated simply, "At Léon, there was a clash between the soldiers of power and the soldiers of a cause. An accidental confrontation . . . one doesn't condemn an accident. We will defend the pursued militants."[141] Yet, according to *Enbata*, "Among the radical *abertzale*, there is dismay. 'All our political action is dead for some time to come.'"[142]

Michel Castaing, writing in *Le Monde*, asked, "Are the Basques like the Corsicans?"[143] His answer: "If, at Bayonne, one tends to minimize what happened [at Léon], it seems that one has the tendency, in Paris, to overestimate the gravity of the events. One exaggerates in both cases."[144] Nonetheless, the concept of "corsification" entered the political vocabulary of the region. A mysterious group calling itself the "Secret Army—Class of Boyer-Rousarie," after the names of the two slain CRS in Baigorri, threatened to take action, "in order to clean the Pays Basque of the terrorist gangrene."[145] They claimed to have Philippe Bidart in captivity and intended to execute him by August 12. While the organization did little other than make threats by phone, the Syndicat Départemental des Policiers en Civil seemed to point a finger at their colleagues when they condemned "any organization of parallel police" engaging in extracurricular retaliation.[146]

Philippe Bidart by this point was well on his way to becoming public enemy number one in France. *Le Monde* called him a "Pyrenean Mesrine," a reference to the modern-day French John Dillinger.[147] Others claimed that IK had descended into "banditry, pure and simple."[148] Bidart became a fugitive in November 1981 after being identified as taking part in the robbery of the Caisse d'Epargne at Saint-Paul-les-Dax on November 7. He was already wanted for the killing of the CRS in Baigorri in March 1982. Now that he had killed again at Léon, he became the subject of one of the most intensive manhunts in French history. Over a period of three years he had participated in two separate killings of French police and was later sentenced twice to life imprisonment without parole. From the time he went into hiding in the fall of 1981, he moved from the homes of sympathizers to *cayolars* in the high Pyrénées to campgrounds to cities outside the region. He stayed for a short time at the abbey of Belloc, where one of his uncles was a priest. ETA also held one of its assemblies there in 1973, and the abbey was known as an asylum for those in need, including flyers during World War II. Perhaps as a consequence of its aid to Basque nationalists, some years ago the abbot of Belloc, Abbé Diharce, was transferred quickly and inexplicably to Benin. If his family did not understand, members of the clergy saw the aid to Bidart and ETA as a pretext and the state's hand in guiding the bishopric to make an example of this "confessor to terrorists."

PHILIPPE BIDART, THE MAN

Saindu mana, otso hazana.
He has the look of a saint and the actions of a wolf.
Basque proverb

Every revolutionary ends as an oppressor or a heretic.
Albert Camus, *The Rebel*

Are there lessons in the background of Philippe Bidart that might explain his progression to a position where he was widely seen in the public mind as the leader of IK, its most deadly militant, and most famous fugitive?[149] Bidart was born in Saint-Etienne-de-Baigorri on April 10, 1953, within three months of Xan Coscarat. He was the eldest of four sons born to Jean-Baptiste Bidart, a local carpenter of modest means. His father had been ten years old at the time of the Spanish Civil War and as a teenager in Baigorri was a member of local dance and chorale groups influenced by the Spanish Basque refugees who settled there in exile. Philippe grew up in a home of modest means near the center of Baigorri, in a solidly Basque family in a solidly Basque village beginning to experience the tensions of economic decline. As we saw in chapter 2, entry into the clerical or religious orders is a historic Basque tradition, especially for the brightest among families with multiple sons. Philippe soon left the village to continue his studies at the Petit Séminaire in Ustaritz (formerly of Larressore), one of the cradles of Basque nationalism in France, where, as we saw in chapter 3, the Chanoine Pierre Lafitte lived and worked until his death in 1985. Apparently Philippe actively intended for a time to enter the clergy. At the same time he was athletically gifted and popular with girls in the village. Moruzzi and Boulaert report that if he had a fault, according to those who remembered him growing up, it was that he had shown early signs of rigidity and intolerance.[150] His contemporaries remembered his anger when others disagreed with him, and some of these disagreements went to the brink of physical blows. He apparently did not seek leadership but was well regarded by others for his strength and solidity. He was not a loner.

Philippe eventually decided to abandon the priesthood, and left the Petit

Séminaire shortly thereafter. In the early 1970s Philippe entered the French Army's 57th Infantry Regiment near Bordeaux in order to fulfill France's requirement of universal military service. While he has been falsely referred to as an army commando, he is said to have shown particular skills with weapons and combat and to have learned the use of explosives and demolitions. He left active duty as a sergeant and continued to fulfill his reserve obligations from 1975 until he went underground in 1981.

THE TRUE BELIEVER

Eric Hoffer, in his classic book *The True Believer*, described the personality factors which compel some individuals to become adherents of mass revolutionary movements. Among those most vulnerable to the appeal of these movements are former soldiers who find their skills unneeded in society and no place for them to fit in:

> The man just out of the army is an ideal potential convert, and we find him among the early adherents of all contemporary mass movements. He feels alone and lost in the free-for-all of civilian life. The responsibilities and uncertainties of an autonomous existence weigh and prey upon him. He longs for certitude, camaraderie, freedom from individual responsibility, and a vision of something altogether different from the competitive free society around him—and he finds all this in the brotherhood and the revivalist atmosphere of a rising movement.[151]

For these ex-soldiers now cut off from the structure, familiarity, and camaraderie of the army, revolutionary movements may offer a similar appeal:

> The similarities are many: both mass movements and armies are collective bodies; both strip the individual of his separateness and distinctness; both demand self-sacrifice, unquestioning obedience and single-hearted allegiance; both make extensive use of make-belief to promote daring and united action; and both can serve as a refuge for the frustrated who cannot endure an autonomous existence. . . . But the differences are fundamental: an army does not come to fulfill a need for a new way of life; it is not a road to salvation. . . . The mass movement, on the other hand, seems an instrument of eternity, and those who join it do so for life. The ex-soldier is a veteran, even a hero; the ex-true believer is a renegade.[152]

One important difference between them, however, is that if the army seeks to protect present-day society, the mass movement seeks to destroy it, focusing instead on an idealized future.

Veterans are only one category of rootless individuals vulnerable to the appeals of radical movements. These people (veterans, adolescents, unemployed college graduates, new immigrants, etc.)—"misfits" in Hoffer's terminology—have not found their place in life but still hope to.[153] We can only speculate on the cultural cleavages between various minorities in the barracks in the 1970s; but, as we saw, at the turn of the century it was a jarring experience for many young ethnic soldiers who were thrown into the common and impersonal cradle of French military and society. In the Third Republic the experience in the barracks was a direct cause of the subsequent assimilation of minority children, whose fathers wanted them spared the embarrassment they had felt in the army with their poor French and country ways. Karl Deutsch reminds us, however, that ethnic nationalism rises up most often not in zones of monolingualism, but in those areas where languages and cultures co-exist and conflict: that it is precisely along the conflict-ridden fault lines of contact and communication that nationalism arises as a reaction to the threatening "other."[154] In this perspective, uprooting a young man from his cultural womb of predominant monolingualism and exposing him to the intensity of outside culture and its implicit hierarchy may make him more Basque, rather than less so. Ethnic identity becomes a familiar harbor which serves as a protection from the winds of widespread and threatening social change. For Hoffer, a minority group is "a compact whole which shelters the individual, gives him a sense of belonging and immunizes him against frustration."[155]

What may be even more important than Bidart's military background is his background as a fallen seminarian. A Catholic vocation is not chosen by accident. Something in the rigidity of that belief system, the comfort of its dualistic choice between good and evil, and the prestige of the priesthood as a guide to others was clearly attractive. Taken out of the priesthood, those other appeals may remain real. As Hoffer describes it:

> He must cling to the collective body or like a fallen leaf wither and fade. It is doubtful whether the excommunicated priest, the expelled Communist and the renegade chauvinist can ever find peace of mind as autonomous individuals. They cannot stand on their own, but must embrace a new cause and attach themselves to a new group. The true believer is eternally incomplete, eternally insecure.[156]

According to the German philosopher Heinrich Heine, what Christian love cannot do is often effected by a common hatred.[157] Hoffer considers the role of hatred against the existing order central to the appeal of mass movements:

Passionate hatred can give meaning and purpose to an empty life. Thus people haunted by the purposelessness of their lives try to find a new content not only by dedicating themselves to a holy cause but also by nursing a fanatical grievance. A mass movement offers them unlimited opportunities for both.[158]

THE ROLE OF FORMER SEMINARIANS

What is so unusual about Iparretarrak is the importance of former seminarians within it. In addition to Bidart, Xan Coscarat, Manex Borda, and G. Lantziri were former seminary students who later withdrew or were forced to leave. Other seminarians, not a part of IK, who were made to leave at the same time included Manex Pagola, now associate curator of the Musée Basque, Jean Etcheverry-Ainchart, nephew of the former deputy, Michel Bendiboure, and M. Sarasola. Borda and Sarasola had already taken their vows. According to one former priest, the bishop of Bayonne is said to have remarked in the mid-1960s that *Enbata* (as a shorthand for Basque nationalism) was his greatest cross to bear. Within three years he moved against the seminarians in an effort to quell the rising tide of nationalism within the priesthood. For these young seminarians were hardly immune from both the nationalist revivalism and the philosophical rootlessness of the time. According to one former priest, between 1965 and 1968 about four-fifths of the seminary students from the region around Baigorri dropped out, victims of an ideological rupture as well as the socioeconomic one afflicting their village as a whole.

It may be this unsettled state as much as any other that explains the appeal of a clandestine movement and recourse to violence against the threat to their way of life. What is the thread which ties their early religious training to their later embrace of violence? Holistic or totalizing value systems seem to have an unusual appeal for these individuals. As another Basque nationalist and former priest put it, they appear to have an unusual susceptibility to Manichaean values—to the certain contrast between black and white, good and evil, right and wrong. One Basque militant outside of IK said, "Politics is the art of compromise. IK didn't ever want to compromise. It's that sort of nihilist rejection of compromise which frightens me."

For one mobilized to see evil and to fight evil, the shift in adversaries from the spiritual world to the secular world is not a great one. As the late twentieth century has demonstrated, the association between Christian idealism and radical Marxism is not as strange as one might believe. For it was in this period beginning in the late 1960s and early 1970s that the Marxist-Christian dialogue emerged on issues of social justice,[159] and the concept of liberation theology was beginning to emerge as a major source of revolutionary social change led by radical local priests in the Third World.[160] By the mid-1980s 15 or 20 of the 150 Basque parish priests had formed an association called Herriakerin (With the country), whose members spoke of the liberation theology of both Father Helder Camara of Brazil and assassinated Archbishop Hector Romero of El Salvador.[161] As one of Herriakerin's members, Father Martin Carrère, put it, "If they had been Basque, they would have been *abertzale*, our combat is the same."[162] In the Basque experience, the thriving cooperative movement at Mondragon was a prime example of the pursuit of a workable economic communalism by radical priests.[163] As Krutwig describes the logic which leads from Christianity to the use of violence, the pursuit of Basque justice easily becomes a holy crusade, and for IK, a holy war: "for we patriots, as for the crusaders in the tenth century, our truth is an absolute truth, and our ideological combat recalls a war of religion."[164]

What these fallen seminarians share with the priesthood is a desire for social control, to guide others, and to be recognized as possessing truth. At base, according to a former member of HT, it was a personality type often given to self-righteousness, which needed to impose its system of values on others. This is a common theme in the literature on terrorism. As Paul Wilkinson points out, "They believe in their total rectitude . . . intolerance, dogmatism, authoritarianism, and a ruthless treatment of their own people who deviate from their own view are common to their mentality."[165] According to Rushworth Kidder, if one can generalize about a terrorist mind-set, it may be said to be characterized by oversimplification of issues, frustration, self-righteousness, utopianism, and social isolation.[166] Psychiatrist Jerrold M. Post writes that for many terrorists the terrorist group "is the only family they have ever had."[167] In short, as one enters into clandestinity, the Basque cause becomes a family and the center of one's emotional and social universe.

As IK's violence accelerated in the 1980s, observers noted a tone of guilt in its declarations, as if its militants were still imbued with the Catholicism so much a part of their Basque roots. *Le Monde*'s Philippe Boggio advanced the theory that:

> the Basque clandestines were mired in a sentiment of guilt, impregnated, even with gun in hand, with strong Catholic values, ill at ease in the skin of desperados, incapable of cynicism.[168]

For Boggio, IK's communiqués came to contain explicit excuses, unconscious apologies for political actions now beginning to alarm the Basque population.

IK Accelerates Its Struggle

The appearance of the eighth issue of *ILDO* in April 1983 is significant because no mention is made of the killings of the CRS in Baigorri more than
a year before.[169] Apart from the initial telephone call the night of the attack,
this is consistent with IK's silence on the event. In August Herri Taldeak reported that Iparretarrak, "probably restructured" in July, had embarked on a
new campaign against tourism.[170] This led to IK's attack against the Office du
Tourisme of Biarritz on September 13, 1983. Claiming to be IK, the three militants evacuated the offices at gunpoint and placed a bomb which detonated
moments later.[171] This made clear IK's refusal to participate in indiscriminate
violence, whether by arms or bombings, and to target political and economic
symbols rather than people. For that reason, IK's bombing attack at Urrugne
against the main SNCF rail line from the Spanish border at Hendaye to Paris
was greeted with dismay. It caused the Madrid to Paris train, the "Talgo," to
derail, miraculously without victims. *ILDO* 9 insisted:

> The armed actions in Euskadi North chosen and carried out by IK have
> always been until present either material actions, . . . or very precise ac-
> tions against people . . . but actions which were limited to giving them
> a good correction without the intention of making an attempt on their
> lives. That means that all of our actions are studied and carried out in
> such a manner as to not create victims.[172]

Even the killing of the gendarmes at Léon was explained as a regrettable
necessity:

> The militants of IK try always to avoid a confrontation with the forces
> of repression, but if it is inevitable they are ready to face off with them.
> That's what happened at Léon the 7th of August 1983. A commando
> of IK discovered by the forces of repression after having tried to avoid
> the confrontation, was obliged to confront them with arms in hand. The
> militants tried to parley with the gendarmes, but they not expecting
> this reaction panicked and opened fire. The militants returned fire and
> retreated after having neutralized the two gendarmes.[173]

On January 3, 1984, IK attacked a barracks of the CRS at Anglet, firing
automatic weapons on the vehicles, but later claiming in a telephone call that
they had done so deliberately so as to avoid firing on the CRS themselves.[174]
While early speculation centered on Grupas Antiterroristas de Liberación
(GAL) as a possible culprit, ultimately the recovery of 9 mm shells from the
scene bearing the same stock numbers as those found both at Baigorri and
Léon convinced police of the authenticity of the call.[175] It was in this climate of

increased police activity that the four militants of Herri Taldeak were arrested the evening of January 10 as they were delivering a group of journalists to a clandestine press conference with IK. Even *Enbata* remarked on the naïveté of the group, which invited the journalists by telephone call.[176] According to *Enbata*, members of the French police intelligence agency, the Renseignements Généraux, then called the journalists later the same afternoon to ask where the press conference would be held.[177]

On March 1, 1984, police stopped a vehicle containing IK militant Gabriel Mouesca, wanted since the previous August for the car bombing at Ascain. According to the police account, Mouesca attempted to flee, gun in hand. As the police opened fire, the driver of Mouesca's car, Didier Lafitte, was shot and killed.[178] It was only following Lafitte's death that IK acknowledged that Popo Larre was still missing, following the shootout at Léon seven months before.[179]

On January 17, 1985, IK claimed responsibility for an attack on the car of the *procureur* of the republic in Bayonne, the same afternoon that the Appeals Court in Pau found the four transporters of journalists arrested in January 1984—Coscarat, Borda, Betti Bidart, and Alain Mateo—guilty and sentenced them to two years in prison and five years of parole.[180] Later that same month the criminal court of Bayonne found IK militants Gabriel Mouesca, Jean-Paul Hiribarren, and Joseph Etcheveste guilty of the firebombing of the tourist property at Ascain in August 1984 and sentenced them to five years in prison.[181] Philippe Bidart, originally a party to the complaint, was found innocent in absentia for lack of evidence. Continuing its string of political targets, IK attacked the gendarmerie of Mauléon in the interior in Soule on January 20, and within ten days police had arrested an IK militant, Jean-Pierre ("Pampi") Sainte-Marie.

In April police discovered a Basque connection with the theft of seventy kilos of dynamite near Foix in the Ariège, several hours south of the Pays Basque, on July 24, 1984.[182] It served to clarify the origins of the dynamite found in a botched bombing attack on the gendarmerie of Saint-Jean-de-Luz on January 30, 1985, when eleven sticks of the stolen dynamite were found. They were identical to those found during an abortive attack on the landing light system of the Biarritz-Parme airport shortly before the arrival of President Mitterrand's plane the previous October 24. Police soon arrested a young IK militant (and member of *Ateka*'s editorial board while an ostensible member of HT), Marie-France ("Maddi") Héguy, and discovered an IK arsenal in her villa in Anglet which included dynamite, detonators, machine guns, and cartridges.[183] With the advent of summer IK again turned to tourist targets, including real estate developments in Saint-Jean-de-Luz and Biarritz,[184] and an attack on Christmas Eve against the Office of Tourism in Biarritz nearly identical to one five years before. This time the justification was the five-year sentence handed down against Gabriel Mouesca on December 5.[185]

The Palais de Justice in Bayonne was a repeat target on August 16, this time motivated by a demand for a release of its prisoners, Marie-France Héguy and Jean-Pierre Saint-Marie.[186] The *International Herald Tribune* reported on September 6 that two bombs fitted with sophisticated timing devices never before seen in the French Pays Basque were found in a truck near Bayonne.[187] On September 12 a violent explosion damaged an annex used by a special unit of thirty members of the Police Judiciare charged with "affaires basques."[188]

Thus, by September 12, 1985, IK already had carried out a total of twelve attacks during calendar year 1985. Claude Jouanne, writing in *Sud-Ouest*, estimated IK's strength at forty militants and asserted that the organization was increasingly divided between those favoring the armed struggle and others who felt the time was right for electoral action, perhaps a candidacy at the upcoming cantonal elections.[189] Moreover, according to Jouanne, the primary effect of the antitourist campaign was to drive away summer tourists, thus hurting the pocketbooks of individual Basque farmers and merchants, without affecting the market for luxury apartments on the coast, which had been IK's main goal. As a result, the organization was forced back on its symbolic targets, the police forces, and the French justice system. Isolated by its own violence, it was difficult to see what Iparretarrak would do next.

Chapter Seven

Iparretarrak, ETA, and GAL: Basque

Violence and the Evolution of

French-Spanish Diplomacy

Without the South, there wouldn't be the North.
Ramuntxo Camblong[1]

They call me the wind of freedom.
Txiki[2]

The greatest influence on Iparretarrak's early violence was the theory and practice of the Spanish Basque movement, in particular several incarnations of Euzkadi Ta Askatasuna or the ETAs. Yet justifiable disagreement exists on the role of ETA in the creation of Iparretarrak, as well as on the impact of IK's violence on ETA's fragile northern sanctuary in France. In this chapter I will examine the complex and tempestuous relationship between Iparretarrak and the ETAs and show how that relationship changed over time. Second, I will chart the participation of French Basques in ETA, particularly in the period from the discovery of ETA's itinerant commando of French Basques in 1990. Third, I will discuss the rise of Spanish intelligence operations directed against ETA's refugee community in France and demonstrate the role of the Spanish government in creating anti-Basque violence in France as an instrument to bring pressure against the French government and force the extradition of ETA members to Spain. I will examine in detail the rise of the Grupas Antiterroristas de Liberación or GAL and the creation of the northern or "dirty" war against ETA's sanctuary in France. Finally, I will examine the success of this joint French-Spanish cooperation in decapitating ETA and the accelerating campaign joined by France on the eve of the 1992 Olympic Games in Barcelona.

The Influence of ETA on IK

The effect of violence on the popular support of the Basque movement was also a concern for ETA in this period and figured in the ideological conflict dividing ETA-m from ETA-pm.[3] ETA-pm in particular was concerned that if the use of violence degenerated into an "elitist" activity cut off from the people, as Francis Jaureguiberry put it, the movement might well risk aborting its own development.[4] According to Jaureguiberry, ETA-pm in 1975 risked "the tactical separation of the military . . . group from the masses, or the risk of falling into an elite activism which doesn't respond to the reality of the people."[5] ETA-m's Commando Txikia, which had carried out the assassination of Admiral Carrero Blanco in Operation Ogro in 1973, took the opposite position: "We consider the armed struggle the supreme form of the struggle of the working class."[6] As one strong critic of Basque nationalism put it, for ETA the embrace of violence was reflective of a higher order of militancy:

> For the militants of ETA the cult of armed action is deep-rooted; it is crowned with the halo of a certain nobility . . . it is above all an affair of men endowed with "balls," that is, of soldiers and no longer simply militants.[7]

The influence of ETA on the French Basque movement was one of the most important elements of Basque political socialization in France beginning in the early 1960s. Even those who rejected the use of violence in the North supported the armed struggle in the South, especially under Franco's rule. According to one Basque scholar of the movement in France, "At one time or another, almost everyone dipped their toes into ETA's water." It was the fear that the North would be a mere "satellite" of the struggle in Spain that concerned many. Moderate French Basque nationalists, of the Christian Democratic tradition, believed that the French movement could have escaped its isolation if not for the contamination of ETA and its theses imported from the South. EHAS, in this view, was fighting an uphill struggle as the image of the *guerrillero* captured the imagination of young French Basque militants tempted by the siren call of the armed struggle. According to this scholar:

> There has always been an odd dance between the militants of North and South. Their relations have been characterized by cooperation then separation, fascination then rejection. . . . Today, IK, having worked with ETA, has now broken with them, rejecting ETA's desire to avoid an armed struggle in the North. There has always been this double move-

ment—courting and then rupture—a love/hate ambivalence. In reality, without the South, there would not have been a movement in the North. There would have been nothing, you understand?

Iparretarrak's fascination with ETA was apparent from the first issue of *ILDO*, its infrequent publication for public consumption, which published a lengthy account by ETA of Operation Ogro, its assassination of the Spanish premier and heir apparent to Franco, Admiral Carrero Blanco, the previous December 20 (1973). This account was followed, in turn, by the press release ETA distributed the day of the killing.[8] (ETA held a press conference in France four days after the killing, on Christmas Eve in 1973, in which the operation was described in detail.) These documents of ETA were inserted in *ILDO* 1 between the justification of Iparretarrak's action against "La Rosée" and Iparretarrak's own statement of strategy. The last article in *ILDO* 1 was the text of ETA's statement of solidarity with the Occitanian farmers on the plateau of Larzac.[9] IK thus devoted more pages to ETA in its first publication than it did to its own militancy. Even *Enbata* noted Iparretarrak's preoccupation with ETA:

> This issue, outside of a fairly brief basic text on the events of Banca, is representative enough of the state of mind of the epoch since, out of sixteen pages, more than half were devoted to ETA, [and] to the attack the previous year against Carrero Blanco in particular.[10]

ETA, for its part, had made clear its sympathy for Iparretarrak and its struggle as early as 1974: "in Euskadi North . . . *our* situation. . . . In order to liberate us, in Euskadi North we count both on the mass struggle and on the armed struggle."[11] By 1975 IK made explicit its support of ETA's struggle:

> For our part, in Euskadi North, there must be an active and total solidarity with our brothers in the South. Because their combat is also our own as members of the same people temporarily divided by this border of shame, but also because capitalists, the bourgeoisie exploit, oppress across frontiers.[12]

This was seconded in a press release in 1978, when IK declared, "We agree with the struggle that ETA is carrying out in the South. For our part, in Euskadi North we have the same goals: an independent Euskadi, reunified and Socialist."[13]

The Theory of the United Front vs. the Single Front

This early period of Iparretarrak's interaction with ETA is characterized by what Moruzzi and Boulaert call "the theory of the united front." [14] In this period of IK's ideological infancy, reflected in the first issue of *ILDO*, IK looked to ETA for doctrinal guidance and identified Basque mobilization on both sides of the frontier as part of the same combat. Yet in short order IK began to try to distance itself from a close identification with ETA in the public mind. This may have been due either to the negative public reaction to the appearance of Basque violence in France or to a developing conflict behind the scenes over ETA's attempt to control IK's development, or both. In either case, by 1980 IK was trying to establish its own identity, insisting, "we don't identify with either ETA-Militar or ETA-Politico-Militar." [15] With the appearance of *ILDO* 6 in March 1981, the friction between IK and ETA was overt, and IK was determined to mark its independence:

> For our part, as an organization of armed struggle, we have decided to count only on our own forces and not to expect the aid of anyone. We are neither controlled, nor even aided by whoever it might be, by any organization, not from Euskadi South, or elsewhere. We intend to keep our autonomy, our freedom of action, our independence. We aren't refusing as such to have relations with other organizations who are pursuing the same goal as us, but on the condition that they respect us and that they don't try to co-opt us and impose on us their point of view.[16]

An even more revealing look at the internal thinking of Iparretarrak vis-à-vis ETA was afforded by the government's seizure of a rare copy of *Erne*, IK's internal newsletter for its militants, in which IK's refusal to take a second seat to the struggle in the South was made clear. IK's objection turned on the distinction between "a single front" and "a united front." [17] IK maintained that at first there was no contradiction between armed struggles in both North and South: if anything, it was the full application of the slogan *Zazpiak bat:* The Seven are one (Euskadi).

It was only after ETA began to insist on the creation of a "single front" (*front unique*) that problems began to surface. As IK framed its dispute: "It's the famous strategy of the single front, the single front of course being the South, and the eternal sacrifice being the North." [18] IK particularly reproached ETA for its attitude as "big brother" seeking to determine the behavior of IK as "little brother." [19] IK should not depend on ETA: "We shouldn't have any illusions; we must not wait for everything from the South. We must organize, struggle, and take our future in our own hands." [20]

In this sixth issue of *Erne* what emerges is a beleaguered and defiant Iparretarrak criticized on all sides for its use of violence in France. The armed struggle in France risked becoming the scapegoat for whatever misfortune befell the French Basque movement or ETA's clandestine refugee community:

> The armed struggle in Euskadi North has become the ideal scapegoat for the partisans of the strategy of a single front: if the refugees have problems, it's because of the armed struggle; if the French government refuses to take into consideration the legitimate demands of the Basque people, it's because of the armed struggle; if new jobs aren't created, it's because of the armed struggle; if the movement is marginalized, it's because of the armed struggle, etc. Certain people have come to reason "end the armed struggle and there will be no more problems" or even "condemn the armed struggle and everyone will agree with us." Unfortunately, that doesn't check out.[21]

To the argument that the population in the North was not ready to accept violence, IK responded that in every case in which the armed struggle was used, even in Spain, its partisans were always a minority at first. For IK, the use of violence was a tool of slow consciousness-raising among the people.

From the time of Marc Légasse's criticism of the attitude of the PNV in exile toward the French Basque movement during World War II (see chapter 3), there existed a sentiment among French Basque militants that Spanish Basque refugees (especially later active-duty ETA members) behaved like conquering heros on R&R in the French Basque sanctuary. On one level, there was undeniably far less interest in events in France because the focus of most of the Basque nationalist camp on both sides of the border had been on events in Spain since the beginning of the Spanish Civil War. Moreover, with the aggravation of ETA's conflict with the Spanish state, it had no reason to want to contaminate its sanctuary in France. In 1984 the tacit if fraying understanding between the refugee community and the French government was that the government would provide a sanctuary for ETA refugees provided that they did not constitute a diplomatic embarrassment with Spain and that they neither practiced violence on French territory nor encouraged violence among the French Basque movement. According to a Spanish press account based on French police sources, part of the understanding over sanctuary was that ETA would try to reason with the "crazies" [*locos*] of Iparretarrak."[22] On November 9, 1990, Inspecteur Dufourg of the Renseignements Généraux (RG), appearing on the "Le Droit de Savoir" (Right to Know) program on television channel TF1, confirmed that the RG had contacted ETA leader

Txomin in order to ask him to exert pressure on Iparretarrak to declare a truce in its violence.[23] The quid pro quo, according to Dufourg, was that "we would protect Txomin against what was going to become GAL in giving him information concerning it." When asked if there had been a positive result from the government's initiative, he responded, "Yes, there was a clear slowing down in the actions of Iparretarrak."[24]

Given the tenuous presence of ETA on French territory, it is understandable if ETA viewed the rise of Iparretarrak's violence as a worrisome development. For ETA, the primary terrain of combat remained in Spain, and IK's fledgling violence threatened to disturb ETA's crucial northern sanctuary. This attitude on the part of ETA's mainstream was as great a source of antagonism for IK as it had been for Légasse forty years before:

> This willingness to limit the demands and the objectives of the struggles of the people in Euskadi North . . . we find in the milieu of the refugees. How is it that these same militants are revolutionary vis-à-vis Euskadi South and reformists in Euskadi North? Do they want to control the struggles in Euskadi North? . . . By what right do they relegate to the second level the struggle in Euskadi North and impose on the militants of Euskadi North the priority of the struggle in the . . . South?[25]

By *ILDO* 9, which appeared in April 1984, IK publicly rejected the theory of a single front (*front unique*) as being unsuited to the reality of the struggles in the North as well as in Navarre: "We challenge the fallacious theory of the single front and we contrast it with one which only realism and our common desire to liberate Euskadi demands: *the strategy of a united front* [*front uni*]."[26] While this publicly revealed the extent of the behind-the-scenes conflict with ETA which had now gone on for several years, IK expressed its hope that "in the acceptance of the autonomy and the liberty of each protagonist, we believe that it is possible to advance and build toward the conclusion of the objects which are common to us: independence, reunification, and socialism for Euskadi."[27]

It was clear by the late 1980s that the conflict between IK and ETA which had lasted for most of the previous decade had sorely divided that segment of the *abertzale* population most sympathetic to the use of political violence. The group Oldartzen, itself highly critical of IK, offered a postmortem of this conflict in 1990:

> The North-South polemic IK/ETA which profoundly divided the *abertzale* movement of the left in Iparralde notably had very concrete and visible effects on the antirepressive struggle. This polemic, among other

things, completely negated the problem of the defense of the refugees in the northern Pays Basque and overshadowed the stakes for the *abertzale* left.[28]

According to Oldartzen, this conflict came to pit many of the French Basque militants who were close to IK against ETA and the struggle in Spain. In a critical open letter to ETA in 1985, Betti Bidart, IK member and brother of Philippe Bidart, complained bitterly:

The refugees want to control the northern Pays Basque totally for they alone are working in its service. They want to prevent all action in Northern Euskadi in order to honor the contract that they passed with Paris. That makes twenty years that they've almost won in the South, twenty years that they tell us that as soon as they take power in the South they'll help us, us poor country bumpkins [*ploucs*] from Northern Euskadi . . .[29]

For one ETA refugee, IK sought to imitate ETA without consultation:

Well, the people from the North want to do the same thing as us, to reproduce here what we've done over there, but without any coordination [with ETA]. Herri Talde wants to be Herri Batasuna just as Iparretarrak wants to be ETA.[30]

For this refugee, the preoccupation with ETA came at the expense of Basque political mobilization in France:

For twenty-five years, the *abertzale* in the North, as a majority, were exclusively preoccupied with ETA's conflict, abandoning their people to the [French right], even going so far as to deliver them up to the Socialist party.[31]

By the time the French government began to move against ETA and deliver some of its militants to the Spanish government beginning in 1984, ETA's basic argument against IK's violence—that it threatened ETA's sanctuary in France—had lost much of its force. By 1987 it was clear that the French government's repression against ETA had taken on a logic and momentum of its own. ETA then muted its criticism of IK's violence in its own preoccupation with survival against the onslaught of French and Spanish pressure.

But it was because of this increased pressure by the French government that ETA opposed IK's movement into clandestinity. For after 1981 the appearance of IK militants seeking refuge within an already restricted population of French Basques willing to risk arrest by hiding a militant of any coloration compounded ETA's problem of hiding several hundred of its own

militants in France. Yet, according to EMA leader Richard Irazusta, his militants (who were sympathizers of IK) pledged to continue sheltering ETA's
militants:

> The Basque problem is not unsolvable. It occurs through negotiation.
> In that which concerns us, we affirm that we will continue to hide the
> refugees so long as the Basque problem will not have found a lasting
> solution. Our position is that of unconditional support in this regard.[32]

One of IK's spokesmen said in 1991 that ETA's desire to block IK's growth
corresponded with the growth of Euskal Batasuna in France as a close affiliate of ETA's front movement Herri Batasuna in Spain. For him, in the wake
of Euskal Batasuna's failure to blunt the rise of IK's analogous front movement, EMA, in the late 1980s, ETA had no choice but to recognize IK/EMA
as a legitimate political force in the North.

The Participation of French Basques in ETA

From the time of the first arrival of ETA refugees in France in the early
1960s little attention was paid to the possibility that French Basques were
active within ETA. This is one reason why Christiane Etchalus's arrest and
conviction for possession of ETA documents and detonators in 1965 was
greeted with such surprise. The reality is that there had been French Basque
members within ETA from the early 1960s. The sequestration of German
Consul General Biehl, following his kidnapping by an ETA commando team
in Donostia and his spiriting over the border, was handled by a group of
French Basques, including at least one priest, who hid him in the village
of Montory in rural Soule. Biehl is said to have escaped from his captors at
one point and to have entered a bar in the village seeking help, only to be
promptly and quietly returned by the villagers to the custody of his captors.
ETA–5th Assembly is reported to have given part of its archives to French
Basque militants for safekeeping. Whatever the role of French Basque militants within ETA, it was clearly one of the deepest secrets of the Basque
community and kept largely from the public eye. According to one informed
observer, "those French Basque militants in ETA seemed to drop out of sight
by the late 1960s."

As we saw in previous chapters, the growth of the refugee community
served as a mobilizing issue for French Basque youth, especially after the
hunger strikes of 1970. During the 1970s, groups such as Jazar, Herriaren
Alde, and Euskal Gogoa were ideologically awakened by the example of

ETA-m, in particular. Some of this translated into the recruitment of IK in the North.

Yet, according to IK, writing in the captured issue of *Erne*, not only were French Basques working for ETA, but:

> The ties were very close between the Basque soldiers of the South and those of the North. Those of the North participated even actively in the struggle in the South. This isn't a secret any longer for anyone. It should be time that we were assuming it. These ties between fighters lasted even after the split between the milis and the poli-milis: relations exist with the soldiers of the two tendencies." [33]

On May 29, 1986, the Spanish weekly *Cambio 16* published an article by journalist Miguel Angel Liso based on the purported contents of an intelligence document delivered to Spanish leader Felipe González that same month, detailing the nature of ties between ETA and Libya. Among the allegations in the article was the claim that in 1978 French Basque militant Koko Abeberry, then editor of *Enbata*, accompanied ETA leader Francisco Javier Aya Zulaica ("Trepa") on a mission to Libya seeking permission from Muammar Khaddafi for ETA guerrillas to use Libyan camps for weapons and explosives training.[34] In early 1987 the Tribunal of Paris found that *Cambio 16* had defamed Koko Abeberry and awarded him 30,000 francs in damages, which *Cambio 16* appealed.[35]

On October 26, 1986, in a demonstration of the increasingly high-tech nature of the counterinsurgency campaign against ETA, Spanish officials aided by the CIA put into effect Operation Clovisse, a sting operation involving selling two sophisticated shoulder-fired missiles in the underground arms market to ETA. Unbeknownst to the purchaser, the missiles were equipped with small radio beacons which permitted the remote tracking of the missiles after their purchase.[36] Spanish authorities tracked the path of the missiles northward, using helicopters at times in order to avoid tipping off ETA through the use of cars, even in remote pursuit. By this time ETA had learned to transport valuable shipments of arms, explosives, and money in loose caravans of cars linked by walkie-talkies and able to warn of roadblocks or pursuit. The missiles crossed the French border and ended their voyage in the border town of Hendaye. On November 5, 1986, based on information provided by Spanish authorities, French police raided the Basque company Sokoa at Hendaye. In a secret compartment in the plant police found an important cache of ETA arms, including the two shoulder-fired missiles which the police had used to track them. The head of Sokoa, longtime Basque militant and former member of *Enbata* in the 1960s, Patxi Noblia, was arrested.

Sokoa was a particularly significant target for the Spanish since they believed that ETA, beginning in 1970, had used a portion of the proceeds from
bank robberies and kidnappings (as a so-called revolutionary tax) to create
an economic infrastructure in France and in Latin America to provide jobs
for ETA refugees.[37] The Spanish, in turn, began to threaten reprisals against
people paying ETA's revolutionary tax, whether voluntarily or not.[38] The
Spanish believed that Sokoa, created in 1971 with 90,000 francs, twenty-five
stockholders, and three employees, was one of ETA's "self-help" network
of cooperatives, bars, bookstores, and Ikastolas. By 1984, of Sokoa's forty-
three employees, one-third were refugees, one-third were French Basques,
and the others indeterminate.[39] Ximun Haran's newspaper *Ager*, close to the
PNV, was particularly bitter about ETA's contamination of Sokoa by using it
as an arms depot:

> ETA's action at Hendaye is an additional blow struck against *abertzalisme*
> in the Northern Pays Basque, and especially to those *abertzale* working
> in the domain of the economy. Already here at home, Basque politics . . .
> and also Basque culture somewhat are sufficiently suspect. We only
> lacked ETA intervening now to compromise the image of the Basque
> economy.[40]

Two years later French police again raided Sokoa but found nothing. But,
as a result of the documents seized in the first raid, the government later
indicted one of ETA's founders, Julen Madariaga, who had lived openly and
legally in France for many years. In the weapons cache was a receipt from
Madariaga's company in Biarritz for material which allegedly was used in the
construction of ETA's car bombs.[41] Madariaga was subsequently sentenced
to four years in prison,[42] and was freed in August 1991.

In May 1987 former *Enbata* founder Ximun Haran accelerated his long-
standing conflict with his former *Enbata* co-founder Jacques Abeberry by
claiming that *Enbata* continued to serve as an apologist for ETA, aiding and
abetting its cause.[43] As we saw previously, within six months Haran intensified the charge, asserting that *Enbata* in reality had been ETA's child since its
creation and had not been fully independent from ETA since its founding at
Itxassou in 1963. Given Haran's role in the creation of *Enbata*, and his closeness with ETA's first generation of refugees, in particular Julen Madariaga,
his assertion after twenty years of silence was a strong one.

On July 7, 1987, Spanish police arrested two ETA militants and a French
citizen, Jean-Philippe Casabonne, who was aiding them in creating an ETA
commando in Andalusia and Seville.[44] Casabonne was the first French citizen to be tried in Spain for complicity with ETA, though he did not come to
trial until December 1988. In early January 1988 French authorities uncov-

ered an ETA explosives factory in Saint-Pee-sur-Nivelle, seizing nearly three thousand pounds of ammonal explosive. Four French citizens were arrested: Christian Echeto, Daniel Derguy, Victor Pachon, and Pierre Abraham.[45]

Then, on December 1, 1989, police raided a residence in suburban Anglet near Bayonne and found an ETA arsenal which included nineteen rocket launchers, 180 kilos of ammonal explosive, ten kilos of "Goma 2" plastic explosive, and other weapons and grenades.[46] The police were disappointed in their intention to arrest important ETA leaders, but did arrest five people, including two French Basques who resided in the house, Odile Hiriart and Pantxika Pagoaga, whose surveillance led to the cache.

It was the arrest of ETA leader José Antonio Urrutikoetxea Bengoetxea ("Josu Ternera") on January 11, 1989, that demonstrated France's effort to "decapitate" ETA.[47] Ternera was caught after police noted the repeated visits of the wife of one of Herri Batasuna's deputies to the European Parliament, José María Montero-Zabala, to the home of former EHAS leader Battitta Larzabal, where Ternera was ultimately found to be sheltered.[48] Earlier on the day of his arrest, the Basque deputy Montero-Zabala himself had visited Larzabal's house, but French police preferred not to arrest him. Reputed to be an important part of the collective leadership of ETA for much of the past decade, Ternera was demanded by ETA as part of the negotiating team to meet with Spanish authorities in Algiers in March 1989.[49] He was also the first refugee targeted by right-wing Spanish assassins in France in 1975. Among the co-defendants put on trial with him in October 1990 were three French Basques who were accused of sheltering Urrutikoetxea Bengoetxea, including the former co-leader of EHAS, Frédéric (Battitta) Larzabal, his wife, Jacqueline, and Didier Dupont.[50] Prosecutors demanded two years of imprisonment for Larzabal, with one year suspended and six-month suspended sentences for both his wife and Dupont. The sentences were upheld on appeal.

According to one French Basque militant, who himself had been imprisoned for aiding ETA, Urrutikoetxea Bengoetxea was one of the "retrograde and Stalinist" wing of ETA who opposed French Basques' being active in ETA. This militant said that, following the arrest of Urrutikoetxea Bengoetxea, the direction of ETA passed to other leaders still free (presumably "Artapalo"), who saw the efficacy of the French Basque role within the organization.

ETA'S ITINERANT COMMANDO OF FRENCH BASQUES

The most important connection between ETA and French Basques was not discovered until 1990.[51] On April 2, 1990, a French traveling salesman attempted to run a roadblock outside of Seville in Spain. When his tires were punctured by the police barricade, he opened fire on the police, wounding one. Following his arrest, Spanish police found 650 pounds of explosives in his car.[52] Though using an alias, the driver soon admitted to being Henri Parot, a French Basque whose confession "stupefied" Spanish authorities. For his confession revealed that the most deadly of all ETA assassination teams over the past decade or more was in fact an itinerant group of French Basque members of ETA.[53] Traveling easily as tourists or businessmen in Spain, Parot and his group are said to have served as the private hit team, "the itinerant commando," of hardline ETA-m leader Francisco Mugica Garmendia ("Artapalo"), whom French police had been seeking for years. Parot's confession led to the arrest of nine other French Basques, none of whom had ever been arrested, listed by intelligence agencies, or even mentioned by either Spanish informers or Spanish Basque refugees during interrogations.[54] Among the others arrested following Parot's confession were Frédéric Haramboure (who ironically had been hit by a stray bullet during an earlier GAL attack on a bar in Bayonne), Jacques Esnal, José Ochoantesana, Jon Parot, Philippe Saez, Jean-Pierre Erramundegui, Vincent García, François Denis, and Esnal's wife, Maïte Duperou.[55] According to Philippe Boggio and Philippe Etcheverry, as many as fifty or a hundred Basque militants were more visible to the authorities than Parot's group, who confined themselves to cultural activities, playing the Basque flute, the *txistu*, or singing in chorales. By the time Parot was arrested, one of his group, Philippe Saez, had become a novice of the Benedictine monastery of Belloc. According to Boggio and Etcheverry, the twelve years of the commando's operation were not without friction. Some were turned off by the killings, others wanted to join Iparretarrak or target GAL; but these remained internal quarrels. What was unusual about this group was that its members were not clandestine. They led normal, open lives and were seen in cafés and at festivals. Even their occasional travels were normal parts of their jobs. For Boggio and Etcheverry, what was more extraordinary was the sheer constancy of the group, its waterproof militancy, despite the climate around it: the beginning of negotiations between ETA and Spain, the rise of Iparretarrak, and so forth: "The explanation is perhaps that these militants could not see the external evolution. The pact concluded with Txomin isolating them; the assassinations bound them a little more to each other with each of the thirty attacks."[56]

By the time police had put together a chronology of Parot's itinerant commando, they attributed to it a total of twenty-eight actions, causing thirty-seven deaths.[57] At the time of Parot's arrest, according to Spanish authorities, the group was preparing a car bombing, targeting either the Spanish minister of the interior or the Audiencia Nacional, both in Madrid.[58]

This French Basque commando had been the most active of ETA's hit teams since its creation in 1978. It flourished in extraordinary secrecy and with a level of compensation far in excess of that of other ETA commandos. According to Parot's confession, he had been recruited in 1978 when mutual friends introduced him to ETA leader Domingo Iturbe Abasolo ("Txomin"). Parot then set up a highly secret group of his friends and his brothers who worked *only* for Txomin, and then only outside the Basque country, for example, in Madrid or Seville. The genius of this itinerant commando was that its members were able to travel freely as tourists or businessmen above suspicion. Following Txomin's deportation to Gabon in June 1986, operational control over Parot's commando passed to Txomin's successor as ETA's head of military operations, Juan Lasa Michelena ("Txikierdi"), and then to Francisco Mugica Garmendia ("Artapalo").[59] Parot's arrest and the subsequent details of his activities provided the greatest proof of the connection between French Basques and ETA. In reality, a month before Parot's arrest Spanish authorities had handed a forty-page list detailing the activity of French citizens within ETA over to French authorities.[60]

At his subsequent trial Parot claimed that his confession had been the result of five days and nights of torture by Spanish interrogators, including the claim that they had injected him with AIDS.[61] The problem with Parot's attempt to withdraw his confession was that several of those he originally implicated had already confessed in turn. In December 1990 the Audiencia Nacional, the Spanish court charged with questions of terrorism, found Parot guilty and sentenced him to ninety-six years and two months of prison.[62] Three of the nine other people accused of membership in Parot's commando were subsequently cleared of charges against them. The unraveling of the Parot group led to open criticism against Artapalo for having used them too frequently and having caused their premature capture.

While ETA had clearly integrated French Basques into the organization at various levels of responsibility, it was also pursuing relations with a number of international terrorist movements and state-sponsors, among them the Tupamaros, IRA, Red Brigades, Red Army Faction, Libyans, and Algerians.[63] The IRA was alleged to have offered to supply ETA arms, though ETA preferred to deal through independent sources.[64] Arrested ETA militants were said to have told the Spanish police that they had been trained in army camps outside Algiers by Cuban military instructors.[65] Terrorist politics makes strange bedfellows, and many of these groups had little in common except the use of armed struggle. None of ETA's relationships was longer lasting or more elaborate than with the Chilean Movement of the Revolutionary Left (MIR).[66] This relationship, which began in 1978, ultimately led ETA to subcontract out several of its kidnappings of Spanish industrialists: the proceeds were split fifty-fifty. As with Parot's group, the advantage of using Chileans was the ease with which they could move as foreigners and serve as intermediaries without arousing suspicion. Among the papers found in the Sokoa arms cache in 1986 were account books showing payments of millions of pesetas under the notation "Chileans." The arrangement lasted until later ETA leaders Artapalo and Santi Potros balked at continuing the 50 percent split originally agreed to by Txomin, and the Chilean connection ceased. For the PNV, these contacts proved that ETA was weakening and that it was drifting away from its Basque roots to terrorism for terrorism's sake.[67]

By early 1991, with more than fifty ETA members or sympathizers in prison in France, more French Basques were thus in jail for helping ETA than for crimes associated with Iparretarrak for the first time since the great increase in IK's violence beginning in the early 1980s. This illustrated IK's continuing difficulty in carving out a legitimate place for its own home-grown violence within the panoply of Basque political action in France. But it also demonstrated the extent of ETA's hold on the hearts and minds of the French Basque movement. As interesting as these arrest records are, they are only the tip of the iceberg, bare suggestions of the extent of the hidden infrastructure of more than five hundred families across France who housed and protected the ETA refugee community from a French government which was now fully cooperating with Spain. For *Ager*, the actions of Parot and the others who were arrested demonstrated ETA's strategy of the "single front" mobilizing both French and Spanish Basques in the service of their dominant struggle.[68]

ETA RETHINKS ITS POSITION ON IPARRETARRAK

By 1984 there were more than eight hundred Spanish Basque refugees seeking refuge in the French Pays Basque, legally or not. French police sources estimated that one out of every three of these refugees was an active member of ETA and that one in every five was gainfully employed, tithing 10 percent of his or her salary to ETA.[69]

Given the presence of several hundred ETA refugees in France by the early 1970s, it would not be surprising if several of them had supported Iparretarrak's creation as individuals, if not officially as an organization. Indeed, among the French Basque milieu, it is universally believed that IK was supported at the beginning by members of both ETA-m and ETA-pm, whether acting as individuals or not. The most radical position claims their ties were organic in nature. In this view, IK was either a creature of ETA or an outgrowth of it.

The contrasting position holds that IK's violence was an annoyance, if not an outright threat, to ETA's sanctuary in France and that ETA had no interest in seeing the rise of a similar violent movement in France. In this view, IK was imitating the militancy of ETA; if certain individual (ex-)members of ETA lent encouragement and expertise, IK still rose despite ETA's own preferences. In either case, ETA served as an important role model for IK's decision to embrace the armed struggle in France.

Whether or not ETA had created IK, it soon had reason to rethink its early support of IK's introduction of Basque violence into France. The resulting intensification of French government measures against the refugee community, which led the Socialist government to rethink France's long-standing tradition of asylum and begin to extradite ETA militants to Spain in the 1980s, was linked in many minds to the French government's perception of the tie between ETA and IK. At the same time ETA was becoming preoccupied with the appearance of GAL hit teams in France, groups of mercenaries and Spanish police agents who were charged with assassinating known ETA leaders. Whatever putative interest ETA as an organization or as individuals might have had in IK now paled before the threat to ETA posed by GAL and the accelerating hostility of the French state. Indeed, some French antiterrorist experts did not rule out the possibility that ETA, acting in self-interest, might deliver IK to the French authorities itself.[70]

While it had become common knowledge that IK's growing violence after 1980 was now injurious to ETA's sanctuary in France, it was not until after IK's February 15, 1984, attack at Urrugne on the main rail line between France and Spain which derailed the Paris to Madrid "Talgo" train, though miraculously avoiding any injuries to passengers, that ETA-m publicly criticized IK's violence. Soon thereafter IK responded by criticizing ETA-m for being revolutionary in the South, but reformist in France. This led Basque observers to the conclusion that IK and the associated Herri Taldeak movement were now more closely aligned with ETA-pm, while Hordago and Laguntza during their existence had probably been closer to ETA-m. Acting in ETA's interest, the Committee of Basque Political Refugees again criticized IK for its attack in July 1986 against the Palais de Justice in Bayonne, which ETA feared might be used to justify the government's decision days earlier to hand over ETA militants to Spain. The committee's denunciation, in a telephone call from an older militant to Agence France Press, was bitter: "When then will this band of little squirts stop injecting their shit every time that a bad plot is hatched against the refugees?"[71]

The hypothesized link between IK and ETA-pm gained important evidence in April 1985, when French authorities arrested four presumed leaders of ETA-pm (due to the quantity of documents seized) in Dax, in the neighboring department of Les Landes. In their possession, the authorities found an official stamp of Iparretarrak, used to mark its communiqués. While its use was not proven, the possession of the stamp was enough to establish the long-suspected organizational tie between IK and ETA-pm. Others suspected that dissident ex-members of ETA-pm were giving IK logistical support, especially training in explosives.[72]

For other critics of IK, the proof of the weak if nonexistent tie between IK and ETA lay in the amateurish nature of IK's attacks. In this view, "if IK had been closely tied to ETA we would have seen a more mature level of political action on their part." IK's attacks generally involved low technology bombings involving gasoline, and later small propane tanks, with little of the sophistication marking ETA's methodology at the time.

EHAS was suspicious about the origins of IK from the beginning. According to one militant with access to the thinking of EHAS's former leaders, there was a strong feeling within EHAS that ETA had created IK to oppose EHAS and that was why EHAS ultimately ended due to IK's threats. One of EHAS's leaders is reputed to have later said to a leader of ETA, "You created them, now they're your responsibility. Manage them yourselves." Some *abertzale* observers wondered whether ETA had released a force in IK now beyond its control. By the mid-1980s, following the death of three policemen in IK attacks, the government was clearly using IK's violence as one justification for the repression of the refugee community. As we will see below, ETA's resulting anger toward IK was attributed by some to a French disinformation operation which intended just that result.

ETA, GAL, and the Reaction of the French Government

I will not let them destroy the fabric of France.
President François Mitterrand

As we saw in chapter 4, the appearance of the first-generation ETA militants in France in the early 1960s, and their potential to foment discontent among the largely passive French Basque population, was a source of early concern to the government. The first wave of ETA militants fled into exile in France in July 1961, following ETA's attack on a train carrying Franco's supporters to a commemoration of the twenty-fifth anniversary of the military rebellion that began the Spanish Civil War.[73] If the attack caused no injuries, and failed to derail a single car, the Spanish response was characteristically harsh. According to Clark, more than one hundred ETA members were subsequently arrested and tortured, and a similar number soon were forced into exile in France.[74]

The early relationships between the founders of *Enbata* and the leadership of ETA in exile, especially Julen Madariaga, were of particular concern to the French government. In 1963 French intelligence reports indicated that almost all of the ETA refugee community in France were present at the creation of the *Enbata* movement at the Aberri Eguna in Itxassou in April. The government believed that ETA was an active force behind the rise of Basque nationalism in France and that the ties began shortly after its first members sought asylum in the Pays Basque Français.

In October 1964 the French government expelled Madariaga, Alvarez Emparanza ("Txillardegi"), Benito del Valle, and Ignacio Irigaray, who had been in charge of ETA's first military front, after police found an arms cache in Irigaray's business.[75] In the wake of their departure, other ETA militants continued to seek refuge in France, including militants like J. J. Etxave; during the 1960s and 1970s ETA slowly consolidated its operation in France, using it as a sanctuary from which to plan and occasionally carry out military operations against Spain. With the successive splinterings of ETA into ETA-V and ETA-VI assemblies, and later ETA-militar (ETA-m) and ETA-poli-mili (ETA-pm), the French government was inclined, if anything, to overestimate the support of the movement and the numbers of militants involved. This was undoubtedly due in part to the reaction to separatism by a jealously unitary state, reinforced by the lessons of the humiliating loss of its colonial empire. According to one old and respected French Basque militant, at the time of ETA-pm's ascendance ETA-m had been reduced to five militants, including two Basque-speaking Basques, one a product of a mixed Basque-Spanish marriage, and two non-Basques. Their early actions were small armed attacks, but never in France, "For you never saw off the limb on which you sit." He said that the process of infiltration of ETA began early, especially by the time of the trial at Burgos. At the time that outspoken French conservative politician and former minister Alexandre Sanguinetti declared for public consumption that France had good information that ETA had six hundred militants and was capable of destabilizing Spain, according to this older militant who sheltered some of them, ETA-m had seven members and four of them did not know how to drive a car: "They were children."

The intensification of the armed struggle in Spain led a steady stream of ETA members, or Etarras, to cross the border to seek sanctuary in France. Many of these militants had not committed "crimes of blood." But the attention of both Spanish and French intelligence was focused on the clandestine inner core of ETA's leaders, especially the military infrastructure, which would ultimately become ETA-m and then simply ETA. Spanish minister of the interior Juan José Roson declared on June 28, 1980, that "all the leaders of ETA live in France."[76] Clark cautiously repeats the suspicion of Spanish government sources that by 1980 the entire 35- to 45-man directorate which controlled ETA lived in secrecy on the French side of the border.[77] If this figure is true, then it casts suspicion on Christian Bombédiac's estimate in *Le Monde* that of five hundred Basque refugees in France at the beginning of 1979 only fifty to eighty were active in ETA.[78] Yet the number of refugees continued to grow as a result of the conflict in the South; by the mid-1980s the figure of eight hundred refugees was cited by the French Ministry of the Interior in discussions with the Spanish government.

THE FRENCH TRADITION OF ASYLUM

More than any other factor, the ETA refugees benefited from the historic French tradition of political asylum, just as the PNV leadership did in the years following the Spanish Civil War. The government attempted to impose on ETA the same conditions of apolitical conduct which the PNV had scrupulously followed after that war. Unlike the bourgeois diplomats of the PNV, the French government found itself confronted in the late 1960s with a growing level of political violence in Spain, planned and carried out by ETA leaders effectively violating the terms of their sanctuary in France. Both ETA and the French state had a tacit agreement in this period to look the other way as long as the Basque violence was not transplanted into France and France could maintain the figleaf of plausible deniability with Spain regarding the use of French territory as ETA's northern sanctuary. As Clark points out, there was little love lost in this era between the French government and the Spanish government of Franco; from the French perspective, giving asylum to ETA may even have balanced the ledger with a Spanish government which was providing refuge for the now-exiled Organisation de l'Armée Secrète (OAS) following the Algerian debacle and its repeated efforts to assassinate de Gaulle.[79]

But with ETA's execution of Admiral Carrero Blanco in Operation Ogro in 1973 and the subsequent news conference held by those responsible upon their return to France, the pressure on the French government began to grow. Since much of the French government intelligence on the Basque movement is gained through informers and illegal wiretaps, and thus never publicly divulged in court, we can only surmise the motives for the French government's attitude in 1974, if it was not the result of Carrero Blanco's assassination. Perhaps the first appearance of violence by Iparretarrak the previous summer was a contributing factor. But, as we saw in chapter 4, the French government banned *Enbata* as first among four ethnic nationalist movements in France, and it was clear that the surrogate target for its action against *Enbata* was ETA itself. While the government continued to defend its policy of political asylum, it began to tighten its control over the issuance of work permits, and the frequent harassment of the refugee community by the French police was an effort to intimidate the refugees into apolitical retirement.[80]

If anything, ETA was increasing its contacts with external groups in this period, seeking arms and technical training. The question of ETA's contacts with the Soviet Union and the world Communist movement have preoccupied its opponents. According to José María Portell, the first ETA militants received training in Cuba beginning in 1964, well before the organization's conversion from nationalism to Marxist revolution.[81] Claire Sterling says that from Cuba ETA militants spread out for training with the Tupamaros, the Montoneros, the Algerians, and later the Libyans; it was in the Libyan camps in 1971 that ETA entered into contact with the IRA.[82] ETA and the IRA were said to have seen each other as allies in the joint struggle against imperialism.[83] Alliances were reported to have been made with Fatah, the largest component of the PLO. Subsequently ETA was trained by the PLO and by Czechoslovakia.[84] By 1974 ETA had entered into an organization of those dedicated to insurrection in Western Europe, which included minority groups like the Bretons and Corsicans and groups like the Red Brigades and Red Army Faction.[85]

In 1975 the *New York Times* reported that ETA had contacted the Soviet Embassy in Paris seeking arms and training.[86] They are said to have voiced unease at dealing with the Spanish Communist party because, like the ultra-French nationalist Parti Communiste Français, it was adamantly opposed to separatism. Following Franco's death, a special ETA assembly in France decided to accelerate its military training; 143 militants were later sent to Algeria at various times for training.[87] In 1978 Spanish police allegedly observed a meeting between KGB agents and ETA-m's Eugenio Etxeveste Arizgura ("Antxon") in Saint-Jean-de-Luz.[88] In January 1979 the Spanish press reported the alleged ties between ETA and both the IRA and the Soviet KGB.[89] Within three years the Basque question figured in the Soviet Union's foreign policy with Spain. During a visit to Madrid in 1979, Soviet foreign minister Andrei Gromyko is said to have offered to settle the Basque insurrection if Spain would pledge not to enter NATO.[90] When the Spanish refused, he is reported to have threatened to exacerbate their struggle. It was at this point that Spain turned to German counterterrorism experts in dealing with the level of Basque violence.

By the mid-1970s Spain was growing exasperated with the mounting campaign of ETA violence. After 1975 Spanish outrage at the killing of Carrero Blanco, combined with growing French discomfort with ETA's violation of the terms of asylum, led to an outbreak of violence against the ETA refugee community that would last until 1987 and exceed in magnitude any domestic violence that France had known since the German occupation of World War II.

The Rise of Anti-ETA Violence

Beginning in 1975, the ETA refugee community in France became the targets of a long series of attacks by various anti-ETA groups which remained active until the French government dropped its policy of asylum in 1986 and adopted a streamlined policy of urgent expulsion of ETA refugees wanted by Spain. In the early years, from 1975 to 1980, the attacks were claimed by a variety of groups, including ATE (Antiterrorism ETA), AAA (Apostolic Anticommunist Alliance), CCAA (Anti-Marxist Commandos), GAE (Armed Spanish Groups), and BVE (Spanish Basque Battalion).[91] In addition, other extreme right-wing Spanish groups came and went under names including ANE, OVAA, OAMES, and Delta Sur. By 1980, while the BVE had become predominant, France had come to believe that the whole pattern of anti-ETA violence was the product of the Spanish police and intelligence services using a variety of cover names. The extent of knowledge and/or complicity by French police and intelligence remained to be proven, but ties at the local level were clear.

The months of March through October 1975 were characterized by an unusual level of political tension in France surrounding the Basque problem, apart from the death of Franco and the vortex of political change in his aftermath.[92] The Spanish undersecretary of state, Luis Peralta España, accused Paris of giving asylum to terrorists. A Basque demonstrator, Jacques Andreu, immolated himself before the Spanish consulate in Pau. Armed undercover Spanish police were apprehended on multiple occasions while attempting to carry out surveillance or operations against the refugee community. French police continued to arrest and prosecute refugees for possession of arms. In a diplomatic signal to both Spain and ETA, French minister of the interior Michel Poniatowski visited Bayonne and the border area and denounced the cycle of violence.

The first act of violence against the refugee community took place on April 6, 1975, with the use of plastic explosives against the Mugalde bookstore in the border town of Hendaye.[93] In May a second bombing of Mugalde took place; three armed Spanish policemen were arrested near the scene and subsequently released at the frontier, without any judicial inquiry.[94] Three days later another armed Spanish undercover agent, masquerading as an antique dealer from Barcelona, was arrested in Bayonne, taken to the border, and released following the intervention of the Spanish consul in Bayonne. Another Spanish agent was arrested two days later in Saint-Jean-de-Luz. In June the Mugalde bookstore was bombed for the third time in three months, and plastic explosives were used against the residences of two Basque refugees, killing one of the perpetrators in the attempt. Following the bombing attack on the restaurant of former ETA military leader J. J. Etxave in Bayonne on June 28, French police arrested François Chabessier, its author, in Perpignan. At his trial Chabessier stated, "The government was bothered by the refugees; we did a work of ecology." [95]

According to the French minister of the interior, Chabessier had been recruited by a former legionnaire named "Yvan" who resided in Madrid and was assigned the task of "recruiting mercenaries in order to form commandos of intimidation against the Spanish political refugees residing in France." [96] Chabessier testified that he had been given a secret code enabling him to find refuge in any Spanish military post. Finally, a communiqué published July 10 and signed "ATE" (Antiterrorism ETA) claimed responsibility for the attacks carried out over the previous months. Claiming to be a "private initiative" having nothing to do with either Spanish police circles or the Guerrilleros de Cristo Rey, the authors of the communiqué said that "Spanish society [was in] a state of legitimate defense." [97] Their stated goal was to assassinate four ETA refugees for each ETA victim.

In August 1975 French police stopped two Spanish citizens in Saint-Jean-de-Luz and found a list of fifty refugees' names and addresses accompanied by photographs. [98] Between 1975 and 1977 this *guerra sucia* or "dirty war" had killed five, wounded thirty-four, and kidnapped two who were never heard from again. A climate of fear settled over the refugee community as this mysterious anti-ETA force acted with seeming impunity. The ease with which the anti-ETA terrorists operated, and the quality of their information (including names, addresses, and photographs of refugees), led the refugee community to believe the hit teams were either paramilitary or parapolice in nature. In this period a new psychological tactic appeared, the use of "political rape," in which the wives or girlfriends of ETA members were abducted and/or assaulted in order to strike a blow against their Etarra relatives. [99]

In 1978 Spanish police services had declared a de facto "right of reply" to ETA actions and recruited mercenaries from the OAS community in exile in Spain or from the organized crime milieu of either Bordeaux or Marseilles. [100] In fact, as the number of attacks against the refugees multiplied, the attacks themselves were attributed to a list which reads like the "who's who" of the European intelligence, mercenary, and soldier-of-fortune circles. In a detailed but highly partisan analysis of the violence against ETA, the Committee of Inquiry into Violations of Human Rights in Europe (CEDRI) draws a complex portrait of the recruitment of the hit teams which served at the direction of the Spanish police.

According to CEDRI, the recruitment of mercenaries for the operation against ETA began in the office of Admiral Carrero Blanco before his death. In restructuring the Spanish intelligence services, Carrero Blanco enlisted trained operatives from a number of backgrounds, including ex-OAS members who had found asylum in Madrid; Italian neo-fascists who fled into exile after the attempted coup of the "Black Prince" Borghese in 1971; Portuguese former secret service agents and members of the ELP (Army for the Liberation of Portugal), including one former Portuguese contract security guard for the American Embassy in Lisbon; Latin Americans, including members of the Argentinian AAA; and finally members of a variety of Spanish extreme right-wing groups, including the Guerrilleros de Cristo Rey. To these were allegedly added members of the Corsican underground and the organized crime syndicates of Bordeaux and Marseilles, as well as agents of the Mossad. From the point of view of the French, the use of ex-OAS agents violated the understanding between France and Spain in 1971 whereby France pledged to control ETA and Spain would control the ex-OAS.

If, in many cases, the killing of ETA refugees was carried out with a brutal efficiency, in other cases there was a clearly indiscriminate and amateurish quality to the bungled attempts. Gayle Rivers attributes many of these early attacks to drunken sprees of retribution by Spanish police and Guardia Civil acting without official approval.[101] Already, however, it was clear that the government was hiring mercenaries whose violence could then be denied by Spanish authorities. In the subsequent trials of those hitmen who were arrested, a classic image of "marginal men" living on the edge of society and engaging in acts of violence not out of principle but for money or thrills often emerged. One GAL member's attorney asked for the court's mercy for his client by describing the formative impact of a loveless alcoholic mother who left home one day to attend a funeral and never returned.[102] Through the camaraderie of GAL's violence, as in other mercenary exploits, he and others found the acceptance and sense of belonging lacking in their personal lives.

By the late 1970s it was clear that the use of multiple names to claim responsibility was simply a figleaf which sought to disguise the source of the attacks. In fact, by 1980 the predominant anti-ETA group had become the Spanish Basque Battalion (BVE). The apprehension of active-duty Spanish police agents in the French Pays Basque as early as 1975 was further corroborated by the subsequent claim of most of the captured mercenaries that they were working for Spanish police or intelligence. The trail of the anti-ETA violence began to point toward the Spanish government.

On June 2, 1977, French police announced the arrest of Miguel Angel

Apalategi-Ayerbe ("Apala"), the chief ETA-pm military commando, after three years of clandestinity.[103] He was suspected most notably of having taken part in the kidnapping of Spanish industrialist M. Arrasate, who was released after paying a ransom of one hundred million pesetas. Police also suspected that Apala was a prime suspect in the disappearance of another ETA leader, Eduardo Moreno Bergareche ("Pertur") the previous summer, in what authorities interpreted as an internal dispute within ETA-pm. By late August Apala was undertaking a hunger strike at the Baumettes prison in Marseilles, and one hundred thousand people marched in Pamplona in his support. He stopped the strike in early September at ETA's demand, expecting a grant of refugee status.[104] *Le Monde* speculated that the Spanish government might be seeking to appease Basque opinion by favoring his receiving refugee status from the French.[105]

In July 1978 former ETA-m leader Juan José Etxave was gravely wounded and his wife killed in an attack on their bar in Saint-Jean-de-Luz, an attack claimed by both AAA and BVE. The alleged leader of the team which struck the Etxaves was Joseph Zurita, who was previously implicated in the assassination of Moroccan opposition leader Ben Barka in France.[106] In December 1978 the BVE accomplished one of its greatest coups in assassinating José María Beñarán Ordeñana ("Argala"), the "electrician" of ETA who had taken part in the killing of Carrero Blanco nearly five years before to the day. Argala was killed by a remote-controlled car bomb, just as he had killed Carrero Blanco in Madrid in 1973. Later in 1978 Italian judge Vitaliano Calabria announced that he had information linking the death of Argala to the Spanish secret services along with Italian elements.[107]

If the purpose of the Spanish state-sponsored violence was to bring pressure on the French government, by 1978 signs began to appear that it was succeeding.[108] First, President Valéry Giscard d'Estaing announced that the Basques would no longer be eligible for refugee status. This policy took effect after a meeting of French and Spanish ministers in January 1979, followed in January and February 1979 by a French government policy of detention and forced relocation of refugees. Madrid expressed particular satisfaction at France's first seizure of twenty refugees, handing seven of them over to Spanish authorities on January 30.[109] This came on the eve of reports that Spanish premier Suárez was preparing strong criticism of the "passivity" of the French on the following day, January 31, before the Council of Europe in Strasbourg. However, this still represented a middle-of-the-road position for the French. According to Clark, between 1977 and 1981 the Spanish demanded twenty-nine extraditions of ETA militants and got none of them, though some militants were handed over at the border on an "unofficial" basis.[110] From the perspective of the Spanish, the French were adding insult to injury in this period with Giscard's public reservations about Spanish entry into the EEC and his expressed "understanding" of the action of French farmers in burning Spanish trucks hauling cheap Spanish produce and wine.[111] In December 1980 Spanish interior minister Roson denounced the French government before the Cortes for permitting the leaders of ETA to "move in complete freedom" and admitted the presence of a small intelligence-gathering function to monitor their movements. His criticism of French policy was soon followed by Jean-François Revel in *L'Express*, and by *El País* in Spain, which denounced the French for their "cynicism." [112]

Failing to convince the French to extradite its most wanted refugees, the Spanish continued their campaign of violence against the refugee community. At the same time ETA embarked on a short-lived "vacation war" along the Spanish coast, as a signal to both the French and Spanish states of its refusal to be bartered between the two.[113] ETA-pm announced its decision to suspend the tourist war in early August because of the public outcry in Spain.[114] The pseudonymous mercenary and counterterrorist Gayle Rivers describes the Spanish government's recruitment in 1979 of a team of high-level international mercenaries in the aftermath of ETA's failed effort, with IRA assistance, to assassinate Spanish premier Suárez with an RPG-7 which failed to explode.[115] Rivers describes operations during late 1979 and 1980 which involved several deaths, including those of Rodrigo Ibarguren ("Zarra") and Julio Larrañaga ("Chempe").[116]

By 1980 the BVE had emerged as the primary vehicle of Spain's violence in France, claiming responsibility for nearly all the attacks that year, which killed nineteen (ten in Spain and nine in France) and wounded more than thirty.[117] In November 1980, following an attack on the Bar Hendayais in Hendaye which killed two and wounded ten, the three attackers, acting for BVE, crossed the French border post and found refuge in the Spanish border police post nearby. According to CEDRI, after calling a high-ranking officer of Spanish intelligence in Madrid, they were transferred to Madrid and then released.[118] After the attack, Giscard d'Estaing declared, "It is intolerable that Spanish police travel to France to settle their disputes." [119] This was the last attack claimed by the BVE, followed by a de facto moratorium on anti-ETA violence for nearly three years. Among the reasons for the truce in the short term were the upcoming French presidential elections in 1981, which offered the possibility of a change in French government policy toward the refugees. From their origins in 1975 until November 1983 on the eve of the appearance of GAL, there were a total of more than sixty attacks against the refugee community carried out in the name of one of the front groups described above.

On December 12, 1980, during his trial for the killing of ETA refugee Periko Elizaran, Maxime Szonek of Bordeaux, reputed to be a contract agent of the Mossad, admitted to working for the Spanish secret services and to having always worked for "the official French secret services whose names are known," which he couldn't identify publicly.[120] His declaration raised the question of the involvement of French intelligence in the anti-ETA campaign, despite government denials. In October 1983 the Spanish weekly *Actual* reported that Szonek was the contact point of the Israeli Mossad's cooperation with the Spanish in attacking ETA in France, due to Israel's concern about the ties between ETA (and the IRA) and the PLO.[121]

While Socialist Laurent Fabius was French premier, he was asked hypothetically about what he would have done about GAL if he had been Spanish premier Felipe González. In a clear statement of *Realpolitik*, Fabius is quoted as saying, "I have never had to give such orders, but if I had had to do it, I would have done it."[122]

The Appearance of GAL: The Northern or "Dirty" War

> *The French Pays Basque has been converted*
> *into a Lebanon by Spain.*
> GAL[123]

> *We will liquidate the terrorists of ETA*
> *who are hiding in France.*
> GAL[124]

In the months following the French presidential elections the Spanish were hopeful that the new administration of François Mitterrand would change long-standing French policy toward ETA, especially its commitment to the nonextradition of political refugees. But Mitterrand and his new minister of the interior, Gaston Defferre, made clear their commitment to the French tradition of asylum.[125] As Defferre stated in July 1981, "Extraditing is contrary to all the traditions of France, especially when it concerns, as there, a political combat."[126] This policy, later called the "Defferre Doctrine,"[127] governed France's policy for the next three years and was not officially reversed until after the next legislative elections in 1986. Not even the victory of the Spanish Socialist Party (PSOE) in the October 1982 Spanish parliamentary elections, and the subsequent appointment of Felipe González as premier, offered enough fraternal Socialist leverage on Mitterrand to convince him to abandon the historic practice of asylum. Defferre reiterated French policy in 1982, saying, "Extradition runs against all France's traditions, especially in questions of political struggles." [128]

The moratorium on anti-ETA violence, which virtually disappeared during 1982, appeared attributable to the dynamics of domestic Spanish politics this time and to the potential change in policy which a change in government might represent. According to Manuel Ballesteros, director of MULA (Mando Unificado de la Lucha Antiterrorista) and a central figure in Spain's efforts against ETA's violence, if ETA's cover in southern France were to disappear or if there existed better collaboration between French and Spanish authorities, ETA would not last six months with the Spanish police. [129] As it was, the Spanish reacted with "bitterness" to Mitterrand's announced antiterrorist plan. Typical was the reaction of the director of Spanish police, José Luis Fernández Dopico, who admitted, "I very much fear that France will continue to be a sanctuary for terrorists who act in their neighbor's [territory], whether they're Spanish, Italian, Germans, or others." [130]

On September 28, 1982, sources close to ETA-pm (Seventh Assembly) revealed their impending decision to renounce the armed struggle and disband. [131] ETA-pm had first declared a ceasefire following the attempted rightist putsch in Spain on February 23, 1981. A year later it was internally divided over the renunciation of violence, and the debate splintered the organization. The majority tendency, the so-called Eighth Assembly, had decided to end the ceasefire. A minority faction, the Seventh Assembly, wanted to continue it. Faced with the inability to reconcile the two positions, the minority group, ETA-pm (Seventh Assembly), decided to disband and to accept government offers of amnesty except for crimes of blood. Ironically, two weeks later, on October 13, French police announced the arrest of Jesús Abrisketa Korta ("Txuxo"), presumed leader of ETA-pm (Eighth Assembly). [132] This came less than three months after the arrest of Domingo Iturbe Abasolo ("Txomin"), ETA-m's leader, who was later deported to Gabon.

In February 1983 a plan emerged from within González's new Socialist administration to neutralize ETA by striking at its rear bases in France. [133] Called the "Damborenena Doctrine," it defined a new "Zone Speciale Nord" (ZEN) in which the Spanish government would implement a broad counterinsurgency plan to end the problem of ETA violence against Spain. For CEDRI, this plan represented a Spanish declaration of "total war" on ETA by mid-1983. [134]

By October 1983 Spanish policemen had embarked on a campaign of abductions against ETA militants. One of its architects declared in a Spanish court in 1989 that the campaign of abductions was created for "humanitarian" reasons. Four Spanish police agents were arrested in October and not released until December 8. One was a member of the antigang forces of the Barcelona police and the other three were part of a special operations unit of the Guardia Civil. At the time of their release on December 8 the police chief of Bilbao posted his personal assurances that they would return to France for their trial.[135] When their trial began in June 1986 none were to be found. All told, more than twenty Spanish policemen were detected around Basque neighborhoods after October 1, to the apparent indifference of the French Police Judiciare.

On December 4, 1983, a Spanish salesman who resided in France, Segundo Marey, was abducted in Hendaye and spirited across the border to Bilbao, where he was held for ten days before being released. Marey apparently came into contact with the refugee community in the context of his job and attracted the attention of Spanish police intelligence. In a communiqué admitting the abduction was an error, the action was claimed by a new and previously unheard of group, the Grupos Antiterroristas de Liberación (GAL). Four days after his kidnapping the four Spanish police detained by the French since October were released; in its subsequent communiqué GAL claimed that it released Marey as a result of France's goodwill gesture, suggesting a tacit trade of hostages. The choice of the name "GAL" was interesting: it has other connotations in Spanish, being both the first three initials of the Spanish word for the French (Gallos) and the name of a popular brand of Spanish detergent, furthering the image of GAL as an act of political cleansing.[136]

Shortly thereafter, French police arrested a Spanish agent named Pedro Sánchez who was found to be in possession of documents coming from the French Renseignements Généraux and the subprefecture in Bayonne.[137] This furthered speculation about a public/private division in French diplomacy in which official public denials were offset by some (perhaps unofficial) cooperation between police at the local level. Then, on December 19, GAL claimed responsibility for the assassination of ETA militant Ramón Oñaederra ("Kattu"), barman of the Café Kayet in Bayonne.[138] Finally, on December 28, GAL succeeded in finding and killing Mikel Goikoetchea ("Txapela"), the brother of historic ETA militant Jon Goikoetchea, killed by the Guardia Civil in 1972.[139] The killing of Txapela was particularly revealing of GAL's thoroughness, since his whereabouts were a closely guarded secret apparently learned from two ETA militants who had just helped him move secretly to Saint-Jean-de-Luz, who were kidnapped by GAL and never heard from again. With Txapela's death, according to the Spanish weekly *Tiempo*, GAL had struck at the heart of ETA's command structure in France.[140]

With these operations, GAL signaled the intensification of the Spanish *guerra sucia* by declaring open season on ETA refugees in their sanctuary in

France. By August 1984, ten months after its creation, GAL had killed nine refugees, wounded five, and kidnapped three, including the two who simply disappeared.[141] In addition, numerous other attempted kidnappings were thwarted, and the persons and property of people outside the refugee community were wounded in the attacks. Among GAL's targets were members of ETA's executive committee, the brother-in-law of ETA leader "Txomin," and Tomás Pérez Revilla, another one of the historic leaders of ETA.[142] Among the techniques perfected by GAL in this period were long-range shootings using telescopic sights, machine-gunnings of bars frequented by the refugee community (including repeat attacks in July and August 1984 against J. J. Etxave's bar in Bayonne), and car bombings.

Between 1983 and 1986 GAL committed a total of twenty-seven assassinations on French soil, as many as Direct Action, the Armenian Secret Army for the Liberation of Armenia (ASALA), and the Support Committee for Arab Political Prisoners (CSPPA) *combined*.[143] For the French news weekly *L'Express*, this was "one of the most beautiful operations ever mounted by the secret services of a European country against a neighboring country, since the end of the Second World War."[144]

With the great increase in GAL's violence during 1983, another school of thought emerged regarding the source. According to this alternative explanation, GAL grew up in the years following ETA's embrace of the so-called revolutionary tax, a process of extortion of contributions from Spanish industrialists and banks in order to avoid kidnapping or ETA attacks. In this view, GAL was the creature of one of Spain's six largest banks, which recruited mercenaries to disrupt ETA's financial apparatus through violence and thus disrupt the collection of the revolutionary tax on banks and their affluent clients.[145] Three of the victims of GAL's violence, José Luis Ansola, Carlos Ibarguren, and José Miguel Lujua, were closely involved with ETA's finances, and Ibarguren was the head of ETA finances at the time.

In January 1984 *Tiempo* reported that a set of offices belonging to a security company on Calle Orense in the northern part of Madrid was in fact the nerve center of GAL. Its activity had become continual in past months, and its employees allegedly were seen in restaurants in Madrid with officials of the Spanish Secret Service or the special operations group of the Guardia Civil. By this point the outlines of what GAL intended were clear. According to a source familiar with its intentions, "GAL, unlike previous efforts, is a total project of direct and psychological warfare, with political objectives within a global plan for the Basque country."[146] Moreover, the genius of any "dirty war" of this kind is the plausible deniability of its existence by the country's leaders. At the same time GAL's violence within France began to exert a serious pressure on the French government to come to some diplomatic settlement with Spain in order to end the state of siege that was gripping the Pays Basque Français.

Iparretarrak's violence seemed to aid GAL's cause since it served to connect in the public's mind the rise of Basque violence in France with the presence of ETA's refugees. For the French Basque movement Laguntza, the purpose of GAL's violence was to isolate the refugee community and prevent any cohesive *abertzale* action.[147] For some, GAL was effecting a needed housecleaning. Even some of those who opposed GAL were afraid to manifest it for fear of lending support to Iparretarrak. For the French government, IK's violence in this period increased the stakes of the conflict and put more pressure on the state to solve both aspects of the problem of violence by moving against the refugee community, which was seen as inspiring the violence of both GAL and IK. As one agent of the Renseignements Généraux described the situation in 1984:

> ETA, that's serious. Note, in passing, that the Spanish [separatists] haven't done anything to facilitate the task of the democracies where they evolve. In using France as a rear base for perpetrating attacks in Spain, they have an odd fashion of thanking us for the welcome that our country gives to political prisoners or militants threatened in their own country. I will go even further, in saying that they pervert their cause in not leaving their new democracy the time to come out of forty years of obscurantism. It suffices just to consider well these two numbers: 50 and 350: 50, that's the number of attacks committed by ETA between the birth of the movement and the death of Franco, that is to say around twenty years. There were 350 attacks since the coming of democracy in Spain, that's to say, in eight years. For me, this needs no commentary.[148]

The issue of Basque violence figured on the agenda of a dinner between François Mitterrand and Felipe González on December 20, 1984, in which France pledged to quell ETA's violence against Spain, and Spain to "attempt" to muzzle the reprisals of GAL in France.[149] Socialist deputy Jean-Pierre Destrade declared in early January, "The GAL is certainly composed of French activists, commanded by certain members of the Spanish police and also supported financially by persons in charge on the other side of the border."[150] Destrade's remarks provoked the immediate ire of the Spanish Socialist Party (PSOE), which demanded proof: "The declarations of M. Destrade are demagogic and without basis."[151]

However, in May *Cambio 16* published a lengthy interview with two purported members of GAL who confirmed many of the suspicions swirling about the organization. They said that GAL had been created the previous October following ETA's assassination of Captain Martín Barrios: "The intelligence services demanded that measures be taken, regardless of the means employed. And since the police couldn't risk working outside of Spanish borders, we decided to form a group which would annihilate ETA on the edge of the law."[152] According to these individuals, GAL was composed of mercenaries of a variety of backgrounds:

> a hundred persons specializing in antiguerrilla warfare and coming from several countries, who fought in the Belgian Congo, in Algeria, in Biafra and the Near East, or who were trained in the French Foreign Legion.[153]

In May 1985 *Le Monde* alleged that there was material evidence of direct contacts between the mercenaries of GAL and the Spanish police.[154] Felipe González referred to the allegations as "errors without basis."[155] Julián San Cristóbal, Spain's director of state security, dismissed *Le Monde*'s allegations as an "insidious accusation, absolutely without foundation." Cristóbal repeated his denials on April 10, 1986, following a similar report by the French television channel Antenne 2.[156] Yet, in late 1987, the Spanish newspaper *Diario 16* named Bilbao police *commissaire* José Amedo Fouce as the organizer of GAL.[157] This corroborated the earlier surfacing of his name during the interrogations of arrested GAL members.

GAL'S "PATRIOTIC TAX"

If GAL sought to end ETA's use of the revolutionary tax levied on Spanish industries and wealthy individuals as a kind of protection money, GAL itself was funded by a patriotic tax allegedly paid by numerous Basque businessmen. For Judge Michel Svahn, president of the court charged with hearing the GAL cases, "the GAL are groups financed by a patriotic tax, voluntarily given, the opposite of the revolutionary tax of ETA, which is extorted. It appears that a nonnegligible number of persons spontaneously gave their collaboration [to GAL] with, to be sure, methods identical to those of ETA."[158]

GAL's members acted "not for ideology nor for sentimentality, but for the money."[159] The fee varied according to the target. In the case of important ETA-m leaders like Domingo Iturbe Abasolo ("Txomin") or Eugenio Etxebeste ("Antxon"), the reported contract was for twenty-two million pesetas or two hundred thousand dollars each.

In early January 1984, several weeks after the meeting between Spanish premier Felipe González and French president Mitterrand, the French stopped granting political refugee status and began to round up ETA militants.[160] Authorities sought to apprehend a list of thirty militants belonging to both ETA-m and ETA-pm, but because of their frequent moves for reasons of security it was only able to apprehend seventeen. Six of these were deported to Guadeloupe on the way to exile in Panama, and seven others were assigned to French residences far from the Spanish border.[161] By July fifty ETA refugees had been expelled from the French Pays Basque, either north of the Loire River or to Latin America, including ETA's presumed military chief as well as the head of its branch of intelligence and infrastructure.[162] As *Herriz Herri* argued, "There is a total reversal of the policy toward the refugees, despite the electoral promises, and this thanks to the assassinations of GAL."[163]

During this same time, between December 1983 and July 1984, GAL killed seven ETA refugees, including the head of ETA's commando groups, and wounded five others. In August *Le Monde* reported that the French police had the team which killed ETA militants Tomás Pérez Revilla and Roman Orbe under surveillance at the time.[164] As part of the subsequent investigation, French authorities identified a departmental police official with close ties to the Front National who was the alleged source of the refugees' photos which had been turned in for identity cards and later found in the possession of the GAL hit teams. For Maître Christiane Fando, lawyer for *abertzale* defendants, the presence of these photos demonstrated the secret ties between the French state and GAL.[165] *Le Canard Enchaîné* reported on April 4 that a list of refugees found on a GAL member was similar to one prepared by the French Renseignements Généraux.[166] The Spanish news weekly *Cambio 16* on June 25 published intelligence files allegedly from the office of Felipe González that included a picture of the assassinated Mikel Goikoetchea ("Txapela") which he had turned into the subprefecture in Bayonne for an official French identity card (*carte de séjour*). In other cases, material seized during an arrest of a refugee did not figure in the trial evidence, but later appeared in the Spanish magazine *Cambio 16* instead.[167] While pursuing the GAL option, Spain also stepped up the application of its year-and-a-half-old program of amnesty and "reinsertion" for ETA militants willing to renounce the use of violence, provided they were not themselves wanted for crimes of blood.[168]

On June 14, 1984, interior minister Gaston Defferre traveled to Madrid to meet with his Spanish counterpart, José Barrionuevo. In response to Spanish assertions that terrorists were finding a refuge in France, Defferre responded, "A terrorist is not a political refugee."[169] *Le Canard Enchaîné* predicted that, as a result of this meeting, the Spanish government would offer an amnesty to those among the eight hundred ETA refugees in France who were not guilty of blood crimes. Both French and Spanish sources estimated that as many as four hundred of the eight hundred would accept the offer. For the four hundred militants who would likely refuse, essentially the clandestine and hard-line faction within ETA-m, the French government would then be free to proceed to measures of distancing or expulsion to South America in order to constrain the organization.[170] Anai Artea (Between Brothers) feared that the next step would be for the French government to consent to extraditions to Spain itself.[171]

With the upcoming visit of President Mitterrand to Aquitaine scheduled for October 1984, there was fear within the refugee community that he would use the occasion to announce a police crackdown on the refugees similar to that before Pope John Paul II's visit to Lourdes in 1983.[172] As of November 1984, nearly one year after GAL's first attack, a total of sixteen of its members indicted by the courts in Bayonne had been set free.[173] By April 1985 the twenty-six members of GAL arrested to date accounted for nearly 60 percent of the GAL attacks. Of the twenty-six, only eight were still in prison.[174]

For Alain Tourré, coordinator of police in the Pyrénées-Atlantiques charged with fighting terrorism, "It is not, far from it, the total dismantlement of GAL, since we can't trace it back into Spain and locate its commanders. But even so these arrests mark a serious reverse for this organization."[175] Socialist deputy Destrade confirmed seeing several of those later found to be part of GAL in political rallies for the Gaullist RPR. He raised the possibility that in following the trail of GAL back to its commanders, "it is possible that one will find persons very highly placed in the *ancien régime* [of Giscard d'Estaing]."[176] The individual Destrade evidently had in mind was former interior minister (Prince) Michel Poniatowski: "this old large and fat sewer rat, who grazed with delight in the used water of the last [seven-year presidential term]."[177]

In a moment of extraordinary candor for a judge concerning a case over which he was presiding, Judge Michel Svahn explained that to eliminate GAL would first mean eliminating ETA:

> There are people who don't like Communists, and one mustn't forget that these Spanish Basques living among us are Communists. One can be a part of GAL for ideological reasons. There are perhaps two hundred and fifty people in the department who would demand but one thing: snare the Spanish Basques. . . . Let's be honest, if you want to suppress GAL, it is necessary to suppress "ETA."[178]

When French police arrested Juan Lorenzo Lasa Michelena ("Txikierdi"), an important leader of ETA-m, on January 30, 1985, police sources called it "the greatest arrest carried out in the Pays Basque Français."[179] Maître Fando later protested the double standard of a French court system which asked for a penalty of seven years against her client Txikierdi, when, in the case of GAL mercenaries arrested with pistols in hand in the process of an attack in Biarritz, the prosecution only asked for five-year terms.[180]

By 1985 the attacks attributed to GAL had taken a different form. While many of the earlier attacks had the marks of thorough and meticulous professionalism, GAL began to use amateurish triggermen who sprayed bars indiscriminately and who in at least one case were caught by outraged witnesses after a stumbling, comic opera flight. On March 8, two young Portuguese mercenaries waited impatiently outside the Bar Batxoki for the patrons to clear out: "But time was passing, and we had our train at 9:25 P.M. So we had to open fire."[181] Six people were wounded, including the widow and daughter of slain ETA militant Juan Otaegui, killed by GAL six months before. On February 17 an old shepherd and a young Parisian girl on vacation were mistakenly killed by two GAL hitmen in the interior town of Bidarray.[182] *Le Monde* referred to these episodes as "ordinary screwups by discount ne'er-do-wells."[183]

French police were alarmed, however, by an emerging pattern of random killing on the part of GAL hitmen, no longer targeting ETA targets, but now firing blindly, killing French citizens and Spanish Basque refugees alike.[184] On September 25, 1985, two GAL members attacked the Hotel Monbar in Bayonne, indiscriminately killing some of its occupants. The perpetrators were apprehended, and at their trial revealed the terms of their contract and bonus clause: 100,000 francs (more than $16,000) and an additional 50,000 francs ($8,000) for every ETA member actually killed in the attack.[185] This bonus clause helped to explain the indiscriminate nature of many of GAL's attacks, since they were paid based on quantity. The two hitmen in the Monbar attack were found guilty and sentenced to life in prison.[186] In other cases, however, suspected GAL members were released due to lack of evidence or because of procedural irregularities.[187] The extent of the GAL violence— twelve deaths in less than fifteen months—contributed to a general climate of insecurity in the region, leading *Le Monde* to speak of "psychological attrition" and to raise the specter of "benevolent vigilantes" joining in the campaign against ETA.[188]

One fascinating element of this period was the appearance between March and August 1985 of a "blonde killer," a coldly efficient female assassin who was credited with six attacks and three deaths before disappearing without a trace in September 1985. In July 1987 *Libération* reported that she might well be a Spanish citizen, Laura Alamar Porta, who was arrested in Biarritz in June 1987 and was then in prison in Pau awaiting trial.[189] Though she tried to pass herself off as an ETA militant collecting a revolutionary tax, her story soon collapsed. Among the names found in her meticulous address book was that of Manuel Ballesteros, long thought to be high in the command structure of GAL. By 1988, however, attention focused on Dominique Thomas, a Frenchwoman who ran a leather and fur shop in Andorra, as a result of a tip by GAL hitman Christian Hitier, a former OAS member arrested in Belgium in March of that year.[190] Though interrogated by French authorities four months before, she had been released for lack of evidence. Then, on July 5, she turned herself in without warning to the Palais of Justice of Bayonne (though Andorra has no extradition treaty with France), allegedly because of anonymous death threats she had received.[191] Thomas was later exonerated, and rumors later surfaced about the wife of another mercenary who had also been active in GAL.

On September 25, 1985, four patrons were killed by two men waiting on the sidewalk as they emerged from the bar of the Hotel Monbar in Petit Bayonne.[192] After a short chase by witnesses, police apprehended the two men, Pierre Frugolie and Lucien Mattei, two criminals who proved to be well known to the authorities in their native Marseilles. GAL claimed responsibility for the attack the next day, and ETA-m acknowledged that the four victims were all former members.[193] A protest march the next day was outlawed by the departmental prefect in order to prevent further attacks by GAL.[194] By this point both the police and public were openly discussing the links between GAL and the Spanish police. As one frustrated *haut fonctionnaire* described his dilemma, "The only means of stopping these murderous waves is to bring political pressure on Spain. That isn't our role, but that of the [French] government." [195]

In 1986 the French government hardened its attitude toward both ETA and GAL. The French legislative elections of that year led to a conservative majority, and a period of awkward "co-habitation" involving a conservative cabinet led by Jacques Chirac and Socialist president François Mitterrand. Chirac moved to implement the law-and-order platform on which he had campaigned and appointed Charles Pasqua, a legislator with a law-and-order reputation, as minister of the interior. Pasqua, condemning GAL's violence, asserted, "We are totally opposed to the activities of persons who are paid by a state to come and settle their accounts on our territory. We will do everything to put them out of a state where they can do harm." [196] By 1986 the sentences handed out to GAL agents had begun to harden. On May 21, 1987, one of the three GAL defendants explicitly stated that they worked for the Spanish government. The following day, before they were sentenced to twenty years in jail, the French state prosecutor said, "You aren't terrorists, you are worse than that, you are mercenaries of terrorism. The terrorists, they have an ideal. You, you only looked for money." [197]

In the spring of 1986, with an attitude of a plague on both their houses, the European Parliament in Strasbourg voted to condemn the violence of *both* ETA and GAL. The vote was 170 to 1, with one abstention. The initiative was jointly sponsored by French Socialist deputy Nicole Péri of the French Pays Basque and Ana Miranda of the PSOE representing Gipuzkoa in Spain.[198]

France Abandons Its Commitment to Asylum: The New Practice of Extraditions in "Absolute Urgency"

It was clear by 1984 that the extent of GAL violence in the Pyrénées-Atlan-tiques had become a source of major political embarrassment for the French government. The government's critics pointed to the inability of the state to quell the anti-ETA violence as proof of either incompetence or complicity with the Spanish state. While continuing to defend the historic tradition of asylum, French authorities nonetheless were casting about for some diplo-matic solution which would lead the Spanish to leash their dogs of war. The previous violence of ATE and BVE had led Giscard d'Estaing's government to end the statute of political refuge for Spanish citizens and on occasion to deliver certain Basque refugees into the hands of the Spanish authorities. This was a lesson that the Spanish learned well. It was therefore as a di-rect result of GAL's violence that the French government began a series of measures which sought to satisfy the Spanish government's objection to the French "sanctuary for terrorists." Among the measures begun in 1984 were the arrest of ETA refugees, assigning them to residences north of the Loire River and exiling many to South America.

The refusal of the Socialist administration to extradite ETA refugees to Spain continued to be a sore point for the two governments and underlay the continued use of anti-ETA violence in France as a lever by the Spanish government. On April 27, 1984, Giscard d'Estaing's former interior min-ister, Michel Poniatowski, advocated "the systematic expulsion of Spanish Basques in the direction of Spain."[199] Poniatowski notably alleged the exis-tence of a close collusion between both Basque and Corsican movements and Libyan secret services, through the intermediary of a "consul general who lived in a large Italian city."[200]

With the advent of Chirac's conservative government in 1986, France's position on extradition was beginning to erode. In early July 1986 the French government decided to deport ETA leader Domingo Iturbe Abasolo ("Txomin"), who had been arrested on April 27 and convicted on June 24 for possession of firearms and violation of his assigned residence.[201] Txomin had resided in France since 1968 and was one of the few refugees to have received the official status of political refugee. The government decided to deport him to Gabon, where he arrived on July 13. His expulsion represented only the last in a series of expulsions of ETA militants to such destinations as Togo, Panama, the Dominican Republic, Cape Verde, Ecuador, Cuba, and Venezuela.

France's policy on deportation had been consistently criticized by Spain; as we have seen, Spain used every tool in its arsenal, from diplomacy to GAL's violence, to change France's policy on ETA's asylum. France's reluctance to extradite ETA militants to Spain was weakened in July when Belgium deported two ETA militants back to Spain, both of whom were then released by Spanish courts.[202] Within a week of Txomin's expulsion, the new government's attitude on the question of expulsions to Spain was reversed. On July 18, 1986, José Barona López ("Txema") was arrested in Saint-Jean-de-Luz, and the government, citing its belief that he was preparing to commit terrorist acts, turned him over to Spanish police at the border.[203]

The government based its decision on a policy permitting the "immediate expulsion" in "absolute urgency" of foreigners not holding the status of political refugees who violated the terms of their residency in France. This policy grew out of article 26 of the *ordonnance* of 1945 on foreigners, modified October 29, 1981 to read: "In case of absolute urgency, [an] expulsion can be pronounced when it constitutes an urgent necessity for the security of the state or for public security." [204] What was different was that France had decided to hand ETA members directly to Spanish authorities rather than continuing to deport them to third countries. While three ETA members had been handed over in 1984 during Pierre Joxe's term as interior minister, the difference between his decision and that made in 1986 was that Joxe had only handed over the three after receiving assurances from the Spanish concerning their physical treatment and safety.[205] With the decision taken in July 1986, the government now appeared to favor the streamlined process of expulsion in "absolute urgency" over the lengthy legal process and appellate layers involved with a formal legal extradition. Interior minister Robert Pandraud denied that the process involved either the abuse of power or procedural error. Rather, he defended the use of the "absolute urgency" procedure in cases like that of Txema where the individual was neither a political refugee nor the subject of a French arrest warrant.[206] French minister of foreign affaires Jean-Bernard Raimond held open the possibility of more extraditions to come.[207] Premier Jacques Chirac pledged his cooperation with Spanish authorities, stating, "France will not be a rear base for terrorists operating on Spanish soil." [208] Felipe González addressed a personal letter of thanks to Chirac within days acknowledging France's pledge of increased cooperation with Spain.[209] On July 26, 1986, *Le Figaro* strongly supported Chirac's decision concerning the new "absolute urgency" policy. Yet, it ironically announced at the same time Chirac's intention to fly to the Hao archipelago in French Polynesia to visit the two French intelligence agents of the DGSE (Direction Générale de la Sécurité Extérieure) who had been arrested, tried, and convicted by New Zealand for their part in the bombing of Greenpeace's *Rainbow Warrior*. As *Le Figaro* explained the inconsistency in its own stand, "These terrorists worked for us." [210]

Between July and August the French seized seven more ETA members and French courts ordered them expelled. The basic charge was "belonging to an organized and armed group which is devoted to terrorist actions." [211] Expulsion was reserved for cases representing "a particularly grave menace to public security." [212] The French government gave its political stamp of approval to the expulsion of three of the seven to Spain and the others to Togo. This sea change in France's attitude toward extradition, and hence in its relationship with Madrid, was confirmed with the visit of interior minister Pierre Joxe to Madrid on August 6.[213] Following France's delivery of two additional ETA members in late August, the Spanish government hailed the measures taken by the French as "very important and positive" and affirmed "the complete identity of views between the two countries." [214] One clear victim of the policy change was an *abertzale* community now isolated by this policy of government cooperation.[215]

It was clear that Paris's greatest interest at this time was ending the cycle of GAL/ETA violence. While publicly denying any role as intermediary between Madrid and ETA, in mid-September the French ambassador to Madrid, M. Guidoni, using his good offices allegedly sent a letter to ETA through Herri Batasuna, asking ETA to declare a sixty-day cease-fire in order to begin negotiations with Madrid and inviting ETA to attend a meeting at the Collège des Jésuites in Bordeaux on September 23.[216] ETA refused to attend the meeting, reasoning that the purpose of the meeting was "to negotiate our surrender in exchange for an end to the extraditions and expulsions." [217] According to *Libération*, "They wanted to force the nationalists to accept surrender . . . nothing more nothing less." [218]

When ETA did not attend the meeting, the French government increased the stakes by announcing the expulsion of three ETA militants to Spain the next day. They were returned to Spain later that month. Ironically, during their trials the following April, one of the three, José Manuel Martínez Beiztegui, was in fact acquitted of the charges against him.[219]

The change in France's policy on extraditions proved to have a radical impact on the condition of life of the refugee community in France. Over the next two years, between 1984 and 1986, nearly two hundred refugees were handed over to Spanish authorities under the "absolute urgency" process.[220] The reaction in the Spanish Basque country was anger and dismay. One response was the targeting of French trucks, buses, car agencies, and stores throughout Spain in protest.[221] This was potentially a serious threat, since France was the second largest source of foreign investment in Spain, following the United States.[222]

In an act of bravado, ETA dismissed the new initiative, claiming it came too late, and that at any rate ETA was prepared for it.[223] Yet, for *Le Monde*'s veteran correspondent in Madrid, Thierry Maliniak, "the measures taken by the French government . . . have incontestably weakened the organization."[224] In perhaps the most telling admission of the de facto "exchange model of politics" existing between France and Spain at this time, anonymous French government sources were quoted on September 25, 1984, as hoping that "the González government would put an end to the GAL activities as a counterpart to the extraditions."[225]

With the reversal of France's position on extradition, the campaign of GAL violence achieved its purpose. Following the agreement between French interior minister Pasqua and his Spanish counterpart José Barrionuevo in 1986, a new era of cooperation between the French and Spanish governments began. With the new French decision to arrest and hand over ETA militants to the Spanish government, the need for GAL's clandestine operations ended. Nevertheless, the trials and appeals of GAL members continued for the next several years.

The only major remaining question concerned the role of the Spanish state in GAL's activity, and public and legal attention centered on the trial of former Bilbao deputy commissioner José Amedo Fouce and inspector Michel Domínguez Martínez, charged with being the masterminds behind GAL. The revelations surrounding their 1991 trial reopened many of the questions first raised during GAL's campaign of violence. Jean-Marc Dufourg, a former inspector of the Renseignements Généraux, the intelligence agency of the French Interior Ministry, made a number of allegations in interviews during the trial. He stated that specific agreements between Felipe González and François Mitterrand led the French Interior Ministry to turn over its records on the Basque refugees, including addresses and photographs, to Spanish Interior Ministry officials.[226] He claimed that this information "was obviously later given to GAL." GAL then used the information to target the refugee community, and pieces of it, including photographs submitted by refugees for government identity cards, were later found on several occasions in the possession of GAL hitmen apprehended in France. He further claimed that Amedo and Domínguez met on several occasions with the late Jean-Pierre Irazabal, head of the Investigations Department of the Central Directorate of the Renseignements Généraux. For Dufourg, Amedo and Domínguez were acting under orders and were later unjustly left by their superiors to take the fall alone. According to Santiago de la Cruz, writing in *Tiempo*, "Hundreds of the prosecution's questions have gone unanswered by Ministry of Interior and Police Officials."[227]

Despite the government's strategy, public opinion polls by OTR/IS in 1991 revealed that 50.4 percent of the Spanish public believed high public officials were behind GAL, 17.8 percent disagreed, and 31.7 percent did not know;[228] 53.4 percent of those polled opposed GAL's methods of fighting terrorism, while 25.9 percent approved. In October 1991 former Portuguese minister of social communication José Sánches Osorio stated that, while he could not prove it, he was sure that both Premier González and interior minister Barrionuevo were aware of GAL's activity and that the Spanish security services were behind it.[229]

After months of testimony Spain's Audiencia Nacional, the National High Court of Justice, rendered its verdict in September 1991. The court found Amedo and Domínguez guilty of six attempted assassinations, serious injuries, illicit association with criminals, falsification of national identity cards, and using aliases. Each man was sentenced to a total of 108 years and eight months in jail. At the same time, the court ruled that Amedo and Domínguez were *not* members of GAL and in fact did not recognize the existence of GAL as an organization. The court declined to hold the Spanish government even secondarily liable for the policemen's actions, ruling that the two men had acted privately and outside the authority of the state. While not found guilty of being members of GAL themselves, Amedo and Domínguez were convicted by the court for having sporadic contacts with "stable elements of GAL."[230] The court's decision was an obvious compromise, limiting its finding of guilt to the two individuals while denying any link between GAL and the government. According to Spanish premier Felipe González, "There is no evidence existing against GAL, nor will any exist."[231]

With the court's verdict known, attention focused on Amedo and Domínguez's likely fate, now ironically tied to the government's talks with ETA. Throughout July and August 1986 the Spanish government steadfastly denied that it was negotiating with "terrorists."[232] Government policy, according to Felipe González, "would not include in any case negotiation with this group of assassins."[233] Yet rumors circulated in Basque circles about government discussions with Txomin even before his arrest in France in April 1986. Then, in the fall of 1986, Spanish intelligence detected the presence in Algeria of as many as forty to fifty ETA members.[234] Sources close to ETA claimed that the Spanish government had in fact been negotiating with Txomin in Algeria until his premature death in an automobile accident in February 1987. As late as August 1987, during his meeting with François Mitterrand at Mitterrand's summer home in Latche in Les Landes, González continued to maintain Spain's official policy of refusing to negotiate with

ETA.[235] Yet within days the Spanish government reversed itself and admitted that it had in fact met in early August in Algeria with ETA, now represented by Eugenio Etxebeste ("Antxon"), who had been brought there from Ecuador at Spain's request to replace the late Txomin.[236]

It was clear that one of the government's olive branches in the negotiations with ETA was the question of pardon for political prisoners. Even ETA's reports from Algeria acknowledged the Spanish effort to offer a reconciliation with dignity and honor. One of the ironies of these negotiations was that Amedo and Domínguez would benefit from the same pardon extended to the ETA militants who had been the original targets of GAL.

Amedo apparently found the linking of his fate to that of ETA distasteful. In an interview with *Cambio 16* in February 1992 he stated his intention to appeal his conviction to the Spanish Supreme Court and to the Constitutional Court if necessary. If neither appeal was successful, he would ask for a government pardon. For an embittered Amedo, "If our country were different, it would bring France to trial. France is to blame for everything that is going on with ETA. No one can tell me otherwise."[237] Having served its purpose, GAL could disappear, though Amedo and the other GAL prisoners were left to pay the price of Spain's strategy. Amedo failed to see GAL as the tool of Spanish *Realpolitik* which it had been from the beginning. What GAL offered was a violent instrument to force a change in French policy, while affording plausible deniability to the Spanish government which created and directed it. As Napoleon III put it, "Whoever serves the state serves an ingrate."[238]

THE ROSE COMMISSION REPORT OF 1986

In June 1985 the Basque regional government in Gasteiz (Vitoria) formed an international commission to study the problem of terrorism and its solutions.[239] The commission was chaired by Clive Rose, former British ambassador to NATO, and included Jacques Leauté, director of the Institut de Criminologie de Paris; Dr. Franco Ferracuti, professor of psychiatry at the University of Rome and a specialist on the Red Brigades; Peter Janke, a British Hispanicist involved with negotiations in Northern Ireland; and Hans Horchem, director of the Department of the Defense of the [German] Constitution at Hamburg and a specialist on the Baader-Meinhof gang. After nine months of study the commission released its report in April 1986. Among its conclusions was that the problem of the Basque country does not originate outside and does not depend on international channels: "its origins are rooted in Basque history." Born during the Franco era, it was considered a legitimate "struggle for national liberation" at a time when "violence seemed justified." For the commission, "the ideological motivation and the allusions to Marxism-Leninism never supplanted the fundamentally nationalist character of the revolutionary action." If the problem of Basque terrorism was a Basque problem, it would be up to the Basques to solve it: "the specificity of Basque terrorism demands that it be combated by Basques themselves." The commission urged that ETA defendants be tried by Basque courts rather than as at present by a special tribunal of the Audiencia Nacional in Madrid. At the same time the commission urged the reinforcement of the Autonomous Basque Police by charging it with all aspects of security and public order in the region. A new Judicial Police would be created to deal with terrorist crimes, and a new intelligence service would report to the regional government.

Part of the challenge of any terrorist situation is a struggle to control the symbolism of political action. In this case, the commission urged a number of steps "to dismantle the image of heroes and patriots which the terrorists seek to conserve." The Rose Commission expressed amazement that no serious study had yet been done on ETA or on the motivations of its militants and urged that ETA not be permitted to define the terms of the conflict:

> The terrorists are living an imaginary war against the system and need to maintain this war mentality in order to justify the deaths. The government must not fall into the trap and convert this fantasy war into a real one.

For the Rose Commission, the bottom line was the need for flexibility and a willingness to negotiate if necessary to end the conflict with ETA: "Given that ETA is an unhappy daughter of dictatorship, and that its members are the offsprings of the PNV, one must never exclude negotiation as a political option." If Madrid still insisted that "there is no more to negotiate with terrorism," that is exactly what the Spanish government and a portion of ETA soon began to do. The problem was not with those willing to negotiate, but with a hard-line faction within ETA which became ascendant after Txomin's death in Algeria. This faction was led by Francisco Mugica Garmendia (known first as "Pakito" or "Paco" and later as "Artapalo"), who had managed to live in clandestinity in France for years despite intense efforts to find him.

EXTENDING THE COOPERATION BETWEEN GOVERNMENTS

In late August 1986, the *New York Times* reported that Spanish premier González had new hopes of success resting on the level of French cooperation.[240] Among Spanish police sources, however, there was a feeling that, even if ETA were weakened, there was still no end in sight. For the *New York Times*'s Edward Schumacher, the energetic measures taken by France and Spain against the refugees only served to aggravate already bitter relations between Madrid and the Basque region.[241] A major reason for this lay in the bedrock of ETA's support within Herri Batasuna.

GAL's Amedo, in his 1992 interview, insisted that ETA was controlled by Herri Batasuna and that the ETA militants sought in France, as well as those negotiating in Algeria, were following a policy line determined by HB leaders. As Amedo put it, "I have enough evidence and reason to say that the HB and ETA are one and the same. . . . All of them are the real ETA. The employees, the ones who plan, manage, direct, and create strategies."[242] Even the PNV saw Herri Batasuna's hand in ETA's strategy, and not vice versa. PNV deputy Ignacio Anasagasti argued that ETA's communiqués were written by what he called the "sociological ETA," the milieu around Herri Batasuna increasingly isolated from the mass of Basque society.[243] By 1992 the PNV believed that ETA was being directed by Herri Batasuna as a result of the climate against ETA's leadership in France.[244] There was the growing belief that ETA's leadership was now isolated in its clandestinity. As Jean-Hébert Armengaud argued in *Libération*, "Isolated in total clandestinity, 'Pakito'—and with him ETA—seem not to have realized that since Franco's death, and with the enactment of the region's autonomy statute, the Basque Country has changed."[245] Uncontrite, Jon Idigoras of Herri Batasuna insisted, "What others consider terrorism is for us an armed response to the Spanish government."[246]

Police admitted to knowing little about ETA's estimated two hundred to five hundred militants or about the eight to ten members of its executive committee and what motivated them. According to one Western intelligence analyst, "One of E.T.A.'s strengths is that it keeps its objectives focused. They don't mess around with this anti-imperialist, anti-American stuff. They go straight for what they say oppresses them—the Civil Guard and the Spanish Government."[247] For one former ETA member, this was "white-glove terrorism" against the oppressor.[248]

In March 1987 *Le Monde* reported that of the seven hundred ETA refugees in France only seventeen had official status as "political refugees" and even this would not protect them from administrative expulsion for continuing political or military activity.[249] The increasing pressure of the French government was being felt by the refugee community. As one refugee put it, "It's even worse than during the GAL attacks. We go out less and less. Some of us have quit our jobs, changing residences several times a week for fear of being arrested."[250] Five hundred families allegedly responded to the "One refugee, one roof" campaign and were housing the refugees in clandestinity in the Pays Basque Français. As Robert Pandraud explained the difficulty confronting France as a result, "France is determined to expel the Basque terrorists from its territory, but the main problem is finding them."[251]

The Government Targets the Refugee Community

By the summer of 1987 the French government was locked in a struggle not only with the ETA refugees, but also with Iparretarrak in the person of Philippe Bidart, whose violence, as we will see below, seemed to unleash a fury of governmental action against the refugees. Bidart's killing of a gendarme in Biscarosse in August 1987 provoked a massive police campaign which fell most heavily on the refugee community. In July 1987 Spanish interior minister Barrionuevo gave a rank-order list of ETA militants sought by Spain to French interior minister Pasqua.[252] Among the fifteen most important names on the list were four individuals believed to be ETA's primary leaders at the time: Francisco Mugica Garmendia ("Artapalo"), Santiago Arrospide Sarasola ("Santi Potros"), José Luis Alvarez Santacristina ("Txelis"), and José Zabaleta Elosegui ("Baldo").[253]

By coincidence, during the intense police searches which followed Bidart's killing of the gendarme in August, police were led to a villa in Anglet, supposedly as a result of a scrap of address found on Gabi Mouesca at the time of his arrest in July near the Tour de France. Instead of finding an IK hideout, the police were surprised to find instead Santi Potros, the leader of ETA's armed commando groups living clandestinely in France.[254]

The claim that it was Iparretarrak which led the government to Santi Potros appeared later to have been a piece of disinformation created by the government to exacerbate the open conflict between Iparretarrak and ETA by this time. Moruzzi and Boulaert go so far as to report the "rumor" that ETA was so infuriated by the report that police found ETA leader Santi Potros through Iparretarrak's lack of skill that they may have taken out a "contract" on Bidart, though soon rescinding it after *abertzale* mediators explained the government's possible ruse.[255]

Soon thereafter, police raided a farm in rural Saint-Pée-sur-Nivelle and found what they believed to be an ETA command post. While they arrested one militant, the two who escaped were believed to have been Artapalo and Baldo, ETA's most important leaders at the time.[256]

According to Clark, at the time of Santi Potros's arrest, police found "in his possession more than 30 pounds of documents with important information about ETA's organizational structure and membership. These documents, together with information gathered in the Sokoa raid the preceding year, enabled French and Spanish authorities to carry out the most massive series of arrests ETA had ever experienced."[257] The most important outcome of these raids was seizure of ETA membership lists totaling more than five hundred names, which included addresses and even car licenses. The minister of state for security, Robert Pandraud, is reported to have called his Spanish counterpart during the evening of October 2, 1987, and the result was a cooperative effort of massive proportions against the Basque milieu.[258] At six o'clock the next morning more than 2,000 government agents moved simultaneously against 150 targets.[259] Within twenty-four hours, French government had carried out 112 searches that produced 67 suspects, growing to 97 by the weekend, only one of them a French citizen.[260] Based on the Santi Potros materials, Spanish police arrested 104 people, of whom 23 eventually went to prison. By mid-November the French government had expelled over 160 refugees to Spain, so that the total number of refugees arrested might have been as high as 300.[261] According to Clark, by June 1988 France had expelled a total of 192 refugees to Spain and more than a dozen other countries.[262] In an interview with the Spanish Catholic daily *Ya*, Pandraud declared:

> France is determined to expel all the Basque terrorists from its territory, but the principal problem is to find them. There is only one limit to our collaboration with Spain; it is to find the terrorists and their support network. . . . It is true that there are still members of ETA as there are in Spain. The two polices are looking for them, and it isn't any more easy to find them in France than in Spain . . . for a long time, the French Socialist Party had an attitude of a certain complacency or of tolerance [toward Basque violence]. . . . The new policy of expulsions in process, carried out at the present time by the government, even if it doesn't always strike the most important head of ETA, still permits the Basque organization to feel itself encircled and thus act with a lot more difficulties than before.[263]

Speaking later before the French National Assembly, Pandraud called ETA the most dangerous terrorist group in Europe, having carried out 2,100 attacks in the previous seven years and a total of more than 600 assassinations.[264] Pandraud claimed that the arrests which took place on October 3 wiped out half of ETA's military structure and would take years to rebuild.

The seized documents permitted the construction of a detailed organizational chart of ETA's leadership, including a seven-man executive committee composed of Francisco Mugica Garmendia ("Artapalo"); Santiago Arrospide Sarasola ("Santi Potros"); José Javier Zabaleta Elosegui ("Baldo"); José Antonio Urrutikoetxea Bengoetxea ("Josu Ternera"); Juan Lorenzo Lasa Michelena ("Txikierdi"); Juan Angel Ochoantesana Badiola; and José Luis Alvarez Santacristina.[265] Santi Potros was in charge of the illegal commandos of ETA's military apparatus, two of which—the Madrid and Barcelona commandos—had been discovered and dismantled.

In a surprise response to this intense French campaign, within a matter of days more than two hundred Spanish Basque elected officials belonging to

Herri Batasuna marched in the streets of Bayonne in protest.[266] As one of the march's leaders, ETA founder and now senator Txillardegi stated, "We are in our home here. The Basque refugees are Basques who have the right to live in the Pays Basque." Calling Txillardegi's statement "detestable" and an imperialistic "diktat," the secretary of the French Social Party for the Pays Basque Français, François Maitia, retorted, "Today, the escalation in out-rageousness continues with this surrealist demonstration of Herri Batasuna in Bayonne." Calling it a "veritable act of suzerainty," Maitia insisted that the Spanish Basque demonstrators were "in the home [of French Basques]" and not "in your home." [267]

As the searches and arrests of October 1987 demonstrated, the cost to French Basques found to be lodging ETA refugees would grow increas-ingly dear.[268] According to Philippe Boggio, the nature of the campaign fur-ther accentuated the cleavage between the Basque movements in France and Spain.[269] He believes that the greatest cost was the psychological self-redefinition of the Spanish Basque movement vis-à-vis the North. As one Basque observer said, "ETA crossed out the North." [270] Herri Batasuna no longer invited its "northern brothers" to its meetings, and ETA's own texts no longer mentioned "the grand Euzkadi." According to Boggio, ETA came to believe that in balancing its books the account of the French Basques was a net deficit. For ETA, according to this theory, the Pays Basque Français was now too French and not sufficiently Basque.

In May 1988 the newly installed French interior minister, Pierre Joxe, made his first official trip abroad to Madrid, during the course of which he is said to have informed the Spanish of the French government's desire to carry out its operations against ETA in a more discreet and selective manner, with-out media spectacles like that of the previous October.[271] At the same time, to the great concern of his Spanish counterparts, he informed them of his opposition to the systematic use of the "absolute urgency" expulsions first enacted by the Chirac government and his preference henceforth for judicial extraditions. This was motivated in part by Joxe's awareness that fully half of the ETA militants expelled to Spain under the "absolute urgency" pro-visions were freed almost immediately. By August 1988 Spanish authorities confirmed the French government's desire to enter into "a different phase" in the fight against ETA by concentrating on its principal leaders and not on secondary militants.[272] As a result, the French announced that the raids and the "absolute urgency" expulsions would become secondary tools. In any case, the Spanish believed that most of the ETA militants who might have been expelled in this manner had already moved secretly to other re-gions of France. By 1988 France and Spain were pledging to coordinate their respective foreign policies regarding Europe. But the Spanish were now clearly critical of Joxe's direction of anti-ETA policy. To dispel those concerns, French foreign minister Roland Dumas visited Madrid in September and assured the Spanish that France's cooperation in the fight against ETA would continue "without mercy."[273] This intergovernmental cooperation continued in a joint ministerial seminar in October which brought together ten Spanish ministers and eight from France.[274] Among the goals of the gathering was to dispel Spanish concerns about Joxe's policies, which contrasted with what the Spanish felt were the "good old days" of his predecessors Charles Pasqua and Robert Pandraud.[275] Joxe, for his part, is said to have reminded the Spanish that they had been promising a solution to the problem of ETA for years. Joxe reportedly told the Spanish that negotiations between them and ETA were doomed to failure so long as the Spanish limited their agenda to amnesty and the reinsertion of ETA militants, while refusing to discuss the problem with ETA in political terms.[276] He reminded them of the costs to France: twenty-seven deaths and an annual police cost of more than five hundred million francs per year in the Pyrénées-Atlantiques.

The government's success in capturing Bidart and moving against the refugee community was costly and incomplete. In a question and answer session before the French National Assembly on October 12, 1988, Pierre Joxe reiterated the government's cooperation with Spain in its antiterrorism campaign. Yet Joxe spoke of a Basque problem which "in my opinion, alas, risks lasting a long time in the Pyrénées-Atlantiques."[277] While declining to reveal the exact strength of the police operation in place in the Pays Basque, Joxe did admit:

> But by itself the annual cost of the police operations in the Pays Basque Français, that is to say half of the Pyrénées-Atlantiques, represents nearly one half billion francs [approximately eight-five million dollars] for an efficiency which is great, but not perfect. But I'm going to multiply again [our] means in the region because it's a question of security for France. And we should organize ourselves in fearing that the Spanish Basque political problem won't be resolved immediately. Four years ago, when I arrived in the government, our Spanish friends told us, "Soon, we're going to succeed." For the moment, I am not sure that that evolution is guaranteed.[278]

In November 1988 Spanish premier González sought to minimize any tensions between the two governments concerning ETA, but still insisted on his government's refusal to undertake political negotiations with an organization to which he attributed "a phenomenon of degeneracy which transformed it into a less and less ideological group, and more and more

fanatical."[279] In December 1988 interior minister Joxe circulated a memorandum to the prefect of the Pyrénées-Atlantiques in which he clarified the
political principles and the rules of law which framed French government
policy toward the Basque problem.[280] Joxe himself sent a copy to his Spanish
counterpart, José Luis Corcuera. Reminding the prefect that he represented
the government in a department whose situation was based on a long historical memory and a contemporary reality without an equivalent in France,
Joxe wrote:

> It is today established, at least for the past, that the influence, in France,
> of the Spanish Basque country was more profound and more grave
> than one imagined, in that which concerned the respect of our sover-
> eignty. . . . I want thus to organize, to equip, and motivate the whole
> of . . . [French public] services . . . susceptible to respond to the evo-
> lution of the most unfavorable hypotheses. It concerns protecting our
> sovereignty and the security of our territory.[281]

Joxe's three specific charges to the *préfet* were:

> 1. To apply French laws in such a way as to protect the security of
> French territory, while respecting the rights of man—whether of French
> or foreigners;
> 2. To aid the Spanish Democracy in overcoming terrorism, and in pro-
> tecting French territory from it; and,
> 3. To assure the tranquillity of those living legally and peacefully in
> your department, but by expelling those whose situation is irregular,
> and those who, accepted as foreigners, don't respect the laws of the Re-
> public, especially when they are engaged in activities likely to trouble
> public order.[282]

Within a month, the capture of ETA leader José Urrutikoetxea Bengoetxea
("Josu Ternera") demonstrated both the sincerity of France's commitment to
cooperate with Spain against ETA and the efficacy of its decision to target
ETA's primary leaders.

Having committed itself in 1986 to an intense campaign against ETA's refugee community, the French government zealously carried out that policy
through a series of extraditions as well as expulsions. Extraditions were a
slower and clearly judicial process involving the exchange of governmental
documents and formal judicial findings. For that reason, between 1987 and
1990 only *fourteen* refugees were formally extradited.[283] The adoption of the
new streamlined "absolute urgency" expulsion process gave the government
the means to circumvent the cumbersome and uncertain legal process and

simply expel the refugees from French territory, either to Spain or to a third country. By July 1991, 197 refugees had been expelled: 26 in 1986; 143 in 1987; 25 in 1988; and only 3 in 1989.[284]

It was in this climate of increased repression and cooperation between France and Spain that negotiations began again between Spain and ETA. The two sides chose to define the agenda in very different ways. For ETA, the only possible basis for the negotiations was the KAS alternative, which called, *inter alia*, for Basque sovereignty and territorial unity.[285] For the Spanish government, the sole question was convincing ETA to lay down its arms. During September and November 1987 meetings occurred in Algeria between "Antxon" Etxebeste representing ETA, and Manuel Ballesteros and later Julian Elgorriaga for the Spanish government. Even ETA acknowledged that throughout the negotiations Elgorriaga offered "a dignified end, incorporation into political and social life with heads held high, as well as the progressive release of prisoners."[286] At the same time, for ETA, he demonstrated, "an intransigent attitude and a profound blindness to the roots of the conflict" and a refusal to discuss the KAS alternative.[287] The two sides were unwilling to overcome the impasse. On December 18 Spain informed the Algerian government of its intention to suspend the negotiations. For ETA, the negotiations were a complement to the armed struggle and only one means to attain its objectives. In reality, the question of negotiating with Spain was a subject of some dispute within ETA. There was a hard-line faction within ETA which had always opposed the negotiations and, with Txomin's death in the automobile accident in Algeria in early 1987, later became ascendant around Artapalo.

THE ASSASSINATION OF "YOYES"

Perhaps the most significant example of the rise of the hard-line faction was the assassination of a former leader of ETA-m, María Dolores González Katarain ("Yoyes").[288] While many members of ETA-pm had accepted amnesty following its decision to disband in 1982, the government had far less success with ETA-m. Yoyes, as a former member of ETA's executive committee, was the most prominent member of ETA-m to accept the Spanish government's offer of amnesty and "social reinsertion." In an operation allegedly carried out by José Antonio López Ruiz ("Kubati") on Artapalo's orders,[289] she was shot thrice in the head by a lone gunman while walking with her four-year-old son during a festival in her native village of Ordizia, where she had lived since accepting amnesty.[290] A former member of ETA's leadership under Txomin, and close to the late José María Beñarán Ordeñana ("Argala"), Yoyes reportedly grew disillusioned with the use of armed struggle and came to believe that political conciliation was necessary to a lasting solution to the Basque struggle.[291] As she later recounted her conversations with Txomin, she said, "I can no longer support a struggle which has degenerated, which has become dictatorial . . . you have become the puppets of a fascist-type militarism. How can I identify with leaders who only know how to applaud attacks and demand even more deaths?"[292] She is reported to have convinced Txomin of the need for negotiations. She subsequently left for Mexico, where she lived for a number of years before deciding to accept the Spanish government's offer of amnesty. As she wrote, she had become a phantom in clandestinity, and "I exist . . . I have a son, I want to live."[293] Although Txomin promised her safety should she accept amnesty, with his subsequent arrest and deportation to Gabon in July 1986, the political culture of ETA shifted dramatically. He was succeeded by Artapalo, who ordered the death of Yoyes two months later. A spokesman for ETA in 1987 explained its decision to assassinate her:

> Yoyes had important responsibilities among us. After a period of personal and ideological degradation, she had chosen the worst of paths: repentance, treason, collaboration with the enemy. The "repentant" are used to legitimate the repression. As a consequence, they are in the service of the enemy.[294]

In telephone calls claiming responsibility for the attack, ETA denounced Yoyes as a "traitor to the Basque people."[295] The killing of Yoyes provoked a broad outcry among former ETA militants and within the *abertzale* community. Seven hundred former members of ETA attended her funeral in a gesture of public protest against this tragic act.[296] Yoyes, before her death, had opposed the ascendance of this hard-line faction within ETA's leadership, referring to Artapalo and his faction as the "hard and irrational section" of ETA.[297] Even GAL's Amedo recognized the different path Txomin represented from that of Artapalo: "In keeping with Txomin's strategy, ETA could have had a different place in Spain's history."[298]

The importance of the hard-line faction around Artapalo grew in influence as other ETA leaders were arrested or killed. One example was the arrest on January 11, 1989 of José Antonio Urrutikoetxea Bengoetxea ("Josu Ternera") in Bayonne, ironically, four days after ETA had declared a unilateral fifteen-day truce in order to press for talks with the Spanish government.[299] As we saw above, his presence had been demanded by ETA as part of its negotiating team with the Spanish in March 1989. With the breakdown of talks with Spain, Antxon was sent from Algeria to the Dominican Republic and held virtually incommunicado. In contrast to those who favored a negotiated settlement with the government—and growing numbers of ETA prisoners were among this group—Artapalo favored an escalation of violence in order to force the government to negotiate. He is quoted as having said, "With the bodies of twelve generals on the table, those people will negotiate on our terms."[300] His policy of car bombings was particularly criticized, as was the rapidity with which he used up ETA's commando groups, including Henri Parot's.

By late 1991 a group of ETA's prisoners in Spain had begun to speak out openly in criticism of Artapalo's strategy of escalation. Isidro Etxabe and Juan Antonio Urrutia, in conversations recorded by their families and later published in excerpts, are said to have described his leadership as a "gang of subnormals" and asked "whether the national sport of the four imbeciles who are up there [referring to ETA's leadership in France] is killing youngsters."[301] They asserted, "They are creating hatred everywhere" by their "savage" attacks.[302] As Urrutia put it, "What needs to be pursued is politics, and the armed struggle should be abandoned."[303] Harsh criticism was also voiced by José Luis Urrusolo Sistiaga ("Joseba"), former member of Txomin's Madrid commando, and later believed by Spanish police to be head of ETA's Tarragona commando.[304] Joseba is said to have called Artapalo a "son of a bitch" and a "cretin" and his followers "toadies" in a letter which other militants later handed to Artapalo himself.[305] Joseba was particularly critical of the life-style of Artapalo's circle in France when compared to the threat and penury of the illegal commandos in Spain: "Pakito has no bloody idea what it is like to be in the interior. . . . He has never been any further than Bayonne. . . . If he moves anymore now, let's see whether it is true that traveling opens the mind and the spirit."[306]

By 1992 the 532 ETA prisoners in Spain were willing to speak openly about their hopes for a negotiated settlement.[307] As one ETA prisoner explained the transformation brought about by incarceration, "It's hard to be a terrorist at age 40."[308] Antxon himself criticized the campaign of car bombings as rendering any further contact with the government impossible.[309] Even Herri Batasuna acknowledged that the violence led to a suspension of contacts between Spain and the ETA prisoners in the Dominican Republic, using the Dominican government as intermediary. In the wake of these public criticisms, Spanish authorities made new offers of special treatment for ETA leaders now willing to abandon the armed struggle.[310]

France Moves against ETA's Leadership

Aurrera bolie.
Let the ball roll.
Oft-quoted saying of ETA leader Domingo Iturbe Abasolo ("Txomin")

The ascendancy of the hard-line faction within ETA seemed to mirror the strategy France had proposed earlier in order to fragment the organization. France favored offering limited amnesty to those ETA refugees willing to return to Spain, while accelerating the repression against the hard-line faction which remained. On April 27, 1987, French police arrested Etarra José Felix Pérez in Bayonne and found a sum of seven hundred million pesetas, or more than six million dollars, in a nearby van, apparently the ransom for wealthy Spaniard Emiliano Revilla, who had been kidnapped in February.[311] By the late 1980s Spain believed that literally hundreds of millions of pesetas were being laundered for ETA's benefit in southern France. Shortly after the arrest of Henri Parot in 1990 Spain proposed that France create a special investigatory unit in which the targeting of ETA's finances might reveal a paper trail leading to ETA's leaders themselves.[312] It was out of these discussions that the French government created a unit in 1992 composed of agents of the Renseignements Généraux and the Criminal Investigation Police to investigate economic and financial crimes and bank fraud. The unit would look closely at large real estate investments, as well as at accounts in banks suspected of laundering ETA's revolutionary taxes. Spain believed that a number of banks were laundering ETA's money in the Pays Basque Français, including the family bank of deputy Michel Inchauspé.[313]

In 1992 Spanish newspapers printed a report to interior minister Philippe Marchand written by French police commissioner Roger Bosle, coordinator of the antiterrorism effort in the Pyrénées-Atlantiques.[314] It was apparently written to furnish rebuttals to Spanish criticism about France's lack of success in moving against ETA's leaders. The report, dated November 21, 1990, explained the difficulties in penetrating the clandestinity which protected Artapalo and other ETA leaders. Bosle argued that finding Artapalo was particularly difficult since he had been living underground for many years and only met with other ETA leaders once or twice a year. Part of Bosle's purpose in the memo was to counter Spanish criticisms of France's ineffectiveness in its campaign against ETA. According to Bosle, there were in fact two thousand agents in the Pyrénées-Atlantiques in 1990, a record number for France, and even more than France had in Corsica at the same time. Rejecting a previous story in the Spanish newspaper *ABC* which claimed that there were only twenty police officers in France devoted to ETA, Bosle claimed, "There are not twenty; there are three hundred."[315] According to one French police source cited:

> It is incredible for someone in Spain to say that we do not want to arrest Artapalo. It shows a lack of information and ignorance about this issue. I can tell you that for some years a number of high-ranking police officers in our country have wanted to arrest him, not only because he is a terrorist, but also because the man who gets Artapalo will win a reputation and a big promotion.[316]

Spanish intelligence reported in 1990 that ETA's primary leaders were Artapalo, Baldo, and Josu Ternera, who had been arrested in Bayonne in January 1989. It was not until September 23, 1990, that police arrested Baldo, thought by Spanish police to be the head of ETA's "legal" commandos, those who were not living in clandestinity.[317] He was succeeded in turn by Jesús Arkautz Arana ("Josu Mondragon"), who was himself arrested on March 18, 1991. Mondragon is alleged to have participated in the creation of the Madrid and Barcelona commandos of ETA and was thought by some to be next in line to succeed Artapalo should the latter be arrested.[318]

The level of pressure being exerted on ETA's clandestine leadership left growing numbers imprisoned in France or Spain. By August 1991 relatively few of ETA's leaders remained at large along with Artapalo. Among them were José Luis Alvarez Santacristina ("Txelis"), its primary ideologue, who was thought to draft ETA's communiqués; José María Arregui Erostarbe ("Fiti" or "Fitipaldi"); Faustino Estanislao Villanueva ("Txapu"); and Miguel Angel Apalategi-Ayerbe ("Apala"), who some thought to be next in line as leader should Artapalo be taken.[319] Spanish intelligence originally believed that Artapalo and Apala had begun to share leadership co-equally in order to ensure succession should one of them be caught. This arrangement recreated the power-sharing between the two men at the helm of ETA-pm in 1976, following the death of Pertur, of which both were accused. The problem was that Apala had been in exile in Latin America for the past decade, and no hard evidence confirmed that he had returned to the Basque country. Later press reports indicated that Apala had subsequently been found living in Cuba, allegedly having severed his ties to ETA.[320]

The number of major figures arrested in recent years had undeniably isolated and weakened the remaining leadership. Those arrested included Santiago Arrospide Sarasola ("Santi Potros"): José Antonio Urrutikoetxea ("Josu Ternera"); Juan José Lasa Michelena ("Txikierdi"); Isidro María Garalde ("Mamarru"); and Eloy Uriarte ("Señor Robles"), ETA's finance man, who was under house arrest in northern France.

With the increasing level of police activity, ETA was slowly forced out of its sanctuary among French Basques and began to spread to other safer areas of France, especially Brittany and Paris.[321] In December 1991 French police arrested one ETA member and twenty other people (five Spanish and fifteen French) in Bayonne, Bordeaux, and Anger in Brittany. All twenty were members of various Basque support groups. At the same time it was reported that Artapalo was seeking refuge in Paris, where he could better avoid police surveillance than in the Pays Basque.[322] Following the discovery of Henri Parot's group in 1990 French and Spanish authorities came to believe that most of ETA's militants either were now hiding in France or were French nationals.[323]

In October 1991 French interior minister Philippe Marchand turned down the request of his Spanish counterpart, José Luis Corcuera, for an increase in the number of Spanish police permitted to work on French territory against ETA.[324] Marchand pointed out the political and legal difficulties the request posed for France until a single legal and police jurisdiction were created as part of the European Community. For Spanish judge Rafael Mendizabal, president of the National High Court, there could be no European union without an authentic European judicial body and so long as terrorists and drug traffickers could find refuge behind other borders.[325] While France maintained its policy of only permitting one Spanish observer on its anti-ETA operations (which Spain criticized for usually taking place on weekends), Marchand did pledge to increase both the quality of its agents and the amount of time devoted to ETA. Spanish authorities believed their point had been made and understood by a French administration which was now aware that the Basque problem was not a Spanish problem alone. Meeting with Felipe González on October 25, 1991, Mitterrand pledged that everything that was necessary would be done.[326] In January 1992 two hundred French police mounted an operation that led to the arrest of eleven people, included Father Pantxu Garat, parish priest in Espelette near the border.

Encouraged by Mitterrand's pledge in October, in early 1992 Corcuera repeated his request for increased cooperation, and this time discussions began concerning the formation of joint French-Spanish Anti-ETA Police Brigades.[327] González told the *Times* of London, "Several weeks ago we began a closer cooperation and I look forward to its realization within the next few days. They are doing a lot to help us."[328] While *Le Figaro* reported in early March that the French ultimately balked a second time at creating joint brigades, apparently a new and secret protocol was signed by both governments increasing their cooperation against ETA.[329] Among the French pledges was its commitment to stepping up surveillance in order to prevent

ETA attacks on the 1992 Summer Olympics in Barcelona. Presumably the new agreement turned on the sharing of intelligence information and more effective action as a result.

The Arrest of Artapalo

Chance is the god of policemen.
A French anti-terrorist commissioner[330]

Within a month, on March 29, 1992, this new level of cooperation between the French and Spanish governments led to the greatest prize of all—the arrest of Francisco Mugica Garmendia ("Artapalo") along with José Luis Alvarez Santacristina ("Txelis") and José María Arregui Erostarbe ("Fitipaldi"). The circumstances of their arrests are still clouded in mystery, but a picture emerges of an ongoing French-Spanish surveillance operation that slowly led them to Artapalo. By one account, the initial break came with the discovery of a small black telephone address book left in a telephone booth by an ETA member. Another maintained that Spanish surveillance of a member of a commando crossing back into France led to Artapalo. According to a long and detailed account in *Cambio 16*, the process leading to the arrests in fact began on September 23, 1990, with the capture of Zabaleta Elosegui ("Baldo").[331] At that time, the joint French-Spanish operation was called "abortive" because Arkautz Arana ("Josu Mondragon") had managed to escape. Unbeknownst to Mondragon, according to police sources, from that time on he was the subject of intense surveillance by dozens of French police and Guardia Civiles who tailed him day and night. For the next six months, Mondragon served as Baldo's successor as head of ETA's legal commandos until his arrest on March 18, 1991. During the surveillance of Josu Mondragon, he was observed with French Basque militant Philippe Lasalle, previously arrested for collaboration with ETA and long thought by the police to have been "burned" as a contact with ETA. Lasalle was followed for the next several months; in January 1992 he was observed taking unusual precautions before meeting another militant who turned out to be José Luis Alvarez Santacristina ("Txelis"), the presumed number two of ETA at that time. Txelis then became the focus of the joint surveillance and was followed and often videotaped in his travels, including trips to Paris. The plan was to make arrests as the militants left one of ETA's biweekly meetings, taking care to let Txelis escape. The operation was aborted twice, in late February and then on March 15, because of concern that Artapalo was not present. On March 29, as police tailed Lasalle, Txelis, and Fitipaldi, the driver of Txelis's car was observed stopping and getting into Lasalle's car. The dressing down he gave Lasalle convinced authorities that he was not just a simple militant and, by a process of deduction, they were led to conclude that this was Artapalo. Police moved in promptly and arrested Artapalo and the others, but it was Artapalo who had been the most earnestly sought of ETA's leaders for the past several years.[332] This 38-year-old had lived in clandestinity for nearly twenty years and was accused of complicity in nineteen deaths, including his participation in Operation Ogro, the assassination of Spanish premier Carrero Blanco in 1973.[333]

Just as they had after the arrest of Santi Potros, police found documents and incriminating information leading to other arrests. At the time of their arrest Artapalo and the others had been frantically trying to shred documents which police later carefully reassembled, including a cashier's check for thirty million pesetas signed by Sabino Euba Cenarruzabeitia ("Pelopintxo"), ETA's treasurer, and presumably intended for arms purchases.[334] Many of these new leads were found on fifteen of Txelis's Macintosh computer diskettes, including information about ETA's effort to set up a network of safe houses in Brittany and Paris to hide its top leadership.

In the wake of Artapalo's capture, police, who had been combing Spanish publications for just such a link, discovered the parallel between the name Txantxangorri ("Robin") which had appeared in a series of odd texts in the campus supplement of the newspaper *El Mundo,* and the name of the hamlet in Bidart, Txantxangorria, where Artapalo was arrested and had been hiding.[335] This explained one of the ways that Artapalo had communicated with his roving commandos in the field and vice versa. The text of the messages discovered seemed to indicate Joseba's desire to cross the border to meet with Artapalo and the threat he was under in Spain. The last appeared on April 1, three days after Artapalo's arrest in Bidart. Police also found evidence of Herri Batasuna couriers on Txelis's diskettes.

On April 28 ETA's treasurer, Sabino Euba ("Pelopintxo"), was arrested as he attempted to board a plane in Paris bound for Mexico. It emerged later that he also had been the subject of covert surveillance during the five months preceding his arrest, in the hope that he would lead police to Artapalo. Police believed he had been responsible for revolutionary taxes totaling two billion pesetas, or more than twenty-one million dollars, since the late 1970s. On May 14, acting on information seized during the arrests of Txelis and Pelopintxo, police indicted thirty-five people in Brittany, including José Luis Ansola Larrañaga ("Peio el viejo") and sixteen Bretons, for their work in creating clandestine safe houses.[336]

Among the other information found was evidence that Herri Batasuna leaders visiting Antxon in the Dominican Republic had communicated with

Txelis by computer modem and international telephone lines from Santo Domingo. Other information led police to believe that ETA had been receiving as much as one hundred million pesetas (one million dollars) per month through its revolutionary tax. Substantial sums of ETA's money were now traced to Swiss banks, where it was alleged to have been laundered, perhaps since 1982.[337]

Madrid called the arrest of Artapalo and the others a "brilliant operation";[338] Luis Roldán, director general of the Spanish Guardia Civil, while denying that it constituted "the end of ETA," nonetheless called it "a very important stage, the beginning leading to pacification."[339] French premier Edith Cresson hailed the arrests as "a great success of French police in the fight against terrorism."[340] French interior minister Philippe Marchand declared, "In three years all the members of ETA's executive committee have been arrested."[341] Yet Felipe González feared reprisals from an organization of those "who don't know how to do anything but kill."[342] As Marchand himself cautioned, "E.T.A. was badly hit, but one can never destroy this group completely."[343]

In the aftermath of the arrests in Brittany in early May French sources leveled harsh criticisms against their Spanish counterparts for their "lack of professionalism" in leaking details about the operation to the press before the arrests were completed.[344] The first Spanish radio reports had in fact been broadcast before noon, while the arrests were still under way.

REGENERATION?

Attention now focused on the question of ETA's ability to reconstitute its leadership. Herri Batasuna cautioned that ETA's leadership has always regenerated itself, and among the names mentioned as succeeding Artapalo were Apala, whose status and even whereabouts were still in doubt; Faustino Estanislao Villanueva ("Txapu"), who had been close to Artapalo; Joseba, who had been his harsh critic; or Iñaki Bilbao Belaskoetxea ("Iñaki").[345] In the wake of Artapalo's capture ETA's newly constituted executive committee was believed to include Txapu; Iñaki; Artapalo's brother Kepa Mugica Garmendia; Achurra Egurola ("Pototo"); Felipe San Epifanio ("Pipe"); Pedro Pikabea Ugalde ("Kepa"); Rosario Picabea ("Errota"); and Galarraga Mendizabal ("Zaldibi").[346] French police sources were reported doubtful about the role of Pototo, Zaldibi, and Txapu. For José Luis Barberia, however, writing in *El País*, ETA's ability to regenerate itself was a self-serving myth.[347] ETA's ability in the past to pass on its leadership had depended on the French sanctuary. With that sanctuary now gone, Barberia argued that ETA would never again be able to create the infrastructure it had previously enjoyed. It was clear that the loss of the French sanctuary led ETA militants to seek refuge elsewhere, including such Latin American countries as Mexico, Cuba, Nicaragua, Venezuela, and Uruguay. The number of militants in these countries, and the businesses which had been created with the revolutionary tax, led them to be called ETA's "embassies" overseas.[348] Particular attention was focused on the link between ETA and the Tupamaros and even the Uruguayan military and police. By May 1992 it was estimated that one thousand former ETA militants had found refuge in Latin America.[349] It was predicted that the number of ETA militants hiding in France would decline to around one hundred, with thirty of them leaving in the wake of Artapalo's arrest. As the French government used the seized documents to roll up the network of clandestine safe houses, many of those who had harbored ETA militants were now said to be unwilling to continue the risk.

On April 2 Artapalo was charged in Paris with criminal association, firearms violations, use of false identity documents, and crimes involving a terrorist enterprise.[350] Spanish politicians called for close cooperation with French judicial authorities in preparing the evidence for his trial, even if preferring that he be turned over immediately by the French. Underscoring the fate that one day might await Artapalo, on April 10, following the completion of his sentence in France, Txikierdi was handed over to Spanish authorities in Madrid.

While both French and Spanish authorities were optimistic that the arrest of Artapalo would finally force ETA to renounce the armed struggle, neither was willing to declare the threat to the World's Fair in Seville and the 1992 Summer Olympics in Barcelona ended. Spain announced plans to guard raillines especially closely and to station 3,000 army troops along the French border in coordination with France to prevent ETA infiltration during the Olympics.[351]

Just one month before the opening of the World's Fair in Seville Spain was bracing for an effort by Basque separatists to disrupt the fair and then, potentially, the Olympic Games in Barcelona. Spain's Interior and Defense ministries therefore spent months preparing a complex security plan in coordination with French, Israeli, and other foreign police and intelligence groups.

The bombing of the Israeli Embassy in Buenos Aires earlier in the month, which killed at least thirty-two people, brought into focus the danger of attacks by Islamic fundamentalist groups. But for Spain the main threat was posed by ETA.

As Spanish interior minister José Luis Corcuera cautioned, "For the moment, we prefer to continue working on the basis of the worst of these two hypotheses. This is not the time to indulge in euphoria that we could end up regretting."[352] Yet documents seized following Artapalo's and Txelis's arrest suggest that ETA had already concluded that attacks on the Olympics and the worldwide criticism they would provoke would be counterproductive to the cause.[353] In early July 1992 ETA proposed a two-month "ceasefire" with "official contacts" ultimately leading to "political conversations." ETA soon insisted that the government respond before the start of the Olympic Games, without success.

Conclusion

The period between 1975 and 1992 constituted a progressive cycle of violence and repression in the Pays Basque Français. The rise of Iparretarrak after 1973 led some government observers to believe that ETA had in fact violated the explicit conditions of its asylum by fomenting a violent Basque movement among the French Basque hosts. In fact, Iparretarrak's appearance greatly threatened ETA's northern sanctuary and risked the lives of its militants, who clung to precarious enough sanctuary without the aggravation of Iparretarrak violence.

The appearance of anti-ETA violence after 1975 revealed an official Spanish governmental policy of striking back at ETA in its rear sanctuary in retaliation for ETA's operations in Spain. For nearly a decade this policy was carried out by mercenaries and contract killers operating under a number of umbrella names. The Spanish use of violence in France represented a deliberate strategy of state-sponsored terrorism in order to blackmail the French government into moving against ETA's northern sanctuary. This Spanish policy culminated in the appearance of GAL in the early 1980s, which pledged to make the gutters in the Pays Basque Français flow red with blood. GAL's violence created a deliberate pressure on the French government, which continued to maintain its historic policy of asylum even after the election of Socialist president François Mitterrand in 1981. With the election of a conservative parliamentary majority in 1986, and the resultant period of "cohabitation" between left and right, the government of Jacques Chirac acquiesced to GAL's violence and adopted a policy of expulsions of ETA refugees in "absolute urgency" to Spain and to third countries. Having succeeded in forcing the expulsion of refugees, and in forcing French action against ETA's northern sanctuary, GAL's purpose was fulfilled and it simply disappeared.

As France's policy toward ETA became more punitive, ETA's own attitude toward Iparretarrak became more moderate, since little was now to be lost by this imitative violence in France. With the advent of ETA's hard-line faction around Artapalo following Txomin's death, ETA once more influenced IK's political strategy of using violence as a tool to force the government to negotiate and its insistence on a series of hard-line and nonnegotiable demands. Lacking the level of ETA's support by either Herri Batasuna or the Basque public in the South, and increasingly rejected for its violence in the North, Iparretarrak began to lose momentum and open the way for the rise of Basque moderate movements which sought to claim leadership of the *abertzale* movement from the legitimate and credible political center.

The arrest of Henri Parot's group in 1990 "stupefied" French and Spanish authorities, demonstrating the extent of French Basque involvement in ETA. In fact, by 1992 there were eighty Basque prisoners in France.[354] Forty-six were Spanish citizens and thirty-seven French. More Basques were in prison for having been either members or supporters of ETA than for having been part of Iparretarrak.

The period from 1986 through 1992 was characterized by an accelerating institutional hostility toward ETA and increased cooperation between the French and Spanish governments. By 1992 it was clear that ETA's northern sanctuary in France was severely reduced. Government successes in this period demonstrated a sophistication and tenacity that included joint French-Spanish surveillances lasting more than six months and stretching across France. This patience led authorities slowly up ETA's organizational chart and culminated in the arrest of what interior minister Marchand called the entire executive committee of ETA by 1992. The level of mistakes being made by ETA by this time, the turmoil which Artapalo's hard-line policies were provoking within ETA and its prisoners, and even the rumors that Apala had been recalled from Latin America after ten years to retake control suggested the extent of its political exhaustion. The events of 1992 raise what Martha Crenshaw calls the question of how terrorism ends.[355] Never have so many voices within the organization, especially among its prisoners, called for genuine negotiation with Spain. Little progress is likely so long as ETA insists on negotiating on the basis of the KAS alternative. With the arrest of Artapalo, ETA may well change his policy of forcing negotiation through an escalation of violence. ETA's offer of a ceasefire and renewed negotiation during the 1992 Olympics may be indicative of the strategy its new leaders will pursue. Spain has sought to offer ETA the chance to lay down its arms with dignity, but both should remember Metternich's dictum that "diplomacy is the art of avoiding the appearance of victory." Both the French and Spanish governments are cautiously optimistic about the future, but Herri Batasuna and others have reminded them pointedly of ETA's historic ability to rise like the phoenix from the ashes of its own destruction.

It has been the repression of the refugee community like no other issue which mobilized the *abertzale* community in France. Iparretarrak essentially failed to win public support for its campaign of violence, leaving the Pays

Basque Français in a period of expectancy. In the 1980s new moderate voices arose which rejected the use of the armed struggle and began to conceive of a political future without borders as part of European unification after 1992. The rise of this moderate Basque center has been the most promising transformation of Basque militancy in the modern era, as we will see in chapter 8, and represents the effort of the French Basque movement to emerge from the ghetto of violence into the mainstream of French Basque political life.

Chapter Eight

The Eclipse of Violence and the Rise of

Basque Moderation

Dembora demmborary darraio.
After one climate comes another.
Basque proverb

In the years following the dissolution of *Enbata* in 1974 the burden of *abertzale* action in France balanced on the far left of the political spectrum. EHAS became the prime vehicle for Basque militancy in the mid-1970s, but remained unable to unite the range of *abertzale* action in France at that time. The reappearance of Iparretarrak's violence in 1977 forced the issue of Basque violence back to center stage and signaled IK's effort to drive EHAS out of existence and to control the landscape of Basque political and cultural action. Apart from the dispute over the use of violence in France, IK and EHAS were ideologically quite close in their overt calls for Socialist revolution. But the twin extremes of socialism and violence marginalized the Basque movement and defined a ghetto cut off from the mainstream of Basque public opinion. With the political center largely unoccupied, new initiatives were begun by Basques who were dissatisfied with the narrow range of ideological choices. Their search for a new political expression signaled the rise of Basque moderation and set the stage for a number of dynamic political and cultural movements in the 1980s.

This chapter examines the rise of Basque moderation and the political and cultural movements which sought to transcend the debate over Basque violence. I will focus on the rise of four Basque political parties—Ezkerreko Mugimendu Abertzalea (EMA), Euskal Batasuna, and Eusko Alkartasuna, and the PNV in France—examine their motives and platforms, and describe their efforts at joint political action. Second, I will describe the rise of a new generation of Basque youth, their values, and their movements, like Patxa, which combined *abertzalisme* with the rhythms of the European alternative music scene. Third, I will examine the accelerating conflict between Iparretarrak and the French state, which led to the arrest and trial of most of its militants by 1991. With the elimination of ETA's northern sanctuary, the question of the armed struggle in France as well as Spain appeared more and more to be a political dead-end. Finally, I will describe the state of the *abertzale* movement in 1992, its growing electoral strength, and the processes of reconciliation and hope which may influence its future development.

The *Abertzale* Movement Emerges from Its Ghetto: The Rise of Basque Moderation

IZAN

In 1977 a group of *abertzale* independents began to meet to discuss the possibility of a new agenda for Basque political activity in France. EHAS remained unsatisfactory to them, and many felt that the focus on a "political party" was impeding tangible achievements on social and economic issues. Between January and June 1978 the lines were drawn for a new political entity—not a movement, much less a party—but more a "work structure" which would seek to enhance Basque economic development through small working groups or "Lan-talde." The early goal was to create 1,500 new jobs by 1985 and ultimately to give the Pays Basque its own "territorial collectivity," as yet undefined. One hundred and twenty-five people took part in its founding assembly on October 28, 1978. Of these, 27 percent were women; 42 percent were less than thirty, and 25 percent less than twenty-five; 62 percent were employed in the service sector, and another 10 percent were students; 72 percent came from the coast, and only 22 percent from the interior. IZAN's goal was to gather together those Basque independents who were not satisfied with the current range of Basque political organizations. IZAN saw itself as a third path between the worn ideologies of the past twenty years—those who were content to say "no" and those using violence.

In the short run IZAN's goals were "partial" in nature, charting realistic goals over the next two years. As one of its leaders put it, "There was a feeling that five hundred *abertzale* working together could accomplish something." By October 1979 IZAN had become "IZAN: Self-Managed Basque Patriotic Collectif." In 1979 it elaborated on a platform with political, cultural, and economic elements.[1] Politically, IZAN sought a Basque "territorial collectivity" in the short run and a unified Basque state in the long run. It called for a Basque cultural statute to save the Basque language and culture. Economically, IZAN embraced the cooperative movement as a model. It sought the total self-management of medium and large industries in the Basque country and the creation of a sister-city relationship between Bayonne and Pamplona to underscore the potential of a united Basque economy. Among its leaders were Patxi Noblia, Ramuntxo Camblong, Michel Burucoa, Jacques Abeberry, Peio Baratxegaray, and Jean Idierer. In September 1981 IZAN reported having 150 dues-paying members.[2]

IZAN supported the election of François Mitterrand during the presidential election in 1981, based on the promises made during his campaign. The hopes mobilized around Mitterrand's election led IZAN to create Hitza Hitz (The Given Word) to hold him to his promises, as we will see below. Its tactical alliance with the local Socialists ultimately foundered when it became clear that Mitterrand and Defferre were in wholesale retreat on the promise of a Basque department. In order to maintain its independence of maneuver, IZAN created Herritarki in 1981 as a vehicle for presenting candidates for the municipal elections in 1983.

HERRI TALDEAK AND THE CREATION OF ATEKA IN 1983

By the fall of 1983 the Herri Taldeak movement had been buffeted by the successive acts of IK's violence, which served to discredit the Basque movement in the eyes not only of the Basque population, but of the mobilized *abertzale* milieu as well. The French have an expression *Reculer pour mieux sauter* or step back to leap higher. In this spirit, Herri Taldeak announced the creation of a new monthly magazine, *Ateka*, which it hoped would serve as an open forum for discussion of ideas and issues across the Basque left.[3] *Ateka* was a fence-mending effort within the *abertzale* leftist milieu. Its editorial team represented a cross-section of opinion on the Basque left. While it did include new faces, such as the eminent Spanish Basque historian of ETA, Professor Jokin Apalategi, it also included the leading voices of HT, such as Xan Coscarat, Eñaut Hartischelhar, Richard Irazusta, Lucien Etxezaharreta, and the former leader of the now outlawed Hordago, Jakes Borthayrou.[4] Within four months of *Ateka*'s founding came Coscarat's arrest (in January 1984) for transporting journalists to IK's clandestine press conference. Coscarat seemed to have been assigned the role of IK's press spokesman and media liaison and performed this role in *Ateka* as well. HT's influence on *Ateka*'s early policies was clear, and a recurring theme in the magazine was the defense of Basque political prisoners. While *Ateka* represented a diversity of Basque leftist thought, a willingness to criticize the armed struggle was clearly out of the question. For, as *Ateka* stated in its first issue, "The struggles of Euskadi North and the often violent or tragic events testify to the reality and to the determination of the *abertzale* movement. . . . [Given] . . . the realities of the struggles of the last few years. . . . With others we have been the actors."[5] Among the rising issues championed by HT was the plight of the refugees, and in December 1984 HT proposed the creation of a Statute of the Political Prisoner in France, including those of IK.[6] By July 1986 *Ateka* reported that the largest single issue in the previous months, with 32 percent of its coverage on the North, was IK and the armed struggle: "in observing the percentages one guesses the importance attributed to each theme."[7]

THE CREATION OF EUSKAL HERRIKO LABORARIEN BATASUNA (ELB)

One of the first efforts to mark its distance from IK's violence was the creation of Euskal Herriko Laborarien Batasuna (United Workers of the Basque Country) in the fall of 1982 by Pierre Iralour, Michel Berhocoirigoin, and others who rejected the spiraling violence which was holding the Basque movement captive. ELB attracted a class of young modern Basque farmers who were perceived as "big thinkers" or Basque nationalists and thus marginalized to a greater or lesser degree in their villages. Indeed, according to one of ELB's founders, if there was a single obstacle to the growth of ELB as a union of Basque farmers, it was the stigma of "nationalism" which made it suspect in the eyes of their conservative rural neighbors: "The fear of nationalism will prevent ELB from being a dominant union in the Pays Basque. We'll always be a minority unless things change greatly." Yet, the future of Basque agriculture depended on these farmer/militants who were willing to try new agricultural crops and techniques in order to revitalize the declining rural interior.

ELB as a political statement grew out of the resentment on the part of these "intellectual farmers" that university-trained intellectuals were "parachuting" down into the rural Pays Basque and trying to herd the mass of Basque farmers with their theoretical discussions and condescension for the reality of farm life. *Enbata* had been the first to attempt this fabian-like strategy of serving as nationalist "clerks" to the masses, and Iparretarrak was only the latest.

ELB's first political text defined its goals, its relations with other parties, and its opposition to the armed struggle.[8] ELB defined itself as the union of all farmers who considered themselves to be workers and thus sought to defend the interests of the majority of Basque farmers.[9] By 1985, ELB claimed (somewhat dubiously) 500 farmers as members, with a goal in sight of 1,000 members in the near future. Yet *Ager* reported in 1985 that ELB represented 30 percent of the farmers in the Pays Basque.[10] If ELB was a union of farmers, it nevertheless rejected the pitfall of corporatist politics (i.e., farmers against everyone else in an economically Hobbesian war of all against all). In progressively larger focus, ELB defined its members as farmers, Basque farmers, and finally as farmers-cum-workers in a chain which tied together all the workers on the planet.

If ELB made no effort to control the political work of its members outside of ELB, it made clear that it would not become the agricultural appendix of any kind of outside group. This was addressed in particular to Herri Taldeak, which, after two unsuccessful efforts to enlist ELB's support in demonstrations, simply sought to co-opt it by announcing publicly that ELB would participate, despite ELB's silence.[11] In the case of the invitation to take part in the antitourist Operation Escargot, ELB explained its refusal to take part: Iparretarrak's campaign at the same time and with the same objectives simply contaminated or eclipsed any other form of action.

The longest single element in ELB's platform was an explanation of its rejection of the use of the armed struggle. During the early 1980s members of ELB became part of the "usual suspects" in Basse-Navarre who were regularly detained and questioned about IK's violence. For ELB, the police profited from IK's violence as the pretext for tainting other militants who had "nothing to do with these actions of IK, [and] the police well knew it."[12] In this way, through guilt by association, ELB was soon called "the union of bomb planters."[13] As a result of experience with both IK and the police, ELB sought to distance itself from IK's violence:

> An armed group in the Pays Basque North, Iparretarrak, has arrived at an elevated degree of violence. This violence apparently is only understood and accepted by an infinite minority of people. . . . The actions of Iparretarrak paralyze all other forms of action . . . everything which is done elsewhere is completely eclipsed by Iparretarrak. . . . *The only trademark of the* abertzale *movement is the violence of Iparretarrak.* . . . Iparretarrak claims to come to the aid of the struggles of the Basque people. If one could measure in terms of efficacy the political violence of IK, it would emerge that it is perceived as an act of demolition.[14]

While *Ateka* sought to bridge the gap between ELB and IK by pointing out the similarities in their recent texts, it was clear that the united front of silence within the mobilized *abertzale* milieu regarding IK's violence was beginning to erode.[15] ELB's experience is significant in that it demonstrated in subsequent months that what IK could not accomplish through co-optation it sought to accomplish through threats and intimidation against those who rejected its violence. Among former militants of ELB, there was a sense that IK's hostility toward ELB came not just from ELB's opposition to violence, but from a general orientation within IK to oppose any initiative it did not control, whether it was Seaska, EHAS, or ELB. ELB thought that others were frightened to do what it attempted. As one former leader of ELB described the climate, "Journalists often asked, 'Aren't you afraid of the consequences?' So you see the climate of intimidation IK sought to create?"

Quite apart from the internal dynamic of the Basque movement at this time, and the ongoing dialogue over violence, the relationship between the Pays Basque and the Socialist administration of François Mitterrand was characterized by dashed hopes, difficult negotiations, and ultimate disillusionment.

THE FATE OF THE BASQUE DEPARTMENT
As part of the development of the Socialist electoral platform for the April 1981 presidential elections, a group of Socialist deputies in the French National Assembly introduced a *proposition de loi,* number 2224, during the 1980–1981 legislative session calling for the creation of a Basque department in France out of the cantons forming the third and fourth legislative *circonscriptions* of the Pyrénées-Atlantiques.[16] Among its articles, number 11 empowered the new department to act in accordance with *proposition de loi* 3401 concerning the safeguarding of minority languages in education and media. In a local press conference on January 31, local Socialist Party officials announced that the creation of a Basque department, as well as a new statute for Corsica, would be proposition 54 of François Mitterrand's "101 Propositions pour la France," the platform of his upcoming 1981 presidential campaign.[17] Proposition 56 called for the preservation of France's minority languages and cultures.

For their part, the Gaullist elected officials (RPR) of the Pyrénées-Atlantiques quickly denounced the Socialist plan as "suicidal" and threatening to the unity of French territory.[18] Bernard Marie, Gaullist deputy from Biarritz until the legislative elections of 1981, expressed his fear that the proposal would lead to the creation of a department as sparsely populated and impoverished as the Creuse or Lozère and ultimately lead to an autonomous and independent Pays Basque.[19] This sentiment was shared by interior minister Christian Bonnet in Oloron on March 5, who also called it "imprudent" to envision creating a Basque department in immediate proximity to Spanish provinces experiencing "grave troubles."[20] He firmly promised that "this government refuses to take measures which . . . would be of a nature one day to threaten the unity of the territory of the Republic."[21] Adding further justification to the government's wariness, the subprefect in Bayonne, Bernard Gérard, declared, "In 1980, the *arrondissement* of Bayonne is the only one in the hexagon where one killed for political reasons."[22]

By March, however, two different associations had been created in support of the idea of a department and an intense debate began, pitting, for the most part, Socialists against their dubious conservative counterparts.[23]

They were quick to pick up arguments for and against a separate department which stretched back to the time of the French Revolution.

Mitterrand's election in 1981 with 51.75 percent of the national vote reflected a clear increase in his support in the Pays Basque and buoyed his supporters' hopes. While his global score in the two Basque *circonscriptions* increased 6.39 percent (from 37.94 percent to 44.33 percent) in comparison to his score in 1974, in Soule the increase was 12.72 percent.[24] In fact, Mitterrand won 57.54 percent in the canton of Tardets, owing to the economic and demographic decline there. As a partial indicator of the importance of the election, the total number of Basque votes cast in the 1981 election was nearly 25 percent greater than in 1974. In the 1981 election alone, the Basque turnout between the first and second rounds increased from 80.9 percent to 88.36 percent, slightly higher than for both the department and the country as a whole.[25]

As expected, Mitterrand dissolved parliament and called for new legislative elections for the following June 14 and 21. If the tinge of socialism continued to manifest itself in Soule, the legislative elections which followed Mitterrand's narrow victory in the presidentials suggested the polarization and anxiety of the traditional Basque electorate. Reflecting its historic political culture, the third *circonscription* in the interior re-elected deputy Michel Inchauspé with a 62.66 percent majority in the first round.[26] In Baigorri, despite the stirrings of economic distress and the rise of IK as a product of the village, Inchauspé received 72.5 percent of the vote in the first round, the highest of any canton in the *circonscription*. On the coast, the Socialist Jean-Pierre Destrade was elected deputy in Bayonne, giving the left a solid foothold in the culturally heterogeneous coast.

HITZA HITZ

On August 20, 1981, the group of forty prominent Basque militants who had originally supported Mitterrand's election constituted themselves as Hitza Hitz in order to try to hold the Socialist administration to the promises Mitterrand had made in his campaign.[27] Within weeks of the election the new Socialist administration began to equivocate by delaying any decision on a Basque department until consideration on its larger restructuring of French local government.

For J.-D. Chaussier, the government's hesitation to honor its own electoral promises revealed the power of the Jacobin idea and the historic sensitivity to any threats to the unity of the French state.[28] While the newly proposed law on administrative decentralization reflected the government's recognition of the need to reform center-periphery relations, it would only do so

if the authority of the state were not challenged. The government's decision to reinforce the role of the departmental *conseils généraux* reinforced a
largely conservative body whose relationship with both the prefecture and
the Parisian ministries was one of mutual dependence. By creating new "feu-
dalities" along ethno-linguistic lines, any change in the territorial status of
either Corsica or the Pays Basque raised the hoary specter of separatism. As
Gilles Darcy put it, "In a state which realized its unity through centralization . . . it is to question that unity, it is to clear the way for every separatism.
In other words, between feudality and centralization, [there's no choice to
be made]." [29]

Speaking in Brittany on October 20, 1981, Gaston Defferre said to a Breton
militant, "You will not be independent . . . you will be one of the regions
of France which will not be in a federal state, but in a unitary state." [30] On
January 9, 1982, the large regional daily *Sud-Ouest* interpreted remarks made
to it by Defferre, the new French minister of the interior and of decentralization, in its headline, "Gaston Defferre à 'Sud-Ouest': Non au département
basque." [31] The same interpretation was picked up and repeated nationally
by *Le Monde*.[32] In acknowledging the emotional reaction of Basque Socialist
deputy Destrade to the story in *Sud-Ouest*, Defferre clarified his remarks
and promised to give the proposal careful study. On February 23, 1982, Defferre announced to an extraordinary meeting of local elected Basque officials
his appointment of a special group, the Ravail Commission, to study the
question of a Basque department in detail.[33] As deputy Michel Inchauspé, a
vocal opponent of a Basque department, remarked on leaving the meeting,
"The best means of burying a project is to create a study commission." [34] By
May 14, in an interview with Marseillaise journalists, Defferre was evoking
the specter of Spanish Basque irredentism and the difficulty of drawing the
borders of a Basque department:

> Finally, I thought that one could make things evolve peacefully, whereas
> if one creates a Basque department, and one day the Spanish Basques
> obtain an independence if not complete, at least something close, and
> that moreover they may want to annex the French Basque depart-
> ment, the government will be confronted by a situation which will not
> be easy.[35]

In reality, the opposition of the departmental *conseil général* to the idea—
still dominated by the right—gave Defferre the excuse to bury a promise
he had never supported in the first place. Hitza Hitz continued its tactical
if open-eyed alliance with local Socialists through the March 1982 cantonal
elections.[36]

Yet by November 1982 it was clear that the idea of a Basque department was dead. In the climate of Basque violence, the government also hardened its positions on related cultural issues like the integration of the Basque primary school movement, Seaska, into the Ministry of National Education. As *Enbata* put it, "Not only is proposition 54 of candidate Mitterrand dead, but now here are the gravediggers to work away at its cadaver."[37] Destrade was unwilling to concede defeat and insisted that Mitterrand was still promising to fulfill his pledge as late as his official visit to Corsica in June 1983.[38] The government moved quickly toward institutional reform in Corsica, but not in the Pays Basque, because of the presence of ETA and the separatist threats it evoked. As Jacques Abeberry editorialized in *Enbata* following the election, "nothing would be more dangerous than betrayed hopes."[39] On February 3, 1984, even the moderate group Hitza Hitz broke with the Socialist Party over its unfulfilled promises and its failure to keep its "given word." Calling this a "fabulous error" on the part of the Socialists, Abeberry argued that the administration had thus discredited the cause of Basque moderation. As Abeberry explained what Mitterrand had done to the moderate Basque camp, "The risk is great of seeing the nationalist left radicalize itself. We, the moderates, partisans of a compromise with the Socialists, we are passing for imbeciles."[40] The president of the association of elected officials in favor of a department announced simply in May 1984, "They lied to us."[41]

Still, Socialist deputy Jean-Pierre Destrade insisted, "It's a project which hasn't been forgotten, but we had to slow it down due to the recurrence of terrorism. We didn't want to continue this project and have it confused with the struggle against terrorism. This was not a project of independence."[42] The *abertzale* opinion was that Iparretarrak's violence had simply given the Socialists the excuse to abandon a promise they had not been enthusiastic about in the first place. Robert Arrambide said, "The PS and François Mitterrand betrayed us and since this decision this has been an open door for [all manner of diversions] including the armed struggle."[43]

In *abertzale* circles, the prevailing opinion was that France had sacrificed the idea of a Basque department on the altar of Spanish-French diplomacy. It was well known that the Spanish government opposed the creation of a Basque department in France for fear of provoking further separatism in the Spanish Basque provinces. Relations between France and Spain had been warming since the French began to extradite ETA refugees back to Spain. In addition to this increasing cooperation in turning over ETA refugees to Spanish authorities, conspiracy theorists pointed to France's decision to withdraw from a joint European fighter plane project and to develop one alone, possibly in conjunction with Spain.[44]

The government's stand lent encouragement to the radical camp. In September 1984 *Ateka* asserted that "in the *abertzale* movement of the left in

Euskadi North, the necessity of armed struggle creates no doubt. By contrast, what poses the problem is the role and the means which the armed struggle must give itself."[45] While confessing to "making mistakes" and "knowing highs and lows," *Ateka* admitted the growing estrangement between those practicing the armed struggle from clandestinity and the majority of *abertzale* militants: "The armed organization must reinforce the legal movement and the legal movement must support the armed organization. Whereas in recent times this solidarity, this support of the legal movement for the armed organization, has been very weak, if not nonexistent."[46] For *Ateka*, this was the problem of any revolutionary struggle, achieving the proper balance between the armed struggle and legal political militancy, the problem which had led to the parting of the ways of ETA-m and ETA-pm nearly a decade before.[47]

FROM THE ISOLATION OF VIOLENCE TO THE POLLS

During the 1983 municipal elections IZAN's initiative led to the creation of a broadly based list of candidates who constituted themselves as Herritarki Bayonne-Capitale. Their goal was to try to create a positive and dynamic image of *abertzalisme* as a political force. Their initiative was based on the belief that "local power is a true power" and that, despite the presence of the *abertzale* movement on the political landscape, it was largely absent from the centers of local decision-making.[48] Herritarki was willing to cooperate with the Socialist Party, provided it kept its promises.

Among its forty-three members were former *Enbata* leaders like Michel Burucoa, former EHAS leaders like Battitta Larzabal, former members of the PSU or Ezker Berri, and such noted cultural figures as Professor Pierre Charritton, member of Euskaltzaindia, the Basque Academy.[49] The effort won a scant 833 votes, or 4.49 percent of the votes cast. Elsewhere in the Pays Basque, a partial list of candidates in Baigorri received more than 13 percent of the votes, confirming the polarization of public opinion in that town. In the 1985 cantonal elections only two *abertzale* candidates presented themselves: Jacques Aurnague in Saint-Jean-Pied-de-Port and Marie Andrée Arbelbide in Iholdy.[50] Aurnague ultimately polled 11.50 percent of the vote and Arbelbide won 16.48 percent, including an important 40 percent in her native village of Hélette. In both cases where Basque candidates were present, the voter turnout substantially exceeded that for the Pays Basque, with 76.9 percent in Saint-Jean-Pied-de-Port and 82.5 percent in Iholdy, compared to 65.5 percent for the Pays Basque as a whole.

The Creation of EMA

By the mid-1980s, and despite self-serving claims to the contrary, the range of difference in *abertzale* political opinion was relatively narrow, apart from the question of violence. For one critic of Iparretarrak:

> What divides the *abertzale*? If I refer to *ILDO* no. 9, I arrive at the conclusion: not very much. The analysis that you, IK, make on the Pays Basque, of its economic reality . . . *is the same*, may it not displease you, as that effected by the movement Enbata, fifteen years ago, taken up later by EHAS, repeated by the Herri Talde, known and admitted by all *abertzale*.[51]

In a hectoring use of parallelism, he repeated the same refrain for repression and for the whole of its political demands. The point was that the Basque political universe was quite narrow by the mid-1980s, and its very fragmentation was a political liability. The cause of that fragmentation was the use of violence. In calling for a deep debate, was IK willing to renounce the use of violence if the moderate majority demanded it?

According to later EMA leader Richard Irazusta, by April 1985 leading militants of Herri Taldeak saw themselves trapped in a political ghetto defined by IK's violence and its prisoners. According to Irazusta, he was joined by Eñaut Haritschelhar and Alain Iriart in wanting HT or its successor to occupy a larger and more important place in the Basque political spectrum, even if it was not yet clear what that would mean. What these leaders of HT were committed to, however, was the moderation of HT if at all possible without leading to internal rupture and conflict.

At the same time they were aware of the intention of Eñaut Etchemendy to create an as yet undefined "cantonal" movement to oppose Iparretarrak and its hold on the Basque political landscape in France. For that reason, the decision was made to accelerate plans for a broader political movement in order to take the wind out of Etchemendy's sails and undercut any potentially competing movement.

In May 1985 Herri Taldeak invited representatives of the range of Basque leftist and independent opinion to Cambo to examine the nature of Basque political militancy in France. Its own general assembly was scheduled for the first morning, followed by a broad political discussion in the afternoon and continuing into the next day.[52] The meeting reflected the need to combine forces, but left unsettled the form that this new political venture would take.[53]

By the end of June HT militants were discussing with other militants the nature of a new Basque political organization and the presentation of candidates at the upcoming legislative elections scheduled for spring 1986.[54] As Richard Irazusta put it, "The absence of *abertzale* candidates in 1981 was a grave error."[55] The proposal to field candidates was not greeted with unanimity. Laguntza was the most skeptical of the idea. For Laguntza, it did not take elections to demonstrate the weakness of the Basque movement: the important question was whether an *abertzale* candidacy could attract new public support for the Basque cause.[56] Laguntza favored a strategy of active abstention from the elections, rather than further marginalizing the Basque movement with a weak turnout for Basque candidates.

The first meeting to discuss participating in the 1986 legislative elections was held in Cambo on August 8, 1985, and brought together forty representatives of HT, Laguntza, and unaffiliated militants. They set the agenda for a larger meeting at Hasparren in September. The more than 150 people who were present in Hasparren represented six Basque cantons. Their discussions produced Ezkerreko Mugimendu Abertzalea (Basque Patriotic Movement of the Left) or EMA.[57] The vote to create a broad Basque political movement was 148 to 3. But the decision to field candidates in the elections was more contentious. Laguntza's strategy of abstention found some support, but in the end, by a vote of 118 to 19 (those favoring active abstention), it was decided to field candidates for the upcoming legislative elections. On December 8 EMA's first general assembly at Macaye attracted two hundred people to discuss the broad lines of the upcoming electoral campaign.

If the precise nature of EMA's platform and strategy remained to be "tied together," some doctrines of faith were considered given: the recognition of the Basque people as one *nation* in two different political contexts; the right of self-determination, as for all peoples; and a self-definition for EMA as being as much *abertzale* as Socialist.[58] Elaborating on this latter point, EMA would later insist:

> Faced with these gravediggers of our people, there remains but one response: the *abertzale* left: two indivisible words for a complementary definition. . . . Neither of these two words taken separately can offer a real solution to the problems of this country. . . . The stakes are enormous and pressing. . . . From whence the necessity of the birth of EMA.[59]

While admitting that it did not represent the whole *abertzale* left, EMA still urged the Basque movement writ large to support it.

The circumstances of EMA's birth, and the fact that the earlier positions of both HT and Laguntza on IK's violence were so near to the surface of the new movement, effectively tied EMA's hands on the question of the armed struggle. While HT remained strongly supportive of the armed struggle and of IK's "political prisoners," as late as December 1985 a former militant of Laguntza continued to criticize some of IK's practice, notably in antagonizing the relationship between the refugee community and the *abertzale* milieu in the North.[60] As a result of this clear internal disagreement, EMA took a position that was neither for nor against the armed struggle.[61] The problem, as EMA leader Richard Irazusta freely admitted, was that on the level of doctrine EMA and IK were developing the same themes. Yet he took pains to contrast the relationship between EMA and IK with that of the contemporary Corsican movement: "Unlike the Corsican movement, where the political branch overtly admits to being under the control of the clandestine branch, that was never the case here. We do not criticize their actions, but we do not depend on them politically either." In fact, EMA's membership was itself divided on the issue of IK's violence. As Irazusta admitted, "Some are favorable, some are neutral, and others are really opposed. Since we were able to overcome these divisions within EMA, we sought to reproduce that spirit in our external evolution with other political groups."

EMA's general assembly effectively sidestepped a pointed debate on the question, which was wise given its contentious nature at the Ipar Euskadi Gaur earlier in the year. Rather, EMA made five points concerning the armed struggle: (1) the first political violence was that of the state; (2) the armed struggle is a political struggle; (3) the means of action are different; (4) EMA would be an exclusively open and public organization; and (5) there was need for a deeper debate on the question of the armed struggle.[62] Given the widespread awareness of the tie between HT and IK, EMA's creation clearly reflected an effort to become more inclusive and to overcome the stigma of association with IK and its violence. Over the course of the next several years EMA and IK evolved on parallel but not wholly congruent paths, diverging on the role of violence as a specific tool of political bargaining. As Irazusta put it:

> Violence may lead to the creation of a new political generation of *abertzale*. The problem, as with ETA or Corsica, is that one never knows if one can stop it, for those capable of ending it may always be overthrown. Thus, it's extremely dangerous for the state to let violence accelerate because after a certain point it risks becoming unstoppable. It finds its own logic, its own life. In letting the situation degrade, one risks aggravating the situation. The government doesn't have that right. We are in the process of creating a generation of youth who have no desire to lead the society in which they find themselves. The risk is to see a generation

who will be taken by a "to the ultimate limit" logic against the present state and society.

Even for critics of EMA, Irazusta's position was a voice of moderation within HT/EMA and reflective of the rise of coastal Labourdin Basques over the more intransigent Basse-Navarrese like Bidart and Coscarat controlling IK.

EMA AND THE 1986 LEGISLATIVE ELECTIONS

At a press conference in mid-January 1986, EMA announced that its campaigns for the upcoming elections would be on the theme of *Atxik* (Hold on, Resist). Its candidates would be Eñaut Haritschelhar for the legislative elections and Richard Irazusta for the regional elections. Both were bright young professionals with long credentials as militants. Haritschelhar had been more visible in the public eye since his hunger strike in 1972 in the cathedral of Bayonne. In the end, neither was successful in distancing himself from the radical shadow of IK and both subsequently lost ground almost across the electoral map of the Pays Basque. Not even *Enbata* was wholehearted in its regard for EMA's candidacy, admitting that its readership and its own editorial team were divided on whether to endorse EMA or not: "the presence of EMA in Sunday's elections involves only a part, admittedly dynamic, of our movement. The results of the election cannot be those of *abertzalisme* in Euskadi North," a position seconded by the newspaper *Ager*, run by Ximun Haran and close to the Basque Nationalist Party in Spain.[63] For an official of the French police charged with combating Basque violence:

> The French [Basque] independentists have committed a heavy political error. They are presenting themselves at the next legislative and regional elections. We'll see then what they represent exactly. That is to say, next to nothing. We will count them, whereas before that, they could project illusions up until that point."[64]

The most disappointing results were in the cities along the coast, where EMA's legislative score ranged from 1.35 percent in Biarritz to 1.78 percent in Anglet to 2.33 percent in Bayonne.[65] Of the coastal cantons, only in Ustaritz (with 5.74 percent) did EMA surpass 5 percent. Its percentage score in the interior was almost twice that of the coast, surpassing 5 percent and being larger in Soule than in either rural Labourd or Basse-Navarre.[66] The highest single concentration of votes for EMA in both the legislative and regional elections came in the now politicized canton of Baigorri, where EMA gained scores of 11.58 percent in the legislative elections and 11.91 percent in the regionals. The result for EMA across the Pays Basque was a vote of 3.77 percent in the legislative elections and 600 more votes and a score of 4.21 percent for the regional elections held at the same time. Yet, in the nineteen cantons of the Pays Basque, the score for EMA made it the third or fourth largest political tendency, surpassing the National Front in seven of the nineteen cantons and the French Communist Party in ten of the nineteen.[67] Moreover, EMA's vote was highest in those cantons where the turnout was highest.

Yet, seen in a longer historical perspective, EMA's 5,111 votes in the 1986 legislative elections seem "mediocre," in Jean-Claude Larronde's words.[68] This is especially true when considering that *Enbata* polled 5,035 votes in 1967, nearly twenty years before, and EHAS got 4,924 eight years before.[69] Comparing *Enbata's* scores in 1967 with EMA's in 1986, one *abertzale* observer commented, "The *abertzale* movement always does the same, [or] even recedes."[70]

For EMA, its vote remained a "militant vote," and it was unable to overcome the marginal image given it by the media, local notables, and tradespeople.[71] As *Le Monde* interpreted the results, "As for the Basque nationalists, their place remains as marginal as in the past."[72] One high school student diagrammed EMA's position in 1986: "EMA = HT = IK."[73] For EMA, the results were encouraging, given that the movement "had appeared on the institutional political scene only 2 or 3 months before the elections, which from a political point of view was fairly radicalized."[74]

THE CREATION OF EKAITZA

In the months following the 1986 elections EMA embarked on a slicker public relations effort, creating a new Basque weekly, *Ekaitza* (Storm), to compete with both *Enbata* and *Ateka*. Its first special issue was distributed at the 1986 Aberri Eguna, and issue number 1 appeared in May 1986. *Ekaitza* was an effort to maintain the mobilization of the recent election and also to continue HT/EMA's efforts at socialization. Denying that it was a tool of EMA alone, *Ekaitza* claimed to be a weekly of "counterpowers" and to represent a forum of discussion.[75] It appeared primarily in French. The highest percentage of articles in Basque was in its first issue, with just over 43 percent. Throughout the first few years of its existence, a consistent average of about 23 percent of its articles were written in Basque.

It was clear by *Ateka's* reaction that *Ekaitza's* appearance had provoked something of a storm within its editorial council. In fact, what was transpiring was a power struggle between HT and Laguntza over the use of violence in France, which played itself out within *Ateka* as a terrain of joint action. As one leader of EMA put it, "*Ekaitza* was created because *Ateka* had become ungovernable, divided between two poles, those supporting the use of violence in the North, the *nordistes* (those close to IK), and the *sudistes* (including Laguntza) supporting ETA in the South." *Ekaitza* was ultimately created by those who supported the armed struggle and were representative of HT and IK. Their departure left the Laguntza contingent within *Ateka* out in the cold. *Ateka* temporarily suspended publication in April 1986, in the throes of a political crisis caused by HT and its new publication. This political conflict only added to *Ateka*'s long-standing deficit.[76] A month and a half later a new editorial team launched *Ateka* anew, but their announcement sounded more like a eulogy than a send-off.[77] It published eight more issues before ending in March 1987.

EMA's theses grew closer to those of Herri Taldeak, though its defense of the armed struggle was now muted. At its general assembly in November 1986, which assembled one hundred of its militants from eleven sections, EMA picked up HT's theme of a statute for Basque political prisoners and for Basque political refugees.[78] Most interestingly, EMA now expressed its support for the positions ETA-m had set forth in 1978 in the KAS Alternative in the South as a set of preconditions for negotiation with the Spanish government. The five points of the KAS Alternative included:

1. Total amnesty for all political prisoners;
2. Legalization of all political parties, including those calling for a separate Basque state, even if illegal under Spanish law;
3. Expulsion of the Guardia Civil and all Spanish forces from Euskadi;
4. The adoption of measures to improve the working and living conditions of the Basque masses and especially the working classes, and the satisfaction of their social and economic aspirations as expressed by their representative organizations;
5. An autonomy statute that encompassed as a minimum these five points:
   a. recognition of the national sovereignty of Euskadi;
   b. The Basque language, Euskera, as the principle official language of Euskadi;
   c. Law enforcement authorities to be under the control of the Basque government;
   d. All military units garrisoned in the Basque country to be under the control of the Basque government;
   e. The Basque people to possess sufficient power to adopt whatever political, economic, and social structures they deem appropriate for their own progress and welfare.[79]

By 1989 EMA claimed to have ten local sections with a total of nearly two hundred militants.[80] Outside observers put the number closer to 100 in 1991. The difference, however, was that EMA's militancy was characterized by a stronger commitment, a stronger degree of voluntarism at the base which set it apart from other movements of older militants. EMA still walked a narrow line regarding IK's use of violence, a position which affected its political credibility. Even with the wave of arrests in the ensuing years, "The position of EMA remains the same: not to support it but not to condemn it."[81] EMA's moderation after 1986 was forced upon it by the weakness of its support even among historic *abertzale* militants. But as one Basque militant put it, "They think they've distanced themselves from IK, but not in the eyes of others."

One of the most detailed political analyses of EMA's strengths and weaknesses was provided in 1990 in an internal document written by Txetx Etcheverry, leader of the competing movement Patxa, discussed below.[82] According to Etcheverry, EMA's strengths included integration of the movement at the base; its presence across the whole *abertzale* movement; a central demand (the creation of Basque institutions); its association with Iparretarrak (seen as a plus with the same Basque youth Patxa was trying to attract); publication of *Ekaitza*, widely read by youth; a greater "protagonism," if not in the streets then in press conferences and public meetings; and good work on the issue of tourism. At the same time Etcheverry identified a number of EMA's weaknesses which Patxa might possibly exploit: a generational gap between its older militants (in their twenties and thirties) and those Patxa was addressing; its political interests; its lack of street presence with Basque youth; a credible leadership-oriented discourse, which turns youth off; fewer militant forces; less humor; and political practices seen as more annoying or bothersome (*chiantes*) to youth.[83]

The Appearance of Three Moderate Basque Political Parties

The major difference in the Basque political landscape in the 1980s, especially in the years following EMA's creation in 1985, was the appearance of three moderate political movements which sought to reoccupy the Basque center in France and expand the support of the Basque idea among the Basque electorate. Each had ties with Basque political parties in Spain. First, the creation of *Ager* in 1981 led ultimately to the creation for the first time of a French Basque section of the Basque Nationalist Party (PNV) in 1991, despite its long presence in France. Second, the creation of Euskal Batasuna (EB) represented the appearance of a French Basque party which was close to the theses of ETA's front-movement Herri Batasuna in Spain, while maintaining its independence. Finally, Eusko Alkartasuna (EA) was the French Basque section of the new party of the same name in Spain created as a result of the splintering of the PNV.

AGER AND THE BASQUE NATIONALIST PARTY (PNV) IN FRANCE

Within three months of the disappearance of EHAS, in July 1981, the first issue of a new Basque monthly, *Ager,* declared its intention to serve as a source of information on the Pays Basque. While pledging to avoid sterile polemics, it declared that the current Basque press was too preoccupied with political sensationalism, violence, and protest. *Ager* was, from its creation, close to the Basque Nationalist Party (PNV) in Spain and a defender of its political positions. Accordingly, *Ager* announced its intention to present information on the activities of the PNV-dominated Basque government in Spain, still poorly understood in France, as well as historical articles on the French Basque country to be contributed by the noted French Basque historian and militant Eugène Goyheneche. Goyheneche, as we saw in chapter 3, had been close to the PNV since the 1930s. The announcement of *Ager's* creation was signed by Jean Etcheverry-Ainchart, Eugène Goyheneche, and Ramuntxo Camblong. From the beginning the effort was underwritten financially by Ximun Haran, who later emerged as the dominant force within *Ager.* The Spanish Basque newspaper *Egin* wrote that among *Ager's* founders were those who twenty years ago were among the first to participate in the first nationalist movement north of the Bidassoa River (the French-Spanish frontier).[84]

Etcheverry-Ainchart served as the director of publication until July 1985, when he was replaced by Bernard Larroulet. With issue number 15 on November 15, 1985, the paper changed its paper and format and began to appear bimonthly. With issue number 57 on January 21, 1986, *Ager* added to its masthead "Pour un Fédéralisme Basque Européen."

In *Ager's* third issue, the PNV stated that the French state had done everything possible to accelerate the loss of Basque identity in France. But the PNV remained frozen in ambivalence about what role to play vis-à-vis the French Basque question. Typical was the vague solution the PNV posed to the French cultural threat: "The PNV wants to formulate clear objectives leading to an authentic unity in conditions permitting the obtainment of an authentic political articulation."[85] A major theme in *Ager* from its beginning was its opposition to the use of political violence and, mirroring the position of the PNV in Spain, its pitched opposition to ETA. In *Ager's* view, ETA's violence had effectively contaminated and sabotaged the development of Basque politics. As we saw above, Haran was bitterly critical of ETA's use of Sokoa as an arms depot. But his greatest criticism turned on ETA's Marxist-Leninist ideology:

> We have always fought . . . with the greatest energy this Marxist-Leninist ideology, outdated and dangerous, always defended by ETA,

an ideology which leads to a "popular" dictatorship even more perni-cious than the fascist dictatorship [of Franco].[86]

Ager's position on IK's violence in France was more nuanced, understand-ing and sometimes sympathizing with the individuals whose use of violence cost them life or freedom, while still opposing violence as a tool of politics in any case.

By 1991 *Ager* and *Enbata* had an ongoing dispute volleying back and forth in their respective publications. A large factor in the dispute was the ten-sion between Haran and Jacques Abeberry, which stretched back to their competition for leadership within *Enbata*. It was in this context that Haran accused *Enbata* and Abeberry of having been a mouthpiece of ETA since its creation. In 1991 *Enbata* riposted by calling the PNV "moribund," a "party of old men," "Leninist" in its style.[87] Haran retorted in *Ager* that the PNV had always been Christian Democratic, in contrast to *Enbata*'s ideological ram-blings: "To the left, to the right, to the center, goes the weathervane *Enbata*, at the will of the wind."[88]

THE CREATION OF A SECTION OF THE PNV IN FRANCE

Despite the creation of *Ager* in 1981, it took more than a decade, until 1990, for the first section of the PNV to be created in France. This is ironic in one sense, since the PNV had first arrived in exile in France following the Span-ish Civil War in the 1930s. But the PNV's steadfast refusal to involve itself in French Basque politics was a consistent pole of its "foreign policy" and an indication of the original deal it had cut with the French government to ex-change neutrality in French politics for government protection and asylum. French Basques who had sought to join the PNV pointed out the irony of the fact that they would have been welcomed as members of the PNV if they had been born in Caracas or Mexico City, but not as Basques born in the three Basque provinces of France. Another irony is that the PNV waited to create its French section until 1990, while parties affiliated with its two pri-mary competitors in Spain—Eusko Alkartasuna and Herri Batasuna—had existed in the Pays Basque Français for several years.

The PNV's announcement appeared in *Ager* in May 1990.[89] The PNV's northern section's executive committee included honorary president Jean Etcheverry-Ainchart, president Ximun Haran, vice-president Michel Eppherre, secretary Jean Barreneche, and treasurer Narkis Diez de Iba-rrondo. By 1991 the PNV's northern section was said to number between fifteen and fifty dues-paying members, but with few elected officials. The circulation of *Ager* was estimated by militants outside the movement at ap-proximately one hundred copies.

The PNV undertook a number of initiatives to improve its image in the North, including financial support for the Basque language primary schools, the Ikastolas. Moreover, when the farm of imprisoned IK militant Pampi Sainte-Marie was threatened with seizure and sale, a major fund-raising campaign succeeded in collecting enough money to save it. The PNV is alleged to have contributed as much as 25 percent of the needed money. The greatest strengths of the PNV section in the North were Haran's political skills and the image of the autonomous government in the South. It appears that the PNV chose to not create a section in the North until EA had already done so. But its influence in 1991 was far more rife in potential than the small number of its militants would suggest. Its position as a spokesman for the dominant Basque political party in Spain and the party dominating the Basque autonomous government put it in a favored position to take part in any future economic or political contacts that unite North and South.

EUSKAL BATASUNA

By the summer of 1984 *abertzale* opinion had become increasingly polarized over IK's use of violence in France. As we saw previously, the killing of the two CRS at Baigorri two years before had led to wholesale resignations within the membership of Herri Taldeak. IK's own refusal to claim responsibility for the attack suggested the disarray which the killings had provoked even within IK itself and raised the possibility that Philippe Bidart was now out of control. With the derailing of the Madrid to Paris "Talgo" train at Urrugne in February 1984, ETA—through the Comité des Réfugiés—criticized IK publicly for the first time. With the rise of GAL violence against the refugee community, and the first delivery of an ETA militant to the Spanish border by French police, supporters of ETA were concerned by IK's violence and its effect on ETA's safety and sanctuary in France.

It was in this climate that Eñaut Etchemendy and others began meeting in the summer of 1984 to discuss the creation of a new cantonal-level movement which would undercut the support for IK and its violence in France. These early meetings continued into the fall of 1985, when five to six people met to flesh out the outlines of a new Basque movement.[90] Etchemendy announced at Renteria in the fall of 1985 his effort to create a "cantonal effort" in the French Pays Basque to support Herri Batasuna (and thus ETA) and to bring together like-minded leftist *abertzale* excluding Herri Taldeak (and thus IK).[91] This effort was taking place at the same time that HT and Laguntza were laying the groundwork for the creation of EMA. In both cases the goal was to create a larger political movement out of the political fragmentation which characterized Basque mobilization in the mid-1980s.

Their vision finally became reality with the constituent assembly of Euskal Batasuna (Basque Unity, EB) in Macaye on June 29, 1986.[92] *Enbata*'s Jacques Abeberry explained why EB was created as a parallel movement to the EMA initiative: "A lot of *abertzale*, however, could not see themselves in this move, which has notably never clearly defined itself regarding the strategy of Iparretarrak. 'Euskal Batasuna,' in return, 'excludes the armed struggle in the current sociopolitical conditions of the Northern Pays Basque.' "[93] EB's criticism of the armed struggle in France emerged less from a philosophical position on violence than from the realistic belief that, unlike the case in Spain, the armed struggle was not appropriate to political conditions within the Pays Basque Français. What was left unsaid was that Euskal Batasuna was created as a pro-ETA and anti-IK political force, whose explicit goal was to try to supplant EMA and whose appearance reflected the race between both groups to occupy the political high ground.[94]

In fact, Euskal Batasuna's creation reflected the desire of ETA-front Herri Batasuna to create an affiliated movement, if not a satellite section, of Herri Batasuna in France. While this was proposed when the discussions over the creation of the new movement were taking place, the French Basque militants ultimately decided not to adopt the name Herri Batasuna, reasoning that to do so would be to deprive themselves of ultimate freedom of maneuver and oblige them to defend possibly unpopular theses decided in the South. It was for that reason that the French Basque movement took the cognate name Euskal Batasuna.

Among the leaders of Euskal Batasuna were former *Enbata* founder Jacques Abeberry and Jacques Aurnague and Claude Harlouchet, both of whom had allegedly left the Socialist Party over the French Socialist administration's failure to stop GAL, which was itself an element of state-sponsored terrorism on the part of the PSOE in Spain. By 1991 EB had between sixty and one hundred militants, depending on the source, most of whom were thirty or older and established in professional careers. EB had more local elected officials than any other active movement in France in 1991. Its economic analysis was done by individuals who were trained in economics, rather than the rote ideological incantations—what the French call the drunken prattle (*gueules de bois*)—of the left. EB sought to play a balancing act between other tendencies and thus serve as the fulcrum of moderate Basque militancy in France.

The broad outlines of its platform were hardly original and situated Euskal Batasuna as a synthesis or natural evolution in the theses of Basque leftist moderation which stretched back to *Enbata*'s socialism in the early 1970s. Among EB's specific goals were:

1. The recognition of Basque national identity.
2. A "Pays Basque" territorial collectivity with a sufficient autonomy to develop a specific politics and leadership.
3. The official status of the Basque language and its use in domains of culture.
4. The establishment of close ties with the Southern Pays Basque in a federal assembly of the Basque people, within a Europe of regions.
5. A free Europe . . . freed of the nationalist supremacies of these old states and artificial frontiers . . .
6. An economy oriented toward the satisfaction of man's fundamental needs, which respects international solidarity, in particular with the Third World. Economic choices developed and put in place with the direct participation of all the actors.
7. A more just society, for the realization of which we want to join together, at the same time, those who demand a progressive democracy and those who profess a clearly defined socialism. To join them not on purely theoretical bases but on concrete stands and struggles against the oppressions and discriminations of all sorts, economic, social, cultural, racial, sexual.[95]

Among the respected and well-known militants who signed its charter were Isabelle Ajuriaguerra, niece of Juan Ajuriaguerra, late leader of the PNV; Jacques (Jakes) Aurnague, who had been a candidate in the 1985 cantonal elections in Saint-Jean-Pied-de-Port; former *Enbata* and EHAS economic theorist Jean-Louis Davant; ex–Mende Berri militant Ellande Duny-Petré, who would soon become responsible for the publication of the weekly *Enbata*; former Herri Taldeak and Jazar militant Augustin Duperou; ELB founder Michel Berhocoirigoin; Claude Harlouchet; ex-Amaia and ex–Mende Berri leader Gabriel Oyarçabal; and former Seaska head Jean-Pierre Seiliez.[96] At the first General Assembly of Euskal Batasuna in Macaye on June 28, 1987, those at the head table included Dominique Bacho, M. Belogui, Frantxoa Dascon, Jacques Aunargue, Eñaut Etchemendy, and Claude Harlouchet. What marked Euskal Batasuna was the diversity of individuals who signed its charter and the different paths which led to its creation.

The movement included approximately 100 militants who diverged from those of EMA in a number of ways. First, they were mostly Christian and Social Democrats who rejected the use of violence and were committed instead to the creation of a just society through peaceful social change. Second, unlike many of the youth of HT and Laguntza, many of these militants were between thirty and fifty years old, in the midstream of their lives and professions. Finally, EB was for many of them the latest institutional home in an *abertzale* commitment that stretched back to the early 1960s.

At its first press conference on July 11, 1986, EB developed the broad outlines of its orientation.[97] It was based on three observations.[98] First, no existing movement was capable of unifying the *abertzale* movement. Second, numerous groups like HT and Laguntza "represent a sense of the *abertzale* world in which numerous militants don't see themselves." Third, EB made explicit a "clearly expressed refusal which served as a principal theme of our campaign: that of the armed struggle in the North in the current sociopolitical conditions." Despite rejecting the armed struggle, EB sought to define an "institutional combat on more radical forms of struggle."[99] In response to a journalist's question concerning the similarity between the names "Euskal Batasuna" and "Herri Batasuna" in Spain, EB called it purely coincidental, though reflecting the need for unity in the contemporary Basque movement. Throughout 1987 EB produced a series of detailed reports on various aspects of Basque life, including the economy, agriculture, culture, and the way its demands would affect the nature of French territory and institutions.[100] While EB acknowledged the similarities between it and some of EMA's economic analyses, some clear differences emerged. First, EB's focus was not on the rhetoric of revolutionary socialism, but rather on the idea of "economic democracy." EB thus retreated from the most radical rhetorical barricades and chose to situate itself in a clear Social Democratic tradition on the eve of European unification. Second, it combined the older theme of *auto-gestion* (self-management) with support for economic groups like ELB, the local cooperative movement, and an independent local press. It favored decentralization and the idea of planning at the cantonal level. Finally, EB reintroduced some of the nineteenth-century federalist P.-J. Proudhon's theses into its economic platform. Specifically, EB borrowed from Proudhon the concept of the respect of private property and the access of all people to its ownership: private property must "serve as the counterweight to public power, to balance the state, by this means to assure individual liberty."[101]

THE CREATION OF EUSKO ALKARTASUNA

In February 1984 the PNV in Spain realized one of its greatest electoral successes in the elections for the Basque Parliament. The architect of that victory was the PNV's charismatic leader, Carlos Garaikoetxea. Yet, barely ten months after the election, growing internal conflict within the PNV and the machinations of the PNV's bureaucracy led to Garaikoetxea's departure from the party in 1985. This provoked one of the greatest internal schisms in the PNV's history. By 1986 Garaikoetxea had assembled his partisans and launched a new Basque political party, Eusko Alkartasuna, to compete in the 1986 Spanish parliamentary elections.

In the fall of 1986 one of Garaikoetxea's close associates, Spanish senator J. J. Pujana, met over lunch with a number of French Basque militants to discuss Garaikoetxea's vision for a party which, like the aspirations of EHAS in the mid-1970s, would be organized in both parts of the Basque regions in Spain and France. Attending the lunch were Pierre Charritton, Ramun-txo Camblong, Jean-Claude Larronde, Isabelle Ajuriaguerra, and Michel Larroulet. Pujana's presence was not coincidental, since Charritton had been one of his former teachers. After being kicked out of seminary studies in Bilbao for the intensity of his Basque nationalism, Pujana came to the Collège de Hasparren in 1963–64, where Charritton was on the teaching staff.

The immediate problem with Garaikoetxea's proposal was that Euskal Batasuna had only been created four months before. Yet, after barely four months of existence, it was clear that there was already an internal division within EB, ironically, over the issue of violence. If there was general opposition to the use of violence in France, there were those within EB who, closer to the theses of Herri Batasuna, supported ETA's use of the armed struggle in Spain. Others, closer to the PNV, were opposed to the use of violence in Spain as well. Among those meeting with Pujana, there was the growing certainty that sooner or later EB would split over this issue.

On November 19, 1986, Eusko Alkartasuna's leader, Carlos Garaikoetxea, held a press conference in Bayonne to reveal the platform and political orientation of the new party.[102] Like EB, Eusko Alkartasuna rejected the violent rhetoric of revolutionary socialism and evoked instead the notion of a freer society based on the principle of equality. EA's refusal of violence was even more explicit than that of EB several months before: "In the context of its political action . . . to . . . obtain the national liberation of Euskadi, EA conforms rigorously to democratic rules, explicitly refusing any path or practice of violence."[103]

Concerning the Northern Pays Basque, EA called for the creation of a Basque department and the elaboration of a statute for the preservation of Basque language and culture in France. It continued: "In the medium and long terms, EA sets the same goals for Euskadi North as those which the party assumes for Euskadi South and this in the context of a Europe where our people will present themselves reunified and with the political role which corresponds."[104] Part of EA's vision of "reunification" concerned the status of the historic Basque province of Nafarroa (Navarra), still treated separately by the Spanish government and a persistent issue for the Spanish Basque movement.

Basque historian Jean-Claude Larronde, who was present on the dais with Garaikoetxea, elaborated on EA's goals for Euskadi North:

First of all, it appeared to us that Eusko Alkartasuna—presenting itself as a democratic, progressive, and modern political party—could define a new *abertzale* political project in which the Pays Basque North would be an integral part.

In particular, such a party condemning violence as a form of political action might represent an alternative for many of the *abertzale* and in particular for many of the young *abertzale* of Euskadi North who resort to extremist practices, violent and even of despair, because they don't encounter reliable political structures, capable of integrating their legitimate aspirations of identity and of social justice.[105]

Another important attraction of EA was its desire to bridge both halves of the Basque experience and include the Pays Basque Français not as an afterthought but as a full partner in the party's deliberations. As Larronde initially reported, "Moreover, it is foreseen that in all the partisan forums of E.A., the Pays Basque will be represented equally, on the same plane and with the same legitimacy as the four provinces of Pays Basque South."[106] In reality, the historic provinces of the Pays Basque Français as a whole would be given the same weight as any *one* of the four historic Basque provinces in Spain. Thus, on the level of structure, the party would be composed of an executive committee of fifteen members, three of which would be elected from Euskadi North.[107] Even at this level, it represented an institutional voice for the French Basque contingent far in excess of that accorded EHAS by its Spanish Basque counterparts.

The reactions of existing groups and observers ranged from moderately positive to moderately critical. Speaking for EMA, Alain Iriart asserted that "the birth of E.A. has as its only context the political struggles of the Pays Basque South. In effect, E.A. is born of the internal conflicts within a party, the PNV."[108] For EMA, the proof of EA's impact would be the upcoming Spanish legislative elections, which would indicate the level of the movement's popular support. Jacques Aurnague of Euskal Batasuna found the move a positive one, but also wondered if it was not an electoral ploy that would have more impact in the South than in the North. Not unexpectedly, Ximun Haran, *Enbata*'s former leader who had grown close to the PNV in his subsequent militancy and led its northern annex, *Ager*, claimed that the political center to which EA aspired was already occupied: by the PNV in the South and by *Ager* in the North. Thus, from their perspective, EA's appearance was a fundamentally "hegemonistic" move. Moreover, *Ager* wondered what impact EA could have without any journalistic support: "Will it be a phantom party in the image of Euskal Batasuna which only shows itself by delicately written communiqués on the burning problems of the moment?"[109] Finally, Jacques Abeberry, writing in *Enbata*, offered a mixed review of the party's creation. According to him, EA might prove to be positive if it turned out to be more than an electoral ploy and if the representatives of the Northern Pays Basque played a serious role of equality in the future of the party. At the same time Abeberry elaborated on the line of questioning he raised at EA's first news conference—the seeming inconsistency of a movement rejecting the use of violence and then making a central issue of its platform the defense of Spanish Basque refugees in France, when the reason the refugees were in France in the first place was because of their use of violence.[110] When Garaikoetxea and the other EA militants responded that it was possible to create a movement of national liberation without violence, Abeberry replied, "If there is in the world an example of a nation which liberated itself by a democratic movement, let them explain it to me. I am ready to understand."[111]

EA gained enormous credibility in the November 1986 Spanish legislative elections, coming in close behind the votes and seats won by the PNV itself. By the 1989 elections to the European Parliament, EA had demonstrated sufficient electoral strength to be the third political force in the Spanish Basque provinces, after the PNV and Herri Batasuna. In the province of Gipuzkoa HB surpassed the PNV's score by 19.71 percent to 14.35 percent. This transformed EA from a dubious enterprise into the vehicle of a "charismatic leader," Carlos Garaikoetxea.[112] EA held its constituent assembly in the North on March 22, 1987, in Hasparren. Eighty people attended, including Garaikoetxea, who led a delegation of twelve from the South. According to Pierre Charritton, by the summer of 1987, EA had forty-three dues-paying members in the North.[113] Among the EA militants singled out for mention by *Ekaitza* were three: Ramuntxo Camblong, Daniele Pilote, and Isabelle Ajuriaguerra.[114] The important new initiative that came out of the meeting was Garaikoetxea's proposal for the creation of a "Peace Table" to which not only ETA would be invited, but, for the first time, Iparretarrak as well.[115] Speaking at the press conference, Jean-Claude Larronde declared that EA wanted to lead the *abertzale* movement out of the "ghettos and chapels in which it currently found itself."[116] Pierre Charritton elaborated on EA's patent refusal of violence, maintaining according to *Ekaitza* that "the violence of ETA, of IK, is no more justified in its essence than that of the 'terrorist Franco,' as long as legal means aren't yet exhausted."[117]

On April 3–5, 1987, Eusko Alkartasuna held its first National Congress in Pamplona with an attendance of nearly one thousand, primarily from the South.[118] Its four preparatory commissions had prepared seven reports that had elicited more than two thousand proposed amendments from local groups during their discussions. In addition to its own militants from the North, Jacques Aurnague attended and spoke on behalf of Euskal Batasuna and was well received. EMA was invited but did not send an observer.

During the voting for members of EA's National Executive Committee, out of forty-two candidates, the only two candidates from the North, Pierre Charritton and Isabelle Ajuriaguerra, were both elected, in second and fifth place, respectively, in terms of total votes. Michel Larroulet was elected to the Council on Conflicts and Discipline. Seven northern delegates were elected to the party's National Assembly: Isabelle Ajuriaguerra, Ramuntxo Camblong, Maïte LaFourcade, Jean-Claude Larronde, Iban Larroulet, Frantxoa Unhassobiscay, and Pierre Charritton. Since Ajuriaguerra and Charritton were each elected to two posts, they were each required to give one up. Most interestingly, owing in part to the talismanic effect of her family name in the history of the PNV, Isabelle Ajuriaguerra was the *top* vote-getter among the 358 candidates for EA's National Assembly.[119] What was important about these votes was that they represented the collective individual will of nearly a thousand Spanish Basque delegates to accord a greater voice to French Basques in the party's councils.

THE POSSIBILITY OF JOINT POLITICAL ACTION

By the spring of 1987 the Basque nationalist movement in France was confronted with an embarrassment of riches. There were now three *abertzale* political parties—EMA, EB, and EA—when there had been none little more than a year before. The three agreed to put aside their sniping and declared a tacit truce in the spring of 1987. The first fruit of their joint action was the decision to co-sponsor the Aberri Eguna of 1987 rather than compete over it. Euskal Batasuna took the initiative of inviting representatives of EMA, EA and centrist *notable* André Luberriaga's group, Goiz Argi, to an organizational meeting, though Luberriaga did not respond.[120] There was a strong minority within EMA from the beginning which opposed EA's role as a co-sponsor, in part because of EA's a priori rejection of violence and because, as a new party, EA stood to gain more in legitimacy and visibility by equal billing as a co-sponsor of the Aberri Eguna.

According to these dissident members of EMA who criticized EA, since 1978 the only Basque political group from Spain officially invited to the Aberri Egunas of the French Pays Basque was Herri Batasuna, "thus showing the left *abertzale* orientation of the most dynamic part of the movement here."[121] Since HB stopped coming to the Aberri Eguna in 1982 and never explained why, the more radical French Basque militants in EMA were confronted with the irony that HB was no longer invited, and EA, the French wing of the Spanish moderate party opposed to ETA, was now one of its official organizers. Moreover, the Spanish Basque organizers of the Southern Aberri Eguna at Gernika that same year invited only Euskal Batasuna from the North and not EMA, another indication of the degree of estrangement between ETA and IK and its supporters within EMA in the North.

Regardless of the jealousies and criticisms of other tendencies, EA was off to a strong start in 1987, riding on Garaikoetxea's coattails, outdistancing Euskal Batasuna, and clearly a viable moderate alternative to EMA's position on violence. As EA confronted the possibility of an electoral campaign, Charritton for one felt that it might be possible to achieve a 10 percent level of public support with a serious effort.

By 1990 the three groups—EMA, EB, and EA—continued to maintain their separate identities and their separate senses of *abertzale* action. The differences that did separate them seemed markers of distinction they jealously guarded. As one of their leaders put it, "Otherwise we would be in the same organization." [122] While EMA and EB continued their militancy, EA's fortunes began to wane along with those of Garaikoetxea in the South. The greatest stigma EA faced was having signed the pact against violence in Spain. EA's northern section also suffered from generational isolation, and by 1991 Charritton was left with a handful of followers. They continued to serve as co-sponsors of the Aberri Egunas in 1991, in a spirit of unity which sought to lend a positive and cooperative image to *abertzale* action.

THE RISE OF MODERATE CULTURAL INITIATIVES

By the early 1980s few observers were more aware of IK's effort to control Seaska and the Ikastola system than was the French state. Indeed, the control over Basque language and culture became an object of political tug-of-war. It appeared that cultural issues came to be held hostage as much by Iparretarrak as by a French state reluctant to make concessions to the radical *abertzale* camp. For the government, concessions over language and culture became part of a carrot and stick strategy for dealing with the outbreak of Basque violence in France.

It was out of the desire to depoliticize these crucial cultural and linguistic questions that Pizkundia was created, holding its first General Assembly in July 1986. [123] Pizkundia was an initiative that brought together thirty-nine different cultural groups united in their desire to preserve and enhance Basque culture and to militate in an avowedly apolitical way. One dimension of this apolitical strategy was the decision to remain silent on the question of violence. Some of the groups were of the *abertzale* camp, but others were far enough away, including groups devoted to pelote or dance. Pizkundia succeeded in getting government approval for the Institut Culturel Basque and in restarting negotiations between the government and Seaska.[124] Other agenda items included bilingual road signs and Basque television. Pizkundia clearly benefited from the government's willingness to modify its cultural strategy.

Other initiatives included IKAS BI, the Association for the Promotion of Bilingual Education in French Public Schools, AEK (the association of evening classes in Basque), and Euskal Herrian Euskaraz, which called for the recognition of Basque as an official language. Several of these initiatives formed an umbrella grouping called Deiadar in 1989 and then again in 1992 in order to support joint initiatives in the area of language and culture.[125] Four Basque-language radio stations were created, including Gure Irratia (Our Radio), Irulegiko Irratia (Radio Iroulégui), Xiberoko Botza (The Voice of Soule), and Radio Adour Navarre.[126] By 1991 the French government had liberalized its position on Basque cultural issues, and the first General Assembly of the Institut Culturel Basque in 1991 was attended by the prefect of the Department of the Pyrénées-Atlantiques.[127] This change led to the creation of a DEUG (Diplôme d'Etudes Universitaires Générales) university cycle in Basque, the opening of a satellite university campus at Bayonne, and a long-hoped-for agreement between the Ministry of National Education and Seaska to integrate its personnel into the ministry over a period of three years. On the level of language policy, while the government had created a chair in Basque language and literature at Bordeaux in 1948, it was not tied to any *license* or undergraduate degree until 1967. Basque is now accepted as an optional elective second living language at the universities of Bordeaux, Pau, and Toulouse.[128]

The Continuation of the Electoral Strategy, 1988–1989

THE 1988 LEGISLATIVE ELECTIONS

With the legislative elections of 1988, the *abertzale* camp united in a rare show of unity to field joint candidates in the Basque *circonscriptions*. Unlike 1986, when EMA had chosen and fielded its own candidates and appropriated the *abertzale* label, the 1988 elections were based on an agreement between EMA, EB, and EA to field joint candidates and to run on a joint platform.[129] EB's Jacques Aurnague ran with EMA's Arnau Thicoipe in the fourth *circonscription* in the interior; EA's Pierre Charritton ran with EB's Jon Parot in the fifth *circonscription* in Bayonne; and EMA's Richard Irazusta ran with EA's Joseph Lahetjuzan in the sixth *circonscription* along the southern coast. The results continued to hover around the 5 percent mark. Irazusta got 2,742 votes or 5.72 percent; Charritton 1,583 or 3.62 percent; and Aurnague got 2,698 or 4.84 percent (8.80 percent in the Basque portion of the district).[130] Yet, while the question of whether it was really an *abertzale* vote remains to be determined, isolated villages registered a greater vote for *abertzale* candidates than ever before: Irazusta, for example, getting 13.78 percent in Ascain and 12.34 percent in Biriatou; Charritton getting 21.36 percent in Ayherre and 22.37 percent in Isturits; and Aurnague getting 13.36 percent in Baigorri and 12.52 percent in Iholdy. What was significant about the results, however, was that while the *abertzale* camp was far behind the electoral scores of either the union of the right or the Socialists, it were nonetheless now the third political force in the Pays Basque Français, surpassing the votes of either the French Communist Party or Jean-Marie Le Pen's right-wing Front National.[131]

THE 1988 CANTONAL ELECTIONS

Within three months of the legislative elections partial cantonal elections were scheduled for September 1988. EMA, EA, and EB continued their commitment to field joint candidates. Out of eleven Basque cantons voting in the 1988 cantonals, joint candidates were ultimately agreed upon in eight cantons. In the canton of Bidache a local candidate could not be found and the *abertzale* camp decided not to "parachute" a candidate into the canton from outside. In two other cantons, Ustaritz and Saint-Jean-de-Luz, for different reasons agreement could not be reached and two *abertzale* candidates ran without joint support.

While the turnout for the cantonals at 54.16 percent was seventeen points less than for the cantonals of 1982, candidates of the French right won 59 percent of the votes and those close to the Socialist party won only 27.46 percent. The *abertzale* candidates won 7.19 percent of the collective vote (7.49 percent not counting the canton of Bidache, which had no *abertzale* candidate).[132] Four of the cantons realized an increase in absolute votes for *abertzale* candidates. In the remaining cantons where the vote declined, the greatest decline was in the two cantons where no agreement was reached on a joint candidate.

THE 1989 MUNICIPAL ELECTIONS

It was not until the 1989 municipal elections that the *abertzale* camp was able to break through the electoral threshold and elect three municipal counselors, one each in the cities of Bayonne, Biarritz, and Hendaye. All three ran as *abertzale* but were members of Euskal Batasuna: Claude Harlouchet ran as an *abertzale* and ecologist in Bayonne and was elected as a municipal counselor with 6.5 percent of the vote. Harlouchet's faction declared before the election that "there is no cultural development possible in Bayonne without a development of Basque culture. We subscribe to the policy advocated by . . . Pizkundea." [133] In Hendaye Robert Arrambide was also elected. Longtime Basque militant Jacques Abeberry led an *abertzale* list in Biarritz and won a seat with 12.32 percent of the vote. Abeberry's case is particularly interesting when one notes that when he first ran as a candidate for *Enbata* during the 1960s he was stigmatized as a "separatist." The evolution in the perception of the *abertzale* camp was such that Abeberry was subsequently made assistant to the mayor of Biarritz for culture, a reward for delivering a significant block of votes which permitted the mayor's position to shift from the right to the Socialist camp in 1991. His role in the election was strongly opposed by the Gaullist camp, who described it as the caricature of immorality with the complicity of the Socialists: "How can one have the indecency to ally oneself with men who threaten the integrity of France? After the Corsican people, why not the Basque people?" [134]

Throughout this electoral period what marked the three primary *abertzale* parties—EMA, EA, and EB—was their willingness to put aside partisan differences and field joint candidates under a common label. This electoral unity represented a clear maturation of the Basque nationalist camp in France, which presented itself as a responsible and electable electoral alternative. Ironically, however, it was this pursuit of credibility on the part of the three parties which opened them up to criticism by the younger Basque radical left. The tensions between the "electoralist" parties and the young insurgents would mark the Aberri Egunas of 1990 and 1991 and fragment the movement again along generational lines. Central to that conflict was the rise of Patxa, a Basque group whose blend of alternative politics and rock music placed it in the context of broader youth protest in Europe.

The Rise of Basque Radical Rock: Patxa

When modes of music change, the fundamental laws of the state always change with them.
Plato, *The Republic*

At the same time as the creation of both Euskal Batasuna and Eusko Alkartasuna, another tendency was coalescing among radical urban youth in Bayonne and the coast who sought to combine their Basque identity with the music and symbols of the European alternative scene. It was in this spirit that Patxa was born in 1986 as a group of *"abertzale* rockers," committed to *rock movida*—the melding of radical rock music and the Basque language.[135]

Patxa grew out of a protest against the visit of ultrarightist National Front leader Jean-Marie Le Pen to Bayonne during the winter of 1986. Shortly after Le Pen's visit the first issue of Patxa's episodic publication *Pacharan* (whose spelling was soon changed to *Patxaran*) appeared, named after the popular Basque alcoholic beverage made from anise and wild plums. In this first issue of *Pacharan*, Patxa fancifully defined its name as coming, "from the Latin *Patxarrus*, a strong alcohol given to lions before they ate Christians, their digestion finding itself perceptibly improved." With a drawing of a Molotov cocktail on the cover, it included articles on the protest against Le Pen and on rock music, as well as illustrations like those in Zap Comics and other alternative comics which first appeared in the United States in the 1960s, which were becoming popular in small alternative comics called *fanzines*. Patxa's first goals included the "antifascist deverminizing" of the Pays Basque Français; social self-reappropriation at all levels; development of the cathedral of Bayonne as a rock music hall; decriminalization of the armed struggle; and an end to closing times for bars in the Pays Basque.[136] From its origins there was a derisive, quasi-anarchistic quality to Patxa's texts, a deliberate refusal to take itself or political action seriously. While Patxa was of the style of May–June 1968, its militants were in fact the children of those who had lived during that time. Explaining what he called the intolerance and close-mindedness of Patxa, one Basque militant said, "They combine the spirit of '68 mixed with the critical and judgmental spirit of the *curé*." Patxa became the vehicle for the latest generation of Basque youth who entered into "rupture," the first way station along the route of politicization for still another generation of "youth in crisis." In this way, Patxa was like Herriaren Alde or Euskal Gogoa before it. Observers estimate its number of militants at around fifty, though even more than in other Basque movements Patxa's membership was naturally fluid and "spontaneous," swelling and receding according to the issues of the moment.

A major focus of Patxa's effort was the mobilization of high school students, similar to Amaia and Mende Berri before it. It created a Komité Lycéen Autonome to mobilize high school students around themes which included antimilitarism, antifascism, and the conditions of education in the schools.[137] In an interview with *Ateka* in June 1986 Patxa claimed that it was "a group which was created, above all, to organize concerts and express the things of youth."[138] As such, it claimed, "We're not on the same terrain as other *abertzale* militants." *Ateka* called *Patxaran* a *fanzine*. Among the *fanzines* popular among Basque high school students are *La Petite Ecolier; Bakalao (Pil Pil)* (from Pau); *Ipurbeltz* (close to Seaska); *La Tueuse au Yaourt; Houlala* (non-*abertzale* anarcho-rock); and *Kalimotxo* (by youth in Cambo).

Patxa embraced a variety of styles of alternative political actions called "provocations," ranging from support for the "Squatt" (squatter) movement, to concerts, carnivals, and the spread of graffiti and *fanzines*. *Actuel* called Patxa a band of "anarcho-independentists" who were

> against everything: nuclear, cops, the army, colonialism, sexism. They refused en masse this empty folklore. Basque culture, that's another thing: well-lubricated festivals, games on all the public squares, songs for fifty people, dances. . . . Patxa is that.[139]

According to Agathe Logéart, "These youths, for the most part unemployed, had taken on the habits of the whole of European marginality."[140] Among the most prominent of the alternative *abertzale* rock groups was KGB, whose name, *kalimotxo gure borroka*, means *kalimotxo* (a mixture of Coca-cola and wine) and *gure borroka* (our struggle). Thus KGB meant roughly "a fierce struggle against foreign drinks."[141] Other groups were named Prima Linea, Beyrouth-Ouest, Aggressive Agricultors, Koktail Molotov, and Begi Xintxo, or "eye of the sage."[142] Patxa began sponsoring a major annual concert of alternative political rock groups at Arcangues in February 1987: "Rock Eguna 1987."[143]

In late February 1988 Patxa organized "Rock Eguna 88" for the benefit of Basque prisoners. *Enbata*, in its issue of March 3, voiced little understanding of Patxa: "a mob let loose, agitated by strange convulsions. Why this *tohu bohu*, why all these Patxa, why these punks and these unwashed [*peu clean*]?"[144] Among *Enbata*'s complaints were the kind of music, the steep 35-franc entry fee, and an estimate of the number attending as a scant 1,000. Patxa in a letter to *Enbata* the following week explained that the entry fee was destined in part for the aid of Basque prisoners and that more than 2,000 people attended.[145] It was clear that Patxa represented the insurgency of an alternative generation of young Basques, eager to blend their commitment to *abertzale* issues with the rock music of their larger generation. They were a major force at the Fêtes de Bayonne of August 1988, selling 1,500 bumper stickers and distributing 20,000 flyers. Patxa's themes of the Basque language and the defense of the refugees and prisoners were prominent during the festival.[146] Patxa also associated itself with other issues, such as family planning and the denunciation of sexual attacks on women.[147] As such, in their own words, "Patxa is not only a part of *abertzale* youth, it's also and above all a manner of being."[148] Patxa in this larger sense was part of a new Basque generation, Euskaldun Berriak (the Basque New Look).[149]

By 1990 Patxa had diversified its causes and become more political in the interim. Its politics were becoming closer to European alternative anarchism than to the other chapels of *abertzale* action in 1990. Thus, in the days leading up to the 1990 Aberri Eguna at Hendaye, tracts appeared promising to disrupt the Basque National Day celebration, in part because of the presence of Eusko Alkartasuna among the organizing groups. Patxa saw EA as a right-wing group and was particularly incensed because of Garaikoetxea's decision to sign the antiviolence pact with Spanish political parties. As early as spring 1988 Patxa called EA

> a rightist party . . . which participated in the repression of social movements . . . wanted to govern with the PSOE and signed a pact legitimating the repression of Paris and Madrid against the prisoners and the refugees. What do we have in common with those people? What do they represent here? [150]

On the day of the celebration Patxa and other groups like Oldartzen, Ajir, and Iega constituted themselves as a countermarch, drowning out the speeches of the organizing parties EA, EB, and EMA through whistles and catcalls.[151] Pierre Charritton, speaking for EA, was physically attacked. The march dissolved as the counterdemonstrators launched rocks over the organizers' heads against the CRS who blocked the bridges to Spain. The march degenerated into confrontations of CRS against Basque, and Basque against Basque as well. In an internal document prepared after the Aberri Eguna, Patxa's leader "Txetx" Etcheverry repeated that the EA's presence had been the primary motive for its decision to disrupt the Aberri Eguna. In contrast, he insisted that Patxa "had everything to gain in working with EB and EMA."[152] For Etcheverry, there were two broad *abertzale* tendencies in 1990: one, characterized by Patxa and its allies, was "rupturist," whose objectives were independentist, anticapitalist, and confrontational. The other tendency, characterized by EB and EMA, was leadership-oriented, reformist, and "credible," though leading toward "Basque regionalism."[153] Etcheverry asserted that Patxa's strength was that it was a militant force which was present on the streets. Its militants were active in such other groups and cultural efforts such as Seaska, AEK, Ajir, KL, EHE, EHLE, the Comité du Soutien des Réfugiés, and the Basque-language radio stations.

According to Etcheverry's *autocritique*, Patxa's greatest weaknesses were that it was not taken seriously, it had no presence in Basse-Navarre, and its magazine *Patxaran* had a weak press run. Moreover, after the Aberri Eguna, Patxa was stigmatized as a divisive force for refusing to cooperate with EA. For Etcheverry, the solution was for Patxa to become an "important rupturist movement" with as many as two to three hundred militants.

In June 1990, following the highly controversial article that *Enbata* collaborator and *Le Monde* stringer Philippe Etcheverry co-authored with *Le Monde*'s Philippe Boggio on Henri Parot and the French Basque commando of ETA (see chapter 7), *Patxaran* published an issue with an elaborate cover of Etcheverry carrying an Antenne 2 television video camera (another of his jobs) and following a hearse. He was followed in turn by two figures measuring him for a tire filled with gasoline. The title on the cover was "Philippe Etcheverry, we'll get you."[154]

By March 1991 Patxa and the other insurgent factions were threatening to break the traditional unity of the Aberri Eguna. As Patxa leader Txetx warned, "There will be at least two [Aberri Egunas] if not three in the future."[155] Thus, in a sad tradition of self-destruction, the Basque movement in 1991 saw itself divided between Patxa and the other insurgent groups, on the one hand, and EMA, EB and EA, on the other. For one Basque critic of Patxa and its ally, *Oldartzen*, both were characterized by "a purity which is nearly puerile in its expression." On the level of political unity, the conflict which Patxa and its allies like *Oldartzen* were waging against the more electorally oriented parties seemed closer to a Hobbesian war of all against all. Yet there was a demonstrable growth of support among Basque youth for Patxa and its theses. In late 1991 more than a thousand youths from both sides of the border responded to Patxa's call for a march in favor of draft evasion.[156]

OLDARTZEN

In October 1989 the first issue of *Oldartzen* appeared announcing the appearance of another Basque movement.[157] In response to the question of why its militants didn't simply join an existing movement, *Oldartzen* asserted that the game of unity involves making unacceptable compromises over principle. The end-product of unity involves a law of strict majority rule and a resulting loss of freedom. At the same time that the imprisoned Philippe Bidart was now calling for the unity of *all* Basque political forces,[158] *Oldartzen* called for the unity of the Basque *left*, which it would support by its "rupturist" political tactics.

Oldartzen was the latest political initiative of Jakes Borthayrou, who had earlier created both Hordago and Laguntza and had been closely involved in *Ateka*. He gathered fifteen or twenty people around him at the beginning. *Oldartzen* was influenced by Herri Batasuna and the Comité des Réfugiés and was thus close to ETA. More important, *Oldartzen* was bitterly opposed to the IK/EMA group (one observer called them "angry to death"), owing in part to the *Ateka/Ekaitza* debacle. At that time, Borthayrou was left with *Ateka*'s debts, which totaled tens of thousands of francs. *Oldartzen*'s support for ETA contrasted with EMA's support for IK. Moreover, Borthayrou worked for AEK, the program of evening courses in Basque, in contrast to EMA, which was close to Seaska. In its opposition to the IK/EMA axis, *Oldartzen* was only the latest incarnation of an ongoing personal and organizational struggle that Borthayrou had waged for years against IK. *Oldartzen's* opposition was not to violence per se. *Oldartzen* called it a historical fact and one useless to discuss on the moral level: "Its use seems to us to be inevitable."[159] Moreover, from its perspective, violence had played an undeniable role in the consciousness-raising of the past fifteen years, especially that of *Oldartzen's* confrontational generation.

Oldartzen's joined Patxa is opposing an alliance with EA for the 1990 Aberri Eguna. For *Oldartzen*, EMA and EB's decision to work with EA reflected their decision to put Basque national unity ahead of leftist ideological unity. The conflict which followed was the worst of nearly thirty years of celebration of the Aberri Eguna in France.[160] Following the Aberri Eguna *Oldartzen* estimated the strength of its and Patxa's supporters at approximately two hundred and fifty that day, but denied responsibility for the fighting which occurred. While denying they were the sole group to shout down EA's Charritton, *Oldartzen* reported that at the Aberri Eguna Charritton had said, "Sozialistak zoazte Errusiarat" (Socialists, go back to Russia).[161]

While lamenting the fragmentation of the *abertzale* movement, *Oldartzen* asserted that given the current political panorama it was not possible to make all groups work together, a situation that would become even more impossible with the appearance of a section of the PNV in the North.[162] For the 1991 Aberri Eguna, Oldartzen offered a platform of demands, including total amnesty for political refugees; a halt to further tourist development; territorial and political recognition of the Pays Basque as a specific institution; the right of the seven Basque provinces to self-determination; the legalization of the Basque language; and the self-organization of those workers with or without a job. In siding with Patxa's decision to organize a separate Aberri Eguna, *Oldartzen* in effect said to EMA, "We're going to organize an Aberri Eguna at Arbonne and you have until March 31 to decide to join us."[163]

IEGA

IEGA (Iparraldeko Euskal Gazteri Abertzalea) is a group of fifteen to twenty high-school-aged youth, many of whom are the children of refugees or have family ties in the South. Their major activity is addressing the problems of high school students.

IEGA's first act was to put up posters in Bayonne saying that ETA's KAS alternative applied to the Pays Basque Français. This angered EMA, in turn, which saw this as an effort to overlay the South's issues on the North and led it to spray paint "IK" over IEGA's posters. IEGA's youthful action centers around "happenings" and gags or hoaxes, like publishing a false letter from Bayonne's Mayor Grenet or calling him "Hirohito II." For more than one not wholly unsympathetic older Basque militant, IEGA's youth were *petits morpions,* annoying young jerks. IEGA's headquarters is now in the headquarters of Euskal Batasuna in Bayonne. Many of their parents are members of EB, and IEGA is close to GARRAI, the youth movement of Herri Batasuna in the south.

The War between Iparretarrak and the French State, 1986–1991

Atzeac escua latz.
Heavy is the hand of foreigners.
Basque proverb

By 1986 there was an acceleration in the cycle of action and reaction between the French government and Iparretarrak. IK was now combining its long-standing attacks against real estate speculation and tourism with attacks against the state and its symbols. IK committed five attacks during the night of March 2–3, including one damaging the home of a farmer in Souraïde, who was denounced as one of these "thugs who cultivate . . . a visceral hatred for *abertzale,* and who inform the police about the activities and motions of militants." [164] On April 12 the government prosecutor, in the trial of Jean-Pierre Sainte-Marie, referred to Iparretarrak as

> fanatics and cowards who are far from creating unanimity in the ranks of Basque nationalists and whose terrorism harms those who seek, in the context of legality, similar objectives. . . . France recognizes the right to difference and to the expression of minorities: violence thus has no reason for being. [165]

In May IK imitated ETA's conduct in the South by targeting a drug trafficker in Chéraute, claiming to act as the defender of Basque moral values and the integrity of Basque youth. [166]

In July IK accelerated its attack on the French state by opening fire on two CRS guarding the Palais de Justice of Bayonne. IK specifically challenged the hardening of French government measures against IK as well as against the refugee community:

> The French government is heavily mistaken if it imagines frightening us with these methods. . . . Repression no matter how brutal will never

make us retreat and the struggle will never end until political solutions will be advanced in response to the legitimate demands of the Basque people.[167]

Not for the first time ETA's Comité des Réfugiés condemned IK's attack on the CRS as being inopportune and unlikely to aid in their efforts to convince the French government to create a statute of political refugees and to permit them to live in the Pays Basque.[168] For *Ekaitza,* "this condemnation taught nothing new, unless that the defense of the refugees belongs exclusively to the Comité des Réfugiés and that it constitutes a private hunting preserve." [169]

By August 1986 the government was ready to appeal the initial court decision to free the four HT members arrested in January 1984 for transporting journalists to IK's clandestine press conference. The government's prosecutor developed a novel line of attack against IK, arguing that IK's crime was "discourse" and that the crimes and attacks of the organization were there to give substance to its terrorist discourse.[170]

In October, following Pope John Paul II's homily in Lyons against violence, the new bishop of Bayonne, Mgr. Pierre Molères, published a pastoral letter urging the abandonment of violence. IK responded within days, justifying its use of violence as a prod for government action:

> If we have taken up arms, it is not for pleasure or to serve some kind of ideology, it's uniquely in order that Euskadi North might live. We are prepared to disarm . . . not just for a day but definitively if political decisions guaranteeing the renaissance of Euskadi North are taken. But we are convinced that only mobilization and struggle will oblige the political powers to make decisions.[171]

THE PRISON BREAK AT PAU

On December 13, in one of the most spectacular and daring events of its kind in recent French history, a team of Iparretarrak commandos calling itself the "Commando Didier" (after IK militant Didier Lafitte, who was killed by the police three years before) succeeded in breaking into the prison of Pau and liberating IK militants Marie-France Héguy and Gabriel Mouesca, who were serving terms of four and thirteen years, respectively, for membership in IK.[172] Héguy in particular had consistently denied membership in IK and would have been released no later than 1988. As a result of this operation, she was now committed to go into hiding like Bidart. For justice officials, the question which was raised was whether she made a spur-of-the-moment decision to escape when first confronted by the IK commando or had been alerted and prepared in advance as investigators believed.[173] As part of the escape plan, the IK militants took three hostages, including the prison director. The choice of the weekend of December 13 was deliberate, since the director of the prison was on call only one weekend in every seven, and it took time to determine which weekend was the one.[174]

In a tightly planned operation apparently led by Philippe Bidart, IK devoted a substantial amount of preparation to locating the prison director's daughter, whose name and phone number appeared in no phone book. After taking the daughter and a friend hostage, she was directed to call her father and summon him from his residence within the prison to her apartment. He arrived unsuspectingly and was taken hostage and, along with his daughter and her friend, driven back to the prison where three IK militants dressed in stolen gendarmes' uniforms faked a transfer of prisoners and quickly overpowered the four guards on duty at that time of night. In order to ensure that the prison director did not have a change of heart, especially when alone before the entry of the prison, a belt with explosives attached to a radio-controlled detonator was attached to his waist. The operation went flawlessly. Before leaving the prison, one of the IK militants dressed as a gendarme signed the clerk's register "IK." Left behind at the prison were five ETA refugees, including four who had been ordered extradited to Spain. Given the evident tightness of preparation, did IK extemporaneously offer to free them? Did they refuse because of a lack of preparation to hide them? Given the recent criticism of IK by ETA's Comité des Réfugiés, was this another chapter in the bruised relationship between the two organizations?[175] Before roadblocks could be established, the group had vanished into the night. Despite the rapid implementation of the police's plan "Autour" (Around), which implemented a close surveillance of the residences of known IK militants in order to assure their presence, no trace of the commandos was found. *Ekaitza* was effusive in its pleasure at the audacity of the operation and summarized the range of attitudes in the local and national press.[176]

IK soon broke its own silence. Once again, in its communiqué concerning the prison break, IK vowed to not give up the armed struggle until the French government embarked on the path of political solutions to the Basque question.[177] For its part, the French government assigned responsibility for the first time to the *procureur général* of Paris and to the Parisian court system, which had been collectively given national responsibility for terrorism by the law of September 9, 1986.[178] Among the IK militants thought to have taken part in the prison break was Xavier Labéguerie, son of the late French senator and *Enbata* founder Michel Labéguerie.[179]

In January 1987 police found explosive charges outside a number of gendarmeries in the Pays Basque as IK accelerated its attacks on the police.[180]

Then on February 28 IK held another clandestine press conference and introduced both liberated prisoners, Marie-France Héguy and Gabriel Mouesca,
to the press.[181] Only *Sud-Ouest, Ekaitza,* and Radio Irouléguy made the rendezvous. Once more *Enbata* was not invited. *Sud-Ouest*'s Christian Aguerre
reported that the press conference took place "certainly" in the forest of the
neighboring Landes. Héguy and Mouesca, who had been hooded until mid-
way through the press conference, took off their hoods, and in a smiling
and relaxed mood proceeded to explain the operation, their militancy, and
their choice of clandestinity as a "total commitment."[182] Héguy made clear
that her decision to escape was made voluntarily, based on her experience in
prison: "My interior self was dying day by day."[183] In the final analysis she
preferred clandestinity to being free: "Morally, I couldn't be satisfied with
this personal outcome."[184] As she later explained in *ILDO,* in a curious way,
had she served her sentence and been freed, she would have been under
surveillance from that point on and even more limited as a militant.[185]

    With the stunning success of the prison break, IK's intention to continue
the armed struggle was greater than ever:[186]

> One must not maintain vain illusions. . . . Only an evolution in the
> relations of force imposed by the struggle will permit arriving at [our
> goals]. As a result, we militants of Iparretarrak will continue to pay the
> costs of the struggle, as long as the violence of the French State and the
> blindness of its leaders necessitate the use of arms.[187]

In the final analysis, for IK, "No, truly, the French State hasn't evidently
learned anything of the lessons of history."[188] As helicopters traversed the
skies over the Basque interior looking for signs of their escape, one nationalist priest spoke of the stakes: "I am Basque, I can't be otherwise. Here it's
the verb 'to be' which is attacked, in the name of the verb 'to have.'"[189]

    If the wheels of justice grind exceedingly slowly, they grind exceedingly
fine: on May 18, 1987, Philippe Bidart was found guilty in absentia by the
seven judges of the Cour d'Assises in Pau for voluntary homicide in the
deaths of the two CRS in Baigorri more than five years before.[190] He was
sentenced to life in prison, as he would be again later for the killing of the
gendarme at Léon. This followed his previous convictions in absentia on
December 5, 1980, in Bayonne for attacks against the Office of Tourism in
Biarritz and the holdup of the Caisse d'Epargne of Saint-Paul-les-Dax. For
the state prosecutor, Bidart was the leader of an Iparretarrak with a "blunt
and ultra-minority ideology."[191] In May 1987, testifying for the defense in
the trial of IK militants Philippe Arruti and Pipo Eyherabide, Xan Coscarat
told the tribunal, "These militants are hostages that you must condemn. But

your decision, if it mortgages their future, will have not any effect on the aftermaths of the struggle and will only reinforce it."[192]

Indeed, between March 30 and June 2, 1987, IK mounted three attacks against the police: against the Gendarmerie of Saint-Jean-Pied-de-Port on the evening of March 29; against the vehicle of a police confidante in Hasparren on May 27; and against the personal car of a gendarme in Mauléon on June 1.[193]

By the end of June IK had returned tragically to the national headlines. On the evening of June 21 border police gave chase to a car later found to contain Betti Bidart, brother of Philippe, and the fugitive Marie-France Héguy and stopped it on a level railroad crossing. After they arrested Héguy and attempted to move the car, it was struck by a Paris-Hendaye train, killing both Héguy and the border policeman, Roger Latasa.[194] Latasa's mourners were led by Robert Pandraud, minister of state for security in the French Ministry of the Interior, and Yvan Barbot, director of the national police.[195] The following day, six hundred people attended the funeral of Héguy in her village of Hélette, which was celebrated by twelve priests.[196] According to one militant who attended the funeral, of the 300 Basque youths who attended, 250 were with Iparretarrak, at least in spirit.

At the funeral services a tape was played of Philippe Bidart, who said, "We have not made this choice for pleasure, nor because we are desperate."[197] For his part in the events which led to Héguy's death, Betti Bidart was indicted by the Parquet of Paris, under the provisions of the antiterrorist law of 1986. The charge included taking part in "an individual or collective enterprise having as goal the troubling of public order by intimidation or terror."[198] IK condemned the "total irresponsibility of the police in this death" and urged all those who wished for the Pays Basque to live to support and participate in the armed struggle.[199]

Within two weeks another IK militant, Christophe Istèque, was killed and his accomplice, Patrick Lembeye, injured when a bomb they were placing exploded during the night of July 5, 1987, outside the tax office of Anglet.[200] The same evening other bombs were placed outside the tax offices in Cambo and Iholdy. Police found Lembeye's companion in the company of Xan Coscarat, by now "the usual suspect" in the police's investigations of IK.[201] Istèque, a native of Baigorri and friend of the Bidarts, was openly a member of EMA, as was Lembeye, and suspected by the Renseignements Généraux of belonging to IK.[202] *Ekaitza*, in an homage to Lembeye, acknowledged that "you weren't a stranger to the recent hard times" and further lauded his work in EMA, in Ipar Euskadi Gaur, and in the support of prisoners.[203] With his arrest, the links between IK and the open arenas of militancy, from HT to EMA, became clear. Yet there was a growing banality, a commonness, about this type of IK militant, who lacked the venom of Bidart. As their friends described them, "They were people from the village." For the police, this was a disquieting sign that IK was beginning to recruit new members previously unknown to them. The police received a break with the discovery of a list of names in the car of Pierre (Betti) Bidart.

The visit of French prime minister Jacques Chirac to Bayonne on July 10 the following week offered the state an occasion to reiterate its belief that violence was not in the Basque temperament and that the Basques as a whole felt themselves profoundly French.[204] Chirac denounced IK's militants as "madmen, misled, manipulated, who sometimes fall into violence.[205] IK, in this match of point-counterpoint, reiterated its own determination to pursue the armed struggle and to enlarge its objectives.[206] The following evening, July 11, an important disposition of French police—as much in place for the security of the upcoming passage of the Tour de France bicycle race as for the search for IK—arrested IK fugitive Gabriel Mouesca and Henri Pérez after finding a suspicious car which they feared was a car bomb parked along the route of the Tour de France in the High Pyrénées. Aerial surveillance by helicopter led police to a hillside campsite three kilometers away where Gabriel Mouesca, thought to be the number two in IK, and Henri Pérez were arrested.[207] Pérez was wanted by the police as a suspect in the prison escape at Pau the previous year. In the tent were found pieces of false identification with Philippe Bidart's picture, leading authorities to believe they had narrowly missed capturing him as well.

THE DISSOLUTION OF IPARRETARRAK BY THE FRENCH COUNCIL OF MINISTERS

As of mid-July 1987 government authorities had attributed more than sixty attacks to Iparretarrak since its appearance in 1973. With the great increase in the level of IK's violence, given the recent death of one IK militant and the arrest of two others who were targeting the Tour de France, the French government apparently would tolerate no more. Accordingly, on July 15 the French Council of Ministers dissolved Iparretarrak.[208] The principal law on which the decision was based was that of January 10, 1936, which the government of Léon Blum had passed in order to combat extreme right-wing leagues during the Popular Front.[209] It was directed against "whoever will have participated . . . in an association or in a group . . . which would have as its goal to bring harm to the integrity of national territory or who will give themselves over to acts in view of provoking acts of terrorism."[210] The official government decree, dated July 17 and published in the *Journal Officiel* of

the French Republic on July 18, contained a number of justifications, among
them, that: (1) Iparretarrak constitutes a combat group; (2) IK is threatening
to the integrity of French territory and to its sovereignty over all or part of
the Department of the Pyrénées-Atlantiques; (3) IK carries out acts of terrorism on or from French territory; and (4) special administrative waivers
would be permitted given the urgency of the case at hand.[211]

For *Sud-Ouest*, the effect of the government's action would probably be
more symbolic or dissuasive than real.[212] For Richard Irazusta, EMA's candidate at the last regional elections, the dissolution was a "psychological
weapon" wielded by the government at a time when IK had suffered important reverses.[213] As Irazusta put it, "One had the impression that . . . they
wanted to give us the coup de grâce. As for me, the coup de grâce decreed in
the Council of Ministers, I don't believe it. It's a very Parisian psychological
weapon. We expected it for a long time."[214] He, among others, expected that
Chirac would do it during his whirlwind visit to Bayonne two weeks earlier:
"They are playing a little more subtly than in Corsica. This time he waited
only until having left in order to throw the oil on the fire."[215] EMA criticized
the government's decision and took up IK's demands for the teaching of the
Basque language, economic development, and the right of the Basques to
determine their own political orientations.[216]

From the perspective of the police, the decision was well timed: "Politically it's astute. The moment was well chosen: taken too soon the measure
could have had a boomerang effect and create more publicity for 'IK' than
harm them. This is the moment where one senses the bankruptcy, the deli-
quescence, that we could go ahead."[217] For another official source, "The goal
is clear, it is a question of cutting off the terrorists from their support and
their means of propaganda. This permits justice to act quickly, often in fla-
grante delicto, and in a very supple fashion. We will be able for example to
demand of anyone of our choice where the documents they possess come
from and how they got them."[218] What effect the dissolution would have
on IK only time would tell. In a communiqué in October IK simply reiterated the same themes which it had developed over the past two years and
ignored the government's dissolution decree altogether.[219] Would it isolate
this movement that *Le Monde* called "the little unloved sister of ETA?"[220] For
Le Monde's Agathe Logéart, "The tourists are there, numerous and indifferent, and Philippe Bidart is still in flight."[221]

THE KILLING AT BISCARROSSE

Aire zahar batean kantore berria.
A new singer to an old tune.
Basque proverb

On August 25, 1987, two gendarmes from Biscarrosse in Les Landes, to the north of Bayonne, were shot during an identity check of a young couple near the beach at Sanguinet-Cazaux.[222] According to the account of the surviving gendarme, the young man—later identified as Philippe Bidart—was smiling and relaxed as he reached into his car to retrieve his papers, revealing a pistol stuck in his belt. When gendarme Guy Chevanton saw the gun and attempted to grab him, Bidart shot him in the leg and then shot and killed the second gendarme, Roger Buschmann, with a bullet in the throat. At this point Bidart and his companion, Lucienne Fourcade, fled with a vacationing and unarmed member of the Police Judiciare from Versailles in hot pursuit. Stealing a car at gunpoint from German tourists, they disappeared into the pine forests of Les Landes. The police quickly implemented the "Plan Eclat," which called for intensive searches by 1,500 police throughout Aquitaine.[223] The following day the government replaced the "Plan Eclat" with the "Plan Epervier" across a larger territory, but canceled it four days later as their trail disappeared. Police believed that Bidart had gone to ground in Bordeaux.[224] The Renault 4L which Bidart had abandoned at the site of the shooting was found to be registered to Lucienne Fourcade, which permitted police to identify her as Bidart's companion. Once more police were surprised to identify an IK militant who, if known for her *abertzale* sympathies, had not been suspected as an active militant.[225] Police soon found their hideaway apartment in Arcachon between Bayonne and Bordeaux and discovered papers which continued to flesh out the organizational charts of Iparretarrak.[226] The police printed two hundred thousand wanted posters, something of an unnecessary expense at least in the southwest, where *Sud-Ouest* featured the story in headlines in its five hundred thousand issues.[227] Soon calls were coming in from throughout France seeking the reward. *Le Monde*, in an article entitled "Philippe Bidart, Lost Basque," captured the public anger and rejection of France's most wanted fugitive, who had now killed for at least the third time.[228] Even for *abertzale* sympathizers, he had become a modern-day Matalas, with the tragic ending at the hands of the state which that story foretold.[229]

Now believing that Bidart had sought refuge at the abbey of Belloc after the killing of the two CRS at Baigorri in 1982, and knowing that he had an uncle there, the police proceeded quickly to a search of Belloc, which proved fruitless.[230] Police also searched the offices of the newspapers *Ekaitza* and

Abil, their printers, and local Basque bookstores without finding his trace. By this point Bidart had been in clandestinity for nearly six years, and the police still had no idea how he had managed to hide himself during that time. Police did find in late September that he had apparently dined the previous evening at one of the finest restaurants in Bordeaux, a fact which appeared in the December regional edition of the French gastronomic guide *Gault et Millau*.[231]

THE CAPTURE OF PHILIPPE BIDART

ETA is the army of the Basques . . . its war [is our war] . . .
Bidart is one of our brothers.
Father Martin Carrère[232]

During the massive police searches in the fall of 1987 it was clear that, while the ETA refugee community was a major target of the government's action, the state was also attempting to isolate Bidart by encircling and indicting his supporters within the Basque community. IK was especially concerned with its security and the problem of informers and intemperate talk in crowded bars. Thus, during the night of December 20, a new IK tract, in the form of a large format French-style business card, cautioned the *abertzale* community:

> Let's be quiet. Silence must be the golden rule among the *abertzale* community. Before the cops, a single response—I have nothing to say. Between friends, at the festivals, at the bistro, the gossip must cease.[233]

On February 19, 1988, the French government announced the capture of Philippe Bidart and four accomplices in a villa in Boucau, an industrial suburb of Bayonne.[234] Ironically, it occurred on the same day that the Spanish government announced the opening of a new dialogue with ETA to end the Basque conflict in Spain. For Bidart, it represented the end of a flight in clandestinity that had lasted nearly six years and three months. For the French public, it represented the capture of the Basque "Jacques Mesrine," the latest in a series of French public enemies number one. For the *abertzale* community, Bidart's arrest represented the capture of a Robin Hood or latter-day Matalas who had thwarted the state for much of the past decade.[235]

He was arrested with fellow militants Joseph Etxebeste (a.k.a. Etcheveste), Philippe Lascaray, Pierre Aguerre, and Jean-Paul Hiribarren. For more than a month local gendarmes had been augmented by six members of an elite group of the Gendarmerie Nationale in a careful surveillance of IK's Hiribarren, who had been freed from prison in May 1987 after being incarcerated for IK's 1984 firebombing in Ascain, an attack for which both Etcheveste and Gabriel Mouesca had been tried in absentia.[236] In the words of the head of the GIGN (Groupe d'Intervention de la Gendarmerie Nationale), Philippe Legorjus, through a careful surveillance, "Very quickly we realized that he had resumed the tics of a clandestine militant. Each day we tried to follow his travels and, after verifications, we advanced the point of observation. We thus arrived at the villa in Boucau." [237] Through electronic bugs installed in his rooms, the police listened in as Patrick Lascaray was formally "inducted," though he had been wounded in a holdup of the Crédit Agricole in Bayonne the previous December and had only just returned from hiding in Spain. Pierre Aguerre had never been identified before by the police. Etcheveste had been a fugitive since 1982.

When the group left the house, Bidart was immediately taken to the ground unharmed. Etcheveste drew his gun and, despite wearing a bullet-proof vest, was hit by two bullets and paralyzed from the waist down.[238] Aguerre was wounded in the arm. Hiribarren was captured unharmed. The whole operation lasted less than a minute. Two days after the arrests IK launched a renewed appeal for Basques to "enlist in the struggle so that the Pays Basque may live and . . . in the support and the participation in the armed struggle." [239]

The government was delighted. President Mitterrand congratulated the gendarmerie for its arrest of Bidart and its struggle against terrorism.[240] The minister of defense, André Giraud, called it "this very important success" obtained in "delicate and often dangerous" conditions.[241] Security minister Robert Pandraud came to Bayonne to congratulate the gendarmes and stated that Iparretarrak was not an isolated group and that it received the support of numerous young Basques within EMA.[242]

With the capture of Bidart and his four accomplices, the government had struck a serious blow to the clandestine wing of Iparretarrak. Bidart represented a tremendous recruitment tool in clandestinity. The most important question at the moment was whether IK would now disappear. With the arrest of its most important members and the level of government operations in the Pays Basque against both ETA and IK, IK's immediate problems were more of survival than of grand strategy.

LUCIENNE FOURCADE'S SMUGGLED LETTER

Otsoak arrapatan dion aragia on zau enbrari xatea.
What the wolf does pleases the wolf's mate.
Basque proverb

In a letter found in Bidart's cell in the Prison de la Santé in April 1988, three months after his arrest, his companion Lucienne Fourcade wrote Bidart of her situation in clandestinity.[243] There remained something of an infrastructure in place, but as she put it, "The 'politicals' [of IK] have made the decision that each group should finance itself." She spoke elliptically of "the actual situation of the organization. It wasn't clear for me either. It is only now that I am perfectly aware of the state of our troops and a new strategy imposes itself. . . . The others must absolutely become actors."[244]

Apparently, IK's remaining militants had decided to mute the use of violence in the face of a massive police presence in the region and to pursue the open political path in the interim: "If the 'politicals' play the game, pushing to the limit the legal actions in their last version, we are going to win points across the board. We [the military wing], during this time, are going to begin again on a more solid basis with [the] advantage [of] the gains of these years of struggle." Fourcade saw Bidart as a symbol of the struggle that those remaining had to nurture:

> We need to absolutely create a dynamism around you . . . you know, it is absolutely necessary that you keep up your myth. Manifest yourself, write. For many people you are still an example to follow and you will have a super-important role vis-à-vis the new strategy . . . you are a soldier, symbol of liberty and because you want so much to get out of those walls, you will get out. We will do everything to aid you and I swear to you I'll be part of the expedition. Above all be strong, endure. There will always be someone here who will love you until death. My heart will only beat for you and for the struggle."[245]

On May 31, 1988, Bidart's lawyer, Jean-Claude ("Koko") Abeberry was indicted for smuggling the letter into the prison, a charge he denied.[246]

IPARRETARRAK REGROUPS

IK appeared again in October 1988, with attacks in Hasparren, Bayonne, and Saint-Jean-de-Luz, ending a silence which stretched back to Bidart's killing of the gendarme at Biscarrosse in 1987. Five of the IK prisoners, including Bidart, undertook a short hunger strike in October without success and repeated it in November. This was coupled with a hunger strike lasting two weeks by five of their family members in the cathedral of Bayonne. For *Enbata*, however, this was part of the strategy Fourcade had described to Bidart in her letter of the previous April.[247] Fourcade herself was captured by police in Bayonne on December 12, 1988,[248] she was provisionally freed in July 1989 because she had not been charged with crimes of violence herself.[249] Finally, with the arrest of Allande Socarros on January 20, 1989, the French authorities had eighteen members of Iparretarrak under detention. IK claimed that its attack on the gendarmerie of Behobie on January 3, 1989, was a direct response to the government's treatment of the prisoners and insisted again that the government, in opting for repression, had not learned anything of the lessons of history.[250] It demanded unconditional amnesty and the release of its "political prisoners." Yet later that year, at a clandestine press conference in November 1989, IK made clear that amnesty alone would not solve the Basque problem, unless it were accompanied by other government policy concessions including a statute for the Basque language, a new form of economic development which would not be based on tourism, the definition of a new institutional entity for the Basque people, and amnesty for its prisoners.[251]

On January 12, 1989, *Herria*, the Basque-language weekly, published a declaration in French by Mgr. Pierre Molères, bishop of the Diocese of Bayonne, condemning the practice of violence. Molères referred in part to "violent terrorism [and] blind . . . because this violence is an impasse which brings tears, death, sterility."[252] Philippe Bidart quickly responded from prison and was most critical of Molères's defense of law and order and his support for the theses of the government:

> The supreme and often advanced argument by the political and administrative "leaders" [is]: "devaluation of the noble and legitimate cultural demands." That means: if the legitimate demands aren't satisfied, it's because of the armed struggle, because of the terrorists. Well, it's exactly the contrary: it's because the "noble and legitimate" demands aren't taken into account that certain *abertzale* are engaged in the armed struggle. And these noble and legitimate demands aren't uniquely cultural but also economic and political. I can assure you that if the legitimate demands of the Basque people are heard, the armed struggle will cease.[253]

In April 1989 Xan Coscarat was again arrested as a suspect in IK attacks in Cambo and Biarritz.[254] Yet, in the months after Bidart's arrest, and with the effective dismantlement of most of the clandestine structure of Iparretarrak, its subsequent attacks were what the Basques call *pétards*, small attacks generally using either small propane tank bombs stolen from service stations or less-effective agricultural explosives.[255] The targets of these attacks were often symbolic: police stations, tax offices, tourist offices, temporary employment agencies, and especially real estate speculation offices.[256] In August 1990, in a series of telephone threats whose authenticity could not be determined, a caller claiming to represent IK and to have Iraqi support threatened to detonate 163 kilos of explosives at diverse locations in the Pays Basque unless Philippe Bidart were released.[257] But nothing transpired.

THE IPARRETARRAK TRIAL OF 1991

Without the tradition of habeas corpus in American law, the French judicial system slowly prepared its cases against the sixteen members of Iparretarrak who remained in custody without trial. It was not until November 1990, coinciding with the release of Xan Coscarat, who had just served nineteen months of a two-year sentence, that the government announced its intention to begin its trial of sixteen militants on January 21, 1991.[258]

If the outcome of the trial was not in doubt, it nonetheless offered the various defendants a public platform to elaborate on the motives of their militancy.[259] In all cases the judge gave the defendants the choice of expressing themselves in French or being removed from the courtroom. Bidart responded, "I accept speaking in French in order to explain the reasons for the struggle and the demands of the Basque people."[260] Bidart first situated his militancy in a Basque history beginning with the time of the Romans and continuing through the night of August 4 during the early French Revolution, before concentrating on the modern Basque movement and its deception with the unkept promises, *hitza hitz* (the given word), of the Mitterrand administration. Bidart declared in part: "We are accused of participation in an association of criminals.[261] Iparretarrak is not an association of criminals, it is a political organization"; and later: "I add that, as a Basque soldier, I am proud to belong to the political organization Iparretarrak."[262] Among the witnesses called for the defense was Richard Irazusta, representing EMA, and by now a frequent contributor of political reflections in *Enbata*'s "Tribune Libre" column. Irazusta declared that EMA was "a holder of the same principles" as those of the accused members of IK."[263] He continued:

> After the year 2000 there will be no more Basques and no one will be on trial. But, before that, the Basques will not be silent and they will pose the problem. Finally, each of the Basque militants must make his/her contribution. The flame must not be extinguished. The [state] must begin the dialogue. It is up to it . . . to solve the problem.[264]

Ironically, within three months, Irazusta himself was arrested by police as the renter of a garage found to contain explosive materials believed used in IK's attacks.[265] His visible role as a spokesman for EMA lent additional evidence to the police assertion that EMA, like Herri Taldeak before it, was the legal "revolving door" through which IK militants passed back and forth between their various choices of militancy.

It was therefore interesting to note the beginning of a dialogue between EMA and the French subprefect in Bayonne in order for each side to explain its position. Neither side would call the series of meetings that began in 1990 a negotiation, but it is clear that the subprefect would not have met with the EMA delegation without approval from Paris. EMA was represented at the meetings by a delegation led by the authors of its moderate electoral strategy, Richard Irazusta and Alain Iriart. According to Irazusta, the sub-prefect asked "a hundred thousand questions" in order to understand EMA's position better.[266] EMA's call for a "Bilçar d'Iparralde" seemed to go too far for the state. It called for powers going beyond the department-region and a special statute for the Pays Basque within France which clearly implied the right of self-determination and reunification with the South.[267] As Irazusta put it, "We didn't go seeking anything. We wanted to make sure that our point of view was communicated by us. We said all we wanted to say." In the same vein, as part of its new diplomatic strategy, EMA began a series of meetings with Herri Batasuna in order to improve relations and repair the rift which had divided IK and ETA.[268] In either case, EMA called itself "the only force making propositions for the future of the Northern Pays Basque."[269]

By the summer of 1991 a major verbal and physical target of IK was the development of Florida-style golf course condominium projects, especially a highly visible one in Bassussarry on the route from Bayonne to Ustaritz. Particularly distasteful was the developer's purchase of the architecturally important ancestral home of the revolutionary deputy Garat. The developer's initial desire to demolish the home soon gave way to public protest and led him to string banners from its façade and use it as a sales office for the condo development.

Despite official pleasure at the arrest and dismantlement of IK's clandestine apparatus surrounding Bidart, what concerned the police was that by 1991 Iparretarrak was now recruiting its *third* generation of militants, most of whom were previously unknown to the authorities. Throughout 1991 Iparretarrak had claimed credit for forty-seven different attacks, fifteen of them failing. According to *Enbata*, since its creation in 1973, IK had never committed so many attacks in a single year.[270] Despite every hope to the contrary, in 1992 IK continued its steady if low-level campaign of violence. Those carrying out its attacks represent still another generation of Basque youth who have been seduced by the path of violence.

Conclusion

By 1991, there were four identifiable generations of Basque militants in France, stretching from those who remembered the Spanish Civil War and had been active in the 1940s to the young alternative scene based on *rock movida* and "rupturist" political tactics. Among these generations, the issue of violence continued to constitute a defining watershed in the nature of Basque militancy in France. What is important in this period, however, is the rise of a number of moderate Basque political parties who rejected the use of political violence and who sought an institutional solution to the political, social, and economic issues threatening Basque cultural survival in France.

The eleventh issue of *ILDO* distributed at the Aberri Eguna of Hendaye in April 1990 vowed to continue the use of violence until a political solution was found to the Basque question. The justification of that violence was based on now-familiar political themes first elaborated in the 1970s. Yet the government's success against the movement, coupled with the rise of the Basque moderate camp, had begun to affect the tone of its demands. By the 1990s, Iparretarrak's growing insistence on a *negotiated* solution with the French government mirrored the on-again, off-again nature of political discussions between ETA and the Spanish government after 1987.

In the case of Iparretarrak, with the imprisonment of most of its leading militants, it seemed as if the French government's ongoing repression had led the movement to reflect on its end-game strategy. For *ILDO* 11, while continuing to press for Basque autonomy and unification in the long run, began to allude to a moderation in its demands, and a willingness to seek a short-run compromise within the context of France:

> Whatever the evolutions may be, the states will remain sovereign on their territory. The French state which governs the Northern Pays Basque will never accept interference on its territory and it will benefit in that from the support of other member states [of the European Community]. An evolution in the Northern Pays Basque depends essentially on action within the French system.

There is within this text both realism and a moderation of ultimate political aims—a search for some middle-range institutional accommodation within the context of France in order to preserve Basque culture in this "urgent situation." With the arrest of Bidart, and the devastation of its clandestine wing, IK now began to speak of the need for a "unitary" front as "indispensable" against French repression and part of a "global" "normalization of this corner of Europe."[271]

As we saw above, the evidence presented at the trial of Xan Coscarat in January 1990 demonstrated the extent of the government surveillance of the Basque movement over the past thirty years.[272] The only modification in his sentence (two years in prison followed by two years of residence outside of the Pays Basque) was the reduction of the government costs charged to him from 94,000 francs to 2,000 francs, with the decision made to not charge him for the costs of the government's long-standing telephone wiretaps.[273] In 1988, in another indicator of the extent of government surveillance of the Basque movement, *Enbata* published a leaked document from the Police de l'Air et des Frontières des Pyrénées-Atlantiques.[274] The document provided statistics on the number of government identity checks of what the Police called "Basque separatists" at the French-Spanish frontier, broken down by organization and citizenship. According to the government figures, out of 3,137 total Basque identity checks during calendar 1987, 1,848 were determined to be sympathizers of ETA-m (including 196 French Basques), 39 of ETA-pm (including 1 French Basque), 27 of the Commandos Autonomes Anticapitalistes (including 3 French Basques), and 1,123 sympathizers of what the government called "Ex-Iparretarrak" following its dissolution that year (including 33 Spanish Basques). The sheer volume of these figures provided another indication of the magnitude of the government's effort to determine the membership of IK as well as ETA and to bracket the movements through physical and electronic surveillance.

Conspiracy theorists within the Basque movement have long maintained in all seriousness that the government had infiltrated Iparretarrak, and several of the same names recur in their recitations. Even those who do not believe that IK itself was penetrated freely discuss the fabric of police informers in the villages who have helped encircle the movement.

As the argument goes, so long as IK's violence was amateurish and did little damage, it actually served the interests of the state by discrediting both the idea of Basque nationalism in France and the presence of ETA refugees within the conservative French Basque population. The cynics' theory asserted that the premature arrest of the four HT militants carrying journalists to an IK press conference—rather than waiting until the conference was actually under way—was because the state did not want to roll up IK at that point. In this view, if IK continued to exist, it was because the state *permitted* it to exist, until Bidart's series of killings forced the state to act. The killing of the CRS in 1982 opened a new phase in France's combat against IK. The appearance of GAL in 1983 meant that three groups committed to political violence were now operating in the Pays Basque Français: Iparretarrak, ETA, and GAL. With the agreement between France and Spain concerning the extradition of ETA refugees, GAL disappeared, as we saw in chapter 7; France then effectively declared open season on both Iparretarrak and ETA at the same time. The one-half billion francs (eighty-five million dollars) that France was spending annually against Basque violence in the Pyrénées-Atlantiques was divided across a host of police and intelligence agencies, from the gendarmerie, Police de l'Air et des Frontières, and Police Judiciare to the Renseignements Généraux and Direction de la Surveillance du Territoire (DST). The DST's counterpart for external intelligence is the DGSE, a functional division like that of the American FBI and CIA. While a decree published in the *Journal Officiel* on April 4, 1982, limited its action to territory outside France, it was clear with the arrest of four DGSE agents in Bayonne in 1985 that even the DGSE was part of the campaign against the Basque movement.[275]

If Iparretarrak found itself in disarray by 1991, the condition of the Basque moderate movements which opposed violence was hardly much improved. The open conflict which characterized the 1990 Aberri Eguna in Hendaye led to two competing Aberri Egunas in 1991.[276] Approximately 1,000 *abertzale* attended EMA's celebration in interior Saint Palpais on the themes of total amnesty and the creation of a specific institution, a Bilçar d'Iparralde in the Pays Basque Français. Another 600–700 attended the competing celebration at Arbonne near Bayonne which was sponsored by Patxa, Oldartzen, ESK, GABE, and IEGA. Their themes included the defense of the prisoners and refugees, the defense of the Basque patrimony, and bilingual road signs. These groups stated their "total solidarity" with Herri Batasuna's Aberri Eguna at Pamplona. For its part, Herri Batasuna diplomatically sent speakers to both. As *Ager* put it, "In waiting for a 'shared political will,' this Aberri Eguna of 1991 was the faithful demonstration of the present division of the forces of the Basque movement. But the enthusiasm of youth was impressive."[277]

As we saw earlier, part of the explanation for the conflict turned on the nature of Eusko Alkartasuna's image and positions and EB's and EMA's willingness to work with them. According to one leader of EMA, the decision to work with EA provoked a real debate within EMA as well. Yet he claimed the same conflict would have existed if the leftist Euzkadiko Ezkerra (EE) had been implanted in the North, because it also had signed the pact against violence in Spain. These latent political tensions grew deeper with the appearance of the PNV on the northern political scene.

In a deeper sense, the conflict within the Basque movement in 1990 reflected a generational division between those older, more credible electoral and leadership-oriented movements like EA, EB, EMA, and the PNV in one camp, and the younger and self-styled "rupturist" movements like Patxa and *Oldartzen* and their allies on the other. If the *abertzale* tendency represented a solid 8 percent of the French Basque electorate in 1991, EMA probably accounted for 5 percent of it and Euskal Batasuna another 2 percent, with the remaining 1 percent divided among movements across the spectrum. French government analyses prepared in 1991 described a Basque movement whose considerable potential was diminished through its fragmentation and internal disarray. The historic nature of this intra-Basque conflict is part of what the late eminent Basque historian Eugène Goyheneche called the tragic Basque tradition of "tribal struggle."[278] The Basque-on-Basque violence of the 1990 Aberri Eguna represented an alien political strategy among

French Basques and led those "rupturist" parties to rethink their position. Yet, in whatever manifestation, for much of the past twenty years, much of the political effort of the French Basque movement has been wasted on personality disputes and internecine warfare.

Within the Basque movement, there was a clear feeling that the French government was continuing a policy of improvisation which dealt with the symptoms and not yet with the causes of Basque discontent. In recent years that policy seems based on a policy of institutional "benign neglect," in contrast to the negotiations and institutional reforms adopted for Corsica. Before the current subprefect arrived in Bayonne the position remained empty for six months. When the interior minister's *conseiller* for the Pays Basque and Corsica was reassigned, a replacement was found for Corsica, but the Basque position went unfilled for several months. When current interior minister Philippe Marchand came to visit the Centre Culturel at Ustaritz, he announced two projects for the Pays Basque—a new subprefecture and a new Commissariat de Police. For many Basque observers, this level of neglect or *maladresse* demonstrates lack of a careful government policy, certainly in contrast to that for Corsica. The explanation is thought to be the declining role of ETA and the now artisanal nature of IK's *pétards*. As one voice close to Iparretarrak explained the government's neglect, "The reason is that there are ten to twenty times fewer incidents of violence in the Pays Basque than in Corsica, and thus the government holds the Basque movement in contempt."

Bidart's arrest at the same time that the Spanish state had reembarked on its effort to negotiate with ETA symbolized for many Basques the intransigence of the French government even on issues of symbolic cultural and linguistic importance, such as the posting of bilingual road signs in Basque and French along highways in the Pays Basque. These issues had indeed been held hostage between IK and the state in the struggle over Basque violence. It was not until May 1988, after the arrest of Philippe Bidart, that the government began to give serious attention to the integration of the Seaska, the Basque primary school movement, into the Ministry of National Education.[279] The state then approved for the 1989–1990 academic year the long-sought advanced DEUG degree in Basque language and culture.[280] The final accord between Seaska and the government was signed on November 23, 1989, after more than a decade of a "dialogue of the deaf."[281] Part of the government's fear was that many of the early parents in the Ikastola movement were Spanish refugees and that Coscarat and Bidart as former Seaska employees were examples of Iparretarrak's effort to take over Seaska. The government's position seemed to reflect the fear that even minimal concessions might be seen as a victory for the armed struggle and lead to an upward spiral in ethnic demands. But in the logic of action and reaction, as Philippe Bidart wrote in his response to Bishop Molères above, from the standpoint of the Basque movement, it was the government's lack of concern for Basque problems—whether political, economic, or cultural/linguistic—which led to the armed struggle and not vice versa. As one militant put it, if the government's inaction had not driven Seaska to the point of financial collapse, there would have been no need for Iparretarrak.

This explanation of the rise of French Basque violence does not account for the attraction of the *guerrillero*—the Robin Hood syndrome—for emerging generations of young Basque militants or the inner psychological drives of individual militants like Philippe Bidart who gravitated from the seminary to violence. Arising well into ETA's middle age, Iparretarrak's analysis was based in part on the belief that only violence would force the attention of the French state. The so-called Watts hypothesis of black urban violence in the United States suggested that violence was necessary to bring ameliorative public policy. At the mass trial in January, Gabi Mouesca declared, "I am of I.K. and proud of it" and while "the armed struggle is necessary in the northern Pays Basque . . . like any soldier I believe in a negotiated solution." [282]

The problem was that the rise of Basque violence in France touched a tender nerve in the history of French political ideas, mixing as it did with visions of Dien Bien Phu, Algeria, and the Commune of Paris. The threat of federalism was one of the heresies which fueled the Terror during the Revolution, and France has guarded its unitary political system and the unity of its territory with unswerving constancy. The rise of Basque violence only hardened the resolve of French Jacobins from the Gaullist right to the Communist left to resist its demands at all costs. In the end, even assuming the armed struggle *could be* contained, would the state then make concessions in the areas of culture, language, and education in order to reinforce the rise of moderate Basque movements and elites?

There *were* moderate voices on both sides seeking a peaceful and face-saving middle ground. As Socialist deputy Jean-Pierre Destrade declared at a press conference in Bayonne on January 28, 1991:

> Beyond the trial of I.K. in Paris, we have the will to appease the situation, to give it its objectivity. Is it that which passes for a negotiation with I.K.? I don't know, but why not? One can imagine, in a certain perspective, a negotiation if it's in order to obtain a truce in the attacks and diverse actions. [283]

One of the strongest traditional arguments against the appearance of Basque violence in France was that it risked alienating this predominantly rural, conservative, and profoundly Catholic French Basque electorate. On the other hand, IK and others have placed their hopes on the generations to come and the belief that growing up in a climate of violence harnessed to national liberation will influence their future political action. While the use of violence has polarized the electorate, it has undeniably led to an increase in the *abertzale* vote. The fruits of this strategy became apparent in the 1992 regional and cantonal elections. The unified Basque list (Abertzaleen Batasuna) included members of both EMA and EB, with members of EA allied with the Occitan movement Entau Païs.[284] Among the elements of the Abertazaleen Batasuna platform was a refusal to condemn the use of violence.[285] The 1992 cantonal elections showed a net increase in the *abertzale* vote, especially in the interior. Basque candidates won 27 percent of the vote in Hasparren, 17 percent in Iholdy, and nearly 27 percent in Saint-Jean-Pied-de-Port, forcing outgoing *conseiller* and deputy Michel Inchauspé into a runoff election.[286] The overall *abertzale* vote in the Pays Basque was 9.98 percent, now stronger in the interior than along the coast. The results of the 1992 cantonals nearly *doubled* the historic iron threshold of 5 percent sought by both *Enbata* and EHAs in the 1960s and 1970s.[287]

What the violence *has* accomplished in the ensuing twenty-five years has been to polarize even the Basque nationalist community in France, just as it has defined the political debate. As one militant sympathetic to the use of violence argued:

> What the violence has done, however, is to change the nature of the political debate. Today, the question is no longer are we for or against a Basque identity. Today we all have been galvanized by the violence and thus define ourselves in terms of it.

The judgment we make about the use of violence is less a question of morality than of efficacy, of the basic *Realpolitik* of violence as an instrument of political change. As Jacques Abeberry explained on Radio Monte-Carlo: "But let's say that violence—I understand political violence— . . . isn't judged from a moral point of view. All causes in . . . history, more or less, have used it and I don't see why the Basques should a priori deprive themselves of it."[288] The question for Abeberry was what would be the outcome of that violence for the Basque people:

> Never will I condemn violence. Not that I am for political violence. But I know that it is part of the arsenal which peoples possess, whether one wants it or not, because there are violences which are first of all institutional. . . . My problem is: "How to escape the violence?" . . . When there is political violence, there must always be political solutions.[289]

Yet, for many *abertzale*, the rise of Basque violence in France was a terrible error and a danger to the cause. Even for those opposed to the use of violence, there was the hope that it would stimulate a rebirth of Basque culture and language that would propel it into the twenty-first century. As one respected Basque militant opposed to violence put it:

> Our hope is that one day our caskets will be covered with the flowers of a new and future hope. The immense evil they do can't prevent our people from their survival. There is an expression in Basque; *Ez da gaitzik hain txarrik zerbait onik berekin ez duenik* (There is no evil so bad that it doesn't carry within it the seeds of good). Without that hope, there is already enough to despair.

Will the French government address the underlying political, economic, and cultural grievances that found expression in violence when all other means had seemingly failed? The state has vacillated, as in Corsica, between policies of repression and accommodation. Yet one remembers that Charles de Gaulle himself called intransigence the arm of the weak. Metternich once defined diplomacy as "the art of avoiding the appearance of victory." The challenge to the French government in 1993 is to find a way to make those face-saving concessions in the areas of culture and political restructuring that will encourage the rise of Basque moderation. To do otherwise may well invite the phoenixlike resurgence of bitter nationalism in later generations, like that of the Armenians, who fight for the honor of their forebears. Certainly much of the bitterness of the 1980s was caused by Mitterrand's failure to keep *hitza hitz*, his given word in his 1981 presidential campaign. With the weakening of Iparretarrak, now is the time for concessions to strengthen the hand of Basque moderation. Government indifference risks encouraging the very rise in nationalism that it seeks to avoid.

Iparretarrak's violence may have cast the Basque movement into a political ghetto, but it has also undeniably increased the population of that *abertzale* ghetto as new generations of Basque youth rise to a political consciousness in an era marked by nationalist violence on both sides of the frontier. The government response to this new generation will determine the nature of political peace in the Pays Basque. As Philippe Bidart's father put it, "I hope that the dialogue is going to begin now. My sons were generous and I hope that their action will accomplish something. This dialogue is necessary, otherwise there will be other Bidarts." [290]

Chapter Nine

Conclusion

There is as much distance between an Auvergnat and a Basque, a Limousin and a Breton, as between a Spaniard and a Slav, an Ostrogoth and a Gaul. . . . France is not "one" in its land and in its race. This highly major country is made of minorities.
Jean Giraudoux[1]

It is [centralization] which permitted the making of France despite the French or their indifference. It is not by chance if seven centuries of monarchy, empire and republic have been centralizers: France is not a natural construction.
Alexandre Sanguinetti[2]

There are ten, twenty Frances, and maybe more.
Pierre Viansson-Ponté[3]

By 1991, the Basque movement in France was divided between poles of violence and electoral moderation which had marked its politics for much of the Fifth Republic. The movement found itself at a crossroads between different constituencies and partners in political dialogue. Today the movement is still preoccupied with problems which have confronted it for much of the past thirty years: its internal fragmentation and the need to attract support from the largely rural, conservative, and Catholic Basque linguistic population in France. Its task has been greatly complicated as the Basque movement has become more secular and moved leftward in its ideology. But the conservative Basque electorate has been unable to ignore the political dynamics swirling around it and has been politicized despite its natural caution. Today it is no longer appropriate to speak of "the Basque church," any more than there is one Latin American Catholic tradition in the context of liberation theology. Here as elsewhere a division between the high and low church has emerged, a political gulf between the cautious *Realpolitik* of the bishopric and the frank nationalism of many village clergy. The Basque nationalism of many of the village clergy, combined with that within the seminaries, has been a major factor in Basque political socialization in France since the 1930s.

From the standpoint of the French Basque electorate, there is a greater support in both relative and absolute terms for Basque nationalist political candidates today than at any other time in history. The political climate in 1992 was marked by both despair and hope: if punctuated by continuing violence and repression, it was also touched by hopes for European unity and the full opening of the Spanish-French frontier. Yet in the 1992 cantonal elections the *abertzale* ticket won nearly 10 percent of the popular vote in the Pays Basque Français, and the *abertzale* vote was now higher in the rural Basque interior, the cradle of Basque culture, than it was along the more assimilated Basque coast. While a figure of 10 percent may seem scant, it was greatly encouraging to the Basque movement for two reasons. First, it nearly doubled the historic "glass ceiling" of 5 percent that Basque candidates had sought to surpass since the 1960s. Second, while this may not appear significant in comparison to support for the French Socialist or Gaullist parties, it should be remembered that Herri Batasuna itself only polls around 15 percent of the Basque electorate in Spain. Yet Herri Batasuna remains a potent partner in the multiparty dialogue over the nature of the political future there.

What is particularly important is the trend in these French electoral figures—the near doubling of the vote for Basque candidacies in recent years, and this in a climate of ongoing government repression and Basque violence. For supporters of Iparretarrak, these figures prove that their use of the armed struggle has succeeded in mobilizing a docile Basque population into a mood of resistance and survival. The opponents of Basque violence believe that Iparretarrak has begun to talk only to itself and has largely contaminated the cultural demands held hostage to government suspicion. Moreover, the violence has clearly fragmented the *abertzale* movement across and within generations and has greatly complicated the growth of a legitimate and successful tradition of Basque political moderation. In this inability to achieve any consensus on the use of violence, the *abertzale* movement has been forced into silence about it—a tactical "least common denominator" designed to hold the coalition together.

Since before the French Revolution the greatest adversary to the growth of Basque nationalism and to the defense of Basque privileges, language, and culture has been the historical ascendance of French nationalism and the public policy apparatus of the French state. As we saw beginning in chapter 1, the history of the Basque people in France has been a history of resistance to central authority and the steady encroachment of French institutions that accelerated in the century before the Revolution. In contrast to the revolutionary myth which grew out of the French Revolution, the Basques were among those peoples who resisted the changes which

the Revolution brought and who sought to defend a Basque cultural reality
bound by the church, their language, and their ties to the soil.

In each period in French history since the Revolution the expression of
Basque particularism has run counter to that of the dominant ideologies of
the time. Thus, in a revolutionary climate of Jacobin centralization and leveling equality, the Basque reaction was one of a religious people who wanted
simply to be left alone. For much of the ensuing century after the Revolution the state lacked the institutional capability to carry out the territorial
and psychological integration of the patchwork quilt that was France in the
nineteenth century. It was not until the advent of the Third Republic in 1871
that the state was able to create a set of institutions to harness to the will
of a Revolution now nearly a century old. The policy initiatives which grew
out of the early Third Republic were a deliberate strategy of state-initiated
nation-building. Through education, the building of tertiary roads and railroads, compulsory military service, and religious laws—to name but a few
examples—the state sought to penetrate the rural interior and effect the geographic and psychological integration of the French people. The Basques
again mobilized behind their clergy and their language in a principled opposition to the threat posed by the radical and anticlerical republic. In this
period the slogan *Eskualdun, fededun* described a political culture in which the
defense of Basque culture and the Catholic faith were intertwined. Basque
resistance to the state culminated in the crisis of separation of church and
state in 1905–1906, which threatened the Basques in their language and in
their faith. Since World War I the chronicle of Basque mobilization in France
has been the slow movement away from conservative clericalism to an expression of true secular Basque nationalism. This process was greatly aided
by the Spanish Basque refugee population that settled in France after the
Spanish Civil War. Allegations of collaboration against Eugène Goyheneche
during World War II revealed the hand of the PNV and a Basque *Realpolitik*
which sought to ensure the best aftermath for the Basques at war's end.

Sensitized by the circumstances of the very birth of the Fifth French Republic, the Basque movement in the 1960s, like other ethnic movements
in France, embraced the language of internal colonialism. It identified the
Basque struggle with that of the Vietnamese, Tunisians, and Algerians,
whose national liberation had so scarred the French political classes and
marked the history of modern political ideas in France. Throughout the
Gaullist Fifth Republic, until the election of François Mitterrand as president
in 1981, Basque nationalism was locked in conflict with French nationalists
whose Jacobinism united such otherwise dissimilar allies as Gaullists and
the French Communist Party.

It was for that reason that the election of François Mitterrand in 1981 was greeted with such enthusiasm among the Basque movement in France, owing especially to the set of promises in his electoral platform, including the creation of a Basque department in France and clear commitments to cultural preservation. But the Socialists' ultimate retreat from their commitments threw the movement into disarray and, suspended between left and right, led to the growth of Basque political parties unwilling to commit the future of Basque language and culture to a largely indifferent or hostile French political system.

One of the greatest obstacles to Basque mobilization in France has been the rise of indigenous Basque violence in Iparralde. It has not only divided the Basque movement from much of the conservative French Basque population, but it has also fragmented the *abertzale* movement into opposing camps. To these indigenous divisions have been added the evolution of Basque political developments in Spain and their impact on the French Basque movement. As a result, the pitched debates over political violence in Spain have bled across the border and marked the debate over Basque nationalism in France. These debates over tactics and strategy have been compounded by schisms within both ETA and the PNV which have been mirrored in the North as well. But the rise of Basque violence in France has also reflected the growing level of frustration of several generations of *abertzale* with the French state and the level of concern of the Basque population regarding the survival of their language and culture into the twenty-first century. If, as the eminent Basque bibliographer Jon Bilbao once said, the rise of Basque nationalism is a reflection of the will of a people unwilling to die, the rise of Basque violence has greatly increased the stakes of the struggle and polarized the *abertzale* community in France as has no other issue.

As a result, by 1991 the French Basque movement was a victim of internal and external fragmentation, torn between competing strategies—violence or moderation—of popular mobilization. Iparretarrak's decision to bring the armed struggle to France has led to twenty years of government encirclement, which has devastated its ranks and effectively isolated it not only from the conservative Basque population, but from supporters of ETA as well. By 1991, 60 Basques were incarcerated in France, 212 refugees had been expelled, 14 extradited, 54 deported, and 24 assigned to residences outside the Pays Basque.[4] Over the past decade 35 Basque militants had died.

Yet the irony of Basque violence in France has been that, while discrediting its own practitioners, it has been largely responsible for the rise of moderate Basque parties which sought to emerge from the ghetto of violence and Socialist revolution into the mainstream of politics. The trend line of their support, now approaching 10 percent in 1992, is a source of encouragement, even if the growth has been exceedingly slow.

One of the greatest obstacles to the growth of Basque nationalism in France has been what Eugène Goyheneche has called the tragic tradition of "tribal struggle" within the Basque movement. From the time of the second *Aintzina* during World War II the Basque movement has been marked by the recurring temptation to fratricide and patricide. The persistent internal conflicts of personalities, ideologies, and generations mostly served to drain the creative force of the nationalist camp and discredited it in the eyes of Basque public opinion.

However important it has been for the Basque movement to assert the contrary, the history of Basque nationalism in France has been a part of the political history of France as well. The nature of Basque political mobilization since before the Revolution has been a reflection of the growth of French institutions and the growth of a national myth which has driven the processes of nation- and state-building in France. In the dialectical relationship between political protest and ameliorative public policy, the relationship between the French state and the Basque movement is central not only to the future of Basque nationalism, but to the survival in France of the Basque culture and language themselves. It is largely owing to the nature of French institutions and society that the development of Basque nationalism in France has differed so much from Basque nationalism in Spain, even within the same historical era.

The fact that France must periodically revisit questions of *being* which lie at the heart of its existence as a community should offer little comfort to other European and Third World societies whose own recent and incomplete processes of nation-building are now punctuated once more by the tumult of ethnic violence. If history has taught us anything, however, it is that the forces of nationalism are at best managed, rarely put to rest. The periodic resurgence of the Armenians, Kurds, Sikhs, Croatians, Serbians, and Azeris demonstrates the phoenixlike potential of ethnic tensions long thought to have died out within the modern state. Yet in the fall of 1993 the tensions of nationalism and communal violence continue to mark the history and stability of the twentieth century more than ever before.

The events in Eastern Europe and the Soviet Union beginning in 1990 have added a further international dimension to the question of ethnic nationalism in both France and Spain. French policy in particular toward the ethnic violence in Yugoslavia is indicative of the historic ambivalence which has guided policy in this area. At the League of Nations in 1925 the French delegate, M. de Jouvenal, refused to vote on the minority treaty concerning the peoples left in the wake of the dissolution of the Austro-Hungarian Empire. He could declare in all sincerity that "France had not signed any minorities treaty because she had no minorities."[5] In 1984 French Communist leader

Georges Marchais harshly criticized a Soviet ethnographic atlas which enumerated France's ethnic minorities, including Basques, Bretons, Alsatians, Corsicans, and Catalans. As Marchais retorted, "We protest with indignation against these ridiculous and odious assertions. For us . . . any man or woman with French citizenship is French. France is not a multiethnic country. It is one country, one nation, one people, the product of a long history."[6]

Yet in 1991 France's early reluctance to see the European Community recognize Croatian and Slovenian independence or to intervene in Yugoslavia's ethnic violence was precisely because it *did* have minorities and feared the precedent that such a European action in Yugoslavia might have on its own restive minorities.[7] French foreign minister Roland Dumas, explaining France's reluctance to act over Yugoslavia, feared that "tomorrow what we have done for Yugoslavia would be applied to other cases."[8] Spain joined in those concerns. The Basques and Catalans have been particularly active in demonstrating for self-determination based in part on the examples of the Soviet republics, especially the Baltics, and the Yugoslavian nationalities.[9] As one ETA spokesman put it, "The Soviet process has given impetus to the search for democratic solutions to the problems of nationality, which in the case of the Basque country means the right to self-determination."[10] The desire for national self-determination and statehood remains a potent dream of empowerment for disenfranchised peoples. As Roger Garaudy put it, "A language is a dialect with an army and a navy."[11] For the Basques, the independence of the Baltics or of the Yugoslavian republics is proof that independence is a viable option and that the vitality of nationalism is far from spent. With the disintegration of Yugoslavia into paroxysms of violence and civil war, the European Community is profoundly divided on what action to take. Germany and Denmark were the first to be willing to recognize the independence of Croatia and Slovenia. A number of countries are prepared to send peacekeeping troops to quell communal violence in Yugoslavia, perhaps under the aegis of the Western European Union. Faced with the Bosnian crisis in 1993, France threatened to intervene alone if need be to end the violence there. But even the most active-minded of the European Community countries recognize that the freedom of Eastern Europe will open up a Pandora's box of ethnic grievances and that Yugoslavia may be a model for other conflicts in coming years. As Karl Deutsch predicted in 1942, "So far as the linguistic factor is concerned, the nationalistic disintegration of mankind may go on with hardly any limit so long as the economic possibilities and the political desires for it remain effective."[12]

In the case of France, the use of force has been a historic tool in the state's effort to tame its society—to create the French nation from which it ostensibly derives its own legitimacy. Yet the use of force is a calculation fraught with risk. For in the relentless logic of politics, the use of repression itself risks becoming the *cause* of Basque political mobilization and not its cure. Still, it is a perennial temptation in French history. It is in this sense that Philippe Boucher spoke of

> the portrait of a society of exclusions, of segregations and of longings, which barely awakens to the demons which it creates: "an ethic of confrontation" reinforced by the religion of the State and the centralizing tradition of Richelieu and the Jacobins.[13]

One explanation for the continuing conflictual nature of French society lies in the imperfect mesh between state and society, in the discrepancy between the myth and reality of the French nation. Whatever that nation is or may be, these cleavages have become exacerbated by the pathology of the Jacobin state, by the conduct and style of French politics. The persistence of self-sustaining and incompatible traditions of thought and action in French politics—of which minority claims of national self-determination are but one—reflects the unfinished will of the Revolutionary Assembly. The fact that ethnic conflicts continue to mark the politics of France—in the Pays Basque, in Corsica, in Brittany—two hundred years later represents still another sense in which it has been said that the Revolution has never fully ended. The persistence of the ethnic factor in French politics seems to reflect the cyclical reappearance of a composite crisis of political development. This crisis defines the nature of persistent questions over identity, political integration, legitimacy, and nation-building which have marked the history of France since the Revolution. France may be the unstable unity of irreconcilable opposites. It is in this light that Pierre Viansson-Ponté suggested that "there are ten, twenty Frances, and maybe more." On the eve of the twenty-first century, with the growing momentum of a united Europe, France finds itself questioning its role in the world and the sense of what it means to be French. While France committed troops to participate in the allied "Desert Storm" campaign against Iraq in 1991, the limited quality of its technology and intelligence-gathering capabilities further demonstrated the marginalization of France as a world power. For the French, far more than for their critics, this era is the heir to the anxieties engendered by the end of its colonial empire and Charles de Gaulle's "certain idea of France." Mitterrand's admission that France is at best a regional power has had a sobering impact on France's own self-image. That image was part of a mythology that anchored France and the French in the world. As François René de Chateaubriand once said of his compatriots, "They must be led by dreams."[14] It is perhaps most revealing of this national self-reappraisal that one of the best-selling books in France in 1991 was conservative commentator Raymond

Soubié's book *Is God Still French?* Soubié's lament was that "We are no longer criticized. Worse, we are ignored." [15] In a climate of self-reappraisal and declining expectations, it is not surprising the government would draw a line beyond which it would not go. Basing its policy on French laws of association first promulgated during the Popular Front in the 1930s, the government has been uncompromising in responding to internal threats to French unity by minority movements which were themselves seen as manifestations of retrograde and illegitimate political demands. One response has been a willingness to use force and repression against ethnic movements. The greatest shortcoming to this policy is that it tends to deal more with the symptoms than with the causes of ethnic discontent.

Yet, in contrast to the use of repression, the state's use of what Daniel Patrick Moynihan called "benign neglect" seems to have been no more successful in quelling ethnic discontent. In reality, in the modern neo-liberal state, ethnic demands are part of the panoply of interest-group politics in which claimant groups seek resources from the government based on group-based criteria, whether as Poujadist shopkeepers and artisans, farmers threatened by EC farm policy, or Le Pen's National Front of those French threatened by the immigrants of empire. The fact that ethnic groups in the Fifth Republic seek government relief should not obscure their basic ambivalence about public authority: resenting the need to seek help in times of misfortune, while denying the very authority of the government in times of good. For itself, the state is also ambivalent: recognizing the potential for policy initiatives to undercut ethnic demands and yet fearful that to do so would be to invite an unending spiral of rising expectations that reinforces the legitimacy of the minority camp. Central to the French government's position has been its long-standing refusal to recognize problems defined ethnically. In this light, former president Valéry Giscard d'Estaing declared: "Contrary to what one often says and writes, there is not a Corsican problem, there are problems in Corsica." [16] To admit otherwise would be to challenge the very linearity of France's self-written history. For Alexandre Sanguinetti and others of the Jacobin persuasion, ethnic militants in modern France were "imbeciles ignorant of all of modern history." [17]

At the same time the government sought to find some middle ground of accommodation to undercut the nature of ethnic political protest while not provoking separatist demands. As then president Giscard d'Estaing described government policy toward the Basques in 1979:

> The rapid growth of these last years, in precipitating changes, has kindled reactions of defense of our cultures and of our regional feelings. These reactions are understandable. But . . . my fundamental

charge, that which prevails over all others, is to maintain the unity of the nation. . . . Diversity doesn't menace national unity. . . . Basque culture has the right to our respect and our support like all the other national cultures. Basque traditions must be faithfully preserved in their authenticity and in their originality. I will help [ensure] it.[18]

By confining government policy to cultural questions, and the sympathy for "regional feelings," the Fifth Republic has sought to depoliticize ethnic demands and to redefine them in a way nonthreatening to French unity. During his unsuccessful reelection campaign in 1981, Giscard d'Estaing vowed to prevent the political contagion of Basque violence on the Spanish model in a region he called the French California.[19]

With the advent of the Socialist administration of François Mitterrand in 1981, a number of changes did occur in the nature of French public policy toward regional minorities, especially in the structure of local government administration, as well as in language policy. In the area of language policy, the government announced the creation in 1985 of a Conseil National des Langues et Cultures de France.[20] According to the Basque cultural umbrella organization Pizkundia, "It's better than nothing, better than the right, which didn't do anything in its 23 years . . . of power."[21]

But it was the subsequent promise of creating new political structures in Corsica and the Pays Basque that was the most controversial part of the government's new initiatives. Their goal was undeniably to undercut the most political demands of the ethnic movements, including the support for ethnic violence in Corsica and the Pays Basque. As Laurent Greilsamer argued, "Incontestably, the policy of decentralization engaged in by the Mauroy government played an appeasing role: the separatist and autonomist movements saw a part of their demands 'defused.' But incontestably as well, this political gain is subsequently losing its weight and is going to dwindle away."[22]—this despite the interior minister's claim to have eliminated domestic terrorism from the map of French politics.

The greatest of these changes concerned the administrative restructuring of Corsica to include two French departments and a separate administrative region. If these promises figured in Mitterrand's platform in 1981, they were not fully implemented until 1990, and then in the face of pitched opposition from the Jacobin camp.[23] Particularly offensive to French senators across the partisan spectrum was article 1 of the Corsican statute, which enshrined the notion of "the Corsican people, component of the French people."[24] Many saw this as opening the Pandora's box of separatist hopes and hence, as the general secretary of the neo-Gaullist RPR Alain Juppé saw it, as "a major political error."[25] National Front leader Jean-Marie Le Pen feared that "Corsica, like the Algeria of old, has entered into a process of revolutionary war: today, the coffin, tomorrow, the suitcase." [26]

If the government moved forward with the idea of a new Corsican statute, the promise of a Basque department was stillborn within weeks after Mitterrand's election in 1981. Much of the deception and disarray of the Basque left after the 1981 election was due to the reversal of the Mitterrand administration's campaign promises to create a Basque department. These dashed hopes were at the heart of the moderate Hitza Hitz initiative, as well as IK's justification for its increase in violence in the early 1980s. As one Basque elected official described the stakes in 1989, "If Paris doesn't listen to these political voices quickly, violence will hardly have any difficulty finding practitioners." [27]

By the mid-1980s, it was clear that the government was holding a series of cultural initiatives hostage in its campaign against both Iparretarrak and ETA, including an accord integrating Seaska's teaching of Basque within the Ministry of National Education and the creation of a DEUG university degree program in Basque. Seaska's president, Jean-Louis Maitia, denounced "the indifference and even the contempt of public powers" toward Basque culture and language. [28]

Yet in December 1988, several months after the arrest of Philippe Bidart and within weeks of the arrest of Lucienne Fourcade (the last of IK's clandestine militants still in flight), interior minister Pierre Joxe made what he called a "nearly accidental" trip after learning of the impending visit of his colleague and minister of industry and development Roger Fauroux to discuss problems of economic development and investment in the Pays Basque. [29] Joxe declared:

> I decided to accompany him. I want to educate myself. My functions are not only the police. In France, we are in a democratic state, and there is no justification for violence, whether it be political or not. The identity of France in Europe cannot occur by forgetting regional identities. In Brittany, in Corsica, in Alsatia, in the Pays Basque, cultural specificities exist. I want to understand the linguistic and cultural problems. There is no reason for these problems to take the form of a crisis. [30]

In the aftermath of the 1989 municipal elections, where the total *abertzale* vote jumped to nearly 10 percent from a score of 4.2 percent during the 1988 legislative elections, it appeared clear that a worried government had a renewed interest in continuing a dialogue with Basque moderates regarding cultural questions. [31] As a result of this renewed dialogue, interior minister Joxe and the minister for economic development, Jacques Chéréque, met on June 30, 1989, with the mayors of the 166 communes making up the Pays Basque Français. Among the series of economic and cultural measures announced that day were several responding directly to the cultural and linguistic concerns raised earlier by moderate Basque leaders: five public teaching posts in Basque; creation of an advanced DEUG degree in Basque; recruitment of teachers for the Ikastola system; and two cultural centers, including one devoted exclusively to Basque culture.[32] Basque militants protested in advance that Joxe's proposals lacked any commitment to the creation of new Basque institutional structures with true decision-making powers. IK blew up the main rail line between Paris and Hendaye the evening before Joxe met with the mayors. A year later, in November 1990, according to presidential advisor Jean Kahn, Mitterrand favored an appropriate administrative entity within the Department of the Pyrenees-Atlantiques, either a syndicate or a community of communes, to advance economic and cultural questions.[33] While Kahn cautioned that his words "should not be read in light of the statute for Corsica," for his neo-Gaullist RPR critics they constituted the impending dismantlement of the state and a threat to republican institutions.[34] In January 1991 the French subprefect in Bayonne, Christian Sapède, confirmed the ongoing discussions that had been occurring with EMA.[35] According to Sapède, as long as the discussion focused on Joxe's proposals to create a community of communes EMA would have interlocutors in the presidential Elysée Palace, and presumably not otherwise.

This dialogue with the state and the potential for government concessions in the areas of culture, economics, and politics make the French government the most important partner in dialogue with the Basque movement. The government has been hesitant to enter into such a dialogue for fear of entering into an unending cycle of rising expectations, with political demands punctuated by endless violence. Critics of the government's reluctance refer to Charles de Gaulle's assertion that "intransigence is the arm of the weak." Moreover, according to bitter critics of Iparretarrak's violence, there is the belief that the creation of a Basque department would have greatly undercut IK's level of public support. A related position holds that the government could have avoided a cycle of successive concessions by granting a package of measures even greater than those demanded. This, so the argument goes, would have taken the wind out of the radicals' sails, if the government had had the wisdom to realize that repression only hardens the resistance in the *abertzale* camp.

The relationship between the French Basque movement and its Spanish Basque counterparts remains one of the primary influences on its doctrine and political organization. This influence has existed since the Spanish Civil War and greatly accelerated after 1963 with the impact of ETA on the French

Basque movement. Today two different Spanish Basque political parties, the PNV and Eusko Alkartasuna, have formal sections in the Pays Basque Français, and Euskal Batasuna is close to, though organizationally distinct from, Herri Batasuna in the South.

Support for ETA and its refugees has been a central element of *abertzale* activity in France since the first appearance of ETA refugees in the early 1960s. As Ramuntxo Camblong put it, "Without the South, there wouldn't be the North."

On the eve of European unification, the French Basque movement has placed great hopes on the economic impact of closer ties with the Spanish Basque provinces. Skeptics believed that the problems of its own aging infrastructure would prevent Spanish Basque industrialists from investing substantially in the North. Even with a growth rate greater than the Spanish average in 1988 and 1989, the 18 percent rate of unemployment in the Spanish Basque region was higher than that of Spain as a whole.[36] Moreover, with the entry of Spain into the EC, there would no longer be a compelling reason to locate in the Pays Basque Français in order to enter into the European market. Even the most traditionally optimistic held that the economic impact would be partial, generally confined to agricultural products and cultural exchanges at the beginning. Moreover, mentalities also have been slow to change on both sides of the frontier. As recently as 1975 a proposed bilingual French-Spanish business school in Bayonne failed for lack of students.[37]

Yet certain trends suggest the growing economic impact of Spanish Basque investment, especially along the coast. Wealthy Spanish Basques have long frequented doctors and specialists in the North, constituting, it is said, as much as three-quarters of some doctors' clienteles.[38] As the exchange rate between the peseta and the franc has changed—making Spain no longer the historic bargain it traditionally was and giving holders of pesetas new buying power in France—French Basques have witnessed a great increase in the number of cars with plates from Donotia on highways and in supermarket parking lots. What was at first a weekend phenomenon has grown in magnitude with the great rise in the purchase of property by Spanish Basques along the French Basque coast.[39] This increased greatly following the Spanish government's decree in 1987 permitting its residents to own secondary residences abroad worth more than $200,000. Whether or not Spanish Basques swell the ranks of vacation home buyers in the Pays Basque Français, that trend will continue unabated. Between 1975 and 1982 the number of secondary residences increased by 44 percent in twelve key communes in the Basque interior, as opposed to an increase of only 16 percent for principal residences.[40] Some observers predict that one-third of the residents of Hendaye will have come from the other side of the border by the end of the century. The mayor of Hendaye claims that already one-half of its population are either refugees from the Spanish Civil War or employed as customs agents or police due to the presence of the border with Spain.[41] For more than twenty years many families in neighboring Irún have sent their children to school in Hendaye. Today there is a growing commuting population of Spanish Basques who live in Hendaye and commute by interstate highway to their jobs in Donostia less than thirty minutes away.

What is important in these trends is the demographics behind them. The proximity of the vibrant Spanish Basque market and Basque-language media just across the border is in clear contrast to the broad expanse of pine forests which separate the Pays Basque from the French regional capital of Aquitaine in Bordeaux, two hours to the north. If the population of the coastal region of the Pays Basque Français including Biarritz and Bayonne is 150,000, the economic region just across the frontier and centered in Donostia includes more than 500,000 people. Adding Bilbao, an hour's drive from the border, increases that figure to 1 million people.[42] In 1991 the Chamber of Commerce of Bayonne estimated that forty companies there had Spanish capital totaling two hundred million francs and that more than half of them had been created within the past two years.[43] As Antton Laffont Madariaga, director of Bayonne's Chamber of Commerce, noted, "The northern Pays Basque remains the most direct path between Paris and Madrid, the necessary passage on the Atlantic arc and the hinge between [the French economic region of] Aquitaine and the Pays Basque of Spain."[44]

For the Pays Basque Français, the opening of the border will create a new source of economic investment that will orient the Basque economy toward a southern market stretching toward Donostia and Bilbao. Its cultural and linguistic impact on the Pays Basque Français is less quantifiable, but will undeniably be a counterforce to the process of francophone cultural assimilation now well in progress along the coast. For the foreseeable future the French Basque movement will continue to look southward for political and cultural support. With the growth of European unification, the question of Basque "independence" may be moot in this interdependent market economy. Yet the vitality of a Basque economy anchored in Spain and extending into the Pays Basque Français would make the Basque country one of the strongest economies in southern Europe, whether as an independent state or as a "standard metropolitan statistical area" (SMSA) or ninety-minute market in a Europe where the sovereignty of existing states is now outmoded as well.

By 1991 there were four identifiable generations of Basque nationalist militants in France. The first and oldest, marked by the events of the Spanish Civil War and World War II, includes Marc Légasse, Pierre Charritton, Jean

Etcheverry-Ainchart, and the late Eugène Goyheneche. Most were active in one of the *Aintzinas* during the 1930s and 1940s. The second generation, that of Jacques Abeberry, Ximun Haran, Jean-Louis Davant, and the late Michel Burucoa, founded *Enbata* and later fragmented over the nationalism/socialism dispute. Abeberry is now a leader of Euskal Batasuna, close to Herri Batasuna. Haran leads the PNV in the North. The third generation of Basque militants grew out of the ferment in the aftermath of the events of May–June 1968, the hunger strikes, and the influence of ETA on the French Basque milieu. It also included the first generation of Iparretarrak militants, such as Philippe Bidart and Xan Coscarat. Today a fourth generation of Basque militants has emerged, with a new generation of IK militants and also an alternative and confrontational tendency reflected in the rise of Patxa and *Oldartzen*. The conflicts which divide them are at the same time about goals, tactics, generations, and personalities. Their inability to transcend these differences and find common cause remains one of the major weaknesses of the Basque movement in France. Theirs is the legacy and tragedy of Goyheneche's "tribal struggle." Government analyses prepared for Iparretarrak's appellate trials acknowledged the potential force of Basque nationalism in France, but pointed to this fragmentation as a major weakness in the present movement.

A major question for the Basque movement in 1993 concerns the potential of violence by ETA and Iparretarrak, both now in disarray. The rise of a hard-line leadership of ETA, and its refusal to compromise or abandon the armed struggle, exposed ETA to growing criticism by both the French and Spanish governments, as well as across the Basque political spectrum. In the case of Iparretarrak, the organization effectively decided after 1986 to pursue two separate strategies of political influence. One, associated with Bidart, Coscarat, and their followers, continued to support the use of violence as a tool to force government negotiations on an agenda IK would define. At the same time, moderate leaders of the movement, including Richard Irazusta and Alain Iriart, created EMA in an effort to pursue a moderate and open electoral strategy, harvesting the votes of Basques politicized by the violence but unwilling to identify directly with it. It is an irony of Basque politics today that EMA's willingness to work with EB and EA has opened it to criticism by the younger generation of Basque militants in Patxa and *Oldartzen* for being leadership- and credibility-oriented. EMA, at the same time, is thus stigmatized by the Young Turks as stodgy and legitimist and by the French state as being the thinly disguised public face of Iparretarrak.

The greatest dilemma which EMA/IK faces today is harnessing the use of violence in order to achieve realistic and attainable political goals. The arrest of Artapalo in 1992 has raised the question of whether ETA's new leader will now be willing to enter into negotiations with the Spanish government and end their struggle. Growing voices within ETA's own prisoner community are calling for genuine dialogue to begin. The danger for ETA and IK—as for other such movements—is that violence takes on a logic and momentum of its own and becomes not a tool of political action but an end in itself, in a familiar descent into nihilistic self-gratification or despair. For EMA leader Richard Irazusta, the real question concerns whether the use of violence can be controlled and whether it can be stopped when pragmatism demands it. For Martha Crenshaw of Wesleyan University, one of the most important questions in the study of terrorism is not why it begins, but how it ends.[45] Crenshaw considers the concept of "defeat" for the terrorists and "victory" for the state too simple to explain the ambiguity of many such situations. In some cases, the very rise of terrorist violence may produce its own decline, by stimulating reaction by the state and/or ultimate disapproval by the public. In other cases, the decline in the climate of legitimacy for such violence may lead some members to rethink their tactics. As Crenshaw describes it:

> As the external legitimacy of violent opposition declines, some members of the organization recognize the signs of failure. Their disillusionment may be moral as well as practical, as terrorism appears both ineffective and unjustified. . . . External pressure and internal dissent grow until it is impossible to sustain terrorism. The organization, now weakened, is destroyed through government arrests, disintegrates through defections, or abandons terrorism in order to preserve its cohesion and identity.[46]

In a rational model, the use of terrorism will continue if it is rewarded, whether by state action or by public support. But there is the danger, according to Crenshaw, that terrorist organizations will "develop a momentum that is independent of environmental goals and constraints. The organization exists to maintain itself more than to accomplish its ostensible purposes."[47] This was the fear within Basque moderate circles that the practitioners of violence were "talking only to themselves." It also explained the growing criticism in the South for Artapalo's hard-line position on negotiations with the Spanish government before his arrest. In 1993 the concerted action of the French and Spanish state has severely limited ETA's northern sanctuary. Indeed, the nature of its post-Artapalo leadership and doctrine remains unclear. Today there is an undeniable opportunity to arrive at a negotiated settlement that will end the armed struggle in Spain and permit political reconciliation there. The question for both ETA and the Spanish government after Artapalo's arrest is whether the negotiating position of either side will move beyond the current "I win, you lose" strategy to one of "I win, you win," which may be the only effective way to end the violence without either side losing face disproportionately. Documents seized at the time of Artapalo's capture suggest that ETA's own leadership recognized that attacks on the 1992 Olympic Games would be self-defeating and a public relations disaster. Yet the Spanish government has chosen to interpret the lack of violence as a sign of weakness on ETA's part, rather than political maturity.

Much of the internal dialogue on violence within the French Basque movement has been a dispute over first principles. For moderate Basque nationalists, the rise of Basque violence in France has been a tragic dead end, destroying the sanctuary of ETA in the North and hardening the attitude of the French government toward even the most moderate linguistic and cultural goals. For Iparretarrak, however, there was a feeling based on the Corsican model that only violence can force true institutional reform by the government. IK's hard-line faction believed that IK's weak and amateurish violence after Philippe Bidart's arrest has not been taken seriously enough to force the state's attention. This in turn becomes the self-fulfilling justification for continuing the struggle. The second justification for the continued use of violence by IK's new militants was the symbol of its prisoners, including Bidart. In November 1992 the government sentenced Bidart to life in prison. His partners received sentences ranging from acquittal to fifteen years in prison. The government demonstrated once more its determination to punish even symbolic violence threatening to the unity of the state. Since the arrest of Bidart and his circle, IK's violence has remained confined to bombings. However, as proof of Iparretarrak's ability to recruit new militants, the number of those bombings continued to grow and in late 1992 included bombings in Paris for the first time.

For the moderate camp, there is the belief that electoral scores for Basque nationalists approaching 10 percent of the electorate will accomplish what violence could not—force the government to take Basque demands seriously and try to preempt the radical camp through a politics of accommodation.[48] Even those Basque nationalists most opposed to violence admit that it has been a factor in the rising Basque political consciousness. For the very rise of Basque moderate parties has been a direct response to the challenge of radical violence. Today both the Basque movement and the government itself have put forth agendas which include institutional change, economic development, and plans for Basque cultural and linguistic preservation.

The resurgence of nationalism in 1993 has redrawn the map of Europe. Events in the former Soviet Union and Yugoslavia demonstrate the continued force of national self-determination and the desire for independence. The rise of nationalism elsewhere in the world has served to undercut traditional criticism of Basque nationalism as an arcane and retrograde phenomenon, a timeworn vestige of romanticism in the modern age. Today the force of nationalism is far from spent and is likely to play a greater role in a European Community now poised to enlarge its membership in Eastern Europe.[49] Indeed, French hesitancy in Yugoslavia was due to fear of creating a precedent for other minorities elsewhere as Europe redefines itself.

If the events of recent years have taught us anything, it is the elasticity of ethnic identity and the sheer staying force of nationalism. Events in the Soviet Union and Yugoslavia underscore once more the futility of government policy based on the forced eradication of nationalist sentiments. The challenge of public policy is to accept peaceful accommodation where assimilation appears unlikely. For as Edmund Burke wrote two hundred years ago, "The use of force is but temporary. It may subdue for a moment; but it does not remove the necessity of subduing again. And a nation is not to be governed which is perpetually to be conquered."[50] As Iparretarrak militant Henri Pérez declared at his trial in Paris in early 1991, "There is not a Basque problem in France but a French problem in the Pays Basque. . . . The struggle of the Pays Basque will endure as long as there are Basques."[51]

Notes

ACKNOWLEDGMENTS

1. Frank Kermode, *The Uses of Error*.

INTRODUCTION

1. See Rodney Gallop, "The Basques: The Oldest People in Europe," *Discovery* (October 1939): 529.

2. On the Roman effort to conquer the Basques, see J. Augustin Chaho, *Voyage en Navarre pendant l'insurrection des Basques, 1830–1835*. Chaho summarizes mention of the Basques in the histories of Florus, Dion, Orose, and Pliny.

3. See W. Boissel, "La légende des douze pairs dans la Chanson de Roland," *Cahiers du Centre Basque et Gascon d'Etudes Régionales*, p. 17; and J. Vodoz, *Roland, Un symbole*.

4. Victor Hugo, *Les Pyrénées*, pp. 65–66.

5. Ibid.

6. Elisée Réclus, "Les Basques: Un peuple qui s'en va," *La Revue des Deux Mondes* 63 (1867): 315.

7. Morton H. Levine, Victoria Von Hagen, Jean-Claude Quilici, and Denise Salmon, "Anthropology of a Basque Village: A New Hemotypological study," *Cahiers d'Anthropologie et d'Ecologie Humaine* 2, nos. 3–4 (174): 169.

8. See also J. Moulinier and A. E. Mourant, "The Rh Factor in Southwestern France: An Examination of the Basque and Bearnaise Population," *C. R. Soc. Biol.* 143 (1949): 393–395; J. N. Marshall Chambers, Elizabeth W. Ikin, and A. E. Mourant, "The ABO, MN, and Rh Blood Groups of the Basque People," *American Journal of Physical Anthropology* 7 (1949): 529–544; and A. E. Mourant, "The Blood Groups of the Basques," *Nature* 4067 (October 11, 1947): 505–506.

9. Mourant, "The Blood Groups of the Basques," p. 505.

10. See Emmanuel Le Roy Ladurie, "Les Basques de baleine à sardine," *Le Figaro*, August 16, 1991; and Alain Echegut and Jean-Jacques Kourliandsky, "L'insoluble question basque," *Témoignage Chrétien* (March 4–10, 1985): 10.

11. Rodney Gallop, *A Book of the Basques*, p. 85.

12. Chambers, Ikin, and Mourant, "The ABO, MN and Rh Blood Groups of the Basque People," p. 530.

13. Jean Haritschelhar, "Dialectes et standardisation: Le cas de la langue basque," *Bulletin du Musée Basque* 131 (1991): 2.

14. From a conversation with Chanoine Lafitte in Ustaritz on July 6, 1973.

15. Haritschelhar, "Dialectes et standardisation: Le cas de la langue basque," p. 9.

16. Ibid., p. 1.

17. Réclus, "Les Basques: Un peuple qui s'en va," p. 316.

18. "L'enquête sociolinguistique sur l'état d'Euskara en Iparralde," *Enbata* 1205 (December 12, 1991): 4.

19. Ibid., p. 4. This compares with Le Roy Ladurie's impressionistic and highly suspect estimate of 120,000 Basque speakers in France ("Les Basques de baleine à sardine").

20. Jean Haritschelhar, "Le Basque: Une langue résistante," in Généviève Vermès, *Vingt-cinq communautés linguistiques de la France*, vol. 1, p. 92.

21. *Hemen* (April 1986).

22. Joseph LaPalombara, "Penetration: A Crisis of Government Capacity," in Leonard Binder et al., *Crises and Sequences in Political Development*, pp. 205–232.

CHAPTER ONE. THE FRENCH REVOLUTION
AND THE BASQUES OF FRANCE

An earlier version of this chapter first appeared as "The French Revolution and the Basques of France," in William A. Douglass, ed., *Basque Politics: A Case Study in Ethnic Nationalism*, pp. 51–101.

1. *Cahier des voeux et instructions des Basques-français pour leurs deputés aux Etats-Généraux de 1789*, new ed. (Bayonne: P. Cazals, 1874), p. 28. This is the oldest known copy of the grievance list of the Third Estate of Labourd following the loss of the original in a fire in the Archives Municipales de Bayonne. It is the only known bilingual text printed in French and Basque. The Basque translation of this prefatory quotation reads: "Ungui aurkhiteen dire tratamendu hortaz; eta beldur luquete gabiantça caltecor luqueten." (p. 29).

2. Cited in Michel de Certeau, Dominique Julia, and Jacques Revel, *Une politique de la langue, la révolution française et les patois*, pp. 10–11.

3. Among the best general sources on the French Revolution are Crane Brinton, *A Decade of Revolution, 1789–1799*; Armand Brette, *Recueil des documents relatifs à la convocation des Etats-Généraux de 1789*; Beatrice Fry Hyslop, *A Guide to the General Cahiers of 1789*; R. R. Palmer, *The Age of Democratic Revolution*; and Georges Lefebvre, *The Coming of the French Revolution*. Among excellent recent sources are Simon Schama, *Citizens: A Chronicle of the French Revolution*; and Emmet Kennedy, *A Cultural History of the French Revolution*.

4. *Lettre du roi pour la convocation des Etats-Généraux, à Versailles, le 27 Avril 1789*.

5. See her *Guide to the General Cahiers of 1789* and her *French Nationalism in 1789 according to the General Cahiers*.

6. Among the best sources on the revolutionary period in the Pays Basque Français are Vicomte de Belsunce, *Histoire des Basques;* Albert Darricau, *France et Labourd;* Eugène Goyheneche, "La révolution," chap. 19 in his *Le Pays Basque;* Pierre Haristoy, *Recherches historiques sur le Pays Basque;* Joseph Nogaret, *Petite histoire du Pays Basque français;* Pierre Yturbide, *Cahiers de doléances de Bayonne et du pays de Labourd,* and his *Petite histoire du pays du Labourd.* English-language sources include the detailed treatment by Helen J. Castelli, "Response of the Pays Basque to the Convocation of the Estates-General in Pre-revolutionary France," in William A. Douglass, Richard W. Etulain, and William H. Jacobsen, Jr., eds., *Anglo-American Contributions to Basque Studies: Essays in Honor of Jon Bilbao;* and Rodney Gallop, *A Book of the Basques.*

7. Cited in Michel Lamy, *Histoire secrète du Pays Basque,* p. 264.

8. A number of important sources exist on the *fors;* among them, E. Dravasa, "Les privilèges des Basques du Labourd sous l'ancien régime"; Etienne Ritou, *De la condition des personnes chez les Basques français jusqu'en 1789;* M. G. B. de Lagrèze, *La Navarre française;* Albert Tessier, *La situation de la femme au Pays Basque et à Bayonne avant la révolution;* Marcel Nussy-Saint-Säens, *Contribution à un essai sur la coutume de Soule;* Eugène Goyheneche, *Le Pays Basque;* and Pierre Haristoy, *Recherches historiques sur le Pays Basque,* who reproduces in great detail a list of the *fors* of the three provinces.

9. See Julien Vinson, *Les Basques et le Pays Basque,* pp. 47ff.; Jacques Descheemaeker, "La frontière pyrénéenne de l'océan à l'Aragon"; and Jean Etcheverry-Ainchart, "Une vallée de Navarre au XVIIIème siècle," *Eusko-Jakintza* 5 (1947): 613–643; 6 (1947): 65–95, 209–228.

10. Cited in Belsunce, *Histoire des Basques,* vol. 3, p. 508.

11. Vinson, *Les Basques et le Pays Basque,* p. 47.

12. See Hyslop, *French Nationalism in 1789,* pp. 186–187.

13. "Exposition de l'état des Basques français du Labourt, pour servoir à regler le traitement particulier qu'ils ont droit d'attendre, et de réponse aux reproches que leur font quelques journaux" (November 18, 1789), in Darricau, *France et Labourd,* p. 49.

14. This account follows Haristoy, *Recherches historiques sur le Pays Basque,* pp. 125ff.; and Tessier, *La situation de la femme.*

15. Haristoy, *Recherches historiques sur le Pays Basque,* pp. 170–193.

16. Ibid., pp. 188–189.

17. See Goyheneche, *Le Pays Basque,* pp. 135ff.

18. Ibid., p. 135.

19. Nussy-Saint-Säens, *Contribution à un essai sur la coutume de Soule,* pp. 23–27.

20. See Goyheneche, *Le Pays Basque,* pp. 275–281; Nogaret, *Petite histoire du Pays Basque français,* p. 48; and the neo-Marxist interpretation of Manex Goyhenetche, *Pays Basque nord: Un peuple colonisé,* p. 41. I am particularly indebted to Professor Eugène Goyheneche for access to his archives and his manuscript under the pseudonym Unatea, "Matalas," probably written for the nationalist newspaper *Aintzina,* ca. 1936–1937.

21. See Gallop, *A Book of the Basques*, pp. 12–14.

22. Goyhenetche, *Pays Basque nord*, p. 31.

23. For a list of the *fors* of Labourd between 1318 and 1692, see M. Haramboure, *Inventaire et description faits en l'année 1713 des privilèges, règlements, titres et aventures qui concernent le pays de Labourt.*

24. It is at the siege of Bayonne that the use of the Basque walking stick, or *makila,* was adapted to modern assault warfare and passed into the military vocabulary as the "bayonet."

25. Darricau, *France et Labourd,* pp. 4–5. It is interesting to note that the Bilçar of Labourd (See note 13 above) erroneously gives the date of the union with France as 1451.

26. "Exposition de l'état de Basques français du Labourd," in Darricau, *France et Labourd,* p. 48.

27. Ibid., p. 45.

28. Ibid., p. 61.

29. Lamy, *Histoire secrète du Pays Basque,* p. 267.

30. Hannah Arendt, *On Revolution* (New York: Viking Penguin, 1977).

31. J. Augustin Chaho, *Voyage en Navarre pendant l'insurrection des Basques, 1830–1835,* p. 321.

32. (Chanoine) Michel Etcheverry, "A Ustaritz en 1789," *Eusko-Jakintza* 2 (1948): 115. Etcheverry attributes his source to the minutes of the meeting recorded by M. Dassance, ex-*greffier* and secretary of Labourd.

33. Pierre Yturbide, *Cahiers des doléances de Bayonne et du Pays Basque.*

34. Barthélemy Jean-Baptiste Sanadon, *Essai sur la noblesse des Basques pour servir d'introduction à l'histoire générale de ces peuples.* For a study of the author, see the series of articles by V. Dubarat, "Sanadon, évêque constitutionnel des Basses-Pyrénées," *Revue du Béarn et du Pays Basque* (September 1905): 407–421; (October 1905): 529–547, who argues (p. 409) that Sanadon published this work based "without doubt" on the notes of Chevalier Jacques de Bela.

35. M. Françisque-Michel, *Le Pays Basque.*

36. Pierre Harispé, *Le Pays Basque.*

37. Sanadon, *Essai sur la noblesse des Basques,* pp. 223ff.; and Françisque-Michel, *Le Pays Basque.* For a recent study of the impact of collective nobility on modern Basque identity in Spain, see the excellent treatment by Davydd J. Greenwood, "Continuity in Change: Spanish Basque Ethnicity as a Historical Process," in Milton J. Esman, ed., *Ethnic Conflict in the Western World,* pp. 81–102.

38. "Plan d'un projet de réunion des Basques français et des Basques espagnols en un ou deux départements de l'Empire," in Darricau, *France et Labourd,* p. 79.

39. Belsunce, *Histoire des Basques,* vol. 3, pp. 488–489.

40. Ibid., p. 486.

41. Sanadon, *Essai sur la noblesse des Basques,* p. 242.

42. Ibid., pp. 242–243.

43. Ibid., p. 243.

44. Goyhenetche, *Pays Basque nord*, p. 31.

45. Sanadon, *Essai sur la noblesse des Basques*, p. 244.

46. Ibid., p. 244. See also Nussy-Saint-Säens, *Contribution à un essai sur la coutume en Soule*, pp. 24–25.

47. Nussy-Saint-Säens, *Contribution à un essai sur la coutume en Soule*, p. 26.

48. Joseph Nogaret, "La noblesse au Pays Basque," in *Hommage au Pays Basque*, p. 83.

49. Tessier, *La situation de la femme*, p. 59.

50. Nussy-Saint-Säens, *Contribution à un essai sur la Coutume en Soule*, p. 24.

51. Goyhenetche, *Pays Basque Nord*, p. 17.

52. Castelli, "Response of the Pays Basque," p. 100.

53. Goyheneche, *Le Pays Basque*, p. 139. See also de Lagrèze, *La Navarre française*.

54. Goyheneche, *Le Pays Basque*, p. 139.

55. Tessier, *La situation de la femme*, p. 38.

56. Nogaret, *Petite histoire du Pays Basque français*, p. 49.

57. I follow the description of Etcheverry-Ainchart, "Une vallée de Navarre au XVIIIème siècle," pp. 71–73.

58. Goyheneche, *Le Pays Basque*, p. 146. See also Nogaret, *Petite histoire du Pays Basque français*, p. 49.

59. Goyheneche, *Le Pays Basque*, p. 146.

60. Etcheverry-Ainchart, "Une vallée de Navarre au XVIIIème siècle," p. 73.

61. Ibid.

62. Haristoy, *Recherches historiques sur le Pays Basque*, p. 127; Nogaret, *Petite historie du Pays Basque français*, p. 48; Goyheneche, *Le Pays Basque*, p. 45.

63. Belsunce, *Histoire des Basques*, vol. 3, p. 498. Haristoy, *Recherches Historiques sur le Pays Basque*, pp. 127ff., bases his account on M. Polverel (syndic of the Estates of Navarre), *Mémoire sur le franc-alleu du royaume de Navarre* (ca. October 1789).

64. Cited in Haristoy, *Recherches historiques sur le Pays Basque*, p. 128.

65. Reproduced in Belsunce, *Histoire des Basques*, vol. 3, p. 507.

66. Ibid., p. 507.

67. Cited in Belsunce, *Histoire des Basques*, vol. 3, p. 502.

68. Ibid., p. 508.

69. Ibid., p. 509.

70. Ibid.

71. Ibid., p. 510.

72. Ibid., p. 511.

73. Cited in M. Sacx, ed., *Bayonne et le Pays Basque, Témoins de l'histoire: Antiquité–1918*, pp. 101–102.

74. Tessier, *La situation de la femme*, p. 58.

75. *Cahier des voeux et instructions des Basques-français pour leur députés aux Etats-Généraux*, p. 36.

76. Darricau, *France et Labourd*, p. 6.

77. Goyheneche, *Le Pays Basque*, p. 132.

78. Ibid., p. 120.

79. Nogaret, *Petite histoire du Pays Basque français*, p. 54.

80. Goyheneche, *Le Pays Basque*, p. 127.

81. Nogaret, *Petite histoire du Pays Basque français*, p. 54.

82. Tessier, *La situation de la femme en Pays Basque*, p. 23.

83. From M. Sacx, *Coutumes générales gardées et observées au pays et baillage de Labourt et ressort d'iceluy*, cited in Sacx, *Bayonne et le Pays Basque*, pp. 65–66.

84. "Exposition de l'état des Basques français du Labourt," in Darricau, *France et Labourd*, p. 48.

85. Ibid., pp. 48–49. The Bilçar lists the following royal letters renewing Labourdin *fors:*

Ainsi François premier dès le 29 novembre 1542 . . . par ses lettres patentes; ainsi Henry II par autres lettres patentes du 5 mai 1554; ainsi François II, par celles du 17 novembre 1559; ainsi Charles IX, par celles du 16 juillet 1565, données à Saint-Jean-de-Luz; par celles du 25 mai 1574 et septembre 1568; ainsi Henri III, le 5 janvier 1575 et le 25 janvier 1576; ainsi Henri IV, par lettres patentes du 22 janvier 1594 et du 4 avril 1598; ainsi Louis XIII, le 11 juin 1606 et 15 septembre 1617; ainsi Louis XIV lui-même, les 20 août 1650, 26 octobre 1668 et 9 septembre 1683.

86. Darricau, *France et Labourd*, p. 78.

87. Goyheneche, *Le Pays Basque*, p. 253.

88. Ibid., p. 263.

89. Cited in Darricau, *France et Labourd*, p. 61.

90. See "Une émeute contre la gabelle, à Hasparren," in Sacx, *Bayonne et le Pays Basque*, pp. 98–99.

91. Cited in Goyheneche, *Le Pays Basque*, p. 270.

92. Cited in Louis Madelin, *La révolution*.

93. For the purpose of convocation, and a history of previous Estates General in France, see Hyslop, *A Guide to the General Cahiers of 1789*, pp. 3–11.

94. R. R. Palmer, *The Age of Democratic Revolution*, pp. 475–476.

95. Brinton, *A Decade of Revolution*, pp. 4–6.

96. The data which follow are from Palmer, *The Age of Democratic Revolution*, pp. 439–440.

97. Ibid., p. 459.

98. Ibid., p. 478.

99. Ibid.

100. Brinton, *A Decade of Revolution*, p. 23–24.

101. Hyslop, *French Nationalism in 1789*, pp. 254–285.

102. Ibid., p. 185.

103. Ibid., p. 189.

104. (Chanoine) Michel Etcheverry, "Les Basques et l'unification nationale

sous la révolution," *Bulletin de la Société des Sciences, Lettres et Arts de Bayonne* 11 (January–June 1933): 75–97.

105. M. Haramboure, "Protestation redigée en vertu du pouvoir ci-dessus" (letter reporting the decision of protest made by the Bilçar the previous day, March 7, 1785), March 8, 1785, in Darricau, *France et Labourd*, pp. 38–39.

106. Cited in Darricau, *France et Labourd*, p. 9.

107. Etcheverry, "A Ustaritz en avril 1789," p. 115.

108. This account of the election follows Goyheneche, "La révolution," chap. 14 in *Le Pays Basque*, pp. 371–372.

109. Haristoy, *Recherches historiques sur le Pays Basque*, p. 213.

110. Ibid., pp. 213–215.

111. Sacx, *Bayonne et le Pays Basque* (p. 115), reports that during the legislative session of January 18, 1793, Meillan, Neveu, Laa, and Dhiriart favored imprisonment and then exile.

112. "Plan d'un projet de réunion des Basques français et des Basques espagnols en un ou deux départements de l'empire," in Darricau, *France et Labourd*, pp. 77–86.

113. *Règlement fait par le roi, pour l'éxecution de ses lettres de convocation aux prochains Etats-Généraux, dans le pays de Soule, du 19 fevrier 1789* (ms. no. P-2951), Musée Basque, Bayonne.

114. Cited in Brette, *Recueil des documents*, vol. 4, p. 149.

115. Hyslop, *A Guide to the General Cahiers of 1789*, p. 86. See also her *French Nationalism in 1789*, pp. 12–13ff.

116. Goyheneche, *Le Pays Basque*, p. 374.

117. Ibid.; Castelli, "Response of the Pays Basque," p. 101.

118. Cited in Castelli, "Response of the Pays Basque," p. 101.

119. The data which follow comes from Castelli, "Response of the Pays Basque," p. 100.

120. Ibid.

121. Ibid.

122. Cited in Belsunce, *Histoire des Basques*, vol. 3, p. 504.

123. Goyheneche, *Le Pays Basque*, p. 374.

124. Cited in Belsunce, *Histoire des Basques*, vol. 3, p. 507.

125. Cited in Goyheneche, *Le Pays Basque*, p. 374.

126. Cited in Belsunce, *Histoire des Basques*, vol. 3, pp. 507ff.

127. Cited in Goyheneche, *Le Pays Basque*, p. 374.

128. Cited in Hyslop, *French Nationalism in 1789*, p. 190.

129. Cited in Belsunce, *Histoire de Basques*, vol. 3, p. 505.

130. Haristoy, *Recherches historiques sur le Pays Basque*, chap. 36, pp. 206–209.

131. Castelli, "Response of the Pays Basque," p. 96.

132. For the details surrounding the opening of the Estates General, see Brinton, *A Decade of Revolution*, chap. 1; and Palmer, *The Age of Democratic Revolution*, pp. 48off.

133. Ferdinand Barbé, "La crise alimentaire à Bayonne pendant la révolution, 1789–1796," *Bulletin de la Société des Sciences, Lettres et Arts de Bayonne* 41 (April–June 1942): 7. It is interesting to note Barbé's implied comparisons to economic problems in Bayonne in wartime 1942.

134. The concept is that of C. Melnik and Nathan Leites, *The House without Windows*.

135. Cited in Darricau, *France et Labourd*, p. 11.

136. Ibid.

137. See the excellent discussion by Georges Lefebvre, "The Problem of the Privileges," chap. 11 in his *The Coming of the French Revolution*, pp. 151–168.

138. Ibid., p. 157.

139. Cited in ibid.

140. Georges Lefebvre, *La révolution française*, pp. 140–141. Palmer, in *The Age of Democratic Revolution* (p. 485), argues that the radicalism of the Breton delegates owed to the fact that the delegates of the Breton Third Estates were "advanced revolutionaries" and that no delegation of Breton nobles attended the Estates General at all. Thus, according to Palmer, the irony was that it was the deputies from Brittany, "in many ways the most privileged province," that took the lead in the abolition of provincial liberties which occurred on the evening of August 4.

141. Lefebvre, *The Coming of the French Revolution*, p. 158.

142. See Madelin, *La révolution*, chap. 4.

143. Cited in Brinton, *A Decade of Revolution*, p. 37.

144. Ibid.

145. Hyslop, *A Guide to the General Cahiers of 1789*, p. 257.

146. Bertrand Barère de Vieuzac, *Mémoires*, vol. 1, pp. 269–270.

147. Among the detailed daily accounts of the parliamentary debates of the early assembly including the night of August 4 are M. J. Madival and M. E. Laurent, eds., *Archives parlementaires de 1787 à 1860* (the account of August 4, 1789 is in vol. 8, pp. 343–350); Bertrand Barère de Vieuzac, *Le point du jour ou ce qui s'est passé la veille à l'Assemblée Nationale*, vol. 3, pp. 25–36; and M. Le Hodey de Saultchevreuil, *Journal des Etats-Généraux*, vol. 3, pp. 365–372.

148. Barère de Vieuzac, *Le point du jour*, vol. 3, p. 34.

149. Cited in Lefebvre, *The Coming of the French Revolution*, p. 166.

150. Cited in Etcheverry, "Les Basques et l'unification nationale sous la révolution," pp. 82–83; Darricau, *France et Labourd*, p. 16.

151. See Philippe Sagnac and P. Caron, *Les Comités des Droits Féodaux et de Législation et l'abolition du régime seigneurial, 1789–1793*.

152. Lefebvre, *La révolution française*, p. 141.

153. See the account in Madival and Laurent, *Archives parlementaires de 1787 à 1860*, vol. 8 (August 4, 1789), p. 348.

154. Cited in Etcheverry, "Les Basques et l'unification nationale sous la révolution," p. 83.

155. "Moyens de la protestation contre l'abolition des privilèges de leur province arrêtée et deliberée par les Basques français du païs de Labourt dans leur

assemblée générale du premier septembre 1789," in Darricau, *France et Labourd*, pp. 39–44.

156. Cited in full in Darricau, *France et Labourd*, pp. 16–17. Darricau reproduces the text of the letter found in the possession of the Garat family.

157. Cited in Goyheneche, *Le Pays Basque*, p. 378.

158. "Exposition de l'état des Basques français du Labourt," in Darricau, *France et Labourd*, p. 56.

159. "18 Novembre 1789—Extract du registre de *Bilçar* contenant les délibérations générales du païs de Labourt," reproduced in Darricau, *France et Labourd*, pp. 44–45.

160. See Etcheverry, "Les Basques et l'unification nationale sous la révolution," pp. 83–85; Goyheneche, *Le Pays Basque*, pp. 378–380; and Castelli, "Response of the Pays Basque," pp. 97–98.

161. Cited in Castelli, "Response of the Pays Basque," pp. 97–98.

162. See the accounts of Le Hodey de Saultchevreuil, *Journal des Etats-Généraux*, vol. 4, pp. 498–505; Barère de Vieuzac, *Le point du jour*, vol. 3, pp. 300–307; and Madival and Laurent, *Archives parlementaires*, vol. 9 (October 12, 1789), pp. 409–411.

163. Cited in Madival and Laurent, *Archives parlementaires*, vol. 9 (October 12, 1789), p. 409.

164. Ibid., p. 410.

165. I have combined the accounts of Madival and Laurent (p. 411) and Barère de Vieuzac, *Le point de jour*, p. 306.

166. M. Polverel, *Tableau de la constitution du royaume de Navarre et de ses rapports avec la France, imprimé par ordre des Etats Généraux du royaume de Navarre*.

167. Cited in Etcheverry, "Les Basques et l'unification nationale sous la révolution," p. 85.

168. A. Mazure, *Histoire de Béarn et du Pays Basque*, p. 362.

169. Cited in Alfred Cobban, "Local Government during the French Revolution," *English Historical Review* 58, no. 229 (January 1943): 18.

170. "Rapport sur la nécessité et les moyens d'anéantir les patois et d'universaliser l'usage de la langue française" (ca. May 1784), in A. Gazier, *Lettres à Gregoire*, p. 293.

171. Ibid.

172. Cited in de Certeau et al., *La révolution française et les patois*, pp. 10–11 (emphasis added).

173. Ibid., pp. 181–185.

174. Cited in Gazier, *Lettres à Gregoire*, p. 5.

175. Cited in Madival and Laurent, *Archives parlementaires*, vol. 11 (January 12, 1790), pp. 170–171.

176. Ibid., p. 171.

177. Ibid., p. 188. Further enabling legislation relative to the creation of the Department of the Basses-Pyrénées passed in the National Assembly on February 8, February 26, and March 4, 1790. See *Collection générale des décrets rendus par*

l'Assemblée Nationale, pp. 12–16, 93–94, 151. The *arrondissement* of Bayonne which administers the Pays Basque was created 28 pluviôse An VIII (February 17, 1800) with subprefectures in Bayonne and Mauléon. The Department of the Basses-Pyrénées became the Department of the Pyrénées-Atlantiques with the advent of the French Fifth Republic in 1958.

178. See Albert Darricau, *Scènes de la terreur à Bayonne et aux environs, 1793–1794.* For the religious impact of the Terror in the Pays Basque, see Roland Moreau, *La religion des Basques: Esquisse historique,* especially chap. 17, "La tourmente révolutionnaire."

179. Cited in ibid., p. 206.

180. See James E. Jacob, "Ethnic Identity and the Crisis of Separation of Church and State: The Case of the Basques of France, 1870–1914," *Journal of Church and State* 24, no. 2 (Spring 1982): 302–303; and Pierre Tauzia, "La IIIème République et l'enseignement religieux en langue basque (1890–1905)," *Bulletin de la Société des Sciences, Lettres et Arts de Bayonne* 129 (1973).

181. Cited in Gazier, *Lettres à Grégoire,* p. 296.

182. *Rapport et projet de décret, presentés au nom du Comité de Salut Public à la Convention Nationale sur les Idiomes Etrangers et sur l'Enseignement de la Langue Française,* par B. Barère, 8 pluviôse, An II (January 28, 1794).

183. Moreau, *La religion des Basques,* p. 198.

184. Goyheneche, *Le Pays Basque,* p. 397; and Lamy, *Histoire secrète du Pays Basque,* p. 269.

185. Cited in Darricau, *France et Labourd,* p. 23.

186. Cited in Etcheverry, "Les Basques et l'unification nationale sous la révolution," p. 92.

187. *Recueil des actes du Comité du Salut Public,* cited in Darricau, *France et Labourd,* p. 25.

188. The following account follows Goyheneche, *Le Pays Basque,* pp. 408–410; Philippe Veyrin, *Les Basques,* p. 187; and René Cuzacq, *Le Comité Revolutionnaire de Bayonne, Sa destitution et son histoire,* 1929.

189. Veyrin, *Les Basques,* p. 187.

190. "Lettre de Garat au premier consul" (7 nivôse An II), in Darricau, *France et Labourd,* p. 64.

191. Eugène Goyheneche, *Notre terre basque.*

192. "Exposé succinct d'un projet de réunion de quelques cantons de l'Espagne et de la France dans la vue de rendre plus faciles et la soumission de l'Espagne et la création d'une maxime puissante," letter from Garat to Savary, duc de Rovigo, 1808, in Darricau, *France et Labourd,* pp. 65–72.

193. Ibid., p. 70.

194. See A. Elorza, "Larramendi: Las conferencias inéditas escritas en 1756," *Revista de Occidente* 2 (1971): 350–355.

195. Cited in Goyheneche, *Le Pays Basque,* p. 382.

196. See J. Augustin Chaho, *Voyage en Navarre pendant l'insurrection des Basques,*

1830–1835, Philosophie des révélations adressée à M. le Professeur Lerminier, and *Histoire primitive des Euskariens basques.*

197. See the sympathetic study by Gustave Lambert, *Etude sur Augustin Chaho.* Though Lambert did not know Chaho personally, his study appeared only three years after Chaho's death in 1858. As an example of Chaho's thought, see J.-B. Orpustan, "Une tentative ambitieuse d'Augustin Chaho: La philosophie des religions comparées (1848)," *Bulletin du Musée Basque* 93 (1981): 127–142.

198. See Jaime del Burgo, *Bibliografía de la guerras carlistas y de las luchas políticas del siglo XIX,* vol. 5, supplemento A–Z, p. 501.

CHAPTER TWO. CLERICALISM, CULTURAL PRESERVATION, AND THE
TENSIONS OF CHURCH AND STATE IN THE PAYS BASQUE, 1870–1906

1. *La Semaine de Bayonne,* May 21, 1890.

2. Pierre Lhande, *Autour d'un foyer basque,* p. 143.

3. Eugen Weber, *Peasants into Frenchmen: The Modernization of Rural France, 1870–1914,* 1976.

4. See the religious sociology of (Chanoine) Fernard Boulard and Jean Rémy, *Pratique religieuse et régions culturelles;* and Gabriel Le Bras, *Etudes de sociologie religieuse.*

5. Consider the words of Charles de Gaulle (grand-uncle of General de Gaulle): "Attacked by sheer force in France, the language of the ancient *vascons* defended itself, resisted, and despite all the efforts of the administration the progress of French was nearly null" (Comte de Charency, H. Gaidoz, and Charles de Gaulle, *Pétition pour les langues provinciales au corps législatif de 1870,* p. 24).

6. Beñat Oihartzabal, "L'enquête socioloinguistique sur l'état de l'Euskara en Iparralde," *Enbata* 1205 (December 12, 1991): 4.

7. Pierre Hourmat, "L'enseignement primaire dans les Basses-Pyrénées au temps de la monarchie constitutionnelle," *Bulletin de la Société des Sciences, Lettres et Arts de Bayonne* 128 (1972): 278.

8. Ibid., p. 201. On this period, see also Pierre Bidart, "L'état et l'enseignement primaire en France d'après l'enquête de 1833: Contribution à l'étude des fonctions historiques de l'école au XIXème siècle" (on file at the Musée Basque, Bayonne).

9. Vincent Wright, "The Basses-Pyrénées from 1848 to 1870: A Study in Departmental Politics," vol. 1, pp. 124ff.

10. Elisée Réclus, "Les Basques: Un peuple qui s'en va," *Revue des Deux Mondes* 78 (1867): 334, n.

11. Prince Louis-Lucien Bonaparte, *Carte des sept provinces basques montrant la délimitation actuelle de l'Euscara et sa division en dialectes, sous-dialectes et variétés.*

12. Vincent Wright, "Religion et politique dans les Basses-Pyrénées pendant la Deuxième République et le Second Empire," *Annales du Midi* 81 (1969): 410. See also P. Charritton, *Petite histoire religieuse du Pays Basque;* and Eugène Goyhen-

eche, "Roland Moreau: Histoire de l'âme basque," *Bulletin du Musée Basque* 29, no. 51 (1971), who insisted: "The vitality of the 'Church of France' took refuge in the ethnic minorities, as the maps of Chanoine Boulard prove."

13. Wright, "Religion et politique," p. 410. See also Lhande, *Autour d'un foyer basque*, chap. 5.

14. Rodney Gallop, *A Book of the Basques*, p. 60, says of their resistance to change:

> There is no more conservative race on the face of the earth. . . . It is no use trying to instill ideas of modern progress into the peasants, for they are always ready with one irrefutable answer: —"what is good enough for my father is good enough for me."

15. Marie-France Chauvirey, *La vie quotidienne au Pays Basque sous le Second Empire*, chap. 2.

16. For the nature of traditional Basque inheritance law, see Albert Tessier, *La situation de la femme au Pays Basque avant la révolution*; Louis Etcheverry, "Les coutumes successorales du Pays Basque an XIXème siècle," in *La Tradition au Pays Basque*, pp. 179–190; Eugène Cordier, *De l'organisation de la famille chez les Basques*, esp. chap. 2, "Le droit Basque, coutumes de Soule, de Labourt et de Basse Navarre"; Pierre Lhande, *Le Pays Basque à vol d'oiseau*; and Lhande, *Autour d'un foyer Basque*, part 1.

17. Etcheverry, "Les coutumes successorales," pp. 181–182. This would not legally change until the law of February 8, 1938, permitted the passing of property to one heir, provided the other heirs received dowries.

18. Tessier, *La situation de la femme*, p. 43.

19. Lhande, *Autour d'un foyer basque*, part 1.

20. Cordier, *De l'organisation de la famille*. See also Louis Etcheverry, "La France est-elle une démocratie?"

21. From the preface to Frédéric Le Play, "La famille basque, la femme basque," in *Les Basques*, p. 14.

22. William A. Douglass, "The Famille Souche and Its Interpreters" (Paper delivered at the Annual Meeting of the Western Society for French History, 1992).

23. Louis Etcheverry, "Monographie de la commune de Saint-Jean-le-Vieux," in *Monographie des communes*, pp. 298–303.

24. Louis Etcheverry, "L'émigration dans les Basses-Pyrénées pendant soixante ans," p. 7.

25. A number of works on the Basques in the Americas have emerged under the auspices of the Basque Studies Program of the University of Nevada at Reno, among them, Douglass and Bilbao, *Amerikanuak*.

26. Professor Eugène Goyheneche noted the impact of the Basques in such varied contexts as Chilean military history and the origins of Mexico's former president Luis Echeverría and that Simón Bolívar himself was a Basque, though from the Spanish province of Bizkaia.

27. Pierre Lhande, *L'émigration basque*, pp. 85–90. During fieldwork in the Pays

Basque in 1975, I met one elderly Basque farmer from Basse-Navarre who spoke at length and fondly in English of his experiences as a shepherd in Nevada before World War I and who, by his own admission, spoke little French.

28. Etcheverry, "L'émigration dans les Basses-Pyrénées," p. 3.

29. Etcheverry, "La commune de Saint-Jean-le-Vieux," pp. 294–297.

30. Wright, "The Basses-Pyrénées from 1848 to 1870," vol. 1, p. 63, and the map in vol. 3, p. 15.

31. Etcheverry, "L'émigration dans les Basses-Pyrénées."

32. Wright offers the following religious breakdown for the department during the Second Empire, out of a total population of 436,640: 430,652 Catholics, 4,750 Protestants, 1,197 Jews, and 41 not stated. What Protestant and Jewish populations did exist were almost exclusively in Béarn ("The Basses-Pyrénées from 1848 to 1870," vol. 1, p. 92).

33. See (Chanoine) Fernand Boulard, *Premiers itinéraires en sociologie religieuse;* and Charritton, *Petite histoire religieuse du Pays Basque.*

34. Roland Moreau, *Histoire de l'âme basque,* pp. 665–668.

35. Ibid., pp. 644–648.

36. Ibid., p. 650.

37. Etcheverry, "La commune de Saint-Jean-le-Vieux," p. 336.

38. H. Descamps de Bragelongne, *La vie politique des Basses-Pyrénées,* p. 7.

39. Pierre Bidart, "Le pouvoir politique dans le village basque: Le cas de Saint-Etienne-de-Baigorry."

40. Lhande, *Autour d'un foyer basque,* pp. 179ff. See also Gaetan Bernoville, *Le pays des Basques,* p. 188.

41. Bernoville, *Le pays des Basques,* p. 104.

42. I am grateful to the late Chanoine Lafitte for pointing this out.

43. See M. G. B. de Lagrèze, *Histoire du droit dans les Pyrénées;* Etienne Ritou, *De la condition des personnes chez les Basque français jusqu'en 1789.*

44. Philippe Veyrin, *Les Basques de Labourd, de Soule et de Basse-Navarre: Leur histoire et leurs traditions,* pp. 111ff.

45. Pierre Tauzia, "La IIIème République et l'enseignement religieux en langue basque (1890–1905)," *Bulletin de la Société des Sciences, Lettres et Arts de Bayonne* 129 (1973): 367.

46. Cited in Bidart, "Le pouvoir politique," p. 188.

47. Cited in M. Sacx, "L'enseignement primaire dans une commune Basque —Bidart (1715–1885)," in Pau et Les Basses-Pyrénées, *Bulletin de l'Association Française pour l'Avancement des Sciences,* session of September 1892, p. 147.

48. Cited in Tauzia, "La IIIème République," p. 373.

49. Tauzia, "La IIIème République, p. 367.

50. René Cuzacq claimed of the elections in the Pays Basque between 1898 and 1914 that "it is the religious and political question which became essential" (*Les élections législatives à Bayonne et au Pays Basque de 1898 à 1914: Radicalisme bayonnais et catholicisme basque,* p. 79). Speaking of an urban-rural electoral split which underscored the persistent conservatism of the countryside, he continued:

These [rural areas] remained shaped by Catholicism and by religion, even in social life, in the image of the old France. In the Pays Basque the clergy kept an influence of this order. . . . Archaism and survivance without any doubt, as is the rule in the Pays Basque; but something else as well; profound agreement of the Basque [*euskarien*] temperament with this political and religious psychology . . . the primordial importance of Catholic life and beliefs.

Cf. Wright, "Religion et politique," pp. 431–435, who argues that while the role of the clergy in most of rural France should not be exaggerated, as even the most religious among them often voted differently, it was true of the Pays Basque that the population voted on the right in defense of the clergy.

51. Bidart, "Le pouvoir politique," p. 187. Cuzacq argues in this same vein that "the force of reaction remained powerful *en terre euskarienne*, classical land of tradition and of the persistent social domination of the Catholic clergy" (*Les élections législatives*, p. 101).

52. The prefect of the Basses-Pyrénées, M. Deffés, wrote to the minister of religion on January 13, 1891:

Any measure which would affect the [clergy] who use the Basque language—and they all use it—would produce the most angering effect on the opinion, not only of our adversaries, but also of our friends. In these conditions, is it possible, is it prudent to act harshly? I do not think so. It would be necessary to strike the whole clergy, and a similar measure would be without efficacy; it would have as an inevitable consequence the resistance of the clergy, encouraged and supported by the faithful; it would raise deep troubles, and that without appreciable results for the government.

Five years later, on the eve of elections in 1896, he advocated putting off such measures in order to avoid an electoral backlash (letter to the minister of religion, E. Combes, April 22, 1896).

53. Letter to minister of religion, May 23, 1901, cited in Tauzia, "La IIIème République," p. 374. Suggesting the advisability of proceeding by successive steps, Francière continues:

There is no doubt . . . at the present time that priests who would preach in French would not be understood by the faithful. Moreover, the abruptly imposed abandonment of certain traditions would stir up a real discontentment of which I have warned of the danger. To the contrary, it seems to me wiser and surer to lead to a new state of affairs by successive stages the fraction of the population of this department which is still backward or hesitant.

54. Consider the disproportionate rightist vote in several coastal and interior towns in that election (from Cuzacq, *Les élections législatives*, p. 26):

Town	Registered	Voting	Rightist-Catholic Candidates	Socialists
Bayonne 2ᵉ (Labourd)	12,477	8,716	8,686	30
Saint-Jean de Luz	3,264	2,385	2,212	17
Hasparren	2,503	2,066	2,060	0
Espelette	1,919	1,505	1,466	5
Bidache	2,660	1,724	1,716	5

55. *La Semaine,* January 14, 1903.

56. It is interesting to note that the same logic, the use of Spanish to teach English, has been institutionalized in American programs of bilingual education in dealing with children of Hispanic origins.

57. Tauzia argued that the ultimate intent of the government was not the suppression of Basque (however desirable from the standpoint of nation-building) but rather the limitation on the influence and authority of the local clergy ("La IIIème République," pp. 383–384).

58. Some priests, while ceasing to teach the catechism in Basque themselves, recruited local women volunteers to continue it in their stead. Another went so far as to suggest that students would be better off learning the catechism in English (cited in Tauzia, "La IIIème République," p. 381).

59. Report of prefect Francière, October 6, 1904, cited in Tauzia, "La IIIème République," p. 381.

60. Cuzacq, *Les élections législatives,* pp. 103–105.

61. Goyheneche, "Roland Moreau," pp. 50–51.

62. Etcheverry, "La France est-elle une démocratie?" p. 16.

63. Pierre Lafitte, "Jean Hiriart-Urruty et les débuts du journalisme en langue basque," *Gure Herria* 6 (1971): 335.

64. Lafitte (ibid., pp. 327–335) offers the following figures for subscriptions to *Eskualduna,* from its founding on March 15, 1887: 1888, 850; 1889, 950; 1890, 1,200; 1891, 1,300; Jan. 1904, 1,700; Dec. 1904, 5,000; 1907 (after the separation), 7,000.

65. Tauzia relates, "Several copies of *Eskualduna,* each week, constitutes the only reading [matter] of Basque village communities. The priests note that the peasants don't have the time to read a daily and that they only buy a paper Sunday or market day" ("La presse dans les Basses-Pyrénées d'après l'enquête diocesaine de 1909," *Bulletin de la Société des Sciences, Lettres et Arts de Bayonne* 130 [1974]: 198). Cuzacq also says, "In the Pays Basque, the Catholic *Eskualduna* became the organ of the now rallied conservatives" (*Les élections législatives,* p. 128).

66. Cuzacq, *Les élections législatives,* pp. 76–77. See also Patrick Brunot, "La droite traditionnaliste dans les Basses-Pyrénées de 1900 à 1950." Ybarnégaray would remain deputy until the end of the Third Republic and, mirroring the later cultural emphasis of *Eskualduna,* would become one of the most rabid critics of

Pierre Lafitte's *Aintzina*, whose calls to political action pale in comparison with *Eskualduna* before the turn of the century.

67. One particularly good source on this period in France is Jean-Marie Mayeur, *La séparation de l'église et l'état*.

68. See the discussion of Pierre Tauzia, "Les inventaires de 1906 dans les Basses-Pyrénées," *Bulletin de la Société des Sciences, Lettres et Arts de Bayonne* 125 (1971), in particular the map on pp. 16–17. It is interesting to note further that Mayeur's map showing areas of particularly grave incidents during the inventories indicates that they occurred nearly exclusively in France's ethnic areas, including Brittany, Alsace, the Pays Basque, and the Occitan interior (see map following p. 198).

69. Cuzacq, *Les élections législatives*, p. 58.

70. One, in particular, who holds this view is Manex Goyenetche, secretary of IKAS, a cooperative movement of private maternal schools dedicated to the teaching of the Basque language to Basque children (from an interview in Bayonne on November 20, 1975).

71. Weber, *Peasants into Frenchmen*, pp. 78–79.

72. According to Jean Duboscq, of Ustaritz, that town lost eighty-five men during World War I and only ten in World War II (from an interview in Ustaritz, on December 2, 1975). The Pays Basque, of course, was not alone. See the impact of the war on the peasantry of Brittany in Olier Mordrel, *Breiz Atao: Histoire et actualité du nationalisme breton*, pp. 65–67.

73. Typical of this view is Jean Duboscq, young (and nominal) director of *Aintzina* in the 1920s.

74. Pierre Bidart, "Une jeunesse en position de rupture: Analyse des effets de l'urbanisation sur la jeunesse scolaire d'un village" (part 2), *Gure Herria* 5 (1974): 293–316.

75. By way of example, one rural Basque who farmed on five hectares (twelve acres) said to me: "What do you want? Our life was hard. This was all we had, because of our limited knowledge of French. I wanted things to be different for my children, and my grandchildren, and that's why I won't speak to them in Basque. French, that's the future."

76. Weber, *Peasants into Frenchmen*, p. 79.

77. Cited in ibid., p. 86.

78. Tessier, *La situation de la femme*, p. 145.

79. Réclus, "Les Basques: Un peuple qui s'en va."

80. See Karl Marx and Frederick Engels, "The Magyar Struggle," *Neue Rheinische Zeitung* 194 (January 13, 1849); reprinted in *Collected Works*, vol. 8, esp. pp. 234–238. For more systematic analyses of Marxism and nationalism, see Hans Mommsen and Albrecht Martiny, "Nationalism, Nationalities Question," in *Marxism, Communism and Western Society*, vol. 6, pp. 20–58; Neil Martin, "Marxism, Nationalism and Russia," *Journal of the History of Ideas* 29 (April–June 1968): esp. 231–241; and Georges Haupt, Michael Lowy, and Claudie Weill, *Les marxistes et la question nationale, 1848–1914*.

81. Marx and Engels, "The Magyar Struggle," p. 238.

82. See, in particular, the extremely rich and detailed contribution of Jean-Claude Larronde, "Le nationalisme basque: Son origine et son idéologie dans l'oeuvre de Sabino de Arana-Goiri," p. 357. Other sources include Milton Manuel da Silva, "The Basque Nationalist Movement: A Case Study in Modernization and Ethnic Conflict," esp. chap. 3, "The Emergence of Spanish Basque Nationalism"; and Stanley Payne, *Basque Nationalism.*

83. In Sabino Arana Goiri, *Obras completas.* For a discussion of the extension of his thought from Bizkaia to the four Basque provinces of Spain, see Larronde, "Le nationalisme basque," chap. 2, "Les implications de la doctrine nationaliste d'Arana-Goiri," pp. 148ff.

84. Da Silva, "The Basque Nationalist Movement," p. 69. One indicator of the spread of Basque nationalism used by Larronde is the number of localities with sections of the party of more than ten members. The province of Gipuzkoa went from five to thirty-five in 1904–1908 (Larronde, "Le nationalisme basque," fig. 7, pp. 315–316).

85. See Pierre Lafitte, *Sabin Arana Goiri: Sa vie, son oeuvre, son influence,* p. 10.

86. Arana wrote in a telegram addressed to President Theodore Roosevelt (for which he was jailed for a time) congratulating him on the independence of Cuba (cited in Da Silva, "The Basque Nationalist Movement," pp. 75–76):

The Basque Nationalist Party congratulates the noble confederation over which you preside for having granted independence to Cuba, which had previously been liberated from slavery. This magnanimous and just example given by your powerful states is unknown and unheard of in the history of European powers, particularly Latin powers. If Europe followed this example, the Basque nation, the oldest people of Europe who have enjoyed centuries of liberty, and whose constitution has been praised in the United States, would also be free.

87. "Fuerismo es separatismo," *Bizkaitarra* 8 (April 22, 1894), cited in Larronde, "Le nationalisme basque," p. 151.

88. "Palabas de Jean Claude Larronde," *Alderi* 260 (February 1971): 28.

89. See his "Españoles y franceses!" excerpted from *Bizkaitarra,* in *Obras completas,* pp. 358–359.

90. "La libertad en Francia," *La Patria* 2, no. 40 (July 27, 1902), cited in *Obras completas,* p. 2203.

91. Larronde, "Le nationalisme basque," p. 87.

92. Eugène Goyheneche, "J. Cl. Larronde: Le nationalisme basque, son origine et son idéologie dans l'oeuvre de Sabino Arana Goiri," *Bulletin du Musée Basque* 58 (4, 1972), 217.

93. Another source on these periodicals is Ceferino de Jemein, *Biografía de Arana-Goiri tar Sabin e historia gráfica del nacionalismo vasco.*

94. I am grateful to Jean-Claude Larronde for this information (from an inter-

view in Bayonne on November 22, 1975). See also his "Le nationalisme basque," pp. 189–196.

95. We find the following:

#4	May 23, 1897	"J. de A."	St.-Jean-de-Luz
#6	June 6, 1897	"M. G."	"
#7	June 13, 1897	"J. de U."	"
#8	June 20, 1897	"M. de M."	"
#11	July 11, 1897	"Mr. S."	"

Again, because of the construction "de" in four of these names, which is uncommon among French Basques, it is reasonable to assume that these subscribers were probably of Spanish Basque origin. Engracio de Aranzadi y Etxeberis ("Kizktza"), *Ereintza, Siembra de nacionalismo vasco, 1894–1912,* pp. 50–57, cites two subscribers each in this period in Germany and the Philippines.

96. From the November 22, 1975 interview with J. C. Larronde.

97. I am grateful to the Chanoine Lafitte for pointing this out during an interview in Ustaritz on October 29, 1975.

CHAPTER THREE. THE "RED" FISH IN THE BAPTISMAL FONT:
CLERICALISM AND NATIONALISM AMONG THE
BASQUES OF FRANCE, 1920–1945

1. "Avant-propos," in Pierre Lafitte ("JEL"), *Eskual-herriaren alde (Pour le Pays Basque): Court commentaire du programme Eskualerriste à l'usage des militants.*

2. Kapito Harri, "Pas de programme politique?" *Aintzina* 1, no. 4 (January 1935): 1.

3. I am grateful to Chanoine Pierre Lafitte for sharing this with me in an interview in Ustaritz on September 29, 1975. "Poisson rouge" (literally, red fish) is French for "goldfish," but the word play is on "red" for communism.

4. See Eugen Weber, *Peasants into Frenchmen: The Modernization of Rural France, 1870–1914;* and Theodore Zeldin, *France, 1848–1945,* vols. 1 and 2.

5. René Cuzacq, *Les élections législatives à Bayonne at au Pays Basque, 1919–1939, l'entre deux guerres.*

6. Bernard Ménou, "Jean Ybarnégaray."

7. See Eugène Goyheneche, "La vie politique et l'économie au Pays Basque Nord," chap. 21 in his *Le Pays Basque.*

8. Zeldin, *France, 1848–1945,* vol. 2, p. 995.

9. Ibid.

10. Ibid., p. 996.

11. Ménou, "Jean Ybarnégaray," p. 14.

12. *Bulletin de L'Association des Anciens Elèves de Larressore, Belloc et Ustaritz, 1930–31.*

13. See J.-B. Orpustan, "Les écrits littéraires basques de Pierre Lafitte," *Bulletin du Musée Basque* 113 and 114 (1986): 163–176.

14. The account which follows is based on an interview with Chanoine Pierre Lafitte in Ustaritz on July 6, 1973.

15. This follows the detailed account of Roland Moreau, "Batailles de jadis au Pays Basque: Le Sillon, le Modernisme, l'Intégrisme, l'Action Française," parts 1 and 2, *Gure Herria* 2 (1972): 65–82; 3 (1972): 182–190.

16. I follow the account of Sillon and Marc Sangnier in the *Encyclopédie Grand Larousse* (Paris: Librairie Larousse, 1960), vol. 9, pp. 579 and 831.

17. Moreau, "Batailles de jadis au Pays Basque," pp. 65–68.

18. Ibid., p. 68.

19. Etienne Salaberry, "L'alienation basque," part 1, *Gure Herria* 5 (1967): 257.

20. I follow Moreau, "Batailles de jadis au Pays Basque," pp. 183–184.

21. Ibid., p. 72.

22. Cited in ibid., p. 74.

23. See Jean-Paul Malherbe, "Aintzina, ou la création du mouvement Eskuale-rriste en Pays Basque français," *Bulletin du Musée Basque* (1977): 193. See also his doctoral thesis, "Le nationalisme basque en France, 1933–1976."

24. Cited in Malherbe, "Aintzina," pp. 193–194.

25. The same Alexandre Marc would later become a major force in the Mouvement Fédéraliste Européen, whose doctrine of ethnic federalism was greatly advanced by interethnic contacts in Paris during the 1930s.

26. Pierre Lafitte, "Les courants de pensée dans la littérature basque contemporaine," *Bulletin de la Société des Sciences, Lettres et Arts de Bayonne* 119 (1968). I am grateful to Chanoine Lafitte for elaborating on these ideas during an interview in Ustaritz on July 6, 1973.

27. Harri, "Pas de programme politique?" p. 1.

28. From an interview with Marc Légasse at his Fuerte Santa Isabel at Pasajes San Juan, Gipuzkoa, on July 28, 1973. It is historically interesting to note that Légasse fort is the site from which the marquis de Lafayette sailed to fight in the American Revolution.

29. Pierre Lafitte, *Sabino Arana Goiri: Sa vie, son oeuvre, son influence.*

30. Ibid.

31. See the sensitive and detailed treatment of Goyheneche's life and militancy by Jean-Claude Larronde, "Eugène Goyheneche, historien," *Bulletin du Musée Basque* 130 (1980): 165–180, and its associated bibliography of Goyheneche's writings; as well as Larronde's "Eugène Goyheneche, un militant basque dans les années 30," *Revista Internacional de los Estudios Vascos* 39, no. 36/1 (1991): 79–160; and his "Eugène Goyheneche, Un compromiso ilustrado por la historia," *Eusko Ikaskuntza, Revista Internacional de los Estudios Vascos* 37, no. 34/2 (July–December 1989): 385–391.

32. The account of Goyheneche's time in Paris which follows is based on a number of interviews with Professor Goyheneche at his home in Ustaritz be-

tween 1973 and 1987. I am greatly indebted to the late Professor Goyheneche for opening his personal archives to me and for his permission to use the excerpts from his correspondence and unpublished manuscripts on which this account is based.

33. Eugène Goyheneche, "Les Basques à Paris," ms., n.d. (ca. 1933), Archives of Eugène Goyheneche (henceforth AEG).

34. Letter from G. Mendiboure to Eugène Goyheneche, July 28, 1932, AEG.

35. See Malherbe, "Aintzina," p. 192.

36. F. D., "Eskual-Ikasleen Biltzarra," *Aintzina* 1, no. 6 (March 1935): 4.

37. From an interview with Eugène Goyheneche in Ustaritz on June 26, 1973.

38. *Le Courrier de Bayonne*, April 7, 1933.

39. Elisée Réclus, "Les Basques, Un peuple qui s'en va," *Revue des Deux Mondes* 78 (March 15, 1867).

40. Eugène Goyheneche, "Lettre aux étudiants basques," ms. (ca. fall 1933), AEG.

41. Goyheneche, "Les Basques à Paris."

42. Ibid.

43. F. D., "Eskual-Ikasleen Biltzarra," p. 4.

44. Eugène Goyheneche, ms. (ca. 1933), AEG.

45. Pierre Lafitte letter to Eugène Goyheneche, n.d. (ca. 1933), AEG.

46. Eugène Goyheneche, ms., n.d. (ca. 1933), AEG.

47. Eugène Goyheneche, "Statut de l'Eskual Ikasleen Biltzarra (Groupe de Paris)," February 23, 1933, p. 2, AEG.

48. Eugène Goyheneche letter to Abbé Urricarriet, June 16, 1933, AEG (emphasis in the original).

49. Abbé Urricarriet letter to Eugène Goyheneche, n.d. (ca. June 1933), AEG (emphasis in the original). Note the Germanic spelling of "culture."

50. Eugène Goyheneche letter to Abbé Urricarriet, June 19, 1933, AEG (emphasis in the original).

51. Deputy Jean Lissar letter to Eugène Goyheneche on Chambre de Députés letterhead, June 20, 1933, AEG.

52. Eugène Goyheneche letter to Deputy Jean Lissar, June 20, 1933, AEG.

53. Ibid.

54. Ibid.

55. Deputy Jean Lissar letter to Eugène Goyheneche, June 23, 1933, AEG.

56. Deputy Jean Lissar letter to Eugène Goyheneche, July 5, 1933, AEG.

57. Comment made in an interview in Ustaritz on September 25, 1975.

58. Eugène Goyheneche, ms. (ca. 1935), AEG.

59. Michel Diharce letter to Eugène Goyheneche, December 29, 1932, AEG. Diharce was a high school student in Bordeaux before later attending the French military academy, St. Cyr. He died during World War II.

60. I refer to Pierre Lafitte's important handwritten manuscripts of this period "Organisation," and "Réponses" (both ca. 1934), AEG. This latter document was signed by the young militant Pierre Amoçain as "JEL" for, as Lafitte wrote in an

attached note to Goyheneche, "my own [signature] would be a little intemperate."

61. "Programme Eskualerriste," in *Eskual-herriaren alde,* pp. 7–8. Lafitte signed the foreword with the pseudonym JEL for *Jainkoa eta lege zaharrak* (God and the ancient laws), which was the slogan of the movement.

62. See the excellent study by Jean-Claude Larronde, *Le mouvement Eskualherriste (1932–1937),* which won the 1991 José Antonio Agirre prize of the Fundación Sabino Arana for the best unpublished manuscript on Basque nationalism.

63. *Eskual-herriaren alde,* chap. 1, pp. 9–10.

64. Ibid., p. 9.

65. Ibid., p. 13.

66. Pierre Amoçain (in reality Pierre Lafitte), "Réponses," AEG, pp. 3–5.

67. Ibid., p. 4.

68. Ibid., pp. 4–5.

69. This follows Eugène Goyheneche, "Askatasun," ms. (ca. 1933), AEG.

70. "Où en sont les Eskualerristes?" *Aintzina* 1, no. 1 (October 1934): 1.

71. "Rèponses," p. 4.

72. E. Goyheneche, ms., n.d. (ca. 1934), AEG.

73. From an interview in Ustaritz on July 6, 1973.

74. "Réponses," p. 5.

75. Ibid.

76. Ibid.

77. Jacques Mestelan letter to Eugène Goyheneche, November 16, 1933, AEG.

78. Jacques Mestelan letter to Eugène Goyheneche, February 16, 1934, AEG.

79. I am grateful to Gorka Aulestia, author of the excellent *Basque-English Dictionary* (Reno: University of Nevada Press, 1989), for pointing this out.

80. Eugène Goyheneche (destined for *Elgar* in Paris?), n.d. (ca. fall 1934), AEG.

81. From an interview in Ustaritz on December 2, 1975.

82. Jacques Mestelan letter to Eugène Goyheneche, December 13, 1934.

83. "S'organiser," *Aintzina* 1, no. 1 (October 1934): 1.

84. "Le balai, la rue n'est pas propre," *Aintzina* 1, no. 1 (October 1934): 1.

85. Untitled Eskualerriste pamphlet, n.d. (ca. 1934), AEG.

86. Pierre Lafitte ("IKAS"), "Etude et action," *Aintzina* 1, no. 11 (August 1935).

87. "Les jeunes et les vieux," *Aintzina* 1, no. 1 (October 1934): 1.

88. From an interview in Ustaritz on December 5, 1975.

89. "Programme Eskualerriste," in *Eskual-herriaren alde,* point one.

90. Jacques Mestelan ("Jakue"), "Feuilles de crèmes," *Aintzina* 1, no. 6 (March 1935): 4.

91. "Le balai, la rue n'est pas propre," p. 1.

92. Ibid.

93. "Programme Eskualerriste."

94. Ibid.

95. *Aintzina* 1, no. 1 (October 1934): 2.

96. Malherbe, "Aintzina," p. 199.

97. Lamina, "Pour faire aimer le Pays Basque à la jeunesse," *Aintzina* 1, no. 12 (September 1935): 1.

98. *Aintzina* 2, no. 22 (July 1936): 2–3.

99. "Les méfaits de la centralisation," *Aintzina* 1, no. 1 (October 1934): 3.

100. Junior, "Décentralisation et syndicalisme," *Aintzina* 2, no. 21 (June 1936): 1.

101. Manech, "Amères vérités," *Aintzina* 3, no. 25 (October 1936): 4.

102. "Où en sont les Eskualerristes?" p. 1. (October 1934), 1.

103. "IKAS," "Etude et action," p. 1.

104. "Parlons net," *Aintzina* 2, no. 17 (February 1936): 1.

105. Léon Lassalle ("News Politic"), "La justice," *Aintzina* 2, no. 14 (November 1935): 1.

106. Junior, "Décentralisation et syndicalisme," p. 1.

107. Ibid.

108. *Aintzina* 3, no. 32 (May 1937): 4.

109. René Cuzacq, *Les élections législatives*, pp. 61–72.

110. Ménou, "Jean Ybarnégaray."

111. Cuzacq, *Les élections législatives*, p. 72.

112. Léon Lassalle ("News Politic"), "Un mystère," *Aintzina* 1, no. 2 (November 1934): 1.

113. "Elections sénatoriales," *Aintzina* 1, no. 3 (December 1934): 1.

114. Manech, "Procédés socialistes," *Aintzina* 2, no. 15 (December 1935): p. 1.

115. Lafitte, "Parlons net," p. 1.

116. *Aintzina* vol. 1, no. 16 (January 1936): 1.

117. Ménou, "Jean Ybarnégaray," p. 92. For this conservative political culture, see also H. Descamps de Bragelongne, *La vie politique des Basses-Pyrénées*.

118. Cited in Ménou, "Jean Ybarnégaray," p. 137.

119. Cuzacq, *Les élections législatives*, p. 90.

120. Ibid., pp. 88–93.

121. Jean Charles-Brun, *Le régionalisme*. See also Edouard Lizop, "Introduction à la pensée de Charles-Brun," *Politique* 37–40 (1967): 103–116; and Jean Charles-Brun, "De la terre natale à l'humanité fédérale," *Politique* 37–40 (1967): 117–172. Among his other works are *L'Europe fédéraliste: Aspirations et réalités; Le principe fédératif;* and his edition of Pierre Joseph Proudhon's *Du principe fédératif et de la nécessité de reconstituer le parti de la révolution,* with introduction and notes by Jean Charles-Brun. For a related exposition on this theme, see Charles Maurras, *L'idée de la décentralisation.*

122. *Aintzina* 1, no. 11 (August 1935): 3.

123. Among the works emanating from the Mouvement Fédéraliste Européen are Guy Héraud, *L'Europe des ethnies, Peuples et langues d'Europe,* and *Les principes du fédéralisme;* and Yann Fouéré, *L'Europe aux cent drapeaux,* and *La révolution fédéraliste.* Presses d'Europe is the publishing affiliate of the Mouvement Fédéraliste Européen.

124. AEG.

125. "Chez les autres: Lyautey régionaliste," *Aintzina* 1, no. 10 (July 1935): 4.

126. Robert Audic letter to Eugène Goyheneche, March 21, 1934, AEG.

127. Eugène Goyheneche, ms., n.d. (ca. 1934), AEG.

128. Letter from Anton Rubbens, chargé des relations étrangères du KVHV, à Eugène Goyheneche, January 24, 1933.

129. AEG.

130. AEG.

131. Among a vast literature on the Spanish Civil War, the best English-language sources are Hugh Thomas, *The Spanish Civil War*; Herbert R. Southworth, *Guernica! Guernica!: A Study of Journalism, Diplomacy, Propaganda and History*; and Gabriel Jackson, *The Spanish Republic and the Civil War, 1931–1939*.

132. José M. Borrás Llop, *Francia ante la guerra civil española: Burguesía, interés nacional e interés de clase*.

133. Géneviève Marre, *La guerre civile en Pays Basque à travers la presse bayonnaise, 1936–37*, p. 59. See also Robert Goldston, *The Civil War in Spain*, pp. 84–85, who argues that by September most of the population of Irún had fled into France.

134. Cited in Marre, *La guerre civile*, p. 63.

135. *La Gazette*, September 8, 1936, cited in Marre, *La guerre civile*, p. 64.

136. Javier Rubio, *La emigración de la guerra civil de 1936–1939*.

137. See Goyheneche, *Le Pays Basque*, chap. 23, pp. 554–555; and Philippe Oyhamburu, *L'irréductible phénomène basque*.

138. Jakes Lahuntze, "Espérances," *Aintzina* 3, no. 25 (October 1936): 2–3.

139. *Aintzina* 3, no. 22 (July 1936): 4.

140. *Débats parlementaires*, Chambre des Deputés, 2ème Séance, July 31, 1936, p. 2341.

141. Cited in J. Bidergaray, "Un jour viendra . . . Peut-être desirerons-nous demain les indésirables d'aujourd'hui," *Euzko Deya* 73 (September 12, 1937).

142. See Bidegaray, "Un jour viendra." Among latter-day critics of Delzangles's attitude are Goyheneche, *Le Pays Basque*, chap. 23, p. 554, who writes, "A 'Basque' elected official went so far as to denounce the presence of the refugees to Minister Yvon Delbos as harmful to tourism. Two years later other [German] tourists would come"; and Philippe Etcheverry, "Un douanier sur la Bidassoa," *Le Monde*, October 4, 1984, p. 28.

143. See the letter of the Fédération Départementale des Contribuables des Basses-Pyrénées, September 15, 1936, reproduced in Borrás Llop, *Francia ante la guerra civil española*, p. 276.

144. Excerpt from the newspaper of Le Comité Mascuraud, cited in Borrás Llop, *Francia ante la guerra civil española*, p. 283.

145. Ibid., p. 285.

146. Cited in ibid., p. 284.

147. Ibid., p. 283.

148. Marre, *La guerre civile*, p. 251.

149. Cited in Ménou, "Jean Ybarnégaray," p. 103.

150. Ibid., p. 115. This image was evidently a favorite of Ybarnégaray's since he also used it in reference to Pierre Lafitte and again in 1956 when he referred

to his opposing party, the MRP, in the election as "devils in a baptismal font." See Descamps de Bragelongne, *La vie politique,* p. 44.

151. *La Presse* would return to this theme virtually word for word in a subsequent editorial on January 29, 1937.

152. Martine Bessière, *Le bombardement de Guernica dans la presse française.*

153. *Débats parlementaires,* Chambre des Députés, 1ère Séance, December 5, 1936, p. 3346. The latter-day leftist critique of Ybarnégaray's position by Spanish Basque militants is acute. See Beltza, *El nacionalismo vasco en el exilio, 1937–1960,* pp. 11–12.

154. Cited in Borrás Llop, *Francia ante la guerra civil española,* p. 310. See also Etcheverry, "Un douanier sur la Bidassoa," p. 28.

155. Goyheneche, *Le Pays Basque,* p. 554; and Oyhamburu, *L'irréductible phénomène Basque.*

156. Gaetan Bernoville, "La guerre civile en Espagne: Le cas des nationalistes basques," *Etudes, Revue Catholique d'Intérêt Général* (October 5, 1936): 83.

157. Pedro Duhalde, *Le nationalisme basque et la guerre civile en Espagne.*

158. Rapport presenté par les Jeunes Nationalistes Catholiques Basques aux Jeunesses Anti-fascistes à l'Occasion du Congrès tenu à Paris, December 19, 1936.

159. Victor Monserrat, *Le drame d'un peuple incompris: La guerre au Pays Basque.*

160. See the document written by Angel Gondra for the Consejo Nacional Vasco, "La democracia vasca: Apuntes sobre el terna que el Consejo Nacional de Euzkadi pasa a conocimiento de las colonias vascas establecidas en paises libres," in Juan Carlos Jiménez de Aberasturi Corta, ed., *Los vascos en la II Guerra Mundial: El Consejo Nacional Vasco de Londres (1940–1944),* pp. 118–120.

161. Pierre Lafitte letter to Eugène Goyheneche (ca. 1936), AEG.

162. Madeleine de Jaureguiberry, "Jacques Maritain et les Basques," *Gure Herria* 3 (1973): 185.

163. I follow the account of Jaureguiberry, ibid., p. 185.

164. Cited in ibid., p. 351. See also Zeldin, *France, 1848–1945,* p. 1022.

165. An example is Universidad de Valladolid, *Informe sobre la situación de las provincias vascongadas bajo el dominio rojo-separatista.*

166. Cited in Thomas, *The Spanish Civil War,* p. 695.

167. I follow Thomas's account, ibid., esp. pp. 695–699.

168. Cited in ibid., p. 696.

169. François Mauriac, "The Victory of the Basques," *Paris Soir,* January 1939.

170. See Beltza, *El nacionalismo vasco en el exilio.*

171. Paul Sérant, "En France comme en Espagne les Basques restent basques," *Monde et Vie* (February 1968): 32. See also Meic Stephens, *Linguistic Minorities in Western Europe.*

172. Autonomous Government of Euzkadi, *The Basque Country and European Peace: An Analysis of the German Domination of Euzkadi.*

173. Consejo Nacional Vasco, "Límites territoriales de Euzkadi (31 julio 1940)," in Jiménez de Aberasturi Corta, *Los vascos en la II Guerra Mundial,* pp. 45–47.

174. Cited in Marre, *La guerre civile,* p. 136.

175. Ibid.

176. "Memorandum of F. K. Roberts of the British Foreign Office to H. Somerville Smith of the Spears Mission," in Jiménez de Abertasturi Corta, *Los vascos en la II Guerra Mundial*, pp. 583–584.

177. "Applicaciones militares del acuerdo franco-vasco del 17 de mayo de 1941," in Jiménez de Aberasturi Corta, *Los vascos en la II Guerra Mundial*, pp. 328–329.

178. See Eduardo Pons Prades, *Republicanos españoles en la II Guerra Mundial*.

179. See the report of Euzko Deya, no. 282 (March 15, 1948), reprinted in Beltza, *El nacionalismo vasco*, pp. 45–46.

180. See Henri Lamarca, *La danza folklórica vasca como vehículo de la ideologiá nacionalista*.

181. Abbé Urricarriet letter to Eugène Goyheneche, March 1943, AEG.

182. M. Olamendia, "Conférence sur le nationalisme basque," (March 3, 1944).

183. Lafitte, *Le Pays Basque*, chap. 23.

184. Abbé Urricarriet letter to Eugène Goyheneche, March 1943, AEG.

185. From an interview with Abbé Pierre Larzabal, in Socoa on July 25, 1973.

186. See conversations with Marc Légasse at his Fuerte Santa Isabel, Pasajes San Juan, Gipuzkoa, July 28, 1973.

187. *Enbata* 1, no. 169 (March 21, 1991): 7.

188. Ibid.

189. Pierre Larzabal (program for *Aintzina*), July 14, 1942, AEG.

190. Ibid., p. 1.

191. Pierre Larzabal, "Notre programme" (ca. January 1943), p. 1, AEG.

192. From the July 25, 1973, interview in Socoa.

193. Pierre Larzabal letter to Eugène Goyheneche, February 18, 1943, AEG.

194. Larzabal (program for *Aintzina*), July 14, 1942, p. 2.

195. Eugène Goyheneche letter to Pierre Larzabal, March 29, 1943, p. 3, AEG.

196. Pierre Larzabal letter to Eugène Goyheneche, April 7, 1943, p. 3.

197. Abbé Urricarriet letter to Eugène Goyheneche, March 1943, AEG (emphasis in the original).

198. Pierre Larzabal letter to Eugène Goyheneche, April 7, 1943.

199. Cited in Charles Barathon, *Le régionalisme d'hier et de demain*, p. 9.

200. In *Revue du Nord et de l'Est* (January 1925), cited in Barathon, *Le régionalisme*, p. 81.

201. Ibid.

202. Pierre Lafitte to Eugène Goyheneche, May 14, 1941, AEG.

203. P. L., "La défense du régionalisme: Pour la réorganisation administrative de la France," *La Presse du Sud-Ouest* 3284 (May 15, 1941).

204. Ibid.

205. Pierre Lafitte, "L'état et l'enseignement de basque," *Aintzina* 2, no. 6 (1942).

206. Goyheneche, *Le Pays Basque*, p. 555.

207. Robert Paxton, *Vichy, Old Guard and New Order*, p. 198.

208. "Anteproyecto del pacto entre el 'Conseil de Défense de l'Empire Français' y el 'Consejo Nacional Vasco,'" in de Aberasturi Corta, *Los vascos en la II Guerra Mundial*, pp. 57 and 185–186.

209. See Olier Mordrel, *Breiz Atao, Histoire et Actualité du nationalisme breton*, p. 214.

210. "Nazi Version of the New Europe," *New York Post*, August 22, 1940.

211. Cited in Moreau, *Breiz Atao*, p. 212.

212. Ibid.

213. J. von Ribbentrop, preface to Frédéric Grimm, *Hitler et la France*, p. 31.

214. Adolf Hitler, *Mein Kampf*, trans. Manheim, p. 636.

215. Ibid., p. 626.

216. Ibid., p. 672.

217. Ibid., p. 617.

218. Ibid., p. 672.

219. Ibid., p. 653.

220. Ibid., p. 627.

221. Cited by von Ribbentrop, preface to Grimm, *Hitler et la France*, p. 15.

222. M. Georges-Anquetil, *Hitler conduit le bal*, esp. pp. 139 and 140, which reproduce the map in question.

223. "Le nonce en Italie Borgongini Duca au Cardinal Maglione," Report no. 7907 (AES 5600/40, orig.) Rome, June 22, 1940, in Pierre Blet, Angelo Martini, and Burkhart Schneider, eds., *Le Saint Siège et la guerre en Europe, mars 1939–aôut 1940*, p. 494. See also Raymond Cartier, *Laisserons-nous démembrer la France?*.

224. Rita Thalmann, *La mise au pas: Idéologie et stratégie sécuritaire dans la France occupée*, p. 22.

225. Cited in ibid.

226. Ibid.

227. Ibid.

228. Cited in ibid., p. 43.

229. "Berlin Recognizes Breton Movement," *New York Times*, July 26, 1940, p. 3. The report was based on a release from the German news agency DNB filed from Berlin. In the same issue, the *Times* reported that the Nazi occupational administration of Alsace had ordered the removal of all signs in French and their replacement with German signs "in view of the reintroduction of the mother tongue of Alsace." See "Nazis Order Strasbourg to Print Signs in German," *New York Times*, July 26, 1940.

230. "Breton Recognition Denied in Berlin," *New York Times*, July 27, 1940, p. 6.

231. Stephens, "The Bretons," in his *Linguistic Minorities in Western Europe*, p. 383.

232. Cited in *New York Times*, July 27, 1940, p. 6. See also "An Independent Brittany: A New German Device," *London Times*, July 26, 1940, p. 3; quoted in *New York Times*, July 27, 1940, p. 6. See, for example, "Germany Plans to Break Up France—Brittany a First Step," *London Times*, July 27, 1940, p. 3, which is based on articles from a German newspaper in Rennes, *Verein für das Deutschtum in*

Ausland, which calls France a "conglomeration of peoples," referring especially to Basques, Catalans, Flemings, "which may indicate Germany's intention sooner or later of making them into separate regions"; cf. Robert L. Koehl, *German Resettlement and Population Policy, 1939–1945: A History of the Reich Commission for the Strengthening of Germandom* (p. 128), who claims that "Himmler toyed with the notion of reconstituting a *Reichsland Burgund* some day as an SS state, but political considerations kept the Nazis from dismembering France as they had Poland."

233. Robert Lafont, "Sur le problème national en France: Aperçu historique," *Les Temps Modernes* 29, nos. 324–326 (August–September 1973): 40.

234. A number of excellent sources exist on the period of Breton collaboration, among them the firsthand account of Olier Mordrel in his *Breiz Atao*. See also Ronan Caerléon, *Complots pour une république bretonne;* Eberhard Jäckel, *La France dans L'Europe de Hitler;* Ronan Roudaut, "Histoire du mouvement breton," *Les Temps Modernes* 29, nos. 324–326 (August–September 1973). For an English-language source that makes extensive use of Caerléon's work, see Jack E. Reece, *The Bretons against France: Ethnic Minority Nationalism in Twentieth-Century Brittany,* chap. 7.

235. *Le Monde,* October 30, 1985, p. 28.

236. George Axelsson, "Separatism Urged for New Brittany," *New York Times,* July 14, 1940, p. 21.

237. Mordrel, *Breiz Atao,* p. 214.

238. Ibid., p. 249.

239. Cited in Roudaut, "Histoire du mouvement breton," p. 181.

240. Mordrel, *Breiz Atao,* p. 229.

241. Ibid., p. 234.

242. Cited in ibid., p. 236.

243. Cited in Jacques Kermoal, "De la chouannerie au F.L.B.," *Le Monde,* August 19–20, 1973, p. 13.

244. Ministre de la Défense, Etat-Major de l'Armée de Terre, Service Historique, *Rapports d'actualité du XXVème corps de l'armée allemande en occupation en Bretagne, 13 décembre 1940–20 novembre 1944.*

245. Roudaut, "Histoire du mouvement breton," p. 182.

246. See Philippe Camby, *La libération de la Bretagne,* pp. 46, 64–67.

247. Kermoal, "De la chouannerie au F.L.B.," p. 13.

248. *Le Monde,* October 30, 1985, p. 28.

249. Kermoal, "De la chouannerie au F.L.B.," p. 13.

250. "Mission en France," confidential report (marked "Secret"), in de Aberasturi Corta, *Los vascos en la II Guerra Mundial,* p. 209.

251. Yann Fouéré letter to Marc Légasse, May 14, 1943, AEG.

252. Yann Fouéré letter to Pierre Lafitte, May 22, 1943, AEG.

253. Yann Fouéré letter to Pierre Landaburu, November 30, 1943, AEG.

254. Eugène Goyheneche, "Réflexions sur le nationalisme breton," ms, n.d. (ca. 1942–1943), AEG.

255. Eugène Goyheneche, ms., n.d. (ca. 1942–1943), AEG.

256. Christian Rudel, *Les guerriers d'Euskadi*, p. 103. Rudel's novel of this period provides a closely accurate if fictionalized account of many of the philosophic debates within the Basque camp over resistance and collaboration. Rudel interviewed Goyheneche at length and his character Professor Henri Etchebarne is only thinly disguised.

257. François Pranzac, "Quand de son action dissolvante, l'Allemagne orchestrait le grand air de la race et de l'autonomie au Pays Basque," *Cette Semaine dans le Sud-Ouest* 2 (July 13, 1946).

258. Ibid.

259. See Pierre Dumas, *Euzkadi: Les Basques devant la guerre d'espagne;* and Georges-Anquetil, *Hitler conduit le bal*, pp. 371–373.

260. Anon., "The Basques as the Germans See Them," n.d. (ca. 1938), Archives of the Basque Studies Program, University of Nevada at Reno, Folio #B5160.

261. Dumas, *Euzkadi*, p. 68.

262. Anon., letter to Eugène Goyheneche, n.d. (ca. 1943) AEG.

263. Pranzac, "Quand de son action dissolvante."

264. Roland Moreau, *Histoire de l'âme basque*, p. 586. I am grateful to Chanoine Lafitte for discussing his Resistance activities with me and sharing his nom de guerre (from an interview in Ustaritz on July 6, 1973).

265. See Colonel Rémy, *La ligne de démarcation: Histoires du Pays Basque du Béarn et de Bigorre*. I am particularly grateful to Eugène Azpeitia, former Basque Resistance fighter, for his long discussions about the Basque Resistance (from interviews in Reno, Nevada, in August 1980).

266. On the interplay of smuggling and terrain, see Daniel Alexander Gómez-Ibáñez, *The Western Pyrénées: Differential Evolution of the French and Spanish Borderland*.

267. Moreau, *Histoire de l'âme Basque*, p. 587. See the poems about the Nazi occupation written by "Iratzeder" (Abbé Jean Diharce of the abbey of Belloc) in Biblioteca de Cultura Vasca, *Acontecimientos del siglo XX en poetas euskéricos* (Buenos Aires: Editorial Vasca Ekin, 1974).

268. From an interview with Chanoine Pierre Lafitte in Ustaritz on July 6, 1973.

269. Rudel, *Les guerriers d'Euskadi*, p. 105.

270. Abbé Urricarriet letter to Eugène Goyheneche, March 1943, AEG.

271. Ibid.

272. Eugène Goyheneche, "Quelques ideés," ms., n.d. (ca. 1942–1943), AEG.

273. In "Carta del Sr. Marc Légasse al Dr. Sr. J. A. Aguirre Lecube," in Fernando Sarrailh de Ihartza ("Krutwig"), *Vasconia*, pp. 536–537.

274. I am grateful to Professor Goyheneche for pointing this out in the interview in Ustaritz on June 26, 1973.

275. Ibid.

276. From the July 6, 1973, interview in Ustaritz.

277. Ibid.

278. One exception is his short chapter in Eugenio Ibarzabal, *50 años de nacionalismo vasco, 1928–1978*, pp. 279–293.

279. Rudel, *Les guerriers d'Euskadi*, p. 104.

280. Ibid., p. 105.

281. Ibid., p. 106.

282. Pranzac, "Quand de son action dissolvante."

283. I am grateful to Professor Goyheneche for his personal account of his arrest and trial during the June 26, 1973, interview in Ustaritz.

284. Beltza, *El nacionalismo vasco en el exilio*, p. 15.

285. From an interview with Marc Légasse at Pasajes San Juan, Gipuzkoa, on July 28, 1973.

286. The official electoral statistics for the Cantonal Election of 1945 are courtesy of the Sous-Préfecture of the Département des Pyrénées-Atlantiques, Bayonne. See also *La Républicaine du Sud-Ouest*, September 28, 1945, and October 2, 1945; and Cuzacq, *Les élections législatives à Bayonne et au Pays Basque, 1944–1956*, pp. 11–12.

287. "Carta del Sr. Marc Légasse al Dr. Sr. J. A. de Aguirre Lecube," pp. 533–537; also in Beltza, *El nacionalismo vasco en el exilio*, pp. 112–117.

288. He described himself as "separatist" to President Aguirre in his letter in 1946 (see Sarrailh de Ihartza, *Vasconia*, p. 534).

289. "Marc Légasse compte sur les enfants pour faire du Pays Basque un état autonome," *Samedi-Soir*, April 22, 1950. See also Marc Légasse, *Paroles d'un anarchiste basque*.

290. "Marc Légasse compte sur les enfants."

291. From an interview at Pasajes San Juan, Gipuzkoa, on July 28, 1973.

292. Gaetan Bernoville, *Le pays des Basques*, p. vii.

293. Philippe Veyrin, *Les Basques*, p. 196.

294. "Le drapeau basque avait été jugé indésirable à Biarritz: De violentes protestations," *Côte Basque Soir* (ca. 1948), AEG.

295. Cited in ibid.

296. "Séparatisme basque: . . . Le ridicule ne tue pas mais il peut conduire en prison," *Résistance Républicaine*, July 1, 1946.

297. Ibid.

298. "Marc Légasse compte sur les enfants."

299. Cuzacq, *Les élections législative à Bayonne et au Pays Basque, 1944–1956*, p. 14.

300. *Le statut du Pays Basque dans la république française, Projet de Loi.*

301. Comments made during the July 28, 1973, interview in Gipuzkoa.

302. Cited in Sarrailh de Ihartza, *Vasconia*, p. 534.

303. Pierre Lafitte, "L'affaire Marc Légasse en correctionnelle," *Herria* 122 (March 20, 1947).

304. See "Bayonne-Préfecture," *Côte Basque Soir*, May 18, 1949.

305. Ibid.

306. Ibid.

307. Reproduced in Sarrailh de Ihartza, *Vasconia*, pp. 533–537.

308. *Four Quartets* (New York: Harcourt, Brace, 1943).

CHAPTER FOUR. THE WIND BEFORE THE STORM: ENBATA AND
SECULAR NATIONALISM, 1960–1974

Earlier versions of this chapter appeared as "Enbata and the Wind before the Storm: Secular Nationalism among the Basques of France, 1960–1974," *European Studies Journal* 6, no. 1 (Spring 1989), and as "Enbata et le vent qui précède la tempête: Nationalisme laïque parmi les Basques de France, 1960–1974," *Enbata* 1000 (November 12, 1987): 3–9. See also my earlier treatment in "The Basques of France, A Case of Peripheral Ethnonationalism in Europe," *Political Anthropology* 1, no. 1 (March 1975): 67–87.

1. Philippe Veyrin, *Les Basques*.

2. "Petit catéchisme de notre mouvement," written as were most of the early editorials by Abbé Pierre Larzabal, editor of *Aintzina II* during the 1940s. The choice of the word *catéchisme* reflects the still incomplete transition from clerical to secular nationalism.

3. In the preface to Gisèle Halimi, *Le procès de Burgos*, p. viii.

4. For the question of internal colonialism, see the works of Professor Robert Lafont, among them *La révolution régionaliste* and *Sur la France*.

5. *Enbata* 74 (June 1967): 8. The song was published in the June 1961 issue under Labéguerie's pseudonym, "Aldategi." See also Léon Boussard, *Jeiki, Jeiki Etxenkoak, ou le défi des Basques*, p. 158.

6. I follow closely the first short history of *Enbata* written by Charles Arribillaga, "Historique d'Embata," *Embata* (June 1958): 4.

7. Ibid.

8. Ibid.

9. *Enbata* 74 (June 1967): 8.

10. I follow *Enbata*'s own account in its twentieth anniversary issue (counting from *Aberri Eguna* on April 15, 1963). See *Enbata* 765 (April 1983): 2. See also Jean-Paul Malherbe, "Le nationalisme basque et transformations sociopolitiques en Pays Basque nord," in Pierre Bidart, ed., *La nouvelle société Basque*, pp. 52–53.

11. Eugène Goyheneche, "Michel Labéguerie," *Revue 64* 5 (October 1980).

12. Jean-Paul Malherbe, "Le nationalisme basque en France, 1933–1976," pp. 54–55.

13. *Enbata* 765 (April 14, 1983): 2.

14. For a discussion of these changes and their impact on the Basque movement, see Malherbe, "Le nationalisme basque et transformations sociopolitiques," p. 53.

15. *Embata* 1 (September 1960): 1. See also Malherbe, "Le nationalisme basque et transformations sociopolitiques," p. 54.

16. A detailed analysis of the history of ETA lies outside the scope of this analy-

sis. A number of excellent sources exist in Spanish, English, and French. In my estimation, the greatest documentary collection is the eighteen-volume collection of material about ETA called *Documentos*. The best English-language sources are Robert P. Clark's excellent books: *The Basque Insurgents: ETA, 1952–1980, The Basques: The Franco Years and Beyond,* and *Negotiating with ETA: Obstacles to Peace in the Basque Country;* and Stanley Payne, *Basque Nationalism.* Among a wealth of Spanish-language sources, several stand out: José Mari Garmendia, *Historia de ETA;* Ortzi, *Historia de Euskadi: El nacionalismo vasco y ETA;* and Jokin Apalategi, *Los vascos, de la autonomía a la independencia.* Among French-language sources are Jean-Louis Davant, "Lutte nationale et lutte des classes dans le mouvement basque," *Temps Modernes* 324–326 (August–September 1973): 238–301; "L'ETA," in Halimi, *Le procès de Burgos,* pp. 149–158; and Jokin Apalategi, *Nationalisme et question nationale au Pays Basque, 1830–1976.*

17. For the effect of the Mouvement Fédéraliste Européen on Enbata, see "Pourquoi Enbata?" *Cahier no. 1* (ca. 1963). Among the most important writings of th Mouvement Fédéraliste Européen are three works by Professor Guy Héraud: *L'Europe des ethnies, Peuples et langues d'Europe,* and *Les principes du fédéralisme.* See also the works of Yann Fouéré, including *L'Europe aux cent drapeaux* and *La révolution fédéraliste.*

18. From an interview in Socoa on November 6, 1975.

19. (Chanoine) Etienne Salaberry, "L'aliénation Basque," part 1, *Gure Herria* 5 (1971): 265.

20. *Enbata* 13 (April 1962): 1.

21. "Echos d'Enbata," minutes of a secret meeting of the movement at Espelette, July 14, 1962.

22. I am grateful to the late Abbé Larzabal and Professor Pierre Charritton for their discussion of this period during interviews.

23. *Enbata* 74 (June 1967): 8. Oddly enough, the effort to mask Larzabal's identity carried over even into *Ekin,* the internal newsletter for *Enbata's* militants only. See no. 3 (1965): 1, in which the three founders were said to include Labéguerie and "a village priest."

24. From an interview in Socoa on November 6, 1975.

25. Txillardegi. "Pierre Larzabal, el cura de Sokoa (entrevista)," *Punto y Hora de Euskal Herria* 179 (June 13–20 1980): 19–22.

26. The image is that of the skirts of the priest's cassock. From the November 6, 1975, interview in Socoa.

27. See Malherbe, "Le nationalisme basque en France," p. 70. See also Pierre Duboscq, "La question basque du nord," in Yves Lacoste, ed., *Géopolitiques des régions françaises,* vol. 25, p. 1071.

28. *Ager* 85 (March 15, 1987): 4.

29. Ibid.

30. Ibid.

31. Cited in Txillardegi, "Pierre Larzabal," pp. 19–22.

32. Cited in Duboscq, "La question basque du nord," p. 1053. Duboscq de-

scribes the interlocking and mutually reinforcing power structure between *curé* and *notables* in the Basque interior.

33. For the role of the parish priest in the Basque village, see Duboscq, "La question basque du nord," pp. 1060ff.

34. "L'aliénation Basque," part 2, *Gure Herria* 1 (1967): 330–331.

35. *Enbata* 24 (April 1963).

36. *Enbata* 765 (April 14, 1983): 2–3. See also Mouvement Enbata, "Pourquoi Enbata?" *Cahier no. 1* (ca. 1963).

37. Mouvement Enbata, "Pourquoi Enbata?"

38. Ibid.

39. Ibid., p. 5.

40. Ibid.

41. Ibid. See also Mouvement Enbata, "L'économie Basque," in *Cahier no. 2*.

42. Cited in ibid., p. 6.

43. *Côte Basque Soir*, April 16, 1963; and *Le Courrier*, April 16, 1963.

44. *Côte Basque Soir*, April 16, 1963.

45. "Le nationalisme d'Enbata," *Le Travail*, April 20, 1963.

46. "Le rassemblement d'Itxassou," *Le Monde*, April 17, 1963, p. 5.

47. Ibid.

48. " 'Enbata' leur promet une préfecture," *Le Travail*, April 20, 1963.

49. "Réflexions après le rassemblement d'Itxassou," *Le Courrier*, April 18, 1963.

50. Cited in ibid.

51. *Enbata* 74 (June 1967): 8.

52. From the archives of Eugène Goyheneche.

53. Cited in *Enbata* 765 (April 15, 1983): 5.

54. Euskal Batasuna, *Projet politique, 1988*, p. 2.

55. Joseph Stalin, *Works*, vol. 2 (1907–1913), p. 307.

56. Ibid., pp. 307–308 (emphasis in the original).

57. Robert P. Clark, "Patterns in the Lives of ETA Members," in Peter Merkl, ed., *Political Violence and Terror: Motifs and Motivations*, p. 289.

58. Ibid., p. 290.

59. Cited in Salaberry, "L'aliénation Basque," p. 265.

60. Cited in *Enbata* 765 (April 15, 1983): 4.

61. Representative of the doctrine of the Mouvement Fédéraliste Européen are the writings of Guy Héraud and Yann Fouéré (see "Pourquoi Enbata?"). For the doctrine of ethnic federalism, see Héraud, *L'Europe des ethnies*, and his *Peuples et langues d'Europe*. See also Fouéré, *L'Europe aux cent drapeaux*, and his *La révolution fédéraliste*.

62. See "Enbata demande la reconnaissance d'une nation basque pour les sept provinces euskariennes," *Côte Basque Soir*, April 16, 1963, pp. 1–2, which estimates the crowd size at 500. Interestingly, an editorial in the same issue by Jean Garat, "L'Europe des matries," estimated the attendance at 1,000. By contrast, the more critical daily *Sud-Ouest* estimated the crowd at 600 in its article on April 16,

1963, entitled "Rassemblement de séparatistes qui demandent la création d'un département basque" (p. 1).

63. René Cuzacq, *Les élections législatives à Bayonne et au Pays Basque, 1961–1965*, p. 108. On the political conservatism of France's ethnic regions, especially the Pays Basque, Brittany, Alsace, and the Occitanian interior, see (Chanoine) Fernand Boulard, *Premiers itinéraires en sociologie religieuse;* and Fernand Boulard and Jean Rémy, *Pratique religieuse et régions culturelles*.

64. Congrès Enbata, "Rapport sur la langue Basque" (April 15, 1963). See also the account in *Le Monde*, April 17, 1963, p. 5, which discusses the demand for a Basque department.

65. The embrace of the doctrine of ethnic federalism by *Enbata* was not new: it was also part of the worldview of *Aintzina* during the 1930s, owing in part to Eugène Goyheneche's contacts in Paris with later MFE militants like Alexandre Marc and Yann Fouéré.

66. See Henri Lamarca, *La danza folklórica vasca como vehículo de la ideología nacionalista*.

67. Perhaps the best example of the French Basques' resentment of the indifference of the Spanish Basque community in exile was the letter from Marc Légasse to the former president of the Basque Republic, José Antonio de Aguirre Lecube, reprinted in Fernando Sarrailh de Ihartza, *Vasconia*, pp. 533–547.

68. See ETA, "A los profesionales de la prensa, radio y televisión: Qué es Euskadi?" and "Qué es ETA y por que lucha?" press release, Caracas (January 1969); and the interview with one of ETA's founders, J. M. Madariaga, in *Elgar* 235 (April 1972): 4–5.

69. For the nature of the motivation of ETA militants and their lives and interpersonal relationships, see Clark, "Patterns in the Lives of ETA Members."

70. Discussing the recent past, its authors spoke of "an epoch when the Basque was ashamed to speak Basque. He didn't yet have pride in his race" (p. 2). Moreover, the imagery of the virtuous mother figure despoiled by foreign men, trees brought to fruit in the benevolent fold of nature, and culture as symbolic mother and father figures demanding the respect and pride of young Basques is found throughout. See also ETA's account in *Zutik* 65 (August 1975).

71. ETA, "A los profesionales de la prensa."

72. I follow *Enbata*'s account in *Enbata* 74 (June 1967): 9.

73. Ibid.

74. Cited in Cuzacq, *Les élections législatives*, p. 108. See also "Un rassemblement de personnalités basques se tient à Itxassou près de Cambo," *Le Monde*, April 16, 1963; and "Le rassemblement d'Itxassou: des Basques demandent que les 'provinces' de la Soule, de la Basse-Navarre et du Labourd forment un département distinct des Basses-Pyrénées," *Le Monde*, April 17, 1963, p. 5.

75. Cited in *Ekin* 1 (January 15, 1966).

76. See Apalategi, *Los vascos*, pp. 266–267. That this antipathy between ETA and the remnants of the PNV in France was of long standing was underscored

in an interview with the son of the late President Aguirre of the Basque Republic in Ustaritz on June 4, 1976.

77. "*Zutik:* Aberri Eguna, 1963," in *Documentos*, vol. 2, pp. 457ff.

78. Emphasis in the original. See also Apalategi, *Los vascos*, p. 269.

79. "Extra *Zutik:* Aberri Eguna, 1963," p. 457.

80. Apalategi, *Los vascos*, p. 267.

81. Ibid.

82. Ibid. See also *Documentos*, vol. 1, pp. 459, 478. Between March and August 1976 the Library of the Basque Studies Program at the University of Nevada at Reno received envelopes postmarked New York (probably sent by CAMBIAS, the Committee of the Americas for Basque Independence and Survival) and stamped ETA. Most contained copies of *Enbata* and solicited contributions to be sent to the account "Askatasuna" (Liberty), at the Crédit Agricole in Saint-Jean-de-Luz, France.

83. Apalategi, *Los vascos*, p. 268.

84. Summarized as part of *Enbata*'s ongoing debate in *Ekin* 9 (November 15, 1966): 9. It was based on Txillardegi's original article in the second issue of *Branka*.

85. *Ekin* (ca. 1965).

86. See *Le Monde*, March 10, 1964. There was a widespread feeling that Etcheverry-Ainchart had done *Enbata* a favor by running under its partisan label. Cynics claimed that Etcheverry-Ainchart was so popular in Baigorri that he could have won on any party list, including that of the perennially marginal French Communist party.

87. Cuzacq, *Les élections législatives*, p. 69.

88. Cited in ibid.

89. Cited in ibid.

90. See Robert Boulay, "Interview avec M. Labéguerie, député de Mauléon: Les Basques veulent avoir leur propre département," *Paris-Presse–L'Intransigeant*, April 17, 1963, p. 2F. For *Enbata*'s interpretation of Labéguerie's decision to turn his back on his former friends, see *Enbata* 74 (June 1967): 8–12.

91. See Malherbe, "Le nationalisme basque en France," pp. 194–200.

92. Boussard, *Jeiki, Jeiki Etxenkoak*, p. 158.

93. Ibid., p. 159.

94. *Ekin* 5 (November 1965): 8.

95. Ibid.

96. Ibid.

97. Ibid., p. 9.

98. Ibid., p. 10.

99. Ibid.

100. *Ekin* 2, 3, and 4 (1965).

101. Ibid.

102. *Ekin* 25 (January 6, 1968): 2.

103. *Enbata* 69 (January 1967): 4.

104. Cited in Malherbe, "Le nationalisme basque en France," p. 78.

105. Cited in *Ekin* 5 (November 1965): 9 (emphasis in the original).

106. The legislative elections of June 1968 are perhaps the best example of the potential electoral response to de Gaulle's choice between order and chaos. See the results in Ministère de l'Economie et des Finances, Institut National de la Statistique et des Etudes Economiques, *Annuaire statistique de la France, 1969,* chap. 10, table 3, "Elections législatives de juin 1968."

107. See the valuable series of electoral analyses by René Cuzacq, especially *Les élections législatives à Bayonne et au Pays Basque de 1958 à 1961.* That the force of Gaullism continued in this area is all the more surprising given Cuzacq's dubious assertion (p. 32) that "the church and the clergy hardly counted any longer on the electoral plane (even in the Pays Basque)."

108. "Rapport de la section Enbata de Bordeaux sur la nouvelle orientation nécessaire au mouvement, Rapport pour le 1965 congrès d'Enbata," ms. (ca. 1965), p. 3.

109. Ibid.

110. Remarks of Chanoine Pierre Lafitte made in an interview in Ustaritz on July 6, 1973.

111. Archives de la Sous-Préfecture du Département des Pyrénées-Atlantiques at Bayonne, Elections Législatives des 5 et 12 mars, 1967, *Récapitulation.*

112. For the third *circonscription,* Etchalus polled 6 percent in Baigorri and 8 percent in Mauléon, the canton with the highest population in the *circonscription.* In the fourth *circonscription,* Haran polled 6 percent in his native coastal canton of Saint-Jean-de-Luz, and a surprising 7 percent in Ustaritz.

113. See the analysis of results in *Enbata* 72 (April 1967).

114. Malherbe, "Le nationalisme basque en France," p. 69.

115. *Ekin* 18 (April 22, 1967).

116. Ximun Haran, "Enbata-ETA-réfugiés," *Ager* 103 (January 1, 1988): 4. This article was written as a response to an earlier version of this chapter which appeared in *Enbata*. See my "Enbata et le vent qui précède la tempête," pp. 3–9.

117. I am indebted to Ximun Haran for his account of this period during an interview in Saint-Jean-de-Luz on July 25, 1973.

118. Aligner, "Le mouvement nationaliste Basque, Enbata," p. 80.

119. For the events of May–June 1968, see Raymond Aron, *The Elusive Revolution: Anatomy of a Student Revolt,* trans. Gordon Clough; Alain Touraine, *The May Movement, Revolt and Reform,* trans. Leonard F. X. Mayhew; Andrew Feenberg, "The May Events," *New Scholar* 4, no. 1 (1973): 51–76; and Jane Elizabeth Decker, "Direct Democracy and Revolutionary Organization in the 1968 French Student-Worker Revolt," *Proceedings of the Western Society of French History* 5 (1977): 406–414.

120. Cuzacq, *Les élections législatives,* p. 63.

121. *Basque-Eclair* (May 25–26, 1968), last page.

122. *Côte-Basque Soir,* May 13, 1968, p. 1.

123. *Côte-Basque Soir,* May 9, 1968, p. 2.

124. *Eclair-Pyrénées,* June 6, 1968.

125. Catherine Mas, "La communauté ethnique et l'Europe: L'exemple basque" ms., Musée Basque, Bayonne.

126. See E. Sprinzak, "France: The Radicalization of the New Left," in Martin Kolinsky and William E. Patterson, eds., *Social and Political Movements in Western Europe*; and Decker, "Direct Democracy and Revolutionary Organization."

127. Beñat Urgarbi, "La gauche française veut récupérer les abertzale du nord," *Branka* 13 (ca. 1970): 24–27.

128. Ibid., p. 24.

129. Ibid.

130. Ibid., p. 25.

131. Yet Aski took on a major importance in the serious and detailed doctoral thesis of Jean-Paul Malherbe. Malherbe's attribution to Aski of 150 militants and a strong ideological platform seems, in retrospect, to have reflected the self-promotion of one of his sources and thus serves as a cautionary note for those of us who toil in the same vineyards ("Le nationalisme basque en France," p. 162).

132. See ibid., p. 169.

133. I am indebted for the discussion which follows to interviews with a number of former Amaia and Mende Berri militants, and I honor their requests for anonymity.

134. *Cahiers d'Amaia* 2 (1969).

135. *Amaia*, ephemeral tract (ca. 1968).

136. Malherbe, "Le nationalisme basque en France," p. 167.

137. Other than Malherbe's thesis, few published sources cover this period of Basque history in France. See, for example, the brief discussion in Meic Stephens, *Linguistic Minorities in Europe*. Most of the material which follows comes from former militants of Amaia and Mende Berri.

138. Malherbe, "Le nationalisme basque en France," p. 169.

139. See Taisne, "Les nationalistes basques et la presse française"; and Malherbe, "Le nationalisme basque en France," p. 169.

140. Malherbe, "Le nationalisme basque en France," p. 169.

141. See Comité de Soutien, "Nouvelles du jour," ephemeral tract, May 22, 1971, Musée Basque, Bayonne; and Euskal Elkargoa, "Dernières nouvelles" (May 1971).

142. *Koska* 1 (January 31, 1973).

143. Ibid., p. 1.

144. *Koska* 2 (February 28, 1973).

145. *Koska* 2 (February 28, 1973).

146. *Enbata* 84 (October 9, 1968): 1.

147. Minutes of the "Réunion du Comité Directeur," October 29, 1966.

148. For a discussion of the generational differences within *Enbata* by the early 1970s and the ideological transformation of Basque movements in Spain and France, see Davant, "Lutte nationale et lutte des classes," pp. 238–301.

149. I follow Malherbe's analysis in "Le nationalisme basque et transformations sociopolitiques," p. 71.

150. Ibid.

151. *Ekin* 26 (February 26, 1968): 8 (emphasis in the original). The slogan *Gora Euskadi Askatuta* dates to the earliest years of this century under the PNV and was subsequently taken up by ETA.

152. *Etorkizuna* 1 (Summer 1967): 1.

153. "Electoralisme," *Etorkizuna* 1 (Summer 1967): 3.

154. Malherbe, "Le nationalisme basque et transformations sociopolitiques," p. 71.

155. *Etorkizuna* 2 (1967).

156. Haran, "Enbata-ETA-réfugiés," pp. 4–5.

157. Ibid., p. 5.

158. Ibid.

159. *Enbata* 94 (October 9, 1968).

160. For a discussion of the ideological and tactical differences which led to the split between ETA (Fifth Assembly) and ETA (Sixth Assembly), see "L'ETA," in Halimi, *Le procès de Burgos;* Clark, *The Basque Insurgents*, pp. 58–70; and Davant, "Lutte nationale et lutte de classes," pp. 260–288.

161. The trial of the six ETA militants at Burgos in 1970 was indicative not only of the interest of the French Basque movement in events in Spain, but of how events in Spain were influencing the nature of French Basque militancy. See Jean Lacouture, "Calme et vigilance dans le Pays Basque français," *Le Monde*, December 15, 1970, p. 2; Halimi, *Le procès de Burgos;* and Maryse Harlouchet, *Le Pays Basque à travers la presse française de septembre à décembre 1970.*

162. I am indebted to Robert Clark's excellent analysis in *The Basque Insurgents*, esp. pp. 58–70.

163. Cited in Clark, *The Basque Insurgents*, p. 58. See his footnote 1 to chapter 3, p. 301.

164. Ibid., p. 59.

165. Ibid., pp. 58–59.

166. Ibid., p. 59.

167. Ibid., p. 61.

168. Ibid.

169. Cited in Davant, "Lutte nationale et lutte des classes," pp. 275–276. See also Madariaga's interview with Jean Lacouture, "La contradiction principale pour nous est au niveau de la nation," *Le Monde Diplomatique* (March 1971): 7.

170. Clark, *The Basque Insurgents*, p. 63.

171. Ibid.

172. Ibid.

173. Ibid., p. 75.

174. On the leftward move of the Occitanian movement in this period, see my "Ethnic Mobilization and the Pursuit of Post-industrial Values: The Case of Occitanie," *Tocqueville Review* 2, no. 2 (Spring 1980); Robert Lafont, *La revendication occitane;* and Gaston Bazalgues, "Les organisations occitanes," *Temps Modernes* 324–326 (August–September 1973): 140–169. On the Breton movement,

see Ronan Roudaut, "Histoire du mouvement Breton"; and Pierre Doridan, "La Bretagne et le socialisme," *Temps Modernes* 324–326 (August–September 1973).

175. For the third *circonscription*, Etchalus polled 6 percent in Baigorri and 8 percent in Mauléon, the latter being the most populated canton. In the fourth, Haran polled 6 percent in his coastal canton of Saint-Jean-de-Luz, and a surprising 7 percent in Ustaritz.

176. Ibid.

177. See the analysis of results in *Enbata* 72 (April 1967).

178. Malherbe, "Le nationalisme basque en France," p. 90.

179. Ibid.

180. It should be added that, according to a content analysis of local newspapers of the epoch, May 1968 in the Pays Basque had little "Basque" character, being essentially characterized here as elsewhere by socioeconomic dislocations brought on by wildcat, union, and other service strikes.

181. Cf. Paxti Mendiale, "La trajectoire du nationalisme basque," *Que Faire* 8–9 (December 1971): 20, who argues that "the lack of internal democracy which blocks ideological debates, the inability to cling to the real struggles of May 1968, and the fundamentally electoral nature of the movement are going to hasten an awakening and enable certain militants to critique Enbata's federalist and petit-bourgeois ideology." See also Davant, "Lutte nationale et lutte des classes," pp. 294–297.

182. Davant, "Lutte nationale et lutte des classes," p. 292.

183. *Ekin* 1 (1971).

184. Malherbe, "Le nationalisme basque et transformations sociopolitiques," p. 71.

185. F. Sarrailh (he would partially alter his name in most of his major writings), *La cuestión vasca*. Sarrailh ("Krutwig") claims to have given the political report at ETA's Fifth Assembly in 1967 which fixed its ideology. See his discussion of this period in Heiko Sagredo de Ihartza ("Krutwig"), *La Vasconie et l'Europe nouvelle*, as well as his interview, "Ayer y hoy de Federico Krutwig," *Muga* 23 (September 1979): 50–78. Davant, in responding to the unusual virulence of Krutwig's attack, claims that it was not personal in nature (for his personal contacts with *Enbata* were cordial), but rather emanated from the rigor of Krutwig's Marxist-Leninist analysis. See Davant, "Lutte nationale et lutte des classes," p. 292.

186. *Enbata* 84 (October 9, 1968): 1.

187. This constant reaffirmation of the commitment to legality (and the rejection of ethnic violence) appears, with hindsight, to have been addressed to certain isolated critics of the movement who argued that the best means for *Enbata* to boost its popularity and legitimacy as a Basque movement would be to "go clandestine" on the ETA model. This same argument was made in public meetings in 1973 and in later interviews with the author by leading militants of HAS in 1975.

188. Aligner, "Le mouvement nationaliste basque, Enbata," pp. 116–117.

189. Ibid.

190. Ibid.

191. Davant, "Lutte nationale et lutte des classes," p. 300.

192. Ibid., p. 171.

193. Cited in *Enbata* 284 (1972): 1.

194. For a discussion of the ideological, and tactical, differences which led to the split between ETA (Fifth Assembly) and ETA (Sixth Assembly), see also "L'ETA," in Halimi, *Le Procès de Burgos.*

195. For the flight of militants to parties of the extreme French left, see Urgarbi, "La gauche française veut recupérer les abertzale du nord," pp. 24–27; and Aligner, "Le mouvement nationaliste basque, Enbata," pp. 8off.

196. "Interview d'E.T.A.," *Enbata* 84 (October 9, 1968): 4 (emphasis in the original).

197. Urgarbi, "La gauche française veut récupérer les abertzale du nord," p. 26. See also Hervé Chabalier, "Un seul pays pour les Basques?" *Nouvel Observateur* 421 (December 4–10, 1972): 104, 109.

198. H. Descamps de Bragelongne, *La vie politique des Basses-Pyrénées*, p. 14.

199. Quoted in Henry Giniger, "French Basque Life Is Peaceful," *New York Times*, January 11, 1971.

200. Christian Rudel, *Les guerriers d'Euskadi*, p. 290.

201. Aligner, "Le mouvement nationaliste basque, Enbata," p. 122.

202. Cited in Lacouture, "Calme et vigilance," p. 2.

203. Aligner, "Le mouvement nationaliste basque, Enbata," p. 126.

204. This was the subject of a mass public meeting I observed on June 18, 1973, at its headquarters, 14 rue des Cordeliers, Bayonne.

205. Cited in *Enbata* 310 (July 1973): 4.

206. Aligner places the number of militants in 1973 at approximately ninety, of which only fifty were paying dues. In contrast, according to its last editor, Koko Abeberry, in an interview in Biarritz on November 25, 1975, the paper was printed in 1,500 copies at that time, with more than 500 subscribers.

207. "Le gouvernement dissout quatre mouvements autonomistes," *Le Monde*, January 31, 1974, pp. 1, 7.

208. See "Après la dissolution du mouvement Enbata: Le Dr. Burucoa affirme sa surprise: Nous n'avous jamais organisé d'action violente—la modération est dans nos méthodes," *Eclair*, January 31, 1974.

209. "Le gouvernement dissout quatre mouvements autonomistes," p. 7.

210. Cited in *Eclair*, February 1, 1974.

211. Ibid.

212. Ibid.

213. *Le Monde*, February 7, 1974.

214. Ministère d'Etat et Ministère de l'Intérieur au président de la 4ème Sous-section de la Section des Contentieux du Conseil d'Etat re: Requête no. 94,477 (June 24, 1974).

215. *Enbata* (October 11, 1973).

216. See Julen Agirre, *Operation Ogro;* and "How Basques Killed Spain's Premier and Almost Got Kissinger," *International Herald Tribune,* September 23, 1974, p. 7.

217. Jokin Apalategi, *Nationalisme et question nationale au Pays Basque,* pp. 235–257.

218. Quoted in Régis Marsan, "Le problème national basque."

CHAPTER FIVE. SOCIALISM AND AUTONOMY: EHAS CONFRONTED BY THE RISE OF YOUNG RADICAL ABERTZALE, 1974–1981

1. "Pourquoi," *Euskaldunak* 1, no. 1 (April 1974): 4.
2. *EHASKIDE* (November 27, 1976): 3.
3. "Une présentation générale de E.H.A.S.," ms. (ca. 1979), p. 2.
4. "Bipolarisation basque," *Euskaldunak* 3 (June 1974): 1.
5. "Pour une politique offensive et unitaire du parti" (ca. 1977), p. 5. This handwritten manuscript was photocopied and sent to militants of the party.
6. Ibid.
7. For elements of Goyhenetche's thought, see his two books in which he develops his thesis of the colonization of the Pays Basque through a reinterpretation of Basque history: *Histoire de la colonisation française au Pays Basque* and *Pays Basque nord: Un peuple colonisé.*
8. At the time of the founding of HAS, Goyhenetche was the secretary of the Basque-language educational group IKAS, parent of the Ikastola Basque maternal school movement and predecessor of Seaska. Goyhenetche's comments are from an interview in Bayonne on November 20, 1975.
9. *EHASKIDE* 2 (May 1976) and 3 (June 1976).
10. From an interview in Bayonne on August 20, 1987.
11. Malherbe, "Le nationalisme basque en France, 1933–1976," p. 172.
12. See also Malherbe's description of the movement and its militants in "Le nationalisme basque en France," p. 172.
13. Ibid.
14. *EHASKIDE* (November 1976): 1.
15. "Bipolarisation basque," p. 1. The use of the phraseology "a certain idea of" is a clear reference to de Gaulle's "certain idea of France."
16. From the August 20, 1987, interview with Larzabal. For the attacks on *Enbata,* see, for example, "Amalgame," *Euskaldunak* 14 (May 1975): 2, which contrasts itself with *Enbata* over the issue of solidarity with the working classes and later in the same issue (p. 7) where HAS attacks the Basque right and extreme right.
17. *Euskaldunak* 2 (April 1974), p. 7.
18. Ibid.
19. From an interview in Bayonne on November 5, 1975.

20. From the German *Schaden* (damage) and *Freude* (joy), a description of the feeling when one is not wholly displeased at the misfortune of one's friends.

21. "L'affaire Enbata," *Euskaldunak* 11 (February 1975): 6.

22. Ibid.

23. According to interviews in 1975 with both Jacques Abeberry and his brother Jean-Claude (Koko) Abeberry, who assumed the position of editor, the decision to reappear as a newspaper was made following the traditional amnesties granted after the presidential elections of 1974. *Enbata*'s appeal of the government's dissolution was denied, but the appellate court in Bordeaux stated that the subsequent amnesty applied to *Enbata* in any case. When the government affirmed that the dissolution was directed at the movement and not the newspaper, it was decided to recreate *Enbata* as a kind of Basque nationalist press service. The paper was now published by a new team of less than ten members, with the Abeberrys dominant.

24. "Socialisme et problème basque," *Euskaldunak* 16 (July 1975): 6. The same point, that it was the question of socialism which divided the two groups, was also made in "Amalgame," p. 2.

25. "Socialisme et problème basque," p. 6. The image of having "their heart to the left" is part of a familiar French saying which says in full: "heart to the left and wallet [i.e., economic self-interest] to the right."

26. Ibid.

27. *Euskaldunak* 1 (April 1974): 2.

28. "Plateforme idéologique," *Euskaldunak* 1 (April 1974): 4.

29. *Euskaldunak* 50 (June 1979).

30. EHAS wrote in *EHASKIDE* (September 1978): 3, "One of the facts of Euskadi Nord risks being an eventual regrouping of elements at the initiative of the old [militants] of Enbata. What will emerge from this exactly? No one knows."

31. "La participation de H.A.S. au 1er mai," *Euskaldunak* 14 (May 1975): 2.

32. From an interview on August 20, 1987.

33. "Pour la création d'un grand mouvement socialiste basque," *Euskaldunak* 5 (August 1974): 3.

34. "La participation au 1er mai," p. 2.

35. Among the most revealing examples of the French nationalist thrust of the Parti Communiste Français was the angry rejection of the definition of France's ethnic minorities as "national minorities" by a new Soviet encyclopedia on minorities. See "French Assail Soviet on Ethnicity," *New York Times*, March 1, 1984, p. A4.

36. "Explication de notre position," *Euskaldunak* 2 (May 1974): 2.

37. Goyhenetche, *Histoire de la colonisation française au Pays Basque*, p. 77.

38. "Pourquoi un parti socialiste basque," *Euskaldunak* 3 (June 1974): 2.

39. *Euskaldunak* 4 (August 1974): 5.

40. Goyhenetche, *Histoire de la colonisation française au Pays Basque*, p. 77.

41. Ibid., p. 79.

42. Ibid. The "hexagon" describes the rough outline of the territory of the French state and is a familiar conceptual shorthand in France for the national territory controlled by Paris.

43. Euskal Herriko Alderdi Sozialista (EHAS), "MANIFESTE," ms. portfolio no. B-9005, Musée Basque, Bayonne (ca. 1976), p. 1.

44. Ibid.

45. See Jokin Apalategi, *Los vascos de la nación al estado*, p. 400.

46. Jokin Apalategi, "Le mouvement basque aujourd'hui," *Les Temps Modernes* 31, no. 357 (1976): 451–452. Cf. Naxto Arregi, *Memorias del Kas, 1975/78*, who argues that in November 1975, at its founding assembly, EHAS in fact positioned itself close to the theses of ETA-m, the issue of support of the armed struggle apparently notwithstanding.

47. "Une information judiciare est ouverte contre le journal 'Enbata,'" *Le Monde*, August 21, 1976, p. 6.

48. I follow Robert Clark's analysis in *The Basque Insurgents: ETA, 1952–1980*, p. 78.

49. Ibid.

50. *Euskaldunak* 21 (December 1975).

51. Euskal Herriko Alderdi Sozialista (EHAS), "MANIFESTE," p. 1.

52. Ibid.

53. ETA, *Zutik* 65 (August 1975): 12.

54. Ibid. See also Apalategi, "Le mouvement basque aujourd'hui," p. 452.

55. I follow Clark's analysis in *The Basque Insurgents*, pp. 79–81.

56. Ibid., pp. 80–81.

57. *Euskaldunak* 37 (May 1977): 3.

58. *EHASKIDE* (November 27, 1976): 4.

59. The figure of 6,500 appears in both *EHASKIDE* (November 27, 1976) and *Euskaldunak* 31 (November 1976): 2.

60. *EHASKIDE* (November 27, 1976).

61. *EHASKIDE* (January 1977) p. 2.

62. Ibid.

63. *EHASKIDE* (February 25, 1978).

64. Cited in Goyhenetche's rejoinder in *EHASKIDE* (December 1977): 2.

65. Ibid.

66. "Une présentation générale de E.H.A.S.," (ca. 1979), p. 2.

67. "Rélations extérieures," insert to *EHASKIDE* (ca. 1976), p. 2.

68. *EHASKIDE* (May 1979).

69. Ibid.

70. Comité Abertzale Socialiste, "Communiqué sur la répression," tract distributed at the demonstrations organized in Bayonne to protest the trial (ca. September 1975). I believe the reference to Garmendia ("Tupa") in the text in place of Paredes Manot ("Txiki") was an inadvertent error, probably due to the haste with which the document and demonstrations were organized (emphasis in the original).

71. Ibid., p. 99. See also Arregi, *Memorias del Kas, 1975/78;* and *Enbata* 396 (March 25, 1976): 8.

72. See, for example, the text in Basque distributed at the mass rally in Pamplona on September 7, 1976: "Komité Abertzale Sozialista," *Euskaldunak* 29 (August–September 1976): 3.

73. Ibid., p. 78. For a discussion of Herri Batasuna's founding and its relationship with other Basque political parties in Spain, including Euzkadiko Ezkerra (EE), its counterpart to ETA-pm (poli-mili), see Clark, *The Basque Insurgents,* pp. 109ff.

74. "Une présentation générale de E.H.A.S.," p. 2.

75. *EHASKIDE* (January 1977): 2. See also Clark, *The Basque Insurgents,* p. 99.

76. *EHASKIDE* (January 1977).

77. Several former militants of HAS are unanimous in making this point. See also Malherbe, "Le nationalisme basque en France," p. 175.

78. I follow Ronan Roudaut's account of the UDB and the MOB in his "Histoire du mouvement breton," *Temps Modernes* 324–326 (August–September 1973): esp. 185–193.

79. Ibid., p. 185.

80. Cited in ibid., pp. 187–188.

81. Ibid., pp. 188–189. For the dissolution of the Breton movements and the charges against them, see "Le gouvernement dissout quatre mouvements autonomistes," *Le Monde,* January 31, 1974, pp. 1, 7.

82. Cited in Roudaut, "Histoire du mouvement breton," p. 188.

83. Y. Deschamps, "FLB: Un mythe subversif," *Politique Brètagne* 1 (1972), cited in Roudaut, "Histoire du mouvement breton," p. 190.

84. FLB, "Communiqué" (April 29, 1972), cited in Roudaut, "Histoire du mouvement breton," p. 189.

85. Ibid.

86. Ibid., p. 192.

87. "Déclaration sur la lutte contre le colonialisme en Europe occidentale," ms. portfolio no. B-9005, Musée Basque, Bayonne (ca. 1976).

88. Ibid., pp. 7–8.

89. Ibid., p. 9.

90. See, for example, *EHASKIDE* November 27, 1976): 1.

91. Goyhenetche, *Histoire de la colonisation française au Pays Basque,* p. 81.

92. *Euskaldunak* 26 (May 1976): 15.

93. Ibid.

94. See Ramuntxo Camblong, who argued in Basque for support of the candidacy of Guy Héraud in the first round in *Herria* (May 1974). Camblong, choosing the lesser of two evils, then supported Mitterrand in the second round. Jean Etcheverry-Ainchart, on the other hand, supported Valéry Giscard d'Estaing. See also the analysis of Pierre Bidart, "Les élections présidentielles de mai 1974 au Pays Basque," *Bulletin du Musée Basque* 66 (1974): 201–220, who attributes the weakness of Héraud's showing to the overly juridical nature of his federalism and

Héraud's own weakness as the "ethnic" candidate compared to a hypothetical candidacy of the Occitanian theorist Robert Lafont (p. 207).

95. Bidart, "Les élections présidentielles," p. 203.

96. "Explication de notre position," *Euskaldunak* 2 (May 1974): 2.

97. "Présidentielles de l'état français," *Euskaldunak* 2 (May 1974): 2.

98. For results of the first round, see the account of *Herria* (May 9, 1974): 7.

99. "Les Basques se sont trompés de droite," *Euskaldunak* 2 (May 1974): 3.

100. *Herria* (May 9, 1974): 7.

101. Ibid.

102. Ibid. p. 203. Bidart also explains the socialist vote in Soule in reference to the tradition of popular resistance in that province and to the relative weakness of the church, which was a major pillar of the conservative social order of the rightist *notables* elsewhere in the Basque interior. For HAS's reaction to the problem of rural depopulation, see F.-B.L. (Battitta Larzabal), "La liquidation des Basques ou la situation démographique du Pays Basque Nord," *Euskaldunak* 28 (July 1976): 4–7.

103. "Les Basques se sont trompés de droite," p. 2.

104. See Bidart, "Les élections présidentielles," p. 217.

105. See "Bipolarisation basque."

106. "Le pourrissement des notables basques," *Euskaldunak* 16 (July 1975): 1–2.

107. "M. Poniatowski: Il est inadmissible qu'une police étrangère intervienne sur notre territoire," *Le Monde*, June 6, 1975.

108. *Euskaldunak* 17 (August 1975): 3.

109. "Le pourrissement des notables basques," p. 2.

110. *Euskaldunak* 17 (August 1975): 1–2 (emphasis in the original).

111. *Sud-Ouest*, January 6, 1976, p. E.

112. "Les élections cantonales: Quatre victoires par K.O.," *Sud-Ouest*, March 9, 1976, p. A.

113. "Cantonales 2ème Tour," *Enbata* 395 (March 18, 1976): 3–4.

114. Ibid.

115. The first two Basque presidents of the *conseil général* were Delissade in 1882 and Inchauspé in 1949.

116. *Enbata* 396 (March 25, 1976).

117. Ibid.

118. "Département Pays Basque," *Euskaldunak* 8 (November 1974): 2.

119. "Nos propositions pour les élections législatives," *Euskaldunak* 42 (October 1977): 5.

120. *Sud-Ouest*, March 11, 1976, p. E.

121. *Le Monde*, March 8, 1977, p. 12.

122. Ibid.

123. *Euskaldunak* 19 (October 1975): 7.

124. *Euskaldunak* 18 (September 1975): 3.

125. "Editorial: E.H.A.S. et les élections," *Euskaldunak* 34 (February 1977): 3.

126. Ibid.

127. Ibid.

128. *Euskaldunak* 35 (March 1977): 5.

129. Ibid.

130. "EHAS aux élections municipales," *Euskaldunak* 36 (April 1977): 4.

131. Ibid.

132. "H.A.S.I.: Herriko Alderdi Sozialista Iraultzailea," *Euskaldunak* 39 (July 1977): 3. See also Clark, *The Basque Insurgents*, p. 78.

133. "Communiqué de HASI," *Euskaldunak* 39 (July 1977): 3.

134. *Euskaldunak* 39 (July 1977): 3.

135. Jakes Eyheramouno, "Une récolonisation politique," *Euskaldunak* 18 (September 1975): 6.

136. "Editorial," *Pindar* (December 1976): 1.

137. Ibid. (emphasis in the original).

138. "Burubateragile," *EHASKIDE* (February 25, 1977).

139. Ibid.

140. Ibid.

141. Ibid.

142. Ibid., p. 4.

143. "Pour une politique offensive et unitaire du parti," p. 6.

144. Ibid.

145. Ibid., p. 3.

146. Ibid.

147. "La possibilité d'évolution à partir du KAS" (ca. 1977), p. 1.

148. *EHASKIDE* (April 1977): 5.

149. *EHASKIDE* (November 1977): 1.

150. Malherbe, "Le nationalisme basque en France," p. 170.

151. Ibid.

152. "Jazar et les législatives de 78," *Pindar* 1 (December 1977).

153. Ibid.

154. "Communiqué de Jazar, 12 novembre 1977," *Pindar* 1 (December 1977).

155. Ibid.

156. Ibid.

157. *Enbata* 495 (February 19, 1978): 2.

158. Ibid.

159. See Jokin Apalategi, "Consolidación del movimiento abertzale, 1976–1978," in his *Los vascos de la nación al estado*, p. 408.

160. *EHASKIDE* (April 1977): 7.

161. "Editorial: E.H.A.S. et les élections," *Euskaldunak* 34 (February 1977).

162. *Euskaldunak* 45 (January 1978): 4.

163. "Editorial: La décolonisation des peuples," *Euskaldunak* 46 (February 1978): 1.

164. *Euskaldunak* 46 (February 1978): 5.

165. *Le Monde* (ca. January 1978).

166. *Le Monde*, February 5–6, 1978, p. 6.

167. *Euskaldunak* 46 (February 1978): 4.

168. *Euskaldunak* 48 (April 1978): 4.

169. *Enbata* (March 12, 1978).

170. J.-C. Larronde, "Elections et forces politiques en Pays Basque Nord, 1848–1979," ms., 1979, Musée Basque, Bayonne.

171. *Enbata* 498 (March 9, 1978).

172. "Analyses post-électorales," *EHASKIDE* (March 1978): 1.

173. *Euskaldunak* 48 (April 1978): 4–5.

174. "Déception," *Enbata* 499 (March 16, 1978): 2.

175. "Analyses post-électorales," p. 1.

176. *Enbata* 495 (February 16, 1978): 3.

177. Ibid. See EHAS's response: "E.H.A.S. ne répond pas des actes d'autres groupes," *Sud-Ouest*, March 17, 1978.

178. Ibid.

179. Ibid. "One way like another" appears to be an oblique reference to EHAS's rejection of the violence supported by Herri Taldeak as a tool of the Basque struggle.

180. E.H.A.S., "Pour l'autonomie du peuple basque," *Euskaldunak* 59 (March 1979): 4.

181. "Editorial: Elections européens interdites aux minorités," *Euskaldunak* 61 (May 1979): 3.

182. J.-L. Davant, "Echec des nationalistes?" *Euskaldunak* 60 (April 1969): 4.

183. "Analyse des résultats par canton," *Euskaldunak* 60 (April 1979): 4.

184. *EHASKIDE* (October 1978): 2.

185. *Euskaldunak* 1 (March 1974). See also 80 (March–April 1981): 14.

186. F.-B.L., "Politique de rupture et violence," *Euskaldunak* 48 (April 1978): 12–13.

187. Ibid.

188. "Moyens de lutte révolutionnaire," chap. 3 in "Déclaration sur la lutte contre le colonialisme en Europe," ms. no. B-9005, Musée Basque, Bayonne (ca. 1976).

189. Ibid.

190. Ibid.

191. Ibid.

192. IK claimed later that the bomb had in fact been planted the night before and, when it didn't explode, its militants were in the process of retrieving it at the hospital when it did explode.

193. "E.H.A.S.," *Enbata* 606 (April 3, 1980). See also "Los muertos de Bayona, Un detonador," *Punta y Hora de Euskal Herria* 170 (April 10–17, 1980): 35–36.

194. *Euskaldunak* 81 (May 1981): 2.

195. Ibid.

CHAPTER SIX. RADICALIZATION AND THE RISE OF BASQUE VIOLENCE
IN FRANCE: IPARRETARRAK OR ''THOSE OF ETA OF THE NORTH''

1. *ILDO* 2 (Summer 1978): 14.

2. *ILDO* 1 (October 1978): 13.

3. *Koska* 1 (January 31, 1973).

4. The text of IK's message to the people of Baigorri is reproduced in *ILDO* 1 (October 1974): 6–7.

5. Surprisingly, the greatest culprit was Basque journalist Philippe Etcheverry, who was *Le Monde*'s primary stringer in the Pays Basque, even while serving earlier as a member of *Enbata*'s editorial team. See, for example, "La lutte armée," *Le Monde*, March 3, 1984. Familiar with the language, and a party to the discussions within *Enbata* over this same question, his persistence in using the minor and contested translation ("Those of the North") seems intended to separate IK from ETA as a political movement. Ironically, by 1983 HT was as hostile to him as it was to *Enbata* as a whole, referring to Etcheverry as "an individual calling himself a journalist," in *Herriz Herri* 139 (July 21, 1983): 2. The choice of the translation "Those of the North" is also the case in a pseudonymous and bitterly hostile critique of Basque nationalism: Gaizki-Ikasi Maketo, *Contre le racket abertzale, ou les insolences anti-patriotiques d'un métèque*, p. 65.

6. See *Enbata* 984 (July 23, 1987): 4.

7. *ILDO* 2 (Summer 1978): 14.

8. *ILDO* 1 (October 1974): 7 (emphasis in the original).

9. Jean-François Moruzzi and Emmanuel Boulaert, *Iparretarrak: Séparatisme et terrorisme en Pays Basque français* (pp. 8off.), quote extensively from *Erne* 6, which the police found in the backpack of Joseph Etcheveste during his arrest.

10. *ILDO* 1 (October 1974): 2.

11. Ibid., p. 4.

12. Ibid., p. 5.

13. Ibid.

14. *ILDO* 2 (Summer 1978): 28.

15. IK, "Réponse d'Iparretarrak à Enbata sur l'affaire Dagorret," *ILDO* 3 (June 1979): 11.

16. IK, "Message au peuple basque, aux travailleurs et peuples opprimés de l'hexagone, au marcheurs de la liberté," ms. November 1, 1975, p. 2. This document was appended to a mimeographed reproduction of *ILDO* 1 which appeared after the attack on the Victoria-Surf in June 1977 and included other tracts written in the interim.

17. Ibid., p. 2.

18. "Vers une stratégie révolutionnaire," ibid., pp. 14–15.

19. From a conversation in Labourd, in August 1987.

20. "French Urban Professionals."

21. *ILDO* 2 (Summer 1978): 37.

22. Jean-Paul Malherbe, "Le nationalisme basque en France, 1933–1976," p. 171.

23. IK, "Zokoa-ko Ekintza," communiqué attached to the reprint of *ILDO* 1 (ca. Summer 1977).

24. Ibid. (emphasis in the original).

25. Ibid.

26. IK, "Communiqué: Pourquoi le Victoria-Surf," in the reprint of *ILDO* 1 (ca. Summer 1977).

27. For a chronological list of IK's violence between 1973 and 1987, see the annex to Moruzzi and Boulaert, *Iparretarrak*, pp. 221–223.

28. See "Communiqué de Matalaz," *Herriz Herri* 163 (January 12, 1984): 2; and Gilles Mermoz, "Pays Basque: L'eta perd ses refuges," p. 29.

29. IK, "Communiqué du 29 décembre 1977," cited in Moruzzi and Boulaert, *Iparretarrak*, p. 64.

30. *Le Monde*, August 25, 1978.

31. *ILDO* 2 (Summer 1978).

32. Position defended by a Herri Taldeak militant before two hundred diverse Basque militants at the Ipar Euskadi Gaur, May 1985, Cambo. At that meeting, participants estimated that one-third of the audience was pro–armed struggle, one-third was against, and the final third undecided.

33. Moruzzi and Boulaert, *Iparretarrak*, p. 65.

34. Ibid.

35. Ibid.

36. "Historique d'Iparretarrak," *Enbata* 987 (July 23, 1987): 4, and Moruzzi and Boulaert, *Iparretarrak*, p. 60.

37. See "Herri Taldeak: Première démarche publique," *Enbata* 703 (February 4, 1982): 5.

38. "Historique de Herri Taldeak," in *Ipar Euskadi Gaur* (ca. 1985), p. 73.

39. Mermoz, "Pays Basque: L'eta perd ses refuges," p. 29.

40. "Historique de Herri Taldeak," p. 73.

41. Ibid. See also "Herri Taldeak: Première démarche publique," p. 5.

42. "Historique de Herri Taldeak," p. 74. See also "Herri Taldeak: Première démarche publique," p. 4.

43. Ibid., p. 74.

44. *Samatsa* (June 24, 1981).

45. See "Le mouvement politique Herri Taldeak Abertzale Socialiste," *Herriz Herri* 65 (February 11, 1982): 8–10; and "Le mouvement Herri Taldeak 'Pour l'autodétermination,'" *Sud-Ouest*, February 1, 1982.

46. "Herri Taldeak: Première démarche publique," p. 5.

47. "Herri Taldeak et les élections présidentielles," *Enbata* 661 (April 23, 1981): 3.

48. Ibid.

49. "Herri Taldeak: Première démarche publique," p. 6.

50. "Herri Taldeak et la lutté armée," p. 70.

51. "Ipar Euskadi Guar," *Herriz Herri* 232 (March 30, 1985): 3.

52. Ibid.

53. "La violence révolutionnaire, pourquoi?" *ILDO* 4 (July 1979): 6–7.

54. "Attentat à Baigorry: Communiqué Herri Taldeak," *Herriz Herri* 72 (April 1, 1982): 2.

55. See "La traque," *Enbata* 805 (January 19, 1984): 6; and "Quatre membres d'Iparretarrak condamnés," *Le Monde*, January 17, 1985.

56. See "Iparretarrak: Un inculpé refuse de parler français," *Sud-Ouest*, January 20, 1984, which describes Jean Borda's refusal to speak French at his subsequent hearing.

57. "La traque," p. 6.

58. See "Manifestation de Bayonne," *Herriz Herri* 168 (February 16, 1984): 9; and "Procès des quatre convoyeurs," *Herriz Herri* 183 (May 31, 1984): 2.

59. "Quatre membres d'Iparretarrak condamnés."

60. "Procès de Xan," *Enbata* 1110 (January 18, 1990): 6.

61. Ibid.

62. Cited in ibid.

63. Moruzzi and Boulaert, *Iparretarrak*, p. 74.

64. I follow Moruzzi and Boulaert, *Iparretarrak*, pp. 73ff.

65. *Le Monde*, August 15, 1978.

66. Moruzzi and Boulaert, *Iparretarrak*, p. 74.

67. Ibid.

68. "Hordago" comes from the card game *mus* and is a bid which literally means "there it is." It is used as the ultimate challenge when a player risks the entire game on a single outcome. The English equivalent is "all or nothing." I am grateful to Professor William Douglass of the University of Nevada at Reno for pointing this out.

69. From an interview in Bayonne on August 20, 1987.

70. "Introduction," *Eduki* 1 (November 1979): 1.

71. Ibid., p. 4.

72. Cited in *Eduki* 1 (November 1979): 12.

73. Ibid., p. 9.

74. Moruzzi and Boulaert, *Iparretarrak*, p. 71.

75. Hordago tract, n.d. (ca. 1979).

76. See *Enbata* 574 (August 23, 1979): 3.

77. *Le Monde*, April 9, 1981.

78. Ibid.

79. See X. Larrabeiti, "Carta blanca a la guerra sucia," *Punto y Hora* 332 (December 16–23, 1984): 17.

80. See its mimeographed publication *Laguntza* (ca. April 1982).

81. "Violence révolutionnaire," in *Laguntza*, tract dated April 20, 1984.

82. Ibid.

83. Ibid.

84. I follow the short history of *Laguntza* included in a tract distributed in

Hendaye on December 11, 1982, and included in *Borroka Azkar* (ca. 1982), pp. 1–2.

85. See "Laguntza: D'un comité anti-répression à l'affirmation d'un courant politique," in *Laguntza*, tract dated April 20, 1984.

86. This group lasted until the mid-1980s and participated in three "squatts" in all. See Squatters du 1er mai, "Ce qu'on nous refuse, prenons le!" ms. (ca. April 1984).

87. I am indebted to Moruzzi and Boulaert (*Iparretarrak*, pp. 74–75) for the list of movements which follows.

88. Ibid.

89. Ibid., p. 75.

90. See chapter 1.

91. See "Communiqué de Matalaz," p. 2; and Mermoz, "L'eta perd ses refuges," p. 29.

92. "Communiqué de Matalaz."

93. *Le Monde*, July 17, 1985, p. 24.

94. Christian Bombédiac, "Le bureau du sous-préfet de Bayonne est détruit dans un attentat," *Le Monde*, July 1–2, 1979.

95. *ILDO* 4 (July 1979): 8 (emphasis in the original).

96. "Deux terroristes basques sont tués par l'explosion d'une voiture qu'ils venaient de 'piéger,'" *Le Monde*, March 28, 1980.

97. HT continued to repeat this position on the subsequent anniversaries of their deaths. See, for example, "26 mars 80: Ramuntxo, Txomin," *Enbata* 762 (March 24, 1983): 3.

98. See "L'agitation au Pays Basque," *Le Monde*, April 1, 1980; and Jean-March Théolleyre, "Le Pays Basque et ses ambiguïtés," *Le Monde*, April 3, 1980.

99. "La cour de sûreté de l'état est saisie de l'affaire de Bayonne," *Le Monde*, March 30–31, 1980.

100. See 'La cour de sûreté de l'état," *Herriz Herri* 22 (April 16, 1981): 8.

101. Cited in Théolleyre, "Le Pays Basque et ses ambiguïtés."

102. "Txomin et Ramuntxo," *ILDO* 6 (March 1981): 2.

103. See the series of communiqués claiming responsibility for the attacks in *ILDO* 7 (June 1981); and "Attentats," *Herriz Herri* 20 (April 2, 1981): 2.

104. IK, "Communiqué," *Enbata* 663 (May 7, 1981): 3. See also *ILDO* 7 (June 1981): 11–12.

105. "Liste des signataires de l'appel," *Enbata* 663 (May 7, 1981): 8.

106. "Communiqué du 24 mai 1981: Réponse à Enbata sur l'article concernant l'action d'Iparretarrak contre L'hélicoptère de M. Etchandy," *ILDO* 7 (June 1981): 11–12.

107. "Conférence de presse d'Iparretarrak," *Enbata* 659 (April 9, 1981): 4.

108. *ILDO* 7 (June 1981).

109. See "Attentat au Pays Basque français: Un C.R.S. est tué et un autre grièvement blessé," *Le Monde*, March 21–22, 1982; and Moruzzi and Boulaert, *Iparretarrak*, pp. 85–89.

110. Moruzzi and Boulaert claim the police thought this call was a hoax as well, since the caller seemed to be speaking in a fake Spanish accent (*Iparretarrak,* p. 87).

111. "Les enquêteurs estiment crédible la revendication de l'attentat par Iparretarrak," *Le Monde,* March 23, 1982.

112. Ibid.; and Moruzzi and Boulaert, *Iparretarrak,* p. 87.

113. Moruzzi and Boulaert, *Iparretarrak,* p. 87.

114. Patricia Gandin, "Un militant français recherché après l'assassinat en mars de deux C.R.S.," *Le Monde,* May 8, 1982.

115. "Nouvelles hypothèses sur le meurtre d'un C.R.S. au Pays Basque," *Le Monde,* April 9, 1982.

116. Cited in *Herriz Herri* (March 25, 1982).

117. Ibid.

118. Cited in "Nouvelles hypothèses sur le meurtre d'un C.R.S. au Pays Basque."

119. "Communiqué Herri Taldeak," *Herriz Herri* 72 (April 1, 1982): 2.

120. " 'Le gouvernement ne cédera pas aux provocations des terroristes', déclare M. Defferre," *Le Monde,* March 24, 1982.

121. "Communiqué de Seaska," *Herriz Herri* (March 25, 1982).

122. *Sud-Ouest,* March 23, 1982.

123. "Le gouvernement ne cédera pas aux provocations des terroristes."

124. Cited in *Enbata* 1110 (January 18, 1990): 6.

125. Ibid.

126. *Le Monde,* April 11–12, 1982.

127. I follow Moruzzi and Boulaert, *Iparretarrak,* p. 90.

128. IK, "Communiqué," *Herriz Herri* 117 (March 31, 1983): 9. See also IK's communiqué of June 29, 1983, in *Herriz Herri* 137 (July 7, 1983): 2.

129. Ibid.

130. IK, "Communiqué du 26 juillet 1983," *Herriz Herri* 141 (August 4, 1983): 2; and *Enbata* 781 (August 4, 1983): 7.

131. Ibid.

132. IK, "Communiqué du 14 septembre 1983," *Herriz Herri* 147 (September 22, 1983): 2.

133. "Corsisation?" *Enbata* 781 (August 4, 1983): 2.

134. Ibid.

135. "L'auteur présumé de l'attentat d'Ascain a été arrêté," *Le Monde,* August 5, 1983. See also "L'escalade de la violence," *Enbata* 782 (August 11, 1983): 4–5.

136. "L'escalade de la violence," p. 4. *Le Monde* on August 5, 1983, reported his sentence as having been twenty months.

137. "L'escalade de la violence," p. 5.

138. Speculation about his fate suggests that he was an intermediary between Bidart, now in hiding for a year and a half, and the outside world. When the gunfight broke out and he was obliged to abandon his car for fear of it being recognized, it was clear that he was suddenly also propelled into clandestinity.

Authorities speculate that in his crisis, he may have wanted to give himself up since he had not fired on the gendarmes. Whether the others killed him to maintain his silence has never been determined.

139. "Iparretarrak accuse la police française de la disparition de J.-C. Larre," *ILDO* 9 (April 1984): 15–16.

140. See "Le mouvement 'Iparretarrak' donne sa version de la fusillade de Léon," *Le Monde*, August 14–15, 1983; and "Communiqué d'Iparretarrak," *Enbata* 783 (August 18, 1983): 5. It is interesting to note that by this time *Enbata* was not invited to IK's infrequent press conferences and was no longer on the distribution list for its communiqués. The text *Enbata* published in this issue was copied from that of another journalist.

141. "Le point de vue d'Herri Taldeak," *Enbata* 783 (August 18, 1983): 4.

142. "L'escalade de la violence," p. 6.

143. *Le Monde*, August 13, 1983, pp. 1, 11.

144. Ibid.

145. "L'escalade de la violence," p. 4.

146. Cited in "Les Basques comme les Corses?" *Le Monde*, p. 11.

147. Ibid.

148. Ibid.

149. I am indebted to the background offered by Moruzzi and Boulaert (*Iparretarrak*, chap. 8, pp. 55–59) and closely follow their account.

150. Ibid.

151. Eric Hoffer, *The True Believer: Thoughts on the Nature of Mass Movements*, pp. 45–46.

152. Ibid., p. 88.

153. Ibid., p. 46.

154. Karl W. Deutsch, *Nationalism and Social Communication*.

155. Hoffer, *The True Believer*, p. 50.

156. Ibid., pp. 127–128.

157. Cited in ibid., p. 91.

158. Ibid., p. 98.

159. Among the earliest texts on the Marxist-Christian dialogue were two French works by Roger Garaudy, whose English translations are *From Anathema to Dialogue* and *The Alternative Future: A Vision of Christian Marxism*, trans. Leonard Mayhew. Among other sources from this period are Paul Oestreicher, ed., *The Marxist-Christian Dialogue*; Thomas W. Ogletree, *Openings for a Marxist-Christian Dialogue*; Leszek Kolakowski, *Toward a Marxist Humanism*; and Milan Machovec, *A Marxist Looks at Jesus* (English translation of the 1972 German edition).

160. Among the classic texts on liberation theology are Gustavo Gutiérrez, *A Theology of Liberation*, trans. and ed. Sister Caridad Inda and John Eagleson; Paulo Freire, *Pedagogy of the Oppressed*, translated from the Portuguese by Myra Bergman Ramos; and José Miranda, *Marx and the Bible: A Critique of the Philosophy of Oppression*, translated from the original 1971 Mexican edition by John Eagleson.

See also S. A. García and C. R. Calle, eds., *Camilo Torres: Priest and Revolutionary;* and José Miguez Bonino, *Doing Theology in a Revolutionary Situation.*

161. See Moruzzi and Boulaert, *Iparretarrak*, p. 146.

162. Ibid.

163. See Henk Thomas, *Mondragon: An Economic Analysis.*

164. Cited in *Contre le racket abertzale*, p. 32.

165. Cited in Rushworth M. Kidder, "The Terrorist Mentality," in Bernard Schechterman and Martin Slann, eds., *Violence and Terrorism 91/92*, p. 27.

166. Ibid.

167. Cited in Kidder, "The Terrorist Mentality," p. 27.

168. Philippe Boggio, "L'automne basque," *Le Monde*, September 29, 1987, pp. 1, 10.

169. See also "Ce que veut Iparretarrak," *Enbata* 785 (September 1, 1983): 6.

170. "Le début de la violence," *Herriz Herri* 143 (August 18, 1983): 2.

171. "L'attaque," *Enbata* 788 (September 22, 1983): 4.

172. "Luttes politiques et lutté armée," *ILDO* 9 (April 1984): 5.

173. Ibid., pp. 5, 6.

174. " 'Iparretarrak' revendique une fusillade contre des C.R.S.," *Le Monde*, January 6, 1984. See also "IK tire sur un cantonnement de CRS," *Enbata* 804 (January 12, 1984): 7.

175. "IK tire sur un cantonnement de CRS," p. 7.

176. "Arrestations de 4 conférenciers d'Iparretarrak," *Enbata* 804 (January 12, 1984): 7.

177. Ibid.

178. Philippe Etcheverry, "Le parquet de Bayonne ouvre une information contre X pour homicide involontaire," *Le Monde*, March 4–5, 1984. It is interesting to note that while *Le Monde* identified Lafitte as a Herri Taldeak militant in a story probably filed on March 3, appearing in the issue of March 4–5, IK identified him as a militant of IK in its press release of March 3. See also "Un militant d'Iparretarrak a disparu depuis sept mois," *Le Monde*, March 8, 1984; and IK, "Communiqué du 3 mars 1984: Iparretarrak accuse l'état français d'assassinat et de tentative d'assassinat," p. 1.

179. "Un militant d'Iparretarrak a disparu depuis sept mois."

180. "Quatre membres d'Iparretarrak condamnés." The article errs in claiming the four were arrested on January 10, 1983.

181. *Le Monde*, January 26, 1985.

182. "Les armes 'ariégeoises' d'Iparretarrak," *Le Monde*, May 23, 1985.

183. Ibid.

184. See *Sud-Ouest*, July 26, 1985, p. 4; and *Le Monde*, August 15, 1985, p. 7.

185. "Iparretarrak revendique un attentat contre l'office de tourisme de Biarritz," *Le Monde*, December 24, 1985.

186. See *Le Monde*, August 18–19, 1985, p. 9; and *Sud-Ouest*, August 17, 1985, p. A.

187. *International Herald Tribune,* September 6, 1985, p. 3.

188. See *Le Monde,* September 12, 1985, p. 7.

189. Claude Jouanne, "Pays Basque: Encore un attentat signé Iparretarrak," *Sud-Ouest,* September 12, 1985, p. 9.

CHAPTER SEVEN. IPARRETARRAK, ETA, AND GAL: BASQUE VIOLENCE AND THE EVOLUTION OF FRENCH-SPANISH DIPLOMACY

1. Cited in Nicolas Beau, "Les Basques dans leur grande famille," *Le Monde,* October 11, 1984, p. 28.

2. One of the last ETA militants to be executed under Franco.

3. See Robert Clark, *The Basque Insurgents,* pp. 70–81.

4. Francis Jaureguiberry, "Question nationale et mouvements sociaux en Pays Basque Sud," p. 224.

5. *Kemen* (internal bulletin of ETA-pm) 5 (April 1975), cited in Jaureguiberry, "Question nationale et mouvements sociaux en Pays Basque Sud," p. 224.

6. Cited in Gaizki-Ikasi Maketo, *Contre le racket abertzale, ou les insolences anti-patriotiques d'un métèque,* p. 65.

7. Ibid., p. 68.

8. "L'execution de Carrero Blanco," ibid., pp. 6–12; and "Communiqué à l'opinion internationale," ibid., p. 13.

9. ETA, "Communiqué lu au Larzac le 18 aôut 1974," *ILDO* 1 (October 1974): 15. For a description of the struggle at Larzac, see my "Ethnic Mobilization and the Pursuit of Post-industrial Values: The Case of Occitanie," *Tocqueville Review* 2, no. 2 (Spring 1980): 67–87.

10. "Historique d'Iparretarrak," *Enbata* 984 (July 23, 1987): 4.

11. ETA, "Communiqué lu au Larzac le 18 aôut 1974," p. 15 (emphasis added).

12. IK, "Message au peuple basque, aux travailleurs et peuples opprimés de l'hexagone, au marcheurs de la liberté," p. 1.

13. IK, "Communiqué de presse," December 23, 1978.

14. Jean-François Moruzzi and Emmanuel Boulaert, *Iparretarrak: Séparatisme et terrorisme en Pays Basque français,* p. 53.

15. "Iparretarrak (ETA del Norte) no se identifica con ETA, aunque persigue el mismo objetivo," *Hoja del Lunes,* February 2, 1980.

16. "Appel au peuple basque," *ILDO* 6 (March 1981): 26.

17. The source is an article entitled, "Batasuna Borrokan" (Unity in Combat) in *ILDO* 9 (April 1984): 2.

18. Ibid.

19. Ibid.

20. Ibid., p. 82.

21. Ibid.

22. "El 'mal español,' " *Actual,* January 23, 1984, p. 12.

23. "Renseignements généraux," *Enbata* 1151 (November 15, 1990): 7.

24. Ibid. See also *Le Canard Enchaîné*, November 15, 1990, p. 6.

25. IK, "Communiqué du 4 octobre 1981," *Enbata* 685 (October 8, 1981): 3.

26. "Batasuna Borrokan," p. 2 (emphasis in the original).

27. Ibid.

28. *Oldartzen* (ca. 1990).

29. See *Enbata* (December 5, 1985); and *Ager* 54 (December 18, 1985): 1.

30. From Christian Rudel, *Euskadi, Une nation pour les Basques*, cited in *Ager* 45 (March 1985), p. 6.

31. Ibid., p. 7.

32. Cited in *Sud-Ouest*, October 10, 1987, p. B.

33. Cited in Moruzzi and Boulaert, *Iparretarrak*, p. 81.

34. See "Diffamation," *Enbata* 925 (June 5, 1986): 3.

35. *Ekaitza*, 41 (February 12, 1987): 8.

36. *Ekaitza* 40 (February 5, 1987): 3.

37. "Objetivo: Las finanzas de ETA," *Actual*, January 23, 1984, p. 9.

38. "Grabbing ETA by the Wallet," *Economist* (November 15, 1983): 48–49.

39. Ibid.

40. *Ager* 77 (November 22, 1986): 2.

41. Philippe Etcheverry, "Un des fondateurs de l'ETA inculpé d'association de malfaiteurs," *Le Monde*, June 2, 1988.

42. *Le Monde*, July 15, 1989.

43. *Ager* (May 1, 1987): 2.

44. "Recrudescence du terrorisme basque," *Le Monde*, July 16, 1987. See also Thierry Maliniak, "Un français soupçonné de collaboration avec l'ETA comparait devant la justice espagnole," *Le Monde*, December 2, 1988.

45. *Sud-Ouest*, January 8, 1988.

46. See "Arrestations du 1er décembre," *Enbata* 1104 (December 7, 1989): 4; and *Le Monde*, December 2, 1989, and December 3–4, 1989.

47. See James M. Markham, "Top Basque Separatist Leader Is Seized in France," *New York Times*, January 13, 1989, p. 4; and Thierry Maliniak, "Paris est resolu à décapiter l'ETA," *Le Monde*, January 13, 1989.

48. "José Urrutikoetxea avait eu la visite d'un député européen basque espagnol," *Le Monde*, January 15–16, 1989.

49. Maurice Peyrot, "Le parquet demande une peine de dix ans de prison contre Josu Ternera," *Le Monde*, October 19, 1989, p. 13.

50. Ibid.

51. See Thierry Maliniak, "Neuf membres de la filière française de l'ETA ont été inculpés et écroués," *Le Monde*, April 10, 1990, p. 40; Claude Jouanne, "Des tueurs qui paraissaient bien tranquilles," *Le Figaro*, April 10, 1990, pp. 1, 9; Thierry Maliniak, "Le jeu sanglant d'Henri Parot," *Le Monde*, April 11, 1990, p. 14; Claude Jouanne, "Henri Parot couvre ses amis," *Le Figaro*, April 13, 1990, p. 8; Philippe Boggio and Philippe Etcheverry, "Le commando secret des Basques français," *Le Monde*, April 14, 1990, pp. 1, 9; Catherine Delsol, "Le commando n'agissait que

pour tuer," *Le Figaro*, April 17, 1990, p. 7; and Philippe du Tanney, "Français de l'ETA: Un lourd 'palmarès,' " *Le Figaro*, April 24, 1990, p. 10.

52. Alan Riding, "French Suspects Held in Basque Terror," *New York Times*, April 11, 1990, p. A3.

53. See Boggio and Etcheverry, "Le commando secret des Basques français"; and Marie-France Etchegoin and Serge Raffy, "ETA, La saga des tueurs fantômes," *Le Nouvel Observateur*, April 26–May 2, 1990, pp. 126–132.

54. Boggio and Etcheverry, "Le commando secret des Basques français," p. 9.

55. Delsol, "Le commando n'agissait que pour tuer," p. 7.

56. Boggio and Etcheverry, "Le commando secret des Basques français," p. 9. It is interesting to note that this article by Etcheverry led to his break with *Enbata*; he had continued to contribute as a member of its editorial team while serving as regional stringer for *Le Monde*. See the bitter reaction of the relatives of the accused to Etcheverry's part in the article in "Mise au point des familles," *Enbata* 1124 (April 26, 1990): 3.

57. "Henri Parot est condamné à quatre-vingt-six ans de prison par la justice espagnole," *Le Monde*, December 21, 1990.

58. *Le Monde*, April 18, 1990.

59. Maliniak, "Le jeu sanglant d'Henri Parot," p. 14.

60. Etchegoin and Raffy, "ETA, La saga des tueurs fantômes," p. 128.

61. *Enbata* 1122 (April 12, 1990): 3.

62. "Henri Parot est condamné à quatre-vingt-six ans de prison par la justice espagnole," *Le Monde*, December 21, 1990.

63. See *New York Times*, August 17, 1975, p. E3.

64. Ibid.

65. *Miami Herald*, July 7, 1978.

66. I follow the account in *Cambio 16*, January 27, 1992, pp. 8–14.

67. Ibid.

68. See *Ager* 156 (April 15, 1990): 6; and 157 (May 1, 1990): 1–2.

69. Gilles Mermoz, "Pays Basque: ETA perd ses refuges," *Valeurs Actuelles*, July 30, 1984, p. 30.

70. Ibid., p. 29.

71. Cited in Daniel Schneidermann, "La solitude des 'abertzale,' " *Le Monde*, August 2, 1986, p. 6.

72. Agathe Logéart, "La routine des expulsions au Pays Basque français," *Le Monde*, March 12, 1987, p. 12.

73. Clark, *The Basque Insurgents*, p. 35.

74. Ibid.

75. See ibid., pp. 39–40.

76. Christian Bombédiac, "La 'guerre des vacances' de l'ETA; Le ministre de l'intérieur met vivement en cause les autorités françaises," *Le Monde*, June 28, 1980.

77. Clark, *The Basque Insurgents*, p. 212.

78. Bombédiac, "La 'guerre des vacances' de l'ETA."

79. Ibid., p. 216.

80. Ibid.

81. José María Portell, *Los hombres de ETA*, p. 88, cited in Claire Sterling, *The Terror Network*, p. 178. According to Sterling (p. 172), Portell had served as an intermediary between ETA and the Spanish government during the 1970s but was assassinated by ETA-pm in 1977 for having moved, in their eyes, from a role of neutral to protagonist. See also Roberta Goren, *The Soviet Union and Terrorism*, pp. 172–175.

82. Sterling, *The Terror Network*, pp. 179–180. I follow Sterling in the section below.

83. Luis Reyes, "IRA y ETA hablan el mismo idioma," *Qué*, December 12, 1977, pp. 22–23.

84. Goren, *The Soviet Union and Terrorism*, p. 173.

85. Ibid.

86. Flora Lewis, "Western Europe's Militant Minorities Find Common Cause in Secret Meeting," *New York Times*, July 8, 1975.

87. Alfredo Semprun in *ABC* (Madrid), August 3, 1978, cited in Sterling, *The Terror Network*, p. 181.

88. *Annual of Power and Conflict, 1978–79*, p. 70, cited in Sterling, *The Terror Network*, p. 184. See also *Cambio 16*, November 24, 1978; and Goren, *The Soviet Union and Terrorism*, p. 173.

89. "La presse dénonce les soutiens étrangers de l'ETA," *Le Monde*, January 30, 1979.

90. Goren, *The Soviet Union and Terrorism*, pp. 174–175, cites *El País*, January 23, 1979; and *London Daily Telegraph*, November 21, 1979.

91. One of the best, if partisan, sources on this period is Comité d'Enquête sur les Violations des Droits de l'Homme en Europe (CEDRI), *Le GAL ou le terrorisme d'état dans l'Europe des démocraties: Rapport d'enquête*.

92. See Léon Boussard, *Jeiki, Jeiki Etxekoak, ou le défi des Basques*, pp. 152–155.

93. A number of chronological sources exist for the attacks against the refugee community in this period. *Le GAL* provides an annual list and analysis of incidents, including the state of French and Spanish political initiatives. Other good chronological sources for anti-ETA violence include *Euskadi, 1975;* "Atentados contra los refugiados políticos," *Punto y Hora* 331 (December 9–16, 1983): 18–19; and X. Larrabeiti, "Carta blanca a la guerra sucia," *Punto y Hora* 332 (December 16–23, 1984): 18–19.

94. Larrabeiti, "Carta blanca a la guerra sucia," p. 18.

95. Cited in *Le GAL*, p. 8.

96. "Des mercenaires seraient chargés d'intimider les réfugiés espagnols en France," *Le Monde*, July 13–14, 1975.

97. "Une organisation 'anti-terrorisme E.T.A.' revendique les attentats dirigés contre les milieux autonomistes basques," *Le Monde*, July 12, 1975.

98. "Un commando espagnol anti-basque est arrêté près de Saint Jean-de-Luz," *Le Monde*, August 28, 1975.

99. Bernard Brigouleix, "In Search of a Future," translated from *Le Monde*, in *Manchester Guardian*, July 6, 1980.

100. Philippe Etcheverry, "La piste du GAL," *Le Monde*, April 19–20, 1987.

101. Gayle Rivers (pseudonym), *The Specialist* (New York: Charter Books, 1985).

102. *Sud-Ouest*, December 5, 1987, p. A.

103. "L'un des dirigeants présumés du mouvement basque ETA appréhendé à Hendaye," *Le Monde*, June 5–6, 1977, p. 24.

104. *Le Monde*, September 4–5, 1977, p. 18.

105. *Le Monde*, August 30, 1977, p. 26.

106. "Cinco años de guerra subterránea contra ETA," *Actual* 84 (October 31, 1983): 17.

107. *Le GAL*, p. 20.

108. I follow Robert Clark, *Negotiating with ETA*, pp. 46–47.

109. Charles Van Hecke, "Madrid se félicite de la coopération français," *Le Monde*, February 1, 1979.

110. Clark, *Negotiating with ETA*, p. 46.

111. "Le ministre de l'intérieur met vivement en cause les autorités françaises," *Le Monde*, June 28, 1980.

112. "La provocation de Roson," *Enbata* 642 (December 11, 1980): 3.

113. "L'ETA vise Madrid et Paris," *Le Monde*, July 3, 1979.

114. "Basque Terrorist Group Vows to End Bombings," *New York Times*, August 2, 1979.

115. See Rivers, *The Specialist*, p. 136.

116. Ibid., pp. 132–201.

117. *Le GAL*, p. 26.

118. Ibid., p. 25.

119. Cited in "Cinco años de guerra subterránea contra ETA," p. 17.

120. "Les assises de Pau," *Enbata* 642 (December 11, 1980): 8.

121. "Cinco años de guerra subterránea contra ETA," p. 12.

122. Cited in *Le GAL*, p. 122.

123. Cited in Luis Reyes, "Los terroristas vascos tienen miedo en Francia," *Tiempo*, November 7, 1983, p. 24.

124. Cited in Philippe Boggio, "L'escalade du 'contre-terrorisme' au Pays Basque," *Le Monde*, March 25–26, 1984, p. 8.

125. Mitterrand's defense of the doctrine of asylum continued to be a major obstacle in French-Spanish relations. See "Madrid: Soulagement chez les Basques," *Le Monde*, August 19, 1982.

126. "Comment la France socialiste favorise le terrorisme," *Le Figaro Magazine* 235 (February 18–24, 1984): 66.

127. See "Cooperation à la hussarde," *Le Monde*, July 22, 1986, p. 1.

128. Cited in Michel Wieviorka, "French Politics and Strategy on Terrorism," in Barry Rubin, ed., *The Politics of Counter-Terrorism: The Ordeal of Democratic States*, p. 75.

129. "Objetivo: Las finanzas de ETA," p. 10.

130. "Madrid: Les autorités accueillent avec scepticisme le plan français," *Le Monde*, August 23, 1982.

131. Thierry Maliniak, "Le secteur minoritaire de l'ETA politico-militaire aurait décidé sa dissolution," *Le Monde*, September 30, 1982.

132. "Le chef présumé de l'E.T.A. (P.M.) est écroué en France," *Le Monde*, October 15, 1982.

133. *Le GAL*, pp. 35–36.

134. Ibid., p. 36.

135. Ibid., p. 41.

136. Xavier Raufer, with Jean-Dominique Padovani, "GAL: Des 'justiciers' bien encombrants," *L'Express*, November 18, 1988, p. 38.

137. Ibid., p. 41.

138. Ibid., p. 39.

139. Ibid.

140. "Las claves ocultas de la 'guerra sucia' contra ETA," *Tiempo*, January 9, 1984, p. 24.

141. Comité pour la Défense des Droits de l'Homme en Pays Basque, communiqué, August 8, 1984, p. 2.

142. *Le GAL*, p. 53.

143. Raufer, with Padovani, "GAL: Des 'justiciers' bien encombrants," p. 38.

144. Ibid.

145. "Objetivo: Las finanzas de ETA," *Actual* 96 (January 23, 1984): 12.

146. "Las claves ocultas de la 'guerra sucia' contra ETA," p. 24.

147. "Analyse politique du G.A.L.," *Laguntza* (July 1985): 20.

148. Cited in "La mort de la contrebande au Pays Basque," *Le Matin*, February 26, 1986, p. 15.

149. "ETA: Il n'y a plus de Pyrénées," *Le Point*, January 22, 1984, p. 61.

150. "Coups de feu contre un C.R.S. au Pays Basque," *Le Monde*, January 5, 1984.

151. Ibid.

152. Cited in Thierry Maliniak, "Le groupe antiterroriste de libération est composé d'une centaine de mercenaires," *Le Monde*, May 19, 1984.

153. Ibid.

154. "Des policiers espagnols auraient été les commanditaires du GAL," *Le Monde*, May 9, 1985.

155. "M. González: Des 'erreurs sans fondement,' " *Le Monde*, May 11, 1985.

156. "M. Pasqua dénonce des personnes 'payées par un état étranger,' " *Le Monde*, May 28, 1986.

157. See *Sud-Ouest*, November 25, 1987, p. 5; and *Le Monde*, July 7, 1988.

158. Cited in *Libération*, January 11, 1985, p. 14.

159. Ibid.

160. John Darnton, "General Is Slain in Madrid: Basque Terrorists Suspected," *New York Times*, January 30, 1984, p. 4.

161. Ibid. See also "ETA: Il n'y a plus de Pyrénées," p. 60.

162. Gilles Mermoz, "Pas Basque: L'Eta perd ses refuges," *Valeurs Actuelles*, July 30, 1984, p. 30.

163. "Collaboration France-GAL," *Herriz Herri* 188 (July 5, 1984): 2.

164. *Le Monde*, August 7, 1984. See also "G.A.L.: Un exécutif français," *Enbata* 830 (August 9, 1984): 4–5.

165. See "Collaboration France-GAL," p. 2.

166. See "Defferre ne veut pas porter le béret," *Le Canard Enchaîné*, April 4, 1984, p. 1.

167. Ibid.

168. Darnton, "General Is Slain in Madrid," p. 4.

169. Georges Marion, "Les Espagnols subventionnent l'exportation de Basques," *Le Canard Enchaîné*, June 20, 1984.

170. Ibid.

171. "Conférence de Presse d'Anai-Artea," *Sud-Ouest*, June 30, 1984.

172. Philippe Etcheverry, "Le GAL sous surveillance," *Le Monde*, October 11, 1984.

173. "Deux membres présumés du GAL remis en liberté," *Le Monde*, November 30, 1984.

174. Philippe Boggio, "Les attentats au Pays Basque français," *Le Monde*, April 11, 1985.

175. Cited in Eric Favereau, "Le cas du juge Svahn," *Libération*, January 11, 1985, p. 13.

176. "M. Destrade et les 'mercenaires' du GAL," *Le Monde*, April 3, 1985.

177. Ibid.

178. Cited in Favereau, "Le cas du juge Svahn," p. 14.

179. "L'Espagne se félicite de la collaboration de la police français au Pays Basque," *Le Monde*, February 2, 1985.

180. Philippe Etcheverry, "L'ETA, organisation de libération, ou association de malfaiteurs?" *Le Monde*, March 2–3, 1986.

181. Cited in "Nous avions notre train à 21 h 25: Il a donc fallu tirer . . . ," *Le Monde*, March 8, 1986.

182. Philippe Etcheverry, "Un berger et une jeune fille sont assassinés par le GAL," *Le Monde*, February 19, 1985, p. 24.

183. "Les 'bavures ordinaires' de truands au rabais," *Le Monde*, March 8, 1986.

184. Boggio, "Les attentats au Pays Basque français," pp. 1–8.

185. *L'Evénement*, December 1, 1987, p. 20.

186. *Pyrénées-Magazine*, December 2, 1987, p. 20.

187. Boggio, "Les attentats au Pays Basque français," p. 1.

188. Ibid.

189. *Libération*, July 28, 1987, pp. 20–21.

190. "La tueuse blonde du G.A.L. se rend à la justice?" *Enbata* 1034 (July 7, 1988): 3.

191. *Le Monde*, July 7, 1988.

192. Philippe Etcheverry, "Quatre réfugiés basques tués à la sortie d'un bar," *Le Monde*, September 27, 1985.

193. "Le GAL revendique l'attentat contre quatre réfugiés basques," *Le Monde*, September 28, 1985, p. 8.

194. Philippe Etcheverry, "Des réfugiés basques ont manifesté malgré l'interdiction préfectorale," *Le Monde*, October 20, 1985, p. 11.

195. Cited in Boggio, "Les attentats au Pays Basque français," p. 8.

196. "M. Pasqua dénonce des personnes 'payées par un état étranger'"; and "Pasqua: Abattre le terrorisme—Guerre contre tous les terrorismes," *Sud-Ouest*, May 26, 1986.

197. Cited in Philippe Etcheverry, "Trois membres présumés du GAL condamnés à vingt ans de réclusion," *Le Monde*, May 22, 1987.

198. *Ager* 61 (March 27, 1986): 7.

199. Cited in Nicolas Beau, "Trêve au Pays Basque français," *Le Monde*, April 29–30, 1984.

200. Ibid.

201. "'Txomin' a été expulsé de France," *Le Monde*, July 15, 1986, p. 2.

202. See Clark, *Negotiating with ETA*.

203. "José Varona López expulsé vers l'état espagnol," *Ekaitza* 12 (July 24, 1986): 2.

204. B. L. G., "Détournement de procédure," *Le Monde*, July 22, 1986, p. 8.

205. "Coopération à la hussarde," p. 1.

206. "Paris et Madrid renforcent la lutte contre le terrorisme," *Le Monde*, July 22, 1986, p. 1.

207. "M. Raimond: 'Il y aura peut-être d'autres expulsions," *Le Monde*, July 22, 1986, p. 8; and "Paris et Madrid renforcent la lutte contre le terrorisme," p. 1.

208. Cited in Edward Schumacher, "Suddenly, Basques Find Haven Full of Hazards," *New York Times*, September 9, 1986, p. 8.

209. Thierry Maliniak, "M. Felipe González a écrit à M. Chirac pour le remercier de sa coopération, *Le Monde*, July 23, 1986, p. 3.

210. Cited in *Ager* 70 (July 31, 1986): 10.

211. Philippe Etcheverry, "Deux réfugiés basques sont expulsés par la France," *Le Monde*, August 29, 1986, p. 26.

212. Ibid.

213. "Plus de sanctuaire pour l'ETA," *Le Monde*, August 8, 1984.

214. Thierry Maliniak, "Madrid remercie Paris pour son comportement envers les militants basques," *Le Monde*, August 31, 1986, p. 3.

215. Daniel Schneidermann, "La solitude des 'abertzale,'" *Le Monde*, August 2, 1986, pp. 1–6.

216. Thierry Maliniak, "L'ambassade de France dément tout contact avec l'ETA militaire," *Le Monde*, December 4, 1984; and *Libération*, February 27, 1986, pp. 26–28. ETA, in an interview with French television channel TF 1 on November 19, 1986, stated that the meeting was at noon on September 22. See "e.t.a.: T.F. 1, 19 novembre," *Enbata* 950 (November 27, 1986): 4.

217. Cited in "e.t.a.: T.F. 1, 19 novembre," p. 4.

218. *Libération*, February 27, 1986, p. 26.

219. Thierry Maliniak, "L'un des membres supposés de l'ETA militaire extradé par la France aurait été acquitté," *Le Monde*, April 19, 1985.

220. *L'Express*, November 18, 1988, p. 38.

221. See Thierry Maliniak, "L'ETA étend son champ d'action," *Le Monde*, December 31, 1986, p. 4; "Nouveaux attentats antifrançais," *Le Monde*, December 30, 1986, p. 4; and "Blast Rips Basque Showroom a Day before Regional Vote," *New York Times*, November 30, 1986, p. 13.

222. Maliniak, "L'ETA étend son champ d'action," p. 4.

223. Thierry Maliniak, "Madrid face au défi de l'ETA militaire," *Le Monde*, August 14, 1985, p. 1.

224. Ibid.

225. *Euskadi 1984*, p. 166, cited in Clark, *Negotiating with ETA*.

226. *Tiempo*, July 8, 1991, p. 51.

227. *Tiempo*, July 1, 1991, p. 36.

228. Ibid.

229. *El País*, October 5, 1991, p. 23.

230. *Cambio 16*, September 30, 1991, p. 36.

231. Ibid.

232. Maliniak, "Le gouvernement dément les rumeurs de negotiation avec l'ETA," p. 3.

233. Thierry Maliniak, "Nous ne negocierons pas avec les assassins de l'ETA," *Le Monde*, October 12–13, 1986, p. 4.

234. "Les services spéciaux de Madrid ont repéré en Algérie des militants de l'ETA," *Le Monde*, October 12–13, 1986, p. 4.

235. See Thierry Maliniak, "MM. Mitterrand et González discutent de la coopération dans la lutte antiterroriste," *Le Monde*, August 26, 1987, p. 4; and his "Contacts entre Madrid et l'ETA?" *Le Monde*, August 27, 1987, p. 4.

236. See Maliniak, "Contacts entre Madrid et l'ETA?" p. 4; and Thierry Maliniak, "Madrid confirme qu'un dialogue est en cours avec l'ETA," *Le Monde*, September 1, 1987, p. 6. Other sources include Paul Delaney, "Basque Terror Grinds on Despite Talks," *International Herald Tribune*, September 5–6, 1987, p. 2; and Thierry Maliniak, "Madrid reste prudent sur les tentatives de dialogue avec l'ETA," *Le Monde*, September 4, 1987, p. 6.

237. *Cambio 16*, February 22, 1992, p. 15.

238. Ibid., p. 19.

239. This section is based on excerpts from the Rose Commission's report contained in Thierry Maliniak, "Le problème de la violence doit être réglé par les Basques eux-mêmes," *Le Monde*, April 8, 1986.

240. Edward Schumacher, "No End in Sight for Basque Terrorism," *New York Times*, August 24, 1986.

241. Ibid.

242. Cited in *Cambio 16*, February 24, 1992, pp. 14–19.

243. From an interview on *ABC*, February 18, 1992, p. 22.

244. See *El País*, February 9, 1992, p. 3.

245. *Libération*, March 31, 1992, p. 29.

246. Ibid.

247. Ibid.

248. Ibid.

249. Logéart, "La routine des expulsions au Pays Basque français," p. 12.

250. Cited in ibid.

251. "Les Espagnols auraient remis aux autorités françaises la liste des membres présumés de l'ETA," *Le Monde*, August 9–10, 1987, p. 6.

252. Ibid.

253. Ramón-Luis Acuña, "Madrid réclame les chefs de l'ETA," *Le Figaro*, August 8–9, 1987, p. 3.

254. Moruzzi and Boulaert, *Iparretarrak*, pp. 195–196.

255. Ibid., p. 199.

256. Ibid., pp. 196–197.

257. Clark, *Negotiating with ETA*.

258. Ibid., p. 197.

259. Frédéric Pons, "Guerre secrète en Euskadi," *Valeurs Actuelles*, October 12–18, 1987, p. 40.

260. Ibid., p. 198.

261. *Deia*, October 22, 1987; and *El País*, November 10, 1987, cited in Clark, *Negotiating with ETA*.

262. Clark, *Negotiating with ETA*. Clark cites as his source *Euskadi 1988*, p. 175.

263. *Ya*, July 12, 1987, cited in "La France est déterminée à expulser tous les terroristes basques," *Le Monde*, July 14, 1987.

264. Pons, "Guerre secrète en Euskadi," p. 38.

265. Ibid., p. 39.

266. *Eclair-Pyrénées*, October 9, 1987, p. 3.

267. Cited in *Sud-Ouest*, October 9, 1987, p. 5.

268. See Philippe Boggio, "L'asile hors la loi," *Le Monde*, February 12, 1988.

269. See Philippe Boggio, "Le temps des ruptures au Pays Basque," *Le Monde*, October 9, 1987, pp. 1, 12.

270. Cited in ibid.

271. Thierry Maliniak, "M. Pierre Joxe plaide pour une coopération plus discrète contre l'ETA," *Le Monde*, May 28, 1988.

272. Thierry Maliniak, "Madrid attend de Paris de nouvelles formes de coopération," *Le Monde*, August 7–8, 1988.

273. Thierry Maliniak, "Français et Espagnols coordonent leur politique européenne pour 1989," *Le Monde*, September 3, 1988.

274. "M. Pierre Joxe a répondu aux critiques dont il est l'objet à propos de la lutte antiterroriste," *Le Monde*, October 11, 1988.

275. Ibid.

276. Ibid.

277. "Assemblée Nationale—Séance du 12 octobre 1988 (Journal officiel: Extraits des déclarations)" cited in *Enbata* 1047 (October 20, 1988): 3.

278. Ibid.

279. "Un entretien avec M. Felipe González," *Le Monde,* November 23, 1988.

280. "M. Joxe veut aider la démocratie espagnole dans un respect scrupuleux des droits de l'homme," *Le Monde,* January 14, 1989.

281. Ibid.

282. Ibid.

283. *Egin* (July 19, 1991).

284. Ibid.

285. See "Communiqué d'E.T.A. au peuple basque," *Enbata* 1012 (February 4, 1988): 4.

286. Ibid., p. 5.

287. Ibid.

288. See Thierry Maliniak, "Le risque de la réinsertion," *Le Monde,* September 12, 1986.

289. *El País,* December 11, 1991, p. 15; *Tiempo,* May 11, 1992, pp. 40–48.

290. Claude Jouanne, "Artapalo, 'général' de l'ETA," *Le Figaro,* July 28–29, 1990, p. 9.

291. *Ager* 73 (September 23, 1986): 3–6.

292. Cited in Etchegoin and Raffy, "ETA: La saga des tueurs fantômes," p. 131.

293. Ibid.

294. Armando Puente, "Trois membres de l'ETA parlent," *Le Point,* May 25, 1987, p. 86.

295. "L'ETA revendique l'assassinat de 'Yoyes,'" *Le Monde,* September 13, 1986, p. 32.

296. Ibid.

297. Ibid.

298. From the interview in *Cambio 16,* February 24, 1992, pp. 14–19.

299. "French Nab ETA Leader Long Sought by Spain," *Washington Post,* January 14, 1989.

300. Cited in *Libération,* March 31, 1992, p. 29.

301. Cited in *Cambio 16,* December 16, 1991.

302. Cited in *El País,* December 2, 1991, p. 15.

303. Ibid.

304. *El País,* May 17, 1992, pp. 1–2.

305. Cited in *Cambio 16,* April 20, 1992, pp. 12–17.

306. Ibid.

307. See *Cambio 16,* April 13, 1992, pp. 16–21.

308. Cited in *Cambio 16,* December 16, 1991.

309. *El País,* March 4, 1992, p. 15.

310. *El País,* December 11, 1991, p. 15.

311. *Enbata* 1024 (April 28, 1988): 3.

312. *Diario 16,* February 24, 1992, p. 5.

313. Ibid.

314. See *Diario 16*, February 16, 1992, p. 7.

315. Cited in ibid.

316. Ibid.

317. *Enbata* 1144 (September 27, 1990): 3.

318. Thierry Maliniak, "Jesús Arkautz a été arrêté au Pays Basque français," *Le Monde*, March 21, 1991.

319. *Ya*, August 19, 1991, p. 3.

320. *El País*, May 17, 1992, pp. 1–2.

321. *El País*, December 13, 1991, p. 19.

322. *Cambio 16*, December 16, 1991.

323. U.S. Department of State, *Patterns of Global Terrorism*, p. 8.

324. *El País*, October 30, 1991, p. 19.

325. *El País*, December 12, 1991, p. 11.

326. *El País*, December 12, 1991, p. 11.

327. See *El País*, February 13, 1992, p. 13; and February 14, 1992, p. 17.

328. Cited in *El País*, February 13, 1992, p. 13.

329. *Le Figaro*, March 2, 1992, p. 28.

330. Cited in Erich Inciyan, "L'ETA militaire est décapitée," *Le Monde*, March 31, 1992, p. 29.

331. I follow the account of *Cambio 16*, April 13, 1992, pp. 16–21.

332. See Alan Riding, "Spain Sees Arrest of Basque Rebels as Easing Threat to Olympics and Fair," *New York Times*, March 31, 1992, p. A7; and "Arrestations à Bidart," *Enbata* 1221 (April 2, 1992): 3.

333. See Philippe Marcovici, "Bande armée," *Le Quotidien de Paris*, March 31, 1992, p. 17.

334. *El País*, May 17, 1992, p. 1.

335. *Cambio 16*, April 20, 1992, pp. 12–17.

336. See "La grande offensive contre ETA," *Enbata* 1228 (May 21, 1992): 4; and *El País*, May 5, 1992, p. 15.

337. "La grande offensive contre ETA," p. 4. See also *Cinco Días*, May 8, 1992, p. 42; and *Le Figaro*, May 16–17, 1992, p. 10.

338. *Libération*, March 31, 1992, p. 29.

339. Cited in Michel Bole-Richard, "Satisfaction prudente à Madrid," *Le Monde*, March 31, 1992, p. 29.

340. Cited in "Top Basque Guerrilla Is Arrested," *New York Times*, March 30, 1992, p. A4.

341. Cited in Michel Bole-Richard, "Le gouvernement n'exclut pas une riposte des séparatistes basques," *Le Monde*, April 1, 1992, p. 3.

342. Ibid.

343. Cited in Riding, "Spain Sees Arrest of Basque Rebels as Easing Threat to Olympics and Fair," p. A7.

344. *El País*, May 5, 1992, p. 15.

345. Ibid. See also *El País*, May 17, 1992, pp. 1–2.

346. Ibid.; and *Tiempo*, May 18, 1992, pp. 48–53.

347. *El País*, May 17, 1992, pp. 1–2.

348. *El País*, May 21, 1992, p. 17.

349. I follow the account in *Tiempo*, May 11, 1992, pp. 40–48.

350. "Les dirigeants présumés d'ETA militaire ont été inculpés à Paris," *Le Monde*, April 4, 1992, p. 15.

351. *El País*, March 4, 1992, p. 13. See also Alan Riding, "Spain Prepares for Offensive by Basque Separatist Group," *New York Times*, March 29, 1992, p. 8.

352. Cited in *Libération*, March 31, 1992, p. 29.

353. John Hooper, "Threat of Basque Rebels to Games Lessens," *Atlanta Journal/ Atlanta Constitution*, July 18, 1992, p. A8 (reprinted from the *London Observer*).

354. *Enbata* 1229 (May 28, 1992): 3.

355. Martha Crenshaw, "How Terrorism Ends."

CHAPTER EIGHT. THE ECLIPSE OF VIOLENCE AND THE RISE OF
BASQUE MODERATION

1. Izan, "Schéma d'orientation autogéstionnaire," n.d. (ca. 1979).

2. *Izan-Hitzak* 15 (September 1981): 2.

3. "Ateka," *Enbata* 780 (July 28, 1983): 7. See also "Iparralde: parón total," *Punto y Hora* 324 (October 21–28, 1983): 43.

4. *Ateka* 2 (November 1983): 2.

5. Cited in *Ateka* 32 (July 1986): 4.

6. "Pour un statut du prisonnier politique: Une campagne en Pays Basque et dans l'état français," *Herriz Herri* 211 (December 28, 1984): 2.

7. *Ateka* 32 (July 1986): 5.

8. See "E.L.B. se définit," *Herriz Herri* 167 (February 9, 1984): 9; and the copy which appeared in the monthly newsletter for Basque and Béarnais farmers in the Pyrénées-Atlantiques, *Laborari Lo Paisan* 14 (January 1984): 15–16.

9. See "Iparralde: parón total," p. 43.

10. *Ager* 50 (October 15, 1985): 3.

11. Ibid.

12. Ibid.

13. Ibid.

14. Ibid. (emphasis in the original).

15. Jean-Marc Cazaubon and Vianney Cier, "IK/ELB: Vers un débat de la gauche abertzale," *Ateka* 5 (February 1984): 3.

16. "Proposition de loi portant création d'un département Pays Basque," *Enbata* 649 (January 29, 1981): 4–5.

17. "Conférence de presse du P.S. Pays Basque," *Enbata* 650 (February 5, 1981): 4.

18. "Tribune libre: Un projet suicidaire," reproduced in *Enbata* 651 (February 12, 1981): 8.

19. "Un département pays basque?" *Le Monde*, September 10, 1981.

20. Cited in "Département P. Basque," *Enbata* 655 (March 12, 1981): 6.

21. Cited in *Le Monde*, March 7, 1981.

22. Cited in *Enbata* 652 (February 19, 1981): 6.

23. For the argument in favor of a Basque department, see "Un nouveau département: Pourquoi?" offprint from *Activités en Pays Basque* 280 (February 1976).

24. "Présidentielles," *Enbata* 664 (April 14, 1981): 3.

25. *Herriz Herri* 26 (May 14, 1981): 1.

26. *Herriz Herri* 31 (June 18, 1981): 1.

27. See Jean-Claude Larronde, "Decepciones y esperanzas: Abertzales en Iparralde (1981–1986)," *Muga* 8, no. 54 (May 1986): 10.

28. J.-D. Chaussier, "L'échec du projet de création d'un département en Pays Basque: L'enfermement du localisme culturel par le pouvoir central," *Bulletin du Musée Basque* 120 (1988).

29. Gilles Darcy, in the foreword to *La libre administration des collectivités locales, réflexions sur la décentralisation*, p. 16, cited in Chaussier, "L'échec du projet de création d'un département en Pays Basque."

30. Cited in "Vous ne serez pas indépendants," *Le Monde Dossiers et Documents* 107 (January 1984): 2.

31. See *Sud-Ouest*, January 9, 1982, p. 1; and *Enbata* 700 (January 14, 1982): 4. For a longer discussion of this issue, see Larronde, "Decepciones y esperanzas," pp. 6–10.

32. "M. Gaston Defferre: Pas de département basque," *Le Monde*, January 10–11, 1982.

33. "Faut voir," *Enbata* 706 (February 25, 1982): 3. See also "Mission interministérielle," *Enbata* 716 (May 6, 1982): 5; "Département basque: Création d'une commission," *Le Monde*, February 25, 1982; and "Des élus du Pays Basque demandent la création d'un département autonome," *Le Monde*, February 23, 1982, p. 12.

34. Cited in *Enbata* 745 (November 25, 1982): 4.

35. "Defferre à la presse marseillaise: Pas de département basque," *Enbata* 718 (May 20, 1982): 6.

36. See Larronde, "Decepciones y esperanzas," p. 10.

37. "Coup de grâce au rapport Ravail," *Enbata* 745 (November 25, 1982): 4.

38. "Département Pays Basque," *Enbata* 776 (June 30, 1983): 2.

39. *Enbata* 664 (April 14, 1981): 2.

40. Cited in Nicolas Beau, "Trêve au Pays Basque français," *Le Monde*, April 29–30, 1984.

41. See "On nous a menti," *Herriz Herri* 183 (May 31, 1984): 10.

42. From an interview in Biarritz on August 22, 1985.

43. Cited in "Iparretarrak revendique d'Hendaye à Pau," *Enbata* 1209 (January 12, 1992): 3.

44. See Axel Krause, "France Drops Out of Fighter," *International Herald Tribune*, August 3–4, 1985, p. 1.

45. "Contribution au débat sur la lutte armée en Euskadi Nord," *Ateka* 12 (September 1984): 11.

46. Ibid.

47. Ibid.

48. "Herritarki: Des orientations pour les municipales," *Sud-Ouest*, August 8, 1982.

49. See Larronde, "Decepciones y esperanzas," p. 12.

50. Ibid.

51. Fina (pseudonym), "Lettre ouverte à I.K.," *Herriz Herri* 185 (June 14, 1984): 2.

52. ". . . Gaur," *Ateka* 20 (May 1985): 8. See also "Ipar Euskadi Gaur: Un rassemblement du mouvement abertzale," *Herriz Herri* 231 (March 23, 1985): 2.

53. "Ipar Euskadi Gaur . . . eta bihar," *Ateka* 21 (June 1985): 9.

54. Jean-Marc Cazaubon, "Démarche pour la constitution d'un mouvement abertzale de gauche," *Ateka* 25 (October 1985): 6.

55. From an interview in Bayonne in August 1991. All quotations here from Irazusta are from this interview.

56. Laguntza, "Par rapport aux élections législatives de 86," ephemeral tract, July 9, 1985, p. 1.

57. "EMA arrive, Atxik!" *Ateka* 26 (November 1985): 12.

58. "E.M.A. ta zabal zazu," *Ateka* 27 (December 1985): 8.

59. "Atxik, l'anti-promesse: Invitation à une lutte," *Ateka* 29 (February 1986): 6.

60. D. D., "Borrokak batasunean," *Ateka* 27 (December 1975): 13.

61. See J.-M.C., "EMA," *Ateka* 28 (January 1986): 6, cited in Larronde, "Decepciones y esperanzas," p. 14.

62. Ibid.

63. See *Ekaitza* 0 (March 30, 1986): 3–4.

64. Cited in "Au Pays Basque," *Le Matin*, February 26, 1986, p. 15.

65. See the results in *Enbata* 914 (March 20, 1986) and 915 (March 27, 1986).

66. I follow Larronde, "Decepciones y esperanzas," p. 14.

67. "Les résultats du scrutin," *Ekaitza* 0, special supplement for the Aberri Eguna of 1986 (March 30, 1986): 1.

68. Larronde, "Decepciones y esperanzas," p. 14.

69. *Ekaitza* 0 (March 30, 1986): 3.

70. Cited in ibid.

71. Ibid., p. 2.

72. Cited in ibid., p. 3.

73. Un Lycéen, "Mathématique au Lycée: EMA = HT = IK," *Ekaitza* 0 (March 30, 1986): 4.

74. Ibid., p. 5.

75. "Ekaitza!" *Ateka* 31 (April 1986): 2.

76. "Ateka: Rideau," *Ateka* 40 (March 1987): 2.

77. "Pour une stratégie de la communication en Pays Basque Nord," *Ateka* 31 (April 1986): 9.

78. "Assemblée générale d'EMA," *Ekaitza* 28 (November 13, 1986): 2.

79. Robert Clark, *The Basque Insurgents*, p. 253.

80. "Iparralde Eguna," *Enbata* 1093 (September 21, 1989): 4.

81. "E.M.A. récentre son action," *Enbata* 1077 (May 18, 1989): 5. See also the interview with Alain Iriart of EMA in *Enbata* 1092 (September 14, 1989): 3.

82. Txetx Etcheverry, "La coordination Patxa/Gabe/Oldartzen et Euskal Batasuna/EMA/IEGA," internal document of Patxa (ca. 1990–91).

83. Ibid.

84. *Egin* (July 15, 1981).

85. *Ager* 3 (September 1981): 5.

86. *Ager* 185 (July 15, 1991): 7.

87. Cited in ibid.

88. Ibid.

89. *Ager* 158 (May 15, 1990): 6.

90. "Proposition du mouvement," handwritten proposal for the creation of EB (ca. October 1985).

91. *Ager* 54 (December 15, 1985): 1.

92. See "Un nouveau mouvement politique: Euskal Batasuna," *Ekaitza* 35 (January 1, 1987): 5; "Euskal Batasuna," *Enbata* 924 (May 29, 1986): 5; and "Euskal Batasuna," *Enbata* 929 (July 3, 1986): 6.

93. Jacques Abeberry, "Mai 86," editorial in *Enbata* 924 (May 29, 1986): 2.

94. *Ager* 169 (November 15, 1990): 6.

95. "Euskal Batasuna," p. 4. *Enbata* 931 (July 17, 1986): 4–6.

96. Ibid.

97. "Euskal Batasuna," *Enbata* 931 (July 17, 1986): 4–6.

98. "Un nouveau mouvement politique: Euskal Batasuna," p. 5.

99. Ibid.

100. See "Une politique économique pour Ipar Euskadi," "Agriculture en Ipar Euskadi," "La culture basque," and "Comment situer notre revendication en ce qui concerne le territoire et les institutions" (all ca. 1987).

101. "Les principes économiques de EB," chap. 2 in "Une politique économique pour Ipar Euskadi" (ca. 1987), p. 3.

102. "e.a.: Bayonne, 19 novembre," *Enbata* 950 (November 27, 1986): 5.

103. Ibid.

104. Ibid.

105. Ibid.

106. Ibid.

107. Bernard Cohen, "Le Pays Basque entre deux voies," *Libération*, November 29–30, 1986, p. 16.

108. "Quelques réactions," *Ekaitza* 30 (November 27, 1986): 2.

109. Ibid.

110. See "Des voies différentes," *Enbata* 950 (November 27, 1986): 2; and "Jakes Abeberry, d'Enbata," *Ekaitza* 30 (November 27, 1986): 3.

111. "Jakes Abeberry, d'Enbata," p. 3.

112. See *Enbata*'s report: "e.a.: Iparralde s'organise," *Enbata* 967 (March 26, 1987): 3.
113. From an interview in Bayonne in August 1987.
114. Ibid.
115. Ibid.
116. "Assemblée générale d'Eusko Alkartasuna," *Ekaitza* 47 (March 26, 1987): 3.
117. Ibid.
118. "e.a.: Premier congrès," *Enbata* 970 (April 16, 1987): 8.
119. Ibid.
120. "A propos de l'Aberri Eguna d'Ascain," *Ekaitza* 49 (April 9, 1987): 5.
121. Ibid.
122. Cited in "Aberri eguna: Le meilleur et le pire renforcent l'unité," *Enbata* 1123 (April 19, 1990): 4.
123. *Ager* 70 (July 31, 1986): 7.
124. "Nouvelle approche," *Enbata* 1181 (June 13, 1991): 4.
125. See "Forum pour l'identité basque," *Enbata* 1225 (April 30, 1992): 4–5; and *Enbata* 1230 (June 4, 1992).
126. *Ager* 45 (March 1985): 7.
127. *Ager* 182 (June 1, 1991): 6.
128. Jean Haritschelhar, "Le Basque: Une langue résistante," in Génévière Vermes, ed., *Vingt-cinq communautés linguistiques de la France*, vol. 1, pp. 98–99.
129. "Elections du 5 juin," *Enbata* 1028 (May 26, 1988): 4–5.
130. *Enbata* 1030 (June 9, 1988): 4–5.
131. *Enbata* 1042 (September 15, 1988): 4.
132. *Enbata* 1044 (September 29, 1988): 4–5.
133. Cited in *Sud-Ouest*, July 1, 1989.
134. Cited in *Le Monde*, March 16, 1991.
135. See Agathe Logéart, "La routine des expulsions au Pays Basque français," *Le Monde*, March 12, 1987, p. 12.
136. *Pacharan* 1 (ca. winter 1986): 8.
137. *Patxaran* 17 (n.d., ca. September 1988).
138. Cited in *Patxaran* (April 1987).
139. *Actuel* (May 1988).
140. Logéart, "La routine des expulsions," p. 12.
141. Ibid.
142. Ibid.
143. P. N., "Rock à Arcangues: Impressions," *Ateka* 38 (January 1987): 20.
144. *Enbata* 1016 (March 3, 1988). See Patxa's response the following issue in "Courrier," *Enbata* 1017 (March 10, 1988): 4.
145. Patxa, "Courrier," p. 4.
146. "Fêtes de Bayonne," *Enbata* 1039 (August 11, 1988): 4–5.
147. "La fête autrement," *Enbata* 1038 (August 4, 1988): 3.
148. Ibid.

149. "Iparraldean, Euskaldun berri," *Ateka* 37 (December 1986): 6.

150. *Patxaran* 15 (ca. Spring 1988).

151. See "Aberri eguna: Le meilleur et le pire renforcent l'unité," p. 4.

152. Patxa ("Txetx" Etcheverry), "La coordination Paxta/Gabe/Oldartzen et EB/EMA/Iega."

153. Ibid.

154. *Patxaran* 27 (June 1990).

155. Cited in *Enbata* 1168 (March 14, 1991): 7.

156. *Enbata* 1207 (December 26, 1991): 2.

157. *Oldartzen* o (October 1989).

158. See his letter in *Ager* 171 (December 15, 1990): 2.

159. *Oldartzen* o (October 1989): 1.

160. "Incidents et divisions lors de la 'Journée de la patrie basque,' " *Le Monde,* April 17, 1990.

161. *Oldartzen* 3 (April 1990).

162. *Oldartzen,* (1990).

163. *Oldartzen* 6 (March 1991): 3.

164. Philippe Etcheverry, "Cinq attentats sont revendiqués par Iparretarrak," *Le Monde,* March 4, 1986, p. 12.

165. Cited in Philippe Etcheverry, "Un séparatiste basque condamné à cinq ans d'emprisonnement," *Le Monde,* April 12, 1986.

166. *Enbata* 923 (May 22, 1986): 4.

167. IK, "Communiqué," *Enbata* 933 (July 31, 1986): 3.

168. "La cassure," *Ekaitza* 35 (January 1, 1987): 5.

169. Ibid.

170. "Iparretarrak et le code pénal à la barre," *Sud-Ouest,* August 12, 1986.

171. *Enbata* 946 (October 30, 1986): 4.

172. See Philippe Etcheverry, "Un commando libère deux indépendantistes basques de la prison de Pau," *Le Monde,* December 16, 1986, p. 11; and "Prison Raid in South France Frees Two Basque Separatists," *New York Times,* December 15, 1986, p. 12. The greatest source of details on the prison break was offered by IK itself in *ILDO* 10 (April 1987): 4–7. See also "Opération commando," *Enbata* 953 (December 18, 1986): 4–5.

173. *Enbata* 953 (December 18, 1986): 1, 4.

174. See the detailed explanation of the planning in *ILDO* 10 (April 1987): 4–5.

175. See the speculation in *Ekaitza* 34 (December 25, 1986): 2.

176. *Ekaitza* (December 18, 1986): 2.

177. IK, "Communiqué d'Iparretarrak," *Enbata* 953 (December 18, 1986): 5.

178. "La quatorzième section va mener l'instruction sur l'évasion de Pau," *Le Monde,* December 24, 1986.

179. *Le Monde,* October 2, 1987, p. 14.

180. "Plusieurs gendarmeries visées par des attentats," *Le Monde,* January 27, 1987, p. 12.

181. See "Mouesca réapparait," *Sud-Ouest*, February 29, 1987; and "Conférence de presse d'Iparretarrak," *Ekaitza* 44 (March 5, 1987): 3.

182. See: "Intervention de Gaby" (p. 4), and "Intervention de Maddi" (p. 5) in *Ekaitza* 44 (March 5, 1987).

183. Cited in Logéart, "La routine des expulsions au Pays Basque français," p. 12.

184. Ibid.

185. *ILDO* 10 (April 1987): 17.

186. See "IK: Les options politiques," *Ekaitza* 45 (March 12, 1987): 4–5.

187. "Ageri," *ILDO* 10 (April 10, 1987): 26.

188. Ibid.

189. Ibid.

190. See *Le Monde*, May 19, 1987; and "Réclusion à perpétuité pour Philippe Bidart," *Enbata* 971 (April 23, 1987): 8.

191. Ibid.

192. "i.k." *Enbata* 974 (May 14, 1987): 7.

193. "Communiqué d'IK," *Enbata* 978 (June 11, 1987): 6.

194. Philippe Etcheverry, "Deux morts au cours de l'arrestation d'un nationaliste basque," *Le Monde*, June 23, 1987. See also *Ager* 92 (July 1, 1987): 1–5.

195. *Sud-Ouest*, June 25, 1987, p. A.

196. "Les obsèques de M.-F. Héguy," *Sud-Ouest*, June 26, 1987.

197. Cited in Agathe Logéart, "Bayonne: 'Des gens du village,'" *Le Monde*, July 9, 1987.

198. *Le Monde*, June 28–29, 1987.

199. Cited in Philippe Etcheverry, "Un poseur de bombes est tué par l'engin qu'il transportait," *Le Monde*, June 7, 1987.

200. Ibid.

201. *Le Monde*, July 8, 1987.

202. Logéart, "Bayonne."

203. "Patrick," *Ekaitza* 63 (July 16, 1987): 5.

204. Paul Bayle, "La violence n'est pas dans le tempérament basque," *Sud-Ouest*, July 11, 1987.

205. Cited in "Le mouvement nationaliste basque Iparretarrak est dissous," *Le Monde*, July 16, 1987.

206. Philippe Etcheverry, "Important dispositif policier pour rechercher les indépendantistes basques en fuite," *Le Monde*, July 14, 1987.

207. Ibid.

208. "Le mouvement nationaliste basque Iparretarrak est dissous."

209. "Effet symbolique et dissuasif," *Sud-Ouest*, July 17, 1987.

210. Agathe Logéart, "La dissolution d'Iparretarrak, une 'arme psychologique' venue de Paris," *Le Monde*, July 17, 1987.

211. Ministère de l'Intérieur, "Décret du 17 juillet 1987 portant dissolution du groupement de fait dénommé 'Iparretarrak,'" *Journal Officiel de la République Française* (July 18, 1987): 8034. The decree was issued over the names of president

François Mitterrand, premier Jacques Chirac, interior minister Charles Pasqua, and minister of state charged with security Robert Pandraud.

212. *Sud-Ouest*, July 18, 1987.

213. Cited in Logéart, "La dissolution d'Iparretarrak."

214. Ibid.

215. Ibid.

216. "Communiqué d'EMA," *Enbata* 984 (July 23, 1987): 5.

217. Cited in Logéart, "La dissolution d'Iparretarrak."

218. Cited in ibid.

219. "Communiqué d'IK," *Enbata* 994 (October 1, 1987): 8.

220. Logéart, "La dissolution d'Iparretarrak."

221. Ibid.

222. I follow the accounts in "Philippe Bidart, l'ennemi no. 1," *Sud Ouest*, August 26, 1987, p. 3; "Bidart tue encore un gendarme landais," *Sud-Ouest*, August 26, 1987, p. 1; Jean-Charles Reix and Pierre Gallerey, "Terrorisme basque: Un nouveau crime," *Le Figaro*, August 26, 1987, p. 8; Jean-François Boulaert and Emmanuel Moruzzi, *Iparretarrak: Séparatisme et terrorisme en Pays Basque français*, pp. 185–188; "Affrontement de Biscarrosse," *Ekaitza* 70 (September 3, 1987): 2–3; and "Philippe Bidart: mythe ou réalité," *Ager* 95 (September 1, 1987): 2.

223. "Affrontement à Biscarrosse," p. 2.

224. See "La cavale en Bordelais du tueur basque," *Sud-Ouest*, August 27, 1987, p. 3; and Claude Jouanne, "Bidart: La piste se perd à Bordeaux," *Le Figaro*, August 28, 1987, p. 7.

225. Ibid.

226. Ibid.

227. "Affrontement à Biscarrosse," p. 2.

228. Philippe Boggio, "Philippe Bidart, Basque perdu," *Le Monde*, August 27, 1987, pp. 1, 8.

229. See Philippe Boggio, "L'automne basque," *Le Monde*, September 29, 1987, pp. 1, 10. For the image of Matalas, see Eugène Goyheneche, "La révolte de Matalas," in his *Le Pays Basque*, pp. 275–281.

230. See Philippe Etcheverry, "Perquisitions dans une abbaye et au siège de deux hebdomadaires nationalistes basques," *Le Monde*, September 5, 1987, p. 10; "Bidart: Perquisition chez les bénédictins," *Le Figaro*, September 4, 1987, p. 10; and "Le monastère perquisitionne," *Sud-Ouest*, September 4, 1987, p. 5.

231. Moruzzi and Boulaert, *Iparretarrak*, p. 192.

232. Cited in *Sud-Ouest*, October 8, 1987.

233. Cited in Moruzzi and Boulaert, *Iparretarrak*, p. 203.

234. "La situation au Pays Basque et la lutte contre le terrorisme: Espagne: Reprise du dialogue avec l'ETA; France: Arrestation du chef d'Iparretarrak," *Le Monde*, February 21–22, 1988, pp. 1, 7; "i.k.: Un revers," *Enbata* 1015 (February 25, 1988): 3; and Philippe Etcheverry, "France's Most Wanted Basque," translated from *Le Monde* in *Manchester Guardian Weekly*, March 5, 1988, p. 15.

235. See Marc Légasse, "Le sursaut d'Iparralde," *Enbata* 1123 (April 19, 1990):

3; and "Philippe Bidart: Une bataille perdue," *Ager* 107 (March 1, 1988): 2.

236. Philippe Etcheverry, "Le temps du dialogue?" *Le Monde*, February 23, 1988, p. 10.

237. Cited in ibid.

238. "i.k.: Un revers," p. 3.

239. Cited in *Enbata* 1015 (February 25, 1988): 3.

240. "Le président de la république et le gouvernement félicitent la gendarmerie," *Le Monde*, February 23, 1988, p. 10.

241. Cited in ibid.

242. Etcheverry, "Le temps du dialogue?" p. 10.

243. *Le Monde*, April 16, 1988.

244. "i.k.: Lettre au prisonnier," *Enbata* 1026 (May 12, 1988): 6.

245. Ibid.

246. *Le Monde*, June 2, 1988.

247. "Un plan suivi à la lettre," *Enbata* 1047 (October 20, 1988): 4.

248. "Lucienne Fourcade arrêtée," *Enbata* 1055 (December 15, 1988): 3; and "La compagne de Philippe Bidart a été arrêtée au Pays Basque," *Le Monde*, December 14, 1988.

249. *Le Monde*, July 30–31, 1989.

250. "Iparretarrak revendique," *Enbata* 1059 (January 12, 1989): 5.

251. "Conférence de presse i.k.," *Enbata* 1102 (November 23, 1989): 7.

252. Cited in *Sud-Ouest*, December 21, 1987.

253. Cited in *Enbata* 1061 (February 10, 1989): 7.

254. *Ager* 132 (April 1, 1989): 3.

255. *Le Quotidien de Paris*, January 12–13, 1991, p. 10.

256. See the recapitulation of the events of 1989, "A travers," *Enbata* 1110 (January 18, 1990): 4–5; the events of 1990, "A travers *Enbata*," in *Enbata* 1158 (January 3, 1991): 4–6; as well as accounts of individual IK attacks in the following issues of *Enbata*: the *syndicat d'initiative* of Cambio in 1135 (July 26, 1990): 8; the tax office of St. Palais in 1139 (August 23, 1990): 4–5, and 1140 (August 30, 1990): 3; the radio transmitter of the gendarmerie on Mt. Jara in 1145 (October 4, 1990): 8; a real estate development in Biarritz in 1155 (December 13, 1990): 8; six attacks during the night of January 10, 1991, against a series of real estate and tourist facilities in 1160 (January 17, 1990): 7; the two attacks against real estate offices in Bayonne and Anglet and the police station of Anglet in 1165 (February 21, 1991): 4; a real estate office in Orthez in 1167 (March 7, 1991): 7; the sales trailer of a real estate development in Anglet in 1172 (April 11, 1991): 3; and attacks on a real estate development in Ciboure and a vacation home in Hélette in 1184 (July 4, 1991): 8.

257. "Des menaces téléphoniques au nom d'Iparretarrak," *Le Monde*, August 22, 1990.

258. *Enbata* 1150 (November 8, 1990): 6.

259. See the accounts of the trial in *Enbata* 1161 (January 24, 1991): 4–5; 1162

(January 31, 1991): 4–6; 1163 (February 7, 1991): 4–6; and *Ager* 174 (February 1, 1991): 6–7.

260. Cited in *Enbata* 1162 (January 31, 1991): 4.

261. The literal translation of "malfaiteurs" is malefactors.

262. Cited in *Enbata* 1162 (January 31, 1991): 6.

263. Ibid.

264. Ibid.

265. See *Enbata* 1174 (April 25, 1991): 3; and "Interpellation du nationaliste basque Richard Irazuta [*sic*]," *Le Monde*, April 23, 1991.

266. From an interview in Bayonne on August 26, 1991.

267. *Oldartzen* 2 (1990).

268. *Ager* 166 (October 1, 1990): 5.

269. Ibid.

270. *Enbata* 1209 (January 9, 1992): 3.

271. "ILDO No. 11," *Enbata* 1126 (May 10, 1990): 6.

272. See the lists of government surveillance of him in "Procès de Xan," *Enbata* 1110 (January 18, 1990): 6.

273. *Enbata* 1135 (July 26, 1990): 7.

274. "Confidential PAF," *Enbata* 1042 (September 15, 1988): 3–4.

275. "Quatre agents de la DGSE interpellés par la police judiciaire," *Le Monde* (November 10–11, 1985).

276. *Ager* 179 (April 15, 1991): 7.

277. Ibid.

278. See *Ager* 166 (October 1, 1990): 5.

279. *Enbata* 1183 (June 27, 1991): 2.

280. *Enbata* 1092 (September 14, 1989): 6.

281. "Seaska: La convention signée," *Enbata* 1102 (November 23, 1989): 2.

282. Cited in *Enbata* 1161 (January 24, 1991): 4.

283. Cited in *Sud-Ouest*, January 29, 1991, and reprinted in *Enbata* 1162 (January 31, 1991): 7.

284. *Enbata* 1220 (March 26, 1992): 4–5.

285. "L'objectif des abertzale, une percée plus large," *Enbata* 1214 (February 13, 1992): 4.

286. Ibid.

287. See the results of the regional and cantonal elections in *Le Monde*, March 24, 1992, and March 31, 1992.

288. Cited in *Enbata* 783 (August 18, 1983): 2.

289. Cited in "L'objectif des abertzale, une percée plus large," p. 4.

290. Etcheverry, "Le temps du dialogue?"

CHAPTER NINE. CONCLUSION

1. From a radio broadcast on November 10, 1939, cited in Paul Sérant, *La France de minorités*.

2. Cited in *Le Figaro*, November 14, 1968, p. 10.

3. Pierre Viansson-Ponté, "Les îles perdues," *Le Monde*, May 2–3, 1976, p. 17.

4. From a poster put up in Bayonne in the summer of 1991 by members of the Association des Jeunes d'Iparralde contre la Repression (AJIR).

5. Cited in the Minutes of the Sixth Committee (Political Questions), Fourth Meeting, Records of the Sixth Assembly, Special Supplement no. 39, *Official Journal*, p. 17.

6. Cited in "French Assail Soviet on Ethnicity," *New York Times*, March 1, 1984.

7. See, for example: Alan Riding, "Separatists in Europe Indirectly Reinforce Unity in Yugoslavia," *New York Times*, September 7, 1991, p. 4; and Alan Riding, "Europeans' Hopes for a Yugoslav Peace Turn to Frustration," *New York Times*, September 22, 1991, p. E3.

8. Cited in Riding, "Separatists in Europe Indirectly Reinforce Unity in Yugoslavia," p. 4.

9. See "Spain's Nationalists, Emboldened by Baltics, Press for Independence," *New York Times*, September 22, 1991, p. 8; "Les Basques et les Catalans se prennent à rever," *Le Monde*, July 10, 1991, p. 3; "ETA Joy at Soviet Split," *European*, August 30–September 1, 1991, p. 6; and Jean-Claude Larronde, "Réveil des nationalités," *Enbata* 1054 (December 8, 1988): 8.

10. Cited in "ETA Joy at Soviet Split," p. 6.

11. Cited in Pierre Viansson-Ponté, "La crise de l'état-nation," *Le Monde*, July 9–10, 1978.

12. Karl W. Deutsch, "The Trend of European Nationalism—The Language Aspect," *American Political Science Review* 36, no. 3 (June 1942): 539.

13. See Phillipe Boucher, "Le rapport sur la violence: Le cri des muets," *Le Monde*, July 29, 1977, p. 1.

14. Cited in James Walsh, "The Search for a New France," *Time*, July 15, 1991, p. 7.

15. Ibid., p. 8.

16. Cited in *Le Monde*, June 11–12, 1978, p. 6.

17. Cited in *Le Monde*, December 11, 1973, p. 11. See also Michel Debré, "Pour l'état-nation," *Le Monde*, February 20, 1980.

18. "M. Giscard d'Estaing: 'Ma charge fondamentale est de maintenir l'unité de la nation,' " *Le Monde*, October 7–8, 1979.

19. *Le Monde*, April 22, 1981, p. 10.

20. *Enbata* 883 (August 15, 1985): 3.

21. Cited in ibid.

22. "La France face aux terrorismes," *Le Monde*, June 25–26, 1982.

23. Jean-Louis Andreani and Thierry Brehier, "Les députés ont adopté le statut de la Corse," *Le Monde*, January 25–26, 1990, pp. 1–6.

24. For an account of the parliamentary opposition to the idea of recognizing "the Corsican people," see the summary of debates in the National Assembly in *Journal Officiel/Débats Parlementaires* 89–91 (November 22–24, 1990). See also Jean-Louis Andreani, "La notion de 'peuple corse' reste au centre du débat," *Le Monde*, November 22, 1990, p. 9; and Nicolas Alfonsi, "Pauvre France!" *Le Monde*, November 22, 1990, p. 2.

25. Cited in "Le 'peuple corse' face à l'unité française," *France-Amérique*, April 13–19, 1991, p. 3.

26. Cited in "M. Jacques Chirac met en cause 'la responsibilité de l'état,'" *Le Monde*, December 22, 1990, p. 13.

27. Philippe Etcheverry, "Les partis nationalistes dénoncent le blocage de leurs revendications culturelles," *Le Monde*, May 14–15, 1989.

28. Cited in Philippe Etcheverry, "Trois mille personnes ont défilé en faveur de la culture basque," *Le Monde*, May 30, 1989.

29. Cited in Georges Marion, "Une invitation du dialogue culturel," *Le Monde*, December 18–19, 1988, p. 8.

30. Ibid.

31. Etcheverry, "Trois mille personnes ont défilé en faveur de la culture basque."

32. Philippe Etcheverry, "MM. Joxe et Chérèque proposent un ensemble de mesures pour le Pays Basque," *Le Monde*, July 2–3, 1989.

33. "M. Mitterand souhaite une 'entité administrative convenable' pour les Basques français," *Le Monde*, November 6, 1990.

34. Cited in "Le RPR dénonce l''attitude démissionnaire' du pouvoir," *Le Monde*, November 7, 1990.

35. Philippe Etcheverry, "Le gouvernement envisage la création d'une communauté de communes au Pays Basque," *Le Monde*, January 8, 1991.

36. Thierry Maliniak, "L'embellie de l'économie basque," *Le Monde*, October 30, 1990.

37. Marc Ambroise-Rendu, "Les voisins basques au quotidien," *Le Monde*, August 4, 1988, p. 7.

38. Ibid.

39. Michel Faure, "Pays Basque: Les nouveaux conquistadores," *Le Monde*, November 8, 1990, pp. 70, 72, 74.

40. Nicolas Beau, "Les Basques dans leur grande famille," *Le Monde*, October 11, 1984, p. 28.

41. Philippe Etcheverry, "Hendaye livrée aux frontaliers," *MAF*, June 25, 1988.

42. Ibid., p. 74.

43. Patrick Busquet, "Les entreprises espagnoles accroissent leurs investissements au Pays Basque français," *Le Monde*, August 24, 1991, p. 18.

44. Cited in ibid.

45. Martha Crenshaw, "How Terrorism Ends."

46. Ibid., p. 33.

47. Ibid., p. 34.

48. "Procès d'IK," *Enbata* 1251 (November 12, 1992): 3.

49. "Goodbye to the Nation-State?" *Economist*, June 23, 1990, pp. 11–12.

50. From his second speech on conciliation with America, in the House of Commons, March 22, 1775.

51. Cited in *Enbata* 1161 (January 24, 1991): 4.

Bibliography

All books, journal, and newspaper articles are listed in alphabetical order.

Abeberry, Jacques. "Mai 86." Editorial in *Enbata* 924 (May 29, 1986).
"Aberri Eguna: Le meilleur et le pire renforcent l'unité." *Enbata* 1,123
   (April 19, 1990).
Actuel (May 1988).
Acuña, Ramón-Luis. "Madrid réclame les chefs de l'ETA." *Le Figaro,* August 8–
   9, 1987.
Ager 3 (September 1981): 5.
——— 45 (March 1985): 7.
——— 54 (December 15, 1985): 1.
——— 54 (December 18, 1985).
——— 61 (March 27, 1986).
——— 70 (July 31, 1986): 7.
——— 73 (September 23, 1986).
——— 77 (November 22, 1986).
——— 85 (March 15, 1987).
——— 95 (September 1, 1987): 2.
——— 107 (March 1, 1988): 2.
——— 132 (April 1, 1989): 3.
——— 156 (April 15, 1990).
——— 157 (May 1, 1990).
——— 159 (May 15, 1990): 6.
——— 166 (October 1, 1990): 5.
——— 169 (November 15, 1990): 6.
——— 171 (December 15, 1990): 2.
——— 174 (February 1, 1991): 6–7.
——— 179 (April 15, 1991): 7.
——— 182 (June 1, 1991): 6.
——— 185 (July 15, 1991): 7.
Agirre, Julen. "How Basques Killed Spain's Premier and Almost Got Kissinger."
   International Herald Tribune, September 23, 1974.
———. *Operation Ogro.* New York: Ballantine Books, 1975.
Alfonsi, Nicolas. "Pauvre France!" *Le Monde,* November 22, 1990.
Aligner, Dominique. "Le mouvement nationaliste Basque, Enbata." Mémoire en
   Histoire, Université de Strasbourg, 1974.

Alvarez Emparanza, José Luis [Txillardegi, pseud.]. "Pierre Larzabal, el cura de Sokoa (entrevista)." *Punto y Hora de Euskal Herria* 179 (June 13–20, 1980).

Amaia. Ephemeral tract (ca. 1968).

"Amalgame." *Euskaldunak* 14 (May 1975).

Ambroise-Rendu, Marc. "Les voisins basques au quotidien." *Le Monde* (August 4, 1988).

"Analyse des résultats par canton." *Euskaldunak* 60 (April 1979).

"Analyse politique du G.A.L." *Laguntza* (July 1985): 20.

"Analyses post-électorales." *EHASKIDE* (March 1978).

Andreani, Jean-Louis. "La notion de 'peuple corse' reste au centre du débat." *Le Monde*, November 22, 1990.

Andreani, Jean-Louis, and Thierry Brehier. "Les députés ont adopté le statut de la Corse." *Le Monde*, January 25–26, 1990.

"An Independent Brittany: A New German Device." *London Times*, July 26, 1940.

Annuaire statistique de la France. Vol. 74. Paris: Institut National de la Statistique et des Etudes Economiques, 1969.

Apalategi, Jokin. "Le mouvement basque aujourd'hui." *Les Temps Modernes* 31, no. 357 (1976).

———. *Nationalisme et question nationale au Pays Basque, 1830–1976*. Bayonne: Elkar, (ca. 1976).

———. "Consolidación del movimiento abertzale, 1976–1978." In *Los Vascos de la nación al estado*. Bayonne: Elkar, 1979.

———. *Los vascos de la autonomía a la independencia*. San Sebastián: Editorial Txertoa, 1985.

"Appel au peuple basque." *ILDO* 6 (March 1981).

"Après la dissolution du mouvement Enbata: Le Dr. Burucoa affirme sa surprise: Nous n'avons jamais organisé d'action violente—la modération est dans nos méthodes." *Eclair*, January 31, 1974.

"A propos de l'Aberri Eguna d'Ascain." *Ekaitza* 49 (April 9, 1987).

Arana Goiri, Sabino. "Fuerismo es separatismo." *Bizkaitarra* 8 (April 22, 1894).

———. *Obras completas*. Buenos Aires: Editorial Sabindiar-Batza, 1965.

Aranzadi y Etxeberia, Engracio de [Kizktza, pseud.]. *Ereintza: Siembra de nacionalism vasco, 1894–1912*. Zarazuz: Editorial Vasco Celaya et Cia, 1935.

Aron, Raymond. *The Elusive Revolution: Anatomy of a Student Revolt*. Translated by Gordon Clough. New York: Praeger, 1969.

Arregi, Naxto. *Memorias del Kas, 1975/78*. Donostia: Ed. Hordago, 1981.

"Arrestations à Bidart." *Enbata* 1221 (April 2, 1992): 3.

"Arrestations du 1er décembre." *Enbata* 1,104 (December 7, 1989).

Arribillaga, Charles. "Historique d'Embata." *Embata* (June 1958).

"Assemblée générale d'Eusko Alkartasuna." *Ekaitza* 47 (March 26, 1987).

"Assemblée Nationale—Séance du 12 octobre 1988 (Journal officiel: Extraits des déclarations)." Cited in *Enbata* 1047 (October 20, 1988).

"Ateka." *Enbata* 780 (July 28, 1983).

Ateka 2 (November 1983): 2.

———— 20 (May 1985).

———— 32 (July 1986): 4.

———— 40 (March 1987): 2.

"Atentados contra los refugiados políticos." *Punto y Hora* 331 (December 1983).

"Attentat à Baigorry: Communiqué Herri Taldeak." *Herriz Herri* 72 (April 1, 1982).

"Attentat au Pays Basque français: Un C.R.S. est tué et un autre grièvement blessé." *Le Monde*, March 21–22, 1982.

"Atxik, l'anti-promesse: Invitation à une lutte." *Ateka* 29 (February 1986).

Autonomous Government of Euzkadi. *The Basque Country and European Peace: An Analysis of the German Domination of Euzkadi*. London: n.p., 1938.

Axelsson, George. "Separatism Urged for New Brittany." *New York Times*, July 14, 1940.

"Ayer y hoy de Federico Krutwig." *Muga* 23 (September 1979).

B. L. G. "Détournement de procédure." *Le Monde*, July 22, 1986.

Barathon, Charles. *Le régionalisme d'hier et de demain*. Paris: Les Oeuvres Françaises, 1942.

Barbé, Ferdinand. "La crise alimentaire à Bayonne pendant la révolution, 1789–1796." *Bulletin de la Société des Sciences, Lettres et Arts de Bayonne* 41 (April–June 1942).

Barère de Vieuzac, Bertrand. *Le point du jour ou ce qui s'est passé la veille à l'Assemblée Nationale*. Vol. 3. Paris: Cussac, 1789.

————. "Rapport et project de décret, presentés au nom du Comité de Salut Public à la Convention Nationale sur les Idiomes Etrangers et sur l'Enseignement de la Langue Française," 8 pluviôse, An II. (January 18, 1794).

————. *Mémoires*. Vol. 1. Paris: Jules Labitte, 1842.

"The Basques as the Germans See Them." Archives of the Basque Studies Program, Folio #B5160. University of Nevada, Reno, n.d. (ca. 1938).

Basque-Eclair (May 25–26, 1968).

"Basque Terrorist Group Vows to End Bombings." *New York Times*, August 2, 1979.

"Batasuna Borrokan." *ILDO* 9 (April 1984): 2.

Bayle, Paul. "La violence n'est pas dans le tempérament basque." *Sud-Ouest*, July 11, 1987.

"Bayonne-préfecture." *Côte Basque Soir*, May 18, 1949.

Bazalgues, Gaston. "Les organisations occitanes." *Temps Modernes* 324–326 (August–September 1973).

Beau, Nicolas. "Trêve au Pays Basque français." *Le Monde*, April 29–30, 1984.

————. "Les basques dans leur grande famille." *Le Monde*, October 11, 1984.

Belsunce, Charles de (Vicomte de). *Histoire des basques depuis leurs établissement dans les Pyrénées occidentales jusqu'à nos jours*. 3 vols. Bayonne: P. Lespés, 1948.

Beltza. *El nacionalismo vasco en el exilio, 1937–1960*. San Sebastián: Ed. Txertoa, 1977.

Béorlégui, General. In *Débats parlementaires*. Chambre des Députés, lère séance, December 5, 1936.

"Berlin Recognizes Breton Movement." *New York Times*, July 26, 1940.

Bernoville, Gaetan. "La guerre civile en Espagne: Le cas des nationalistes basques." *Etudes, Revue Catholique d'Intérêt Général* (October 5, 1936).

———. "Rapport presenté par les jeunes nationalistes catholiques basques aux jeunesses anti-fascistes à l'occasion du congrès tenu à Paris," December 19, 1936.

———. *Le pays des Basques*. 2nd ed. Paris: J. de Gigord, 1946.

Bessière, Martine. "Le bombardement de Guernica dans la presse française." Diplôme Technique de Documentaliste, Institut Nationale des Techniques de Documentation, Conservation Nationale des Arts et Métiers, 1974.

Bidart, Pierre. "L'état et l'enseignement primaire en France d'après l'enquête de 1833: Contribution à l'étude des fonctions historiques de l'école au XIXème siècle." Ms. Université de Paris, VIIIème. Musée Basque, Bayonne, n.d.

———. "Les élections présidentielles de mai 1974 au Pays Basque." *Bulletin du Musée Basque* 66 (1974).

———. "Une jeunesse en position de rupture: Analyse des effets de l'urbanisation sur la jeunesse scolaire d'un village." Part 2. *Gure Herria* 5 (1974).

———. "Le pouvoir politique dans le village basque: Le cas de Saint-Etienne-de-Baigorry." Thèse de doctorat de Troisième Cycle, Ecole des Hautes Etudes en Sciences Sociales, Paris, 1975.

———. *Le pouvoir politique à Baigorri, village basque*. Bayonne: IPAR, 1977.

———. *La nouvelle société basque, ruptures et changements*. Paris, 1980.

Bidergaray, J. "Un jour viendra . . . Peut-être desirerons-nous demain les indésirables d'aujourd'hui." *Euzko Deya* 73 (September 12, 1937).

"Bipolarisation basque." *Euskaldunak* 3 (June 1974).

"Blast Rips Basque Showroom a Day before Regional Vote." *New York Times*, November 30, 1986.

Boggio, Philippe. "L'automne basque." *Le Monde*, September 29, 1987.

———. "Le temps des ruptures au Pays Basque." *Le Monde*, October 9, 1987.

———. "L'asile hors la loi." *Le Monde*, February 12, 1988.

Boggio, Philippe, and Philippe Etcheverry. "Les attentats au Pays Basque français." *Le Monde*, April 11, 1985.

———. "Le commando secret de basques français." *Le Monde*, April 14, 1990.

Boissel, W. "La légende des douze pairs dans la Chanson de Roland." In *Cahiers du centre basque et gascon d'etudes régionales*. Bayonne: Editions du Musée Basque, 1935.

Bole-Richard, Michel. "Satisfaccion prudente à Madrid." *Le Monde*, March 31, 1992.

———. "Le gouvernement n'exclut pas une riposte des séparatistes basques." *Le Monde*, April 1, 1992.

Bombédiac, Christian. "Le bureau du sous-préfet de Bayonne est détruit dans un attentat." *Le Monde*, July 1–2, 1979.

———. "La 'guerre des vacances' de l'ETA: Le ministre de l'intérieur met vivement en cause les autorités françaises." *Le Monde*, June 28, 1980.

Bonaparte, Prince Louis-Lucien. *Carte des sept provinces basques montrant la délimitation actuelle de l'euscara et sadivision en dialectes, sous-dialectes et variétés.* London: Stanford's Geographical Establishment, 1863.

Bonino, José Miguez. *Doing Theology in a Revolutionary Situation.* Philadelphia: Fortress Press, 1975.

Borràs Llop, Jose María. *Francia ante la guerra civil española: Burguesía, interés nacional e interés de clase. Colección Monografías*, no. 43. Madrid: Centro de Investigaciones Sociológicas, 1981.

Borroka Azkar (ca. 1982).

Boucher, Phillippe. "Le rapport sur la violence: Le cri des muets." *Le Monde*, July 29, 1977.

Boulard, Fernand [Chanoine, pseud.]. *Premiers itinéraires en sociologie religieuse.* Paris: Editions Ouvrières, 1954.

Boulard, Fernand, and Jean Rémy. *Pratique religieuse et régions culturelles.* Paris: Editions Ouvriéres, 1968.

Boulay, Robert. "Interview avec M. Labéguerie, député de Mauléon: Les basques veulent avoir leur propre département." *Paris-Presse-L'Intransigeant*, April 17, 1963.

Boussard, Léon. *Jeiki, jeiki etxenkoak, ou le défi des basques.* Paris: Editions Albatros, 1975.

"Breton Recognition Denied in Berlin." *New York Times*, July 27, 1940.

Brette, Armand. *Recueil des documents relatifs à la convocation des Etats-Généraux de 1789.* 4 vols. Paris: Imprimerie Nationale, 1894–1915.

Brigouleix, Bernard. "In Search of a Future." Translated from *Le Monde. Manchester Guardian*, July 6, 1980.

Brinton, Crane. *A Decade of Revolution, 1789–1799.* New York: Harper and Brothers, 1934.

Brunot, Patrick. "La droite traditionnaliste dans les Basses-Pyrénées de 1900 à 1950." Ms., Institut des Etudes Politiques, Université de Bordeaux, 1969.

Bulletin de l'Association des Anciens Elèves de Larressore, Belloc et Ustaritz, 1930–31. Bayonne: Imprimerie La Presse, 1931.

Burgo, Jaime del. *Bibliografía de las guerras carlistas y de las luchas políticas del siglo xix.* Vol. 5, Supplement A-Z. Diputación Foral de Navarra, Institución Príncipe de Viana, 1966.

"Burubateragile." *EHASKIDE*, February 25, 1977.

Busquet, Patrick. "Les entreprises espagnoles accroissent leurs investissements au Pays Basque français." *Le Monde*, August 24, 1991.

Caerléon, Ronan. *Complots pour une république bretonne.* Paris: Editions de la Table Ronde, 1967.

Cahiers d'Amaia 2 (1969).

Cambio 16, November 24, 1978.

———, December 16, 1991.

———, April 13 and 20, 1992.

Camby, Philippe. *La libération de la Bretagne*. Rennes: Ouest-France, 1980.

"Cantonales 2ème tour." *Enbata* 395 (March 18, 1976).

Cartier, Raymond. *Laisserons-nous démembrer la France?* Paris: Fayard, 1939.

Castelli, Helen J. "Response of the Pays Basque to the Convocation of the Estates-General in Pre-revolutionary France." In *Anglo-American Contributions to Basque Studies: Essays in Honor of Jon Bilbao*, edited by William A. Douglass, Richard W. Etulain, and William H. Jacobsen, Jr. Desert Research Institute Publications on the Social Sciences, no. 13, University of Nevada, Reno, 1977.

Cazals, P. *Cahier des voeux et instructions des basques-français pour leurs deputés aux Etats-Généraux de 1789*. New ed. Bayonne: P. Cazals, 1874.

Cazaubon, Jean-Marc. "Démarche pour la constitution d'un mouvement abertzale de gauche." *Ateka* 25 (October 1985).

———. "EMA." *Ateka* 28 (January 1986).

Cazaubon, Jean-Marc, and Vianney Cier. "IK/ELB: Vers un débat de la gauche abertzale." *Ateka* 5 (February 1984).

Certeau, Michel de, Dominique Julia, and Jacques Revel. *Une politique de la langue, la révolution français et les patois*. Paris: Gallimard, 1975.

Chabalier, Hervé. "Un seul pays pour les Basques?" *Nouvel Observateur* 421 (December 4–10, 1972).

Chaho, J. Augustin. *Philosophie des révélations adressée à M. le Professeur Lerminier*. Paris: Librairie Orientale de Mme. Vicomtesse Dondey-Dupré, 1835.

———. *Voyage en Navarre Pendant l'Insurrection des Basques, 1830–1835*. Paris: Arthurs Bertrand, 1836.

———. *Histoire primitive des Euskariens basques*. Bayonne: Librairie de la Vicomtesse de Bonjou, 1847.

Chambers, J. N. Marshall, Elizabeth W. Ikin, and A. E. Mourant. "The ABO, MN, and Rh Blood Groups of the Basque People." *American Journal of Physical Anthropology* 7 (1949): 529–544.

Charency, Hyacinthe Comte de, H. Gaidoz, and Charles de Gaulle. *Pétition pour les langues provinciales au corps législatif de 1870*. Paris: Alphonse Picard et Fils, 1903.

Charles-Brun, Jean. *Le régionalisme*. Paris: Bloud et Cie., 1911.

———. *L'Europe fédéraliste: Aspirations et réalités*. Paris: W. Giard, 1927.

———. Edition of Pierre Joseph Proudhon's *Du principe fédératif et de la nécessité de reconstituer le parti de la révolution*, with introduction and notes by Jean Charles-Brun. Paris: Editions Bossard, 1921.

———. *Le principe fédératif*. Paris: P.U.F., 1940.

———. "De la terre natale à l'humanité fédérale." *Politique* 37–40 (1967).

Charritton, Pierre. *Petite histoire religieuse du Pays Basque*. Bayonne: Editions Euskal Herria, 1946.

Chaussier, J.-D. "L'échec du project de création d'un département en Pays

Basque: L'enfermement du localisme culturel par le pouvoir central." *Bulletin du Musée Basque* 120 (1988).

Chauvirey, Marie France. *La vie quotidienne au Pays Basque sous le Second Empire.* Paris: Hachette, 1975.

"Chez les Autres: Lyautey Régionaliste." *Aintzina* 1, no. 10 (July 1935).

"Cinco años de guerra subterránea contra ETA." *Actual* 84 (October 31, 1983).

Clark, Robert P. *The Basques: The Franco Years and Beyond.* Reno: University of Nevada Press, 1980.

————. *The Basque Insurgents: ETA, 1952–1980.* Madison: University of Wisconsin Press, 1984.

————. "Patterns in the Lives of ETA Members." In *Political Violence and Terror: Motifs and Motivations,* edited by Peter Merkl. Berkeley: University of California Press, 1986.

————. *Negotiating with ETA: Obstacles to Peace in the Basque Country.* Reno: University of Nevada Press, 1990.

Cobban, Alfred. "Local Government during the French Revolution." *English Historical Review* 58, no. 229 (January 1943).

Cohen, Bernard. "Le Pays Basque entre deux voies." *Libération,* November 29–30, 1986.

"Collaboration France-GAL." *Herriz Herri* 188 (July 5, 1984).

Collection générale des décrets rendus par l'Assemblée Nationale. Paris: Baudouin, Imprimeur de l'Assemblée Nationale, 1790.

Comité Abertzale Socialiste. "Communiqué sur la répression." Bayonne (ca. September 1975).

Comité d'Enquête sur les Violations des Droits de l'Homme en Europe (CEDRI). *Le GAL ou le terrorisme d'état dans l'Europe des démocraties: Rapport d'enquête.* Basel, Switzerland: CEDRI, February–June 1979.

Comité de Soutien. "Nouvelles du jour." Ephemeral tract, May 22, 1971. Musée Basque, Bayonne.

Comité pour la Défense des Droits de l'Homme en Pays Basque. Communiqué, August 8, 1984.

"Comment la France socialiste favorise le terrorisme." *Le Figaro* 235 (February 18–24, 1984).

"Communiqué de HASI." *Euskaldunak* 39 (July 1977).

"Communiqué de Jazar, 12 novembre 1977." *Pindar* 1 (December 1977).

"Communiqué de Matalaz." *Herriz Herri* 163 (January 12, 1984).

"Communiqué de Seaska." *Herriz Herri* (March 25, 1982).

"Communiqué d'e.t.a. au peuple basque." *Enbata* 1, no. 1,012 (February 4, 1988): 4.

"Communiqué d'Iparretarrak." *Enbata* 783 (August 18, 1983).

"Communiqué du 24 mai 1981: Réponse à Enbata sur l'article concernant l'action d'Iparretarrak contre L'hélicoptère de M. Etchandy." *ILDO* 7 (June 1981).

"Conférence de presse d'Anai-Artea." *Sud-Ouest,* June 30, 1984.

"Conférence de presse du P.S. Pays Basque." *Enbata* 650 (February 5, 1981).

"Contribution au débat sur la lutte armée en Euskadi Nord." *Ateka* 12 (September 1984).

"Cooperation à la hussarde." *Le Monde*, July 22, 1986.

Cordier, Eugène. "Le droit basque, coutumes de Soule, de Labourt et de Basse Navarre." In *De l'organisation de la famille chez les basques*. Paris: Auguste Durand et Pédone-Lauriel, 1869.

Côte-Basque Soir, May 9, 1968; May 13, 1968.

"Coup de grace au rapport Ravail." *Enbata* 745 (November 25, 1982).

"Coups de feu contre un C.R.S. au Pays Basque." *Le Monde*, January 5, 1984.

Crenshaw, Martha. "How Terrorism Ends." Paper presented at the 1987 Annual Meeting of the American Political Science Association, Chicago, September 3–6, 1987.

Cuzacq, René. *Le Comité Revolutionnaire de Bayonne, Sa destitution et son histoire*. Bayonne: Imprimerie du Courrier, 1929.

———. *Les élections législatives à Bayonne et au Pays Basque, L'Avènement de la république modérée, 1871–1898*. Bayonne: Chez l'Auteur, 1951.

———. *Les élections législatives à Bayonne et au Pays Basque de 1898 à 1914: Radicalisme bayonnais et catholicisme basque*. Mont de Marsan: Editions Jean-Lacoste, 1952.

———. *Les élections législatives à Bayonne et au Pays Basque, 1919–1939, l'entre deux guerres*. Mont de Marsan: Jean-Lacoste, 1956.

———. *Les élections législatives à Bayonne et au Pays Basque de 1958 à 1961*. Bayonne: Chez l'Auteur, 1971.

———. *Les élections législatives à Bayonne et au Pays Basque, 1961–1965*. Bayonne: Chez l'Auteur, 1971.

D. D. "Borrokak batasunean." *Ateka* 27 (December 1975).

D. F. "Eskual-Ikasleen Biltzarra." *Aintzina* 1, no. 6 (March 1935).

Darcy, Gilles. *La libre administration des collectivités locales, réflexions sur la décentralisation*. Paris: Economica, 1984.

Darnton, John. "General Is Slain in Madrid: Basque Terrorists Suspected." *New York Times*, January 30, 1984.

Darricau, Albert. *Scènes de la terreur à Bayonne et aux environs, 1793–1794*. Bayonne: A. Lamaignère, 1903.

———. "Exposition de l' état des basques français du Labourd." In *France et Labourd*. Dax: H. Labéque, 1906.

da Silva, Milton Manuel. "The Basque Nationalist Movement: A Case Study in Modernization and Ethnic Conflict." Ph.D. diss., Department of Political Science, University of Massachusetts at Amherst, 1972.

Davant, Jean-Louis. "Echec des nationalistes?" *Euskaldunak* 60 (April 1969): 4.

———. *Histoire du Pays Basque: Le peuple basque dans l'histoire*. 4th ed. Bayonne: Editions Goiztiri, 1970. Donostia: Elkar, 1986.

———. "L'ETA." In *Le procés de Burgos*, edited by Gisèle Halimi. Paris: Gallimard, 1971.

———. "Lutte nationale et lutte des classes dans le mouvement basque." *Temps Modernes* 324–326 (August–September 1973).

———. *Histoire du peuple basque: Le peuple basque dans l'histoire.* 4th edition. Donostia: Elkar, 1986.

Débats parlementaires. Chambre des Deputés, July 31, 1936.

Debré, Michel. "Pour l'état-nation." *Le Monde*, February 20, 1980.

"Déception." *Enbata* 499 (March 16, 1978): 2.

Decker, Jane Elizabeth. "Direct Democracy and Revolutionary Organization in the 1968 French Student-Worker Revolt." *Proceedings of the Western Society of French History* 5 (1977).

"Déclaration sur la lutte contre le colonialisme en Europe Occidentale." Ms. portfolio no. B-9005, Musée Basque, Bayonne (ca. 1976).

"Defferre ne veut pas porter le béret." *Le Canard Enchaîné*, April 4, 1984.

Deia, October 22, 1987.

Delaney, Paul. "Basque Terror Grinds on Despite Talks." *International Herald Tribune*, September 5–6, 1986.

———. "Basques in Spain Tense after Ousters by France." *New York Times*, October 11, 1987.

Delsol, Catherine. "Le commando n'agissait que pour tuer." *Le Figaro*, April 17, 1990.

"Département Pays Basque." *Euskaldunak* 8 (November 1974).

Descamps de Bragelongne, H. *La vie politique des Basses-Pyrénées.* Pau: Marrim-pouey, 1958.

Deschamps, Y. "FLB: Un mythe subversif." *Politique Bretagne* 1 (1972).

Descheemaeker, Jacques. "La frontière pyrénéenne de l'ocean à l'Aragon." Thèse de doctorat, Université de Paris, 1946.

"Des élus du Pays Basque demandent la création d'un département autonome." *Le Monde*, February 23, 1982.

"Des menaces telephoniques au nom d'Iparretarrak." *Le Monde*, August 22, 1990.

"Des mercenaires seraient chargés d'intimider les réfugiés espagnols en France." *Le Monde*, July 13–14, 1975.

"Des policiers espagnols auraient été les commanditaires du GAL." *Le Monde*, May 9, 1985.

"Des voies différentes." *Enbata* 950 (November 27, 1986).

Deutsch, Karl W. "The Trend of European Nationalism—The Language Aspect." *American Political Science Review* 36, no. 3 (June 1942).

———. *Nationalism and Social Communication.* Cambridge: MIT Press, 1966.

"Deux membres présumés du GAL remis en liberté." *Le Monde*, November 30, 1984.

"Deux terroristes basques sont tués par l'explosion d'une voiture qu'ils venaient de 'piéger'." *Le Monde*, March 28, 1980.

"Diffamation." *Enbata* 925 (June 5, 1986).

Documentos. 2 vols. Donostia/San Sebastián: Hordago, 1979–1981.

Doridan, Pierre. "La Bretagne et le socialisme." *Temps Modernes* 324–326 (August–September 1973).

Douglass, William A. "The Famille Souche and its Interpreters." In *Proceedings of the Annual Meeting of the Western Society for French History* 19 (1992).

Douglass, William A., and Jon Bilbao. *Amerikanuak: Basques in the New World.* Reno: University of Nevada Press, 1975.

Douglass, William A., Richard W. Etulain, and William H. Jacobsen, Jr., eds. "Response of the Pays Basque to the Convocation of the Estates General in Pre-revolutionary France." In *Anglo-American Contributions to Basque Studies: Essays in Honor of Jon Bilbao.* Desert Research Institute Publications on the Social Sciences, no. 13, University of Nevada, Reno, 1977.

Dravasa, E. "Les privilèges des basques du Labourd sous l'ancien régime." Thèse de doctorát de l'Etat en Droit, Université de Bordeaux, 1950.

Dubarat, V. "Sanadon, évêque constitutionnel des Basses-Pyrénées." *Revue du Béarn et du Pays Basque* (September and December 1905).

Duboscq, Pierre. "La question basque du nord." In *Géopolitiques des régions françaises,* edited by Yves Lacoste. Vol. 2. Paris: Fayard, 1986.

Duhalde, Pedro. *Le nationalisme basque et la guerre civile en Espagne.* Paris: n.p., 1937.

Dumas, Pierre. *Euzkadi: Les Basques devant la guerre d'espagne.* Paris: Editions de l'Aube, 1938.

du Tanney, Philippe. "Français de l'ETA: Un lourd 'palmarès'." *Le Figaro,* April 24, 1990.

"E. A.: Bayonne, 19 novembre." *Enbata* 950 (November 27, 1986).

Echegut, Alain, and Jean-Jacques Kourliandsky. "L'Insoluble question basque." *Témoinage Chrétien,* March 4–10, 1985.

Eclair-Pyrénées, June 6, 1968 and October 9, 1987.

"Editorial." *Pindar* (December 1976).

"Editorial: E.H.A.S. et les élections." *Euskaldunak* 34 (February 1977).

"Editorial: Elections européens interdites aux minorités." *Euskaldunak* 61 (May 1979): 3.

"Editorial: La décolonisation des peuples." *Euskaldunak* 46 (February 1978): 1.

Egin, July 19, 1991.

"E.H.A.S." *Enbata* 606 (April 3, 1980).

"EHAS aux élections municipales." *Euskaldunak* 36 (April 1977).

"E.H.A.S. ne répond pas aux actes d'autres groupes." *Sud-Ouest,* March 17, 1978.

EHASKIDE (November 27, 1976).
———— (January 1977): 2.
———— (April 1977): 5.
———— (November 1977): 1.
———— (December 1977): 2.
———— (February 1978).
———— (September 1978): 3.

—— (October 1978): 2.

—— (May 1979).

"Ekaitza." *Ateka* 31 (April 1986): 2.

Ekaitza 0 (March 30, 1986): 2–5.

—— 33 (December 18, 1986): 2.

—— 34 (December 25, 1986): 2.

—— 40 (February 5, 1987).

—— 41 (February 12, 1987).

—— 44 (March 5, 1987): 4–5.

—— 45 (March 12, 1987): 4–5.

—— 63 (July 16, 1987): 5.

—— 70 (September 3, 1987): 2–3.

Ekin 1, 2, 3, 4, and 5 (1965).

—— 25 and 26 (1968).

"E.L.B. se définit." *Herriz Herri* 167 (February 9, 1984).

"Elections Sénatoriales." *Aintzina* 1, no. 3 (December 1934).

Elgar 235 (April 1972): 4–5.

"El 'mal español'." *Actuel*, January 23, 1984.

El País, January 23, 1979.

——, November 10, 1987.

——, October 5 and 30, 1991

——, December 11, 12, and 13, 1991.

——, February 9, 13, 14, 1992.

——, March 4, 1992.

——, May 4, 5, 17, and 21, 1992.

Elorza, A. "Larramendi: Las conferencias inéditas escritas en 1756." *Revista de Occidente* 2 (1971).

"EMA arrive, Atxik!" *Ateka* 26 (November 1985).

"E.M.A. ta zabal zazu." *Ateka* 27 (December 1985).

Embata 1 (September 1960).

"Enbata demande la reconnaissance d'une nation basque pour les sept provinces euskariennes." *Côte Basque Soir*, April 16, 1963.

Enbata 13 (April 1962).

—— 69 (January 1967).

—— 74 (June 1967).

—— 84 (October 9, 1968).

—— 284 (1972): 1.

—— (October 11, 1973).

—— 396 (March 25, 1976): 8.

—— 495 (February 16, 1978): 3.

—— 498 (March 9, 1978).

—— 652 (February 19, 1981): 6.

—— 655 (March 21, 1981): 6.

—— 659 (April 9, 1981).

———— 664 (April 14, 1981): 2, 3.

———— 700 (January 14, 1982): 4.

———— 716 (May 6, 1982): 5.

———— 718 (May 20, 1982): 6.

———— 745 (November 25, 1982): 4.

———— 765 (April 14, 1983).

———— 776 (June 30, 1983): 2.

———— 781 (August 4, 1983).

———— 782 (August 11, 1983).

———— 783 (August 18, 1983): 2.

———— 785 (September 1, 1983).

———— 788 (September 22, 1983).

———— 804 (January 12, 1984).

———— (August 9, 1984).

———— 883 (August 15, 1985).

———— (December 5, 1985).

———— 914 (March 20, 1986).

———— 915 (March 27, 1986).

———— 923 (May 22, 1986): 4.

———— 924 (May 29, 1986): 5.

———— 929 (July 3, 1986): 6.

———— 931 (July 17, 1986): 4–6.

———— 946 (October 30, 1986): 4.

———— 953 (December 18, 1986): 1, 4.

———— 967 (March 26, 1987): 3.

———— 970 (April 16, 1987): 8.

———— 971 (April 23, 1987): 8.

———— 974 (May 14, 1987): 7.

———— 978 (June 11, 1987): 6.

———— 984 (July 23, 1987): 5.

———— 994 (October 1, 1987): 8.

———— 1,015 (February 25, 1988): 3.

———— 1,016 (March 3, 1988).

———— 1,017 (March 10, 1988): 4.

———— (April 28, 1988).

———— 1,026 (May 12, 1988): 6.

———— 1,028 (May 26, 1988): 4–5.

———— 1,030 (June 9, 1988): 4–5.

———— 1,039 (September 21, 1988): 4.

———— 1,042 (September 15, 1988): 3–4.

———— 1,044 (September 29, 1988): 4–5.

———— 1,047 (October 20, 1988): 4.

———— 1,055 (December 15, 1988): 3.

———— 1,059 (January 12, 1989): 5.

—— 1,061 (February 10, 1989): 7.

—— 1,077 (May 18, 1989): 5.

—— 1,092 (September 14, 1989): 3, 6.

—— 1,102 (November 23, 1989): 7.

—— 1,110 (January 18, 1990): 4–5.

—— (April 12, 1990).

—— 1,126 (May 10, 1990): 6.

—— 1,135 (July 26, 1990): 8.

—— 1,139 (August 23, 1990): 4–5.

—— 1,140 (August 30, 1990): 3.

—— (September 27, 1990).

—— 1,145 (October 4, 1990): 8.

—— 1,150 (November 8, 1990): 6.

—— 1,155 (December 13, 1990): 8.

—— 1,158 (January 3, 1991): 4–6.

—— 1,160 (January 17, 1991): 7.

—— 1,161 (January 24, 1991): 4–5.

—— 1,162 (January 31, 1991): 4–6, 7.

—— 1,163 (February 7, 1991): 4–6.

—— 1,165 (February 21, 1991): 4.

—— 1,167 (March 7, 1991): 7.

—— 1,168 (March 14, 1991): 7.

—— 1,172 (April 11, 1991): 3.

—— 1,174 (April 25, 1991): 3.

—— 1,181 (June 13, 1991): 4.

—— 1,183 (June 27, 1991): 2.

—— 1,184 (July 4, 1991): 8.

—— 1,207 (December 26, 1991): 2.

—— 1,209 (January 12, 1992): 3.

—— 1,214 (February 13, 1992): 4.

—— 1,220 (March 26, 1992): 4–5.

—— 1,225 (April 30, 1992): 4–5.

—— (May 28, 1992).

—— 1,230 (June 4, 1992).

"Enbata leur promet une préfecture." *Le Travail*, April 20, 1963.

ETA. "A los profesionales de la prensa, radio y televisión: Qué es Euskadi?"
/"Qué es ETA y por que lucha?" Press release, Caracas, January 1969.

ETA. "Communiqué lu au Larzac le 18 août 1974." *ILDO* 1 (October 1974).

ETA. *Zutik* 65 (August 1975).

"Eta: 'Il n'y a plus de Pyrénées." *Le Point*, January 22, 1984.

"ETA Joy at Soviet Split." *European*, August 30–September 1, 1991.

"E.t.a.: T. F. 1, 19 novembre." *Enbata* 950 (November 27, 1986): 4.

Etchegoin, Marie-France, and Serge Raffy, "ETA, La saga des tueurs fantômes."
Le Nouvel Observateur, April 26–May 2, 1990.

Etcheverry, Louis. "L'émigration dans les Basses-Pyrénées pendant soixante ans." In *Proceedings of the Association Française pour l'Avancement des Sciences*. Pau. September 21, 1892.

———. "Monographie de la commune de Saint Jean-le-Vieux." In *Monographie des communes*, concours offert par la Société des Agriculteurs de France (1897). Paris: J. Lefort, 1898.

———. "La France est-elle une démocratie?" XVIIIème Congrès Annuel de la Société d'Economie Sociale et des Unions de la Paix Sociale. Paris: Au Secrétariat de la Société d'Economie Sociale, 1899. Also reprinted in *La Réforme Sociale* (August 16, 1899).

———. "Les coutumes successorales du Pays Basque au XIXème siècle." In *La tradition au Pays Basque*. Paris: Bureaux de la Tradition Nationale, 1899.

Etcheverry, Michel (Chanoine). "Les basques et l'unification nationale sous la révolution." *Bulletin de la Société des Sciences, Lettres et Arts de Bayonne* 11 (January–June 1933).

———. "A Ustaritz en avril 1789." *Eusko-Jakintza* 2 (1948).

Etcheverry, Philippe. "La lutte armée." *Le Monde*, March 3, 1984.

———. "Le parquet de Bayonne ouvre une information contre X pour homicide involontaire." *Le Monde*, March 4–5, 1984.

———. "Un douanier sur la Bidassoa." *Le Monde*, October 4, 1984.

———. "Le GAL sous surveillance." *Le Monde*, October 11, 1984.

———. "Un berger et une jeune fille sont assassinés par le GAL." *Le Monde*, February 19, 1985.

———. "Des réfugiés basques ont manifesté malgré l'interdiction préfectorale." *Le Monde*, October 20, 1985.

———. "Quatre réfugiés basques tués à la sortie d'un bar." *Le Monde*, September 27, 1985.

———. "L'ETA, organisation de libération, ou association de malfaiteurs?" *Le Monde*, March 2–3, 1986.

———. "Un séparatiste basque condamné à cinq ans d'emprisonnement." *Le Monde*, April 12, 1986.

———. "Deux réfugiés basques sont expulsés par la France." *Le Monde*, August 29, 1986.

———. "Un commando libère deux indépendantistes basques de la prison de Pau." *Le Monde*, December 16, 1986.

———. "La piste du GAL." *Le Monde*, April 19–20, 1987.

———. "Trois membres présumés du GAL condamnés à vingt ans de réclusion." *Le Monde*, May 22, 1987.

———. "Un poseur de bombes est tué par l'engin qu'il transportait." *Le Monde*, June 7, 1987.

———. "Deux morts au cours de l'arrestation d'un nationaliste basque." *Le Monde*, June 23, 1987.

———. "Important dispositif policier pour rechercher les indépendantistes basques en fuite." *Le Monde*, July 14, 1987.

————. "Le temps du dialogue?" *Le Monde*, February 23, 1988.
————. "France's Most Wanted Basque." Translated from *Le Monde* in *Manchester Guardian Weekly*, March 5, 1988.
————. "Un des foundateurs de l'ETA inculpé d'association de malfaiteurs." *Le Monde*, June 2, 1988.
————. "Hendaye livrée aux frontaliers." *MAF*, June 25, 1988.
————. "Les partis nationalistes dénoncent le blocage de leurs revendications culturelles." *Le Monde*, May 14–15, 1989.
————. "Trois mille personnes ont défilé en faveur de la culture basque." *Le Monde*, May 30, 1989.
————. "M. Joxe et Chérèque proposent un ensemble de mesures pour le Pays Basque." *Le Monde*, July 2–3, 1989.
————. "Le gouvernement envisage la création d'une communauté de communes au Pays Basque." *Le Monde*, January 8, 1991.
Etcheverry, Txetxe. "La coordination Patxa/Gabe/Oldartzen et Euskal Batasuna/EMA/IEGA." Internal Document of Patxa (ca. 1990–1991).
Etcheverry-Ainchart, Jean. "Une vallée de Navarre au XVIIIème siècle." *Eusko-Jakintza* 5–6 (1947).
Etorkizuna 1 and 2 (1967).
Euskadi, 1975. Euskaldunak Danok BAT. Bayonne: Editions Euskal-Elkargoa, 1976.
Euskadi, 1984. San Sebastián: Anuario EGIN, 1984.
Euskal Batasuna. *Projet politique, 1988*.
Euskaldunak 1 (April 1974): 2.
———— 4, 5 (August 1974): 5.
———— 16 (July 1975): 1–2.
———— 17 (August 1975): 3.
———— 31 (November 1976): 2.
———— 37 (May 1977): 3.
———— 39 (July 1977): 3.
———— 42 (October 1977): 5.
———— 43 (November 1977): 3.
———— 45 (January 1978): 4.
———— 46 (February 1978): 4.
———— 48 (April 1978): 4.
———— 50 (June 1979).
———— 80 (March–April 1981): 14.
———— 81 (May 1981): 2.
Euskal Elkargoa. "Dernières nouvelles." (May 1971).
Euskal Herriko Alderdi Sozialista (EHAS). "Manifeste." Ms., portfolio no. B-9005, Musée Basque, Bayonne (ca. 1976).
"Explication de notre position." *Euskaldunak* 2 (May 1974).
"Extra *Zutik*: Aberri Eguna, 1963." In *Documentos*. Donostia/San Sebastián: Hordago, 1979–1981.

Eyheramouno, Jakes. "Une recolonisation politique." *Euskaldunak* 18 (September 1975).

F.-B. L. (Battitta Larzabal [Larçabal]). "Politique de rupture et violence." *Euskaldunak* 48 (April 1978): 12–13.

Faure, Michel. "Pays Basque: Les nouveaux conquistadores." *Le Monde,* November 8, 1990.

"Faut voir." *Enbata* 706 (February 25, 1982).

Favereau, Eric. "Le cas du juge Svahn." *Libération,* January 11, 1985.

Feenberg, Andrew. "The May Events." *New Scholar* 4, no. 1 (1973).

"Fêtes de Bayonne." *Enbata* 1039 (August 11, 1988).

Fina [pseud.]. "Lettre ouverte à I.K." *Herriz Herri* 185 (June 14, 1984).

Fouéré, Yann. *L'Europe aux cents drapeaux.* Paris: Presses d'Europe, 1968.

——— . *La révolution fédéraliste.* Paris: Presses d'Europe, 1969.

Freire, Paulo. *Pedagogy of the Oppressed.* Translated from Portuguese by Myra Bergman Ramos. New York: Seabury Press, 1968.

"French Assail Soviet on Ethnicity." *New York Times,* March 1, 1984.

"French Nab ETA Leader Long Sought by Spain." *Washington Post,* January 14, 1989.

"G.A.L.: Un exécutif français." *Enbata* 830 (August 9, 1984).

Gallop, Rodney. "The Basques: The Oldest People in Europe." *Discovery* (October 1939): 529.

——— . *A Book of the Basques.* London: Macmillan, 1930. Reprint. Reno: University of Nevada Press, 1977.

Gandin, Patricia. "Un militant français recherché après l'assassinat en mars de deux C.R.S." *Le Monde,* May 8, 1982.

Garat, Jean. "L'Europe des matries." *Côte Basque Soir,* April 16, 1963.

Garaudy, Roger. *From Anathema to Dialogue.* Translated by Leonard Mayhew. New York: Vintage Books, 1968.

——— . *The Alternative Future: A Vision of Christian Marxism.* Translated by Leonard Mayhew. New York: Simon and Schuster, 1974.

García, S. A., and C. R. Calle, eds. *Camilo Torres: Priest and Revolutionary.* London: Sheed and Ward, 1968.

Garmendia, José Mari. *Historia de ETA.* 2 vols. Madrid: Siglo Veintiuno, 1981.

Gas, Christian. *Regiones y autonomías en europa occidental desde 1918, carácter éthnico, regionalismo, subnacionalismo.* Instituto de Desarrollo Regional, Universidad de Granada, 1979.

Gaurhuts. "Sobre nacionalismo revolucionario." In *Socialismo Abertzale y marxismo nacional vasco.* Hendaye: Mugalde, 1976.

Gazier, A. "Rapport sur la nécessité et les moyens d'anéantir les patois et d'universalier l'usage de la langue française." In *Lettres à Gregoire sur le les patois de France, 1790–1794.* Paris: A. Durand et Pedone-Lauriel, 1880.

Georges-Anquetil, M. *Hitler conduit le bal.* Paris: Editions de Lutèce, 1939.

——— . "Breton Recognition Denied in Berlin." *New York Times,* July 27, 1940.

"Germany Plans to Break Up France—Brittany a First Step." *New York Times,* July 27, 1940.

Giniger, Henry. "French Basque Life Is Peaceful." *New York Times,* January 11, 1971.

Goldston, Robert. *The Civil War in Spain.* London: Phoenix House, 1966.

Gómez-Ibáñez, Daniel Alexander. *The Western Pyrénées: Differential Evolution of the French and Spanish Borderland.* Oxford: Clarendon Press, 1975.

"Goodbye to the Nation-State?" *Economist,* June 23, 1990.

Goren, Roberta. *The Soviet Union and Terrorism.* Boston: Allen and Unwin, 1984.

Goyheneche, Eugène. "Askatasun." Ms. (ca. 1933), Archives of Eugène Goyheneche.

———. "Statut de l'Eskual Ikasleen Biltzarra (Groupe de Paris)." February 23, 1933, Archives of Eugène Goyheneche.

———. "Les basques à Paris." Ms., n.d. (ca. 1933). Archives of Eugène Goyheneche.

———. "Lettre aux étudiants basques." Ms. (ca. fall 1933). Archives of Eugène Goyheneche.

———. "Où en sont les Eskualerristes?" *Aintzina* 1, no. 1 (October 1934).

———. "Le drapeau basque avait été jugé indésirable à Biarritz: De violentes protestations." *Côte Basque Soir* (ca. 1948). Archives Eugène Goyheneche.

———. *Notre terre basque.* Bayonne: IKAS, 1961, 1964.

———. "Réflexions sur le nationalisme breton." Ms., n.d. (ca. 1942–1943). Archives Eugène Goyheneche.

———. "Quelques idées." Ms., n.d. (ca. 1942–1943). Archives Eugène Goyheneche.

———. "Roland Moreau: Histoire de l'âme basque." *Bulletin du Musée Basque* 29, no. 51 (1971).

———. "J. Cl. Larronde: Le nationalisme basque, son origine et son idéologie dans l'oeuvre de Sabino Arana Goiri." *Bulletin du Musée Basque* 58 (1972).

———. "La révolte de Matalas." In *Le Pays Basque.*

———. "La révolution." Chap. 19. In *Le Pays Basque.*

———. "La vie politique et l'economie au Pays Basque Nord." In *Le Pays Basque.*

———. *Le Pays Basque.* Pau: SNERD, 1979.

———. "Michel Labéguerie." *Revue 64* 5 (October 1980).

Goyhenetche, Manex. *Histoire de la colonisation française au Pays Basque.* Collection Oldar. Bayonne: Editions ELKAR, 1975.

———. *Pays Basque nord: Un peuple colonisé.* Bayonne: Editions ELKAR, 1979.

Greenwood, Davydd J. "Continuity in Change: Spanish Basque Ethnicity as a Historical Process." In *Ethnic Conflict in the Western World,* edited by Milton J. Esman. Ithaca: Cornell University Press, 1977.

Greilsamer, Laurent. "La France face aux terrorismes." *Le Monde,* June 25–26, 1982.

Grimm, Frédéric. *Hitler et la France*. Paris: Plon, 1938.

Gutierrez, Gustavo. *A Theology of Liberation*. Translated and edited by Sister Caridad Inda and John Eagleson. New York: Orbis Books, 1972.

Halimi, Gisèle. *Le procès de Burgos*. Paris: Gallimard, 1971.

Haramboure, M. (Syndic-Général de Labourd). *Inventaire et description faits en l'année 1713 des priviléges, règlements, titres et aventures qui concernent le pays de Labourd*. Bayonne: Fauvet Duhard, 1785.

Haran, Ximun. "Enbata-ETA-réfugiés." *Ager* 103 (January 1, 1988).

Harispé, Pierre. *Le Pays Basque*. Paris: Payot, 1929.

Haristoy, Pierre. *Recherches historiques sur le Pays Basque*. 2nd ed. Marseilles: Laffitte Reprints, 1977 (originally published 1883).

Haritschelhar, Jean. "Le basque: Une langue résistante." In *Vingt-cinq communautés linguistiques de la France* by Généviève Vermès. Vol. 1. Collection Logiques Sociales. Paris: L'Harmattan, 1988.

——— . "Dialectes et standardisation: Le cas de la langue basque." *Bulletin du Musée Basque* 131 (1991): 2.

Harlouchet, Marysee. "Le Pays Basque à travers la presse française de septembre à décembre 1970." Rapport rédigé en vue de l'obtention du Diplôme Technique de Documentation, Institut National des Techniques de Documentation. Paris: Conservatoire National des Arts et Métiers, 1972.

Hårri, Kapito [Abbé Pierre Lafitte, pseud.]. "Pas de programme politique?" *Aintzina* 1, no. 4 (January 1935).

"H.A.S.I.: Herriko Alderdi Sozialista Iraultzailea." *Euskaldunak* 39 (July 1977).

Haupt, Georges, Michel Lowy, and Claudie Weill. *Les marxistes et la question nationale, 1848–1914*. Paris: François Maspero, 1974.

Hemen (April 1986).

"Henri Parot est condamné à quatre-vingt-six ans de prison par la justice espagnole." *Le Monde*, December 21, 1990.

Héraud, Guy. "Chez les autres: Lyautey régionaliste." *Aintzina* 1, no. 10 (July 1935).

——— . *L'Europe des ethnies*. Paris: Presses d'Europe, 1963.

——— . *Peuples et langues d'Europe*. Paris: DeNoel, 1968.

——— . *Les principes du fédéralisme*. Paris: Presses d'Europe, 1968.

Herria (May 9, 1974): 7.

"Herri Taldeak et la lutte armée." *Ipar Euskadi Gaur* (1985).

"Herri Taldeak et les élections présidentielles." *Enbata* 661 (April 23, 1981).

"Herri Taldeak: Première démarche publique." *Enbata* 703 (February 4, 1982).

"Herritarki: Des orientations pour les municipales." *Sud-Ouest*, August 8, 1982.

Herriz Herri 26 (May 14, 1981): 1.

——— 31 (June 18, 1981): 1.

——— 231 (March 23, 1985): 2.

Hiriartia, J. de. *Le cas des catholiques basques*. Paris: Peyre, 1938.

"Historique de Herri Taldeak." In *Ipar Euskadi Gaur*. Bayonne: Imprimerie Artisanale (ca. 1985).

"Historique d'Iparretarrak." *Enbata* 984 (July 23, 1987).

Hitler, Adolf. *Mein Kampf.* Translated by Ralph Manheim. Boston: Houghton Mifflin, 1971.

Hoffer, Eric. *The True Believer: Thoughts on the Nature of Mass Movements.* New York: Harper and Row, 1951.

Hooper, John. "Threat of Basque Rebels to Games Lessens." *Atlanta Journal/ Atlanta Constitution,* July 18, 1992 (reprinted from the *London Observer*).

Hourmat, Pierre. "L'enseignement primaire dans les Basses-Pyrénées au temps de la monarchie constitutionnelle." *Bulletin de la Société des Sciences, Lettres et Arts de Bayonne* 128 (1972).

"How Basques Killed Spain's Premier and Almost Got Kissinger." *International Herald Tribune,* September 23, 1974.

Hugo, Victor. *Les Pyrénées.* Paris: Editions La Découverte, 1984.

Hyslop, Beatrice Fry. *A Guide to the General Cahiers of 1789.* New York: Octagon Books, 1968.

———. *French Nationalism in 1789 according to the General Cahiers.* New York: Octagon Books, 1968.

Ibarzabal, Eugenio. *50 años de nacionalismo Vasco, 1928–1978,* San Sebastián: Ediciones Vascas, 1978.

"IKAS." "Etude et action." *Aintzina* 1, no. 11 (August 1935).

"IK: Les options politiques." *Ekaitza* 454 (March 1987).

ILDO 1 (October 1974).

——— 2 (1978).

——— 4 (July 1979).

——— 7 (June 1981).

——— 9 (April 1984).

——— 10 (April 1987): 4–7.

"Incidents et divisions lors de la 'Journée de la patrie basque'." *Le Monde,* April 17, 1990.

Inciyan, Erich. "L'ETA militaire est décapitée." *Le Monde,* March 31, 1992.

"Interpellation du nationaliste basque Richard Irazuta [sic]." *Le Monde,* April 23, 1991.

"Introduction." *Eduki* 1 (November 1979).

"Ipar Euskadi gaur." *Herriz Herri* 232 (March 30, 1985).

"Iparraldean, euskaldun berri." *Ateka* 37 (December 1986).

"Iparralde: Parón total." *Punto y Hora* 324 (October 21–28, 1983).

Iparretarrak. "Message au peuple basque, aux travailleurs et peuples opprimés de l'hexagone, au marcheurs de la liberté," November 1, 1975.

———. "Zokoa-ko Ekintza." Communiqué attached to the reprint of *ILDO* 1 (ca. 1977).

———. "Communiqué: Pourquoi le Victoria-Surf." In the reprint of *ILDO* 1 (ca. 1977).

———. "Communiqué de Presse." N.p., December 23, 1978.

———. "Reponse d'Iparretarrak à Enbata sur l'affaire Dagorret." *ILDO* 3 (June 1979).

———. "La violence révolutionnaire, pourquoi?" *ILDO* 4 (July 1979).

———. "Communiqué du 4 octobre 1981." *Enbata* 685 (October 8, 1981).

———. "Communiqué." *Herriz Herri* 117 (March 31, 1983): 9.

———. "Communiqué." *Herriz Herri* 137 (July 7, 1983): 2.

———. "Communiqué du 26 juillet 1983." *Herriz Herri* 141 (August 4, 1983).

———. "Communiqué du 14 septembre 1983." *Herriz Herri* 147 (September 22, 1983).

———. "Communiqué." *Enbata* 933 (July 31, 1986).

———. "Les options politiques." *Ekaitza* 454 (March 12, 1987).

———. "Communiqué du 3 mars 1984: Iparretarrak accuse l'etat français d'assassinat et de tentative d'assassinat." *Herriz Herri* (n.d.): 1.

———. "Message au peuple basque, aux travailleurs et peuples opprimés de l'hexagone: Au marcheurs de la liberté." Ms., December 23, 1978.

———. "Communiqué du 29 decembre 1977." In *Iparretarrak: Séparatisme et terrorisme en Pays Basque français* by Jean-François Moruzzi and Emmanuel Boulaert.

"Iparretarrak accuse la police française de la disparition de J.-C. Larre." *ILDO* 9 (April 1984).

"Iparretarrak (ETA del norte) no se identifica con ETA, aunque persigue el mismo objetivo." *Hoja del Lunes*, February 2, 1980.

"Iparretarrak et le code pénal à la barre." *Sud-Ouest*, August 12, 1986.

"Iparretarrak revendique un attentat contre l'office de tourisme de Biarritz." *Le Monde*, December 24, 1985.

"Iparretarrak: Un inculpé refuse de parler français." *Sud-Ouest*, January 20, 1984.

IZAN. "Schéma d'orientation autogestionnaire." N.p., n.d. (ca. 1979).

Izan-Hitzak 15 (September 1981).

Iztueta, Paulo, and Jokin Apalategi. "El marxismo y la cuestión nacional vasco." Translated from Basque by Paulo Izteuta. Zorauz: Editorial Itxaropena, 1977.

Jäckel, Eberhard. *La France dans L'Europe de Hitler*. Paris: Fayard, 1968.

Jackson, Gabriel. *The Spanish Republic and the Civil War, 1931–1939*. Princeton: Princeton University Press, 1965.

Jacob, James E. "The Basques of France, A Case of Peripheral Ethnonationalism in Europe." *Political Anthropology* 1, no. 1 (March 1975).

———. "Ethnic Mobilization and the Pursuit of Postindustrial Values: The Case of Occitanie." *Tocqueville Review* 2, no. 2 (Spring 1980).

———. "Ethnic Identity and the Crisis of Separation of Church and State: The Case of the Basques of France, 1870–1914." *Journal of Church and State* 24, no. 2 (Spring 1982).

———. "The French Revolution and the Basques of France." In *Basque Politics: A Case Study in Ethnic Nationalism*, edited by William A. Douglass. Basque

Studies Program Occasional Papers, Series No. 2. Reno: University of
Nevada, 1985.

————. "Enbata and the Wind before the Storm: Secular Nationalism among
the Basques of France, 1960–1974." *European Studies Journal* 6, no. 1 (Spring,
1989); published by Enbata as "Enbata et le vent qui précède la tempête:
Nationalisme laïque parmi les basque de France, 1960–1974." *Enbata* 1000
(November 12, 1987).

"Jakes Abeberry, d'Enbata." *Ekaitza* 30 (November 27, 1986).

Jaureguiberry, Francis. "Question nationale et mouvements sociaux en Pays
Basque sud." Thèse de doctorat du Troisiéme Cycle, Ecoles des Hautes
Etudes en Sciences Sociales, Paris, December 1983.

Jaureguiberry, Madeleine de. "Jacques Maritain et les Basques." *Gure Herria*
3 (1973).

"Jazar et les législatives de 78." *Pindar* 1 (December 1977).

Jemein, Ceferino de. *Biografía de Arana-Goiri tar Sabin e historia gráfica del
nacionalismo vasco.* Bilbao, n.p., 1935.

Jiménez de Aberasturi Corta, and Juan Carlos, eds. *Los vascos en la II Guerra
Mundial: El consejo nacional Vasco de Londres (1940–1944).* Centro de Docu-
mentación de Historia Contemporánea del País Vasco, no. 6. San Sebastián:
Eusko Ikaskuntza, 1991.

"José Urrutikoetxea avait eu la visite d'un député européen basque espagnol."
Le Monde, January 15–16, 1989.

"José Varona López expulsé vers l'état espagnol." *Ekaitza* 12 (July 24, 1986): 2.

Jouanne, Claude. "Pays Basque: Encore un attentat signé Iparretarrak."
Sud-Ouest, September 12, 1985.

————. "Bidart: La piste se perd à Bordeaux." *Le Figaro,* August 28, 1987.

————. "Des tueurs qui paraissaient bien tranquilles." *Le Figaro,* April 10, 1990.

————. "Henri Parot couvre ses amis." *Le Figaro,* April 13, 1990.

————. "Artapalo, 'général' de l'ETA." *Le Figaro,* July 28–29, 1990.

Journal Officiel/Débats Parlementaires 89–91 (November 22–24, 1990).

Junior. "Décentralisation et syndicalisme." *Aintzina* 2, no. 21 (June 1936).

Kemen (internal bulletin of ETA-pm) 5 (April 1975).

Kennedy, Emmet. *A Cultural History of the French Revolution.* New Haven: Yale
University Press, 1989.

Kermoal, Jacques. "De la chouannerie au F.L.B." *Le Monde,* August 19–20, 1973.

Kermode, Frank. *The Uses of Error.* Cambridge: Harvard University Press, 1991.

Kidder, Rushworth M. "The Terrorist Mentality." In *Violence and Terrorism 91/92,*
edited by Bernard Schechterman and Martin Slann. Guilford: Bushkin, 1991.

Koehl, Robert L. *German Resettlement and Population Policy, 1939–1945: A History of the Reich Commission for the Strengthening of Germandom.* Cambridge:
Harvard University Press, 1957.

Kolakowski, Leszek. *Toward a Marxist Humanism.* New York: Grove Press, 1968.

"Komité Abertzale Sozialista." *Euskaldunak* 29 (August–September 1976).

Koska 1 (January 31, 1973).

————— 2 (February 28, 1973).

Krause, Axel. "France Drops Out of Fighter." *International Herald Tribune,*
    August 3–4, 1985.

Labéguerie, Michel [Aldategi, pseud.]. *Enbata* 74 (June 1967): 8.

Laborari Lo Paisan 14 (January 1984).

"La cassure." *Ekaitza* 35 (January 1, 1987).

"La cour de sûreté de l'Eta." *Herriz Herri* 22 (April 16, 1981).

"La cour de sûreté de l'Eta est saisie de l'affaire de Bayonne." *Le Monde,*
    March 30–31, 1980.

Lacouture, Jean. "Calme et vigilance dans le Pays Basque français." *Le Monde,*
    December 15, 1970.

Ladurie, Emmanuel Le Roy. "Les basques de baleine à sardine." *Le Figaro,*
    August 16, 1991.

"L'affaire Enbata." *Euskaldunak* 11 (February 1975).

"La fête autrement." *Enbata* 1,038 (August 4, 1988).

Lafitte, Pierre (Abbé) [JEL, pseud.]. *Eskual-herriaren alde (Pour le Pays Basque):
    Court commentaire du programme Eskualerriste à l'usage des militants.* Bayonne:
    Imprimerie La Presse, 1933.

—————. "Programme Eskualerriste." In *Eskual-herriaren alde (Pour le Pays Basque):
    Court commentaire du programme Eskualerriste à l'usage des militants.* Bayonne:
    Imprimerie La Presse, 1933.

—————. "Le balai, la Rue n'est pas propre." *Aintzina* 1, no. 1 (October 1934).

—————. "S'organiser." *Aintzina* 1, no. 1 (October 1934).

—————. "Les jeunes et les vieux." *Aintzina* 1, no. 1 (October 1934).

—————. "Les méfaits de la centralisation." *Aintzina* 1, no. 1 (October 1934).

—————. "Parlons net." *Aintzina* 2, no. 17 (February 1936).

—————. "La défense du régionalisme: Pour la réorganisation administrative de
la France." *La Presse du Sud-Ouest* 3284 (May 15, 1941).

—————. "L'état et l'enseignement de basque." *Aintzina* 6 (1942).

—————. "L'affaire Marc Légasse en correctionnelle." *Herria* 122 (March 20,
1947).

—————. *Sabino Arana Goiri: Sa vie, son oeuvre, son influence.* Editions Gure Herria.
Bayonne: Imprimerie des Cordeliers, 1967.

—————. "Les courants de pensée dans la litérature basque contemporaine."
Bulletin de la Société des Sciences, Lettres et Arts de Bayonne 119 (1968).

—————. "Jean Hiriart-Urruty et les débuts du journalisme en langue basque."
Gure Herria 6 (1971).

Lafont, Robert. *La révolution régionaliste.* Paris: Gallimard, 1967.

—————. *Sur la France.* Paris: Gallimard, 1971.

—————. "Sur le problème national en France: Aperçu historique." *Les Temps
Modernes* 29, nos. 324–326 (August–September 1973).

—————. *La revendication occitane.* Paris: Flammarion, 1974.

"La France face aux terrorismes." Le Monde, June 25–26, 1982.

"L'agitation au Pays Basque." *Le Monde*, April 1, 1980.

"La grande offensive contra ETA." *Enbata* 1228 (May 21, 1992): 4.

Lagrèze, M. G. B. de. *Histoire du droit dans les Pyrénées*. Paris: Imprimerie Imperiale, 1877.

———. *La Navarre française*. Paris: Imprimerie Nationale, 1881.

"Laguntza: D'un comité anti-répression à l'affirmation d'un courant politique." In *Laguntza*, tract, April 20, 1984.

Laguntza. "Par rapport aux élections législatives de 86." Ephemeral tract, July 9, 1985.

Lahuntze, Jakes. "Espérances." *Aintzina* 3, no. 25 (October 1936).

"L'aliénation Basque." Part 2. *Gure Herria* 1 (1967): 330–331.

Lamarca, Henri. *La danza folklórica vasca como vehículo de la ideología nacionalista*. Bayonne: Ed. Elkar, 1977.

Lamare, Pierre. "La frontière franco-espagnole en Pays Basque." Grupo de Ciencias Naturales "Aranzadi," Real Sociedad Vascongada de Amigos del País. San Sebastián: Museo de San Telmo, 1956.

Lambert, Gustave. *Etude sur Augustin Chaho*. Paris: E. Dentu and Bayonne: L. Andre, 1861.

Lamina. "Pour faire aimer le Pays Basque à la jeunesse." *Aintzina* 1, no. 12 (September 1935).

"La mort de la contrebande au Pays Basque." *Le Monde*, February 26, 1986.

Lamy, Michel. *Histoire secrète du Pays Basque*. Paris: Albin-Michel, 1980.

La Palombara, Joseph. "Penetration: A Crisis of Government Capacity." In *Crises and Sequences in Political Development* by Leonard Binder, et al. Princeton: Princeton University Press, 1971.

"La participation de H.A.S. au 1er Mai." *Euskaldunak* 14 (May 1975).

"La possibilité d'évolution à partir du KAS." (ca. 1977).

"La presse dénonce les soutiens étrangers de l'ETA." *Le Monde*, January 30, 1979.

"La provocation de Roson." *Enbata* 642 (December 11, 1980): 3.

"La quatorzième section va mener l'instruction sur l'évasion de Pau." *Le Monde*, December 24, 1986.

La Républicain du Sud-Ouest, September 28 and October 2, 1945.

Larronde, Jean-Claude. "Le nationalisme basque: Son origine et son idéologie dans l'oeuvre de Sabino de Arana-Goiri." Thèse de Doctorat en Droit, Faculté de Droit et des Sciences Economiques, l'Université de Bordeaux I, 1972.

———. "Elections et forces politiques en Pays Basque nord, 1848–1979." Ms., 1979. Musée Basque, Bayonne.

———. "Eugène Goyheneche, historien." *Bulletin du Musée Basque* 130 (1980): 165–180.

———. "Decepciones y esperanzas: Abertzales en Iparralde (1981–1986)." *Muga* 8, no. 54 (May 1986).

———. "Réveil des nationalités." *Enbata* 1054 (December 8, 1988).

————. "Eugène Goyheneche, Un compromiso illustrado por la historia." Eusko Ikaskuntza, *Revista Internacional de los Estudios Vascos* 37, nos. 34/2 (July–December 1989): 385–391.

————. "Eugène Goyheneche, un militant basque dans les années 30." *Revista Internacional de los Estudios Vascos* 39, nos. 36/1 (1991): 79–160.

————. *Le mouvement Eskualerriste, 1932–37.* (Winner of the first José Antonio Agirre Prize.) Bilbao: Fondación Sabino Arana, 1933.

Larzabal, Pierre (Abbé). "Petit catéchisme de notre mouvement." *Aintzina II* (ca. 1942).

————. "Notre programme." *Aintzina II* (ca. January 1943). AEG.

Larzabal (Larçabal), Battitta. "La liquidation des basques ou la situation démographique du Pays Basque Nord." *Euskaldunak* 28 (July 1976).

"Las claves ocultas de la 'guerra sucia' contra ETA." *Tiempo*, January 9, 1984.

"Las finanzas de ETA." *Actual* 96 (January 23, 1984): 12.

"La situation au Pays Basque et la lutte contre le terrorisme; Espagne: Reprise du dialogue avec l'ETA; France: Arrestation du chef d'Iparretarrak." *Le Monde*, February 21–22, 1988.

Lassalle, Léon (Abbé) ("News Politic"). "Un mystère." *Aintzina* 1, no. 2 (November 1934).

————. "La justice." *Aintzina* 2, no. 14 (November 1935).

"La traque." *Enbata* 805 (January 19, 1984).

"La tueuse blonde du G.A.L. se rend à la justice?" *Enbata* 1,034 (July 7, 1988).

"L'auteur présumé de l'attentat d'Ascain a été arrêté." *Le Monde*, Aug. 5, 1983.

Le Bras, Gabriel. *Etudes de sociologie religieuse.* Paris: Presses Universitaires de France, 1975.

Le Canard Enchaîné 169 (November 15, 1990).

"Le chef présumé de l'E.T.A. (P.M.) est écroué en France." *Le Monde*, October 15, 1982.

Le Courrier, April 16, 1963.

Le Courrier de Bayonne, April 7, 1933.

"Le début de la violence." *Herriz Herri* 143 (August 18, 1983): 2.

Lefebvre, Georges. *La révolution française.* Paris: Presses Universitaires de France, 1951.

————. *The Coming of the French Revolution.* Translated by R. R. Palmer. Princeton: Princeton University Press, 1971.

Lefebvre, Th. *Les modes de vie dans les Pyrénées atlantiques orientales.* Paris: Librairie Armand Colin, 1933.

Le Figaro, November 14, 1968.

————, March 2, 1992.

"Le GAL revendique l'attentat contre quatre réfugiés basques." *Le Monde*, September 28, 1985.

Légasse, Marc. "Paroles d'un anarchiste basque." *Aintzina* 4 (1943).

————. "Le statut du Pays Basque dans la République française, Projet du Loi."

Saint-Jean-de-Luz: Gargains, n.d. (ca. 1940s).

———. "Séparatisme basque: . . . Le ridicule ne tue pas mais il peut conduire en prison." *Résistance Républicaine,* July 1, 1946.

———. "Le séparatisme basque est-il un existentialisme?" In *Cahiers Internationaux d'Etudes Humanistes.* Bayonne: n.p., 1951.

———. "De la contrebande considérée comme une obligation de conscience." *Gure Herria* 24 (1952).

———. "Le sursaut d'Iparralde." *Enbata* 1,123 (April 19, 1990).

"Le gouvernement dissout quatre mouvements autonomistes." *Le Monde,* January 31, 1974.

"Le gouvernement ne cédera pas aux provocations des terroristes,' déclare M. Defferre." *Le Monde,* March 24, 1983.

Le Hodey de Saultchevreuil, M. *Journal des Etats-Généraux.* Vol. 3. Paris: Devaux et Gattey, 1789.

Le Matin, February 26, 1986.

"Le ministre de l'intérieur met vivement en cause les autorités françaises." *Le Monde,* June 28, 1980.

Le Monde, December 11, 1973.

———, February 7, 1974.

———, March 8, 1977, p. 12.

———, August 30, 1977.

———, September 4–5, 1977, p. 18.

———, August 15, 1978.

———, August 25, 1978.

———, February 5–6, 1978, p. 6.

———, June 11–12, 1978.

———, March 7, 1981.

———, April 22, 1981.

———, January 10–11, 1982.

———, February 23, 1982.

———, February 25, 1982.

———, August 13, 1983.

———, August 7, 1984.

———, January 26, 1985.

———, September 12, 1985.

———, August 15, 1985.

———, July 17, 1985.

———, August 18, 1985.

———, November 10–11, 1985.

———, March 4, 1986, p. 12.

———, April 12, 1986.

———, December 24, 1986.

———, January 27, 1987, p. 12.

——— , May 19, 1987.

——— , June 23, 1987.

——— , June 28–29, 1987.

——— , July 8, 1987.

——— , August 27, 1987, pp. 1, 8.

——— , September 5, 1987, p. 10.

——— , October 2, 1987, p. 14.

——— , February 21–22, 1988, pp. 1, 7.

——— , July 7, 1988.

——— , December 2, 1988.

——— , December 14, 1988.

——— , July 15, 1989.

——— , July 30–31, 1989.

——— , December 2, 1989.

——— , December 3–4, 1989.

——— , April 18, 1990.

——— , March 6, 1991.

——— , April 23, 1991.

——— , March 24, 1992.

——— , March 31, 1992.

"Le mouvement Herri Taldeak 'Pour l'autodétermination'." *Sud-Ouest,* February 1, 1982.

"Le mouvement 'Iparretarrak' donne sa version de la fusillade de Léon." *Le Monde,* August 14–15, 1983.

"Le mouvement nationaliste basque Iparretarrak est dissous." *Le Monde,* July 16, 1987.

"Le mouvement politique Herri Taldeak Abertzale Socialiste." *Herriz Herri* 65 (February 11, 1982).

"Le nationalisme d'Enbata." *Le Travail,* April 20, 1963.

"Le Nonce en Italie Borgongini Duca au Cardinal Maglione." Report no. 7907 (AES 5600/40, orig.) Rome, June 22, 1940. In *Le Saint Siège et la guerre en Europe, mars 1939, août 1940,* edited by Pierre Blet, Angelo Martini and Burkhart Schneider. Vol. 1 of *Actes et documents du Saint Siege relatifs à la Seconde Guerre Mondiale.* Vatican City: Libreria Editrice Vaticana, 1965.

"L'enquête sociolinguistique sur l'état d'euskara en iparralde." *Enbata* 1205 (December 12, 1991): 4.

"Le 'peuple corse' face à l'unité française." *France-Amérique,* April 13–19, 1991.

Le Play, Frédéric. "La famille basque, la femme basque." In *Les Basques.* Saint-Jean-de-Luz: Eskualduna, 1897.

"Le point de vue d'Herri Taldeak." *Enbata* 783 (August 18, 1983).

"Le pourrissement des notables basques." *Euskaldunak* 16 (July 1975).

"Le président de la république et le gouvernement félicitent la gendarmerie." *Le Monde,* February 23, 1988.

"Le rassemblement d'Itxassou." *Le Monde,* April 17, 1963.

"Le RPR dénonce 'l'attitude démissionnaire' du pouvoir." *Le Monde*, November 7, 1990.

"Les armes 'ariégeoises' d'Iparretarrak." *Le Monde*, May 23, 1985.

"Les assises de Pau." *Enbata* 642 (December 11, 1980).

"Les Basques comme les Corses?" *Le Monde*.

"Les Basques et les Catalans se prennent à rêver." *Le Monde*, July 10, 1991.

"Les Basques se sont trompés de droite." *Euskaldunak* 2 (May 1974).

"Les 'bavures ordinaires' de truands au rabais." *Le Monde*, March 8, 1986.

"L'escalade de la violence." *Le Monde*, August 5, 1983.

"Les dirigeants présumés d'ETA militaire ont été inculpés à Paris." *Le Monde*, April 4, 1992.

"Les élections cantonales: Quatre victoires par K.O." *Sud-Ouest*, March 9, 1976.

"Les enquêteurs estiment crédible la revendication de l'attentat par Iparretarrak." *Le Monde*, March 23, 1982.

"Les Espagnols auraient remis aux autorités françaises la liste des membres présumés de l'ETA." *Le Monde*, August 9–10, 1987.

"Les obsèques de M.-F. Héguy." *Sud-Ouest*, June 26, 1987.

"L'Espagne se félicite de la collaboration de la police française au Pays Basque." *Le Monde*, February 2, 1985.

"Les principes économiques de EB." Chap. 2. In *Une politique économique pour Ipar Euskadi*. (ca. 1987).

"Les résultats du scrutin." *Ekaitza* 0, special supplement for the *Aberri Eguna* of 1986 (March 30, 1986).

Le statut du Pays Basque dans la république française: Projet de loi. Saint-Jean-de-Luz: Imp. Dargain, 1946.

"L'Eta perd ses refuges." *Valeurs Actuelles*, July 30, 1984.

"L'ETA revendique l'assassinat de 'Yoyes'." *Le Monde*, September 13, 1986.

"L'ETA vise Madrid et Paris." *Le Monde*, July 3, 1979.

Lettre du Roi pour la convocation des Etats-Généraux, à Versailles, le 27 avril 1789. Document #P-2951 Musée Basque. Paris: Imprimerie Royale, 1789.

L'Evénément, December 1, 1987.

Levine, Morton H., Victoria Von Hagen, Jean-Claude Quilici, and Denise Salmon. "Anthropology of a Basque Village: A New Hemotypological Study." *Cahiers d'Anthropologie et d'Ecologie Humaine* 2 nos. 3–4 (1974): 169.

Lewis, Flora. "Western Europe's Militant Minorities Find Common Cause in Secret Meeting." *New York Times*, July 8, 1975.

L'Express, November 18, 1988.

Lhande, Pierre. *Autour d'un foyer basque*. Paris: Nouvelle Librairie Nationale, 1907.

———. *L'émigration basque*. Paris: Nouvelle Librairie Nationale, 1910.

———. *Le Pays Basque à vol d'oiseau*. 8th ed. Paris: Gabriel Beauchesne, 1931.

Libération, January 11, 1985, 14.

———, February 27, 1986, p. 26.

———, July 28, 1987, pp. 20–21.

————, March 31, 1992.

"Liste des signataires de l'appel." *Enbata* 663 (May 7, 1981).

Lizop, Edouard. "Introduction à la pensée de Charles-Brun." *Politique* 37–40 (1967).

Logéart, Agathe. "La routine des expulsions au Pays Basque français." *Le Monde*, March 12, 1987.

————. "Bayonne: 'Des gens du village.'" *Le Monde*, July 9, 1987.

————. "La dissolution d'Iparretarrak, une 'arme psychologique' venue de Paris." *Le Monde*, July 17, 1987.

London Daily Telegraph, November 21, 1979.

"Los muertos de Bayona, Un detonador." *Punta y Hora de Euskal Herria* 170 (April 10–17, 1980).

"Lucienne Fourcade arrêtée." *Enbata* 1055 (December 15, 1988).

"L'un des dirigeants présumés du mouvement basque ETA appréhendé à Hendaye." *Le Monde*, June 5–6, 1977.

"M. Destrade et les 'mercenaires' du GAL." *Le Monde*, April 3, 1985.

"M. Gaston Defferre: Pas de département basque." *Le Monde*, January 10–11, 1982.

"M. Giscard d'Estaing: 'Ma charge fondamentale est de maintenir l'unité de la nation." *Le Monde*, October 7–8, 1979.

"M. González: Des 'erreurs sans fondement." *Le Monde*, May 11, 1985.

"M. Jacques Chirac met en cause 'la responsibilité de l'état." *Le Monde*, December 22, 1990.

"M. Joxe veut aider la démocratie espagnole dans un respect scrupuleux des droits de l'homme." *Le Monde*, January 14, 1989.

"M. Mitterrand souhaite une 'entité administrative convenable' pour les basques français." *Le Monde*, November 6, 1990.

"M. Pasqua dénonce des personnes 'payées par un état étranger'." *Le Monde*, May 28, 1986.

"M. Pierre Joxe a repondu aux critiques dont il est l'objet à propos de la lutte antiterroriste." *Le Monde*, October 11, 1988.

"M. Poniatowski: Il est inadmissible qu'une police étrangère intervienne sur notre territoire." *Le Monde*, June 6, 1975.

"M. Raimond: 'Il y aura peut-être d'autres expulsions.'" *Le Monde*, July 22, 1986.

Machovec, Milan. *A Marxist Looks at Jesus.* English translation of the 1972 German ed. Philadelphia: Fortress Press, 1976.

Madariaga, Julen. "La contradiction principale pour nous est au niveau de la nation." *Le Monde Diplomatique* (March 1971): 7.

Madelin, Louis. *La révolution.* Chap. 4. Paris: Hachette, 1914.

Madival, M. J., and M. E. Laurent, eds. *Archives parlementaires de 1787 à 1860.* Paris: Paul DuPont, 1875.

"Madrid: Les autorités accueillent avec scepticisme le plan français." *Le Monde*, September 30, 1982.

"Madrid: Soulagement chez les basques." *Le Monde*, August 19, 1982.

Maketo, Gaizki-Ikasi. *Contre le racket Abertzale, ou les insolences anti-patriotiques d'un métèque.* Biarritz: Editions Distance, 1981.

Malherbe, Jean Paul. "Aintzina, ou la création du mouvement Eskualerriste en Pays Basque français." *Bulletin du Musée Basque* (1977).

———. *Le nationalisme basque en France, 1933–1976.* Thèse du doctorat de IIIème Cycle, Sciences Politiques, Université des Sciences Sociales, Université de Toulouse I, 1977.

———. "Le nationalisme basque et transformations sociopolitiques en Pays Basque nord." In *La nouvelle société basque,* edited by Pierre Bidart. Paris: L'Harmattan, 1980.

Maliniak, Thierry. "Le secteur minoritaire de l'ETA politico-militaire aurait décidé sa dissolution." *Le Monde,* September 30, 1982.

———. "Le groupe antiterroriste de libération est composé d'une centaine de mercenaires." *Le Monde,* May 19, 1984.

———. "L'ambassade de France dément tout contact avec l'ETA militaire." *Le Monde,* December 4, 1984.

———. "L'un des membres supposés de l'ETA militaire extradé par la France aurait été acquitté." *Le Monde,* April 19, 1985.

———. "Madrid face au défi de l'ETA militaire." *Le Monde,* August 14, 1985.

———. "Le problème de la violence doit être réglé par les basques eux-mémes." *Le Monde,* April 8, 1986.

———. "Nous ne negocierons pas avec les assassins de l'ETA." *Le Monde,* July 24, 1986.

———. "Le gouvernement dément les rumeurs de négotiation avec l'ETA." *Le Monde,* August 14, 1986.

———. "Madrid remercie Paris pour son comportement envers les militants basques." *Le Monde,* August 31, 1986.

———. "Le risque de la réinsertion." *Le Monde,* September 12, 1986.

———. "L'ETA étend son champ d'action." *Le Monde,* December 31, 1986.

———. "MM. Mitterrand et González discutent de la coopération dans la lutte antiterroriste." *Le Monde,* August 16, 1987.

———. "Contacts entre Madrid et l'ETA?" *Le Monde,* August 27, 1987.

———. "Madrid confirme qu'un dialogue est en cours avec l'ETA." *Le Monde,* September 1, 1987.

———. "Madrid reste prudent sur les tentatives de dialogue avec l'ETA." *Le Monde,* September 4, 1987.

———. "M. Pierre Joxe plaide pour une coopération plus discrète contre l'ETA." *Le Monde,* May 28, 1988.

———. "Madrid attend de Paris de nouvelles formes de coopération." *Le Monde,* August 7–8, 1988.

———. "Français et Espagnols coordonent leur politique européen pour 1989." *Le Monde,* September 3, 1988.

———. "Un français soupçonné de collaboration avec l'ETA comparait devant la justice espagnole." *Le Monde,* December 2, 1988.

———. "Paris est resolu à décapiter l'ETA." *Le Monde,* January 13, 1989.

———. "Neuf membres de la filière française de l'ETA ont été inculpés et écroués." *Le Monde,* April 10, 1990.

———. "Le jeu sanglant d'Henri Parot." *Le Monde,* April 11, 1990.

———. "L'embellie de l'économie basque." *Le Monde,* October 30, 1990.

———. "Jesús Arkautz a été arrêté au Pays Basque français." *Le Monde,* March 21, 1991.

Manech. "Amères verités." *Aintzina* 3, no. 25 (October 1936).

———. "Procédés socialistes." *Aintzina* 2, no. 15 (December 1935).

"Manifestation de Bayonne." *Herriz Herri* 168 (February 16, 1984).

"Marc Légasse compte sur les enfants pour faire du Pays Basque un état autonome." *Samedi-Soir,* April 22, 1950.

Marcovici. M. "Bande armée." *Le Quotidien de Paris,* March 31, 1992.

Marion, Georges. "Les Espagnols subventionnent l'exportation de basques." *Le Canard Enchaîné,* June 20, 1984.

———. "Une invitation du dialogue culturel." *Le Monde,* December 18–19, 1988.

Markham, James M. "Top Basque Separatist Leader Is Seized in France." *New York Times,* January 13, 1989.

Marre, Généviève. *La guerre civile en Pays Basque à travers la presse bayonnaise.* Mémoire de maìtrise, Institut d'Etudes Ibériques et Ibero-Americaines, Université de Bordeaux III, 1973.

Marsan, Régis. "Le problème national basque." Mémoire de DES, Université de Paris I, La Sorbonne, 1975.

Martin, Neil. "Marxism, Nationalism and Russia." *Journal of the History of Ideas* 29 (April–June 1968).

Marx, Karl, and Frederick Engels. "The Magyar Struggle." *Neue Rheinische Zeitung* 194 (January 13, 1849). Reprinted in *Collected Works,* vol. 8 (1848–1849). New York: International Publishers, 1977.

Mas, Catherine. "La communauté ethnique et l'Europe: L'exemple basque." Ms. Musée Basque, Bayonne.

"Mathématique au lycée: EMA-HT-IK." *Ekaitza* 0 (March 30, 1986).

Mauriac, François. "The Victory of the Basques." *Paris Soir,* January 1939.

Maurras, Charles. *L'idée de la décentralisation.* Paris: Editions de la Revue Encyclopédique, 1898.

Mayeur, Jean-Marie. *La séparation de l'église et l'état.* Collection Archives, Paris: René Julliard, 1966.

Mazure, A. *Histoire du Béarn et du Pays Basque.* Pau: E. de Vignancour, 1839.

Medhurst, Kenneth. *The Basques and the Catalans.* Report no. 9 (new edition). London: Minority Rights Group, 1977.

Melnik, C., and Nathan Leites. *The House without Windows.* Evanston: Row, Peterson, 1958.

Mendiale, Paxti. "La trajectoire du nationalisme Basque." *Que Faire* 8–9 (December 1971).

Ménou, Bernard. "Jean Ybarnégaray." Ms., Institut d'Etudes Politiques, Université de Bordeaux, France, n.d.

Mermoz, Gilles. "Pays Basque: ETA perd ses refuges." *Valeurs Actuelles,* July 30, 1984.

Mestelan, Jacques [Jakue, pseud.]. "Feuilles de crèmes." *Aintzina* 1, no. 6 (March 1935).

Miami Herald, July 7, 1978.

Michel, Françisque Xabier. *Le Pays Basque.* Paris: Firmin Didot, 1857.

Ministère de la Défense, Etat-Major de l'Armée de Terre, Service Historique. *Rapports d'actualité du XXVème corps de l'armée allemand en occupation en Bretagne, 13 décembre 1940–20 novembre 1944.* Chateau de Vincennes, 1978.

Ministère de l'Economie et des Finances, Institut National de la Statistique et des Etudes Economiques. *Annuaire statistique de la Franc, 1969.*

Ministère de l'Intérieur. "Décret du 17 juillet 1987 portant dissolution du groupement de fait dénommé 'Iparretarrak'." *Journal Officiel de la République Française* (July 18, 1987).

Ministère d'ètat et Ministère de l'Intérieur au président de la 4ème Sous-section de la Section des Contentieux du Conseil d'Etat re: Requête no. 94,477, June 24, 1974.

Minutes of the Sixth Committee (Political Questions), Fourth Meeting. Records of the Sixth Assembly, Special Supplement no. 39. *Official Journal,* Geneva League of Nations, 1925.

Miranda, José. *Marx and the Bible: A Critique of the Philosophy of Oppression.* Translated from the original 1971 Mexican edition by John Eagleson. New York: Orbis Books, 1974.

"Mission interministérielle." *Enbata* 716 (May 6, 1982).

Mommsen, Hans, and Albrecht Martiny. "Nationalism, Nationalities Question." In *Marxism, Communism and Western Society,* edited by C. D. Kernig. New York: Herder and Herder, 1972–1973.

Monserrat, Victor. *Le drame d'un peuple incompris: La guerre au Pays Basque.* Preface by François Mauriac. 2nd ed. Paris: H. Peyre, 1937.

Mordrel, Olier. *Breiz Atao: Histoire et actualité du nationalisme breton.* Paris: Alain Moreau, 1973.

Moreau, Roland. "La tourmente révolutionnaire." Chap. 17. In *La religion des basques: Esquisse historique.* Bayonne: Imprimerie des Cordeliers, 1964.

———. *Histoire de l'âme basque.* Bordeaux: Taffard, 1970.

———. "Batailles de jadis au Pays Basque: Le Sillon, le Modernisme, l'Intégrisme, l'Action Française." Parts 1 and 2. *Gure Herria* 2 (1972) and 3 (1972).

Moruzzi, Jean-François, and Emmanuel Boulaert. *Iparretarrak: Séparatisme et terrorisme en Pays Basque français.* Paris: Plon, 1988.

"Mouesca réapparait." *Sud-Ouest,* February 29, 1987.

Moulinier, J., and A. E. Mourant. "The Rh Factor in Southwestern France: An

Examination of the Basque and Bearnaise Population." *Comptes Rendus des Seances. Societe de Biologie et de Ses Filiales* 143 (1949): 393–395.

Mourant, A. E. "The Blood Groups of the Basques." *Nature* 4067 (October 11, 1947): 505–506.

Mouvement Enbata. "L'économie basque." In *Cahier no. 2.* Bayonne: Mouvement Enbata, 1967.

"Moyens de lutte révolutionnaire." Chap. 3. In "Déclaration sur la lutte contre le colonialisme en Europe." Ms. no. B-9005. Musée Basque: Bayonne, (ca. 1976).

"Nazis Order Strasbourg to Print Signs in German." *New York Times,* July 26, 1940.

"Nazi Version of the New Europe." *New York Post,* August 22, 1940.

New York Times, August 17, 1975.

Nogaret, Joseph. *Petite histoire du Pays Basque français.* Bayonne: A. Foltzer, 1923.

———. "La noblesse au Pays Basque." In *Hommage au Pays Basque.* Bayonne: Editions du Musée Basque, 1933.

"Nos propositions pour les élections législatives." *Euskaldunak* 42 (October 1977).

"Nous avions notre train à 21 h 25: Il a donc fallu tirer . . ." *Le Monde,* March 8, 1986.

"Nouvelles hypothèses sur le meurtre d'un C.R.S. au Pays Basque." *Le Monde,* April 9, 1982.

Nussy-Saint-Säens, Marcel. *Contribution à un essai sur la coutume de Soule.* Bayonne: Le Lebre, 1942.

"Objetivo: Las finanzas de ETA." *Actual,* January 23, 1984.

Oestreicher, Paul, ed. *The Marxist-Christian Dialogue.* London: MacMillan, 1969.

Ogletree, Thomas W. *Openings for a Marxist-Christian Dialogue.* Nashville: Arlington Press, 1969.

Oihartzabal, Beñat. "L'enquête sociolinguistique sur l'état de l'Euskara en Iparralde." *Enbata* 1205 (December 12, 1991): 4.

Olamendia, M. "Conférence sur le nationalisme basque." Ms., Paris, March 3, 1944.

Oldartzen 0 (October 1989).

——— 3 (April 1990).

——— 6 (March 1991): 3.

"On nous a menti." *Herriz Herri* 183 (May 31, 1984).

Orpustan, J.-B. "Les écrits littéraires basques de Pierre Lafitte." *Bulletin du Musée Basque* 113 and 114 (1986): 163–175.

Ortzi. *Historia de Euskadi: El nacionalismo vasco y ETA.* Paris: Ruedo Ibérico, 1971.

Oyhamburu, Philippe. *L'irréductible phénomène basque.* Paris: Editions Entente, 1980.

P. N. "Rock à Arcangues: Impressions." *Ateka* 38 (January 1987).

Pacharan 1 (ca. winter 1986): 8.

"Palabas de Jean Claude Larronde." (On the occasion of his receipt of the 1970 Prize "Sabindia Batza.") *Alderi* 260 (February 1971).

Palmer, R. R. *The Age of Democratic Revolution.* Princeton: Princeton University Press, 1959.

———. "Une tentative ambitieuse d'Augustin Chaho: La philosophie des religions comparées (1848)." *Bulletin du Musée Basque* 93 (1981): 127–142.

"Paris et Madrid renforcent la lutte contre le terrorisme." *Le Monde,* July 22, 1986.

Patxa. "Courrier." *Enbata* 1017 (March 10, 1988).

Patxaran (April 1987).

——— 15 and 17 (1988).

Paxton, Robert. *Vichy, Old Guard and New Order.* New York: Knopf, 1972.

Payne, Stanley. *Basque Nationalism.* Reno: University of Nevada Press, 1975.

Peyrot, Maurice. "Le parquet demande une peine de dix ans de prison contre Josu Ternera." *Le Monde,* October 19, 1989.

"Plateforme idéologique." *Euskaldunak* 1 (April 1974).

"Plus de sanctuaire pour l'ETA." *Le Monde,* August 8, 1984.

Polverel, M. *Tableau de la constitution du royaume de Navarre et de ses rapports avec la France, imprimé par ordre des Etats Généraux du royaume de Navarre.* Paris: Desaint, 1789.

Pons, Frédéric. "Guerre secrète en Euskadi." *Valeurs Actuelles,* October 12–18, 1987.

Pons Prades, Eduardo. *Republicanos españoles en la II Guerra Mundial.* Barcelona: Editorial Planeta, 1975.

Portell, José María. *Los hombres de ETA.* Barcelona: Dopesa, 1974.

"Pour la création d'un grand mouvement socialiste basque." *Euskaldunak* 5 (August 1974): 3.

"Pour l'autonomie du peuple basque." *Euskaldunak* 59 (March 1979): 4.

"Pourquoi." *Euskaldunak* 1, no. 1 (April 1974).

"Pourquoi Enbata?" In *Cahier no. 1.* Bayonne: Mouvement Enbata, (ca. 1963).

"Pour une politique offensive et unitaire du parti." Report prepared for the 1977 General Assembly of EHAS. Ms. (ca. 1977).

"Pour une stratégie de la communication en Pays Basque nord." *Ateka* 31 (April 1986).

"Pour un statut du prisonnier politique: Une campagne en Pays Basque et dans l'état français." *Herriz Herri* 211 (December 28, 1984).

Pranzac, François. *La républicaine du Sud-Ouest,* September 28, 1945, and October 2, 1945.

———. "Quand de son action dissolvante, l'Allemagne orchestrait le grand air de la race et de l'autonomie au Pays Basque." *Cette Semaine dans le Sud-Ouest* 2 (July 13, 1946).

"Présidentielles de l'état français." *Euskaldunak* 2 (May 1974).

"Prison Raid in South France Frees Two Basque Separatists." *New York Times,* December 15, 1986.

"Procès des quatre convoyeurs." *Herriz Herri* 183 (May 31, 1984).

"Procès de Xan." *Enbata* 1110 (January 18, 1990).

"Proposition de loi portant création d'un département Pays Basque." *Enbata* 649 (January 29, 1981).

"Proposition du mouvement." Handwritten proposal for the creation of EB (ca. October 1985).

Puente, Armando. "Trois membres de l'ETA parlent." *Le Point*, May 25, 1987.

Punto y Hora 331 (December 9–16, 1983).

Pyrénées-Magazine, December 2, 1987.

"Quatre agents de la DGSE interpellés par la police judiciaire." *Le Monde*, November 10–11, 1985.

"Quatre membres d'Iparretarrak condamnés." *Le Monde*, January 17, 1985.

"Quelques réactions." *Ekaitza* 30 (November 27, 1986).

"Rapport de la section Enbata de Bordeaux sur la nouvelle orientation nécessaire au mouvement, Rapport pour le 1965 Congrès d'Enbata." Ms. (ca. 1965).

"Rapport sur la langue basque." *Congrès Enbata*, April 15, 1963.

"Rapport sur l'necessité et les moyens d'anéantir les patois et d'universaliser l'usage de la langue française." In *Lettres à Gregoire sur palois de France, 1790–1794* by A. Gazier. Paris: A. Durand et Pedone-Lauriel, 1880.

"Rassemblement de séparatistes qui demandent la création d'un département basque." *Sud-Ouest*, April 16, 1963.

Raufer, Xavier, with Jean-Dominique Padovani. "GAL: Des 'justiciers' bien encombrants." *L'Express*, November 18, 1988.

Réclus, Elisee. "Les basques: Un peuple qui s'en va." *Revue des Deux Mondes* 68 (March 15, 1867).

"Réclusion à perpétuité pour Philippe Bidart." *Enbata* 971 (April 23, 1987).

"Recrudescence du terrorisme basque." *Le Monde*, July 16, 1987.

Reece, Jack E. *The Bretons against France: Ethnic Minority Nationalism in Twentieth-Century Brittany*. Chap. 7. Chapel Hill: University of North Carolina Press, 1977.

"Réflexions après le rassemblement d'Itxassou." *Le Courrier*, April 18, 1963.

Réglement fait par le roi, pour l'exécution de ses lettres de convocation aux prochains Etats-Généraux, dans le pays de Soule, du 19 fevrier 1789. Paris: Imprimerie Royale, 1789.

Reix, Jean-Charles, and Pierre Gallerey. "Terrorisme basque: Un nouveau crime." *Le Figaro*, August 26, 1987.

"Rélations extérieures." Insert to *EHASKIDE* (ca. 1976).

Rémy, Colonel. *La ligne de démarcation: Histoires du Pays Basque du Béarn et de Bigorre*. Paris: Perrin, 1973.

"Renseignements généraux." *Enbata* 1,151 (November 15, 1990).

Reyes, Luis. "IRA y ETA hablan el mismo idioma." *Qué*, December 12, 1977.

———. "Los terroristas vascos tienen miedo en Francia." *Tiempo*, November 7, 1983.

Riding, Alan. "French Suspects Held in Basque Terror." *New York Times,* April 11, 1990.

————. "Separatists in Europe Indirectly Reinforce Unity in Yugoslavia." *New York Times,* September 7, 1991.

————. "Europeans' Hopes for a Yugoslav Peace Turn to Frustration." *New York Times,* September 22, 1991.

————. "Spain Prepares for Offensive by Basque Separatist Group." *New York Times,* March 29, 1992.

————. "Spain Sees Arrest of Basque Rebels as Easing Threat to Olympics and Fair." *New York Times,* March 31, 1992.

Ritou, Etienne. *De la condition des personnes chez les basque français jusqu'en 1789.* Bayonne: Imprimerie A. Lamaignère, 1897.

Roudaut, Ronan. "Histoire du mouvement breton." *Les Temps Modernes* 29, nos. 324–326 (August–September 1973).

Rubio, Javier. *La emigración de la guerra civil de 1936–39.* Madrid: Librería Editorial San Martín, 1977.

Rudel, Christian. *Les guerriers d'Euskadi.* Paris: J. C. Lattès, 1974.

————. *Euskadi, une nation pour les basques.* Paris: Encre, 1985.

Sacx, M. *Coutumes générales gardées et observées au pays et baillage de Labourd et ressort d'Iceluy.* Bordeaux: P. Mastre, 1770.

————. "L'enseignement primaire dans une commune basque—Bidart (1715–1885)." In Pau et les Basses-Pyrénées, *Bulletin de l'Association Française pour l'Avancement des Sciences,* session of September 1892.

————, ed. *Bayonne et le Pays Basque, témoins de l'histoire: Antiquité—1918.* Bayonne: IKAS, 1968.

Sagnac, Philippe, and P. Caron. *Les Comités des Droits Féodaux et de Legislation et l'abolition du régime seigneurial, 1789–1793.* Paris: Imprimerie Nationale, 1907.

Sagredo de Ihartza, Heiko [Krutwig, pseud.]. *Vasconia.* Buenos Aires: Editions Norbait, 1962.

————. *La cuestión vasca.* Madrid: n.p., (ca. 1965).

————. *La Vasconie et l'Europe nouvelle.* Bayonne: Editions Elkar, 1976.

————. "Ayer y hoy de Federico Krutwig." *Muga* 23 (September 1979): 50–78.

Salaberry, Etienne (Chanoine). "L'aliénation basque." Part 1. *Gure Herria* 5 (1971).

Salaberry, Etienne. "L'aliénation basque." Part 1. *Gure Herria* 5 (1967).

Samatsa, June 24, 1981.

Sanadon, Barthélemy Jean-Baptiste. *Essai sur la noblesse des basques pour servir d'introduction à l'histoire générale de ces peuples.* Pau: E. de Vignancour, 1785.

Schama, Simon. *Citizens: A Chronicle of the French Revolution.* New York: Alfred A. Knopf, 1989.

Schneidermann, Daniel. "La solitude des 'Abertzale'." *Le Monde,* August 2, 1986.

Schumacher, Edward. "No End in Sight for Basque Terrorism." *New York Times,* August 24, 1987.

"Seaska: La convention signée." *Enbata* 1,102 (November 23, 1989).

Semprun, Alfredo. *ABC* (Madrid), August 3, 1978.

Sérant, Paul. *La France de minorités.* Paris: Robert Laffont, 1965.

———. "En France comme en Espagne les basques restent basques." *Monde et Vie,* February 1968.

Soboul, Albert. "De l'ancien régime à la révolution: Problème régionale et réalités sociales." In *Régions et régionalisme en France du XVIIIème siécle à nos jours,* edited by Christian Gras and Georges Livel. Paris: Presses Universitaires de France, 1977.

"Socialisme et problème basque." *Euskaldunak* 16 (July 1975).

Southworth, Herbert R. *Guernica! Guernica!: A Study of Journalism, Diplomacy, Propaganda and History.* Berkeley: University of California Press, 1977.

"Spain's Nationalists, Emboldened by Baltics, Press for Independence." *New York Times,* September 22, 1991.

Sprinzak, E. "France: The Radicalization of the New Left." In *Social and Political Movements in Western Europe,* edited by Martin Kolinsky and William E. Patterson. London: Croom Helm, 1976.

Squatters du 1er mai. "Ce qu'on nous refuse, prenons le!" Ms. (ca. April 1984).

Stalin, Joseph. *Works.* (1907–1913). Moscow: Foreign Languages Publishing House, 1953.

Stephens, Meic. *Linguistic Minorities in Western Europe.* Llandysul (Dyfed), Wales: Gomer Press, 1976.

Sterling, Claire. *The Terror Network.* Berkeley Books, New York: 1982.

Sud-Ouest, January 6, 1976.

———, March 11, 1976.

———, July 9, 1981, p. 1.

———, March 23, 1982.

———, July 26, 1985.

———, August 17, 1985.

———, June 25, 1987, p. A.

———, July 18, 1987.

———, August 26, 1987, pp. 1, 3.

———, August 27, 1987, p. 3.

———, September 4, 1987, p. 5.

———, October 8, 1987.

———, October 9, 1987.

———, October 10, 1987, p. B.

———, November 25, 1987.

———, December 5, 1987.

———, December 21, 1987.

———, January 8, 1988.

———, July 1, 1989.

———, January 29, 1991.

Taisne, Edith de. "Les nationalistes basques et la presse française." Rapport pour le Diplôme de Documentaliste, Institut National des Techniques de la Documentation, Conservatoire Nationale des Arts et Métiers, Paris. Ms., n.d. Musée Basque, Bayonne.

Tauzia, Pierre. "Les inventaires de 1906 dans les Basses-Pyrénées." *Bulletin de la Société des Sciences, Lettres et Arts de Bayonne* 125 (1971).

——. "La IIIème République et l'enseignement religieux en langue basque (1890–1905)." *Bulletin de la Société des Sciences, Lettres et Arts de Bayonne* 129 (1973).

——. "La presse dans les Basses-Pyrénées d'après l'enquête diocesaine de 1909." *Bulletin de la Société des Sciences, Lettres et Arts de Bayonne* 130 (1974).

Tessier, Albert. *La situation de la femme au Pays Basque et à Bayonne avant la révolution.* Bayonne: Foltzer, 1918.

Thalmann, Rita. *La mise au pas: Idéologie et stratégie sécuritaire dans la France occupée.* Paris: Fayard, 1991.

Théolleyre, Jean-Marc. "Le Pays Basque et ses ambiguïtés." *Le Monde,* April 3, 1980.

Thomas, Henk. *Mondragon: An Economic Analysis.* London: Allen and Unwin, 1982.

Thomas, Hugh. *The Spanish Civil War.* Rev. ed. New York: Harper and Row, 1977.

Tiempo, July 1, 1991, p. 36.

——, July 8, 1991, p. 51.

——, May 11, 1992, pp. 40–48.

——, May 18, 1992, pp. 48–53.

"Top Basque Guerrilla Is Arrested." *New York Times,* March 30, 1992.

Touraine, Alain. *The May Movement, Revolt and Reform.* Translated by Leonard F. X. Mayhew. New York: Random House, 1971.

"Tribune libre: Un projet suicidaire." Reproduced in *Enbata* 651 (February 12, 1981).

"26 mars 80: Ramuntxo, Txomin." *Enbata* 762 (March 24, 1983).

"Txomin a été expulsé de France." *Le Monde,* July 15, 1986.

"Txomin et Ramuntxo." *ILDO* 6 (March 1981).

"Un commando espagnol anti-basque est arrêté près de Saint-Jean-de-Luz." *Le Monde,* August 28, 1975.

"Un département Pays Basque?" *Le Monde,* September 10, 1981.

"Une information judiciare est ouverte contre le journal 'Enbata.'" *Le Monde,* August 21, 1976.

"Un entretien avec M. Felipe González." *Le Monde,* November 23, 1988.

"Une organisation 'anti-terrorisme E.T.A.' revendique les attentats dirigés contre les milieux autonomistes basques." *Le Monde,* July 12, 1975.

"Une présentation générale de E.H.A.S." Ms. (ca. 1979).

United States Department of State. *Patterns of Global Terrorism.* Washington D.C.: Government Printing Office, 1991.

Universidad de Valladolid. *Informe sobre la situación de las provincias vascongadas bajo el dominio rojo-separatista*. Vallodolid: Talleres Tiffograficos "Cuesta," 1938.

"Un militant d'Iparretarrak a disparu depuis sept mois." *Le Monde*, March 8, 1984.

"Un nouveau département: Pourquoi?" Offprint from *Activités en Pays Basque* 280 (February 1976).

"Un nouveau mouvement politique: Euskal Batasuna." *Ekaitza* 35 (January 1, 1987).

"Un rassemblement de personnalités basques se tient à Itxassou près de Cambo." *Le Monde*, April 16, 1963.

Urgarbi, Beñat. "La gauche française veut récupérer les abertzale du nord." *Branka* 13 (ca. 1970).

Van Hecke, Charles. "Madrid se félicite de la coopération française." *Le Monde*, February 1979.

"Verein für das Deutschtum in Ausland." *London Times*, July 30, 1940.

Veyrin, Phillippe. "La révolution de 1789 et les basques." *Bulletin du Musée Basque* 18, nos. 1–4 (1941).

——— . *Les Basques de Labourd, de Soule et de Basse Navarre: Leur histoire at leurs traditions*. Grenoble: Arthaud, 1947.

——— . *Les Basques*. Bayonne: Arthaud, 1955.

Viansson-Ponté, Pierre. "Les îles perdues." *Le Monde*, May 2–3, 1976.

——— . "La crise de l'état-nation." *Le Monde*, July 9–10, 1978.

Vinson, Julien. *Les basques et le Pays Basque*. Paris: Cerf, 1883.

"Violence révolutionnaire." In *Laguntza*, tract dated April 20, 1984.

Vodoz, J. *Roland, un symbole*. Paris: Librairie Ancienne Honoré Champion, 1920.

von Ribbentrop, J. Preface to Frédéric Grimm, *Hitler et la France*. Paris: Plon, 1938.

"Vous ne serez pas indépendants." *Le Monde Dossiers et Documents* 107 (January 1984).

Walsh, James. "The Search for a New France." *Time*, July 15, 1991.

Weber, Eugen. *Peasants into Frenchmen: The Modernization of Rural France, 1870–1914*. Stanford: Stanford University Press, 1976.

Wieviorka, Michel. "French Politics and Strategy on Terrorism." In *The Politicals of Counter-Terrorism; The Ordeal of Democratic States*, edited by Barry Rubin. Lanham: University Press of America, 1990.

Wright, Vincent. "The Basses-Pyrénées from 1848 to 1870: A Study in Departmental Politics." 3 vols. Ph.D. diss., University of London, 1965.

——— . "Religion et politique dans les Basses-Pyrénées pendant la Deuxième République et le Second Empire." *Annales du Midi* LXXXI (1969).

Ya, July 12, 1987.

——— , August 19, 1991.

Ybarnégaray, Jean. "Elections sénatoriales." *Aintzina* 1, no. 3 (December 1934).

Yturbide, Pierre. *Cahiers de doléances de Bayonne et du pays de Labourd*. Bayonne: Foltzer, 1912.

————. *Petite histoire due pays du Labourd.* Pau: G. Lescher-Moutoué, 1914.

Zeldin, Theodore. *France, 1848–1945.* 2 vols. Oxford: Clarendon Press, 1973.

"Zutik: Aberri Eguna, 1963." In *Documentos.* Vol. 2, Donostia/San Sebastián: Hordago, 1979.

Index

AAA (Apostolic Anticommunist Alliance), 288

Abasolo, Domingo Iturbe ("Txomin"), 281, 294, 298, 303, 319

Abeberry, Abbé, 133

Abeberry, Jacques: among IZAN leadership, 331; on Basque goals, 141, 144; Basque political thought defined by, 183; candidacy (1967) of, 158; conflict between Ximun Haran and, 278; on creation of EA, 354; elected to office (1989), 359; influenced by Spanish refugee issue, 135, 149; as liaison between ETA/*Enbata*, 151; questions need for armed struggle, 243; on renewal of *Enbata*, 179; responses to attacks from HAS, 188

Abeberry, Jean-Claude ("Koko"), 180, 277, 375

Abeberry, Maurice, 180

Aberri Eguna: of 1963, 139–41, 144, 151, 153; of 1964, 154; of 1971 and 1972, 230; of 1987, 355; of 1990, 359, 364, 381, 382; of 1991, 356, 359, 364, 381

Abertzale movement: analysis of splintering of, 210, 339; becomes political force, 358–59, 387, 395–96; creation of EB to unite factions of, 348–51; criticism of HT by, 246; defining as Socialist, 217; denounces assassination of Yoyes, 317; France's expulsion policy impact on, 305; hunger strikes as focus for, 230; IK/ETA split impact on, 274–76; impact of Bidart's arrest on, 373; impact of EHAS demise on, 226; impact of GAL's violence on, 297; internal dissent over violence within, 284, 333, 348, 384–85, 389, 401; IZAN focus on issues of, 251; on loss of Basque department, 337; mobilization around trial of ETA militants, 198–99; Patxa as "*abertzale* rockers" of, 359–63; protest against Baigorri attack by, 257; reaction to CRS killing, 260; reaction to KAS proposal, 214–16; rise of moderation in, 330–31; united efforts during 1988 elections by, 357–58. *See also* French Basque nationalism; French Basques

Abetz, Otto, 110

Abrisketa Korta, Jesús ("Txuxo"), 294

"Absolute urgency" policy, 304–5, 313, 315–16

Académie Basque, 66

Actual (weekly), 293

Adema, Chanoine, 39

AEK (Alfabetatze Euskalduntze Koordinakundea), 357

"Affaire Stawisky," 86

Ager (newspaper), 172, 278, 282, 346–47

Aggressive Agricultors, 361

Aguerre, Christian, 368

Aguerre, Pierre, 373–74

Aguirre, José Antonio de, 95, 118, 125, 133